# Commercial Equity
# Fiduciary Relationships

*For S M V-G*

| AUSTRALIA | BUTTERWORTHS   271-273 Lane Cove Road, North Ryde 2113 |
| | 111 Gawler Place, Adelaide 5000 |
| | King George Tower, 71 Adelaide Street, Brisbane 4000 |
| | 53-55 Northbourne Avenue, Canberra 2601 |
| | 461 Bourke Street, Melbourne 3000 |
| | 178 St Georges Terrace, Perth 6000 |
| CANADA | BUTTERWORTHS CANADA LTD   Toronto and Vancouver |
| IRELAND | BUTTERWORTH (IRELAND) LTD   Dublin |
| MALAYSIA | MALAYAN LAW JOURNAL SDN BHD   Kuala Lumpur |
| NEW ZEALAND | BUTTERWORTHS OF NEW ZEALAND LTD   Wellington and Auckland |
| PUERTO RICO | BUTTERWORTH OF PUERTO RICO INC   San Juan |
| SINGAPORE | BUTTERWORTHS ASIA   Singapore |
| SOUTH AFRICA | BUTTERWORTH PUBLISHERS (PTY) LTD   Durban |
| UNITED KINGDOM | BUTTERWORTH & CO (PUBLISHERS) LTD   London and Edinburgh |
| USA | BUTTERWORTH LEGAL PUBLISHERS   Carlsbad, California; Salem, New Hampshire |

National Library of Australia Cataloguing-in-Publication entry

Glover, John, 1954- .
Commercial equity: fiduciary relationships.

Includes bibliographical references and index.
ISBN 0 409 30498 0.

1. Equity — Australia. 2. Fiducia. 3. Trusts and trustees — Australia. I. Title.

346.94059

# Commercial Equity

# Fiduciary Relationships

John Glover

BA (Hons) (Melb), LLB (Hons) (Melb), BCL (Oxon)
*Barrister*
*Senior Lecturer in Law, Monash University*

*Butterworths*
*Sydney   Adelaide   Brisbane   Canberra   Melbourne   Perth*
*1995*

# Contents

## Part 2   The Fiduciary Relation of Influence

## Part 3   Fiduciary Relations and Confidential Information

# Preface

Fiduciary relationships in commerce were once thought to be an improbable thing. The heart of commerce was conceived as certainty and despatch—which left little room for conscientious obligations and the balancing of rival equities. A different view is presented in this book. Modern commerce is shown to be based on structures of *trust*, a phenomenon to which the fiduciary relationship gives modern expression. Breach of fiduciary relationship has undoubtedly become the fastest-growing commercial wrong of the 1990s, reflecting North American developments and supplying another reason, perhaps, why North American jurisprudence has become more persuasive in our private law.

*Commercial Equity: Fiduciary Relationships* has a purely functional methodology. Fiduciary relationships are analysed by type and then under the rubrics: When do fiduciary relationships exist? What is their scope? When are fiduciary rules breached? and What remedy is appropriate? Categories used are those which have served for generations in the positive law. Possibilities for future development are measured according to the applicable policy, the logical inclusion of concepts and what utilitarian philosophy there may be implicit in the common law. This is the plane on which most judges justify their decisions. No legal theory is promoted. Practitioner orientation tends to proscribe the meta-languages of economists and the English restitutionary scholars.

The work had its genesis in research into the Australian reception of the unjust enrichment and restitution ideas, which provides some of the perspectives that this book adopts. I am grateful to the Australian Research Council for funding the endeavour. I am also grateful to Monash University for enabling me to teach Restitution and Commercial Equity over the last few years. On fiduciary relationships, the author's judgment is that the existing law cannot be adequately explained by restitutionary doctrine. No one needs to be enriched before a breach of fiduciary duty occurs. Much of *Commercial Equity: Fiduciary Relationships* is taken up with discussing the shortcomings of personal remedies and examining the interaction of proprietary relief and insolvency: a level of analysis that equity illumines and restitution does not reach.

Finally, I would like to thank Mrs Gretchen Kewley of Monash University for preparing the index and the table of cases, and Mrs Margaret Rose of Butterworths for good-humoured editorial assistance.

Clayton
January 1995

*John Glover*

xi

# Table of Cases

**References are to paragraphs**

**References are to paragraphs**

**References are to paragraphs**

**References are to paragraphs**

**References are to paragraphs**

**References are to paragraphs**

**References are to paragraphs**

**References are to paragraphs**

**References are to paragraphs**

**References are to paragraphs**

**References are to paragraphs**

**References are to paragraphs**

**References are to paragraphs**

**References are to paragraphs**

**References are to paragraphs**

**References are to paragraphs**

**References are to paragraphs**

**References are to paragraphs**

# Abbreviations

| | |
|---|---|
| Birks | P Birks *Introduction to the Law of Restitution* (Clarendon Press 1985) |
| Burrows | *Essays on the Law of Restitution* A Burrows (ed) (Clarendon Press 1991) |
| Burrows *Restitution* | A Burrows *Law of Restitution* (Butterworths 1993) |
| Evans | M Evans *Outline of Equity and Trusts* 2nd ed (Butterworths 1993) |
| Finn *Equity* | *Essays in Equity* P D Finn (ed) (Law Book Co 1985) |
| Finn *Fiduciaries* | P D Finn *Fiduciary Obligations* (Law Book Co 1977) |
| Finn *Relationships* | *Equity and Commercial Relationships* P D Finn (ed) (Law Book Co 1987) |
| Finn *Restitution* | *Essays on Restitution* P D Finn (ed) (Law Book Co 1990) |
| Ford | *Ford and Austin's Principles of Corporations Law* 7th ed H A J Ford and R P Austin (Butterworths 1995) |
| Ford & Lee | H A J Ford and W A Lee *Principles of the Law of Trusts* 2nd ed (Law Book Co 1990) |
| Goff & Jones | Goff and Jones *Law of Restitution* 4th ed G Jones (Sweet & Maxwell 1993) |
| Gower | L C B Gower *Gower's Principles of Modern Company Law* 5th ed (Sweet & Maxwell 1992) |
| Gurry | F Gurry *Breach of Confidence* (Clarendon Press, 1984) |
| Hayton | *Cases and Commentary on the Law of Trusts* 9th ed D J Hayton (Sweet & Maxwell 1991) |
| Jacobs | *Jacobs Law of Trusts in Australia* 5th edn R P Meagher and W M C Gummow (eds) (Butterworths 1986) |
| Laws | *Laws of Australia* (Law Book Co 1993) |
| McKendrick | *Commercial Aspects of Trusts and Fiduciary Obligations* E McKendrick (ed) (Clarendon Press 1992) |
| McLean | D M McLean *Trusts and Powers* (Law Book Co 1989) |
| MGL | R P Meagher, W M C Gummow and J F Lehane *Equity: Doctrine and Remedies* 3rd ed (Butterworths 1992) |
| Ricketson | S Ricketson *Law of Intellectual Property* (Law Book Co 1984) |
| Scott | A W Scott and W Fratcher *Law of Trusts* 4th ed (Little, Brown & Co 1989) |
| Shepherd | J C Shepherd *Law of Fiduciaries* (Carswell 1981) |
| Spry | I C F Spry *Equitable Remedies* 4th ed (Law Book Co 1990) |
| Tilbury | M J Tilbury *Civil Remedies* Vol 1 ( Butterworths 1990) |
| Underhill | Underhill and Hayton *Law Relating to Trusts and Trustees* 14th ed D J Hayton (Butterworths 1987) |
| Waters | *Equity, Fiduciaries and Trusts* D Waters (ed) (Carswell 1993) |
| Youdan | *Equity, Fiduciaries and Trusts* T G Youdan (ed) (Carswell 1989) |

# Chapter 1

# Introduction

**[1.1]**  Over the past few decades, commercial law in common law countries has changed in form. Standards and principles have largely supplanted rules. Reasoning from purposes has become the dominant mode of creative reasoning, with reasoning by analogy and defined prescriptions in consequent decline.

In Australia and New Zealand, as in the United States, Canada and, to a lesser extent, the United Kingdom, the formal reflection of a once robust individualism has gone. Courts no longer draw sharp distinctions between the interests of one party and those of others: a preference for one's own interests no longer legitimates action, and a right to selfishness is no longer endorsed. Altruism has taken its place—both commercial norms and the private law generally have a more 'good-neighbourly' aspect. People are enjoined to make sacrifices and to share.

Belief in the neutrality of systems of rules is also in decline. Justice is thought more to inhere in outcomes reached than in any principle for social action that decisions may imply. There is a term used to describe these phenomena generally: 'anti-formalism'.[1]

**[1.2]**  Anti-formalism in the law has had different vehicles in different countries. Equity has been the spearhead of the movement in Australia, while, in the United States, anti-formalism has been almost exclusively powered by statute. Throughout this century, the American Law Institute has presented restatements of the private law. One of these, the Institute's Uniform Commercial Code, was enacted in 51 jurisdictions between 1953 and 1966.[2] It embodies many of the anti-formalist trends, as we will see. In Australia and Canada the orientation has been more towards case law. The law's retreat from formal rules in those countries has been mainly through equitable doctrines, judicially applied. To some extent also, the principles of equity have been put in codified form.

Equity was kept prominent in Australia for an historical reason. It was an obvious candidate to be formality's corrective when the need for one arose.

---

[1] D Kennedy 'Form and Substance in Private Law Adjudication' 89 *Harv LR* 1685, 1713–17, 1776–7 (1976); P S Atiyah 'From Principles to Pragmatism: Changes in the Function of the Judicial Process and the Law' 65 *Iowa LR* 1249, 1259 (1980).

[2] W Twining *Karl Llewellyn and the Realist Movement* 1973, 270.

Equity and the common law were anomalously separated in New South Wales until 1970 and, during that time, a lot of equity appeals from New South Wales were made to the High Court. This had the effect of 'fertilising' the other Australian jurisdictions. Equitable doctrine in Australia was kept alive at a time when it was in decline in the United Kingdom.[3]

**[1.3]**   Another commentator has attributed the 'renaissance' of Australian equity to a moral development inherent in the common law.[4] For whatever reason, commercial problems have undoubtedly suggested equitable solutions in Australia. Observing this, Sir Anthony Mason remarked that distinctive concepts, doctrines, principles and remedies, developed by the old Court of Chancery—

> have extended beyond old boundaries into new territory where no Lord Chancellor's foot has previously left its imprint . . . Equitable doctrines and relief have penetrated the citadels of business and commerce, long thought, at least by common lawyers, to be immune from the intrusion of such principles.'[5]

## Equity

**[1.4]**   The idea of equity is traditionally understood in relation to the common law—as a supplement, or corrective—but not another description of law itself.[6] Equity or some similar dispensing power was seen to be needed because the law had an inevitable defect. It arose out of the law's general application: characteristic of a just system of law. Application of the law to particular persons and circumstances will sometimes be unfair. What is intended by the rules will often be frustrated by the facts. Exceptions must be accommodated, or the reverse of the rules' intentions may be achieved. These are imperatives.

When the truism is added that it is not possible to frame general rules which are just for all situations, then the need for an equity appears.[7] Were it not for equity, judges would need to have, in cases where they saw fit, a general discretion not to apply the law. This is undesirable, especially in a democracy. Equity's genius may be that it has systematised this necessary dispensing power. The process functions predictably and according to precedent, (as it were) like the common law corrected.[8]

**[1.5]**   Equity is morally charged with this corrective function. But it operates on a different level from that of the common law. Equity is not normally concerned with the universal good: the scope of its attention is usually limited to the circumstances in which individual actors are placed. This is where the law needs correcting.

Equity concerns itself with questions of how a person positioned in a certain way should act. Perhaps for reasons to do with equity's religious beginnings, this concern is expressed in terms of that person's *conscience*. With what rival

---

[3] See MGL [215]–[247].

[4] P Finn 'Commerce, the Common Law and Morality' (1989) 17 *MULR* 87, 89.

[5] A Mason 'The Place of Equity and Equitable Remedies in the Contemporary Common Law World' (1994) 110 *LQR* 238, 238.

[6] Eg, *Ashburner's Principles of Equity* 2nd ed by D Browne (1933), 3; *Pomeroy's Equity Jurisprudence* 5th ed by S Symons (1941), §§43–4.

[7] See Aristotle *Nichomachean Ethics* Book 5, Chapter 10; *Rhetoric* Book 1, Chapter 13.

[8] *Equity in the World's Legal Systems: A Comparative Study* ed R Newman (1973), 15–29.

claims is this conscience affected? Should a person's action be restrained or enjoined? Should property in one person's name be held for someone else's benefit?

A salient fact about equitable principles is that they allow the law-giver a lot of leeway to consider the justice of the case. Equity, despite its moralism, is not as prescriptive as it may seem. Rather than dictating the appropriate law, equity empowers judges to provide it. Some commentators suggest that equitable principles, or certain of them, are only rationalisations—that real outcomes are reached on other grounds.[9] Let us consider the maxims of equity. Two or more of these compendious principles will often apply to the same facts and justify opposing outcomes. Contradictory, this seems, but individuation of justice may require as much. In equity the facts of every transaction must be closely examined. Modern decisions, as a rule, are long on the facts. 'A Court of Law' Lord Stowell said in *The Juliana*,[10] 'works its way to short issues, and confines its view to them.'

> A Court of Equity takes a more comprehensive view, and looks to every connected circumstance that ought to influence its determination on the real justice of the case.

**[1.6]**  Equity is not only a corrective. Apart from ameliorating common law rules, equity has built a structure on its interventions—a parallel legal regime has emerged from equity's corrective beginnings.[11] Among the building blocks for this structure are the individual legal actors and the relationships they have formed.

Invention of the 'trust' concept was the regime's largest step. Trusts developed out of the gaps which lay between ownership and obligation at law.[12] Formal trust relationships eventually became quite rule-bound, in an equitable kind of way. The equitable rules were not as rigid as those at common law, but resembled them.

'Fiduciary relationships'—the subject of this book— are another equitable creation. The fiduciary concept is at an earlier stage of development than the trust. No body of rules has yet formed around it. Fiduciary status has still a largely remedial, or corrective, function. Although fiduciary relationships which involve property often resemble trusts, in all cases they fall short of the requirements of the trust-constitutive rules. We shall examine the fiduciary relationship shortly, after a note on equity's interventions in commercial relationships.

## Equity and commercial relationships

**[1.7]**  A view developed in the nineteenth century, particularly in England, that some inherent incompatibility existed between equity and commerce. On this view, commercial law protects 'self-advancement and self-protection':

---

[9] See Spry 4.

[10] (1822) 2 Dodds 504, 521; 165 ER 1560, 1567, quoted in *Jenyns v Public Curator (Q)* (1953) 90 CLR 13, 119, curiam.

[11] Cf P Finn 'Equity and Contract' in P Finn ed *Essays on Contract* (1987), 104, 105.

[12] F Maitland *Equity: A Course of Lectures* 2nd ed by J Brunyate (1949), 23.

To say that a man is to trade freely, but that he is to stop short of any act which is calculated to harm other tradesmen, and which is designed to attract business into his own shop, would be a strange and impossible counsel of perfection.[13]

Speed and certainty were called for, which did not permit a close examination of the actors' behaviour.[14] Commercial documents were said to require detachment from surrounding circumstances—to be freed of equities—in order to be readily transmissible.[15]

It has been remarked as an unlikely thing to put equity to work at the task of regulating commercial relationships. A body of law originating in 'family and friendship' and 'love-oriented contexts' is introduced into the world of work and exchange.[16] Conceptualists would say that this is some kind of category mistake.[17]

**[1.8]** An alternative school of thought exists. Jurisprudence of the United States *Uniform Commercial Code* ('the UCC') is its famous expression. Theoretical underpinnings, though, were long ago expressed by the German political economist, Max Weber.[18] Writing between 1910 and 1914 on the formal qualities of modern law, Weber observed that:

> the system of commodity exchange, in primitive as well as in technically differentiated patterns of trade, is possible only on the basis of far-reaching personal confidence and trust in the loyalty of others. Moreover, as commodity exchange increases in importance, the need in legal practice to guarantee or secure such trustworthy conduct becomes proportionally greater.

Formal rules, Weber says, will be replaced by categories which express *meanings* and *intention*. 'Trusting' characterises the modern exchange— something which is only susceptible to 'ethical rationalisation'. Weber's logic of historicism shows the commercial law moving from rule-based categories to ones based in 'attitude-evaluation'. Characteristics of the modern legal system described are in fact quite harmonious with the present functioning of equity; though such a possibility may have surprised Weber, given the 'formalistic' qualities that he ascribed to the 'Anglo-American common law' (at 889–92).

**[1.9]** The UCC proceeded from a rather more practical philosophy. Karl Llewellyn, chairman of the codifiers, gave the project these objectives:[19]
(a) to simplify, clarify and modernise the law governing commercial transactions;

---

[13] *Mogul Steamship Co Ltd v McGregor and Co* (1889) 23 QBD 598, 614, Bowen LJ (CA), affirmed [1892] AC 25.

[14] *Re Wait* [1927] 1 Ch 606, 635–40, Atkin LJ (CA); *Scandinavian Trading Tanker Co Ltd v Flota Petrolera Ecuatoriana* [1983] 2 AC 694, 703–4, Lord Diplock; *Hospital Products Ltd v United States Surgical Corp* (1984) 156 CLR 41, 118–19, Wilson J.

[15] P Devlin *The Enforcement of Morals* (1965), 44; H Lucke 'Good Faith and Contractual Performance' in P Finn (ed) *Essays on Contract* (1987), 155, 172.

[16] P Gardiner *An Introduction to the Law of Trusts* (1990), 17; G Moffatt 'Pension Funds: A Fragmentation of Trusts Law' (1993) 56 *MLR* 471, 480.

[17] See R Unger 'The Critical Legal Studies Movement' 96 *Harv LR* 563, 564–5, 648–56.

[18] *Economy and Society*, G Roth and C Wittich ed (1978), 884.

[19] 'Memorandum for NCC executive: Re Possible Uniform Commercial Code' (1940), extracted in W Twining *Karl Llewellyn and the Realist Movement* (1973), Appendix E, 524–9.

(b) to permit the continued expansion of commercial practices through custom, usage and agreement of the parties;
(c) to make uniform the law amongst the various jurisdictions.

The subject of the code was to be legal affairs of a distinct sub-community within the United States, comprising 'merchants', or commercial actors, whose group mores were said to be evident.[20] Merchants had ways of negotiating (bargaining), ways of settling disputes, attitudes to the state, and other things in common. Traditional commercial law had to be 'discovered' within these mores and the code then made responsive to it.

The role of the code was not to reveal the law to the judges: commercial law was immanent in the commercial community, and the judges' job was to discover it . Lord Mansfield in the eighteenth century had a similar idea. He believed that 'merchants' might conveniently form specialist juries, trying traders' disputes according to 'the law merchant'.[21] Llewellyn acknowledged the debt to Mansfield. Formal characteristics of the UCC are illuminated by the correspondence. Llewellyn and the codifiers eschewed what was elsewhere called the 'mechanical jurisprudence' of rules.[22] Instead of law as a 'machine-manual' or a 'fire-drill' set of regulations, the codifiers used many more 'situation-specific', ethical standards. 'Unconscionability' in §2-302 represents this idea:

> (1) If the court as a matter of law finds the contract or any clause in the contract to have been unconscionable at the time it was made the court may refuse to enforce the contract, or it may enforce the remainder of the contract without the unconscionable clause, or it may so limit the application of any unconscionable clause as to avoid any unconscionable result.

The court is 'chartered', as it were, to use its own insight to find anything 'unconscionable' in the deal before it.[23] The standard of 'unconscionability' to be applied in this was the prevailing sense of commercial unfairness.

**[1.10]** Commercial equity, the UCC and Mansfield's 'law merchant' all function comparably. Justice of the legal (not of the political) kind is dispensed; good faith is mandated; reasonable expectations are satisfied;[24] values inherent in capitalism are found. These are moral imperatives, relevant to the use of financial power,[25] and they find expression in equity's conscience.

The special place of 'honesty' should be noted. It is possibly the most basal of all the values mentioned. Not all societies and legal systems attach the same value to honesty in commercial dealings. Mainland China, for example, is busily drafting a corpus of commercial legislation in light of the current investment levels. Corruption is said to be a great force in contemporary China,

---

[20] See R Danzig 'A Commentary on the Jurisprudence of the Uniform Commercial Code' 27 *Stanford LR* 621, 622–3 (1975) quoting from K Llewellyn *The Common Law Tradition* (1960), 122.

[21] C Fifoot *Lord Mansfield* (1936), 104–17.

[22] K Llewellyn *The Common Law Tradition* (1960), 122; phrase from R Pound 'Mechanical Jurisprudence' 8 *Colum L Rev* 605 (1908).

[23] R Danzig 'A Commentary on the Jurisprudence of the Uniform Commercial Code' *27 Stanford LR* 621, 629 (1975).

[24] P Freund 'Social Justice and the Law' in R Brandt (ed) *Social Justice* (1962), 93, 94–6.

[25] *Contra* G Brennan 'Commercial Law and Morality' (1989) 17 *MULR* 100, 103.

affecting almost all substantial commercial decisions:[26] perhaps it is endemic to authoritarian states. Widespread dishonesty would make a commercial equity regime, or any other rule of law, difficult to sustain: legal categories are devalued, and they do not reflect the way that decisions are taken. If more than a cynical form of commercial regulation is to apply, there must be consensus about honesty and the proper role of legal categories.

The fiduciary relationship, to which this book is devoted, is only one of equity's remedial instruments; but it is the point on which our plumb of analysis drops. Claims that can be made before an equity court are the subject of our concern.

# Legal uses of the fiduciary relationship

**[1.11]** Invocation of fiduciary relationships may put claimants in a most advantageous position. They may become entitled to specific relief, to restitution of benefits that defendants have obtained, or to compensation. The whole range of equitable personal and proprietary remedies may be available. Use of these may entail the advantages of a claimant's priority in the defendant's insolvency, or of subtraction of a defendant's gains which are incidental to a wrong committed. Equity makes three quite separate uses of this door-opening fiduciary concept.

It is important to distinguish between the several categories of fiduciary relationship existing in each of these. The character of each reflects the way it is used.

### Fiduciary relationships of trust and confidence

**[1.12]** This is easily the most important category of fiduciary relation, the one which has grown exponentially in recent years. Nearly all of this book will be concerned with it.

Fiduciary relationships of trust and confidence arise where one person reposes trust in another—or, alternatively, where a person is entitled to trust another, whether the other is actually trusted or not. Sometimes this relationship is called one of 'confidence' instead—trusting and confidence mean much the same. Relationships between partners, between agents and principals, trustees and beneficiaries, companies and directors, employers and employees and solicitors and clients are all accepted examples of the trusting relation.[27] One party to the relationship assumes an obligation to act in the other's interests. Alternatively, equity may decree that one party should act in the other's interests, whatever is done in fact. A gain derived through breach of this trust may be reversed, as we said, through equity's full range of gain-stripping remedies. For convenience, we will say that obligations under this type of relation are imposed upon 'the fiduciary', or sometimes 'the trusted party'. The party to whom the obligations are owed we will call 'the beneficiary', or sometimes, 'the party trusting'—although the word 'beneficiary' is not entirely apt. No formal trust relationship is implied.

---

[26] P Kennedy 'Corruption is Contagious' *Guardian Weekly* 23 January 1994, 24.
[27] *Hospital Products Ltd v United States Surgical Corp* (1984) 156 CLR 41, 96, Mason J and [3.10].

## Fiduciary relationships of influence

[1.13]   The second type of fiduciary relationship is concerned with influence, and has a longer pedigree. Equity looks jealously at any influence that the trusted party has over a party trusting. Trusted parties are sometimes assumed to use influence unduly if they are shown to be in a position to do so. Examples of this are in the relationships between parent and child, priest and parishioner and, problematically, between solicitor and client. When transactions between these parties occur, the parent, priest or solicitor is presumed to have exercised influence over the child, parishioner, client or customer, and the trusted party bears the onus of establishing that the influence has not been exercised or misused.

Breach of this influential fiduciary relation is easier to prove than breaches of the trusting one; remedial consequences, however, are more limited. A transaction brought about by influence in breach of the relation will usually only be rescinded and/or equitable remedies will be withheld from the influencing party. Some gains made by the trusted party in breach of the relation of influence may be beyond the trusting party's reach.

The wrong of 'undue influence' is another name for this doctrine. Presumptive effect may be given to a wrong and the burden of proof will be reversed where the influence derives from a pre-existing relationship. This is what interests us—where the wrong requires proof of a relationship. We will not be as much concerned with 'actual' undue influence, which is established on a purely transactional basis.

[1.14]   Pre-existing 'relationships of influence' describe an attribute of one of the parties. 'Influence' refers particularly to one party's control over the motives of the other. To have control over another's motives is not of itself wrongful: the control may be exercised entirely for the good, as it usually is, by parents over their children.

Whether an influenced party can be said to have acted voluntarily is not conclusive as to whether 'undue influence' is present. Undue influence looks more to want of good conscience on the part of the influencer than to want of consent on the part of the influenced.[28]

Nor is it particularly relevant whether the influenced party is reasonably entitled to follow the influencer's design. Reasonableness and expectations are more the stuff of the trusting relationship.

A party influenced unduly has simply been subjected to an improper motive for action. For example, a wife might agree to guarantee her husband's business when he persuades her by threatening to commit suicide;[29] or, a young musician at the beginning of his career might be influenced to agree to unfavourable management terms by an experienced operator.[30] Both the wife threatened and the musician imposed upon acted voluntarily. Obligations were freely undertaken. But pre-existing relations existed in both cases. Equity has

---

[28] W Winder 'Undue Influence and Coercion' (1939) 3 *MLR* 97, 100; 'Undue Influence and Fiduciary Relationship' (1940) 4 *Convey.* (NS) 274, 282: see [8.3].

[29] See *Fairbanks v Snow* 13 NE 596 (1887).

[30] See *O'Sullivan v Management Agency & Music Ltd* [1985] QB 428 (CA).

intervened in these undue influence cases, it may be said, because it disapproved of how the influenced party's motive was induced.

Where 'undue influence' applies presumptively, it takes an explicitly relational form. Influence is seen to flow from a pre-existing association. Further distinction between those relationships which equity is, from their nature, prepared to give presumptive effect to, and those where the presumption arises only if they are shown to be of influence, will not concern us here. It is treated in Chapter 8. The category of 'fiduciary relationships of influence' is enlarged on here as part of a corrective to fiduciary reasoning. Dangers lie in mixing the 'trusting' with 'influential' and 'confidential' relations.

### Fiduciary relationships and confidential information

**[1.15]**  If secrets or confidences are received by persons who are aware or may be taken to be aware of their confidential nature, those persons may come under a duty to maintain the confidentiality of what they learn.

Confidential information may be received pursuant to a fiduciary relationship. Trusted employees may learn their employer's trade secrets through the circumstances of their employment; a manufacturer may discover the confidential idea of an inventor, who approached the manufacturer to do a deal. Equity in these cases has an established jurisdiction to relieve the employer and the inventor if their confidences are breached. Relief is often grounded in the fiduciary nature of the relation whereby the confidence was passed. Injunctive or restitutionary remedies are allowed against a person who misuses the confidential information of another, or discloses it to a third party.

For example, during negotiations for a co-operative business venture between a small mining company and a larger one, details of a mineral discovery were revealed. A duty for the larger company to respect the smaller company's confidence arose and was broken when the larger company decided to exploit the discovery alone.[31] Or a former employee of an importing company might start up his own business and use the same network of suppliers that the former employer found by experience to be reliable.[32] Yet again, a dishonest employee of a geophysical survey company might sell confidential data of a client oil company to a third party.[33] Confidentiality is breached in each case.

**[1.16]**  The equitable 'duty of confidentiality' thus arises where the information was originally imparted in confidence. It may also arise if the information was improperly obtained.[34]

Equitable intervention to protect confidences has several jurisdictional bases and the Corporations Law imposes a comparable duty in s 232(5). Contract between the parties underpins much of the general law regime and there is limited fiduciary potential in that. Or protection may be given because circumstances of communication of the information are such that a 'reasonable man' would accept an obligation of confidence. Nothing is particularly

---

[31]  See *Lac Minerals Ltd v International Corona Resources Ltd* [1989] 2 SCR 574 and [9.38].

[32]  See *Wright v Gasweld Pty Ltd* (1991) 22 NSWLR 317 (CA): [9.2].

[33]  See *Ohio Oil Co v Sharp* 135 F 2d 303 (1943): [9.15].

[34]  *Commonwealth of Australia v John Fairfax & Sons Ltd* (1980) 147 CLR 39, 50 Mason J: [9.10].

relational (or fiduciary) about this, either—non-fiduciaries like strangers[35] and thieves[36] are equally bound.

Confidentiality cases which concern us are where equity intervenes to protect confidences because of the nature of the relationship between the parties at the time confidences were imparted.[37] The field of interrelation between fiduciary duties and duties of confidentiality lies here.[38] Only this form of the equitable jurisdiction over confidential information, and the relation it supposes, has the potential for being assimilated into the fiduciary canon.

[1.17] Relationships importing duties of confidentiality and fiduciary relationships both regulate similar investments of trust.[39] Where confidential information is acquired in an established fiduciary relationship, the duty of confidence will readily be inferred.[40] Overlapping fiduciary and confidentiality duties can exist. Directors of a company, for example, or persons occupying executive positions may be alleged to have misused corporate information. Where the corporate information was confidential, the same wrong may be argued to be both a breach of fiduciary duty and a breach of confidence. Normally a company claimant will choose to rely upon breach of the fiduciary duty. There is less to prove, and nothing has to be demonstrated to be of nature confidential.[41]

Employer and employee relationships are also an example. Similarity between fiduciary and confidentiality duties has prompted some to courts to express the view that the duty of confidentiality is a species of the fiduciary obligation.[42] Both sorts of equitable duty have been said to express the one fiduciary standard of 'good faith'.[43] The view of the High Court in *Moorgate Tobacco Co Ltd v Philip Morris Ltd*,[44] though, seems to be quite opposed. Philip Morris was argued to have acquired confidential information 'by use of or by reason of ... a fiduciary position or of opportunity or knowledge resulting therefrom'. Relief was sought, alternatively, for breach of fiduciary duty and breach of confidential duty. Even though no fiduciary duty was found to exist (at 436), Deane J still went on to examine the possibility that the confidentiality duty applied. Possible breach of confidence and possible breach of fiduciary duty were treated as separate things.

---

[35] *Ashburton v Pape* [1913] 2 Ch 469 (CA); *De Beer v Graham* (1891) 12 NSWR (E) 144; *Commonwealth of Australia v John Fairfax & Sons* (1980) 147 CLR 39.

[36] *Franklin v Giddins* [1978] Qd R 72.

[37] R P Austin 'Fiduciary Accountability for Business Opportunities' in Finn *Relationships* 141, 142.

[38] Suggested by Gowans J in *Ansell Rubber Co Pty Ltd v Allied Rubber Industries Pty Ltd* [1967] VR 37, 40 and Finn *Fiduciaries* 136–51.

[39] Wolinski and Enocome 'The Need for a Seller's Fiduciary Duty Towards Children' (1977) 4 *Hast Const L Q* 249, 266.

[40] P Finn *Fiduciary Obligations* 142.

[41] Suggested by R P Austin 'Fiduciary Accountability for Business Opportunities' in Finn *Relationships* 141, 143.

[42] *Fractionated Cane Technology Ltd v Ruiz-Avila* [1988] 1 Qd R 51, 62, McPherson J, affirmed FC (1988) 13 IPR 609; *Schering Chemicals Ltd v Falkman Ltd* [1982] 1 QB 1, 27, Shaw LJ (CA); *Westminster Chemical NZ Ltd v McKinley and Tasman Machinery & Services Ltd* [1973] 1 NZLR 659, 667; *Ohio Oil Co v Sharp* 135 F 2d 303 (1943), 306, Murrah J.

[43] Ricketson 850–1.

[44] (1984) 156 CLR 414, Deane J, Gibbs CJ, Mason, Wilson and Dawson JJ agreeing.

**[1.18]** So it is probably incorrect to say that fiduciary relationships subsume the equitable duty to maintain the confidentiality of confidential information. To speak of an *overlap* between duties of the fiduciary and confidential kind is more appropriate. Whatever the similarity of the confidential and trusting relations, the whole of confidentiality liability cannot be reduced to relational terms.[45] Meagher, Gummow and Lehane observe in relation to the equitable obligation of confidence that:

> in some cases the information has passed between the parties already linked by a pre-existing fiduciary relationship and [then] that relationship controls the extent of fidelity owed by one party to another.[46]

Obligations regarding confidences are conceived then as matters of 'fidelity' and said to flow from the 'nature and content of the fiduciary relation in question'. Protection of confidences is conceived as partly relational in this way.[47] Fiduciary linkage is problematic.

## Reasoning from one type of fiduciary relationship to another

**[1.19]** Can a fiduciary relationship of *influence* (with its attendant presumptions) be argued to exist because the parties were found in a relation of *trust and confidence?* Or can a fiduciary relationship of *trust and confidence* (with its enhanced remedies) be argued to exist because *confidential information* has passed between the parties? A formal 'No' is suggested as the answer to both of these questions. The fiduciary types of *trust and confidence*, *influence* and *confidentiality* each refer to distinct bodies of equitable doctrine. Each doctrine has its own functions and objectives. Separate modes of reasoning to the existence of the relations have developed accordingly. It is an error not to discriminate between them.

The important relationship of *trust and confidence* is inferred in connection with the preservation of trusting institutions, it will be suggested at [2.2]–[2.3]. Commercial advisers, brokers, solicitors, partners and agents are examples. Others, like unfair competitors, parties to failed joint ventures and disloyal ex-employees, may have the trusting requirements thrust upon them. Fiduciary obligations of the trusting relation may be said to express the ground rules of commercial interaction.

**[1.20]** Fiduciary relations of *influence* have a much less exalted function. Undue influence is more purely remedial in its focus. It is in this like 'unconscionable dealing' wrong, with which it is often associated. When a presumption of influence is raised in a transaction, the person who takes a benefit is assumed to take the benefit by its undue exercise—unless the contrary is proved. Concern for establishing the 'undueness' of influence is

---

[45] At [1.15]; also *Finn Fiduciaries* 143–51, Shepherd 324 and M Richardson 'Breach of Confidence, Surreptitiously or Accidentally Obtained Information: Theory versus Law' (1994) 19 *MULR* 673, 684–7.

[46] At [4107]; also noted in *Smith Kline & French Laboratories (Aust) Ltd v Secretary, Department of Community Services and Health* (1990) 22 FCR 73, 86, Gummow J.

[47] S Wright 'Confidentiality and the Public/Private Dichotomy, [1993] 7 *EIPR* 237, 338–9; R Dean *Law of Trade Secrets* (1990), 179–81.

with the stronger party's conscience—a much more limited horizon than the fiduciary relation of trust and confidence.

**[1.21]** The fiduciary relation involving *confidential information* is more limited again. It is the least prescriptive of the fiduciary types. Assuming that the rationale of respecting confidences is a corollary of a duty of good faith, confidentiality is simply a matter of enlightened reciprocity. Commercial actors are obliged to maintain confidences in their dealings with each other. This is a quite minimal fulfilment of another's trust. Respecting the confidence of confidential information is no reflex of the trusting and confidential duty.

## Distinguishing the influential relationship from the trust and confidence relationship

**[1.22]** Despite the separateness that most commentators perceive,[48] the influential and trusting relationships are the types most commonly confused.

Solicitors and clients, for example, are regulated according to the trusting and confidential regime for some commercial purposes and the influential regime for others. A 'fair dealing' obligation is imposed on solicitors contracting with their clients,[49] although nothing reprehensible is implied about solicitors doing business with clients who are within the trusting relation. There is also a large body of older authority that treats the solicitor and client relation as one of the 'accepted categories' of the relationship of influence. Presumed undue influence hence will flow.[50] No categorical answer may be possible as to whether the fiduciary relation between solicitors and clients should be one of influence, or one of trust. Equally, whether breach of a solicitor's duty to his client should be presumed, or be such as the client bears the burden of proving, may be 'instance-specific'. It depends on the circumstances of the transaction impugned.[51]

Where the effect of influence is a prominent feature in the relationship—for example, if a solicitor receives from the client a gift[52] or loan,[53] or the subject-matter of litigation is purchased,[54] then the influential relation should apply. Otherwise and for different commercial interactions, the relation may be treated as an ordinary fiduciary one of trust and confidence. There is little reason in principle why a client who negotiates with a solicitor from a position

---

[48] See, for example, MGL, [501]–[555] and [1501]–[1531]; F Jordan *Chapters on Equity in New South Wales* 6th ed (1947), 112–15, 136–9; *Ashburner's Principles of Equity* 2nd ed D Browne (1933), 299–305, 306–32; Finn *Fiduciaries* 82–8; W Winder 'Undue Influence and Fiduciary Relationship' (1940) 4 *Convey* (NS) 274 and cf R Flannigan in 'The Fiduciary Obligation' (1989) 9 *Ox Jo Legal Studies* 285, 286–7.

[49] *Farrington v Rowe McBride & Partners* [1985] 1 NZLR 83 (CA); *Day v Mead* [1987] 2 NZLR 443 (CA); *Brown v Inland Revenue Commissioners* [1965] AC 244; Finn in McKendrick, 37–9; *Laws* 15.2 [17]; but cf *Cordery's Law Relating to Solicitors* ed F T Horne (1988), 10–11.

[50] *Allisons v Clayhills* (1907) 97 LT 709; *Wright v Carter* [1903] 1 Ch 27 (CA); *Tomson v Judge* (1855) 3 Drewry 306; 61 ER 920; *Gibson v Jeynes* (1801) 6 Ves 267; 31 ER 1044 and authorities cited in MGL [1511].

[51] Finn in McKendrick, 39; *Laws* 15.2 [17].

[52] *Wright v Carter* [1903] 1 Ch 27 (CA); *Liles v Terry* [1895] 2 QB 679.

[53] *Law Society of New South Wales v Moulton* [1981] 2 NSWLR 736 (CA).

[54] *Pitman v Prudential Deposit Bank Ltd* (1896) 13 TLR 110; *Simpson v Lamb* (1857) 7 El & Bl 84, 119 ER 1179; *Wood v Downes* (1811) 18 Ves Jun 120, 34 ER 263, 1202.

close to equality should receive the protection of the influential relation's presumption.

**[1.23]**  The relationship of agent and principal is another ambiguous area. The House of Lords decision in *Tate v Williamson*[55] denied a fiduciary agent the right to retain a purchase he made from his principal. Lord Chelmsford LC at 61 justified this with the following passage, which signally confuses the ideas that we are trying to separate.

> Wherever two persons stand in such a relation that, while it continues, confidence is necessarily reposed by one, and the influence which naturally grows out of that confidence is possessed by the other, and this confidence is abused, or the influence is exerted in order to obtain an advantage at the expense of the confiding party, the person so availing himself of his position will not be permitted to retain the advantage.

The agent in that case did have a measure of trust and confidence reposed in him. But this could barely support the inference that the agent was in a position to wield influence. Confidence abused would have been a perfectly satisfying rationale of the duty.[56] It is not possible to treat all fiduciary obligations imposed on agents as of one or other type. The answer again must be 'instance-specific'. Some agents are in influential relationships with their principals.[57] Others are not.[58] What these two relationships suggest is the problems which may exist with the undiscriminating use of fiduciary rhetoric. Justifications drawn from authorities dealing with the influential relation are likely to confuse when called in aid of the relationship of confidence.[59]

A useful corrective is provided by dicta in *Re Coomber*.[60] A 'fiduciary agent' there received a gift from his principal while administering a deceased estate on her behalf. The disposition was later argued to attract the presumption of undue influence for him to rebut. In separate judgments, each member of the Court of Appeal denied this contention and drew a distinction between the influential and the 'normal' type of fiduciary relation. Fletcher-Moulton LJ generalised this, saying at 729 that:

> [the argument] illustrates in a most striking form the danger of trusting to verbal formulae. Fiduciary relations are of many different types; they extend from the relation of myself to an errand boy who is bound to bring me back my change up to the most intimate and confidential relations which can possibly exist between one party and another where the one is wholly in the hands of other because of his infinite trust in him. All these are cases of fiduciary relations, and the Courts have again and again, in cases where there has been a fiduciary relation, interfered and set aside acts which, between persons in a wholly independent position, would have been perfectly valid. Thereupon in some minds there arises the idea that if there is

---

[55] (1866) LR 2 Ch App 55.

[56] Suggested by W Winder 'Undue Influence and Fiduciary Relationship' (1940) 4 *Convey* (NS) 274, 282.

[57] Eg, *McKenzie v McDonald* [1927] VLR 134; *Grantwell Pty Ltd v Franks* (1993) 61 SASR 390 (FC).

[58] Eg, *Walden Properties Ltd v Beaver Properties Pty Ltd* [1973] 2 NSWLR 815 (CA); *Walker v Corboy* (1990) 19 NSWLR 382 (CA): see [3.80].

[59] See *Hospital Products Ltd v United States Surgical Corp* (1984) 156 CLR 41, 141–2, Dawson J; *Chan v Zacharia* (1984) 154 CLR 178, 192–204, Deane J; *James v Australia and New Zealand Banking Group Ltd* (1986) 64 ALR 347, 391, Toohey J.

[60] [1911] 1 Ch 723 (CA); also *Cowen v Piggott* [1989] 1 Qd R 41.

any fiduciary relation whatever any of these types of interference is warranted by it. They conclude that every kind of fiduciary relation justifies every kind of interference. Of course that is absurd. The nature of the fiduciary relation must be such that it justifies the interference.

## Distinguishing the fiduciary relationship constituted by receipt of confidential information from that of trust and confidence

[1.24]   Confidentiality exerts less 'gravitational pull' over the trusting relation than does influence. There is a more significant difference between the two fiduciary types. Most texts and commentaries keep the relationships distinct.[61] However, in fiduciary rhetoric, being undisciplined as it sometimes is, the two are often conflated. Combination of the two fiduciary types sometimes affects formal analysis, as happened in *Boardman v Phipps*.[62]

The majority in that case found that Tom Phipps was a fiduciary and liable to account because of a 'position that he assumed' regarding the plaintiff's affairs. Phipps and Boardman had taken it upon themselves to intervene gratuitously in the conduct of a family settlement. At 102 and 107 respectively, Lords Cohen and Hodson said that confidential information acquired by interveners acting in the interests of the settlement supplied a link between it and profits that the interveners made. Agents had acquired 'information and opportunity' while acting in a fiduciary capacity and were made accountable for profits earned thereby. If the category really stretched here was 'property', the confidentiality of the confidential information was a still confusing factor. The majority derived a fiduciary relationship of trust and duty to account for a private profit from the circumstances whereby Tom Phipps acquired confidential information. A constructive trust was impressed on the defendants' profit in the settlement's favour. This, on the face of things, is to assimilate the proprietary sanctions of the trusting relationship with the normally personal sanctions of a breach of confidence. No reason pertaining to confidentiality was advanced to justify the constructive trust, which, like all other proprietary remedies, may have been strictly speaking unavailable in the case.

---

[61] Eg *Snell's Equity* 29th ed P V Baker and P Langan (1990), 95, 251; *Hanbury and Maudsley: Modern Equity* 12th ed J Martin (1985), 579–85; Finn *Fiduciaries* 130–68; Shepherd 319–38.

[62] [1967] 2 AC 46; also *Lac Minerals Ltd v International Corona Resources Ltd* [1989] 2 SCR 574, 658, LaForest J: see [9.38].

# Part One

# Relationships of Trust

# Chapter 2

# Theory and Method

## Growth of the trusting relationship

**[2.1]**   It is the *trusting* type of fiduciary relationship that has grown so rapidly in recent years. With only a little hyperbole, Tamar Frankel said of modern society that 'the predominant social and legal relations' through which people interact are 'fiduciary relations'.

'Law should reflect the changes in societal structure ... a major reason for recognizing and developing a separate body of fiduciary law is that our society is evolving into one based predominantly on fiduciary relations.'[1]

The trusting relationship has led to the concepts of 'fiduciary' and 'fiduciary relation' being pressed into so many services. A great many more people seem now to be trusted. Writers vie with one another to find the elusive common feature of human interaction by which the 'fiduciary relation' can be defined. Breach of fiduciary obligation is becoming a standard wrong in commercial dealings—a phenomenon, we have noted at [1.1], to be connected with the contemporaneous decline of legal formalism and rise of equity in the private law.

A number of reasons have been suggested for why the fiduciary development has occurred. One view is that fiduciary law is just a remedy-driven device. If the courts are able to determine a person to be a 'fiduciary', they have at their disposal a newly fashionable instrument with which to restrain emerging forms of self-interest.[2] Another view suggests that it is an alteration in society's commercial values that has caused the 'fiduciary' to emerge. Commercial interaction is now investigated more critically and the rightness of marketplace outcomes is no longer passively accepted. A majority of people, it is thought, find the uncorrected morality of the marketplace unacceptable. 'Welfarist and communitarian views' may have supplanted earlier beliefs in self-reliance and individual responsibility.[3] A third view sees

---

[1] 'Fiduciary Law' (1983) 71 *Calif LR* 795, 798.

[2] D De Mott 'Beyond Metaphor: An Analysis of Fiduciary Obligation' [1988] *Duke LJ* 879, 915; also L A Sheridan *Fraud in Equity* (1957), 107–24.

[3] N Seddon 'Compulsion in Commercial Dealings' in Finn *Restitution* 138, 141; P Finn 'Commerce, the Common Law and Morality' (1989) 17 *MULR* 87; P Finn 'Conflicts of Interest' in *Professional Responsibility* (1987) 9, 9–16.

the development of fiduciary relationships as part of a structural change in modern economies—a theme which we shall pursue a little further.

**[2.2]**  In the view of some distinguished commentators, the increased presence of a particular type of economic actor is a feature of modern economies. This is the professional fiduciary, or, as perhaps better known, 'the professional'.[4] It has been said that an—

> increase in the number of professionals and the growth of professionalism has been generally accepted by social scientists as a major if not a defining characteristic of industrial societies.[5]

Professionals are persons who perform functions for others and are trusted by them. They attend to various interests of their clients or customers. Professionals expect to receive value in return for the discharge of their trust. It is uncommon for clients to give specific directions as to how their interests should be served.

**[2.3]**  In areas such as manufacturing, investment, banking and litigation, client interests served by professionals are in large part economic.[6] Very often professionals employ a skill for the purpose based on theoretical knowledge. It is something which may be competence tested and based on education and training. 'Professions', or sub-groups of professionals, in many cases have a fixed code of standards, which require that they supply impartial services in defined client relationships. Markets for professionals exist. Within and between the fiduciary professions there is marketplace competition. Out of this societal development, the rise of the professional, a distinct fiduciary 'ideology' has been said to have evolved.[7] It resembles an ethic for the professional relation which can be described as 'altruism'.

**[2.4]**  Relations between modern professionals and their clients have an important characteristic. Professionals are *paid* for what they do. Their motivation to act is the promise of financial reward. Professionals are not disinterested persons performing superogatory or selfless acts. The bulk of fiduciary relationships are now entered by people in commerce for commercial reasons and for profit. Within such relationships there are benefits to be had on both sides. The party trusting and the party trusted each expect gains—but of a different sort. The relation has a recognisable value to each. Law's role may be to 'protect the utility' of the fiduciary institution as a means of doing business. It has value both for fiduciaries and the people who use them.[8] As Ernest Weinrib says:

> Examination of the activities of fiduciaries involves, above all, an inquiry into the propriety of profit-making. What is at stake is whether the court should sanction or stigmatize a particular act performed by a businessman in a commercial context. Given the acceptance by the courts of the value inherent in a capitalist social

---

[4] Eg, E Durkheim in 1900 in his essay *Professional Ethics and Civic Morals* (1957 edn), 1-41; T Johnson *Professions and Power* (1972), 9.

[5] Johnson ibid, at 9.

[6] G Millerson *The Qualifying Associations: A Study in Professionalisation* (1964), 5.

[7] At 6–10; R Cooter and B J Freedman 'The Fiduciary Relationship: Its Economic Character and Legal Consequences' (1991) 66 *NYUL Rev* 1045, 1046–8.

[8] See P Finn 'Fiduciary Principle' in Youdan 1, 26.

order ... certain forms of profit may be regarded as acceptable without any assessment of the reasonableness of the profit-making activity and indeed the profit motive itself may be regarded as the element that purifies the transaction and clothes it with a legal justification.[9]

Many fiduciaries do make profits out of the relation. That they have a legitimate profit-motive must be an assumed condition of the world. Both fiduciaries and those trusting them have legitimate financial interests to be protected.

## Fiduciary rhetoric[10]

[2.5] Judicial expression of the fiduciary relation has traditionally been highly moralistic. Nineteenth century rhetoric exercises a continuing and perhaps distorting influence over the central questions in fiduciary law. It lies rather incongruously beside the profit-making practices of modern fiduciaries. Judges from the Victorian era delighted in extolling superogatory behaviour. They often did this in high-blown and aphoristic phrases. It was an age of moral certitude. The time has passed, but dicta in Victorian cases continue to exert a strong force over reasoning in today's fiduciaries cases. The following is typical, referring to–

> an inflexible rule of a Court of Equity that a person in a fiduciary position ... is not, unless otherwise expressly provided, entitled to make a profit; he is not allowed to put himself in a position where his duty and interest conflict.[11]

The fiduciary task has been described as 'unbending and inveterate', whereby fiduciaries are held to 'a punctilio of an honour the most sensitive', to enable 'the level of conduct for fiduciaries [to be] kept at a level higher than that trodden by the crowd'.[12] Equity's fiduciary rule is said to be 'inflexible ... and must be applied inexorably by this court'.[13] The suggested consequence of the same 'inflexible' rule of equity is that no fiduciary may profit from his role as fiduciary. No man 'who stands in a position of trust towards another, [can], in matters affected by that position, advance his own interests (eg, by making a profit) at that other's expense'.[14]

[2.6] In 1942 Lord Russell delivered his speech in *Regal (Hastings) Ltd v Gulliver*.[15] The world had largely assumed its modern shape by then. Nevertheless, he said there was:

> a rule of equity which insists on those, who by use of a fiduciary position make a profit, in no way depends on fraud, or absence of *bona fides*; or upon such questions or considerations as whether the profit would or should otherwise have gone to the plaintiff, or whether the profiteer was under a duty to obtain the source of the profit

---

[9] 'The Fiduciary Obligation' (1975) *UTLJ* 1, 2.

[10] P Finn 'Contract and the Fiduciary Principle' (1989) 12 *UNSWLJ* 76, 85.

[11] *Bray v Ford* [1896] AC 44, 51, Lord Herschell.

[12] *Meinhard v Salmon* 164 NE 545 (NY CA), 546, Cardozo CJ (1928).

[13] *Parker v McKenna* (1874) LR 10 Ch 96, 124–5, James LJ.

[14] *Robins v Randfontein Estates Gold Mining Co Ltd* 1921 AD 168, 179, Innes CJ; further examples in G Jones 'Unjust Enrichment and the Fiduciary's Duty of Loyalty' (1968) 84 LQR 472, 472–4.

[15] (1942) [1967] 2 AC 134n, 144–5.

for the plaintiff, or whether he took a risk or acted as he did for the benefit of the plaintiff, or whether the plaintiff has in fact been damaged or benefited by his action. The liability arises from the mere fact of a profit having, in the stated circumstances, been made. The profiteer, however honest and well-intentioned, cannot escape the risk of being called to account.

A strict antithesis is maintained—between fiduciary relationships, on the one hand, and the making of profits, on the other. *Regal (Hastings)* concerned the secret profits of company directors made 'by reason or by use of their positions'—an important phrase that we will discuss at [5.56]. In order to reach his decision in that case, Lord Russell needed only to refer to the making of a wrongfully *undisclosed* profit. Profit that the principal did not accept or consent to before it was made was all that had to be proscribed. A profit had been made by some company directors through a sale of shares they had purchased in the company's subsidiary. That company was arguably the proper entity to make the profit, unless it was disclosed to and ratified by the company in general meeting. The absence of evidence of disclosure noted at 140 was fatal to the directors' case. Dicta in the speech reveal the overblown characteristic. It is noted (at 145) that 'the strictness of the [no profits at all] rule in equity' is illustrated by the authorities of *Keech v Sandford*,[16] a common source of misleading analogies, and *Ex parte James*.[17] Appropriately uncompromising things are quoted from what was said in the judgments of Lord King LC and Lord Eldon LC respectively, although in quite distinguishable contexts. The same type of reasoning as that of Lord Russell in *Regal (Hastings) Ltd v Gulliver*[18] was employed in several of the speeches made in *Boardman v Phipps*.[19] Status of the defendants as fiduciaries in that case was not in question.

**[2.7]**   Commercial fiduciaries simply do not fit a stereotype of voluntariness and self-abnegation. Fiduciary rewards—say, fee remuneration—may be the subject of open negotiation with the beneficiary. A mercantile agent seeking goods for sale on commission may be persuaded to reduce his commission rates, or a solicitor may be induced to reduce his quoted fee for service. Hourly rates may be compromised. Quasi-contractual recovery may be applicable.[20] Fiduciaries may be entitled by rule of law to a reasonable remuneration for what they have done, assuming that it constitutes a benefit to the beneficiary concerned.[21] Sharing of profits is even less structured. Solicitors' contingency fees, where permissible, are at large. In a fiduciary distributorship or business franchise agreement the distributor's percentages may be the subject of hard bargaining before agreement is struck.

Consider the first instance judgment delivered by McLelland J in *United States Surgical Corporation v Hospital Products International Pty Ltd*.[22] It

---

[16] (1726) Sel Cas Ch 61; 25 ER 223.

[17] (1803) 8 Ves 337; 32 ER 385.

[18] (1942) [1967] 2 AC 134n, 140–1.

[19] [1967] 2 AC 46.

[20] Explained by Deane J in *Pavey and Matthews Pty Ltd v Paul* (1986) 162 CLR 221, 250–64; see also S J Stoljar *The Law of Quasi-Contract* 2nd ed (1989), 185–219.

[21] Birks, 266–76, 286–90; cf A S Burrows 'Free Acceptance and the Law of Restitution' (1988) 104 LQR 576 and J Beatson *The Use and Abuse of Unjust Enrichment* (1991) 31–44.

[22] [1982] 2 NSWLR 766.

was, as we shall see, a difficult case. The fiduciary issue arose from the terms of a dealership agreement. At first instance, the distributor argued that there could be no fiduciary relationship between the parties because the distributor had a profit interest distinct from that of the supplier. McLelland J considered this submission at length before, at 811, rejecting it. He held that a fiduciary relation did exist 'in relation to such of USSC's interests as were represented by the market for its products in Australia'. The distributor's power combined with the supplier's vulnerability, he thought, counted too far in the fiduciary direction. The conclusion was reached, though, only after a general inquiry ranging over some nineteen authorities, including *Re Coomber*[23] and *Boardman v Phipps*.[24] Together, the authorities spanned widely different factual problems and at least two different types of fiduciary relationship.[25] *Re Coomber*, for one, is usually quoted when a fiduciary element is being denied.[26] Fletcher Moulton LJ in that case would likely have disapproved of the first instance reasoning in *Hospital Products* and have thought that it resembled the unsuccessful fiduciary argument before him. For at first instance the existence of a fiduciary relationship between the distributor and the supplier in *Hospital Products* was supported by authorities dealing with the exercise of undue influence. Different *types* of fiduciary relationship must be kept distinct, as Fletcher Moulton LJ said at 728-9. The matter–

> illustrates in a most striking form the danger of trusting to verbal formulae . . . [that] every type of fiduciary relation justifies every type of interference. Of course that is absurd.

Other fiduciary solecisms abound. It would be invidious to list them. The point is that the undisciplined use of fiduciary rhetoric is apt to cause analytic problems. Doctrinal ballast should be used sparingly. One purpose of this book is to highlight that fact by suggesting a taxonomy of reasoning types.

## Academic theories of the relation

[2.8] Some academic writers have developed a theoretical structure for the relationship. Conceived to be a practical task,

> the theoretical challenge . . . [is] to develop an account of fiduciary obligation that is more than merely descriptive and is sufficiently analytic to permit its predictable application to a variety of diverse relationships and practical circumstances.[27]

Doctrinal 'theories' in the private law are usually intended to have some predictive utility. The idea is to assist litigants and judges in hard cases. Writings on the fiduciary relationship fall within two broad classes. First, there are those accounts which base their predictive utility on a finding as to the nature of a fiduciary relationship. These accounts lead usually to a reduction of the fiduciary phenomenon to definitional form: perhaps a species of 'undertaking' or 'reliance'. Secondly, there is a body of accounts which describe what a fiduciary relationship is, without defining it. Descriptions

---

23 [1911] 1 Ch 723.
24 [1967] 2 AC 46.
25 [1982] 2 NSWLR 767, 809–11.
26 [1911] 1 Ch 723, 728–9, Fletcher Moulton LJ—in a passage quoted at [XX]
27 D De Mott 'Beyond Metaphor: An Analysis of Fiduciary Obligation' [1988] *Duke LJ* 879, 909.

differ according to the standpoints their authors choose. Some, like Finn in
*Fiduciary Obligations*, are written from the standpoints of the fiduciary rules.
Others distil 'categories' from where fiduciary relationships have been found
in the past.[28] Others again analyse the subject from the standpoints of fiduciary
remedies—'unjust enrichment' theories, as sometimes they are called.[29] We
shall examine the main writings on fiduciaries, beginning with accounts of the
type leading to definitions of what a fiduciary is.

### Definitional theories

**[2.9]** Definitional theories attempt to isolate the essential nature of the
fiduciary relationship in one dominant idea. This may be the fiduciary's
undertaking certain things, or a beneficiary's entrusting of property to him or
her. Alternatively, the definitive idea may be the power or discretion that a
fiduciary enjoys and/or the fact that the other party relies on the fiduciary.
Even mere inequality between two persons has been a pretender to this
definitional status. As will be seen, no theory can explain all contexts where
courts find fiduciary relationships. Probably because of this fact, several
writers and jurists have advanced 'blended' concepts, drawing on more than
one theory. For example, David Ong embarks on a search for an 'element
common to and definitive of all those situations that produce the fiduciary'.[30]
He suggests that he has found that element in the notion of 'implicit
dependency'. J C Shepherd explicitly sets out to define. He says at the outset,

> 'The intent of this paper is to consider and define the central concept being used
> when we identify any relationship or duty as "fiduciary".'[31]

The definition Shepherd proposes is a bundle of elements entitled 'transfer of
encumbered power'.[32] It is a sort of cocktail of the things he isolates and
describes as 'property theory', 'reliance theory', 'unequal relationship theory',
'contractual theory', 'unjust enrichment theory', 'commercial utility theory',
'power and discretion theory' and 'rule or dualistic theory'. The 'essential'
elements of each are said to be encapsulated in the notion of 'transfer of
encumbered power'. This is scientific method taken to an extraordinary degree.
Unlike academics, few judges have the time or, perhaps, see the need to
provide a definition of a 'fiduciary relationship'. Canadian judges are
sometimes an exception.[33] Most others are like judges deciding *Hospital
Products Ltd v United States Surgical Corporation*[34] in the High Court: content
to note the absence of any definition of 'fiduciary', in a way that suggests that
one might have been expected. Sir Anthony Mason has recently remarked,
extra-curially, that:

---

[28] L Sealy 'Fiduciary Relationships' (1962) Camb LJ 69, 74–9; D Waters *The Constructive Trust*
(1964), 341–3, 'Excursus A: The Classification of Fiduciaries'.

[29] J C Shepherd 'Towards a Unified Concept of Fiduciary Relationships' (1981) 97 *LQR* 51,
53–6.

[30] 'Fiduciaries: Identification and Remedies' (1986) 8 *U of Tas L Rev* 311, 315, 317.

[31] J C Shepherd 'Towards a Unified Concept of Fiduciary Obligation' (1981) 97 *LQR* 51, 51.

[32] J C Shepherd *The Law of Fiduciaries* (1981), 93–110.

[33] Eg Wilson J in *Frame v Smith* (1987) 42 DLR (4th) 81, 99 and Sopinka J in *Lac Minerals Ltd
v International Corona Resources Ltd* [1989] 2 SCR 574, 599.

[34] (1984) 156 CLR 41, 68, Gibbs CJ; 96, Mason J; 141, Dawson J.

The quest for a precise definition which identifies the characteristics of the fiduciary relationship, in particular other relationships which attract equitable relief, continues without evident signs of success.[35]

**[2.10]**   Is it right to expect a definition? Perhaps the true functioning of language precludes the possibility of there ever being a definitional answer to this equity problem. We deal with this point below in connection with how the *existence* of a fiduciary relationship is to be inferred. Here an observation of the philosopher Ludwig Wittgenstein is relevant. 'Modern man', he said, has a 'craving for generality': an urge to find common 'properties or ingredients' in the things that general terms refer to.[36] Ancient philosophers thought the search for these properties to be among the primary philosophic tasks. Instead, Wittgenstein's theory runs, many general terms refer to no more than 'family resemblances' between things. Nothing actually in common between them need be supposed.

Perhaps fiduciary relationships are by their nature not susceptible of definition. In this event the relationships can only be described. Detection of various resemblances between relations which are potentially fiduciary may be what the exercise of judging is about. It is a judicial function. There is no convenient fiduciary template which can be applied in its place.

## Descriptive theories

**[2.11]**   When describing fiduciaries, as opposed to defining them, jurists and writers are not concerned with the 'essence' of the fiduciary relationship. Nor are they concerned with the 'common qualities' inherent in each of the things to which the word 'fiduciary' refers. Rather, description is concerned with uses of the term that the law makes. This can be done in a number of ways.

### 1. Factual categories

**[2.12]**   Description by 'factual categories' is a type of generalisation concerning the form of a fiduciary relation drawn from the facts of cases where fiduciary relationships have been found. For instance, partners are usually found to be fiduciaries. There might on this approach therefore be a category of 'partnership' within the fiduciary canon. Categories of relationship might for present purposes include bankers, business advisors or any other identifiable person or entity in a trusted position. However most writers choosing this approach have opted to pitch their categories at a much higher level of abstraction. So Len Sealy, writing in 1962, advanced four categories of decided cases—some of which sound a little abstract. They were 'Property-based', 'Obligation-based', 'Accretions to the estates of life tenants', and 'Undue influence'.[37] Donovan Waters, writing *The Constructive Trust* two years later, was even more abstract. He advanced at 341–2 just the two abstract categories of 'control of property' and 'holding of an office'. A big problem with this approach is that 'factual categories' are of almost no use in characterising fact situations which arise for the first time. This is where theory

---

[35] 'The Place of Equity and Equitable Remedies in the Contemporary Common Law World' (1994) 110 *LQR* 238, 246.

[36] *The Blue and Brown Books* (1969), 17.

[37] L Sealy 'Fiduciary Relationships' [1962] Camb LJ 69, 74–81 and 'Some Principles of Fiduciary Obligation' [1963] *Camb LJ* 119.

of the relation is most needed: in determining hard cases. A factual approach cannot discriminate between novel fiduciary arguments for which there is no obviously applicable authority. It cannot be used creatively.

## 2. Rule-based descriptions

**[2.13]** Some descriptions assume that a different fiduciary relationship exists for each fiduciary rule. Most 'rule-based' description are like this. They deny that one can generalise beyond the individual fiduciary rules. So, a rule regulating the exercise of directors' discretions is said to generate one kind of relationship and a rule regulating the self-interest of product distributors generates another. There is said to be no point in speculating on the common characteristics in both relationships. Such likenesses are only accidental. Instead, with fiduciaries, we are said to be dealing with self-contained obligations, or 'fiduciary obligations', as Paul Finn described them in 1977. As a mode of classification, 'rule-based descriptions' is only one step less general than the 'factual categories' we have just examined. The central organising principle of 'rule-based descriptions' is not the cases decided; rather, it is those cases divided into the individual fiduciary rules to which they relate. But predictive value is as restricted.

**[2.14]** One of the principal exponents of this 'atomistic' type of theory is Paul Finn.[38] He begins his work *Fiduciary Obligations* with the declaration that:

> the modern usage of 'fiduciary' . . . is not definitive of a single class of relationships to which fixed rules and principles apply. Rather its use has generally been descriptive, providing a veil behind which individual rules and principles have developed.

*Fiduciary Obligations* then makes a primary division of fiduciary rules into 'fiduciary powers' and 'standards of loyalty and fidelity'. 'Powers' are further subdivided into five main rules. 'Standards' are subdivided into eight rules. Description from the perspective of individual rules is really a species of classification, as Finn concedes. 'In the end result', he says at p 2, 'we will be left with categories of fiduciaries.' It is claimed that these categories are not amenable to expansion through the use of analogy. This is because they are rule-specific and the rules must expand first.

> Each category . . . exists only for the purposes of its own particular obligation. A fiduciary for one obligation is *not* ipso facto a fiduciary for all, or indeed any, other obligations.

**[2.15]** Rule-based approaches have a limited usefulness. Categories of fiduciary are only explicable in terms of the rules that apply to fiduciaries. But why do lawyers want to know whether a category exists?—to see whether the rule applies. The question that the rule begs is as big as the one the category begs. To say that the category depends on the rule is to say nothing. Fiduciary rules and fiduciary categories are not concomitant, as Finn's analysis suggests. The category question, or 'who is a fiduciary', is primary. It is this that practical lawyers look to theory for—the thing which Tamar Frankel said must adjust to the condition of post-industrial society (at [2.1]).

---

[38] 'Atomistic' is the description of D De Mott in 'Beyond Metaphor: An Analysis of the Fiduciary Obligation' [1988] *Duke LJ* 879, 915.

### 3. 'Reasonable expectations'

[2.16]   Consider the following description of a fiduciary. Although the possibility of such generalisation had been denied in the earlier *Fiduciary Obligations*, the descriptions are part of a further theory provided by Paul Finn at the end of his 1989 essay, 'The Fiduciary Principle'.[39] 'A person', he says,

> will be a fiduciary in his relationship with another when and insofar as the other is *entitled to expect* that he will act in that other's or in their joint interest to the exclusion of his own several interest. [emphasis added]

The fiduciary idea is like the duty of care. For–

> all one can ask for is a description of a fiduciary—a description which suggests the essence of the fiduciary idea but which is no more precise than is a description of the tort of negligence.

'Reasonable expectations' are proposed as 'the essence' of the fiduciary idea. Doctrine from the United States authorities is developed (pp 33–54): fiduciary relationships as a 'legal phenomenon' are distinguished from fiduciary relationships as a 'factual phenomenon.' In the 'legal' or 'core' fiduciary relationships, it is said, courts find the fiduciary expectation as a matter of course. 'Partnership', 'principal and agent' and 'director and company' are cited (p 33) as within this class. On the other hand, in merely 'factual' or ad hoc fiduciary relationships, the fiduciary expectation is generated by proof of various fiduciary indicia. At pp 46–7 these are said to include the familiar series of 'ascendency', 'influence over another's affairs', 'vulnerability', 'trust', 'confidence' and 'dependency'.

[2.17]   A similar scheme is proposed in 15.2 The Laws of Australia, [14-32]. 'Status-based' and 'fact-based' categories of fiduciary are distinguished. 'Status-based' categories resemble 'legal' categories and they are referred to sometimes as 'nominate'. The idea seems to be that familiar categories of fiduciary can be distinguished by the fact that they have a name. Examples of this type given at [15-25] are trustees, company directors, solicitors, promoters, partners, agents and employees. 'Fact-based' categories are, at [26], said to 'depend on the particular facts of the case and the circumstances governing the relationship between the parties.' No examples are given. Instead, it is said that the answer in any particular case is 'difficult to determine' and three areas of difficulty are listed.

[2.18]   The upshot of the 'legal' and 'factual' distinction seems to be that courts infer the existence of a fiduciary relationship more readily in some cases than in others. Where parties are in a relation which is usually fiduciary, what results is called a 'legal' or 'status-based' relationship. If more has to be shown, the fiduciary relationship which is found is called 'factual', implying that further facts were needed. But then, the troublesome cases are all 'factual'. What we need is a methodology for determining which further facts in these cases can be decisive. It is not useful to dwell on the fiduciary characterisation of 'legal' or 'status-based' categories because the issue is simply not contentious. No one disputes that the partnership relation is a fiduciary one.

---

[39] In Youdan, 1, 54; also see P Finn 'Contract and the Fiduciary Principle' (1989) 12 *UNSWLJ* 76, 93 and 'Fiduciary Law in the Modern World', in McKendrick, 8, 9.

**[2.19]**   Although a 'core', 'legal' or 'status-based' relationship of partnership is a better example of mutual confidence and trust than a particular ad hoc relation in the form of a retail distributorship, both relationships may be found to be fiduciary. 'Reasonable expectations' directs us to the unsurprising fact that courts will require more cogent proof that the retail distributorship has the necessary trust and confidence than the archetypal partnership. The distinction is reminiscent of that between 'presumed' undue influence and 'actual' undue influence: elements of both wrongs may be the same and difference relates only to the burden of proof.[40]

**[2.20]**   Methodology behind the 'reasonable expectations' theory may involve an exercise in relationship 'characterisation'.[41] Whose *interests* does the relationship exist to serve? A mutual interest, or the interests of the beneficiary only? Consider how this might apply to commercial fiduciaries. Their dealings with beneficiaries are almost invariably structured in contract form. Assume that the contracting beneficiary is not under a disability, or under a special susceptibility, and is not acting charitably. Each party to the contract has a separate interest to promote, or a joint interest, if the parties are partners. On 'reasonable expectations' theory, the fiduciary regime is said to be about a particular type of protection for the interests of one of the parties. Interests of the beneficiary in the relationship are said to be entitled to a paramountcy over the interests of the fiduciary.[42] Fiduciaries, the trusted ones, must wholly subordinate their own interests to beneficiaries. Mere 'mediations' between contending interests and the lesser protections afforded by the doctrines of 'unconscionability' and 'good faith' are (at 6–10) dismissed. They fall well short of the 'paramountcy' that fiduciaries ought to give to their beneficiaries' interest.

**[2.21]**   'Reasonable expectations' as a test may function not dissimilarly to 'reasonable foreseeability' in the law of torts. For just as 'reasonable expectations' is proposed as the basis of a duty under equitable principles, 'reasonable foreseeability of risk of injury to others' is the basis of the tortious duty of care. Each test purports to be a legal inference from the facts of a given case. There are echoes of Lord Atkin in *Donoghue v Stevenson*:[43]

> Who, then, in law is my neighbour? The answer seems to be—persons who are so closely and directly affected by my act that I ought reasonably to have them in contemplation.

Both tests are in form extremely general and open-ended—one could almost say, vacuous. Of the tortious test, Glass JA has recently said in *Minister Administering the Environmental Planning and Assessment Act 1979 v San Sebastian Pty Ltd*:[44]

> A recognition has emerged that the foreseeability inquiry . . . raises issues which . . . decline from the general to the particular. The proximity upon which a

---

[40] See *Johnson v Buttress* (1936) 56 CLR 113, 136–7, Dixon J; MGL [1521]–[1523] and below at [8.6].

[41] P Finn 'Fiduciary Principle' in Youdan, 54 and his 'Contract and the Fiduciary Principle' (1989) 12 *UNSWLJ* 76, 85–9.

[42] P Finn 'Fiduciary Principle' in Youdan, 1, 27.

[43] [1932] AC 562, 580.

[44] [1983] 2 NSWLR 268, 295–6.

*Donoghue* type duty rests depends on proof that the defendant and plaintiff are so placed in relation to each other that it is reasonably foreseeable as a possibility that careless conduct of *any kind* on the part of the former may result in damage of *some kind* to the person or property of the latter.

**[2.22]**  Perhaps the analogy could be pursued a little further. An interesting prognostication on the fate of a 'reasonable expectations' test in fiduciary law is suggested by the fate of the 'reasonable foreseeability' test in tort.[45] In the decades which followed *Donoghue v Stevenson*,[46] the 'reasonable foreseeability' idea as the basis of liability became unable to provide a working solution in several classes of case. Most notably, this was in the area of recovery for pure economic loss. 'Reasonable foreseeability' had runaway potential. Authority then emerged which restricted tortious recovery by a further factual inference.[47]

Several variants of 'reasonable foreseeability' developed, depending on which type of duty was alleged to have been breached. In this way, reasonable foreseeability, the test, came to be encumbered with a variety of restrictions— restrictions which had a certain artificiality about them for the fact that they could not be justified in terms of the principle itself. Most recently, Australian authority rationalised the same into the legal control device of 'proximity'. In its original form, 'proximity' as a legal control device was combined with the old reasonable foreseeability formulation as the second part of a two stage test. It seems to have been the work of Deane J, developing it particularly in the cases of *Sutherland Shire Council v Heyman*[48] and *Jaensch v Coffey*.[49] Proximity, as a test of law, may have come initially to augment the 'reasonableness' inference from fact, but had the obvious capacity to supplant it. In *Gala v Preston*, Mason CJ, Deane and McHugh JJ said:[50]

> The requirement of proximity constitutes the general determinant of the categories of case in which common law negligence recognizes the existence of a duty to take reasonable care to avoid a reasonably foreseeable and real risk of injury.

**[2.23]**  A realist, perhaps a cynic, might say that the tortious inference from fact came to be treated as the empty thing it always was. Looking explicitly to policy considerations, 'proximity', the rule of law, can be made more responsive to new and difficult categories of case. This corresponds to the emerging classes of fiduciary relationships. But prediction of liability in these novel cases is then as much a matter of political science as law. This is what is suggested will be the fate of any factual expectations test for fiduciary relations. Fiduciaries' 'expectations' would be unable to provide any more than a rationalisation for determining liability in hard cases. Because it could be applied very broadly to include many undesirable liabilities, a limiting device of law will be needed. Some cognate to 'proximity' for fiduciaries would have to be found.

---

[45]  See J G Fleming *The Law of Torts* 8th ed (1992), chapters 8, 9; M Davies *Torts* (1992), 61–7.

[46]  [1932] AC 562.

[47]  Eg, *Hedley Byrne & Co Ltd v Heller & Partners* [1964] AC 465 (negligent misstatement) and *Caltex Oil (Australia) Pty Ltd v The Dredge 'Willemstadt'* (1976) 136 CLR 529 (negligent acts).

[48]  (1985) 157 CLR 424, 495.

[49]  (1985) 155 CLR 549, 584–5.

[50]  (1991) 172 CLR 243, 253.

Another parallel comparable to 'reasonable expectations' in fiduciary law may exist. This time the field is administrative law: specifically, the implication test for finding that the rules of natural justice apply. The decision of the High Court in *Kioa v West*[51] may mark the same critical point as where 'reasonable foreseeability' was ousted in the tortious duty of care. A 'legitimate expectation' test may, after that case and those which followed it, be imposed directly onto the facts of a case as a rule of law.[52]

### 4. Relationship as instrument

**[2.24]** 'Reasonable expectations', which we have just examined, may eventually function as though the relationship had no content. The legal fiction of 'reasonable expectation' has important remedial corollaries. Fiduciary relationships are just a means to an end—'instruments' to achieve something, justifiable in terms of the end itself. Yet to recognise that a relationship is 'instrumental' is a strange sort of a description. Instrumental description describes a process whereby fiduciary relationships are found so that the gain-based remedies of equity can be used. Courts reasons backwards, as it were, from the desired remedial outcome to a finding about the parties' mutual relation. Relationship is predicated on remedy.

**[2.25]** De Mott is a remedial theorist. In one article she makes a detailed theoretical investigation of the fiduciary obligation, particularly as it is interpreted in the United States, and including some reference to Australian cases. The conclusion is reached that 'instrumental description is the only general assertion about fiduciary obligation that can be sustained.'[53] In fact, she says, the fiduciary obligation is–

> a device that enables the law to respond to a range of situations in which, for a variety of reasons, one person's discretion ought to be controlled because of characteristics of that person's relationship with another.

Characterisation of a relation may be perceived to give access to the gain-stripping remedies of equity. In the words of a Canadian commentator,

> Fiduciary relief is far more powerful (and far more discursive) than a remedy in contract or negligence ... the relief seeks primarily to protect a party owed a duty of utmost good faith from deleterious action by the party owing the fiduciary duty.[54]

**[2.26]** A consequence said to follow from the remedial view is that the fiduciary obligation is 'situation-specific'. There are, it is said, no 'short-cuts' in the judicial task. The facts of each case potentially involving a fiduciary must be appraised in terms of the appropriateness of equitable relief.[55] Or as another remedial theorist says: 'the concept of fiduciary duty is relevant only in terms of remedy'.[56] This would seem to deny even the possibility of general jurisprudence of the fiduciary relation.

---

51  (1985) 159 CLR 550.
52  M Allars *An Introduction to Australian Administrative Law* (1990), [6.19]–[6.26].
53  D De Mott 'Beyond Metaphor: An Analysis of Fiduciary Obligation' [1988] *Duke LJ* 879, 915.
54  M Ellis *Fiduciary Duties in Canada* (1988), 20–2.
55  D De Mott 'Beyond Metaphor: An Analysis of Fiduciary Obligation' [1988] *Duke LJ* 879, 923.
56  J R M Gatreau 'Demystifying the Fiduciary Mystique' (1989) 68 *Can Bar Rev* 1, 17; also G Jones 'Unjust Enrichment and the Fiduciary's Duty of Loyalty' (1968) 84 *LQR* 472.

**[2.27]** Remedial theory may face a logical difficulty, notwithstanding its theoretical austerity. Weinrib put it in these terms:

a definition in terms of the effect produced by the finding of a fiduciary relation begs the question in an obvious way: one cannot both define the relation by the remedy and use the relation as a triggering device for the remedy.[57]

Does it beg the question? The remedial theory of description assumes that a fiduciary relationship is of nature instrumental rather than substantial. There are, according to remedial theory, no substantial attributes to describe, or to define. Quite properly in its own terms, the fiduciary relationship is analysed by what it is an instrument to.

**[2.28]** Remedial theory is sometimes implicit in the caselaw. This sort of approach was taken in 1879, in *Ex parte Dale*.[58] Despite its age, the case involved a commercial insolvency problem of the modern type. A bank had been entrusted as agent to regularly collect certain moneys and send them on to its client. Insolvency of the bank intervened when some of the money had been collected but not sent. The client argued that the entrusting gave rise to a fiduciary relation between itself and the bank, with the client having a consequent right to trace the moneys, its property, into the liquidators' hands. Fry J upheld this—to the degree that the client's money could be 'followed and separated' from the bank's own money. Perhaps because the argument had a little bit of novelty about it, he said at 778,

What is a fiduciary relationship? It is one in respect of which if a wrong arise, the same remedy exists against the wrongdoer on behalf of the principal as would exist against a trustee on behalf of the cestui que trust.

Although this was the unreserved dictum of a (then) first instance judge, it may have represented the intuitive understanding that many judges had of what a fiduciary relationship was. It was a 'remedy-trigger'. The relationship was inferred from the wrongful act of the fiduciary and not anything which preceded it. Deane J (dissenting) in *Hospital Products Ltd v United States Surgical Corporation* said something almost equivalent.[59] He was, he said, 'not persuaded' that a fiduciary relationship existed in a case before him between a product distributor and its supplier. However, where a flagrant breach of contract had occurred, he thought that the factual basis of a fiduciary relationship could be dispensed with altogether. The distributor might be still liable as constructive trustee for profits that it made in flagrant breach of contract. Fiduciary remedies were directly accessible for the injured party. Deane J thought that this flowed from—

the principles under which a constructive trust may be imposed as the appropriate form of equitable relief in circumstances where a person could not in good conscience retain for himself a benefit, which he had appropriated to himself in breach of his contractual or legal or equitable obligations to another.

**[2.29]** Deane J's fiduciary equivalence may be a species of fiduciary instrumentalism. A constructive trust was clearly the desired outcome. Factual

---

[57] E J Weinrib 'The Fiduciary Obligation' (1975) 25 *UTLJ* 1, 5; cf L Sealy 'Fiduciary Relationships' [1962] *CL* 69, 72.

[58] (1879) 11 Ch D 772.

[59] (1984) 156 CLR 41, 124–5: see [8.6].

problems with the orthodox fiduciary relationship stood in its way. So 'principles' of the constructive trust were invoked, although they were not set out. Yet it may be that there are no such 'principles', whereby the victim of a contract-breaker is entitled to a constructive trust over the wrongdoer's gain. That this is true in Anglo-Australian law was confirmed by Gareth Jones in 1991, at pp 83–4 in his *Restitution in Public and Private Law*.

**[2.30]** Two more cases from the United Kingdom instance a latent instrumental theory. Examples of the remedial fiduciary relationships from Canada and the United States are more common.[60] In *English v Dedham Vale Properties Ltd*,[61] a husband and wife negotiated the sale of their home to a property developer. Everyone knew that the price of the property would be affected by what planning approvals could be obtained for it. Before the contract was signed, the developer made a secret planning application as the vendors' 'agent'. News that the application had been successful came to the developer after it had signed the contract, but before settling it. Still the developer maintained secrecy about the application. The vendors discovered what had happened some time after settlement had been completed. They then made claim to the increased value of the land consequent on a successful planning application. The developer was argued to be liable to account in equity for the profit it made by misusing the vendors' names and failing to disclose the outcome of the application. For this some equitable jurisdiction was needed. So the vendors alleged that the developer had misconducted itself 'as a fiduciary'. Slade J upheld this at 110, stating that the relationship had to be a 'fiduciary' one. But in finding that the relationship was fiduciary on the facts, he disregarded authorities cited to him which required the fiduciary element to pre-exist the relevant wrong. Instead, at 111 he held that the fiduciary relationship could sufficiently arise from the developer's misconduct itself—that is, in the absence of undertakings, reliance, property or meaningful discretions at all.

**[2.31]** *Chase Manhattan Bank NA v Israel-British Bank (London) Ltd*[62] is an even more striking example of the occasional insubstantiality of the fiduciary relation. Chase Manhattan was a New York bank which mistakenly paid another New York bank some $2m for the credit of the British bank. Before Chase was able to recover the money, the British bank petitioned the court for a winding-up order. So Chase Manhattan claimed that it was entitled to the money in equity. The liquidator of the British bank was said to be a constructive trustee for it of the sum mistakenly paid and Chase could trace the money into the liquidator's hands. Before upholding this claim, Goulding J noted that the law relating to tracing claims in equity required a fiduciary relationship to exist between the payee and the recipient.[63] This doctrinal requirement was satisfied by his finding at 119 that a fiduciary relationship arose from mere payment into the wrong hands. The fiduciary

---

[60] Eg, (Canada) *Burns v Kelly Peters & Associates Ltd* (1987) 41 DLR (4th) 577 (BCCA); *Plaza Fibreglass Manufacturing ltd v Cardinal Insurance Co* (1990) 68 DLR (4th) 586 (Ont HC); (US) *Jordan v Duff Phelps Inc* 815 F 2d 429 (7th Cir 1987); *Committee on Children's Television Inc v General Foods Corporation* 673 P 2d 660 (SC Ca 1983).

[61] [1978] 1 WLR 93, Slade J.

[62] [1981] Ch 105, Godding J.

[63] At 118–20, citing *Sinclair v Brougham* [1914] AC 398 and *Re Diplock* [1948] 1 Ch 465 (CA).

relation was again the instrument which facilitated the availability of equitable remedies. It was accorded no further status. Lord Denning used an 'instrumental' fiduciary relationship, too, in at least two cases.[64]

## Proposed methodology

[2.32]   We are concerned in this part only with the *trusting* type of fiduciary relationship—the species which has undergone the most dramatic development. There should be several stages to its analysis. The largest question with it is *who* is, or can be, a fiduciary? What are the established (and emerging) pathways of judicial reasoning leading to a fiduciary relationship?

The importance of this central question should not be allowed to obscure the other steps along the way to fiduciary relief. Fiduciary liability is not the simple concomitant of fiduciary status once it is found. For as Frankfurter J observed, in 1943:[65]

> To say that a man is a fiduciary only begins analysis; it gives direction to further inquiry. To whom is he a fiduciary? What obligations does he owe as a fiduciary? In what respects has he failed to discharge those obligations? And what are the consequences of his deviation from duty?

[2.33]   Laskin J in *Canadian Aero Service Ltd v O'Malley*[66] stated the standard issues arising in a fiduciary case in a similar way. Concern, as he expressed it, was first with the constitution of the relationship. Was it a fiduciary one or not? Concern then moved to the scope of the duties owed, thence to breach of the fiduciary duties and, finally, to what ought to be the appropriate remedy. Mason J in *Hospital Products Ltd v United States Surgical Corporation* adopted a similar outline in his dissenting judgment.[67] We will adopt that outline here:

- Does a fiduciary relationship exist?
- What is the scope of the relationship?
- Has the relationship been breached?
- What is the appropriate remedy?

---

64  *Reading v R* [1948] 2 KB 268 (1st instance) and *Phipps v Boardman* [1965] 1 Ch 992 (CA).

65  *Securities and Exchange Commission v Chenery Corporation* 318 US 80 (1943) (SC), 85–6.

66  (1973) 40 DLR (3d) 371, 381 (judgment of the court).

67  (1984) 156 CLR 41, 96, 102, 104, 107, using the words of Laskin J in *Canadian Aero Service Ltd v O'Malley* (1973) 40 DLR (3d) 371, 391.

# Chapter 3

# Existence of a Fiduciary Relationship

**[3.1]** 'Who is a fiduciary?' is a notoriously uncertain question in the private law. Judicial method for determining the answer is quite unsettled, as even is what is relevant to argument on either side. Yet relationships are increasingly found to be of a fiduciary nature. Much has now been written about this. At a very high level of generality one could say that persons in trusting relationships are identified as fiduciaries on account of what they agreed to, undertook, or are taken to have assumed. Beyond that there is no consensus. What a 'trusting relationship' is and what 'taken to have assumed' may include are matters which have virtually defied explanation.

## Accepted categories of relationship

**[3.2]** Fiduciaries of the familiar sort are said to be within the 'accepted categories' of fiduciary relationship. Partners, agents and principals, employers and employees, companies and directors, and solicitors and clients are 'accepted fiduciary relationships' listed by Mason J in *Hospital Products Ltd v United States Surgical Corporation*.[1] To this number one might add trustees and beneficiaries, receivers in bankruptcy and creditors, liquidators and contributories, and a few more. Calling the relationships 'accepted' refers to the fact that the courts accept that they have a fiduciary consequence. Existence of a trusting relationship in these situations is easily established. Accepted categories are situations where courts make a ready inference to the existence of a fiduciary relationship. No more than that is meant. Being 'accepted' does not mean that presumptive effect is given to the relationship. The claim of a beneficiary who stands within an accepted category of relationship is just like the claim of any other fiduciary beneficiary. In this the fiduciary relationship of trust is unlike the relation of influence. A person alleging 'accepted' fiduciary status simply brings the defendant within the court's range of reliable inference—unless special circumstances exist. So, for example, a principal suing an agent who makes a wrongful gain in the course of his or her agency has still to make out a case that the agency was a fiduciary one at the relevant time. Only then will equity provide its remedies to subtract the gain and pass it to the principal. Something of a formality in 'accepted' cases, the existence

---

[1] (1984) 156 CLR 41 at 96.

of a fiduciary relationship stage in the reasoning process is still there.[2] Fiduciary aspects of the relationship must be isolated and precedent cited to justify a fiduciary conclusion. One commentator refers to an 'accepted category' relationship as a fiduciary 'legal phenomenon'.[3] The forensic consequence of this is the same. Courts' fiduciary characterisation of accepted relationship categories may be so much a matter of course that it is virtually a rule of law. When an 'accepted category' of relationship is present on the facts, the claimant need not do much more than present a case based on prima facie evidence.

**[3.3]** Recognition that there are accepted categories of fiduciaries does not take one far towards identifying the non-standard fiduciary relations. Accepted categories serve as a kind of analogical core when reasoning to further categories. But the fact analogies are available does not suggest any directions that the process of inference might take. Nor do the accepted categories supply any limits to the process. The traditional approach to identification of non-accepted categories will now be explained, after some prefatory observations about 'interests'.

### Identification of a fiduciary: 'interests analysis'

**[3.4]** 'Interests' that merit judicial protection are, on one view, the raw material upon which the trusting relationship is based. The phenomenon has been described in this way:

> A fiduciary relationship arises on the concurrence of two factors and the interaction between them. The first is the existence of an interest as a beneficiary in the subject-matter of the alleged trust, of such nature that it merits judicial protection. The second is an interference with that interest by an intervenor who owed the beneficiary a duty to support the interest.[4]

This makes an obvious point, as well as more doubtfully assimilating the fiduciary relationship to a trust. Speaking in terms of 'interests' possessed by beneficiaries objectifies discussion of the relation. The price of this is a little ambiguity, for 'interests' are also the subject of the fiduciary relationship of influence, of the law of torts and much else in the private law. It is difficult to distinguish between the trusting fiduciary relationship and the fiduciary relationship of influence by virtue of the interests each relationship protects: the interests are much the same.

'Interests analysis' is a term which we will use to describe a particular modern approach to the identification of fiduciaries.[5] This is an a priori attempt to make the task of identification easier, by restricting the amount of judgment that the traditional approach involves. The theory starts with an uncontentious assumption. Equity intervenes to sanction the trusted party where a breach of trust or confidence threatens to violate the interests of beneficiaries. A breach of fiduciary duty occurs where the interests of the trusting party have collided

---

2  *United States Surgical Corporation v Hospital Products International Pty Ltd* [1983] 2 NSWLR 157 at 204–5 (CA).
3  See P Finn 'The Fiduciary Principle' in Youdan, 1at 33–41.
4  *Evans v Anderson* (1977) 76 DLR (3d) 482 at 506, Clement JA, Haddad JA agreeing (Alta CA).
5  See, eg, 'Fiduciary Principle' in Youdan, 1 at 3–6; 'Contract and the Fiduciary Principle' (1989) 12 UNSWLJ 76 at 88–96; 'Fiduciary Law' in McKendrick 7 at 8–10.

or threaten to collide with interests of the trusted party. Equity, in these circumstances, will treat the trusted party as though he or she were formally acting on the trusting party's behalf. Dishonest or disloyal behaviour is proscribed. This includes where equity intervenes because of the trusted party's uncommercial handling of the trusting party's interests and where the trusted party has been supine, or negligent as well.[6]

Equity's purpose in promoting the beneficiaries' interests is thought to give shape to the trusting relationship. Its form is thought to be implicit in the interests governed. 'Interests analysis' reasons to the content of fiduciary categories by looking backwards to the scope of the interests which they protect. The idea has an interesting pedigree. It is mainly associated with the United States and the law of torts, in which it has provided a purposive check or 'touchstone' to limit the proliferation of doctrine.[7] For what interests does one want to protect?

> The law protects only those interests of an individual which have social value. It does not protect the factual interest which one may have in doing an act in revenge or hatred or with a desire to harm. Nor does it protect the interest which one may have in achieving an unlawful result or in using unlawful means.'[8]

'Interests analysis' as a mode of fiduciaries reasoning is particularly evident in the North American authorities. The majority judgment of the Supreme Court of Canada in *Cansons Enterprises Ltd v Boughton & Co*[9] assimilated the rules of equitable compensation with the law of tort. This was justified on account of the 'interests protected' by each regime being seen to be identical. The same 'policy considerations' could be applied to both. Reasoning from 'interests protected' and reasoning from the policy of the law is much the same thing.

**[3.5]**   The 'interests analysis' of Paul Finn begins from the premiss of what he calls an 'agreed' concern of the law. This is the imposition of—

> standards of acceptable conduct on one party to a relationship for the benefit of the other where one has a responsibility for the preservation of the other's interests.[10]

The process continues (at 4):

> 'Unconscionability' [the standard] accepts that one party is entitled to as of course act self-interestedly . . . [but] proscribes excessively self-interested or exploitative conduct. 'Good faith' [the standard] . . . qualifies this by positively requiring that party, in his decision and action, to have regard to the legitimate interests therein of the other. The 'fiduciary' standard for its part enjoins one party to act . . . selflessly and with undivided loyalty. There is, in other words, a progression from the first to the third: from selfish behaviour to selfless behaviour.

'Graduated progression' through the standards of 'unconscionability' and 'good faith' is said to lead to the 'fiduciary principle'. Interests of the

---

[6] *Nocton v Ashburton* [1914] AC 932; *McKenzie v McDonald* [1927] VLR 134; *Day v Mead* [1987] 2 NZLR 443: see [6.17]–[6.20].

[7] R Pound 'Interests of Personality' 28 *Harv LR* 343 (1915); W A Seavey 'Principles of Torts' 56 Harv LR 81–7 (1942); K Lipstein 'Protected Interests in the Law of Torts' [1963] *CLJ* 85; J G Fleming *The Law of Torts* 8th ed (1992)3–4.

[8] Ibid, Seavey at 81.

[9] (1991) 85 DLR (4th) 129 at 135–53, LaForest J.

[10] P Finn 'Fiduciary Principle' in Youdan 1 at 2.

fiduciary, or trusted party, are progressively denied along the way. By the time that the fiduciary principle is reached, the fiduciary is said to be obliged to subordinate *all* his or her interests the trusting party. A 'fine loyalty' is said to be required of a fiduciary, to ensure the 'paramountcy' of the beneficiary's interests.

**[3.6]** Interests analysis may have commercial problems. Logical narrowing of a fiduciary's own legitimate interests until they become non-existent is not consistent with the character of the professional fiduciary that we noted at [2.7]. Commercial fiduciaries are always legitimately concerned with their own interests. Fiduciaries' remuneration, their fees and profits may without any disloyalty be the uppermost things in their minds. Compare the quite different 'interests' approach taken by Mason J in *Hospital Products Ltd v United States Surgical Corporation.*[11] Mason J as well as the judge at first instance and the New South Wales Court of Appeal found a fiduciary relationship to exist on facts where the fiduciary was not at all disinterested. A product distributor company and its supplier were involved. Ordinarily in this relationship, a distributor's interest is in its sales margin, while the supplier looks more to sales volume. Financial returns to each party are not produced in the same way. Parties to the relationship have separate interests which do not always coincide. Mason J said at 101:

> Although [the trusted party] was entitled to prefer its own interests to the interests of [the trusting party] in some situations where those interests might come into conflict, this entitlement was necessarily subject to the requirement that [the trusted party] act bona fide and with due regard to the interests of [the trusting party]. In no circumstance could it act solely in its own interests without reference to the interests of [the trusting party].

This sounds more like a business arrangement than a 'fine' or 'selfless' loyalty. Commercial fiduciaries mostly act, as noted, in order to promote interests of their own. From each fiduciary's perspective, their own separate interests may be and usually are the dominant 'purpose' of their entering the relationship.[12] Fiduciaries, as Finn acknowledges, are not expected to be charitable institutions. So lawyers are properly interested in their fees; estate agents are interested in their commissions; bankers are interested in their percentages and so forth. There is no wrong in this. It is how the engine of a capitalist society functions. Why should an 'interests' approach to relationship characterisation deny fiduciary status to relations which contain a healthy self-interest? Commercial fiduciaries who act 'selflessly and with an undivided loyalty' appear to function without commercial motives.

## Traditional identification

### Analogies and purposes

**[3.7]** Anglo-Australian law has traditionally had an empirical approach to the characterisation of facts.[13] In finding whether particular facts fall within one category or another, theory is not relevant. Economics is not relevant. Morals are not relevant. A form of deductive reasoning is employed instead, which

---

11 (1984) 156 CLR 41 at 99–101.
12 Cf P Finn 'Contract and the Fiduciary Principle' (1989) 12 *UNSWLJ* 76 at 87.
13 See *Hallstroms Pty Ltd v FCT* (1946) 72 CLR 634 at 646, Dixon J.

usually permits of direct and simple answers. Assume that a question arises about whether a particular person became auditor of a particular corporation. It is answered by seeing whether that person was appointed by the company in general meeting, or by the Commission pursuant to s 327 of the *Corporations Law*. Judges ask whether the facts of the case exhibit the distinguishing characteristic of the category—in this case, compliance with the legislative formalities for appointment.

Traditional characterisation of whether a particular relation is a fiduciary one proceeds on similar lines. Actual or implicit reference is made to some fiduciary hallmark in the decided cases. Whether the facts of a case fall within the accepted categories of fiduciary is then decided deductively. A person either did or did not serve as a company director, a receiver in bankruptcy, or a solicitor, etc at a particular place and time. There are appropriate tests to establish this. Some of them are statutory. Whether the facts of a case are to fall within a new or emerging category of fiduciary relation is determined inductively. An analogy is made from the accepted categories of fiduciary relationship and/or previously decided cases. Analogy, the familiar technique, the engine of equity's development, is pressed into a service which has been sanctioned over hundreds of years.

**[3.8]** We should pause here. Analogies can be misleading. Quite irrelevant likenesses may establish a common link between two things: sticks of dynamite and candles have several common features. There may be coincidences of shape, size and age that have no bearing on why the two things are being compared. To use a fiduciaries example: whether a particular investment banker is a fiduciary may have nothing to do with his clients' eminence or their level of income. It may not relate to the way the banker dresses or the clubs that he has joined. Yet all these things may be thrown up in an undiscriminating process of analogy moving from bankers who have been found to be fiduciaries to ones who have not.

Some 'criteria of sameness' must exist to control the process of analogy and make it useful. The analogiser must seek one or more common characteristics possessed by each of the subjects being compared. Purpose is the correcting focus. The existence of a purpose in the selection of common characteristics is critical. Analogy without purpose has no direction and will lead to arbitrariness.

*Common characteristics*

**[3.9]** Consider the four following situations where fiduciary relationships have been found to exist. A number of decisions have been based on the theory in each. But remarkably different 'primary characteristics' of the fiduciary relationship are suggested. The first situation is no doubt already familiar.

1. A company was the distributor of certain products in Australia on behalf of an overseas supplier. The distributor was obliged by contract with the supplier to act in its best interests and develop the supplier's market. Contrary to this, the distributor established its own company with a view to pirating the supplier's market position.

**[3.10]** In *United States Surgical Corporation v Hospital Products International Pty Ltd*[14] the New South Wales Supreme Court at first instance

---

[14] [1982] 2 NSWLR 766, McLelland J.

held that this distributor, by doing what it did, was a fiduciary in breach of limited fiduciary relationship with the supplier. The relation found at 811 covered 'such of the supplier's interests as the market represented'—a decision upheld in the New South Wales Court of Appeal, where the significantly enlarged remedy of constructive trust was imposed.[15] Part of its reasoning on that appeal, the Court of Appeal noted of fiduciary characterisation (at 205) that:

> it is necessary to find some criterion which the facts must satisfy. Since, as we have said, any fiduciary relationship which existed here did not fall within any established category, some principle or requirement must be found which is common to all or, at least, most, categories, it being likely that some may represent a particular response to special situations eg the cases of undue influence and confidential information.

The notion of *undertaking* was seen to be this criterion. After noting this to be the view in a number of authorities and commentaries, the court continued at 206:

> it follows that if F has undertaken to act in the interests of B, F will be a fiduciary: and, conversely, a fiduciary relationship cannot exist unless F has undertaken to act in the interest of B, it being understood that such an undertaking precludes F from acting in his own interest in the same matter, that is, in the matter in respect of which the undertaking was given.

'Undertaking' in this formulation is the pivotal element and sine qua non of fiduciary relationships. It may now be something of an orthodoxy in Australia. For when *Hospital Products* reached the High Court on appeal, Gibbs CJ disagreed with the lower courts on the facts, but found that the test proposed by the Court of Appeal was 'not inappropriate in the circumstances'. Mason J in that case proposed a test to determine the existence of a fiduciary relationship which was not much different.[16]

**[3.11]**   The second situation may also be familiar.

2. An army sergeant was on overseas duty. Wearing his army uniform, he on several occasions rode through a city in a truck carrying contraband goods. This was so inspection of the truck by the local police might be evaded. Substantial amounts of money were received by him for these services. In *Reading v R*, the United Kingdom Court of Appeal held that the sergeant was a fiduciary. Being such, Reading was liable to account to the British Crown for moneys he received.[17]

Judgment of the Court of Appeal was given by Asquith LJ. Assuming that a fiduciary relationship was a necessary part of the Crown's case to retain the confiscated moneys, he reasoned at 236 that:

> such a relationship subsisted in this case as to the user of the uniform and the opportunities and facilities attached to it; and that the [sergeant] obtained the sums by acting in breach of the duties imposed by that relation.

This fiduciary relation was a consequence of something entrusted by the trusting party—specifically, (at 236) entrusted *property*, in the sergeant's

---

[15] [1983] 2 NSWLR 157 (CA), curiam: see [6.87].

[16] (1984) 156 CLR 41 at 72, Gibbs CJ; 96–7, Mason J.

[17] *Reading v R* [1949] 2 KB 232, affirming [1948] 2 KB 268, Denning J, on different grounds.

uniform, and an entrusted 'job to be performed'. In this way, the *Reading* fiduciary liability proceeded from a quite different theory from that in the above *Hospital Products* judgments. A different side of the relation is relied upon. For it was the corrupt distributor, the alleged fiduciary, who made the undertaking in *Hospital Products*. In *Reading*, the entrusting was an act of the Crown. The Reading relationship was generated by the party alleging it.

**[3.12]**  The third situation is one of reliance between parties.

3.  Defendant was a finance company. It joined with a promoter and a third company in a joint venture to develop a shopping centre. Prior to the project commencing, and without the knowledge of the third company, the promoter gave the finance company a mortgage over all the joint venture land. This was to secure other borrowing that the promoter had made. The venture proved to be successful. But the finance company claimed a right to enforce that mortgage for the promoter's other borrowing in priority to the third company's profit share. The third company was in danger of missing out, for the finance company had thus taken a prior charge over all the venture's profits. In *United Dominions Corporation Ltd v Brian Pty Ltd* the High Court of Australia held that the finance company was in breach of fiduciary obligation by so doing.[18]

The trusting relation here was characterised by *reliance*. The reliance being that of one party to the joint venture on another. Reliance such as this can be described as being of the 'mutual' kind. All parties to the joint venture relied upon each other. The element of reliance proceeded from each party. In this respect it is unlike both of the foregoing bases of the relationship. For the *undertaking* of the party trusted and the *property* entrusted by the party trusting moved from only one of the parties in each case. Reliance here proceeded from both. 'Mutual confidence' or reliance as a mode of fiduciary reasoning was originally specific to the accepted category of partnership. In this context it is acknowledged in the strongest terms to base a fiduciary characterisation. For example, in *Birtchnell v Equity Trustees Executors and Agency Co Ltd*,[19] Dixon J approved this dictum of Bacon VC in *Helmore v Smith*:

> If a fiduciary relation means anything, I cannot conceive of a stronger case of fiduciary relation than that which exists between partners. Their mutual confidence is the life blood of the concern. It is because they trust one another that they are partners in the first instance; it is because they continue to trust one another that the business goes on.[20]

**[3.13]**  In *United Dominions*,[21] the idea was applied to the analogous joint venture. The fiduciary nature of this association was stated in the joint judgment of Mason, Brennan and Deane JJ, with which Gibbs CJ and Dawson J agreed. Beginning with the note (at 10) that '[T]he term ... joint venture ... is not a technical one with a settled common law meaning', hence no necessary characteristics were implied by the term, the justices concluded (at 10–11) that:

---

[18]  (1985) 157 CLR 1.
[19]  (1929) 42 CLR 384 at 407.
[20]  (1886) 35 Ch D 436, 444 (1st instance, affirmed on appeal).
[21]  (1985) 157 CLR 1.

the most that can be said is that whether or not the relationship between the joint venturers is fiduciary will depend upon the form which the particular joint venture takes and upon the content of the obligations which the parties to it have undertaken.

Characterisation of the relationship was said to depend on the 'form and content' of the venture. Evaluation of the joint venture's contract terms was how the fiduciary question was resolved. Two criteria were selected: first, whether the profits were 'mutual', or to be shared, and secondly, whether, and if so, how the joint venture property was held by the promoter for the other two. The second criterion may beg the question to be determined. What sort of a venture between the mortgagor and the other two was this? If the property was held on trust, then the financier could not do as it did. The first, the profit-sharing or mutuality of gain criterion, was more critical.

**[3.14]**    The judgment of Gibbs CJ in that case was concerned with a further extension of the partnership analogy which the facts required. This was to impose fiduciary obligations at a time prior to the commencement of the joint venture. For this purpose he used two more or less parallel principles:

the 'obligation to perfect fairness and good faith' is not confined to persons who actually are partners, but 'extends to persons negotiating for a partnership, but between whom no partnership as yet exists[22]

and

a person who is negotiating for himself and his future partners as an agent for the intended partnership, and who clandestinely receives an advantage for himself, must account for that advantage to the partnership when it is formed.

Gibbs CJ also referred to the kind of duty to be imposed on one who seeks the 'co-operation' of others. Such a person, 'an intending partner, like a partner, owes a duty of the utmost good faith.'[23] This brand of fiduciary is one of whom reciprocity is expected, not undertakings. No 'property entrusted' is relevant at all. On the facts of the case, the shopping centre property was at all times held by the promoting venturer, which gave the mortgage to the financier. It was never owned or entrusted by the third venturer plaintiff.

**[3.15]**    The fourth situation involves the exercise of discretions.

4. The defendant was the Canadian government. Pursuant to the Indian Act 1952 (Can), a band of Indians had surrendered to the government land from a reserve. This was done so that the government could arrange a lease of the land to a golf club. Terms of the lease obtained by the government were much less favourable than those approved by the band when the land was surrendered. In *Guerin v R* the Supreme Court of Canada found that the government owed a fiduciary duty to the band arising from its control over the use to which the lands could be put.[24]

Power of the Canadian Crown to affect the Indians' interests was the basis of the court's decision in *Guerin*. Courts in Canada particularly have chosen to invest the power characteristic with fiduciary consequences. A fertile source

---

[22] At 5, quoting from *Lindley on Partnership* 15th ed (1984), 480.

[23] At 6, quoting from *Directors Etc of the Central Railway Co of Venezuela v Kisch* (1867) LR 2 HL 99 at 113.

[24] [1984] 2 SCR 335.

of abuses for equity to control is envisaged. It applies where, by exercise of powers (or discretions), the party trusted can alter the legal or practical interests of another.

**[3.16]**   Specifically in *Guerin*, powers under a federal Indian Act 1952 were the source of fiduciary obligations that bound the government. On the majority view (at 348) the Indian Act gave the government a 'historic responsibility' to—

> act on behalf of the Indians so as to protect their interests in transactions with third parties, Parliament has conferred on the Crown a discretion to decide for itself where the Indians' best interests really lie. This is the effect of s 18(1) of the Act. This discretion on the part of the Crown, far from ousting, as the Crown contends, the jurisdiction of the courts to regulate the relationship between the Crown and the Indians, has the effect of transforming the Crown's obligation into a fiduciary one.

This is distinct from each of the other fiduciary bases. The *Guerin* relationship arose unilaterally from the trusted party's possession of a power to affect another, just as though the trusted party had given an undertaking. But no undertaking was necessary. It might have been denied. The relation is more imposed on the trusted party than assumed by him. This fiduciary relation functions more as a tort. It regulates governments, whether they act through federal Departments of Indian Affairs, or otherwise.

**[3.17]**   Looking, therefore, for 'one common characteristic' in fiduciary relationships, the courts have ended up with four. Undertaking, (entrusted) property, reliance and power have been exemplified. There may well be more, for the law of fiduciaries does not at this point seem beyond expansion. To a varying degree, each characteristic has the capacity to explain the others. Quite often, the different characteristics are blended. Consider the somewhat eclectic formulation of Mason J in *Hospital Products Ltd v United States Surgical Corporation.*[25] He said of the 'accepted categories' that:

> The critical feature of these relationships is that the fiduciary undertakes or agrees to act for or on behalf of or in the interests of another person in the exercise of a power or discretion which will affect the interests of that other person in a legal or practical sense. The relationship between the parties is therefore one which gives the fiduciary a special opportunity to exercise the power or discretion to the detriment of that other person who is accordingly vulnerable to abuse by the fiduciary of his position.

Mason J's formulation thus incorporates both the 'undertaking' characteristic, used by the New South Wales Court of Appeal in that case, and the Canadian 'power or discretion' formulation of Wilson J in *Frame v Smith.*[26] He continued:

> The expressions 'for', 'on behalf of', and 'in the interests of' signify that the fiduciary acts in a representative character in the exercise of his responsibility'

**[3.18]**   The judgment of Dawson J in *Hospital Products* also mentions the difficulty of 'identifying and classifying those qualities in individual

---

[25] (1984) 156 CLR 41 at 96–7.
[26] In terms strikingly similar to those she used: (1987) 42 DLR (4th) 81, 99 (SC).

relationships which give rise to fiduciary obligations'.[27] He states at 142 that there is –

> the notion underlying all the cases of fiduciary obligation that inherent in the nature of the relationship itself is a position of disadvantage or vulnerability on the part of one of the parties which causes him to place reliance upon the other and requires the protection of equity acting upon the conscience of that other.

Dawson J cites for this the authority of *Tate v Williamson*.[28] This is a case usually referred to in the context of its 'undue influence' facts. A harsh bargain was extracted by a moneylender from a financially distressed heir. This was the context in which the 'disadvantage or vulnerability' quality was relevant. Another type of fiduciary relationship was present: the fiduciary relationship of influence. One distinguished commentator has argued that the reasoning of Lord Chelmsford LC in that case was really about the trusting relation, because it is based in the moneylender's 'undertaking'.[29] Undue influence, disadvantage and vulnerability will all be irrelevant in this event. Disadvantage or vulnerability, in fact, may either be (unstated) corollaries of 'power or discretion', or, with respect, a doctrinal mistake. The fiduciary relation of trust has been confused with the fiduciary relation of influence. Yet the element of 'vulnerability' is bracketed with 'reliance' in innumerable United States and Canadian authorities. Possibly the suggestion is that reliance implies vulnerability. It should be remembered that the paradigm of reliance was noted above as the relation which subsists between equal partners. The matter is one which will require further investigation below.

**[3.19]** Testing the traditional approach through a selection of cases, there are signs of serious inconsistency. No definition of the 'fiduciary relationship' is forthcoming. 'One common element' looks like several. Each of the 'common' elements we have seen resists explanation in terms of each other. What is contended now is that the confusion is implicit in the traditional approach. This, though, is still the approach of many commentators. J C Shepherd, for example, considers that the academic task is to–

> define the central concept being used when we identify any concept being used when we identify any relationship or duty as 'fiduciary'.[30]

Or, as put by another, there must be an 'element common to and thus definitive of all those situations which produce the fiduciary'.[31] This is the type of reasoning which we have called 'definitional'. It supposes that when the term 'fiduciary' is applied to different categories of relationship, there must be some subsisting common element, a 'golden thread', which unites them. Perhaps a majority of judges share this view—although it is not commonly articulated. The existence of a common element may be assumed in the search for definitions. However, it should not be thought that the view is universal. The judgment of Gibbs CJ in *Hospital Products Ltd v United States Surgical*

---

[27] (1984) 156 CLR 41 at 142.

[28] (1866) 2 Ch App 55 at 60–1.

[29] W Winder (1940) 4 *Convey* (NS) 274 at 282.

[30] J G Shepherd 'Towards a Unified Conception of Fiduciary Relationships' (1981) 97 LQR 51 (opening line); see also his *Law of Fiduciaries* (1981) pp 3–12.

[31] D S Ong 'Fiduciaries: Identification and Remedies' (1986) 8 U of *Tas L Rev* 311 at 315.

*Corporation* does not seem to share it.[32] Nor does it follow from the approach of the Canadian Supreme Court in *Canadian Aero Services Ltd v O'Malley*.[33]

### 'Family resemblances'

**[3.20]**    Difficulties of logic with the traditional understanding of fiduciary relationships may be part of a wider problem in the philosophy of language. General terms used in any discourse may not function in the same way as specific ones. Ludwig Wittgenstein propounds a view which would emphatically deny the logical premises which we have alluded to. A general concept, such as 'fiduciary relationship', would not, for him, entail the existence of any 'common element' when it is used.[34] This is the epistemology of the ancients. Searching for the common properties of general terms is a facile search for easy answers. It yields no useful knowledge. Rather, general terms entail nothing more than a series of 'family resemblances' between their particular instances.[35] 'Men', he says 'have a craving for generality':

> There is [a] tendency to look for something in common to all the entities which we commonly subsume under a general term. We are inclined to think that there must be something in common to all games, say, and that this common property is the justification for applying the general term 'game' to the various games.; whereas games form a *family* the members of which have family likenesses. Some of them have the same nose, others the same eyebrows and others again the same way of walking; and these likenesses overlap. The idea of a general concept being a common property of its particular instances connects up with other primitive, too simple, ideas of the structure of language. It is comparable to the idea that *properties* are *ingredients* of the things which have the properties; eg. that beauty is an ingredient of all beautiful things as alcohol is of beer and wine.

**[3.21]**    When this is related to the 'who is a fiduciary?' question, it suggests that no one of the elements of 'undertaking', 'property', 'reliance' and 'power' should be expected in every fiduciary relationship. Some relationships, of course, may have several of these elements in common. The facts of the *Hospital Products Ltd v United States Surgical Corporation*[36] relationship had features in common with the 'undertaking' and 'power' based relationships, cited by Mason J (at 96–7), and the 'reliance' based relationships, cited by Dawson J (at 142). When other relationships are placed side by side they may appear to have virtually no common features. Consider what the fiduciary relationship found in *Reading v R* (the army sergeant entrusted with the Crown's 'property')[37] had in common with the fiduciary relationship in Guerin v R (the Indian band liable to the government's 'power').[38] Are both cases talking about the same thing? So it may be that there is no essential undertaking, or property entrusted, or any other element, separately or in combination, to be uncovered in each fiduciaries case. Judging such a case, or

---

[32] (1984) 156 CLR 41 at 67–75.

[33] (1973) 40 DLR (3d) 371, curiam (Laskin J), discussed at [3.83]–[3.86].

[34] See L Wittgenstein *Preliminary Studies for the Philosophical Investigations Generally Known as 'The Blue and Brown Books'* (B Blackwell edn 1969) pp 17–19; cf *Tractatus Logico-Philosophicus* tr D F Pears and B F McGuiness (Routledge edn 1974), ¶3.322–¶3.325.

[35] *Blue and Brown Books*, 17.

[36] (1984) 156 CLR 41.

[37] [1949] 2 KB 232 (CA).

[38] [1984] 2 SCR 335 (Can SC).

arguing it, is therefore not easy. No key is easily found to what Mason J described as the fiduciary 'gateway to relief in specie'.[39]

**[3.22]** Perhaps the facts of a novel case should be examined with one primary question in mind. Can the facts justify an analogy from any of the fiduciary characteristics drawn from previous cases? Fiduciary characterisation is a substantial exercise of legal judgment. No necessarily right or wrong answer to the question will appear. A judicial determination must be made of what is an acceptable degree of resemblance. Four primary characteristics are offered here: undertaking, property, reliance and power. A 'resemblances' approach built on these characteristics may be conformable to the newly result-oriented jurisprudence of equity in overseas jurisdictions. Policy considerations consulted by the House of Lords in *Barclays Bank plc v O'Brien*[40] and *CIBC Mortgages plc v Pitt*[41] and the Canadian Supreme Court in *Canson Enterprises Ltd v Boughton & Co*[42] and *Norberg v Wynrib*[43] can serve as an express direction in the formation of fiduciary analogies. Fiduciary characterisation may only be made if it advances a judicial purpose. This is doctrinally possible, though, only within the boundaries of acceptable resemblance. It is the purpose of this chapter to describe those boundaries.

**[3.23]** The resemblances methodology is not new. A little theoretical flexibility in the conception of a fiduciary has been suggested, that is all. Courts, or some courts, have been using a similar approach for some time: closely analysing the facts of a case while keeping in mind various identified criteria. In *Hospital Products Ltd v United States Surgical Corporation* these were the criteria described by Gibbs CJ as relevant 'circumstances' to be considered, in making the fiduciary characterisation. Was there a 'relation of confidence' [ie trust], he asked, or any 'inequality of bargaining power'? What was the effect of the relationship being argued for in a 'commercial transaction'?[44] Fiduciary status was denied on the combination of these circumstances. Mason J, in the same case, rather eclectically listed eight 'factors' and came to the opposite conclusion.[45] Namely—

> (1) there [being] a valuable market for USSC's products in Australia [viz an *interest* at stake]; (2) USSC, by appointing HPI, *entrusted* HPI with the exclusive responsibility of promoting that market . . . (3) the manner in which the market was to be promoted was left to HPI's discretion [viz a *power or discretion*]; (4) the exercise of that discretion provided HPI with a special opportunity of acting to the detriment of the market for USSC's products, rendering USSC *vulnerable* to abuse by HPI . . . ; (5) [no agency of HPI for USSC]; (6) although HPI's actions would not alter or affect USSC's legal rights vis-a-vis others, its actions could and did adversely affect in a practical sense the market in Australia for USSC's products and consequently its product goodwill in this country [viz an *adverse legal or practical effect*]; (7) in the circumstances mentioned in (1-6) above USSC relied on

---

[39] *Hospital Products* (1984) 156 CLR 41 at 100.

[40] [1994] 1 AC 180 at 188–9, Lord Browne-Wilkinson, other Lords agreeing.

[41] [1994] 1 AC 200 at 211, Lord Browne-Wilkinson, other Lords agreeing.

[42] (1991) 85 DLR (4th) 129 at 155–6, Sopinka J; 146–9, LaForest J, other JJ agreeing.

[43] (1992) 92 DLR (4th) 449 at 287–93, McLachlin J.

[44] (1984) 156 CLR 41 at 69.

[45] At 98–9; cf 'factors' in *Canadian Aero Service Ltd v O'Malley* (1973) 40 DLR (3d) 371, 391, Laskin J (judgment of the court).

HPI to protect and promote USSC's product goodwill in Australia [viz *reliance*]; (8) [market responsibility subject to contract term] [emphasis added]

Several of these factors have 'family resemblance' potential in terms of the criteria of undertaking, entrusted property, reliance and power suggested.

**[3.24]**   The methodology of fiduciary 'resemblances' can accommodate itself to another conception of the trusting element in the relation between two parties. It may take two forms. Either the beneficiary actually trusts the other, or the beneficiary possesses a legally protected right to trust. Whether the beneficiary actually trusts the fiduciary is not critical. He or she can still be in a 'structure of trust' and have a right to trust. Either 'trust in fact' or the 'right to trust' have as their subject one or more of the beneficiary's interests. In structure, a fiduciary relationship resembles many other relationships recognised by law. One party's interests are under the control of another as, say, one's vehicle might be under the control of a vehicle-repairer, or one's children's education under the control of their teachers. Sometimes the controlling party is trusted and sometimes not. To the degree that the features of a relation resemble the features of relationships in earlier cases found to be fiduciary, the relation is fiduciary. The matter is one of evaluation. Its boundaries are those of acceptable analogy. Just as legal discourse never contains 'essences', except as a figure of speech, there is no essence in the fiduciary relation. It is just another form of language. Theories which attempt to draw rigorous distinctions between verbal phenomena on a scientific paradigm are destined to produce endless inconsistency.[46] Language is more like fashion than the data of science. No a priori characterisation of the fiduciary relation from within the kaleidoscopic variety of human interaction is possible. Nor should formal classification of persons' 'interests' be expected to yield a more precise result.

In an empirical way, we have gathered below under four headings the salient criteria of characterisation used in modern fiduciaries cases. Analogical possibilities of 'undertaking', 'entrusted property', 'reliance' and 'power' are investigated. Workings of each criterion are then illustrated by specific commercial relations. Relations like trusts, partnership or solicitor and client have not been chosen. It would be obvious to say that fiduciary relations deriving from trusts are based in trustees' undertakings, or that partners are fiduciaries for each other because of a mutual reliance. Instead, the illustrations for each characteristic are chosen because they are problematic. First, however, three more general points will be made.

*Multiple resemblance*

**[3.25]**   Fiduciary relationships may be identified, we say, by showing that the characteristics of any one criterion exist on particular facts. Reliance, therefore, may form a sufficient basis for a fiduciary relationship. Or, one party may have undertaken something to the other. Sometimes the characteristics of several criteria are combined in the same case. We saw how *Hospital Products* evinced this phenomenon.[47] Relationships can be fiduciary for more than one reason. So reliance can be combined with undertaking. In fact, an undertaking

---

[46]  See L Wittgenstein *Blue and Brown Books* (1969) pp 16–21.
[47]  (1984) 156 CLR 41; see [3.17]–3.18].

by the fiduciary can usually be spelt out of the dealings of commercial fiduciaries. Any person who knowingly assumes a role where another trusts him, or the control of another's property or interests, can be said to have undertaken the obligations of so doing. Partnerships are an example. Partners undertake a responsibility towards the promotion of a mutual interest which includes the interest of another. Such an undertaking could form the basis of a fiduciary relationship between partners. Yet the courts have long chosen to articulate the fiduciary nature of this relation by the characteristic of reliance instead.[48] Deciding which resemblance in a relation is the salient, or outstanding, one is part of the exercise of judgment. Cases can be justified in more than one way. Alternative justifications may just be different, rather than wrong.

### Contract terms

[3.26]   Although the Privy Council has recently said that the 'essence' of a fiduciary relationship is that 'it creates obligations of a different character from those deriving from the contract itself',[49] evaluation of contract terms between the parties is still the primary consideration in determining whether a relation is fiduciary.[50] If there is a contract, and the contract allocates rights and duties between its parties, then fiduciary characterisation may be simple. One or other of the criteria may be clearly attracted. For example, sufficient evidence of a real estate agent's undertaking to serve the vendor's interests will usually exist in the terms of a retainer agreed between the parties. Or a partnership deed may make mutual reliance unequivocal. Somewhat less clearly, a disqualifying factor may arise from the terms of a contract. For example, in *Rickel v Schwinn Bicycle Co*[51] a reliance-based fiduciary relation was argued to exist between a bicycle supplier and its dealer. It was said to be negatived by terms of the dealership agreement which indicated that there was no exclusivity on either side of the transaction and that any profits made were non-mutual.

[3.27]   Interrelation of fiduciary relations and contract is a difficult thing to generalise about. There have been dicta in effect treating a fiduciary relationship as subordinate to anything agreed.[52] Certainly where parties are bound by contract, and the contract is breached, the appropriate remedy for a wrong described by the breach derives from the contract itself. Contracts must be enforced. Otherwise the value of the institution will be eroded.[53] A fiduciary relationship should, it is said, 'accommodate' itself to a contract between the parties, in the sense of being consistent with it.

> The fiduciary relationship cannot be superimposed on the contract in such a way as to alter the operation which the contract was intended to have according to its true construction.[54]

---

[48] Eg, Dixon J in *Birtchnell v Equity Trustees Executors and Agency Co Ltd* (1929) 42 CLR 384 at 407–9 and cases there cited.

[49] *Re Goldcorp Exhange Ltd* [1994] 2 All ER 806 at 821 (PC).

[50] P Finn 'Contract and the Fiduciary Principle' (1989) 12 *UNSWLJ* 76 at 89–92.

[51] See 144 Cal Rptr 732 (1983): see further [3.49].

[52] Eg, *United Dominions Corporation v Brian Pty Ltd* (1985) 157 CLR 1, 11, Mason, Brennan, Deane JJ; *Noranda Australia Ltd v Lachlan Resources NL* (1988) 14 NSWLR 1, 17, Bryson J.

[53] *Peso Silver Mines Ltd v Cropper* (1966) 58 DLR (2d) 1, 8; *Jirna v Mister Donut of Canada* (1971) 22 DLR (3d) 639, 644–6.

[54] *Hospital Products Ltd v United States Surgical Corporation* (1984) 156 CLR 41, 97, Mason J.

**[3.28]** This raises the traditional competence of equity and its rules in the face of the common law. It is not the subject of any serious dispute. The common law of contract will have priority over equitable obligations to the extent that both regimes apply to the same facts. This was discussed by Brennan J in *Daly v Sydney Stock Exchange Ltd*.[55] A loan was made by a client to a stockbroker personally, in circumstances where the broker had acted in breach of fiduciary duty. It was held that the fiduciary remedy of a constructive trust over the loan proceeds should not be allowed because an underlying loan contract had not been avoided. A common law debtor-creditor relationship excluded fiduciary relations so long as it subsisted. Brennan J cited principles stated in *Latec Investments Ltd v Hotel Terrigal Pty Ltd*.[56] In that case, mortgaged property was improperly sold by the mortgagee to a company associated with it. Although the mortgagee had been entitled to sell when it did, the mode of the sale gave the mortgagor a right to have the transaction set aside. For priority purposes, it was argued by the mortgagor that equity would at all times accord it an interest in the property and one in priority to property interests created by the purchaser. This was not accepted. Particularly in Kitto J's analysis, the beneficial interest in the property sold was ascertainable by the contract of sale, until it was set aside. Contract was primary. It was not overreached by equity.

So transactions with a fiduciary may not be set aside, or claims made to an enrichment in the fiduciary's hands, until a relevant contract between the parties is rescinded. This is a matter of significance in relation to remedies, as well as to our present concern with the existence of a fiduciary relation. Remedies for breaches of fiduciary relationship are necessitated by hidden frauds, impositions and profiteering under the surface of contracts.[57] Legal structures of business are not threatened. They are reinforced. Two more directed questions arise here.

*Can the existence of a fiduciary relation be negatived by express contract term?*

**[3.29]** Pre-emption or overriding of an equity court's characterisation of a specific relation is not normally enforceable. Parties might agree, though, to exclude themselves from the protection of equity. A number of principles are applicable here. First, liability for fraud at law cannot be excluded by contract term. As Lord Shaw said in *Boyd and Forrest v Glasgow & South Western Railway Co*:[58]

> ... it is a sound principle ... that the terms of a contract, however far they may extend in putting a burden of risks and speculations upon the contractor, cannot be founded on as a protection from fraud of either contracting party.

Secondly, fiduciary obligations involve equitable fraud, a widely defined term which includes negligence.[59] Thirdly, it is clear that liability for the negligent

---

[55] (1986) 160 CLR 371 at 389–90.
[56] (1965) 113 CLR 265 at 277–8, Kitto J.
[57] L Sheridan *Fraud in Equity* (1957) pp 189–92.
[58] [1915] SC (HL) 20 at 35–6, Lord Shaw; also *S Pearson & Son Ltd v Dublin Corporation* [1907] AC 351.
[59] L Sheridan *Fraud in Equity* (1957) pp 115–16 and 169–72, citing *Nocton v Lord Ashburton* [1914] AC 932 at 953–4, Lord Herschell.

type of equitable fraud is excludable by contract.[60] Fourthly, if a fiduciary discloses to the trusting party that he has already breached a fiduciary duty, a trusting party with knowledge can consent to or ratify the breach. Fifthly, the trusting party might agree to give the same consent to the breach in advance. Some fiduciary duties implied by law may be contractually waivable.[61]

**[3.30]** In theory at least, a contract term might exclude liability for breach of a particular fiduciary duty. It might be arguable that terms to a similar effect should be implied in an appropriate case. However, courts would be slow to give such provisions the effect that a fiduciary might intend for them. On contractual principles, it would need to be shown that the beneficiary, at the time of agreeing, knew the material facts with sufficient particularity to make an informed waiver or consent. Drafting a waiver clause to cover more than the simplest breaches of fiduciary duty would be difficult. Ignoring the fact that distribution agreements are usually drafted by suppliers, consider what sort of clause would be needed for the supplier to waive in advance the *Hospital Products* type of wrong.[62] That is, a claim by a supplier that a distributor appropriated its market. Comparable problems have arisen with the sufficiency of directors' interest declarations for the purposes of 'interested director' company articles.[63] Contract terms at most might be allowed to negative some particular fiduciary obligation otherwise obtaining. A company's articles of association, for example, might include a provision that a fiduciary director should be remunerated at a certain rate. This perhaps was what was meant by Lord Herschell's dictum in *Bray v Ford* that:

> It is an inflexible rule of a Court of Equity that a person in a fiduciary position . . . is not, *unless otherwise expressly provided*, entitled to make a profit.[64] [emphasis added]

## Can a fiduciary relationship be imposed by contract term?

**[3.31]** Just as parties cannot decide to attract equitable jurisdiction by agreement, they may be unable to impose fiduciary relationships on themselves. For courts will not readily enforce a contractual pre-emption of judicial discretion to characterise a relation as fiduciary or not. It is for the court and not the parties to decide upon intervention. The building contractor in *Mac-Jordan Construction Ltd v Brookmount Erostin Ltd (in rec)*[65] recently became liable to this tendency. He was not permitted to obtain the insolvency advantages which flow from fiduciary status by the device of making a developer hold project retention moneys 'as fiduciary'.

The question also arose in *Noranda Australia Ltd v Lachlan Resources NL*,[66] where the court was concerned with construction of the assignment conditions

---

[60] *Re City Equitable Fire Insurance Co Ltd* [1925] Ch 407 (CA); in *Hedley Byrne & Co Ltd v Heller & Partners Ltd* [1964] AC 465 at 486, Lord Reid; 500–1, Lord Morris; 508–9, Lord Hodson and 518–19, Lord Devlin.

[61] A Anderson 'Conflicts of Interest: Efficiency, Fairness and Corporate Structure' 25 *UCLA Law Review* 738 (1978) at 755–6.

[62] (1984) 156 CLR 41.

[63] Ford [1509]–[1514] and the Corporate Law Reform Act 1992 (Cth), ss 243LA–243MA.

[64] [1896] AC 44 at 51–2.

[65] [1992] BCLC 350 at 356–7, Scott LJ (CA).

[66] (1988) 14 NSWLR 1, Bryson J.

of a joint venture agreement. A continuing venturer argued that a venturer assigning its interest was in breach of fiduciary duty by failing to observe an applicable term. On the face of things, this looked like a mixture of obligations. Existence of the fiduciary duty was based on a provision of the agreement that the 'general nature' of obligations created should 'be fiduciary in nature and neither [venturer] shall act in a manner calculated to derive an unfair advantage from the joint venture at the expense of the other.'

It was held that this general implication of a fiduciary relation between the parties did not affect the assignment conditions. Assignment was a matter involving construction of the agreement only. The 'scope' of the fiduciary relation was 'ordinarily to be expected' to be 'in relation to a defined area of conduct'—areas of 'mutual concern'. This exempted the separate property interests of the venturers in their shares. Bryson J's analysis expressly adverted to the characteristic of reliance as the appropriate criterion of a joint venture relation, citing the reliance paradigm of *Birtchnell v Equity Trustees, Executors and Agency Co Ltd*.[67]

### Commercial and 'arm's length' transactions

**[3.32]** Is it inherent in the nature of commercial relations that they should not be fiduciary? This was long thought to be the case and we examined the rationale of such a proposition in Chapter 1. *Keith Henry & Co Pty Ltd v Stuart Walker & Co Pty Ltd*[68] is an authority which exemplifies this once orthodox thinking. A licensed importer of hog casings claimed to have been wronged when one of the firms it supplied obtained an import licence in its own name. The importer alleged that a fiduciary relationship between the parties had thereby been breached and the firm should be debarred from enjoying the licence. However, the court said of this allegation that:

> there is no room here for the application of any [fiduciary] rule. It cannot be suggested that the plaintiff and the defendant at any stage stood in any fiduciary relationship to the other. The position is simply that business men—or business firms—were engaged in ordinary commercial transactions with each other, dealing with each other, as the saying goes, at arm's length.[69]

**[3.33]** Three members of the High Court majority in *Hospital Products Ltd v United States Surgical Corporation* were also influenced by the 'commerce excludes the fiduciary' canon, but they stopped short of endorsing it fully.[70] Wilson J said (at 118–19):

> In a commercial transaction of the kind here under consideration where the parties are dealing at arm's length and there is no credible suggestion of undue influence, I am reluctant to import a fiduciary obligation.

Dawson J observed at 149 that 'to invoke the equitable remedies sought in this case ... would be to introduce confusion and uncertainty into commercial dealings.' Gibbs CJ was less circumspect. The commerciality point was central to his determination of the case. After rejecting the supplier's (unlikely)

---

[67] (1929) 42 CLR 384, cited at 15: generally on joint ventures, see [3.90]–[3.96].

[68] (1958) 100 CLR 342.

[69] At 350–1, Dixon CJ, McTiernan J and Fullagar J; also *Jones v Bouffier* (1911) 12 CLR 579 at 599–600, 605; *Dowsett v Reid* (1912) 15 CLR 695 at 705 and *Para Wirra Gold & Bismouth Mining Syndicate NL v Mather* (1934) 51 CLR 582 at 592.

[70] (1984) 156 CLR 41.

position of inequality with its distributor as the basis of a fiduciary characterisation, he said:

> the fact that the arrangement between the parties was of a purely commercial kind and that they had dealt at arm's length and on an equal footing has consistently been regarded by the Court as important, if not decisive, in indicating that no fiduciary relationship arose.

**[3.34]** The antinomy that Gibbs CJ suggests, between commerce and fiduciary relations, is contended never to have existed and not to do so now. 'Accepted' partnership and agency categories of fiduciary relationship have been conceived to exist between merchants for centuries. Now the majority of all kinds of fiduciary relations coming before the courts are commercial.[71] Persons in business are relied upon to keep faith and sometimes this confidence is not honoured. Commercial partnerships, dealerships, mercantile agencies and other such relations are institutions, as it were, expressing the trust of parties dealing within and through them. Banking is similar. It was recently said that–

> the whole global banking system works on trust. Every day we take each other's unsecured credit pledges for vast amounts. This system has stood the test and is based on the expectation that another bank will 'do the right thing' and honour its obligations. Naive maybe, but given the minute by minute volume of interbank transactions that occur, it is clearly not possible to formally and fully document each transaction.[72]

**[3.35]** What about the metaphors of 'at arm's length' and 'on an equal footing'? Are not transactions described by these phrases also held to be of a non-fiduciary nature? It is suggested here that both terms are essentially vacuous. No identifiable category or quality is highlighted by them. They are just a value judgment. Consider the following series of transactions involving commercial fiduciaries: banking, buying a business, distributing a branded product and using a broker to sell shares. To say of each transaction in the series that the parties to it are 'arm's length' does not indicate any feature they have in common. It is only a rationalisation of why fiduciary characterisation was once denied for each.

The same rationalisation often combines the descriptions 'commercial', 'arm's length' and 'on an equal footing'. Together they are ways of expressing the conclusion that a given relationship is not fiduciary because it does not satisfy the fiduciary criteria. The terms are not themselves criteria. A similar point has been made by J Lehane in 'Fiduciaries in a Commercial Context' in P Finn (ed) *Essays in Equity*.[73]

**[3.36]** Undertaking is the criterion which is most commonly referred to when the language of 'commercial' or 'arm's length' disqualification is used. It was

---

71. See R Flanigan 'The Fiduciary Obligation; (1989) 9 *Ox Jo Legal Studies* 285, 305 and dicta in *Bluecorp Pty Ltd (in liq) v ANZ Executors & Trustee Co Ltd* (1994) 13 ACSR 386, 399 Mackenzie J (SC (Qld)).

72. (Unnamed) delegate to the *Banking Law and Practice* 9th Annual Conference (1992), *Proceedings*, at 332–3.

73. At 104, noting, in a way that eludes the writer, how Deane J makes this 'very clear' in *Hospital Products Ltd v United States Surgical Corporation* (1984) 156 CLR 41 at 122–3.

used implicitly in *Keith Henry & Co Pty Ltd v Stuart Walker & Co Pty Ltd*[74] and was the 'common denominator' of majority High Court judgments in *Hospital Products Ltd United States Surgical Corporation*.[75] Parties to a relationship are perceived to be acting for themselves and not assuming to act for the others. When an undertaking by its alternative name of 'representative element' is denied, the expression 'arm's length' will also describe the transaction which results. It is not fiduciary, but no specific disqualification of it is implied. See how the High Court majority in *Hospital Products Ltd v United States Surgical Corporation* distinguished the reasoning of the New South Wales Court of Appeal in *United States Surgical Corporation v Hospital Products International Pty Ltd*. The Court of Appeal had found a fiduciary relation to exist between the distributor HPI and its supplier USSC. It was held by the majority that in the absence of an implied term in the contract between the parties about HPI not harming USSC's market in Australia, the 'representative element' assumed by HPI lost its basis. 'Arm's length', as an epithet, was then used by each member of the majority to describe the type of relation which resulted.[76]

**[3.37]**    When 'reliance' is the criterion for a fiduciary relation, a finding of an 'arm's length' transaction functions similarly. 'Arm's length' dealings usually follow where the presence of reliance in a situation has been either factually denied;[77] or the 'reasonable expectation' that the claimant might have protected its interest by contract has not been met. On the relation between the 'arm's length' metaphor and the 'contractual' expectation, see the judgment of Sopinka J in *Lac Minerals Ltd v International Corona Resources Ltd* (McIntyre and Lamer JJ agreeing).[78] That part of the fiduciary reasoning of Dawson J in *Hospital Products Ltd v United States Surgical Corporation* which was based on the 'reliance' criterion is comparable.[79] 'Power' as a criterion makes similar use of the metaphors. 'Power' analysis may treat an 'arm's length' attribution as likely to flow from a situation where a contract might have been expected, but has not resulted.[80] Again, the 'arm's length' epithet is quite inconsequent. 'Arm's length' and 'commercial' descriptions of a relation subject to fiduciary characterisation cannot be expected to stand in the way where the court bases its reasoning on 'instrumental' considerations. Where a fiduciary relationship is inferred to satisfy doctrinal requirements, no factual consideration can displace it.[81] The metaphors are equally irrelevant to the 'remedial' fiduciary relation. If a particular outcome is desired, the rationalisations are not wanted.[82] The entire exercise is result-oriented.

---

[74] (1958) 100 CLR 342 at 350–1.

[75] (1984) 156 CLR 41 at 71–2, Gibbs CJ; 96–7, Mason J; 122, Deane J; 142, Dawson J; 116, Wilson J.

[76] (1984) 156 CLR 41, on appeal from [1983] 2 NSWLR 157 (CA): at 70, Gibbs CJ; 118, Wilson J; 149, Dawson J.

[77] *James v Australia and New Zealand Banking Group Ltd* (1986) 64 ALR 347 at 391, Toohey J.

[78] [1989] 2 SCR 574 at 607–8 (Can SC).

[79] (1984) 156 CLR 41 at 142.

[80] *Lac Minerals* [1989] 2 SCR 574 at 607–8, Sopinka J (Can SC).

[81] As in *E Pfeiffer Weinkellerei-Weinenkauf Gmbh v Arbuthnot Factors Ltd* [1988] 1 WLR 150 and *English v Dedham Vale Properties Ltd* [1978] 1 WLR 93.

[82] See, eg, *Deonandan Prashad v Janki Singh* (1916) LR 44 Ind App 30 (PC) and *Plaza Fibreglass Manufacturing Ltd v Cardinal Insurance Co Ltd* (1990) 68 DLR (4th) 586.

# Fiduciary characteristics

## 1. UNDERTAKING

[3.38] This is probably the most accepted characteristic of commercial fiduciary relationships in Australia. Identification of fiduciary status is based in a representation by one party that he or she will act on behalf of another, or in that party's best interests. It is analogous to the express trustee's acceptance of trusteeship. Austin Scott, writing in 1949, thought that the nature of a fiduciary could be expressed in these terms:[83]

> Who is a fiduciary? A fiduciary is a person who undertakes to act in the interests of another person. It is immaterial whether the undertaking is in the form of a contract. It is immaterial that the undertaking is gratuitous.

Or, as another has said, 'a fiduciary' is 'simply someone who undertakes to act for or on behalf of another in some particular matter or matters.'[84]

The *undertaking* conception of the relationship has its genesis in the acceptance by one party of another party's trust. Strict fiduciary liabilities are implied from that acceptance. Len Sealy in 1962 saw that undertakings were characteristic of, at least, the most important categories of fiduciary relationships.[85] An eminent practising lawyer in Canada has recently affirmed that all fiduciary relationships can be defined by the undertaking of one party.[86]

[3.39] Australian importance of undertaking theory is underlined by the fact that it was the one which gained the preponderance of judicial support in the *Hospital Products* litigation. As noted, the facts there concerned the possible fiduciary liability of the Australian distributor of surgical products manufactured by a United States supplier.[87] McLelland J at first instance found that the distributor was in a limited fiduciary relationship towards the supplier. Scope of this relationship was limited to the supplier's market for its goods. McLelland J based his finding on two things. First, a 'recognised analogy' with the trust, as paradigm of fiduciary relationships, constituted by the *undertaking* that the distributor had contractually assumed to act in the interests of the supplier (at 810-811). Secondly, the finding was based in the power that the distributor had to detrimentally affect the supplier's market. On appeal, the New South Wales Court of Appeal agreed with the fiduciary finding generally and explicitly with McLelland J's first basis for it, observing:[88]

> it is necessary to find some criterion which the facts must satisfy. Since ... any fiduciary relationship which existed here did not fall within any established category, some principle or requirement must be found which is common to all or, at least, most categories.

---

[83] A Scott 'The Fiduciary Principle' (1949) 37 *Calif LR* 539 at 540.

[84] Finn *Fiduciaries* [467].

[85] Sealy 'Fiduciary Relationships' [1962] *Camb LJ* 69 at 76I7 'where the fiduciary has undertaken or been under an obligation'.

[86] J Gautreau 'Demystifying the Fiduciary Mystique' (1989) 68 *Can Bar Rev* 1 at 7.

[87] [1982] 2 NSWLR 766 at 810.

[88] [1983] 2 NSWLR 157 at 205, curiam.

**[3.40]**   In this way the court sought a 'common element' for all or most 'categories' of fiduciary relationship. Counsel in that case had suggested a number of categories which, 'omitting the confidential information cases', were said to encompass the whole phenomenon. In each of these, the court said (at 206), 'F is acting for or on behalf of B'. Hence—

> if F has undertaken to act in the interest of B, F will be a fiduciary; and, conversely, a fiduciary relationship cannot exist unless F has undertaken to act in the interest of B, it being understood that such an undertaking precludes F from acting in his own interest in the same matter, that is, in the matter in respect of which the undertaking was given.

Undertaking was the one criterion that the Court of Appeal found in each fiduciary relationship. McLelland J's references to power as also one of the springs of a fiduciary relationship were jettisoned. Holding out of an undertaking to a beneficiary was a sufficient 'representative element' by which the person should be bound as a fiduciary. In the absence of such an undertaking, it was incorrect to describe a person as a fiduciary. On the facts of the case, the distributor's undertaking was at 198 held to arise from an implied contractual promise to 'do nothing inimical' to the supplier's market interests.

**[3.41]**   When, on further appeal, *Hospital Products* reached the High Court, the whole court denied the contractual basis of the 'representational element'. All but one judge found that no fiduciary relationship existed on any other basis.[89] Chief Justice Gibbs, in so finding, remarked at 72 that the 'undertaking' criterion for a fiduciary relationship was a 'not inappropriate' one. For the major difference between the Gibbs CJ judgment and the judgment of the Court of Appeal was that Gibbs CJ (at 63–7) did not find the implied term upon which the Court of Appeal's undertaking had been based. The other majority judgment of Dawson J treated fiduciary relationships as based in a different dominant idea—namely, the vulnerability and reliance characteristic, which will be discussed at [3.89]–[3.137].

Mason J wrote a dissenting judgment which essentially agreed with the Court of Appeal, apart from not finding the implied term. Beginning with generalities about the fiduciary relation at 96–7, he saw that the 'critical feature' of all fiduciary relationships was that:

> the fiduciary undertakes or agrees to act for or on behalf of or in the interests of another person in the exercise of a power or discretion which will affect the interests of that other person.

Applying this conception, at 101–2 he found that a fiduciary relation was appropriate in this case, but should be limited to the supplier's market for its products.

**[3.42]**   Undertaking has had currency in Anglo-Australian law under various guises. For example, in *Walden Properties Ltd v Beaver Properties Pty Ltd* an 'undertaking' was spelt out of the obligations which a self-appointed agent imposed upon himself.[90] When a company's receiver accepts appointment, he

---

[89] (1984) 156 CLR 41, Gibbs CJ, Wilson, Deane and Dawson JJ; Mason J dissenting.
[90] [1973] 2 NSWLR 815 at 833, Hope JA (Kerr CJ agreeing) (CA).

or she is said to do the same.[91] In *Noranda Australia Ltd v Lachlin Resources NL*[92] an 'undertaking' for the purpose was provided by an express contract term.

Problems with this approach are manifold and will emerge in the course of this chapter. Undertaking, the theory, cannot explain those cases where the facts are directly inconsistent with a 'representative' or voluntary element. Too many fiduciary relationships have been found where fiduciaries have been entirely ignorant of their beneficiaries. In other cases, persons found to be fiduciaries have obviously been acting only on their own behalves.[93] These fiduciaries represented nobody. They did not accept any trust, they merely abused it. In other cases again, it is difficult to imagine how the putative fiduciary had any option of accepting or declining a trust thrust upon them.[94] We shall now examine some specific relationships where application of the theory has been discussed.

## Managers and agents of syndicated loans

**[3.43]** 'Syndicated loans' are arrangements whereby several lenders combine their resources to lend to a single borrower.[95] 'Difficult credits' and refinancings of the 1980s, it has been observed, were often achieved thereby.[96] Syndication of lenders is often resorted to because a loan is 'too large or too risky' for a single bank or lending institution to finance by itself, or the collateral is insufficient to satisfy any one bank.[97] In its common form, the first step in a loan syndication is for a 'manager' bank to be appointed. Then the manager is authorised by the borrower to obtain a loan for it on terms it outlines in a 'mandate letter'.[98] When it acts pursuant to this authority, the manager serves expressly as the borrower's agent. The manager seeks to interest other banks (or lenders) in participation on the mandated terms. Other banks which express an interest are supplied by the manager with an 'information memorandum'. This describes the borrower's affairs in more detail. Thereafter a formal set of loan documents is signed by each participating lender. One of those participants is appointed by the others as their 'agent', to receive and distribute information about the borrower and to represent the participants in regulating the borrower's performance. Managers and agents are very often the same party. Both are paid. Remuneration of the agent will usually be a term of the initial loan agreement.

---

91  *Cape v Redarb Pty Ltd* (1992) 8 ACSR 67 at 80 (Higgins J, ACT SC); also *Chittick v Maxwell* (1993) 118 ALR 728, Young J (SC (NSW)) (concerning a self-appointed legal adviser).

92  (1988) 14 NSWLR 1, Bryson J: see Finn *Fiduciaries* [398] and the (unlikely) case of *Deonanandan Prashad v Janki Singh* (1916) LR 44 Ind App 30 (PC), cited by the NSW CA in *Hospital Products* at 207–8.

93  *Reading v R* [1949] 2 KB 232 (CA) is an example, above at [3.21].

94  Eg, *Moore v Regents of the University of California* 793 P 2d 479 (SC of Calif 1990); *Plaza Fibreglass Manufacturing Co Ltd v Cardinal Insurance Co* (1990) 68 DLR (4th) 586.

95  P Gabriel *Legal Aspects of Syndicated Loans* (1986) p 2.

96  'Banking Law and Practice' 9th annual conference (1992), 'Comment' by N T Cleary: *Proceedings*, 328 at 331.

97  (Note) 'Liabilities of Lead Banks in Syndicated Loans under the Securities Acts' 58 *BULR* (1978) 45 at 45.

98  P Wood *Law and Practice of International Finance* (1980), 256–63 and J O'Sullivan 'The Roles of Managers and Agents in Syndicated Loans' [1992] *Jo of Banking and Finance Law and Practice* 162 at 163–4.

**[3.44]**   Two fiduciary relationships have been argued to arise from the above facts. These are as between the participating banks and the manager and as between the participating banks and the agent.[99] We shall deal with the manager first. Commentators associated with the finance industry have strenuously denied that managers assume fiduciary duties in the performance of their function.[100] The process of bringing participants into a syndication is said to be an archetypal 'arm's length' transaction, which attracts no fiduciary consequence. This has been justified because participants in banking syndicates 'are highly sophisticated parties ... Participants understand and expect that the manager will have his own interests to protect.'[101]

Participants have been said to–

'buy' a product developed, marketed, and serviced by the manager/agent ... the relationship is not fundamentally different from the relationship between IBM and the purchaser of a large computer system.[102]

R C Tennekoon in *The Law and Regulation of International Finance*,[103] is more balanced. He says that:

Some writers [referring to the above] have taken the view that fiduciary duties ... will not be imposed on a lead manager for the benefit of co-lenders in a syndicate in respect of the negotiation of loan documentation. It is submitted that the risk that a court will impose fiduciary duties cannot altogether be ruled out.

**[3.45]**   Should the courts find this relationship to be fiduciary? Consider then the facts of *UBAF Ltd v European American Banking Corporation*,[104] keeping in mind the possibility that the manager had acted outside the bounds of any acceptable commercial behaviour. The defendant was a United States bank that had lent a considerable sum to a shipping company. Later, when that company encountered financial difficulties, the bank approached various lenders including an English bank and suggested that a syndicated loan be made to its problem customer. An information memorandum about the shipping company was duly circulated and agreements were executed. The United States bank as manager was also appointed the participants' agent. It turned out later that the information memorandum had contained false information. Contrary to the fact, the shipping company had been said to have a cash flow sufficient to service the loans. Its ships were described as much more valuable than they were. Eventually the shipping company defaulted and the English bank suffered loss. On one view, what the manager may have done in this case was to abuse its position of trust in the financial community. It had shifted a large part of its loss onto the backs of smaller banks which trusted it. When the English Court of Appeal came to deal with the facts on an (interlocutory) appeal, it held (at 518) that the United States bank was potentially under a fiduciary liability to the participants at all stages of the syndication. Both as syndicate manager and as syndicate agent, the defendant

---

[99] O'Sullivan, ibid, at 173–7 and 180–1.

[100] Eg O'Sullivan id, following L Clarke and S Farrar 'Rights and Duties of Managing and Agent Banks in Syndicated Loans to Government Borrowers' [1982] 1 *Univ of Illinois Law Rev* 229 at 233–5.

[101] O'Sullivan, ibid, at 177.

[102] Clarke and Farrar, ibid, at 234.

[103] (1991) p 56.

[104] [1984] 2 WLR 508 (CA), curiam (Ackner LJ).

was the participants' fiduciary. The court did not in this seem to have considered the terms of the loan agreement and whether it contained any exclusion of an agent's fiduciary liability.

[3.46] In the *UBAF* case, a syndicate manager's alleged breach of fiduciary duty flowed from the terms of the information memorandum. The manager should have disclosed what it knew of the borrower's financial difficulties. In *Natwest Australia Bank Ltd v Tricontinental Corporation Ltd*[105] a loan manager was held to be in breach of 'common law or fiduciary duty' by failing to disclose that it possessed undischarged guarantees from the borrower relating to an earlier transaction. As has been pointed out, the background facts of this and the previous case are not particularly uncommon. Syndicate managers have often been previous lenders to the borrower. No liability for the manager is usually incurred on that account.[106] It has been suggested in this connection that a manager's having interests of its own which conflict with its duties to participants need not entail 'fiduciary liability' if the manager makes adequate disclosure.[107] Perhaps this is so. However it does not supply any answer to the characterisation question. The relationship between participants and manager may be fiduciary notwithstanding.

[3.47] Now the fiduciary position of the agent appointed by the loan syndicate will be considered.[108] Several relevant differences between syndicate agents and managers exist. Agents are appointed pursuant to the terms of syndication agreements and these agreements are typically voluminous. They may purport to delegate only ministerial tasks to the agent and otherwise exhaustively regulate the agent's powers and duties.[109] It may be argued by the agent that the agreement is an 'entire code' of agent liabilities;[110] or that the courts' fiduciary characterisation is pre-empted by an exemption clause. It is said to be quite normal for provisions to be inserted in the loan agreement to the effect that:

> [t]he relationship between the Agent and each Bank is that of principal and agent only. Nothing herein shall constitute the Agent a Trustee or Fiduciary for any Bank ... [111]

What effectiveness such provisions can have is considered elsewhere in this book.[112] Or again, the agent might be expressly permitted to conduct separate loan business with the borrower, including reconstruction of liability.[113] This last possibility, though, is more relevant to negativing the occurrence of a breach of duty than the existence of the relationship wherefrom it flows.

---

[105] (SC (Vic), McDonald J, 26 July 1993, unreported); see [1993] ACL Rep 45 Vic 5.

[106] P Gabriel ibid, 174–5.

[107] P Gabriel, ibid, 174–5.

[108] See B W Semkow 'Syndicating and Restructuring International Financial Transactions' 18 *International Lawyer* (1984) 869 at 869–86.

[109] O'Sullivan ibid, at 182–3.

[110] cf *Noranda Australia Ltd v Lachlan Resources NL* (1988) 14 NSWLR 1.

[111] Gabriel ibid, 164–5.

[112] See [3.29]–[3.30] and J F Lehane (note) [1982] *Int Fin Law Rev* 241.

[113] O'Sullivan ibid at 182, citing the surprising NZ case of *NZI Securities Ltd v Bank of New Zealand* (HC (NZ), Wylie J, 11 February 1992, unreported).

## Distributor and supplier

**[3.48]**  Relations between distributors and suppliers are ordinarily not of a fiduciary nature. Even where these parties possess a common interest in expoiting a market for the supplier's products, the separate interests of the distributor and the supplier are usually more significant and they need not coincide at all. They often conflict. This can be illustrated with reference to those interests associated with pricing policy, explained by Dawson J in *Hospital Products* in the High Court. He said:[114]

> where there is no agreement to the contrary ... and the distributor resells his supplier's products, [the distributor] must determine the price at which he will market them. Whilst it may be in the supplier's interest that the products should be sold at a price which is as close as possible to the wholesale price, the distributor's interest may dictate a higher price. Whilst it is in the supplier's interest that the distributor should purchase and sell as many of the supplier's products as the market will absorb, there may be considerations which the distributor must take into account in his own interest which will involve a lesser achievement ... such matters as the distributor's capacity to finance its operations, to give credit and to promote the product.

Accordingly, what has been termed the 'interests analysis', when applied to the relation, might point away from a fiduciary characterisation. Distributors, it could be said, cannot in law or in fact be expected to subordinate their own financial interests to those of the supplier. They have irreducibly separate concerns which are not reconciled by the overarching common interest.[115]

**[3.49]**  Fiduciary characterisation of distributorships is the subject of much United States authority. Emphasis there tends to be placed on the relationship's economic character. Distributorships are analysed in terms of profit-making. So, to the extent that the profit interests of supplier and distributor conflict, those parties are said not to be engaged in a fiduciary relationship.[116] 'Interests analysis' is commonly accorded the power of decision. Sometimes the same distinction is drawn in terms of whether the parties derive 'mutual' or 'non-mutual' profits out of the relation. If important marketing decisions may be taken by either the distributor or the supplier without regard to the other, then the profit may not be 'mutual' enough to be fiduciary.

The Californian case of *Rickel v Schwinn Bicycle Co*[117] used the mutuality of profit test. A bicycle distributor claimed that his supplier was in breach of fiduciary duty. In defence, the supplier denied that the relationship between the parties was fiduciary at all. Because there was a distribution agreement between these parties, the primary focus of the court was to construe the relationship that the agreement defined. Examination of the agreement's terms indicated that Rickel was free to sell Schwinn bicycles or any other brand of bicycle he chose. The Schwinn Co was able to make entirely 'unilateral' pricing decisions. Primarily from these features, it was concluded that only

---

[114] *Hospital Products Ltd v United States Surgical Corporation* (1984) 156 CLR 41 at 143, Dawson J.

[115] *Hospital Products* also at 99, Mason J.

[116] See *St Joseph Equipment Co v Massey-Ferguson Inc* 546 F Supp 1245 (1982); *Worldvision Enterprises Inc v American Broadcasting Co Inc* 191 Cal Reptr 148 (1983) and *C Pappas Co Inc v E & J Gallo Winery* 610 F Supp 662 (1985).

[117] 144 Cal Reptr 732 (1983).

'non-mutual' profits in the relation could be made by either party. Rickel and Schwinn were not for this reason in a fiduciary relationship. Hence the Schwinn Co did not owe Rickel a fiduciary duty not to hamper the sale of his bicycle shop, as he alleged.

[3.50]   United States cases treat the relation between franchisee and franchisor analogously to that between distributor and supplier.[118] This is not surprising, given the economic emphasis of the American cases. Franchises and distributorships have a similar economic character. Making of cooperative profits is central to both. Franchises are said to be 'interdependent or co-operative business relationships', not of themselves generative of fiduciary relationships.[119] Or, as said in another case: '[a] franchise relationship is inherently a business relationship, not a fiduciary relationship.'[120]

The effect of this is is to pose the doubtful antithesis between fiduciary relationships and commerce that we have discussed at [2.7]. The better view may be to apply the indicium of 'mutuality'. This tends to negate fiduciary status for franchises for the same reasons as it does for distributorships.

[3.51]   There is some authority that reasoning from undertakings or other fiduciary characteristics *can* succeed in turning a distributorship or franchise into a fiduciary relation.[121] This is despite an 'interests analysis' pointing in the other direction. Not in all fiduciary distributorships or franchises is there a confusion between 'good faith' and fiduciary obligations, of the kind said sometimes to occur in United States cases.[122] First, we need to set aside the assumption we have previously made for the purposes of exposition—namely, that there is some paradigm of a 'distributorship' or 'franchise' relationship, with an objective 'nature,' amenable to dissection and analysis. The world being a various place, a great many, probably most, relations have at least one exceptional feature. Few conform to the paradigmatic form. For example:

1. The distributor might undertake to protect a *specific interest* of the supplier; or, the distributor might undertake to act in a particular joint interest. A specific interest of the supplier could exist in the market goodwill of its products. Terms of an agreement and mutual dealings of the parties might indicate that the distributor undertook to protect and 'do nothing inimical' to this goodwill. Such an undertaking, and a fiduciary relationship so based, was found by a majority of judges who heard the *Hospital Products* litigation in its various stages.[123]

2. A different type of reasoning toward fiduciary characterisation could be used in conjunction with undertaking. A multiple resemblance may occur. The supplier might, for example, entrust property to the distributor. See the

---

[118]  See H Brown 'Franchising— A Fiduciary Relationship?' 49 *Texas Law Rev* 650 (1971).

[119]  *Chmieleski v City Products Corporation* 660 SW 2d 275 (1983), 292–3; also *Bach v Friden Calculating Machine Co Inc* 155 F 2d 361 (1946); *Power Motive Corporation v Mannesman n Demag Corporation* 617 F Supp 1048 (1985).

[120]  *Picture Lake Campground v Holiday Inns Inc* 497 F Supp 858 (1980).

[121]  *Impala Platinum Ltd v Impala Sales (USA) Inc* 389 A 2d 887 (1978), *Arnott v American Oil Company* 609 F 2d 873 (1979).

[122]  P Finn 'Fiduciary Principle' in Youdan, p 1 at pp 20–4.

[123]  See McLelland J, at first instance, [1982] 2 NSWLR 766 at 811, a unanimous NSW CA, [1983] 2 NSWLR 157 at 206–8 and Mason J in the High Court (1984) 156 CLR 41 at 101–2.

alternative reasoning of Mason J in *Hospital Products Ltd v United States Surgical Corporation*, where he observed:[124]

> HPI's position as custodian of USSC's product goodwill in Australia may be likened in a general way to that of a bailee whose duty is to protect and preserve a chattel bailed to him.

3. One party, usually the supplier, might unduly influence the other. A different *type* of fiduciary relation might be invoked. Undue influence may be exerted during the course of reaching agreement. A stronger party might require the servient party to surrender all his or her independence in the relationship.[125] This was the way that a fiduciary relationship was found in *Dunfee v Baskin-Robbins Inc*.[126] The claimants were the small-town proprietors of a store in the 'Baskin-Robbins' chain. When a shopping mall opened nearby, their business declined dramatically. Baskin-Robbins, however, high-handedly refused to consider the plaintiffs' request that it permit a relocation of the store. A breach of fiduciary duty resembling undue influence was seen to flow from this—inferred explicitly out of the parties' unequal bargaining strength (at 1151). Similar argument was made for the variety store proprietor in *Chmieleski v City Products Corporation*.[127]

The finding of an 'exceptional' distributorship in one of these, or some other, ways can be a sort of 'late-gate' to a distributorship's fiduciary status.

### Business promoter and prospective investor

**[3.52]** Equity protects fiduciary undertakings here, by way of analogy with more established fiduciary relations. Fraudulent promoters of businesses have been seen to commit wrongs similar to those committed by fraudulent promoters of companies. Sameness of wrong has suggested sameness of remedy and brought the fraudulent business promoter within the fiduciary canon. Fraudulent company promoters are archetypal fiduciary rogues. Their pedigree dates from the unregulated days of the nineteenth century. For over one hundred years, boards of companies representing subscribers have sued to set aside disadvantageous bargains made with persons who promoted their incorporation. A well-established fiduciary relation between promoters and companies has been the result. One early case put it that the promoters of a bank and their solicitor were 'trustees' for the bank in respect of a sale of their own property to it.[128] Fiduciaries as 'trustees' for their companies will be considered further at [5.90]. The idea has faded in significance. A more modern example of the errant company promoter was in *Tracy v Mandalay Pty Ltd*.[129] A company was established in that case with the object of building a block of flats in a housing shortage. After the venture was thwarted for want of a building permit, the company's promoters were disciplined as fiduciaries for having made to it an undisclosed sale of their own property.

---

[124] (1984) 156 CLR 41 at 101.

[125] See P Finn 'Fiduciary Principle' in Youdan, 1 n 234.

[126] 720 P 2d 1148 (1986).

[127] 660 SW 2d 275 (1983).

[128] *Tyrrell v Bank of London* (1862) 10 HLC 26; 11 ER 934; see also *Directors of Central Railway Co of Venezuela v Kitsch* (1867) LR 2 HL 99 at 113, Lord Chelmsford LC.

[129] (1953) 88 CLR 215.

**[3.53]** *Erlanger v New Sombrero Phosphate Co*[130] is an authority which establishes fiduciary principles for promoters generally. The facts involved a huge gain made by the promoters on a secret sale of their own property to a newborn company. A majority of the House of Lords allowed the company the right to rescind the purchase. Lord Cairns LC (at 1236) said of company promoters generally that:

> They stand, in my opinion, undoubtedly, in a fiduciary position. They have in their hands the creation and moulding of the company; they have the power of defining how, and when, and in what shape, and under what supervision, it shall start into existence and begin to act as a trading corporation.

Where promoters do all this 'creating', 'moulding' and 'defining how' just in order to sell their own property to the company, as Lord Cairns said in the following paragraph, acquitting their fiduciary duty requires a further act. A proper board of directors for the company must be constituted. It must be a body which can exercise an 'independent and intelligent judgement' on whether to make the purchase or not.

**[3.54]** According to the scheme of some 'rule-based' theories of the fiduciary relation, considered at [2.16], the fiduciary wrong here is an aspect of the conflict of duty and interest rule—an application, more particularly, of the rule which prohibits persons in a fiduciary position from selling their own property to the trusting party without proper disclosure.[131] Analogical genesis of the 'business promoter' category also involved the self-purchasing agent—the agent, that is, who undertakes to purchase property on behalf of a principal and who fulfils the commission by purchasing his own property. Explained in this context by Lord Parker in *Jacobus Marler Estates Ltd v Marler*,[132] this is the particular wrong of the company promoter. Self-dealing of this kind denies the heart of the engagement that the putative fiduciary *undertakes* to discharge. Fiduciaries in corresponding relationships have included agents who act as advisors to their principals on contemplated purchases,[133] and those who give particulars of a property to interest a trusting purchaser.[134]

**[3.55]** *Catt v Marac Australia Ltd*[135] is an extension of this reasoning to the world of tax-minimisation in the 1980s. An entrepreneur named Winter promoted and sold schemes which involved the financier, Marac. Pursuant to one scheme, Marac was to purchase a jet aircraft in the United States and then sell it to the nominee company of a partnership of medical practitioners. A taxation benefit would be obtained by the company and passed on to the medical practitioners. Jet Charterers was then to take the aircraft on lease from the nominee company. Marac only set the transaction in motion. Its sole function was to provide bridging finance. However, Marac was the entity sued when a particular scheme failed and the individual partners suffered loss. Each of Winter, Jet and Marac were said to be in breach of fiduciary obligation owed to the medical practitioners. Because Marac was the only defendant

---

130  (1878) 3 App Cas 1218 (HL).
131  Finn *Fiduciaries*, [519].
132  (1913) 114 LT 640n (HL), and see Finn *Fiduciaries* [519].
133  *Tyrrell v Bank of London* (1862) 10 HLC 26; 11 ER 934.
134  *Regier v Campbell-Stuart* [1939] Ch 766.
135  (1986) 9 NSWLR 639.

which remained solvent by the time of action, only its fiduciary status was in question.

[3.56]   Before the Supreme Court of New South Wales Marac argued that it was protected from fiduciary liability by two things. The parties were said to be at 'arm's length' and the transaction was of a commercial nature. To this, Rogers J said at 654:

> The reason why Marac is not protected . . . is precisely because it was not at arm's length from the other parties. Its arm was firmly linked into Jet's and Winter's. In the plaintiff's submission, on a true analysis, Marac's position was more akin to a promoter's.

After citing Dawson J's disapproval of fiduciary liabilities being applied to 'commercial' and 'arm's length' transactions in *Hospital Products Ltd v United States Surgical Corporation*,[136] Rogers J ruled that the same was inapplicable to the case before him. At 655 he found that Marac had had all its dealings for the scheme with 'the pliant Winter', to the disadvantage of the practitioners scattered all over Australia. This paralleled the wrong of a self-dealing promoter. Namely, negotiation of the terms of a sale of one's own property to a company with pliant directors installed for the purpose of consenting. Winter, too, was anxious to earn his commission. There was no one independent who 'looked at documents, asked questions, and exercised judgement' to protect the partners' interests. As Rogers J said (at 655), a fiduciary obligation akin to that of a promoter was 'thrust upon' Marac. Which is to strike a discordant note in the largely consensual theory of this characteristic. Undertakings are assumed, not imposed.

[3.57]   *Hill v Rose*[137] is a not dissimilar case. Hill was introduced to an apparently prosperous crayfish business. He invested a substantial sum of money in the venture without being told anything of its financial structure, or a large debt that it had incurred. Mr and Mrs Rose had previously conducted the business. They knew that it was in extreme financial difficulty at the time Hill became interested. Tadgell J held at 138–9 that Hill and the Roses were in a fiduciary relationship—one which 'resembled' that between a company and its promoter. The Roses and company promoters were both 'insiders'. Superior knowledge possessed by each was said to mean that the insiders must, as Tadgell J put it at 141, 'lay bare the essentials of the business' to the reliant investor.

### Is 'undertaking' stretched too far?

[3.58]   It might be doubted whether the linguistic kinship of Marac's liability with that of a company promoter was a sufficient 'family resemblance' for the promoter principles to be attracted. The same might be thought of the resemblance between the Roses and Hill relationship and that of a promoter and a company he promotes. Meagher Gummow Lehane (at [503]) find it 'difficult to see' why the relationship in either of these cases was fiduciary, having regard to 'established principles'. Judgments that we have outlined above are indeed a little difficult to follow. What undertaking did Marac or the Roses give to those who trusted them? According to traditional,

---

136  (1984) 156 CLR 41, 149.
137  [1990] VR 129.

undertaking-centric, accounts of the fiduciary relation of trust, the facts would seem quite inadequate.[138]

[3.59]  In *Marac's* case there was possibly no undertaking at all. Quite rightly, with respect, the fact that Marac was both purchaser and on-seller of the aircraft was treated as having no equitable significance.[139] It was only a transactional device for the avoidance of stamp duty. Marac had never any interest in capital profits. It only had its financier's claim to interest on money advanced. Marac was said to become a 'promoter' with fiduciary liabilities only because of its 'insistence' on dealing only with the deceitful Winter, rather than the twenty practitioners scattered around Australia. Fiduciary liability, it could be said, and the relationship wherefrom it flowed, was imposed as a remedial sanction—in court and well after the event.

[3.60]  Undertakings are scarce also in *Hill v Rose*.[140] Tadgell J said at 141 that a business promoter who seeks out another to take an interest in his enterprise attracts a fiduciary obligation as one who 'sets the stage and entices the [investor] to walk upon it.'

But is this not equally done by the vendor of a farm, or the assignor of patent rights, or one who sells a fruit shop in the suburbs? It is submitted that there is nothing in the metaphors of 'setting of the stage' or the 'invitation to walk upon it' to justify the fiduciary finding. Nothing, therefore, is assumed by the vendor comparably to a company promoter upon which to base the relation.

[3.61]  There may have been a doubtful analogy made in these cases. The business promoter and investor relation inadequately correlates with the company promoter and company relation. Neither of the business promoter cases seems to have established the common characteristic of undertaking needed to make the analogy sustainable. There was inadequate evidence for the purpose in each of *Catt v Marac* and *Hill v Rose*. Possibly the fiduciary relation would have been more sustainable from the existence of known reliance, in each case, of the investor on the promoter. Although this, too, is doubtful. The promoter of the proposed leveraged buyout in *Amendola v Bayer*[141] was not found to be a fiduciary on the reliance characteristic either.

Finn in 'The Fiduciary Principle' expresses a different critical view. He has called the type of remedial obligation here an 'imposition of duties of information disclosure simply for the purpose of informing another's decision'.[142] Partly on the basis of an 'interests analysis', he reaches the conclusion (at 24) that this is a matter not appropriate for the 'fiduciary' standard at all. Regulation of the business promoter he says should not go beyond a contractual standard of good faith. Academically the conclusion may have some appeal. However it is of little interest to the person who tries to reach beyond the limited remedies that follow from contractual wrongs.

---

[138] See Finn *Fiduciaries* [541].
[139] (1986) 9 NSWLR 639, 655.
[140] [1990] VR 129.
[141] 907 F 2d 760 (Ill 7th circ 1990).
[142] In Youdan, p 1 at pp 16–21.

**Broker and client**

**[3.62]**   Only some aspects of the relations between brokers and clients can be fiduciary. Brokers are sometimes outside the fiduciary scheme altogether. In this event brokers are liable to their clients only on a tortious basis, or pursuant to the terms of the broker and client retainer. Lush J put this in a rather minimalist way in *Option Investments (Aust) Pty Ltd v Martin*.[143] 'A broker's duty', he said–

> is to execute the orders that a client gives to him. He is under no duty to give advice, though if he does he must of course do so honestly and with appropriate skill and ability. He is under no duty, and has no general authority, to initiate transactions, for instance, the sale of securities held without his client's instructions. The relationship has fiduciary aspects relating to moneys and securities held by the broker, but otherwise the broker's duty is to execute orders . . .

**[3.63]**   Such a conception is inconsistent with dicta in other authorities which confer fiduciary incidents on the normal relationship between broker and client.[144] However, it does highlight a difference between the brokerage relation and other putatively fiduciary relationships we have considered: franchises and distributorships, in particular. Construction of the terms of the retainer is unlikely to yield a fiduciary characterisation. A client's contract with a broker is unlikely of itself to imply fiduciary status. A broker classed as an errant fiduciary will ordinarily have committed some trustee-like wrong—like purchasing his principal's property.[145] Only a contractual relationship may obtain where brokers do no more than execute their clients' orders.[146] But this does not preclude the possibility of fiduciary intervention. Brokers are apt to undertake responsibilities beyond a broker's retainer, which include:

1. giving advice upon which the client is reasonably believed to rely;
2. initiating transactions without the client's instructions; or
3. receiving money, securities or other property in the course of the retainer on behalf of the client.

**[3.64]**   The whole transaction between the client and the broker must be examined to see whether any of these further responsibilities have been undertaken. Fiduciary potential of (3) will be reviewed at [3.72]–[3.81], in connection with the property characteristic. Close examination of both the other possibilities was made in the United States case of *Merrill Lynch Pierce Fenner & Smith Inc v Boeck*.[147] A client had invested in commodity futures through the broker Merrill Lynch. Loss was suffered, allegedly in reliance on advice which the broker 'undertook' to give. When the broker was later shown to know that advice it had given was incorrect, it was said to come under a fiduciary duty to tender the corrected information. The duty so expressed was generated by the existence of a fiduciary relationship between the parties. This in turn was held to depend on the nature of the 'account' which the client maintained with the broker. This could take two forms. A 'discretionary

---

[143] (1980) 5 ACLR 124 at 128 (SCV).
[144] Eg, *Jones v Canavan* [1972] 2 NSWLR 236 at 246, Asprey JA.
[145] Eg, see *Estate Realties Ltd v Wignall* [1991] 3 NZLR 482.
[146] See *McIntyre v Okurowski* 717 F Supp 10 (Mass 1989).
[147] 377 NW 2d 605 (1985) (SC (Wisconsin)).

account' is one, where the broker determined which purchases and sales to make and assumed control of the investment decision. Or it could be a 'non-discretionary account' where the client made decisions as to which commodities to buy and sell and the broker's advice was not relied upon. Only the discretionary account had fiduciary potential. As the investor was 'an experienced commodities trader who was aware of the risks and uncertainties of the market', the court found that the facts of the case more resembled the non-discretionary form. Accordingly (at 609), no fiduciary relationship was found.

**[3.65]** In this way the *Merrill Lynch* analysis separated the ministerial and the fiduciary aspects of a broker's role. The Canadian case of *R H Deacon & Co Ltd v Varga*[148] did likewise. The stockbroker there was instructed by its client to purchase a stipulated number of shares in a stipulated corporation for a price within a stipulated range. As it happened, the broker itself owned a large interest in the stipulated corporation and was aware that the corporation was in an unsatisfactory financial position. However the broker made no disclosure of what it knew and 'the broker's advice was not sought'. The client's investment proceeded and a substantial loss was incurred. Later the client alleged that it was in a fiduciary relationship with the broker and that a breach of fiduciary duty occurred when the broker failed to disclose what it knew. The court's characterisation of the relationship emphasised the ministerial nature of the broker's role and, adopting a description of a broker's duties from an earlier Canadian case, it held that the 'primary duty' of this broker was to carry out instructions. A fiduciary duty could only arise[149] 'when there is a conflict of interest between the principal and agent or where the principal has imposed such a term in the agency agreement'.

This may be to say that a fiduciary relation with a broker exists either as agreed between the parties or to remedy an explicitly *equitable* wrong. Tortious or contractual misdeeds do not attract the relationship.[150] The broker's instructions were carried out in the Varga case and there was no conflict of interest. So no fiduciary relationship needed to be implied.

**[3.66]** Whether the relation between broker and client was fiduciary was also considered by the High Court in *Daly v Sydney Stock Exchange Ltd.*[151] The facts of the case occurred when a share broker was nearly insolvent. Dr Daly did not know of this at the time and was persuaded to make a loan of money to the broker personally. The broker had allegedly given incorrect and self-interested advice which prevented Dr Daly from evaluating the risks that the loan entailed. A constructive trust was argued to be impressed on the proceeds lent, to facilitate a claim on a fidelity fund established by the Sydney Stock Exchange Ltd. The fund provided compensation if the client could show that the broker received the money claimed 'as trustee'.[152] Thus the fiduciary status

---

[148] (1972) 30 DLR (3d) 653 (CA (Ont)), affirmed SC (Can) (1973) 41 DLR (3d) 767, discussed by E J Weinrib in 'The Fiduciary Obligation' (1975) 25 *UTLJ* 1 at 4.

[149] At 659, McRuer CJHC, following of Riddell J in *Johnson v Birkett* (1910) 21 OLR 319; also adopted in *Scherer v Zacks* [1952] 4 DLR 503 at 505–7.

[150] A position approved by W Gummow in 'Compensation for Breach of Fiduciary Duty' in Youdan p 57 at 75–9.

[151] (1986) 160 CLR 371.

[152] Securities Industry Act 1975 (NSW) s 97(1).

of the broker and client relationship was relevant in a particularly remedial kind of way. Particularly as Gibbs CJ saw the matter, the important question in the case was whether the constructive trust remedy was available.[153] If it was, then the broker was obviously a 'trustee' of sorts, satisfying the legislation, and so the relationship might be characterised accordingly. Whether the constructive trust was itself based in a fiduciary relationship was a matter of little consequence on this approach, although Brennan J said at 385:

> Whenever a stockbroker or other person who holds himself out as having expertise in advising on investments is approached for advice on investments and undertakes to give it, in giving that advice the adviser stands in a fiduciary relationship to the person whom he advises.

Although restricting his remarks more to the facts, Gibbs CJ (at 377) expressed himself to a similar effect:

> It was right to say that [the broker] owed a fiduciary duty to Dr Daly and acted in breach of that duty. The firm, which held itself out as an adviser on matters of investment, undertook to advise Dr Daly, and Dr Daly relied on the advice which the firm gave him. In those circumstances it had a [fiduciary duty to disclose].

Gibbs CJ at 380–1 (Wilson and Dawson JJ agreeing), went on to hold that it was not necessary to find that a constructive trust existed in order to ensure that the firm was not unjustly enriched. A purely contractual right for Dr Daly as creditor to be repaid by his debtor would suffice to right the wrong. For the reasons discussed, this had no direct bearing on the nature of the broker and client relationship in that case. Brennan J at 390–1 came to decide the case on an even narrower basis. He found that the word 'defalcation' was not satisfied in s 97(1) of the Securities Industry Act 1975 (NSW).

**[3.67]** Brennan J's broad description in *Daly's* case of a stockbroker's fiduciary status is a problematicly wide dictum. It would make nearly all investment brokers fiduciaries. The broker in *Option Investments (Aust) Pty Ltd v Martin*[154] would seem to be included, despite Lush J's minimalism. Option Investments had been in the business of purchasing and selling contracts for the future delivery of various commodities. At 128 it was observed that:

> The [broker's] enterprise was new; the idea of an Australian futures exchange was relatively new; clients were few and likely to be uninformed.

At least some of the clients must have sought the broker's advice. At least some must have been known to rely on it. But nothing seemed to depend on this and the reasons for judgment ignored it. Dispute concerned the practice of a broker 'closing out' and reselling a client's partly paid contracts when 'margin calls' were not paid. The client alleged that the broker caused loss by not 'closing out' until after the value of the contracts had substantially fallen. Lush J then discussed the bases on which brokers could be liable to their clients. In the first place, he said, a broker could be liable by the terms of a contract with the client. Any contract here was to be implied from telephone conversations between the parties and the 'rule or custom of most exchanges'.

---

153   (1986) 160 CLR 371 at 378–80.
154   (1980) 5 ACLR 124 (SC (Vic)).

No restrictions were seen to be placed on the 'closing out' times that the broker might choose to use. Lush J went on to say (at 128) that brokers were under no duty to give advice, but, if they did advise, then the advice had to be honest and not negligent. That these were only contractual or tortious sanctions was evident from the authorities referred to, only *Surman v Oxenford*[155] and *Hogan v Shaw*[156] on the interpretation of brokerage agreements. Little room was left for fiduciaries.

**[3.68]**  Despite *Option Investments*, the better view may be that brokers often do enter fiduciary relationships with their clients when they undertake to advise. The advisory function may transform a non-discretionary brokering account into a discretionary one. Brokers are in this way analogous to bankers. By advising a client, as well as acting dishonestly, a broker may, to use Sachs LJ's expression from *Lloyds Bank Ltd v Bundy*,[157] have 'crossed the line' into a fiduciary relationship. Anticipating the later characteristic of *reliance*, liability is attracted in two stages. A broker, first, must usually have undertaken to advise a client, whether pursuant to contract or otherwise. Then there must be circumstances where the broker knows that the client will rely on that advice. Fiduciary liability can be built on such a foundation. In *Reed v McDermid St Lawrence Ltd*[158] the British Columbia Court of Appeal took this approach to a broker's liability. The client was an unsophisticated old woman living on a disability pension, and stock in the corporation invested in was volatile. This did not automatically mean that the broker was under a duty to warn of potential risks. Ordering that the case be re-tried, the Court of Appeal held at 622 that the extent of the duty of broker to client beyond the bare agent's duty of executing instructions was a question of fact in each case:

> the client's relationship with the broker may give rise to higher obligations on the part of the broker if the client, by words or deeds, makes such obligations part of the relationship and the broker accepts those obligations.

A nexus between reliance and undertakings here is not a matter of law. Indeed, reliance may be conspicuously absent. This could be where there is evidence that the client had already made his or her own mind up before consulting the broker. In *James v Australia and New Zealand Banking Group Ltd*[159] the bank recommended to one of its customers that a particular mortgage-broker be employed to satisfy the customer's finance needs. That broker then carelessly predicted that funds would be available and the customer suffered loss when they were not. One of the bank's several successful defences to a consequent breach of fiduciary duty claim made against it was that the client would have proceeded with the transaction which caused the loss regardless of the broker's predictions. It might alternatively be argued, as we have seen, that the broker was used only in a ministerial way.[160]

---

[155] (1916) 33 TLR 78.
[156] (1889) 5 TLR 613.
[157] [1975] QB 326 at 342.
[158] [1991] 2 WWR 617, curiam.
[159] (1986) 64 ALR 347, Toohey J: discussed further at [3.122].
[160] *R H Deacon & Co Ltd v Varga* (1972) 30 DLR (3d) 653 and see P Finn 'Fiduciary Law' in McKendrick, p 7 T pp 10–11.

## 2. PROPERTY

**[3.69]**  'Property' is a sort of meta-language for the identification of fiduciary relationships. It is a shorthand for describing one type of a beneficiary's interests which can be the subject of trust in another. Commercial fiduciaries are entrusted with the various proprietary interests by their beneficiaries. Property might exist, for example, in share scrip left with a broker when the shares are bought or sold. Or the title deeds to land might be entrusted to the custody of a solicitor. Equipment to be sold, or the proceeds of its sale, may be possessed by a mercantile agent. Situations like these are examples of where property interests are held by one person on behalf of another. At a higher level of abstraction, the property of beneficiaries might exist in business opportunities or profitable contracts that come under another's control.

**[3.70]**  Trusted persons such as agents, employees, brokers or solicitors will sometimes acquire legal title to the entrusted property. This may be to facilitate the performance of tasks with that property, or its safe-keeping. The prime example of legal title being held for another is the institution of the trust itself. Fiduciaries who hold the legal title to fiduciary property may be treated indistinguishably from trustees.[161] In other cases, beneficiaries will retain the legal title to the property and be able to assert 'pure proprietary' claims to regain possession of the property.[162] Entrusting or the existence of equitable jurisdiction will not need to be established for the purpose of a 'pure proprietary' claim.[163] Fiduciary law will often act in aid of the common law relation of agency. Principals who delegate to agents the power to manage their property may be saved the trouble of devising a contract with a list of prohibitions against the agent misappropriating that property. Fiduciary law does the job for them. Equity implies appropriate prohibitions into the relationship.[164]

Both equitable and 'pure proprietary' rights are subject to the terms of any contract between the parties. Equitable rights are subject also to contrary mutual intention in the entrusting itself. Both of these may occur in certain types of agency, where the property held by the agents is in their own names.[165] Equitable interests of beneficiaries in this kind of property may be identified simply as the beneficiary's 'property'.

**[3.71]**  'Property theory' is not often cited as a justification by the courts where the existence of a fiduciary relationship is contested. Nor is it much espoused by legal writers advocating the systematisation of fiduciary law. This may be because of property's observed tendency to obscure substantive issues:

> what argument over property finally reduces to, as do most arguments about property, is what are the legitimate interests that call for the protection of the law.[166]

---

[161] J G Shepherd 'Towards a Unified Concept of Fiduciary Relationships' (1981) 97 *LQR* 51 at 63.

[162] Goff and Jones, pp 75–83.

[163] See *Walker v Corboy* (1990) 19 NSWLR 382: below, at [3.80].

[164] See R Posner *Economic Analysis of Law* 3rd ed (1986), 384, n.2; Anderson 'Conflicts of Interest: Efficiency, Fairness and Corporate Structure' (1978) 25 *UCLA Law Rev* 738; Shavell 'Risk Sharing and Incentives in the Principal and Agent Relationship' (1979) 10 *Bell J Econ* 55; Brudney and Clark 'A New Look at Corporate Opportunities' (1981) 94 *Harv LR* 997 at 999.

[165] *Bowstead on Agency* 15th edn, ed F M B Reynolds (1985) pp 162–3.

[166] S Beck 'The Quickening of Fiduciary Obligation: Canadian Aero Services v O'Malley' (1975) 53 *Can Bar Rev* 771 at 781.

Fiduciary characterisation arising from the entrusting of property may raise important policy questions. Should equity deprive persons of gains they make for themselves in the course of producing gains for those who trust them? Should profits belong to those who provided the profit-maker with the initial opportunity or introduction to make them? Property language is ill-adapted to resolve them. While inquiries should be made into such things as the nature of the wrong committed, the fairness of the transaction to both parties, and the commerciality of the facts, all else tends to be submerged when a 'claimant's property or not' determination is made.[167] Nor is one directed to the issue of the appropriateness of the sanction in view of the gravity of the wrong. 'Property' language is to some degree a distraction from proper fiduciary analysis. Nevertheless, the courts dealing with the following relations have used 'property' as a convenient reasoning tool for the characterisation exercise and the idea may not be beyond being used analogically.

### Agents receiving money for their principals[168]

**[3.72]** Suppose a mercantile agent has just sold a cargo of grain on his or her principal's account. The proceeds of sale are banked with the day's takings into the agent's account. Or suppose that a manufacturing business has sold some of its equipment through the offices of a trade auctioneer. Is either the agent or auctioneer in a fiduciary relationship with the client? Will equitable remedies be available in respect of the moneys collected? This might become important if the agent were to become bankrupt in the period intervening between collection of the money and payment of it over to the principal.

**[3.73]** Equity attaches considerable significance to the *way* in which an agent receives his principal's property. Money paid by third parties to agents on behalf of principals is treated differently from money that the principal directly receives.[169] There is no rule that equity will regard money as possessing the same character as the underlying property that it represents. Further to the preceding illustrations, prices received for the consigned cargo or the equipment sold are not themselves entrusted. Proceeds received in either case are not given by the principal into the agent's care, because they are not the principal's to give at the relevant time. The money came from a third party. The point of the the transaction for the principal was to use the agent to *get* the money from someone else. Nor is the money entrusted by the third party who pays it. It is simply the consideration in an ordinary commercial exchange: the price of grain or equipment purchased. In another example, I might send my car to a dealer to sell on my behalf.[170] The dealer is then in a fiduciary relationship with me, at least to the extent of my property interest in the car. Our fiduciary association derives from an undertaking the dealer made, actually or impliedly, when receiving the car. This is to act in my interest. A fiduciary relation may be constituted by the dealer's acceptance of the property that I entrust in the car. He may not thereafter take a bribe from a would-be

---

[167] T Frankel 'Fiduciary Law' (1983) 71 *Calif L R* 795 at 829.

[168] See P Finn 'Fiduciary Principle' in Youdan, p 1 at pp 35–7; Finn 'Fiduciary Law' in McKendrick p 7 at 17–18; *Bowstead on Agency* 15th edn, ed F M B Reynolds (1985) 156–64 and 193–200.

[169] See Brunyate *Limitation of Actions in Equity* (1932) 86–7.

[170] See L S Sealy 'Fiduciary Relationships' [1962] *Camb LJ* 69 at 80.

purchaser of the car,[171] or secretly buy the car himself.[172] Up to the time of sale, the agent holds the car on my behalf. However the picture changes after the car is sold. The dealer ceases to hold the car, or any other specific property which I have entrusted. Instead, the dealer very often becomes my debtor in respect of the price received and equitable remedies are displaced.[173] It may follow that equitable intervention is unavailable, either in the ordinary case or where the agent is insolvent.[174]

**[3.74]** Agency transactions may sometimes have both fiduciary and non-fiduciary aspects, and at other times not be fiduciary at all. Intention of the parties, particularly the trusting party, is decisive on this. What was intended is taken to be indicated by certain things. Most particularly, obligations that the trusting party may have placed the agent under in dealing with the subject property. It was said by Slade J in *Re Bond Worth Ltd*[175] that:

> where an alleged trustee has the right to mix tangible assets or moneys and to deal with them as he pleases, this is incompatible with the existence of a *presently* existing fiduciary relationship in regard to such assets or moneys.

A submission based upon the indications approach of this passage was made in *Clough Mill Ltd v Martin*.[176] Robert Goff LJ said there that it–

> is a submission which I am unable to accept. In every case, we have to look at the relevant documents and other communications which have passed between the parties, and to consider them in the light of the surrounding circumstances, in order to ascertain the rights and duties of the parties inter se, always paying particular regard to the practical effect of any conclusion concerning the nature of those rights and duties. In performing this task, concepts such as bailment and fiduciary duty must not be allowed to be our masters, but rather be regarded as our tools of trade.

Robert Goff as Lord Goff has since referred to the fiduciary characterisation of an agency. He used it as an analogy in *Napier v Hunter*,[177] a case concerned with whether an insurer's subrogatory rights gave it an equitable proprietary lien. Authorities on the point were old and inconclusive. The question, he thought, should be resolved functionally, just like the characterisation of an agency. Both agency and insurance relationships are alike in that they are governed by contracts. Agents who receive money from a third party in an agency capacity may also hold it as trustee for the principal. In agency or insurance, he said, the question is what is appropriate in the commercial circumstances of the transaction.[178] Was it more appropriate that the agent's money should be held separately from his own resources, or should it be treated as part of the agent's normal cash-flow? Perhaps in this–

> a central question, too often overlooked (because not directly an issue), is *whether the rights of the principal are sufficiently strong, and differentiable from other*

---

[171] See *Lister & Co v Stubbs* (1890) 45 Ch D 1; *Metropolitan Bank v Heiron* (1880) 5 Ex D 319.

[172] *Haywood v Roadknight* [1927] VLR 512 at 521.

[173] *Bowstead on Agency* 15th edn, ed F M B Reynolds (1985) 193.

[174] See *Daly v Sydney Stock Exchange Ltd* (1986) 160 CLR 371at 378–80, Gibbs CJ.

[175] [1980] Ch 228, 261 and see *Stephens Travel Service International Pty Ltd v Qantas Airways Ltd* (1988) 13 NSWLR 331 at 348, Hope JA (CA).

[176] [1984] 3 All ER 982 at 987 (CA).

[177] [1993] AC 713 at 744.

[178] At 744, quoting *Bowstead on Agency* 15th edn (1985), ed F M B Reynolds 162.

*claims*, for him to be entitled to a prior position in respect of them on the agent's bankruptcy.[179] [emphasis added]

The rights of the insurer were strong enough in the *Napier* case to give it the proprietary right sought.

[3.75]  Fiduciary characterisation of the agency is one way for a principal to attract the enhanced remedies of equity against an agent who has misappropriated a sale price. This involves establishing that the agent is at the same time a fiduciary, as well as a debtor, in respect of the money received. The exercise does not involve any general principle relating to agencies and fiduciary relationships. Whether a given agency is a fiduciary one is the sort of question from which the editor of the last edition of *Bowstead on Agency* would probably have recoiled. Agency was there said to be regulated by the law in several different ways, according to its form.[180] Not every person who can be described as an 'agent' is also a fiduciary and not every fiduciary agent owes comparable equitable duties. Fiduciary agents may owe equitable duties in regard to some parts of the relation and not others, which describes the possibility of a partial fiduciary relation that authorities have confirmed.[181] *Bowstead* generally takes a 'rule specific' view of the fiduciaries. Litigants in each case are said to have the task of arguing for the precise fiduciary duty or duties which the facts attract, then the remedy or remedies the principal may have if those duties are breached should be justified. It is a methodology earlier described as 'atomistic'.[182]

[3.76]  One line of authority on agents' money receipts is quite favourable to a fiduciary characterisation. These are the cases dealing with the species of commercial financing known as 'factoring'.[183] Factoring is an arrangement whereby books debts are assigned, in effect, as security for advances from the assignee as lender. Problems have arisen where this security takes the form of agreements to assign future debts. The factoring agreements then can only be effective in equity.[184] Typically, by term of agreements, assignors constitute themselves the assignees' agents to deal with the debts after they had been assigned. This enables the debts to be collected in the ordinary way. It confirms the assignees' entitlement to all moneys the assignors receive from the debtors. Arrangements parallel the above examples dealing with the proceeds of grain and equipment sales. Factoring assignees possess rights over the debts assigned comparable to the rights that grain and equipment sellers have over their property before it is sold. For the factored debts have in theory been 'purchased' by the assignee lenders, pursuant to the equitable assignments. The assignor 'agents' are often referred to as actual trustees. Money received

---

179   [1993] AC 713 at 744, quoting from *Bowstead*.

180   *Bowstead on Agency* 15th edn, ed F M B Reynolds (1985) 156.

181   *New Zealand Netherlands Society 'Oranje' Incorporated v Kuys* [1973] 1 WLR 1126 at 1130 (PC); *Hospital Products*, [1982] 2 NSWLR 766 at 810 (at first instance); [1983] 2 NSWLR 157 at 206 (CA); (1984) 156 CLR 41 at 97–8, Mason J (diss).

182   At [2.14]: *Bowstead* op cit, 156–64.

183   See *Holroyd v Marshall* (1862) 10 HLC 191; 11 ER 999; *Tailby v Official Receiver* (1888) 13 App Cas 523.

184   See *Re Lind* [1915] 2 Ch 345 at 360, Swinfen Eady LJ (CA); *Norman v FCT* (1963) 109 CLR 9 at 24, Windeyer J; *FCT v Betro Constructions Pty Ltd* (1978) 20 ALR 647 at 650–1; *Re Puntoriero* (1991) 104 ALR 523 at 528–30, Einfeld J.

by them pursuant to the arrangement is referred to as 'trust property'.[185]

**[3.77]**   Dixon J's judgment in *Palette Shoes Pty Ltd v Krohn*[186] instances how property rights are extended in this type of arrangement. A fiduciary conception of the assignment of future debts was appealed to in order to characterise the debt proceeds later in the agent's hands. *Palette* involved a shoe manufacturing company which agreed to sell all the boots and shoes that it manufactured to a financier. The shoe manufacturer agreed to act thereafter as the financier's agent in selling the goods on its behalf. It would deliver to the financier invoices for goods sold on credit and receive from it a discounted cash balance in return. The manufacturer agreed to pay to the financier all money it later received from purchasers on account of credit sales. This money was by then due to the financier. It had already been discounted and paid to the manufacturer. We will not be concerned with the actual question appealed to the High Court concerning registration of assignment formalities. Relevantly to this, Dixon J held at 32–3 that the factoring agreement did not have to be registered as an assignment of book debts because nothing was presently assigned. Assignments were only contemplated by the procedure established.

**[3.78]**   Our consideration of *Palette Shoes* will be restricted to the effect which the majority of the court gave to the agreement of the manufacturer to sell shoes as agent of the financier. Dixon J at 30 said of this that:

> In equity the relation of agent would carry with it a duty to account, and, as a rule, a duty, if moneys are received in the course of the agency, to hold them specifically for the principal. At law the relation would be that of debtor and creditor. Even when the agent received under the authority of the principal the price of the latter's property, his obligation to pay it over at law was a personal obligation only. The importance which has been given to the question whether property in the manufactured shoes vested in the [principals] before it passed to the customers who bought them seems to be mistaken. As I have said, even if the goods sold were their property at law, the [principals] would gain no property in the proceeds. The company would at law still be no more than their debtor. In equity [it is different] . . . The reason why in equity the proceeds of property may be followed by the owner and treated as a fund held upon a constructive trust in his favour is that his beneficial ownership of the thing gives him prima facie an equitable interest in the proceeds.

Trust obligations are thus imposed on parties to a factoring ageement. They regulate a situation whereby a mercantile agent holds proceeds for remission to a principal. From an 'agent's duty to account', beneficial ownership of the subject of the account can be inferred in the person owed the duty. Such beneficial ownership may subsist inside a trust or fiduciary relation. Or it may not. There is no distinction in relation to the proceeds of sale between an express trustee, a constructive trustee and an agent. If the proceeds are to be accounted for in an equitable way, then the relevant relation between the parties has been characterised as fiduciary.

**[3.79]**   A methodology for examining this type of case will now be suggested, based in the principle that all consensual transfers of property rights are

---

[185] *Bowstead* op cit p 157: see the cases there cited—said to be 'inappropriate' and 'unsatisfactory'.
[186] (1937) 58 CLR 1.

exercises of intention.[187] This principle ultimately determines the fiduciary status of an agent's monetary receipts. Ownership of money as a species of property depends on what obligations the agent undertook. Where the intention is express, characterisation of the receipts may be straightforward. A term of the parties' agreement may provide that the agent will be debtor to the principal for money due on account between them. Alternatively, the parties may agree to impress a trust in favour of the principal on moneys received by the agent. Where parties are silent on the capacity in which an agent receives moneys for the principal, the relevant intention must be inferred from constitutive documents of the agency and its surrounding circumstances. An important consideration is whether the agent is under an express obligation to keep the moneys separate from the agent's own resources. If the agent is so obliged, fiduciary characterisation is more likely. The agreement may provide for the monthly notification of the agent's receipts and payment of that balance into a designated bank account. Such a 'running account' is suggestive of a contractual, purely legal relationship between agent and principal. On the other hand, the agent may be obliged to bank moneys received to the credit of a special account on the day that they are received. This counts more in favour of a fiduciary characterisation.

[3.80] Concerned with factoring finance for a shoe manufacturer, Dixon J drew inferences as to intention as between principal and agent in *Palette Shoes Pty Ltd v Krohn*.[188] Contract documents and surrounding circumstances were examined in order to reach a fiduciary conclusion.[189] In *Westpac Banking Corporation v Savin*[190] the court interpreted standard form auction contracts for the same purpose. An auctioneer of boats was found liable to account for auction proceeds as fiduciary and not as a debtor. *Walker v Corboy*[191] involved construction of a public statute. A farm produce agent at a wholesale market became insolvent before paying the proceeds of produce sales to his principals. In New South Wales, the Farm Produce Act 1983 regulates the affairs of agents who sell farm produce on behalf of growers. Indicia of a non-fiduciary relation were argued to exist in the absence of any requirement in the Act for the keeping of separate accounts for each grower. Nor did the Act prohibit mixing of the proceeds of agency sales with the licensed person's own moneys. Despite these indications, the New South Wales Court of Appeal confirmed that the produce agent held proceeds of sales as a fiduciary. Meagher JA expressed the view (at 398) that general usage, or 'industry-wide practice', in respect of the receipts also counted in the fiduciary direction. Although not discussed in that case, the sufficiency of remedies that an applicable statute gives the principal for an agent's non-performance would also be relevant. An insufficiency might be used to rebut the argument that provisions of the statute

---

[187] Also in *Westpac Banking Corporation v Savin* [1985] 2 NZLR 41 at 45 (CA), Richardson J: also eg *The 'Tiskerei'* [1983] 2 Lloyds Rep 658 and *Walker v Corboy* (1990) 19 NSWLR 382 at 395, Meagher JA.

[188] (1937) 58 CLR 1 at 18–36.

[189] At 31–3: a 'prima facie rule' of construction, per Meagher JA in *Walker v Corboy* (1990) 19 NSWLR 382 at 396; see also Cohen v Cohen (1929) 42 CLR 91at 101–2, Dixon J.

[190] [1985] 2 NZLR 41 at 45, Richardson JA; at 58, McMullin JA (CA).

[191] (1990) 19 NSWLR 382 (CA).

are an 'entire code' for the default in question.[192] The retention fund in a construction contract was treated analogously in *KBH Constructions Pty Ltd v Lidco Aluminium Products Pty Ltd.*[193]

**[3.81]** In this way a fiduciary relationship between principal and agent can be derived from a principal's beneficial interest in moneys that the agent receives. However, in commercial situations a finding that an agency is of a fiduciary nature will often not be made. The matter is more purely remedial. A constructive trust over the proceeds in favour of the principal's remedy is often sufficient. This is how the fiduciary entitlement is vindicated. A constructive trust may be awarded when the agent, in breach of fiduciary duty, fails to account for the proceeds.[194] Courts may award constructive trusts without adverting to the fiduciary relationships which facilitate them.[195]

## Officers of a company and 'corporate opportunities'

**[3.82]** 'Corporate opportunity' doctrine has developed in connection with a particular breach of fiduciary obligation committed by directors and other senior officers of corporations. Those persons may usurp or improperly divert business opportunities of the corporation for their own benefit.[196] Cases under this heading are not often about the *existence* of a fiduciary relationship between the parties. This is assumed from the fact of directorship of or seniority in the corporation at the relevant time. Dispute is rather over whether the scope of a director's or officer's duties to the corporation includes making the disputed gain. Or, putting this as we will later at [4.35]–[4.43], the issue is whether the duty and its breach establishes a sufficient nexus between the plaintiff corporation and the defendant's gain. In the leading case of *Cook v Deeks*[197] a profitable construction contract was appropriated by fiduciary directors who were in undisputed control of the company at material times. Although unquestioned, the fiduciary relationship might be reasoned to exist from the directors' previous undertaking to serve it. No property language needs to be used at all. However, for various reasons, it sometimes intrudes.

**[3.83]** In *Canadian Aero Service Ltd v O'Malley*[198] it was factually difficult to establish a *Cook v Deeks* fiduciary relationship based on undertakings. Facts constituting the breach of duty, in the defendants' submission, occurred after the undertakings had ceased to have effect. Senior employees of Canadian Aero resigned from their positions before acting against the corporation's

---

[192] See *Stephens Travel Service International Pty Ltd (receivers and managers appointed) v Qantas Airways Ltd* (1988) 13 NSWLR 331 (CA).

[193] (1990) 7 BCL 183 ( SC (NSW)) Giles J).

[194] The outcome in *Palette Shoes Pty Ltd v Krohn* (1937) 58 CLR 1 at 30, Dixon J; *Walker v Corboy* (1990) 19 NSWLR 382; *Stephens Travel Service International Pty Ltd (receivers and managers appointed) v Qantas Airways Ltd*, supra.

[195] Evident particularly in Canadian cases: see *Ontario Wheat Producers' Marketing Board v Royal Bank* (1982) 145 DLR (3d) 663 (HC (Ont)) affirmed (1984) 46 OR (2d) 362 (CA); *United Association etc v J Neilson & Sons (Mechanical) Ltd* (1982) 6 WWR 763 (Albta QB); *Re Ontario Egg Producers' Marketing Board and Clarkson Co Ltd* (1981) 33 OR (2d) 657 (HC); *Re Haina (HB) & Assoc. Inc* (1978) 86 DLR (3d) 262 (BCSC).

[196] Ford [9.230].

[197] [1916] 1 AC 554 (PC); also *Regal (Hastings) Ltd v Gulliver* (1942) [1967] 2 AC 134n, *Peso Silver Mines Ltd v Cropper* (1966) 58 DLR (2d) 1.

[198] (1973) 40 DLR (3d) 371 (SC).

interests. This was done so that the former employees might pursue a profitable tender through a company of their own. The same tender had been actively sought by the employees, prior to their departure, for Canadian Aero itself. Eventually the tender was let to the former employees' company, whereupon Canadian Aero alleged that fiduciary obligations had been breached. 'Damages' were claimed, equal to the value of the benefit that the former employees' company appropriated. The matter reached the Supreme Court of Canada on appeal, where obligations flowing from the relationship were found (at 382) to go 'at least this far':

> a director or senior officer like [the defendants] is precluded from obtaining for himself, either secretly or without the approval of the company . . . any property or business advantage either belonging to the company or for which it has been negotiating.

**[3.84]**   In *Canadian Aero* the plaintiff claimed that the tender represented 'the fruits of a corporate opportunity'. An 'interest' of Canadian Aero was said to be directed by the disloyal officers to a company of their own. The court agreed (at 372) and found that the opportunity did 'belong to the corporation' in the requisite sense. In this the court made a deliberate use of property language. Appropriation of that opportunity by the corporation's former employees would be the thing sanctioned.[199]

Existence of a fiduciary relation between officers and the company was not specifically adverted to in the course of the *Canadian Aero* appeal. No specific obligation or role of the officers was relevant. Nor was reliance, power or any other non-proprietary mode of fiduciary reasoning called in aid. Instead, both relationship and its breach were treated as evident from the finding of which person rightfully 'owned' the appropriated opportunity. Opportunities within a corporation's line of business, like this tender, were said (at 386) to 'belong' to the corporation in some quasi-property sense. One commentator has doubted how satisfactory it was for a company to 'own' as against a fiduciary an opportunity which is not susceptible of division into legal and beneficial estates.[200] Only after ignoring the existence of a fiduciary relation stage in its reasoning did the court in *Canadian Aero* appraise the substantial fairness issue—namely, the justice of imposing a fiduciary standard on the (former) officers. This was achieved with notable clarity: examining (at 391) whether the fiduciary duties implied had been breached in the context of applicable 'factors'. The same evocative 'property' language is similarly used in Australia only in connection with the 'scope' inquiry.

**[3.85]**   The *Canadian Aero* mode of property reasoning to the relation seems to fall within the celebrated criticism of this made by Lord Upjohn in *Boardman v Phipps*.[201] This was also a case which did not involve any question as to whether a fiduciary relation existed. Boardman conceded that he was a fiduciary and his co-defendant sought no better treatment. As solicitor, Boardman had made a substantial private profit from the handling of his client's affairs. On appeal the issue was whether the fiduciary relationship

---

199  At 385 (judgment of the court delivered by Laskin CJ), approving the approach in the note 'Corporate Opportunity' 74 *Harv LR* 765 (1961).

200  J G Shepherd 'Towards a Unified Concept of Fiduciary Relationships' (1981) 97 *LQR* 51 at 64.

201  [1967] 2 AC 46 at 127–8 (dissenting).

extended to and prohibited the making of that profit. Lord Cohen, hearing the case, reasoned (at 102–3) from the existence of a property interest in certain information about shares. He said that a misuse of property in the information had occurred. Lord Hodson agreed (at 106–7). This was in fact the view of a majority of the majority of Lords deciding the case. Boardman the solicitor had misused his client's property by using it to generate profits for himself. Lord Upjohn explicitly disagreed with this analysis and it was not shared by the other Lords. It could not be allowed, said Upjohn at 127, that a fiduciary relation was extended by this interest. 'Information', he said,

> is not property at all. It is normally open to all who have eyes to see and ears to hear. The true test is to determine in what circumstances the information has been acquired.

**[3.86]**  Criticism of the Upjohn kind can be applied to the *Canadian Aero* analysis. It highlights one point particularly in reasoning to the existence of a fiduciary relation. The language of property obscures consideration of the link between the quality of the wrong committed and its perpetrator. Focus for this should be on what corresponds to Upjohn's 'circumstances' in which 'the information has been acquired'. Proprietary analysis has the usual self-evidency about it. A 'corporate opportunity' is, of course, an interest of a corporate claimant. To call it a 'property' interest leads to the inference that the defendant is a fiduciary in breach of duty if it can be shown that the defendant has diverted the opportunity. The reason why has not been satisfactorily explained. Calling the interest 'property' takes the analysis no further.

### 3. RELIANCE

#### Reliance in fact and the entitlement to rely

**[3.87]**  A reliance characteristic may include two things. Either a person may *rely in fact* on another, or, in the circumstances, the person may be *entitled to rely*.[202] Reliance in fact occurs where a person has actual trust or confidence in another. Business partners usually have this sort of confidence in one another. Or a businessman may actually place trust in the judgment of his financial advisor, or his bank manager. Entitlement to rely occurs by operation of law. The entitlement arises in those relationships which the law recognises as inherently confidential and worthy of protection. Fiduciary status is then given without much argument. A client, say, may be entitled to rely on the integrity of a solicitor he has consulted, according to fiduciary standards. This is so regardless of whether the client actually trusts the solicitor or not. An important thing to note about the different types of reliance is that they substantially overlap. Each example of reliance given in this paragraph of either kind, involving partners, bank managers, business advisors and solicitors, could probably be argued for as an example of the other type. Partners and bank managers might be such as one is entitled to rely upon. Or, in many cases, a solicitor is one who is actually relied upon. Almost all instances of 'entitlement to rely' are also 'reliances in fact'. Partners are entitled to rely on each other and usually do. Repeated instances of factual reliance move towards the 'entitlement to rely'. Proof that the plaintiff must

---

[202] Cf P Finn 'Fiduciary Principle' in Youdan 1 at 33–54.

adduce in court changes accordingly. Much of the reliance characteristic here is illustrated by these ambivalent relationships: joint venture participants, bank managers and the like. They are midway between actual and expected reliance.

[3.88]  The 'actual' and 'entitled' distinction can be put in other ways. Forms of reliance could be classed as actual or hypothetical to the same effect. Or reliance can be seen as a 'factual phenomenon' or 'legal phenomenon', as some have · put it.[203] The distinction sheds little light on fiduciary characterisation and erects a classification with little present relevance. It is tautologous to say that one trusts or reposes confidence in a fiduciary, at least as we have understood the term. Of course one trusts a person trusted. Identity of who by the reliance characteristic is a 'fiduciary' cannot be developed by repeating the word 'trust'. Elucidation will more likely come about by distinguishing different ways in which trust can be relied on. Hence a general division of the characteristic is proposed. Reliance in a fiduciary relation may be either 'two-sided' or 'one-sided'. This reflects the different ways in which reliance may be placed. Two-sided reliance is where the parties rely on each other, mutually. One-sided reliance is where one party relies on another, often from a position of vulnerability or inequality. We shall examine reasoning processes under each heading separately.

### Two-sided reliance (the partnership analogy)

[3.89]  Equity has recognised several relations where each party places trust and confidence in the other. This reliance is mutual, or 'two-sided'. Partnership is its paradigm and the main source of analogies for reasoning in novel cases. Originally an equitable idea, 'partnership' defined in the uniform partnership legislation now subsumes the whole sense of the term.[204] It is–

> the relation which subsists between persons carrying on business in common with a view to profit.[205]

Carrying on business for profit defines the relation. The canonical definition of partnership is explicitly commercial. Dixon J said of partnership's equitable nature in *Birtchnell v Equity Trustees, Executors and Agency Co Ltd*[206] that:

> The relation between partners is, of course, fiduciary. Indeed, it has been said that a stronger case of fiduciary relationship cannot be conceived than that which exists between partners.

We have noted that the mutual trust and confidence of partners is one of the 'accepted categories' of fiduciary relation. A 'stronger case of the fiduciary relationship cannot be conceived', Dixon J says, and he continues by making a quotation from the judgment of Bacon VC in *Helmore v Smith*.[207] This was a case where a partner temporarily went insane. His co-partner allowed the sheriff to proceed to execution against the insane partner's partnership share for a very small sum. The co-partner then purchased the share from the sheriff

---

[203] P Finn 'The Fiduciary Principle' in Youdan 1 at 33–54; 36A *Corpus Juris Secundum* (1961), 381-9; 37 *Am Juris* 2d (1968), 16.

[204] 'Commentary' by R A Ladbury in Finn *Relationships*, 45–6.

[205] Partnership Act: UK s 1(1); NSW s 1(1); Vic s 5(1); Qld s 5(1); WA s 7(1); SA s 1(1); Tas s 6(1).

[206] (1929) 42 CLR 384 at 407.

[207] (1886) 35 Ch D 436 at 444.

at a bargain price. It was an act of great disloyalty. When the insane partner recovered, he successfully brought action to have the transaction set aside, as entered in breach of fiduciary duty. Bacon V-C observed:

> [partners'] mutual confidence is the life blood of the concern. It is because they trust one another that they are partners in the first instance; it is because they continue to trust one another that the business goes on.

A point is made about the nature of partners' trust. Partners trust 'one another', Bacon V-C says, in a mutual way. Trust proceeds from each party, both in deciding to join the relation in the first place and in deciding to stay in it. We see below how analogies from such a characteristic have fared.

### Joint ventures[208]

**[3.90]**   A joint venture has been described as an association of two or more persons engaging in or about to engage in a common business enterprise.[209] Oneness in that enterprise usually marks off a joint venture from a partnership, though 'joint venture is not a technical [term] with a settled common law meaning'.[210] Joint ventures are often partnerships as well. Both are cooperative associations for profit and are entered for similar reasons. But not all the 'accepted' aspects of a partnership may be present in a given joint venture. Sometimes a joint venture will be no more than a contractual relation between its members—like the 'farm-in' arrangement in *Diversified Mineral Resources NL v CRA Exploration Pty Ltd*.[211] 'Contract only' and 'fiduciary' ventures are the antitheses in the characterisation of joint ventures. 'Contract only' characterisations are made in a considerable number of joint venture cases.

**[3.91]**   What distinguishes joint ventures that are fiduciary from merely contractual ventures is the question here. At least one commentator believes that an a priori answer is possible, arguing that whether a joint venture is of a fiduciary character or not is an is an identifiable aspect of the venture's formal structure.[212] The opposite is contended here. Fiduciary characterisation of a joint venture is an instance of the same characterisation exercise as with any other non-accepted relation. It is a matter of resemblances: persuasive analogies, judgment and degree. The sufficiency of mutual trust and confidence that a joint venture exhibits is important in this context. Judgment on the resemblance between the mutual trust in joint venture and the partnership paradigm is made.[213] Assessment of the rights and duties of the participants in a particular joint venture must be made.[214] Things held out about

---

[208] See B H McPherson 'Joint Ventures' Finn Equity p 19; J D Merralls 'Mining and Petroleum Joint Ventures in Australia: Some Basic Legal Concepts' (1981) 3 *AMPLJ* 1; G Ryan 'Mining Joint Venture Agreements' (1982) 4 *AMPLJ* 101.

[209] B H McPherson 'Joint Ventures' in Finn *Relationships* p 19 at 20.

[210] *United Dominions Corporation Ltd v Brian Pty Ltd* (1985) 157 CLR 1, 10, Mason, Brennan, Deane JJ.

[211] (Fed Ct), 3 February 1995, Whitlam J, unreported. See [3.26]–[3.31].

[212] R A Ladbury 'Mining Joint Ventures' (1984) 12 *ABLR* 312.

[213] See S Ongley 'Joint Ventures and Fiduciary Obligations' (1992) 22 *VUWLR* 265 and L Griggs 'Joint Ventures, Partnerships and Fiduciary Obligations' (1994) 24 *Qld Law Soc Jo* 77.

[214] See *United Dominions Corporation Ltd v Brian Pty Ltd* (1985) 157 CLR 1 at 10, Mason, Brennan, Deane JJ.

the joint venture to third parties are not relevant.[215] Construction in the first place must be made of the formal terms of the association which appear in the joint venture agreement. As Mason, Brennan and Deane JJ in *United Dominions Corporation Ltd v Brian Pty Ltd* said:[216]

> whether or not the relationship between joint venturers is fiduciary will depend on the form which the particular joint venture takes and upon the content of the obligations which the parties to it have undertaken.

Construction is a matter of substance. In *Noranda Australia Ltd v Lachlan Resources NL*[217] a term of a joint venture agreement expressly used the 'fiduciary' word, but in the result, a contract-only characterisation was made. An obligation imposed by the fiduciary provision was subordinated to the agreement's substantial form.

**[3.92]** Some joint ventures may not be fiduciary because of their formal structure alone. Statutory definition of 'partnership' in the partnership Acts contains three main features: 'carrying on a business', 'in common' and 'with a view to a profit'. Each of these features should be embodied to follow the equitable partnership paradigm. Australian joint ventures, particularly in the mining industry, may specifically negate the 'in common' aspect. This usually appears from the terms of the constituent documents. Ventures like this are said to be, structurally, not of a fiduciary nature.[218] In some joint venture agreements it is provided that each participant will be rewarded for its contribution by a proportionate share in what is produced. Say, each venturer gets one-third of the coal extracted from a certain mine. The raising of the coal part of this venture is obviously 'in common', whatever the agreement may provide. Perhaps the operator is a separate entity which manages the daily functions of the mine on behalf of all the venturers. It may be directed by them in committee. Or one participant in the venture undertakes the mining work and is indemnified by the others. Venturers have a common interest in raising the mine's product. Extractive, or production, parts of the venture are of a fiduciary nature. However, the balance of the venture may be otherwise. The agreement might provide that subsequent stages of the venture will not involve any common interests. Justified reliance through the reposition of trust and confidence can be negated in this way. Disposal of proportionate product shares in the coal may be left unregulated. Fiduciary responsibility may thereby be excluded from the marketing of the venturers' shares. Venturers might compete for the same customers and undercut each other. The whole undertaking apart from the raising of the coal can be expressed to be the independent interest of each participant.[219]

---

[215] *Walker v Hirsch* (1884) 27 Ch D 460 at 467–8, Cotton LJ.

[216] (1985) 157 CLR 1, 10–11.

[217] (1988) 14 NSWLR 1, at 13–16, Bryson J; and see above at [3.31].

[218] R Ladbury 'Commentary' in Finn *Relationships* 38–47 and J Jackson 'Fiduciary Relationships in Australian Joint Ventures' (1986) 14 *ABLR* 107.

[219] See M Crommelin 'The Mineral and Petroleum Joint Venture in Australia' (1986) 4 JENRL 65 at 73–4; P Finn 'Fiduciary Obligations of Operators and Co-Venturers in Resource Joint Ventures in Australia' [1984] *AMPLA Yearbook* 160; N Tole and J Waite 'Fiduciary Obligations in Resource Joint Ventures in Australia' (1985–6) 4 *Oil & Gas Law and Taxation Review* 160.

In *Erewhon Exploration Ltd v Northstar Energy Corporation Ltd*,[220] the operator, which managed a Canadian oil and gas venture, was held to stand in a fiduciary position towards non-operators. The 'contractual context' of the venture implied duties of the fiduciary kind. Difference in nature of ventures may thus be reduced to a drafting matter. Constitutive documents can be phrased to achieve a desired fiduciary or purely contractual outcome. This is subject to the absence of any factual inconsistency upon which the courts might base a different characterisation. A fairly crisp means of deciding the characterisation question would appear possible. But the reality is usually much more ambiguous. Even identification of a feature of a venture as 'in common' or 'not in common' will probably involve the same balancing of resemblances as a fuller analysis.

[3.93]　Joint ventures are sometimes treated in a less a priori way and are argued to be fiduciary to the extent that they resemble partnerships. B H McPherson makes this suggestion,[221] generalising from *Canny Gabriel Jackson Advertising Pty Ltd v Volume Sales (Finance) Ltd*[222] and *United Dominions Corporation Ltd v Brian Pty Ltd*.[223] There is no equitable difference between a fiduciary joint venture and a partnership. 'Mutual trust and confidence' of partners is in this way as much the hallmark of a fiduciary joint venture as of a partnership. 'Trusting' and 'mutual' are the evaluative criteria.

[3.94]　Two recent decisions of the High Court show how the trusting indicia in a relationship are isolated and viewed. The first is *Canny Gabriel Jackson Advertising Pty Ltd v Volume Sales (Finance) Ltd*.[224] Volume Sales financed the performance of contracts by the singers Cilla Black and Elton John. In return, the promoter of the singers agreed to assign to the financier 'a one half interest in the contracts and to perform the contracts as a joint venture'. There was a provision for equal sharing of profits (but not losses) and the loan was to be repaid before any distribution of profit. Box office proceeds were paid into an account in the financier's name. The financier later submitted in court that this 'joint venture' was in equity a partnership. As such it entitled the financier to an equitable interest in the box office proceeds before payment. The interest was needed because of an equitable charge over the proceeds that the promoter subsequently gave to an advertising agency. If the financier had a pre-existing interest, it had priority over the charge.

At 326–7 the High Court accepted the financier's submission and concluded that the joint venture was a partnership in equity, as equally it was under the Partnership Act 1892 (NSW). The following factors were said to require it.

1. The parties became joint venturers in a commercial enterprise with a view to profit;
2. Profits were to be shared;

---

[220] (1993) 108 DLR (4th) 709 at 757, Hunt J.

[221] 'Joint Ventures' in Finn *Relationships*, p 19 at pp 32–6.

[222] (1974) 131 CLR 321.

[223] (1985) 157 CLR 1.

[224] (1974) 131 CLR 321 curiam; see also *Marr v Arabco Traders Ltd* (1987) 1 NZBLC 102,732, Tompkins J (SC (NZ)), citing at 102,743 the partnership case of *Birtchnell*, per Dixon J, quoted at [3.12].

3. The policy of the joint venture was a matter for joint agreement and it was provided that differences relating to the affairs of the joint venture should be settled by arbitration;
4. An assignment of a half interest in the contracts for the appearances of Cilla Black and Elton John was unsuccessfully attempted; and
5. Each party was concerned with the financial stability of each other in a way which is common with partners.

**[3.95]** *United Dominions Corporation Ltd v Brian Pty Ltd*[225] is the second decision. The High Court was concerned in that case with a joint venture which had as its object the development of land in a Brisbane suburb. Three companies participated: Brian, UDC and SPL. Brian had the idea, UDC was the financier and SPL owned the land. Prior to the venture commencing, SPL gave a mortgage over this land to UDC. This was to secure lending for the project. However, without Brian's knowledge, then or later, the mortgage terms contained a 'collateralisation clause', securing over the land a liability of SPL which was unrelated to the joint venture. When the venture was completed, a substantial profit appeared likely for each of the participants. The profit was represented by an increase in the value of the joint venture land, then about to be sold and the proceeds divided. UDC, however, refused to discharge the mortgage it held over the land even after it had been repaid the loan it made to the joint venture. UDC asserted a right to set off the amount of SPL's other liability against the venture profit pursuant to the 'collateralisation clause', of which Brian had been unaware. What UDL proposed to do was to diminish Brian's profit share in order to recoup SPL's extra-venture borrowing. Mason, Brennan and Deane JJ disallowed this, in a leading judgment. They found (at 11) that the relationship between each of UDL, SPC and Brian was fiduciary at the time that SPL gave the mortgage to UDC. The 'collateralisation clause' was an advantage that UDC had obtained in relation to the venture without the 'knowledge and informed consent' of Brian. It followed in the joint judgment that the clause could not be relied on to the extent of Brian's profit share.

**[3.96]** The joint judgment in *United Dominions* determined the venture's fiduciary status by first construing the terms of the formal venture agreement, though these were not the only consideration, nor were they even critical to the case. For SPL gave the mortgage to UDC with its 'collateralisation clause' prior to execution of the formal agreement. Characteristics of an inchoate relation, shortly to be examined, were involved, as well as a joint venture. Nevertheless, the majority's approach to construction of the constituent document was significant. Generalisations about joint ventures were eschewed. From the terms of the agreement two fiduciary indicia of status were elicited (at 11): each an indicator of mutuality. First, any profits of the venture were to be shared. Secondly, the joint venture property was held on trust for the participants by SPL. Gibbs CJ (at 7–8) and Dawson J (at 16) agreed, Gibbs CJ saying that there was–

> in the circumstances of the present case, a relationship between UDC and Brian based on the same mutual trust and confidence, and requiring the same good faith

---

[225] (1985) 157 CLR 1 and see *Biala Pty Ltd v Mallina Holdings Ltd* (1993) 11 ACSR 785at 831–2, Ipp J (SC (WA)).

and fairness, as if a formal partnership deed had been executed.

Assimilation of the fiduciary joint venture to a partnership was fairly explicit. Indicia of partnership in the venture were evident to the court, even if the mutual obligations were inchoate at the time that the fiduciary duty was breached.

### Inchoate relations[226]

**[3.97]** A fiduciary relationship exhibiting the characteristic of mutual reliance may exist even at a very early stage of the parties' dealings. This can be before the making of any final undertaking by the putative fiduciary, or an anticipated transfer of property has occurred. Nevertheless, at that time the requisite element of reliance to base the relation may be found. Fiduciary reliance can be evident where reasoning from other characteristics is premature. It exists where each party trusts, confides in and relies on the loyalty of the other. On the partnership paradigm, the resultant fiduciary obligations then bind the parties mutually, whatever project they have in view.

**[3.98]** Inchoate facts occurred in the joint venture case of *United Dominions Corporation Ltd v Brian Pty Ltd*.[227] Judgments in that decision illustrate the derivation of a fiduciary relation and mutual reliance in circumstances of incompleteness. The High Court, as we saw at [3.94], accepted that a joint venturer in the position of UDC owed each other participant in the venture a fiduciary duty not to obtain a collateral advantage without its consent. It was argued that, even if such a duty did exist, it was inapplicable prior to the signature of the joint venture agreement. The venture was, it was said, only a prospect at the time when SPL gave UDC the mortgage with the contentious 'collateralisation clause'. Hutley JA said of the point in the New South Wales Court of Appeal:[228]

> [UDC] made much in argument of the incomplete specification of the interests of the parties and of their failure to have agreed on vital terms. This seems to me to have confused the case. I see nothing legally objectionable in a number of people subscribing money for the purpose of a joint venture to be further defined. I would also consider that persons so clubbing together as joint venturers had obligations, inter se, analogous to those of partners at will. In other words, I do not see the changes which were made in the objects of the joint venture from time to time as showing that all that was intended was that the relationship between [UDC] and each contributor was that of debtor and creditor, and that each person admitted to the joint venture had no responsibilities to his fellows.

Dawson J said in the High Court (at 16):

> Whilst a concluded agreement may establish a relationship of confidence, it is nevertheless the relationship itself which gives rise to the fiduciary obligations. That relationship may arise from circumstances leading to the final agreement as much as from the fact of the final agreement itself.

**[3.99]** All judgments reported in the *United Dominions* litigation dismissed the 'incompleteness' defence. A fiduciary relationship might be based on

---

[226] See generally, G Hammond 'Equity and Abortive Commercial Transactions' (1990) 106 *LQR* 207.

[227] (1985) 157 CLR 1.

[228] *Brian Pty Ltd v United Dominions Corporation Ltd* [1983] 1 NSWLR 490 at 493 (CA).

mutual reliance existing between persons who intend to enter a fiduciary relation of a different kind. In confirming the Court of Appeal on this, however, two of the three judgments in the High Court added a small qualification. By the relevant time, it was said, the stage of 'mere negotiation' had passed. In the joint words of Mason, Brennan, Deane JJ at 12:

> arrangements between the prospective joint venturers had passed far beyond the stage of mere negotiation. Each had, by then, agreed to be, and been accepted as, a participant in each of the proposed joint ventures, if both or either of them went ahead. Each had made or agreed to make financial contributions towards the cost of the project or projects in which it or he had agreed to participate.

Gibbs CJ noted:

> it is unnecessary to decide whether persons negotiating for a partnership always stand in a fiduciary relationship . . . [here] the parties had . . . proceeded beyond the stage of mere negotiation. UDC at the time of the mortgage was in a relationship with [SPL and Brian] which, if not one of partnership, was one between persons who, intending to become partners, had already embarked on the partnership venture, of which the execution of the mortgage was an incident.[229]

**[3.100]**   Can a fiduciary relationship arise during 'mere negotiations'? Finn suggests that the fiduciary relationship might play an 'instrumental' role at the negotiating stage—purposively 'protecting opportunities' from the 'pre-emptive strike of one of the parties'.[230] Judges deciding *United Dominions Corporation Ltd v Brian Pty Ltd*[231] failed to endorse this possibility. In the next year, the Queensland Supreme Court decision in *Fraser Edmiston Pty Ltd v AGT (Qld) Pty Ltd*[232] was handed down. It was held there that a fiduciary relationship arose out of 'mere' negotiations for a partnership. The plaintiff had been entitled to a 'priority lease' in a shopping centre and negotiated to take this in partnership with the defendant. Before negotiations had proceeded very far, the defendant appropriated the tenancy to itself. Plaintiff cited the authority of *United Dominions*, apparently without challenge, for the proposition that a fiduciary relationship could arise out of 'negotiations'. The same finding was made also, following *United Dominions*, by the majority on the appeal in *Ravinder Rohini Pty Ltd v Krizaic*.[233] Parties made plans to demolish a hotel just purchased by one of them and redevelop the land with the expertise of another. An architect was instructed to prepare plans, development approval was obtained and engineers, plumbers and financiers were consulted. Then the parties fell out. Thereafter the party which owned the hotel was able to sell it with an 'approved development plan' for a considerable profit. Because there had been an 'informal arrangement to assume a partnership', at 311–14 a sufficient basis for fiduciary duties was found.

---

229   At 6, referring to *Lindley on Partnership* 15th ed (1984) p 480 and *Fawcett v Whitehouse* (1829) 1 Russ and M 132; 39 ER 51.

230   P Finn 'Fiduciary Law' in McKendrick, 7 at 18–19 and see his 'Good Faith, Unconscionability and Fiduciary Duties' (1990) *Energy Law* 103 at 118–19.

231   (1985) 157 CLR 1.

232   (1986) 2 Qd R 1, Williams J.

233   (1991) 30 FCR 300 (Fed Ct, FC), Davies and Wilcox JJ, Miles J not deciding.

The Ontario Court of Appeal in *International Corona Resources Ltd v Lac Minerals Ltd*[234] also cited *United Dominions* with approval on this point. It was held that a fiduciary relation based in mutual reliance existed where negotiations for a business association had not proceeded very far at all. Like the *Fraser Edmiston* facts,[235] the opportunity the subject of the *Lac* negotiations was specific to one party. Corona had made a mineral discovery and Lac Minerals negotiated with it for a joint development. But while negotiations were still at an early stage, Lac seized the opportunity for itself. It acquired the mineral-rich land that Corona had told it of before Corona had a chance to purchase the land: either for itself, or for the parties jointly. Negotiations had been so preliminary that not even the legal form of the proposed relationship had been agreed upon.

**[3.101]**     The *Lac Minerals* fiduciary finding was not upheld on appeal in the Canadian Supreme Court.[236] Sopinka J, with whom a majority agreed, at 599–608 based his reasons for denying a fiduciary relation on the absence of an appropriate 'power' in Lac and 'vulnerability' in Corona. Recovery for the defrauded prospecting company was allowed by the majority on account of Lac's 'breach of confidence' by misusing the critical information.[237] One of the majority, Lamer J, agreed with the minority on remedy, and they together formed a majority to sanction Lac with a constructive trust. The authority stands for an anomalous series of propositions. Sopinka J wrote the leading majority judgement. At 602–3 he considered the inchoate aspect of the argued fiduciary relation and the lower court's opinion on the applicability of the *United Dominions*[238] decision. Sopinka J distinguished the case, as being one concerned with a 'de facto partnership or joint venture'. Whereas, as he observed in *Lac* (at 603):

> The parties [in *Lac Minerals*] had not advanced beyond the negotiation stage. Indeed, they had not identified what precisely their relationship should be.

This built on what Holland J had said at first instance, before finding a fiduciary relationship—namely, that—

> The most that can be said is that the parties came to an informal oral understanding as to how each would conduct itself in anticipation of a joint venture or some other business arrangement.[239]

La Forest J wrote the leading minority judgment. Finding at 653–5 for the existence of a fiduciary relation, he was not concerned that the inchoate nature of the parties' relationship might disqualify it from fiduciary status. Wilson J, also in the minority, described the relation between Corona and Lac (at 631) simply as 'ongoing'.

**[3.102]**     A few common themes emerge from these judgments. For one thing, the type of mutual relationship negotiated for is not important. It might be the

---

[234] (1987) 62 OR (2d) 1, 44, (judgment of the Ont CA).

[235] (1986) 2 Qd R 1.

[236] *Lac Minerals Ltd v International Corona Resources Ltd* [1989] 2 SCR 574.

[237] 'Breach of confidence' was treated independently, as it is in this book. See P Finn 'Fiduciary Principle' in Youdan 1 at 50.

[238] (1985) 157 CLR 1.

[239] *International Corona Resources Ltd v Lac Minerals Ltd* (1986) 25 DLR (4th) 504, 538.

partnership in *Fraser Edmiston Pty Ltd v AGT (Qld) Pty Ltd*,[240] or the joint venture in *United Dominions Corporation Ltd v Brian Pty Ltd*.[241] It could be an agency, as in *Amalgamated Television Services Pty Ltd v Television Corporation Ltd*,[242] or the 'other business arrangement' in *Marr v Arabco Traders Ltd*.[243] It may not be critical that the negotiated relationship never eventuates.[244] Courts may be more disposed to find negotiations fiduciary where they deal with an opportunity specific to one of the parties, like the mineral discovery in *Lac Minerals Ltd v International Corona Resources Ltd*.[245] It is of general significance that the prospective relationship and the negotiations which precede it embody mutual trust.

### One-sided reliance

[3.103] Several legal and equitable regimes compete to regulate the consequences of one-sided reliance. Sometimes the phenomenon is referred to as vulnerability or inequality. First, there is the fiduciary relationship of trust, which concerns us here. A person relies on another, as he may be entitled to do, and, if the other disappoints that reliance, the trusting relationship will have been breached. Secondly, there are the sorts of facts which the fiduciary relation of influence attends to. A vulnerable or unequal party in a relationship places his trust in someone stronger or more competent. If the reliance is exploited by the stronger party, a series of remedial obligations is available. The reliant party may have been unduly influenced. The 'unequal' or 'vulnerable' type of reliance does not often attract the trusting relationship in Australia. It is much more common in the North American cases.[246] In Australia the trusting relation is only one of several resources to remedy the untoward consequences of this type of reliance, and is not always the most appropriate resource.[247]

[3.104] Anglo-Australian case law tends to class 'one-sided' forms of reliance where the parties are unequal as instances of 'undue influence'[248], or 'unconscionability'.[249] This may not be always so. Authorities are increasingly affected by competing strains of theory coming from Canada and the United States. Dawson J in *Hospital Products Ltd v United States Surgical Corporation*,[250] for example, said in 1984 that 'inherent in the nature' of the fiduciary relation, was—

> a position of disadvantage or vulnerability on the part of one of the parties which causes him to place reliance on the other and requires the protection of equity.

---

[240] (1986) 2 Qd R 1.

[241] (1985) 157 CLR 1.

[242] [1969] 2 NSWR 257: see 265–7, Jacobs JA (dissenting).

[243] (1987) 1 NZBLC 102,732.

[244] *Fraser Edmiston Pty Ltd v AGT (Qld) Pty Ltd* (1986) 2 Qd R 1 and *Lac Minerals Ltd v International Corona Resources Ltd* [1989] 2 SCR 574; but cf *Vroon BV v Foster's Brewing Group Ltd* [1994] 2 VR 32, 86–7, Ormiston J.

[245] [1989] 2 SCR 574, or the priority lease in *Fraser Edmiston Pty Ltd v AGT* (1986) 2 Qd R 1; see P Finn 'Fiduciary Law' McKendrick, 7 at 18.

[246] In the United States, see *Broomfield v Kosow* 212 NE 2d 556 (1965) and in Canada, *Morrison v Coast Finance Ltd* (1966) 55 DLR (2d) 710 (CA (BC)).

[247] See P Finn 'Fiduciary Principle' in Youdan, p 1 at pp 27–30.

[248] Eg, *Bank of New South Wales v Rogers* (1941) 65 CLR 42.

[249] Eg, *Commercial Bank of Australia Ltd v Amadio* (1983) 151 CLR 447.

[250] (1984) 156 CLR 41 at 142.

This is close to some celebrated words used by E J Weinrib in an article approved in the Canadian Supreme Court.[251] Fiduciary types are conflated. Multi-national corporations or departments of state, wronged by their fiduciary agents, are made to conform to a claimant's profile designed for the disadvantaged.

**[3.105]** Under this 'one-sided' heading we shall deal with the claim of a party to a relationship who either relies in fact on another, or who is legally entitled to do so. We will not be specifically concerned with parties who are specially disadvantaged or vulnerable. These are matters for undue influence. An example of the current type of fiduciary relation is that between employer and employee. An employer is entitled to expect that employees in their employment will be acting in the employer's and not their own interests. At least, this is true until the employer is informed otherwise. The employer is 'vulnerable' to the extent that an employee may act otherwise than he is relied upon to do.

## Banker and customer

**[3.106]** Bankers' relationships with their customers are now recognised to be of a fiduciary nature in at least some of their aspects. This is a recent phenomenon, but there is Australian and Canadian authority to this effect[252] and even *Halsbury's Laws of England* now regards it so.[253] Traditionally, things were different. The relationship of banker and customer was treated as that of debtor and creditor and thought to be defined by the terms of the contractual retainer subsisting between the parties. Or more specifically, as Bankes J observed in 1921 in *N Joachimson v Swiss Bank Corporation*,[254]

> In the ordinary case of banker and customer, their relations depend entirely or mainly on implied contract.

Despite the customer's 'deposit' of money with the banker, the formal relation of trustee and cestui que trust in respect of that money is still thought to be absent. No obligation lies on the banker to account specifically for the money. Mutual obligations of the parties in respect of that money are determined on a 'running account' basis.[255]

**[3.107]** Some debtor and creditor authority describes the relation referred to as that of 'banker and *customer*'. Both old[256] and more modern[257] United Kingdom cases tend to do this. It is probably significant that in each of these cases the relation of a bank was with a customer who was also a *depositor*. Being a depositor is one of the several characters that a bank customer may

---

[251] 'Fiduciary Obligation' (1975) 25 *UTLJ* 1, 6–7, specifically approved by Wilson J in *Frame v Smith* (1987) 42 DLR (4th) 81, 99 (SC).

[252] *Commonwealth Bank of Australia v Smith* (1991) 102 ALR 453 (Fed Ct (Full Court)) and the Canadian cases of *McBean v Bank of Nova Scotia* (1981) 15 BLR 296 and *Hayward v Bank of Nova Scotia* (1984) 45 OR (2d) 542: also G A Weaver and C R Craigie *Law Relating to Banker and Customer in Australia* 2nd ed (1990), [6.10]–[6.24].

[253] Vol 3(1), 4th ed (1989), [251].

[254] [1921] 3 KB 110 at 117, Bankes J.

[255] *Re Metway Bank Ltd* [1991] 1 Qd R 120; G A Weaver and C R Craigie, op cit, [6.40].

[256] Eg, *Devaynes v Noble (Sleech's Case)* (1816) 1 Mer 539 at 568; 35 ER 771 at 780.

[257] Eg, *R v Davenport* [1954] 1 WLR 569 (CCA).

assume. Customers might also be borrowers, or persons seeking commercial advice. United States authorities have specifically distinguished the 'banker and depositor' relation from other types of customer relationships.[258] Consider the traditional British case of *Foley v Hill*.[259] A bank had argued that the Statute of Limitations gave it a defence to its customer's action for the return of a sum deposited. The deposit had been made many years before. To evade the defence, the customer claimed the deposited sum in equity. Equitable jurisdiction was claimed both in the 'complication of accounts' and from a 'fiduciary relationship' on the facts. As the account had only three entries and was entirely expressed in the pleadings, the first argument was unsuccessful. The second argument amounted, in present terms, to a property-based claim of a relationship based in the entrusted sum. The 'supposed fiduciary character existing between the banker and his customer' was argued to be analogous to that whereby 'agents', 'factors' and 'stewards' are entrusted with the property of their principals and employers.

**[3.108]** All members of the House of Lords in *Foley v Hill* confirmed the non-fiduciary finding of Lord Lyndhurst LC in the court below. After examining the facts of banking business, Lord Cottenham LC held at 1005 (and other members of the House agreed) that a banker in the course of his trade was not intended to be a trustee of specific money deposited. Banking business would not allow it. Instead,

> the banker is bound to return an equivalent by paying a similar sum to that deposited with him when he is asked for it.

In a separate concurring speech Lord Brougham also examined a banker's ordinary trade, adding a significant remark. 'Certain acts', he said at 1008, 'that are often performed by a banker',

> put [the banker] in a totally different capacity. He may in addition to his position of banker, make himself an agent or trustee towards a cestui que trust.

This might be an expression of fiduciary liability in the terms of 1848. Lord Brougham gave the example of the brokerage of exchequer bills, suggesting that a fiduciary relation based in property might follow. Other, different, acts, he said, may also attract obligations of a fiduciary character.

**[3.109]** One hundred and fifty years after the House of Lords decision in *Foley v Hill*, the 'trade of a banker' with his or her customers has grown considerably. Banking has developed in new directions beyond the acceptance of deposits. Now perhaps,

> modern banking practices involve a highly complicated structure of credit and other complexities which often thrust a bank into a role of an advisor, thereby creating a relationship of trust and confidence which may result in a fiduciary duty thrust upon the bank.[260]

---

258  *Bank of Marin v England* 385 US 99 at 101 (1966) (SC); *Klein v First Edina National Bank* 196 NW 2d 619 (1972); *Stewart v Phoenix National Bank* 64 P 2d 101 (1937); *Klatt v First State Bank* 220 NW 318 (1927) and (Annot) 'Existence of a Fiduciary Relationship Between Bank and Depositor or Customer so as to Impose Special Duty of Disclosure upon Bank' 70 ALR 3d 1344 (1976), 1349–50.

259  (1848) 2 HLC 28; 9 ER 1002.

260  *Deist v Wachholz* 678 P 2d 188; 193 (1984).

There are several activities normally now undertaken by banks where customers rely on the bank. Reliance is the thing which injects an equitable element into the banker and customer relation. In the 1958 case of *Woods v Martin's Bank Ltd*,[261] Salmon J was concerned with whether a bank owed a customer a duty to give a customer sound investment advice. At 70 he said:

> In my judgment, the limits of a banker's business cannot be laid down as a matter of law. The nature of such a business must in each case be a matter of fact.

After then considering some exhibited advertising brochures of a bank, which had in excess of 600 branches, Salmon J concluded at 71 that 'it was and is within the scope of the defendant bank's business to advise on all financial matters'.

Fiduciary relations associated with reliance, we have noted, may be of more than one type. For instance, if a bank wrongfully exercises its influence over customers, it will be in the context of a 'fiduciary relation of influence', dealt with in Chapter 8. Or the bank may be liable for its misconduct in unconscionable dealings with customers. We are only concerned here with reliance in the context of the trusting type of fiduciary relation.

**[3.110]** We will not be dealing under this heading with a bank's improprieties in obtaining the consent of its customers to various dealings. These are matters for undue influence and related wrongs. Consider the analysis in *Woods v Martin's Bank Ltd*.[262] A bank counselled an inexperienced young man to make an unwise investment in one of the bank's problem customers. The bank was seen to have unduly influenced its customer by so doing. For this, the bank's conduct in dealing with its customer was directly evaluated. It was conduct which disclosed the exercise of influence and might have been unconscionable. The bank had acted unfairly in taking security or a guarantee from a customer for an advance to another: unconscionably shifting a bad risk from itself to the customer providing the guarantee or security.[263]

Concern with the bank's behaviour, where it is the salient feature of the case, is treated below at [8.24] under the 'Unconscionability' sub-heading of 'Undue Influence'. It is not our current focus. Under this heading, we look more from the position of a different party. Customers, rather than bankers, and the consequence of customers' reliance are our specific concern. United Kingdom authority is of little assistance here. It still regulates the banker in the banker and customer relation within the terms of the 'undue influence' category, including what in Australia is referred to as the 'unconscionable dealing'.

**[3.111]** Customer reliance on a bank may occur where financial advice has been taken in connection with a loan. Advice may relate to details of the lending transaction itself, or to the use of its proceeds. Alternatively, customers may rely on the bank's loyalty to a particular investment purpose of which they have advised the bank. Customers might be on one or other side in a

---

[261] [1959] 1 QB 55.

[262] [1959] 1 QB 55.

[263] D Waters 'Banks, Fiduciary Obligations and Unconscionable Transactions' (1986) 65 *Can Bar Rev* 37 at 43.

corporate takeover war. Not only then a source of funds for one party, the bank may be in the position of being that party's confidant. As discussed further at [3.129], customers in this position may claim an 'entitlement to rely' on the bank not to frustrate their takeover plans.

**[3.112]**    Doctrinal as well as policy questions arise in these cases. Why should a bank's liability for the disappointed reliance of its customer be founded on a fiduciary relationship? Would not a breach of an express or implied term of the banker and customer contract, or the commission of a tort, lead to a more satisfactory solution? Or, in policy terms, why should the enhanced 'gain stripping' and 'insolvency prioritising' remedies of equity be available when other more measured avenues to relief are open? It is not easy to express exactly what it is in the banker and customer relation that should attract equity's intervention. Others have done this at greater length.[264] Equitable intervention might be justified as tortious simulacra needed to protect a customer's 'reasonable expectation' that his bank will act in his interest. Donovan Waters, though, has suggested that this rationale is empty and only restates the problem.[265]

**[3.113]**    Bankers' 'reliant' customers may on occasions be corporations larger than themselves, perhaps with in-house lawyers and an abundance of advisors. Will such customers as readily be seen to repose reasonable or justifiable trust in the bank? The reliance question must be considered in the light of the customer's experience and resources.[266] A finance director, say, applying for a loan on behalf of a large corporation, might be expected to have greater knowledge of loan transactions than a sole trader acquiring a taxi licence. Fiduciary characterisation of relationships may not be the same even where the bank on each occasion commits what in Chapter 5 is classified as a fiduciary wrong. It is less reasonable for the director of the large corporation to claim to have relied upon and reposed trust in the bank. Fiduciary relationships should be invoked to protect the trusting aspects of customers' dealings. The boundaries of where the banker ceases to be the customer's 'arm's length' debtor and becomes liable for the consequences of reliance may shift. At the same time, it may also be wrong to restrict bankers' fiduciary liability for reliance to where they 'chance their arms' to advise. Bankers will then be able to insulate themselves from adverse fiduciary consequences by the use of well-drawn disclaimers. Trusting and reliance should be seen as an integral and non-excludable part of modern banking. Fiduciary standards of loyalty should apply in any trusting aspect of the relationship and appropriate remedies should be available accordingly.

## Bankers' advice

**[3.114]**    Where a banker gives a customer advice on financial affairs, the banker and customer relation may be found to imply, in addition to any

---

[264] T T Kitada 'Emerging Theories of Banking Liability—The Breach of Covenant of Good Faith and Fair Dealing' (1986) 103 *Banking LJ* 80 and E L Symons 'The Banker-Customer Relation' (1983) 100 *Banking LJ* 220 and 325.

[265] D Waters 'Banks, Fiduciary Obligations and Unconscionable Transactions' (1986) 65 *Can Bar Rev* 37 at 41.

[266] See *First National Bank of Hopkins v International Machines Corporation* 156 NW 2d 86, 88-9 (1968) (Minn SC), Murphy J and K W Curtis 'The Fiduciary Controversy: Injection of Fiduciary Principles into the Bank-Depositor and Bank-Borrower Relationships' 20 *Loyola of LA L Rev* 795 838-9 (1987).

contractual rights, both common law duties of care and a fiduciary duty.[267] Remedies in contract, tort and equity may all be called in aid when defective advice is given. We shall consider what the specifically 'fiduciary' wrongs and their remedies are in Chapter 5. Here we seek to isolate the element of reliance in characterisation of the banker's fiduciary status.

*Investment advice*

**[3.115]** Investment advice is about the employment of money (or its equivalent) for profit. Funds of money advised upon may be the customer's own, or funds which the bank lends. The 'crucial circumstance' giving rise to an advisor's fiduciary status has been said to be whether the bank knows, or reasonably ought to know, that its advice is being relied upon by the customer. As Donovan Waters puts it,[268]

> Knowing, actually or constructively, of this reliance, the bank may have been negligent in the advice it gave, or in the preparation of documentation it put before the client. It does not need the duty of care in tort law to make the bank liable. *The confidence reposed in the bank, the reliance, and the bank's knowledge of that situation may justify the imposition of an express trustee standard of behaviour upon the bank.* [emphasis added]

**[3.116]** Fiduciary liability for defective advice may arise only where the bank knows that it is being relied upon. For characterisation of relation, it does not matter whether the bank's advice to the customer was based on facts within the bank's knowledge. This is a fact more relevant to the duty's breach than its existence.[269]

Factual reliance of the customer on the bank's investment advice may occur if the customer has been a customer for a substantial length of time. In *Commonwealth Bank of Australia v Smith*,[270] where the relation was found to be fiduciary, the Commonwealth Bank had been banker and financial adviser to the Smiths for 24 years. In the United States case of *Stewart v Phoenix National Bank*[271] the parties had had a '25 year association'. Or the customer may be inexperienced in finance or in business.[272]

Where 'special disadvantage' in the nature of age, infirmity, poor education or difficulty with the English language affects the customer, the trusting relationship is usually inappropriate. This is because if the bank benefits from the customer's consent in these circumstances, the matter is dealt with as 'undue influence and unconscionable dealing'. A hallmark of 'special disadvantage' facts leading to the present kind of relation based on reliance is some factor which should alert the 'properly perceptive banker' to the fact that his advice was being relied upon.[273]

---

[267] *Halsbury's Laws of England* 4th ed, vol 3(1), [251].

[268] 'Banks, Fiduciary Obligations and Unconscionable Transactions' (1986) 65 *Can Bar Rev* 37 at 59–60.

[269] Cf *Kabwand Pty Ltd v National Australia Bank Ltd* (1989) 11 ATPR 50,367; *Commonwealth Bank of Australia v Smith* (1991) 102 ALR 453.

[270] (1991) 102 ALR 453.

[271] 64 P 2d 101 (1937).

[272] *Commonwealth Bank of Australia v Smith* (1991) 102 ALR 453.

[273] D Waters 'Banks, Fiduciary Obligations and Unconscionable Transactions' (1986) 65 *Can Bar Rev* 37 at 59.

**[3.117]**   It would be the very height of altruism for a bank in its relation with a customer to look *only* to the customer's interests. It is uncommercial to expect a bank to advise and lend money with the sole interest of the customer in mind, no matter how much the customer may rely. A bank, as we are reminded in *National Westminster Bank plc v Morgan*, 'is not a charitable institution'.[274] The United States decision in *Klein v First Edina National Bank*[275] was concerned with an alleged fiduciary duty to disclose. It expressed the matter as follows.

> We believe the correct rule to be that when a bank transacts business with a depositor or other customer, it has no special duty to counsel the customer and inform him of every material fact relating to the transaction—including the bank's motive, if material, for the transaction—unless *special circumstances* exist, such as where the bank knows or has reason to know that the customer is placing his trust and confidence in the bank and is relying on the bank. [emphasis added]

A customer's reliance cannot be expected to elicit complete selflessness from the bank. *Klein's* case defines the inquiry in a helpful way. Was there a 'special circumstance' in the case which can justify a fiduciary response?

**[3.118]**   Bankers who advise customers on the acquisition of a business or investment are like stockbrokers who tender investment advice. Both have defined non-fiduciary roles in accepting deposits, and buying or selling shares, respectively. Bankers and stockbrokers may each create a fiduciary element in the relation with a customer or client by assuming to advise a person who is known to rely. In *Daly v Sydney Stock Exchange*[276] a stockbroker acting as an 'investment adviser' was found to be a fiduciary to the extent of his advice. Brennan J, as we noted at [3..66], expressed at 385 the principle that:

> Whenever a stockbroker or other person who holds himself out as having expertise in advising on investments is approached for advice on investments and undertakes to give it, in giving that advice the adviser stands in a fiduciary relationship to the person whom he advises.

**[3.119]**   A corresponding principle was applied to an advising banker in *Commonwealth Bank of Australia v Smith*.[277] Fiduciary relations were seen to be created between a customer deciding whether to purchase a country hotel and a local bank manager who offered his advice on the prospect. The 'interests analysis' inherent in the relation was expressed by the court at 476:

> A bank may be expected to act in its own interests in ensuring the security of its position as lender to its customer but it may have created in the customer the expectation that nevertheless it will advise in the customer's interest as to the wisdom of a proposed investment. This may be the case where the customer may fairly take it that to a significant extent his interest is consistent with the bank in financing the customer for a prudent business venture.

Both the vendor of the hotel and its prospective purchaser were customers of the bank. All parties anticipated that the purchase would be financed by a substantial bank loan. In these circumstances the bank was argued to have an

---

[274] [1983] 3 All ER 85 at 91, Dunn LJ (CA).
[275] 196 NW 2d 619 at 623 (1972), curiam.
[276] (1986) 160 CLR 371.
[277] (1991) 102 ALR 453 at 476 (Fed Ct (FC)), Davies, Gummow and Shepherd JJ.

'apparent commercial self-interest' in facilitating the transaction. The loan was lending business. When the bank adopted the role of 'investment adviser' through its manager, the bank had to think beyond its own interest and discharge a duty owed to the customer. In this case the duty owed was an obvious spring to the fiduciary relationship. Described at 478, this was the duty to avoid a conflict of interest arising from the bank having the vendor also for its customer. Although the fact that the vendor was also a customer was disclosed to the purchaser, a recommendation was not given that the purchaser take independent advice. A potential conflict of duties owed by the bank to each client precluded the merits of the transaction being advised to either one. This is one fiduciary duties analysis of the facts. The 'interests' dicta above seem to go further. They suggest that the customer's fiduciary expectation could be defeated by the bank offering no more than 'unwise', careless or inadequate advice.

*Transactional advice*

**[3.120]** Transactional advice refers to finance deals between the customer and the bank, taken individually. Advising on details of the lending transaction and their significance is integral to the business of banking. Retail banks enter commercial relations with their customers every day. A businessman, for example, may take out a loan, or parents may guarantee an overdraft extended to a son or daughter. Before entering those undertakings, the bank will usually explain to the businessman and the parents what their rights and liabilities in the transaction are. Sometimes the wisdom of the deal from the customer's perspective is touched on and, at other times, the correlative positions of the bank and third parties are explained. Fiduciary relationships are not the normal way that the law regulates this aspect of the banker's business. Prima facie, and following the principle in *Shaddock & Associates Pty Ltd v Council of the City of Paramatta*,[278] if a bank through its proper officer takes it upon itself to explain the mechanics of a transaction, the bank is under a tortious duty of care not to misstate the position. Alternatively, the persons advised may be able to avoid the transaction in equity by alleging a misrepresentation, or conduct contrary to the Trade Practices Act 1974 (Cth). If the 'fiduciary' idea is used in this context at all, it is usually as part of a non-trusting type of claim. Customers advised may claim that the bank has acted 'unconscionably', or that the bank or its agent advising have exercised 'undue influence' in the deal.

**[3.121]** *James v Australia and New Zealand Banking Group Ltd*[279] involved a fiduciary relationship of trust claim arising from 'transactional advice' given in a wider 'investment advice' context. It underlined the importance of demonstrating a customer's factual or justified reliance before a 'transactional advisor' will be found to be a fiduciary. Bank customers claimed that they received defective transactional advice when about to make a substantial rural investment. Loan funds were desperately needed to meet commitments that the customers had already undertaken. The manager of the bank indicated that he could not lend the customers what they wanted and recommended that they apply to a particular Perth mortgage-broker instead. The customers went to the

---

[278] (1981) 55 ALJR 713.
[279] (1986) 64 ALR 347 (Fed Ct, Toohey J).

broker, who turned out to be an unlicensed incompetent and they suffered loss as a consequence. The bank manager who recommended the broker was argued to be the customers' fiduciary, who caused the loss by his breach of duty. Toohey J noted (at 353) that the customers claimed that:

> they had come to rely upon the bank for advice in financial matters relating to the conduct of their farming operations.

False representations by the manager concerning the availability of bridging finance and loan servicing were also alleged as a cause of loss. Alternatively to the fiduciary claim, negligence and conduct contrary to s 52 of the Trade Practices Act 1974 (Cth) were argued.

[3.122] In a detailed judgment in *James v Australia and New Zealand Banking Group Ltd*, Toohey J described the following additional facts. The customers were members of an established grazing family in Western Australia. They had several farms and were said (at 351) to be 'amongst the biggest landholders in the Katanning district'. While the customers had banked at a local branch of the bank for several years, it was not their only source of finance. They sought the assistance of the bank only from time to time and in order, usually, to fund what had already been purchased. The bank argued that its advice concerning the decision to invest was never requested, either generally or in relation to the transaction in this case. Toohey J said at 353, concerning fiduciary reliance:

> I do not accept that [the customers] looked to the bank for advice as to what properties they should buy or how they should conduct their farming operations. Indeed, given the long farming history of the James family, it would be surprising if they looked to the branch manager of a bank for farming advice.

Accordingly, at 350–2 he found that the banker and customer relation there was not fiduciary. Reliance was negatived, both in fact and as a reasonable expectation.

[3.123] Use of the language of fiduciaries to regulate the banker and customer relation in the United Kingdom has been disciplined by the House of Lords in *National Westminster Bank Plc v Morgan*.[280] The *Morgan* facts concerned a bank manager who obtained a customer's execution of a mortgage after offering her a transactional explanation. The customer alleged that the circumstances surrounding the advice put pressure on her to sign—a fact, she said, which should have been evident to the manager at the time. In the English Court of Appeal the customer was allowed to avoid the mortgage by reason of the fact that it was obtained in breach of a banker's 'fiduciary duty of care'.[281] Reversing this conclusion and introducing a new requirement of 'manifest disadvantage' for the claimant in a (presumed) relation of influence, Lord Scarman said of fiduciary relationships generally (at 703):

> My Lords, I believe that the Lords Justices were led into a misinterpretation of the facts by their use, as is all too frequent in this branch of the law, of words and phrases such as 'confidence', 'confidentiality', 'fiduciary duty'. There are plenty of confidential relationships which do not give rise to the presumption of undue influence.

---

[280] [1985] 1 AC 686: see [8.6] for a fuller discussion.
[281] [1983] 3 All ER 85, Dunn and Slade LJJ.

Lord Scarman seemed to conceive that banks might become liable in a 'confidential relationship' where he says that the plaintiff's claim might be a fiduciary one without having presumptive effect. The presumptive wrong of undue influence is distinguished and the reference must be to the fiduciary relationship of trust. The possibility was taken up also by Lord Browne-Wilkinson in *CIBC Mortgages plc v Pitt*[282]—again discussing limitations on the wrong of undue influence. A 'wholly separate doctrine of equity' was noted, being one which binds 'those in a fiduciary position who enter into transactions with those to whom they owe fiduciary duties'.

The upshot of the United Kingdom authority seems to be that a bank's breach of fiduciary relationship is usually proven by the customer satisfying the undue influence requirements. But this is not the only possibility. When the requirements of undue influence cannot all be proven against a bank and a customer's trust has still been breached, the customer need not be without an equity. A fiduciary relationship of the trusting kind may be breached as well.

**[3.124]**   This is not the approach of the North American authorities. Relief is forthcoming within the confines of the solely trusting relationship in both Canada and the United States. The Supreme Court of Arizona in *Stewart v Phoenix National Bank*,[283] for example, used a fiduciary relationship to prevent a bank from enforcing a particular mortgage covenant against its customer. The customer had dealt with the bank for 23 years and came to habitually rely on the bank's advice, which included, relative to one transaction, a representation that the bank would not rely on the covenant. The bank was seen to be taking advantage of its customer's trust when it sought to resile from this representation. A fiduciary relationship of trust had grown up between the parties. *Klein v First Edina National Bank*[284] was a similar case. A customer of 20 years gave a stock mortgage to the bank to assist her employer in securing a new advance of working capital. In fact the bank used the advance to retire the employer's earlier debt. All the elements of a fiduciary relationship (and its breach) were found to be established in these circumstances, except proof that the bank knew of its customer's reliance. The decision in *Deist v Wachholz*[285] was a little less helpful. Its facts concerned a bank customer of 24 years standing, who was advised to sell a ranch which he owned. The ranch's purchaser was the secret partner of the bank vice-president. A breach of fiduciary duty was found to be committed without any evidence of fiduciary reliance being received. The banker and customer relation was just what was evident on the facts. No presumptive effect was accorded to the claim in any of these United States instances of the fiduciary banker and customer relationship.

**[3.125]**   We have noted how in the United Kingdom the elements of the undue influence wrong must be found in order to relieve a reliant bank

---

[282] [1994] 1 AC 200 at 209, Lords Templeman and Lowry agreeing.

[283] 64 P 2d 101 (1937).

[284] 196 NW 2d 619 (1972).

[285] 678 P 2d 188 (1984); see also *Pigg v Robertson* 549 SW 2d 597 (1977).

customer.[286] In Australia there is a preoccupation with the bank's conduct and not the client's reliance. The same wrong-centred approach is taken, giving rise to a search for 'unconscionability' or 'unconscionable dealing' on the bank's part. We note at [8.24] that the difference between undue influence and unconscionability is small. The Australian position seems to imply that if a bank ventures to give transactional advice a fiduciary relationship may not always follow. Rather, the giving of bad or self-interested advice is an occasional wrong. Authorities which clearly base fiduciary relationships in a customer's reliance and not the bank's wrong come from North America. But, as a straw in the wind, consider the 1991 Martin Committee report on banking deregulation.[287] Australian case law was said to be inadequate in relation to the 'fairness' of customers' guarantee liabilities. Advice and disclosure requirements for banks were not sufficient. To rectify this the report proposed a 'code of banking practice'—a cooperative scheme to regulate this and other aspects of the bank–customer relationship. Inspection of this code indicates that it replicates the decided law in one part and emulates the North American cases in others.[288] Could fiduciary doctrine be fertilised by these recommendations?

[3.126] If a bank could be bound by fiduciary liabilities to a borrower who relies on the bank's transactional advice, a fiduciary relation might equally arise between a bank and a reliant customer who guarantees the borrowing of another. A bank which gives a self-interested or incomplete explanation of the transaction should perhaps be potentially liable on the fiduciary standard in either case. Once the explanation is relied upon by the customer to the knowledge of the bank, a type of ordinary, 'arm's length' lending is arguably transformed into a fiduciary dealing. Even though no fiduciary obligation to disclose transactional details was imposed where a bank had no reason to believe that a corporate officer was relying on it for advice, the reasoning in *Mackenzie v Summit National Bank*[289] may be persuasive.

[3.127] Consider also the Californian case of *Barrett v Bank of America*.[290] The Barretts were the principal shareholders in a small electronics company. The company had obtained from the Bank of America a $250,000 loan guaranteed by the Small Business Administration ('SBA') and a $400,000 'line of credit'. To secure this accommodation, the Barretts gave the bank two personal guarantees secured by mortgages over residential properties. One was for the SBA loan and one was for the line of credit. Less than a month after this was done, the bank informed the Barretts that they were in 'technical default' because the borrower's assets to liability ratio no longer conformed to the bank's requirements. An officer of the bank suggested to the Barretts that they could cure the default by introducing new capital to the company

---

[286] *CIBC Mortgages plc v Pitt* [1994] 1 AC 200 at 207–9, Lord Browne-Wilkinson, explaining *National Westminster Bank plc v Morgan* [1985] AC 686.

[287] *A Pocket Full of Change*: Banking and Deregulation report of the House of Representatives Standing Committee on Finance and Public Administration (1991), [20.152-79]; I am grateful to E V Lanyon for this point.

[288] Australian Bankers Association *Code of Banking Practice* (1993): Part B 'Principles of Conduct' 7.0–19.1.

[289] 363 NW 2d 116 (Minn App 1985), Leslie J.

[290] 229 Cal Rptr 16 (1986).

through a merger or acquisition. Specifically, the Barretts were advised that when a new, merged company became responsible for the loans, the personal guarantees would be released. So a merger was consummated with another company and the bank accepted the new entity as its customer. However the new entity filed for bankruptcy before the guarantees had been released. The bank assigned all its securities to the SBA, including the guarantees and supporting mortgages. The Barretts were eventually forced to sell their home and turn over the proceeds to the SBA. Action was commenced against the Bank of America, alleging, inter alia, an entitlement to damages for its 'constructive fraud' in breaching a relationship of trust and confidence. The Court of Appeal (4th Dist) upheld the submission made on behalf of the Barretts that the bank was in breach of fiduciary obligation. Wiener Ass-J at 20–1 said (the rest of the court concurring):

> a relationship of trust and confidence exists between a bank and its loan customers which gives rise to a duty of disclosure of facts which may place the bank or a third party at an advantage with respect to the customer ... Here there is substantial evidence to support the constructive fraud theory. Ronald Barrett perceived his relationship with [the bank officer] as very close and he relied on [the officer's] financial advice implicitly.

**[3.128]** It may be appropriate to draw a line here. Further extension of fiduciary liability within the banker and customer relation may be to descend into 'categories of illusory reference'. The notion of 'fiduciary', indeed, looks like a 'device permitting a secret and even unconscious exercise of ... a creative choice.'[291] Hyperbole in *Commercial Cotton Co v United California Bank*[292] may well amount to this. A corporate customer informed its bank that some of its cheque forms were missing. The bank failed to act promptly and stop payment on the relevant cheques and the customer's account was debited for payment of cheques which had been forged. Despite the customer's protests the bank declined to admit its negligence in this and relied on a statute of limitations defence. The court thereupon said (at 554):

> The relationship of bank to depositor is at least quasi-fiduciary and depositors reasonably expect a bank not to claim nonexistent legal defences to avoid reimbursement when the bank negligently disburses the entrusted funds.

Which is somewhat questionable. Faulty or incomplete handling of a 'checking transaction' which does not produce an obvious benefit to the bank may be beyond the margins of the fiduciary sanction. The possibility has been discussed and conservative views have been expressed by at least one academic commentator.[293]

*Loyalty to customers' purposes: takeovers*

**[3.129]** Two sets of hypothetical facts explain this sub-heading.

1. *The Target Company*. A Co is a bank customer and commences negotiations to obtain a new line of credit. Bank receives from A Co certain non-public information about A Co's corporate health and forward plans. D Co, another customer of the bank, applies to the bank for a loan. D Co

---

291 J Stone *Legal System and Lawyers' Reasonings* (1968) p 241.
292 209 Cal Rptr 551 (Cal App 4th dist 1985).
293 K W Curtis 'The Fiduciary Controversy' 20 *Loyola of LA Law Rev* 795 at 836–40 (1987).

reveals to the bank that the purpose of the loan is to enable it to make a
bid to acquire a voting majority in A Co. In deciding whether to extend
credit to D Co and to finance its plans, the bank makes use of the
confidential information that it acquired from A Co. Can A Co, the target
company, complain of a breach of fiduciary obligation by the bank?[294]

2. *The Offeror*. B Co is an large investment company. While not a long-
standing bank customer, the bank actively sought B Co's business. This
occurred at the highest levels. B Co's board of directors met a director of
the bank and outlined the long-term plan of B Co to take over C Co, another
large investment company. The bank supported the plan. It promised all the
help it could give. However the chairman of the bank, who was not at the
meeting with B Co, had already committed the bank to invest in C Co on
the bank's own behalf. Over the following years, both B Co (with the
bank's loans), and the bank itself, built up substantial minority
shareholdings in C Co. In doing this the bank was not interested in taking
over C Co. B Co, however, did have a rival intent on taking over C Co.
This was a company which was still another customer of the bank. The
rival had also been engaged in building up a minority shareholding in the
investment company. Matters came to a head. The bank ended up selling
its minority shareholding in C Co to the rival so that that company became
the majority shareholder. As a result, the market value of B Co's minority
shareholding in C Co plunged by 50 per cent. B Co, the takeover offeror,
was aggrieved. It claimed to be entitled to fiduciary relief against the bank
for not disclosing its conflict of interest in relation to the takeover target.[295]

[3.130]   If the parties in each example were found to be in a fiduciary relation,
the problem for the bank then was one of conflicting duties.[296] A bank must
be loyal to all its customers.

We will explore the breach of duty question in Chapter 5—whether, that is,
if the bank in each example had remained neutral and made full disclosure of
its interests and loyalty to the adverse party, no breach of fiduciary duty would
have occurred.

Our concern now is with how an initial fiduciary relationship might be
established. A notable fact in both the cases on which the examples are based
is that a fiduciary relation was argued to flow from the customer's reliance
and imparting of confidential information to the bank.

[3.131]   In the case of the target company, North American policy seems to
dictate that any need to protect A Co's confidentiality should be overridden
by the interest of the bank in making lending decisions on all information
available to it. In a robust way, this was expressed by the United States
court:[297]

---

[294] See *Washington Steel Corporation v TW Corporation* 602 F 2d 594 (1979).

[295] See *Standard Investments Ltd v Canadian Imperial Bank of Commerce* (1985) 22 DLR (4th)
410 (Ont CA).

[296] Suggested by D Waters 'Banks, Fiduciary Obligations and Unconscionable Transactions' (1986)
65 *Can Bar Rev* 37 at 40.

[297] *Washington Steel Corporation v TW Corporation* 602 F 2d 594, 603 (1979) (3rd Circuit New
Jersey), curiam; see also the different reasoning in *American Medicorp Inc v Continental Illinois
National Bank and Trust Company of Chicago* 475 F Supp 5 (1977).

We do not believe that a bank violates any duty that it may owe to one of its borrowers when it uses information received from that borrower in deciding whether or not to make a loan to another prospective borrower ... the promulgation of a rule restricting the dissemination of confidential information within the loan department of a bank is neither the proper province of a court nor the appropriate subject for state law adjudication ... the adoption of such a rule would make unwise banking policy. To prohibit a bank from considering all available information in making its own loan decisions might engender one or both of two undesirable outcomes. First, it might force banks to go blindly into loan transactions, arguably violating its duties to its own depositors. Alternatively, such a rule might discourage banks from lending money to any company which expresses an interest in purchasing shares of stock of another of the bank's customers. The adverse implications for the free flow of funds [is why the target Co's argument has to fail]. Bank credit is, after all, the largest part, by far, of the national money supply.

It would, the court continued at 601, be too easy for target companies to develop a 'shark repellant' against takeovers. Loans might be taken from all the major banks. The court was not prepared to treat A Co's relation with the bank as fiduciary at all. It refused to 'draw a fiduciary rabbit from a commercial loan agreement hat' for fear that to do so might 'wreak havoc with the available funding for capital ventures'. As the court said, ordinary commercial borrowers, without more, are just customers.[298]

[3.132]   In the case of the offeror, *Standard Investments Ltd v Canadian Imperial Bank of Commerce*,[299] the loss of confidentiality in B Co's plan left reliance as the only spring to a fiduciary relationship. Seven years had elapsed between B Co's disclosure to the bank of its takeover intention and the rival's assumption of control over the target company. Initial confidentiality had simply evaporated. The final result achieved for the offeror in that case was much more promising than for the above target company. Stating the law to be 'clear' that 'in certain circumstances a fiduciary relationship may be created between a bank and its customer', the court approved the trial judge's dictum that a 'special circumstance' was necessary before a fiduciary relationship could be found.[300] The judgment at 434–5 went on to list ten factual findings which led to a fiduciary conclusion. Paraphrased, it is worth setting them out. They indicate the type of facts that were treated as significant. (1) Standard Investments was not an old customer; (2) its controllers planned to acquire control of the target company; (3) the controllers decided that they would need the 'assistance, advice and financial support' of the bank; (4) the Standard Investments account was then taken to the bank; (5) the bank was gratified to get this and other 'excellent business' through Standard Investments connections; (6) it was obvious that takeover plans of importance to the customer were being disclosed; (7) the identity of the target company and a crucial player in the drama were made known; (8) it was common knowledge that the bank was also banker to the target company, that the crucial player was a common director of the bank and the target company, and that the good offices of the crucial person were essential; (9) the bank came to realise

---

[298] At 600–1; see (Note) 'Bank Financing of Involuntary Takeovers of Corporate Customers: A Breach of Fiduciary Duty?' 53 *Notre Dame Lawyer* 827 (1978).

[299] (1985) 22 DLR (4th) 410, curiam.

[300] At 432, approving (1983) 5 DLR (4th) 452 at 481.

precisely what the controllers wanted; and (10) the bank offered encouragement and assistance for the plan.

**[3.133]** Listing of fiduciary 'factors' is the same methodology as that of Mason J in *Hospital Products Ltd v United States Surgical Corporation*[301] and Laskin J in *Canadian Aero Service Ltd v O'Malley*.[302] At the end of its enumeration in *Standard Investments* at 435, the court said that there could be 'no doubt' that the controllers of the offeror 'were relying on the advice, assistance and guidance of [the bank] and that [the bank] through [its manager] was aware of the reliance.'

Ergo, the relationship was fiduciary. This is a finding which has been disapproved. Paul Finn, for one, makes the point that there was nothing especially 'fiduciary' about the *Standard Investments* relationship at all. It could, he said, have been as adequately justified on the basis of 'good faith' and 'fair dealing'.[303] The outcome is said by another commentator to be inconsistent with the way that modern banking business must be conducted—a view on which there is no unanimity.[304]

## One-sided reliance and inequality

**[3.134]** Justifications of a trusting relation based in the reliance of a fiduciary relationship's weaker party are common in Canadian cases. To a lesser degree, this is also so in the United States. As a form of reasoning, one-sided reliance is apt to shade into the hereunder characterisation of the relationship based on one party's *power* over another. It is also problematic and we shall simply sketch how this use of the characteristic might function, without endorsing it.

**[3.135]** Unequal reliance was the sort of phenomenon described by Wilson J in *Frame v Smith*.[305] Dealing specifically with a matrimonial dispute, as she was, Wilson J described a principle to cover fiduciary characterisation in all contexts. It is mainly concerned with *power* in the relation and will be considered below. However it includes as one of the three 'characteristics' of a fiduciary relationship that one party is 'peculiarly vulnerable' to another. This is what happens with the unequal type of reliance. Whether or not a beneficiary is 'entitled' to rely in an accepted relationship, the beneficiary does rely and may become vulnerable for that reason.

Reliance here may be not so much a defining characteristic of a relationship, as we have treated it until now, as the relationship's result. Reliance causing inequality is implied from the fact that power is held.[306] How it was acquired is irrelevant. 'Inequality' combined with one-sided reliance and vulnerability may thus be another fiduciary characteristic. 'Reliance' in this formulation functions more as part of a fiduciary conclusion than a syllogistic middle term.

---

[301] (1984) 156 CLR 41 at 98–9.

[302] (1973) 40 DLR (3rd) 371 at 391.

[303] P Finn 'Fiduciary Principle' in Youdan, 1 at 22–3.

[304] P Graham 'Statutory Regulation of Financial Services in the United Kingdom and the Development of Chinese Walls in Managing Conflicts of Interest' in McKendrick 43 at 49–53; cf Herzl and Colling 'The Chinese Wall and Conflict of Interest in Banks' 34 *Bus Law* 73 at 100 (1978) and Lipton and Mazur 'The Chinese Wall Solution to Conflict Problems of Securities Firms' 50 *NYUL Rev* 459 at 475 (1975).

[305] (1987) 42 DLR (4th) 81 at 99 (dissenting).

[306] J R M Gautreau 'Demystifying the Fiduciary Mystique' (1989) 68 *Can Bar Rev* 1 at 5.

It is not a fact to be established. Sopinka J in *Lac Minerals Ltd v International Corona Resources Ltd* was persuaded by the idea.[307] He gave judgment for the majority of justices on the fiduciaries point, expressly adopting Wilson J's three characteristics. Fiduciary relationships based in reliance and inequality between the parties are also found in United States authorities.[308]

**[3.136]** Deducing a fiduciary relationship from the 'vulnerability' criterion in *Frame v Smith*[309] overlooks the justice of imposing a fiduciary relation on the stronger party. Should an expert, say, by virtue of his expertise, be attributed with fiduciary responsibilities to those who rely on him?[310] Responsibility as a fiduciary may have been rejected or ignored by the stronger party. Or a responsibility to take care of the weaker party may have been effectively disclaimed through an exemption clause.[311] Characterisation of the trusting relation should not be the same in all these events. The law has other and perhaps better suited devices to regulate the inequality phenomenon.

**[3.137]** Reliance of the unequal type has a specially uncertain place in the commercial law. If a party to a commercial transaction wishes to be sure that the promises of another can be relied upon, the reliance may be protected by contract. As much was said by Dawson J in *Hospital Products Ltd v United States Surgical Corporation*.[312] A fiduciary relationship does not arise where one party has accepted inadequate contract terms to protect his interest. In *Jirna v Mister Donut of Canada Ltd*[313] the court held that no fiduciary relationship arose out of the franchise before it, as 'there was no disparity amounting to a serious inability on the part of one of the parties to effectively negotiate and so protect his interest.'

**4. POWER (OR DISCRETION)**

**[3.138]** This is the last characteristic of the fiduciary relation that we shall examine. It provides that a fiduciary relation may exist where the party trusted has a power (or discretion) to change the legal or practical interests of the party trusting. Expressed by Toohey J in *Mabo v The State of Queensland [No 2]*,[314] 'the source of the [fiduciary] obligation . . . is precisely the power to affect the interests of a person adversely'.

The word 'power', in strictness, may imply for its possessor a discretion in whether to exercise it or not. So it may be unnecessary to speak separately of a 'discretion'. Sometimes the two words are used interchangeably.[315] The idea here is that fiduciary relationships are about the control of unregulated discretions. The purpose of the category is to curb abuses of power.

**[3.139]** The power-based conception has been particularly influential in Canada. In significant ways the Canadian fiduciary relationship appears to

---

307 [1989] 2 SCR 574 at 599–600.
308 Eg *Chmieleski v City Products Corporation* 660 SW 2d 275 (1983).
309 (1987) 42 DLR (4th) 81 at 99, Wilson J.
310 *Hutton v Klabal* 726 F Supp 1154 (NY 1989).
311 See *Hedley Byrne & Co Ltd v Heller and Partners Ltd* [1964] AC 465.
312 (1984) 156 CLR 41 at 147.
313 (1971) 22 DLR (3d) 639 at 645 (Ont CA), affirmed [1975] 1 SCR 2.
314 (1992) 175 CLR 1 at 201.
315 J C Shepherd 'Towards a Unified Concept of Fiduciary Relationships' (1981) 97 *LQR* 51 at 68.

function as a tort.[316] Ernest Weinrib in his influential 1975 article[317] wrote that the 'primary policy' of the fiduciary relation was to regulate situations where–

> the principal's interests can be affected by, and are therefore dependent on, the manner in which the fiduciary uses the discretion which has been delegated to him. The fiduciary obligation is equity's blunt tool for control of the discretion. . . . Two elements thus form the core of the fiduciary concept and these elements can also serve to delineate its boundaries. First, the fiduciary must have scope for the exercise of discretion, and, second, this discretion must be capable of affecting the legal position of the principal.

**[3.140]** A fiduciary relationship may therefore arise unilaterally where the power characteristic is invoked. On the Canadian view, all that need be shown is that one party possesses the indicia of a discretion, or power or control in relation to another. Nothing need proceed from the party affected by these things. 'Discretion', 'power' or 'control' over the interests of the trusting party is taken to imply reliance from that party's perspective.

Apart from Weinrib, Justice Wilson of the Supreme Court is another important source of Canadian fiduciary law. Her dissenting judgment in *Frame v Smith*[318] has been much approved.[319] The case involved an unlikely damages claim by a husband against his former wife. The wife's liability was argued to arise from her denial of his legal right to access to children of their former marriage. Finding that the wife was a fiduciary, she said at 99 that there has been no definition of the concept 'fiduciary', although the contexts where it arose had the following common features:

(1) The fiduciary has scope for the exercise of some discretion or power.
(2) The fiduciary can unilaterally exercise that power or discretion so as to affect the beneficiary's legal or practical interests.
(3) The beneficiary is peculiarly vulnerable to or at the mercy of the fiduciary holding the discretion or power.

**[3.141]** 'Features' described by Wilson J in *Frame v Smith* seem to be cumulative, or rather, to be the premises of a syllogism leading to a fiduciary conclusion. There are problems with this, as with Weinrib's formulation, when the idea is universalised. 'Power or discretion' as a unified conception of the fiduciary relationship is at the one time not wide enough, and too wide. It is not wide enough to explain the bribery and secret commissions cases. In *Reading v R*,[320] Sergeant Reading was scarcely able to change the Crown's legal or practical interests in any sensible way, but he was a fiduciary all the same. Nor could a bribed sergeant of the Metropolitan Police in *Attorney-General v Goddard*[321] affect the interests of the Attorney-General. The vendor of land after sale and prior to settlement holds the land as fiduciary for the purchaser without having any ability to affect the purchaser's interests.[322]

---

[316] J R M Gautreau 'Demystifying the Fiduciary Mystique' (1989) 68 *Can Bar Rev* 1 at 15.
[317] (1975) 25 *UTLJ* 1 at 4.
[318] (1987) 42 DLR (4th) 81 (SC (Can)), 98–9.
[319] Eg, by Sopinka and La Forest JJ (dissenting) in *Lac Minerals Ltd v International Corona Resources Ltd* [1989] 2 SCR 574 at 599, 645 and La Forest JJ and McLachlin (dissenting) in *Canson Enterprises Ltd v Boughton & Co* (1991) 85 DLR (4th) 129 at 155, 136.
[320] [1949] 2 KB 232 (CA).
[321] (1929) 98 LJKB 743.
[322] J C Shepherd 'Towards a Unified Concept of Fiduciary Relationships' (1981) 97 *LQR* 51 at 70.

Think also of the cases where the parties' relations are inchoate. Could the sitting tenant and prospective partner in *Fraser Edmiston Pty Ltd v AGT (Qld) Pty Ltd*[323] be at the mercy of the proposed partner's 'power or discretion'? The only harm that could come to the sitting tenant at the point which negotiations had reached was by the proposed partner doing wrong. And if a fiduciary relationship is constituted by the wrong it remedies, the nakedness of the device is exposed. 'Fiduciary' relations are just instruments to a desired conclusion.

**[3.142]** The 'power or discretion' idea is at the same time too wide. The conception would attach fiduciary sanctions to those legal powers which have no correlative duties. Consider, for example, a lessor's power to renew a lease. Should the power that this affords the lessor over the lessee turn the lessor into a fiduciary? Something more is needed. Most franchises embody power in the franchisor, but as was seen at [3.50], this is not enough. Additional trusting or mutuality must exist. Something similar was found in those United States cases where a non-renewing franchisor is found to be a delinquent fiduciary. In *Arnott v American Oil Co*,[324] for example, a franchisee service station proprietor was held to be in a fiduciary relationship with his an oil company franchisor only after cogent evidence was received of the parties' common interests and profit. The decision may well be wrong. Consider also the mortgagee's power of sale. A mortgagee's exercise of this will often detrimentally affect the mortgagor's interests. But orthodoxy in *Henry Roach (Petroleum) Pty Ltd v Credit House etc*[325] and *Australia and New Zealand Banking Group Ltd v Bangadilly Pastoral Co Pty Ltd*[326] is that this power exists only to serve the mortgagee's interest.

Perhaps the 'power or discretion' characteristic is unsuited to the resolution of fiduciary disputes in the private law. The 'power' idea may be too open-ended and general to be reduced to the categories that the private law works with. Power is not and cannot be a characteristic element in a fiduciary relationship because it only describes a relationship's result. A fiduciary relationship may, but need not always, confer power on the stronger party to it. This should not be confused with how the relationship is constituted in the first place. Workable applications of the 'power-based' fiduciary characteristic may only be where the power is an unanalysable raw fact. Governmental power is of this type.

## Government and native

**[3.143]** Authorities under this sub-heading concern the distinctly non-commercial relation between governments and indigenous peoples. It is a category of interest rather than direct use to commercial equity. 'Government and native' relations test the integrity of fiduciary 'rhetoric' in the power-based approach to characterisation. In *Guerin v R*[327] the Supreme Court of Canada found that the federal government administering the Indian Act 1952

---

[323] (1986) 2 Qd R 1, above at [3.100].
[324] 609 F 2d 873 (1979).
[325] [1976] VR 309 at 313, Lush J.
[326] (1978) 139 CLR 195.
[327] [1984] 2 SCR 335, at [3.15].

(Can) was under a fiduciary obligation to the Musqueam Indian band of British Columbia. The *Guerin* litigation had arisen out of that band's surrender of some of its reserved land to the Crown (Indian Affairs Branch) for development as a golf club. The Indians alleged that the Crown did a very bad deal for them. A claim for compensation was framed in terms of the Crown's breach of fiduciary obligation to the band. Unanimously the court decided that this claim should succeed.

**[3.144]** In the view of four of the eight justices who heard the appeal in *Guerin*, it was the surrender of previously Indian land which was critical to the case's fiduciary characterisation (at 383). An intended exchange of the Indians' previous title for money was what elicited the Crown's duty to prevent the Indians from being exploited. The surrender was seen (at 384) to give rise to a 'discretion', which served to 'transform the Crown's obligation into a fiduciary one.' For this, a general proposition was announced:

> where by statute, agreement or perhaps by unilateral undertaking, one party has an obligation to act for the benefit of another, and that obligation carries with it a discretionary power, the party thus empowered becomes a fiduciary.

The interpretation of the Dickson judgment in *Guerin* adopted here was given by McEachern CJBC in *Delgamuukw v The Queen in right of British Columbia*.[328] Aboriginal land rights were again involved, but this time no title claim was made. Rather, 'fiduciary rights' to use unoccupied Crown land were upheld. Dickson J's formulation of the power characteristic is inconsistent in some respects from the way we have presented it. There may be a latent ambiguity. What was the connection between the Indians' previous title to the land and the Crown's fiduciary duty in respect of it? Did title play any part in the inference of fiduciary duties? On first principles of the 'power or discretion' justification, it is hard to see what this connection could be.

**[3.145]** *Mabo v The State of Queensland [No 2]* was a High Court decision in which opposing views were taken of a 'government and native' fiduciary relation.[329] Fiduciary issues were only discussed by Toohey J and Dawson J (dissenting). Mason CJ (at 15) and McHugh J (at 73–4) agreed with Brennan J that the fiduciary or 'remedial' issue did not arise. Deane and Gaudron JJ in a joint judgment did not deal with the fiduciary claim. However the possibility of 'compensatory damages' on a similar rationale was referred to by them at 119–20. Only the reasoning of Toohey J brought out the fiduciary issue. It also raised the titleholding ambiguity in *Guerin* that we have just seen.

**[3.146]** In *Mabo*, an Aboriginal people sought a declaration that title to certain islands was vested in them and that the Queensland Coast Islands Declaratory Act 1985 (Qld) wrongly purported to confirm title in the Crown. With Dawson J dissenting, the High Court held that native title of the Meriam people existed and had never been validly extinguished. The title aspect of the case and its compensatory ramifications are what *Mabo* is generally associated with. But there was also a fiduciary duty claim made, intended to be operative

---

328 (1991) 79 DLR (4th) 185 at 480–1.
329 (1992) 175 CLR 1.

in the event that the Aboriginal people failed to establish title. Dawson J phrased it at 163:

> the Crown, whether trustee or not, owes [the Aboriginal people] a fiduciary duty to deal with those lands in such a manner as to have regard to their traditional rights in them. They argue that this duty arises from the unilateral assumption of control by the Crown over the native inhabitants on annexation, the policy of protection of native inhabitants adopted by the Crown and the creation of a reserve (later put under the control of a trustee) for the use and benefit of the native inhabitants.

This is a 'power or discretion' claim to a fiduciary relationship on the Weinrib model.[330] After referring to the E J Weinrib article specifically, Toohey J said that it was the 'power' of the Crown and the 'corresponding vulnerability' of the Meriam people which–

> gave rise to a fiduciary obligation on the part of the Crown. The power to destroy or impair a people's interests in this way is extraordinary and is sufficient to attract regulation by Equity to ensure that the position is not abused. The fiduciary relationship arises, therefore, out of the power of the Crown to extinguish traditional title by alienating the land or otherwise; it does not depend on an exercise of that power.

[3.147]   Toohey J sought legitimacy for this relationship by connecting it with the principle that Mason J described in his oft-quoted dictum in *Hospital Products*.[331] An alternative basis for the fiduciary finding was expressed as well. If, as Toohey J continued at 203,'the relationship between the Crown and the Meriam people with respect to traditional title alone were insufficient to give rise to a fiduciary relation', then the Crown's 'course of dealings' with the indigenous people could be substituted. Examples of the course of dealing that Toohey J suggested were 'the creation of reserves in 1882 and 1912 and the appointment of trustees in 1939'. These are unilateral occurrences, each of them. Origins of the fiduciary relationship were expressed in terms reminiscent of Wilson J in *Frame v Smith*.[332] No nexus between the relation and native title to the lands was necessary.

[3.148]   Dawson J denied that the facts of the Mabo case gave rise to the 'power or discretion' type of fiduciary relationship. His fiduciaries dictum in *Hospital Products Ltd v United States Surgical Corporation*[333] should be remembered here. Namely, that:

> underlying all the cases of fiduciary obligation ... inherent in the nature of the relationship itself is a position of disadvantage or vulnerability on the part of one of the parties which causes him to place reliance upon the other and requires the protection of equity acting on the conscience of that other.

This was said to be inapplicable for a reason specific to the cases concerning indigenous peoples. Dawson J at 165–7 examined the United States and

---

[330] See E Weinrib 'Fiduciary Obligation' (1975) 25 *UTLJ* 1 at 4–8 also R Blowes 'Governments: Can You Trust Them with Your Traditional Title?' (1993) 15 *Syd LR* 254 and C Hughes 'The Fiduciary Obligation of the Crown to Aboriginies: Lessons from the United States and Canada' (1993) 166 *UNSWLJ* 70.

[331] *Hospital Products Ltd v United States Surgical Corporation* (1984) 156 CLR 41 at 96–7.

[332] (1987) 42 DLR (4th) 81 at 98–9.

[333] (1984) 156 CLR 41 at 142.

Canadian authorities on fiduciary relations between governments and Indian tribes, concluding that the existence of Indian title to land was essential to their fiduciary reasoning. He quoted Dickson J in *Guerin v R*[334] on the above. Not finding for the existence of aboriginal title was seen by Dawson J to preclude a fiduciary finding as well. Yet, according to the method of resemblances, there may be no necessary connection between property considerations and the 'power or discretion' characteristic. It is not at all evident why a property criterion like title should be a limitation on the 'power or discretion' characteristic.

## Public officials and persons affected

**[3.149]** This analogy is concerned with decisions made by society's administrators. These are administrative decisions of the type made in government departments. Decision-making responsibilities may be referred out of these departments to boards, tribunals, advisory councils, bureaux, commissions, local councils and individuals holding public offices. All these entities may exercise delegated, decision-making power.[335] Our inquiry here is whether the North American fiduciary characteristic of 'power or discretion' could apply to persons (and their delegates) making decisions within administrative departments in Australia. For brevity we will call these persons 'public officials'. The question is whether public officials can be characterised as fiduciaries, with power over persons affected by their decisions. A position like this obtains in the United States, as we will see. The desired corollary might be that when a fiduciary duty is breached by a public official, the beneficiaries affected will always have standing to complain and the gamut of equitable remedies will be awarded for their relief.

**[3.150]** A large body of specialist law has grown up in the Australian and other common law jurisdictions to regulate the relationship between government and the governed. Under the title of 'administrative law', it specifically regulates the decision-making function of public officials and their exercise of public discretions. Public officials possess a degree of autonomy in the judgmental aspect of their roles. Discretions are implied from the freedom that public officials have to choose the standards which justify their decisions.[336] A standard-choosing, discretionary, activity will be the focus of the power-based fiduciary characterisation here.

**[3.151]** Administrative law is primarily concerned to nullify or avoid unsatisfactory exercises of discretion by public officials. Validity of decisions tends to be what prerogative writs and the Federal and State statutory systems of review are concerned with. 'Remoter economic consequences' of the type that concern the fiduciary regime are generally outside the scope of administrative law.[337] Subject to the tort about to be considered, the forms of action in administrative law are only a very limited basis for awards of

---

334 [1984] 2 SCR 335 at 375.
335 M Allars *Introduction to Australian Administrative Law* (1990) at [1.2].
336 See D J Galligan *Discretionary Powers* (1986) 8-11.
337 *Calveley v Chief Constable of the Merseyside Police* [1989] 2 WLR 624 at 629, Lord Bridge; P Hogg *Liability of the Crown* 2nd ed (1989) pp 186–8.

damages or other civil liability.[338] The tort is 'misfeasance in a public office'—
a 'new' tort, which can only be committed by public officers.[339] A public
official causing unauthorised loss is liable under it, where the action is
malicious, or performed in the official's knowledge that he or she has acted
without authority. In most cases, either malice or wilful excess of authority is
difficult to prove. Aronson and Whitmore suggest (at p 121) that the main
significance of the tort is exemplary. It quietens the 'special sense of outrage
when a public official wilfully abuses his power.' Damage is the gist of
liability. The tort is not attracted where the officer makes a personal gain
through information acquired from the claimant, unless the claimant is able to
show that a corresponding loss has been suffered. Its tortious nature is
compensatory. Public wrongs in the nature of 'insider trading' escape proper
sanction.

**[3.152]** Commodity producers in Australia are sometimes compelled by
statutory schemes to 'pool' their product for marketing purposes. Could it be
argued that a power-based fiduciary relationship could be inferred to sanction
public officials administering such a scheme? Primary producers, for example,
might wish to argue that an individual or board owes them fiduciary duties
pursuant to the Wool Marketing Act 1987 (Cth) s 64, or the Wheat Marketing
Act 1989 (Cth) ss 60–61.

The United States decision in *Nussbaum v Weeks*[340] concerned a purchaser
of agricultural land who was at the same time the general manager of the local
water district. As purchaser he failed to disclose to the land's vendor that the
district's irrigation policy was about to change. This enabled him to buy the
land at a comparatively low price. When the vendor discovered what had
happened, he commenced an action which alleged that the purchaser was his
'fiduciary' and in breach of duty by what had been done. On appeal, the court
(at 365) accepted this part of the claim. It saw it to amount to an allegation
of 'insider trading'. A public official had used information acquired in a public
capacity to make a private profit. The status of the manager of the water district
as a 'fiduciary' for those affected by his decisions was found without much
elaboration. The proposition 'that a public office is a public trust', was
described as a 'universal truism.'[341] Trust had been placed in the water district
manager as a public official. In the event, the appeal court (at 365) reversed
a finding of liability at first instance for the (perhaps doubtful) reason that the
purchase was made in a sufficiently private capacity to negate the duties of
office.

**[3.153]** Another decision to the same effect was *Creech v Federal Land Bank
of Wichita*.[342] A farmer had mortgaged his land to the 'Federal Land Bank
Association of Colorado'. This was an institution formed pursuant to the Farm
Credit Act of 1971, which was federal legislation exempting farm credits from

---

[338] E Campbell 'Liability to Compensate for Denial of a Right to a Fair Hearing' (1989) 15 *Mon LR* 383 at 404–5.

[339] M Aronson and H Whitmore *Public Torts and Contracts* (1982) pp 120–31; R Sadler 'Liability for Misfeasance in a Public Office' (1992) 14 *Syd LR* 137.

[340] 263 Cal Reptr 360 (4 Dist 1989).

[341] At 364, quoting *People v Harby* 125 P 2d 874, 881 (1942), Moore PJ.

[342] 647 F Supp 1097 (D Colo 1986), Finesilver CJ.

the Securities Act of 1971. When the farmer went into default, he raised the claim that the Land Bank was in breach of duty under a fiduciary relationship with him. Although the farmer did not succeed on the facts of this case, the court (at 110) specifically approved of the 'theory' of the claim brought and observed that in a deserving case 'those who implement the provisions of the Farm Credit Act of 1971' would be liable as fiduciaries to the farmers affected. In *Pope v Propst*[343] a former house owner succeeded against a county housing inspector. This public official used his position to acquire the house at an undervalue by threatening to have it condemned. There are other examples of this use of fiduciary reasoning.

---

[343]  345 SE 2d 880 (Ga App 1986).

# Chapter 4

# Scope of the Relationship

---

**[4.1]** *Scope* defines the reach of a fiduciary relationship. It describes the subject matter over which its obligations extend.[1] As a step in fiduciary reasoning, considerations of scope come next after establishing the existence of a fiduciary relationship and before seeing whether a fiduciary obligation has been breached. It was said by Bryson J in *Noranda Australia Ltd v Lachlan Resources NL* 'ordinarily' to be the case that:

> a person under a fiduciary obligation to another should be under that obligation in relation to a defined area of conduct, and exempt from the obligation in all other respects. Except in the defined area, a person under a fiduciary duty retains his own economic liberty.[2]

We are now describing and setting limits upon the area over which the fiduciary relationship extends.

**[4.2]** Speaking of the 'scope' of a fiduciary relationship is to express a link between abstract fiduciary obligations, on the one hand, and a specific transaction impugned, on the other. Cardozo J in *Meinhard v Salmon*[3] was concerned with this when he sought to define the fiduciary responsibilities of property developers who were engaged in a 'joint adventure'. The managing adventurer was offered and accepted a new development in his own name. Whether or not this 'new development' was an 'asset of the venture', which the manager had appropriated, or something personal to the manager, was said to depend on the 'scope' of the fiduciary relationship subsisting between the adventurers. Cardozo J described this as an inquiry to find–

> the nexus of relation between the business conducted by the [fiduciary] and the opportunity brought to him as an incident of [that business].

Indeed, the implied scope of the fiduciary obligations in such cases as *Birtchnell v Equity Trustees Executors and Agency Co Ltd*[4] and *Boardman v*

---

[1] See generally Finn *Fiduciaries* 234–2; MGL [514]–[521]; P D Maddaugh and J D McCamus *Law of Restitution* (1990), 588–91; 15.2 Laws [33].

[2] (1988) 14 NSWLR 1 at 15.

[3] 164 NE 545, 249 NY 458, 464 (1928) (CA (NY)).

[4] (1929) 42 CLR 384, esp at 408, Dixon J.

*Phipps*[5] was the critical consideration. At the same time, it is difficult matter to generalise about. In almost in every case where the scope of fiduciary obligations has been significant, some aspects of it are peculiar to the facts. Judgment is involved.

**[4.3]** When the scope of a fiduciary obligation is examined in the context of an undertaking-based fiduciary relationship, it is relatively straightforward. Scope of the relationship is equal to the parameters of what the defendant *undertook* to do.[6] It is not so easy with the other characteristics. When they arise, the scope question may be subsumed in the breach of duty inquiry. For in logic it may be that the concept of 'breach' of fiduciary duty includes what is here referred to as the 'scope' of a duty. A fiduciary obligation can only be breached in circumstances where the impugned transaction is within the scope of the obligation. The scope idea is nevertheless worth pursuing, whatever its subordination to breach of duty. It highlights what is within a relationship's ambit—what is its reach—apart from the content of the fiduciary rules.

**[4.4]** *McLeod and More v Sweezey*[7] is a Canadian authority which illustrates how the 'scope' of a relation can be critical in determining whether fiduciary obligations are breached or not. The case concerned a prospector named Sweezey, whose expertise had once enjoyed a high reputation in Manitoba. The plaintiffs were mining speculators interested in a remote area of that province. Sweezey agreed with the plaintiffs to stake and explore certain 'asbestos mining claims'. On his return, Sweezey said that he had staked the claims as instructed and that there was no evidence of asbestos. So the plaintiffs let applications for the claims lapse. Sweezey later went back to the area and staked 24 claims for himself. Four years later, chromium was discovered in the same remote area. Sweezey was able to sell his claims for a substantial sum. The plaintiffs alleged that the further claims Sweezey had staked for himself were held by him as trustee for them. In consequence, a constructive trust was said to be impressed on his sale proceeds in the plaintiffs' favour. Deciding for the plaintiff speculators, the Supreme Court found that the scope of what Sweezey undertook to do extended beyond the staking of claims according to instructions. The speculators had given Sweezey a description of the location, a small sketch and told him the whereabouts of a cache of mining tools. They had also promised him an interest in any claims of value that he found. In return for this, as the Supreme Court said at 148,

> [the plaintiffs] bargained for [Sweezey's] mature judgement and for that not only on the prospect of the discovery of asbestos. The expression in the memorandum of agreement, 'asbestos mining claims', was descriptive of what had been originally staked. The plaintiffs desired an expert opinion on those claims in the totality of their possibilities and not on one of them only. That, therefore, was the measure of his duty as the fiduciary of the plaintiffs in acting on the disclosure of all the plaintiffs had of value; he undertook to apply his experience to everything found in

---

5  [1967] 2 AC 46 at 110, Lord Hodson, 127, Lord Upjohn (dissenting); and similar reasoning in *Hospital Products Ltd v United States Surgical Corporation* (1984) 156 CLR 41 at 97, Mason J.

6  See Finn *Fiduciaries* p 243; D Waters *Law of Trusts in Canada* 2nd ed (1984) p 714.

7  [1944] 2 DLR 145; see also *Pine Pass Oil & Gas Ltd v Pacific Petroleums Ltd* (1968) 70 DLR (2d) 196 (SC (BC)).

the area of the claims and, on the strength of the opinion so formed, to stake, if that was called for, and to advise the plaintiffs of that opinion.

**[4.5]**  Sweezey's staking claims on his own behalf was in breach of fiduciary duty if that duty was conceived to extend to the mineralisation of an entire area. This was how his advisory and claim-staking undertaking was interpreted. The facts are to be compared with those of the earlier Canadian mining decision in *Tombill Gold Mines Ltd v Hamilton.*[8] It dealt with a prospector who was only employed occasionally by a company. He agreed to 'try' and stake claims for the company in a particular area when he was there for another reason. Subsequently, the prospector did stake valuable claims in the area—but purportedly only on his own behalf. When the company brought a similar claim to that in *Sweezey's* case, it was allowed no recovery.

**[4.6]**  Agent and principal is another fiduciary relation based on the undertaking characteristic where scope analysis is straightforward. What the agent has *undertaken* to do defines the scope of the relationship. So stockbrokers, a species of the agent, will be bound by fiduciary obligations flowing from the type of agreement which subsists between them and their clients. Brokers will have undertaken whatever is expressly or impliedly provided in the terms of their retainers to purchase or sell shares. In cases of a 'non-discretionary' instruction to purchase shares of a specific number and type, there may be no reason why the broker cannot engage in various undisclosed practices which do not prejudice the client. Brokers may 'marry' the orders of different clients—that is, bring together the buying and selling requests of clients in their own offices, rather than purchase and sell on the exchange floor. This was said to be acceptable by Jacobs JA in *Jones v Canavan.*[9] In other circumstances, brokers might permissibly make purchases on their own accounts of the same shares that they are instructed to purchase for clients.[10] Dixon CJ dealt with an analogous situation in *Van Rassel v Kroon.*[11] In that case, a fiduciary had been commissioned to purchase a lottery ticket on behalf of other persons. At the same time the fiduciary purchased a ticket on his own account. His own ticket proved to be the winning ticket, but he came under no obligation to the other persons thereby.

> The fiduciary is at perfect liberty before the drawing to acquire for himself beneficially any number of tickets in the same lottery as that in which he holds a ticket on behalf of others or of himself and others.

As members of the High Court observed in *Daly v Sydney Stock Exchange Ltd,*[12] only when brokers assume the role of advisors, in addition to that of broker or agent, will the scope of fiduciary obligations extend beyond the buying and selling transaction.

**[4.7]**  Where the possible reach of fiduciary obligations is broad, some jurists, notably Upjohn J in *Boulting v Association of Cinematograph, Television and*

---

[8] (1956) 5 DLR (2d) 561 (SC).
[9] [1972] 2 NSWLR 236 at 245 (CA).
[10] *Merrill, Lynch, Pierce, Fenner & Smith v Boeck* 377 NW 2d 605 (1985); *Scott & Horton v Godfrey* [1901] 2 KB 727 at 739, Bigham J.
[11] (1953) 87 CLR 298 at 303.
[12] (1986) 160 CLR 371 at 377, Gibbs CJ; at 385, Brennan J.

*Allied Technicians*[13] and later as Lord Upjohn in *Boardman v Phipps*,[14] have urged that the courts take a reasonable and commonsensical approach to their jurisdiction. Fiduciaries law has a 'runaway potential'. Paul Finn in his *Fiduciary Obligations* recommends (at p 234) a judicial 'narrowing' of the scope of the wider duties, according to reasonableness criteria. For 'some fiduciary relationships', Austin Scott observed in 1949,[15] 'are undoubtedly more intense than others. The greater the independent authority to be exercised by the fiduciary, the greater the *scope* of his fiduciary duty.' [emphasis added]

Varying 'intensity' in relationships is one description of differences in scope which arise. Discrimination between the scopes of different fiduciary relations by the discretions that they embody has a practical use. Fiduciary relationships in commerce, once found, might stifle industry or discourage invention if they are given a uniform reach. The three headings which follow are specific to issues of 'scope' as they arise in different commercial contexts. Fiduciary liability of varying stringency is inferred from each.

## Fiduciary relationships in commerce

### 1. EMPLOYERS AND EMPLOYEES

**[4.8]**   Scope issues arising in the employees' fiduciary relations with their employers assume some prima facie propositions. Employees are not entitled to make undisclosed use of their employers' property for their own benefit. Secrets or processes that employees learn of from employers, or that they are employed to derive, will normally belong to employers. In a 'secret process' case, the scope of the fiduciary relationship between the parties will typically be argued to comprehend the secret in question. Fletcher Moulton LJ in *Rakusen v Ellis, Munday & Clarke*[16] dealt with such a problem. He observed that there are some confidential relations between employees and employers, in which–

> knowledge which [the employees] acquire is not knowledge at their own disposal but consists substantially of the secrets of their employer. Such employments come to an end sometimes at the choice of the master, sometimes at the choice of the servant, and thereupon difficulties necessarily arise, because the person who is no longer in employment still has in his breast secrets which are the property of his past employer. The view that the law takes of the rights of the parties in that position is too clear to be disputed. The employee is quite free to go into the service of people who may be the rivals or opponents of his former master. He may go into employment quite inconsistent with the employment he has had in the past. All that the law says is: You shall not disclose or put at the service of your new employer the secrets that belong to your old employer.

**[4.9]**   The language of property and 'ownership' is often used to describe the 'scope' nexus between an employer's interest infringed and the fiduciary relationship between employer and employee. The employee's action is said necessarily to be within the scope of the relationship because the employee

---

[13] [1963] 2 QB 606.
[14] [1963] 2 QB 606 at 637–8 and (1942) [1967] 2 AC 46 at 133–4.
[15] 'The Fiduciary Principle' (1949) *Cal L J* 539 at 541.
[16] [1912] 1 Ch 831 at 839.

has appropriated the employer's property: an approach which should be taken with caution.

Where the interest has been physically subtracted (or stolen), it is straightforward. But there are other remedies for something so direct. The police might be called and a restitution order applied for. Obligations deriving from fiduciary relationships are usually invoked where the wrongdoing is more subtle. There is, then, much authority to say that interests, say, in information, should not be reduced to property terms.[17] In the decision of the New South Wales Supreme Court in *AWA Ltd v Koval*[18] a 'property' approach to questions of scope was the one used. Breach of an employee's fiduciary duty not to make secret use of his employer's property was the argued basis of an order to make the employee disgorge his gains. It was important to the claim that it was established that the scope of the fiduciary relation included the following situation, which had developed prior to the employment ending. Koval was employed by AWA in Sydney as its senior foreign exchange dealer and money market manager. In that capacity, Koval was initially very successful and made a large profit for his employer. As a consequence, he applied to the general manager for some remuneration additional to his salary. Koval alleged that he then received verbal authority from the manager to use a small part of AWA's overall yearly dealing limit to enter transactions on his own account. Resulting profits were to be split between Koval and AWA. 'Naturally', Koval alleged, this arrangement was kept secret from the AWA directors. As the 'split' profits were made, they were paid in to various bank accounts which Koval and an associate opened. AWA's board eventually discovered what was going on. Koval's profits were sought and his story of the arrangement was disbelieved. It was found by Rogers J that Koval had breached a fiduciary obligation within the scope of the duty that he he owed AWA as employee. Specifically, it was found that this duty extended to the part of the dealing limit which Koval had used to make profits for himself. The dealing limit was AWA's 'property' and Koval had used it for his own gain. His claim to have used it as of right was disbelieved.

**[4.10]** More meticulous examination of 'scope' was made in *McLeod and More v Sweezey*[19] and the Canadian mining cases. The inquiry there began with examination of the express and implied terms of the employees' contracts of employment. Did the scope of the 'undertakings' assumed extend to the opportunities in question? Only if so, in the Canadian analysis of Maddaugh and McCamus, could the employers be said to possess 'expectations' which it would be unconscionable to deny.[20] Unconscionability was said to affect Sweezey and justify the court order because of the part in the creation of such an expectation which he had played.

**[4.11]** The High Court decision in *Consul Development Pty Ltd v DPC Estates Pty Ltd*[21] is also of relevance in this area, although its authority is

---

[17] See, eg, *Boardman v Phipps* [1967] 2 AC 46 at 126, Lord Upjohn and *Pancontinental Mining Ltd v Commissioner of Stamp Duties* [1989] 1 Qd R 310 at 312, de Jersey J (FC).

[18] (1993) 35 *Ind L R* 217 (SC (NSW), Rogers J).

[19] [1944] 2 DLR 145 (SC).

[20] P D Maddaugh and J D McCamus *Law of Restitution* (1990) p 591.

[21] (1975) 132 CLR 373.

mainly quoted on the equitable liability of third parties. The facts of the case began with a wrong done by an employee to an employer within a fiduciary relation of employment. One employee served as the manager of his employer's property investment company. This person secretly enabled another company to take the benefit of investment opportunities of which the manager had learnt in course of his employment. Breach of fiduciary duty by the manager within the scope of his employment was consequently inferred. The other company, DPC Estates Pty Ltd, was controlled by the employer's articled clerk. Through this company the clerk took the proceeds of the manager's deception and shared them with him. Stephen J (at 402–3), with whom Barwick CJ agreed, treated as being irrelevant to a determination of the scope of the manager's employment that the employer's company had insufficient resources to make the investment itself. Although no advantage was or could have been subtracted from the investment company, its entitlement to fiduciary loyalty was unaffected. Different approaches of the United States authorities on this point will be noted below at [4.44]–[4.50]. All the reported judgments in *Consul Development Pty Ltd v DPC Estates Pty Ltd* found that the manager's breach was within the scope of his duties to his employer.[22] Perhaps the pleadings made it unnecessary, but it was not found by any judge that the articled clerk had misconducted himself within the scope of his employment. The clerk had been the manager's partner in fraud and provider of the profit-making vehicle. It may be that the scope of an articled clerk's employment relationship does not preclude his competition with his master's sideline investments. When the case was before the Court of Appeal, Jacobs P said (at 455) short of finding fiduciary liability–

> I think that [the articled clerk] continued to believe that there may well have been something wrong in relation to the transactions . . . based on a feeling that it was wrong for him, an articled clerk of [the solicitor] and [the manager], an employee working for [the solicitor's] companies, to be arranging behind [the solicitor's] back and in his own office to enter into profitable transactions of the same character that [the solicitor] entered into.

### Employees' inventions

**[4.12]**    Much litigation has surrounded the question of who is entitled to an employee's inventions and their associated patent rights. Certain basic principles are clear.[23] Entitlement to patent rights in Australia is regulated by equity and the common law and not by statute.[24] Where employees are employed to make inventions and they make them during the course of their employment, the inventions are prima facie the property of their employer. In such a case,

> the employer will be the inventor and the workman or employee will be a mere instrument through which he realizes his ideas, if the employer had a conception of the result embraced in the invention or the general idea of a machine upon a particular principle and then, to carry his conception into effect, employed the

---

[22]  Ibid and (1974) 1 NSWLR 443 (CA).

[23]  See generally S Ricketson *Law of Intellectual Property* (1984), 1014–17 and *Lipscomb's Walker on Patents* 3rd edn, ed E Lipscomb (1984), 3.5.

[24]  It is the same in the United States; cf UK Patents Acts 1949, s 56 (apportionment) and 1977, ss 39–42 (compensation).

manual dexterity of an employee mechanic in the mechanical details and arrangements requisite for carrying the original conception into practice.[25]

**[4.13]** Consequently, if patent rights have already been obtained in the employees' names, they will hold them on trust for their employers. This was the result in *Edisonia Ltd v Forse*.[26] An employee of a phonograph company had invented an improved recording cylinder. Although he took out a patent in his own name, the employee was found to have no beneficial interest in it. Warrington J stated the relevant duties at 551–2:

> [the employee] must be taken to be placed under the obligation of using the utmost of his skill and knowledge and inventive powers to produce in the business of the company the best possible [result] . . . his part in these inventions was performed in the execution of that duty.

*Adamson v Kenworthy*[27] was another such case. An employee draughtsman patented a new form of brake for cranes. The idea had evolved through the instructions and directions of his employer and the employee was consequently found to possess no beneficial interest in what he had discovered. In *Timber Engineering Co Pty Ltd v Anderson*[28] the defendants were sued to account for profits which had been made by pirating their employer's business. By way of defence they asserted an entitlement to 'just allowances' for originating the 'concept and design' of certain products. This was disallowed—for the reason that the defendants had developed the products within the scope and course of their employment. It was an employment for which they had 'presumably been remunerated on a proper basis'. So the inventions or designs were said to be the property of the employer.

A contrary result may follow where the employees are not employed to make the inventions they did and their field of employment is general. Where inventions are conceived by employees in the course of such general employment, the inventions prima facie belong to the employees. An employer is not entitled to his employees' inventions simply because they were made in the employer's time, nor because they were made by virtue of what the employees had the opportunity to observe in the course of their employment.[29]

**[4.14]** Employees' inventions may be the subject of express terms of the employees' contracts of employment. If the inventions are thereby provided to belong to the employer, this will usually be conclusive. Entitlement is established, assuming that the term is not invalid as an unreasonable restraint of trade.[30] As Powell J suggested in *On The Street Pty Ltd v Cott*,[31] a term may even be implied to the same effect. This will depend on whether the employees' fiduciary obligations or common law duties of fidelity to their

---

[25] *Lipscomb's Walker on Patents*, §3.5, citing inter alia *Standard Parts Co v Peck* 264 US 52 (1924).

[26] (1908) 25 RPC 546.

[27] (1931) 49 RPC 57, Farwell J and see *Triplex Safety Glass Co Ltd v Scorah* (1938) 20 RPC 41.

[28] [1980] 2 NSWLR 488 at 506–7, Kearney J: see [6.86] below.

[29] *Re Charles Selz Ltd's Patent Application* (1953) 71 RPC 158; *Aas v Benham* [1891] 2 Ch 244 at 256 (CA).

[30] See *Sterling Engineering Co Ltd v Patchett* [1955] AC 534; *Electrolux Ltd v Hudson* [1977] FSR 312.

[31] (1990) 10 FLR 234, 242; 3 ACSR 54 (NSW SC)— re an executive director.

employer are seen to require it. The following principle was stated by the United States Supreme Court in *United States v Dubliner Condenser Corporation*.[32]

> One employed to make an invention, who succeeds, during his term of service, in accomplishing that task, is bound to assign it to his employer any patent obtained. The reason is that he has only produced that which he was employed to invent. His invention is the precise subject of the contract of employment. A term of the agreement necessarily is that what he is paid to produce belongs to his paymaster.

In the United States, it may be, fiduciary obligations are liable to be imposed by contract terms and implied ones at that. This is contrary to the usual position in Australia that we have described above.[33] What follows now is a methodology for establishing entitlement to employees' inventions—apart from the effect of express or implied contract provisions.

**[4.15]**  In establishing entitlement, it is necessary to see, first, whether the making of inventions is within the course of the employee's ordinary duties, or whether the inventions are in some way exceptional and beyond the call of duty. For this the employees' contracts of employment should be examined, as is illustrated by the United States case of *Moore v American Barmag Corporation*.[34] The inventor there was a 'service engineer', employed by a manufacturer of machinery for the textiles industry. There was considerable argument about what the inventor's employment duties precisely were. The parties agreed that those duties definitely included the 'start up of texturing machines', 'troubleshooting on texturing machines' and 'reporting on customer trials'. The employer unsuccessfully alleged further that the employee's duties required him to 'design adaptations on certain machine parts' as well. On the facts of the case, the employer's sales manager asked the employee to visit the textile plant of a customer in a different part of the state. The customer had experienced a problem with 'the feed path on a yarn texturing machine', which the sales manager had claimed to have a solution for. When the employee arrived and put the sales manager's solution to the customer, it was rejected. After this (recorded at 400),

> [the] plaintiff eventually returned to his hotel room where, in a state between waking and sleeping, he conceived of a novel way of feeding yarns through an air texturing machine which would greatly increase the speed at which quality yarn could be produced.

On the next day, the employee tried the idea at the customer's plant. It proved highly successful. The employee then returned to his employer, disclosed the idea, and requested some 'compensation for his invention'. But it appears from the report that the only extras on the excursion that the employer would pay the employee for were his hotel room, meals and travel expenses. Shortly afterwards the employer filed an application for a patent on the invention, with the employee's consent. In these circumstances, the court found that the employee had at least an arguable entitlement to the patent rights and the matter should proceed to trial. The employee was not one who had been 'hired to invent'. Invention was the province of the employer's separate 'research

---

32  289 US 178 at 187 (1933).
33  See [3.31] and Ricketson 1015–16.
34  693 F Supp 399 (WDNC 1988).

and development arm'. Coming from the employer's 'sales and service arm', inventions were outside the tasks which the employee was required to perform. No term in the employee's contract of employment prevented his claim. The result would presumably have been different had the employee been employed as a designer, a draughtsman, or in the 'research and development arm'.

**[4.16]** Next, the status that the employee occupies in the employer's organisation should be determined. If the employee is a director of the employer company, his obligations as director may prevent him from taking advantage of his fiduciary position to gain a financial advantage for himself which the company might have enjoyed. Referring to *Cook v Deeks*[35] and *Regal (Hastings) Ltd v Gulliver*,[36] further discussed at [5.71]–[5.73], Danckwerts J in *Fine Industrial Commodities Ltd v Powling*[37] made a managing director a constructive trustee for his company of a patent that he had taken out for himself. The director was able to raise some evidence of his purchase of the patent rights from the company. However, at 262, he was found not to have discharged the burden that rests upon fiduciaries contracting with their principals. The bargain was not shown to be a fair one, upon which the principal was fully advised and given full knowledge of all relevant facts.

Application of comparable common law principles in *Worthington Pumping Engine Company v Moore*[38] reached a similar conclusion. The employee who had made inventions and had taken out patents in his own name there was described as the English 'agent and manager' of an American corporation. Employed at a high salary, the agent was said (at 46) to be 'in effect, the alter ego of the Plaintiff Corporation outside the United States'. When dismissed, the agent asserted a right to restrain the company from using the inventions he had patented. The court held (at 49) that the agent was a trustee of the patents for the company, pursuant to obligations of good faith imposed by the relevant contract of employment.

## 2. PARTNERS (AND JOINT VENTURERS)

**[4.17]** Partnerships, as we saw at [3.89], are the paradigm of fiduciary relationships based in the parties' *mutual reliance*. Either this reliance existed in fact, or the partners and those analogous to them had a right to expect it. Commercial partnerships are continuing arrangements, usually businesses, whereby the parties agree to work together towards a particular object and/or share profits earned thereby. Joint ventures have a similar purpose, but without the element of continuity. Profit-making objectives in a joint venture are limited to a single purpose or group of purposes, usually specified in the joint venture agreement.[39] Partnerships and joint ventures hence involve similar business relations, but of differing specificity and purpose. But the scope of the mutual fiduciary obligations in either a partnership or a joint venture is ascertained in the same way. Whether a one-time or a continuing arrangement,

---

[35] [1916] AC 654.

[36] (1942) [1967] 2 AC 134n.

[37] (1954) 71 RPC 253, see esp 262.

[38] (1903) 20 RPC 41.

[39] See *Noranda Australia Ltd v Lachlan Resources NL* (1988) 14 NSWLR 1, *Hunter Engineering Co Inc v Syncrude Canada Ltd* [1989] 1 SCR 426; *Midcon Oil & Gas Ltd v New British Dominion Oil Co Ltd* (1958) 12 DLR (2d) 700.

the ambit of the business limits the nature of the relationship which flows from it. The business of the partnership or joint-venture defines the subject-matter over which fiduciary obligations extend.

[4.18] An obvious first place to look in order to see what matters and activities a mutually reliant business extends to is its constitutive document. A partnership deed or joint venture agreement is the first place for inquiry. In *Birtchnell v Equity Trustees, Executors and Agency Co Ltd*[40] a firm of estate agents brought action against the estate of a deceased partner. This was to compel the estate to account for profits made by the partner deceased from an alleged 'transaction concerning the business of the firm'. The deceased had received a share in the profits of certain land speculation—a business that the partner had engaged in secretly, through the medium of a customer who had made purchases and sales through the firm in the ordinary way. The question before the High Court was whether the business scope of the firm included the carrying on of a general business in land speculation. Irving CJ in the Supreme Court of Victoria had held that speculation would be an extension and variation of a 1913 partnership deed. As this had never been agreed between the partners, it was therefore not an authorised activity of the firm. The High Court majority took a contrary view, holding that it was wrong to look simply at formalities. Agreement was not the only way to establish the partners' mutual duties. Instead, in the words of Dixon J at 408:

> The subject matter over which the fiduciary obligations extend is ... to be ascertained, not merely from the express agreement of the parties, whether embodied in written instruments or not, but also from the course of dealing actually pursued by the firm.

In the pages following, Dixon J treated the nature of the firm's course of dealing as primarily discoverable from its balance sheet, accounts and cash book. Examination of these disclosed that the firm's business involved occasional departure from the terms of the partnership articles. Sometimes the firm acted in concert with a client on a speculative basis, earning a profit share in addition to a selling commission. The secret advantage which the deceased partner had derived was, as Dixon J said at 418, 'an advantage, the pursuit of which fell within the scope of the partnership business'. His estate was liable accordingly.

[4.19] An opportunity is not within the scope of the partnership or joint venture business simply because it is through the business that the fiduciary learns of it. As Lord Hodson said in *Boardman v Phipps*:[41]

> it does not necessarily follow that because an agent acquired information and opportunity whilst acting in a fiduciary capacity he is accountable to his principals for any benefit which comes his way as the result of the use he makes of that information and opportunity.

As well as being shown to have discovered the opportunity in the course of partnership or joint venture activities, the fiduciary must make a certain use of the opportunity in order to be liable. The use must be one related to the business of the firm and also separate from it.

---

[40] (1929) 42 CLR 384.
[41] [1967] 2 AC 46 at 102–3.

**[4.20]**   A common example of an opportunity's related use is competition with the partnership business. Or the use might be the pursuit of some undertaking that could easily have been pursued in conjunction with the business, or in addition to it. The partnership case of *Aas v Benham*[42] is of relevance here. A partner in a shipbroking firm was sued by the firm to account for profits that he made in the formation of a ship-building company. The ship-building opportunity was shown to have come through the shipbroking connection and the broker's name and letterhead were used in all correspondence. However it was held by the United Kingdom Court of Appeal that the business of shipbroking was separate from that of ship-building and could not reasonably include it. Profits made were outside the scope of the fiduciary relationship that the firm entailed and, accordingly, the partner did not have to account for them to the firm. Lindley LJ at 256 used the following illustration.

> Suppose a partner to become, in the course of carrying on his business, well acquainted with a particular branch of science or trade, and suppose him to write and publish a book on the subject, could the firm claim the profits thereby obtained? Obviously not, unless, by publishing the book, he in fact competed with the firm in their own line of business.

**[4.21]**   In a comparable way, an opportunity can be 'related' or not to a joint venture business. In *Trimble v Goldberg*,[43] for example, a 'joint adventure' was agreed for three speculators to acquire shares and land from a particular vendor. The same vendor sold further land to two of the speculators, upon which those speculators made separate profits. When those speculators were sued for an account by the excluded speculator, no liability was found as the profits were not within the scope of the joint adventure.

**[4.22]**   There may be what Paul Finn has described as an 'ill-defined exception' to the rule on the scope of partnership liability here described.[44] A partner or joint venturer who *wrongfully* uses a fiduciary position to exploit an opportunity may be liable upon proof only of the wrong and the fact that the opportunity was exploited in a fiduciary context. Liability will arise whether or not some use of the opportunity within the scope of the fiduciary business is made. *Trimble v Goldberg*[45] distinguished this exception as requiring an abuse of fiduciary position which caused a loss or injury, not found in the facts of that case. The principle was distinguished also in *Jenkins v Bennett*,[46] where a partner had been sued on account of occasional advice he had given to his wife, who operated a competing business. No injury to or competition with the partnership business was found. Finn in *Fiduciary Obligations* refers (at p 236) to a 'misuse' of position as partner or joint venturer in this context, which may be apt to cover the separately wrongful use as well. The exception in fact accords with the authorities on the liability of corporate officers for corporate opportunities, which we shall see at [4.47] below.

---

[42] [1891] 2 Ch D 244 (CA), esp at 255–6, Lindley LJ.
[43] [1906] AC 494 (PC).
[44] Finn *Fiduciaries* 236, citing *Russell v Austwick* (1826) 1 Sim 52.
[45] [1906] AC 494, 500 (PC), see below at [5.75].
[46] [1965] WAR 42.

## 3. CORPORATIONS AND CORPORATE OFFICERS

**[4.23]**  Fiduciary principles may apply to the relation between a corporation and its directors, executives, managers and any other person authorised to act or do business on its behalf. Equity is concerned with what people *do* in relation to the corporation, not with the titles that companies or statutes may give them. Following the Corporations Law s 232(1), we shall describe as 'officers' of a corporation the directors, executive officers, receivers, administrators, liquidators, trustees of compromises and others who can act on a corporation's behalf. The term will be given an equitable purview, which, unlike the Corporations Law, includes agents generally.[47] Also, one proposition is generally true. Once a fiduciary relationship has extended to an officer of a corporation so understood, its obligations cannot be avoided by relinquishment of the office.[48]

Scope of the fiduciary duties of corporate officers has been often litigated. Much of the courts' time has been spent setting the boundaries of the defined area of conduct to which a corporate fiduciary's obligations extend. Much more time, in fact, than has been required to establish the equivalent boundaries of both the employer and employee relation and the relation between partners. We shall begin our attempt to establish the regulated domain of the corporate fiduciary by outlining the duties to which corporate fiduciaries are liable. There will be in this way an unavoidable anticipation of the next heading.

**[4.24]**  A corporate officer is in the first place under a fiduciary duty to act in good faith.[49] This is the duty of officers to act 'bona fide in what they consider—not what a court may consider—is in the best interests of the company.'[50] We will only consider here the fiduciary duties which corporate fiduciaries may owe to their corporation, not those which may be owed to creditors, contributories and others, considered at [5.90]–[5.99]. This 'good faith' duty owed to a corporation implies a standard of conduct for the taking of management decisions. Attainment of the standard involves something more than mere honesty.

**[4.25]**  The 'good faith' duty is connected with another fiduciary duty which is management-related. This is the duty that corporate officers only exercise powers conferred on them for the purposes for which they were conferred. We will call it the 'proper purposes' duty.

The proper scopes of each of the two duties together raise policy questions as to the standards that should be reached in decision-taking on behalf of corporations. Yet *boundaries* in the scope of each duty are usually

---

[47]  See *Canadian Aero Service Ltd v O'Malley* (1973) 40 DLR (3d) 371 at 381 (SC); *Green and Clara Pty Ltd v Bestobell Industries Pty Ltd* [1982] WAR 1 (FC).

[48]  *Green and Clara Pty Ltd v Bestobell Industries Pty Ltd* [1982] WAR 1 (FC); *Balston Ltd v Headline Filters Ltd* [1990] FSR 385, 410–11; *Island Export Finance Ltd v Umunna* [1986] BCLC 460 at 480; *Industrial Development Consultants Ltd v Cooley* [1972] 1 WLR 443 and *Palmer's Company Law* 25th ed (1992) at [8.501].

[49]  P Finn *Fiduciary Obligations*, 78–80; *Gower's Principles of Modern Company Law* L C B Gower 5th ed (1992), 553–6; *Ford and Austin's Principles of Corporations Law* H A J Ford and R P Austin 7th ed (1995) [8.070], [8.290]–[8.300]; *Palmer's Company Law* 25th ed (1992), [8.505]–[8.515]; cf Corporations Law s 232(2), duty to 'act honestly'.

[50]  *Re Greene & Fawcett Ltd* [1942] Ch 304, 306, Greene MR (CA).

uncontentious—it is not normal to suggest, say, that a director's personal decision on which school to send his children to should be taken according to the standard of a reasonable director. The views of a majority of shareholders are thought to be irrelevant in such a matter, and to suggest otherwise would be to wildly expand the scope of the management duties.

Sometimes it is clear what is corporate management and what is not. But there are areas in which the scope of management duties is less plain. The same director might have secretly organised payment of the school fees by diversion to the school of a monetary receipt which the corporation would have received otherwise. As member of the school council, the director might have assisted the school to drive a very hard bargain with the corporation's sales department. Boundaries of fiduciary law are now concerned. In the first case, the director might claim that the monetary receipt was entirely personal to him or her and could never have been obtained by the corporation. Scope is then the question. *Was* the receipt of money personal, or was it not? Is it relevant that the corporation could not have sued for the money? In the second case, the director might say that the deal was with an entirely separate sales arm of the corporation. His or her duties as a director were limited to research. What, then, was the true scope of the directorship?

**[4.26]**     Fiduciaries law has some specific duties to regulate wrongdoing of the type just discussed. For present purposes we will be concerned with two of these, conflicts of interest and secret profits, respectively. Sometimes they are called fiduciary sub-rules.[51] The former is the obligation that corporate fiduciaries must avoid entering engagements which would involve *conflict* between their personal interests and their duties to the corporation. We will call it the 'conflicts rule'. The latter is a rule which prohibits corporate officers from making secret *profits* for themselves from the use of corporate assets, information or opportunities.[52] We will call this the 'profits rule'.

We will anticipate the next chapter with a word about the content of each of these duties. The conflicts rule here is substantially as stated in *Ford's Principles of Corporations Law*,[53] *Palmer's Company Law*[54] and *Gower's Principles of Modern Company Law*.[55] The formulations seem liable to the criticism that they proscribe the wrong act.[56] For, looking from a remedial perspective, equity is not so much concerned with entry into engagements containing a conflict of interest as with the actual pursuit of the personal interest conflicting. The following part of Sir Frederick Jordan's *Chapters on Equity in New South Wales* has been approved for making this point.[57]

---

[51] R P Austin 'Fiduciary Accountability for Business Opportunities' in Finn *Relationships* 141 at 142; Finn *Fiduciaries* 246–51.
[52] As stated in *Palmer's Company Law* 25th ed (1992), [8.536].
[53] H A J Ford and R P Austin 7th ed (1995) [9.060]–[9.100].
[54] 25th ed (1992), [8.516] ('. . . directors are required not to put themselves in a position . . . ').
[55] L C B Gower 5th ed (1992) p 559 ('. . . directors must not place themselves in a position . . . ').
[56] Made in *Chan v Zacharia* (1984) 154 CLR 178 at 198, Deane J and *Hospital Products Ltd v United States Surgical Corporation* (1984) 156 CLR 41 at 103, Mason J.
[57] 6th ed, ed F C Stephen (1947) p 115; approved by Deane J in *Chan*, ibid.

It has often been said that a person who occupies a fiduciary position ought to avoid placing himself in a position where his duty and his interest ... conflict. This is rather a counsel of prudence than a rule of equity; *the rule being that a fiduciary must not take advantage of such a conflict if it arises.* [emphasis added]

**[4.27]**　R P Austin says of the conflicts and the profits rules that, 'For the most part [they] cover the same ground and a conclusion expressed in terms of one of them can usually be restated in terms of the other.'[58]

Nevertheless, many jurists and writers have been anxious to accord priority to one or other rule. This may be from a desire to find symmetry in the pattern of corporate fiduciary duties, or in fiduciary duties generally. In the celebrated speech of Lord Upjohn in *Boardman v Phipps*,[59] the explanatory possibilities of the conflicts rule were much extended, perhaps for this reason. As R P Austin says,[60] the conflicts rule assumes a straightforward 'duty' for the private interest to conflict with. But it has no mechanism to assist it where the scope of the duty is ambiguous. The scheme of Finn in *Fiduciary Obligations* accords a similar prominence to the conflicts rule. Conflicts of duty and interest and conflict of duty with duty are there called fiduciary 'rules'. The secret profits prohibition, on the other hand, is accorded the status only of a 'sub-rule'.[61]

**[4.28]**　Apart from usual citation of the foregoing rules, there is no agreed list in works of authority of what other fiduciary rules apply to corporate officers. A measure of this uncertainty is as follows. In the latest edition of *Ford and Austin's Principles of Corporations Law*[62] the following fiduciary duties, distributed over two chapters, are said to bind directors at general law:
* Duty to act in good faith for the benefit of the company as a whole (pp 259–69);
* Duty not to fetter discretions (pp 269–71);
* Duty to act for proper purposes (pp 272–80);
* The conflicts rule (pp 305–9);
* Duty not to misappropriate company property and information (pp 317–19); and
* The profit rule and corporate opportunities (pp 320–28)

*Gower's Principles of Modern Company Law*[63] states only four duties, phrased so as to include all of Ford's list. Authority differs on whether the conflict and profit rules are separate. *Palmer's Company Law*[64] strongly maintains their separate status and the rules are treated apart in R P Austin's account of the subject.[65] Other works, including the seventh edition of *Principles of Corporations Law*, treat the conflicts rule as the primary one and relegate the profits rule to the status of a sub-rule. Gibbs CJ said as much in

---

[58] R P Austin 'Fiduciary Accountability for Business Opportunities' in Finn *Relationships* 141 at 146.

[59] [1967] 2 AC 46 at (diss) 126–7.

[60] In 'Fiduciary Accountability for Business Opportunities' in Finn *Relationships*, 141—7.

[61] Finn *Fiduciaries* Chapters 18, 21 and 22.

[62] 7th ed (1995).

[63] L C B Gower 5th ed (1992), 551–71.

[64] 25th ed (1992) at [8.536].

[65] In Finn *Relationships*, 141, 147.

*Consul Development Pty Ltd v DPC Estates Pty Ltd*,[66] as did Lord Upjohn in *Boardman v Phipps*.[67] Paul Finn in *Fiduciary Obligations* is of this view and says (at 246) that the profits rule is a 'not very illuminating' formulation of the conflicts rule.

**[4.29]**   Deane J in *Chan v Zacharia*[68] took a position adopted in none of these authorities. He said that there was 'a general principle of equity requiring a person in a fiduciary relationship to account for personal benefits or gain' and this general principal had 'two themes', resembling the conflicts rule and the profits rule respectively. 'Whilst overlapping', the rules were acknowledged at the same time to be 'distinct'. Justice Deane continued (at 199):

> Stated comprehensively in terms of the liability to account, the principle of equity is that a person who is under a fiduciary obligation must account to the person to whom the obligation is owed for any benefit or gain (i) which has been obtained or received in circumstances where a conflict or a significant possibility of conflict existed between his fiduciary duty and his personal interest in the pursuit or possible receipt of such a benefit or gain or (ii) which was obtained or received by use of or by reason of his fiduciary position or of the opportunity or knowledge resulting from it.

We shall further consider this inclusionary statement in the next chapter. Its doctrinal upshot for now is that the rules should be treated as having independent pedigrees. The profits rule is not another expression of the conflicts rule. Nor is it subordinate to it. Scope problems arising out of one or other rule deserve separate treatment. No significance is meant here by the fact that the conflicts rule is the one treated first.

## Corporate officers: scope of the conflicts rule

**[4.30]**   Conflicts between corporate officers' personal interests and their corporate duties are proscribed by this rule. Officers are forbidden to enter circumstances either where actual conflict exists or where it might arise in the future. The duties that their interests may conflict with are those which derive from the offices they hold in the corporations. Scope of the conflicts rule is in a way quite straightforward. It is something that must equal and cannot exceed the scope of the officers' corporate duties.[69] The exercise is then to see what those duties entail.

Within this limitation, though, the mere *possibility* of conflict between personal interests and officers' duties has a potential application which is very wide. All sorts of unlikely combinations of personal interest and duty might conceivably conflict. Wisely, the reach of this has been judicially curtailed. Mere contingent conflict is said not to attract the rule unless the conflict is

---

[66] (1975) 132 CLR 373 at 393, citing *Aberdeen Railway Co v Blaikie Bros* (1854) 1 Macq 461, 471; [1843–60] All ER 249.
[67] [1967] 2 AC 46 at 127; see also *NZ Netherlands Society 'Oranje' Inc v Kuys* [1973] 2 All ER 1222 at 1225, Lord Wilberforce (PC).
[68] (1984) 154 CLR 178 at 198.
[69] Cf Finn *Fiduciaries* pp 238–44.

'real and sensible' and more than purely hypothetical.[70] Common sense is vindicated. Nevertheless, if a conflict within the scope of the rule is found to exist, actually or potentially, the main defence left for the corporate officer is to pass this step and deny the breach of duty itself. The conflicting interest, it might be said, was a minor thing and not such as to affect or be incompatible with the officer's duty.

[4.31] The following examples may show that establishing the scope of a corporate officer's duty may not be straightforward. This is preliminary to finding the applicable scope of the conflicts rule. We have just noted that the scope of the conflicts rule and the relevant officer's duty are much about the same thing. Assume first a company, one which carries on a business of printing banknotes. Conduct of this business is the primary object of this company in its memorandum of association. After a number of years, the managing director discovers some suitable printing presses going cheaply. So he buys the presses on his own account and then resells them to the company for three times the price. When this is discovered, the company seeks to impress a constructive trust over the managing director's profit. Such a claim was disallowed by the Privy Council in *Burland v Earle*.[71] In order to establish it, the board said that it had to be shown by the company that the managing-director's purchase of the (cheap) presses was such as should have been made for the company. The court found that Burland as managing director had no 'commission or mandate' from the company to purchase the presses at the time when he did. Hence Burland could not be treated as the company's trustee in making the purchase. The scope of Burland's duties as managing director did not include the making of this obviously advantageous purchase. Hence Burland's profit on the deal was made in a private capacity and the company had no equity to disturb it.

[4.32] Reasoning in *Burland v Earle*[72] was followed by the High Court in *Peninsular and Oriental Steam Navigation Company v Johnson*.[73] Again the scope of a managing-director's duties was used to establish the scope of the fiduciary rule. One Johnson was managing director of a colliery company. He was also managing director of another company which bore his name and carried on business as a mining agent, and which was substituted for Johnson himself as the mining company's managing agent just prior to the events in the case. Johnson arranged for the agent to purchase some second-hand mining equipment at a bankruptcy sale. Most of this equipment was then resold to the colliery company at a 100 per cent profit. The other directors of the colliery company were shown a book entry of the transaction, which referred only to the purchase of 'stores'. Facts about the deception eventually came to light. However, by that time the colliery company was unable to return the equipment and rescind the transaction. So a different claim in equity was brought instead, to have Johnson's company account to the colliery company

---

[70] *Hospital Products Ltd v United States Surgical Corporation* (1984) 156 CLR 41 at 103, Mason J; *Chan v Zacharia* (1984) 154 CLR 178 at 205, Deane J; *Queensland Mines Ltd v Hudson* (1978) 18 ALR 1 at 3; *Consul Development Pty Ltd v DPC Estates Pty Ltd* (1975) 132 CLR 373 at 399, Gibbs CJ.

[71] [1902] AC 83.

[72] [1902] AC 83 (PC).

[73] (1938) 60 CLR 189.

for the profits it made. Johnson was an officer who had caused an interposed entity to make a handsome private profit at the colliery company's expense. Members of the High Court were unanimous in disallowing the claim, for much the same reason that the claim in *Burland v Earle*[74] failed. Mining equipment, when purchased at the bankruptcy sale, was not, in the words of Latham CJ, 'the property in equity of the colliery company'.[75] He observed that there was–

> no evidence to show that the machinery was bought on behalf of the colliery company. The evidence, on the other hand, shows that the machinery was bought as a speculation, with the intention of selling it at a profit to any willing purchasers. It was resold to various purchasers, including the colliery company.

**[4.33]**   The managing director and his vehicles were allowed great latitude in the conduct of their own affairs, even where these verged upon the company's needs—a point also justified by Dixon J. 'No doubt', Dixon said,

> it was within the scope of the managing-director's authority to buy second-hand mining machinery for the company if he considered that it was required. If, therefore, he determined that the . . . machinery was needed and should be acquired by [the colliery company] and had caused [the other company] to buy simply for the purpose of intercepting an intermediate profit upon the acquisition of the machinery by the former company upon which he had so determined, it may well be that, inasmuch as [the other company] were represented in the transaction by [Johnson], they would be saddled with a constructive trust arising from his abuse of authority as managing-director of [the colliery company]. But there is no satisfactory proof . . . that [Johnson] had determined that the machinery should be acquired by [the colliery company].

So the scope of a managing director's duty was limited to that officer's assumption of a particular responsibility in the transaction. This required the colliery company to prove that Johnson, the rogue, had 'determined' upon the purchase of specific equipment for the company in order to give content to the duty with which his personal interest was so clearly in conflict.

**[4.34]**   Reasoning in the *P and O* case may seem a little artificial to many modern readers. How, in the circumstances, could the company have established liability? Why should it depend on proof that the wrongdoer set a task for himself? It is not very likely that Johnson would have left any evidence of incriminatory 'determinations' lying around. Such reasoning on the scope of duties (leading to a fiduciary outcome) may be why the conflicts rule has fallen into disuse. Earlier authorities, like *Burland v Earle*,[76] *Bell v Lever Bros*[77] and the dicta in *Bray v Ford*[78] had all used the conflicts rule exclusively in this context—that is, to determine whether company directors were entitled as against their companies to keep the private profits that they made. Then the 1942 case of *Regal (Hastings) Ltd v Gulliver*[79] marked a change of direction. All the law lords in that case, excepting Viscount Sankey, based their breach

---

[74] [1902] AC 83 (PC).

[75] (1938) 60 CLR 189 at 213; see also 247, Dixon J.

[76] [1902] AC 83.

[77] [1932] AC 161.

[78] [1896] AC 44 at 51, Lord Herschell.

[79] (1942) [1967] 2 AC 134n.

of fiduciary duty reasonings on only the profits rule. The conflicts rule was thereafter ignored in most United Kingdom corporate profits cases, such as *Industrial Development Consultants Ltd v Cooley*.[80] Only the views of Lord Upjohn stand against the trend. See, for example, what he said in *Boulting v Association of Cinematograph, Television and Allied Technicians*[81] and his dissenting speech in *Boardman v Phipps*.[82]

Decline of the conflicts rule has been reflected in Australia, too. Compare the reasoning in the *P & O case* with, for example, *Es-Me Pty Ltd v Parker*[83] and with *Green and Clara Pty Ltd v Bestobell Industries Pty Ltd*.[84]—even though both rules were referred to in the latter case. 'Conflict of interest and duty' has now a limited usefulness in drawing down equitable sanctions upon profiteering corporate officers. In the United States, as will be seen at [4.47]–[4.50], the strict and prophylactic aspects of the conflicts rule are entirely eschewed. Scope of rule and consequent scope of duty inquiries are pursued much more flexibly there and with greater openness to considerations of policy.

### Corporate officers: scope of the profits rule

[4.35]    The profits rule has a different scope as between honest and dishonest fiduciaries.[85] If corporate officers act dishonestly or in bad faith, they will be liable for *any* secret profit made either whilst serving as an officer, or as a consequence of so serving. So in *Cook v Deeks*,[86] serving company directors who had 'deliberately designed to exclude' the company from obtaining a profitable contract in order to pass it to a company of their own had clearly done wrong within the scope of this rule. In *Canadian Aero Service Ltd v O'Malley*,[87] the senior executives of a company found liable had resigned, but in order, it was accepted, to tender in competition with the company. This was to enable them then to win a profitable contract in the name of a company of their own.

[4.36]    By contrast, honest fiduciaries may not be within the scope of the profits rule if they do no more than profit while serving as corporate officers. Nor, often, will they be within the scope of the rule if they profit by what they learn in the course of fiduciary office. To make an honest fiduciary liable, there needs to be a further link between the corporate claimant and the gain made. Corporate assets, information or opportunities must have been *used* in the making of the private profit. Evidence of profit-making user is needed to make the honest fiduciary liable.[88] Wilberforce J, though, in deciding to make a fiduciary liable for profits innocently made in *Phipps v Boardman*,[89] expressed the principle with reservations. 'It would', he said,

---

[80] [1972] 1 WLR 443, Roskill J.

[81] (as Upjohn LJ) [1963] 2 QB 606 at 637–8 (CA).

[82] [1967] 2 AC 46 at 123–5.

[83] [1972] WAR 52 (FC).

[84] [1982] WAR 1 (FC).

[85] See *Palmer's Company Law* 25th ed (1992) [8.536].

[86] [1916] 1 AC 554 (PC).

[87] (1973) 40 DLR (3d) 371 (SC).

[88] See Palmer's *Company Law* 25th ed (1992) [8.536].

[89] (at first instance) [1964] 2 All ER 187 at 203.

be unsafe to say that the mere use in any circumstances of any knowledge or opportunity which came to the trustee or agent in the course of his trusteeship or agency made him liable to account . . . it is necessary to consider . . . whether the action which brought about the profit was either within or without the scope of the duties of the office or the employment.

**[4.37]**     There have been several statements of the scope of the profits rule as it applies to honest corporate officers. Perhaps still the most celebrated of these was that made by Lord Russell in *Regal (Hastings) Ltd v Gulliver.*[90]

The case concerned the directors of a company which owned a cinema. They decided to take leases of two other cinemas in the same town, with a view to selling all the cinemas as one concern. A subsidiary was formed to lease the other cinemas. However, the lessor of the other cinemas would not lease them to the subsidiary unless either the rent was guaranteed by the directors, or the subsidiary's shares were paid up to at least £5000. The directors were unwilling to guarantee the rent of a business about to be sold and the company had only £2000 to pay up the subsidiary's shares. This shortfall affected the only available way of getting the cinemas. In the event, a solution was arrived at. The shortfall was made up by directors and the company solicitor acting personally. They provided £3000 of their own money to pay for the extra paid-up shares.

Some features of the transaction later became significant and should be noted. One of the directors did not purchase the shares personally, but nominated outsiders and the solicitor, although a fiduciary, was not a corporate officer. The directors, the solicitor and others were accordingly issued 3000 £1 shares in the subsidiary at par. Shortly afterwards, all the shares in the company and the subsidiary were sold for a price that had been agreed before the shortfall became apparent. It put a nominal value on the subsidiary's shares of some £4, resulting in the directors and the solicitors making an apparent profit of about £3 on each of the shares in the subsidiary. It was the way that the price was paid. It might otherwise have been represented by the purchaser paying more for the shares in the holding company. In the hands of its new controllers, however, the holding company thereafter brought action to recover the nominal profit that the obliging directors and solicitor made on their short-lived shareholding in the subsidiary.

It was a remarkably unmeritorious claim. A large part of the price agreed was 'clawed back' on a technicality. The company as claimant alleged that the profit on sale of the subsidiary's shares was one which the holding company itself should have made. The profit, it was said, had been wrongfully diverted.

**[4.38]**     All members of the House of Lords who heard *Regal Hastings* found that the directors were in good faith. Together with others, the directors had facilitated a profitable transaction for the company which it would have been unable to enter otherwise. However the House was also unanimous in finding that the directors were liable to account to the company in the hands of its new controllers. The invalidating effect of the profits rule was found to include the profit the directors made on the subsidiary's shares. For this profit the

---

[90] (1942) [1967] 2 AC 134n at 144–5.

directors were obliged to account. What was contentious here was not the content of the profits rule; nor was it questioned that a private profit had in fact been made. Defences of the company's implied ratification and consent were abandoned. Scope was the remaining issue. What the directors denied was that the profits rule extended as far as this transaction in their private capacities. One of several formulations in the case of the scope of director's fiduciary liability was given by Lord Russell. His statement of the rule in *Regal* is the one most commonly cited. It was specifically followed, for example, by the Canadian Supreme Court in *Peso Silver Mines Ltd v Cropper.*[91] In *Regal*, at 147, Lord Russell said that the directors had acquired the shares 'by reason of and only by reason of the fact that they were directors and in the course of the execution of that office'.

The 'link', or nexus, between profit and duty was constituted by the holding of corporate office. This is expressed as a twofold requirement. The profit must be derived both *causally* ('by reason of' the directorship) and *temporally* ('in the course of' the directorship). Directors, as and when directors, are thereby disallowed from taking secret profits. It is notable that the effect on the corporation of what the directors did is irrelevant. Also, whatever the directors' state of mind was is irrelevant. Instead, the rule has a prophylactic, or cautionary, message. The making of secret profits being regarded, perhaps, as an inherently wrongful thing, the scope of the rule prohibiting it has an inexorable operation.

**[4.39]** Lord Macmillan's speech in *Regal Hastings*[92] expressed a slightly different view on the scope of a director's fiduciary duty to observe the profits rule. As he said (at 153), conduct is within the scope of the rule if–

> (i) what the directors did was so related to the affairs of the company that it can properly be said to have been done in the course of their management and in utilisation of their opportunities and special knowledge as directors, and (ii) what they did resulted in a profit for themselves.

This passage embodies the causal and temporal elements of Lord Russell's formulation and expands them to refer to *use* made of the opportunities and knowledge in question. For this reason it may be a formulation of greater value, as we will suggest below.

**[4.40]** The possibility that a corporate officer might resign in order to enjoy a secret profit and thus avoid the temporal element in both of the *Regal Hastings* 'scope' formulations has since emerged in 'corporate opportunity' cases. Profits in these cases might not then literally be made 'in the course of' a fiduciary office. So the officers' conduct arguably fell outside the ambit of the profits rule. One such case was *Industrial Development Consultants Ltd v Cooley.*[93] Cooley was an architect who had long worked for a regional gas board. He was later appointed the managing director of an architectural consultancy company—a move apparently designed to assist the company in getting public sector work. On behalf of the company, Cooley tried to get

---

[91] (1966) 58 DLR (2d) 1 at 6–7, curiam.

[92] (1942) [1967] 2 AC 46 at 134n.

[93] [1972] 1 WLR 443; also *Canadian Aero Services Ltd v O'Malley* (1973) 40 DLR (3d) 371 (SC); *Green and Clara Pty Ltd v Bestobell Industries Pty Ltd* [1982] WAR 1 (FC); *Island Export Finance Ltd v Umunna* [1986] BCLC 460.

consultancies with various gas boards. But in all cases he was met with opposition to the principle of a company, rather than an individual, acting as consultant. Later one of the boards approached Cooley personally. It was proposed that Cooley be retained as architect in his individual capacity. Cooley made no mention of this proposal to the company. Shortly after, he resigned from his office as managing-director on a plea of ill-health. Cooley then entered a consultancy contract with the gas board in form very similar to what he had formerly sought on the company's behalf. Roskill J found that Cooley was liable to account to the company for the profits he made on the gas board contract and this notwithstanding that the opportunity to profit did not come to Cooley as director. Also, the opportunity was unavailable to the company. Roskill J said (at 451) that:

> Information . . . came to [Cooley] while he was managing director and which was of concern to [the company] and was relevant for [the company] to know . . . information which it was his duty to pass on to [the company].

**[4.41]** *Cooley's case* has the salient feature that the former director found liable was appointed to his corporate office to obtain just the sort of opportunity which he took for himself. At 445 Roskill J described the resignation plea of ill-health as a 'dishonest pretext', thereby coming close to making Cooley account as a dishonest fiduciary. This may explain the indeterminacy of the chosen words 'concern' and 'relevance' to describe the scope of the rule.

In *Green and Clara Pty Ltd v Bestobell Industries Pty Ltd*,[94] Burt CJ in the Supreme Court of Western Australia was concerned with a similar question. It was another case of corporate officers resigning to take up opportunities. Was it a sufficient basis of liability, he asked, for officers merely to acquire knowledge of the profit-making opportunity through their corporate office? Or did some *use* of that opportunity have to be demonstrated as well? Concluding that there was evidence of both things in the case, he said that the answer did not much matter. But he added (at 5):

> The single legal proposition . . . that it is enough to show that the fiduciary obtained within the relationship the opportunity to make the profit or knowledge that the profit was there to be made.

This would suggest, contrary to the cases we have seen above, that evidence of the officer's knowledge of the opportunity without use of it is sufficient.

**[4.42]** Scope of the profit rule is illustrated in a slightly different way in *Pacifica Shipping Co Ltd v Anderson*.[95] The New Zealand High Court dealt with a 'corporate opportunity' type of private profit, which was argued to attract equitable intervention on two bases. The first was of present concern: to enforce fiduciary duties which surrounded the profit being made. The second basis was in the protection of the confidential information that the opportunity was said to represent, which we will not consider here. The claimant in *Pacifica Shipping* was a company which conducted a prosperous shipping service between two New Zealand ports. One of the company's employees was sent to Europe to find a ship suitable for a slightly different

---

[94] [1982] WAR 1 at 5–6 (FC).
[95] [1986] 2 NZLR 328, Davison J.

route. The board of the company believed that an expansion to this route would be successful, too. When the employee found an appropriate ship, he did not make his discovery known to the company. Instead, the employee and one of the company's directors purchased the ship through a company of their own. It was intended by them to commence a shipping service over the new route. Was the shipping company entitled to an injunction preventing the other company and/or the employee and the director from operating a route it had proposed for itself? The court allowed the company's claim made along 'corporate opportunity' lines. The company was seen (at 338) to have engineered what was a 'maturing business opportunity' in respect of the new route and this was developed, it was said, to a stage sufficient for it to be protected. Proper competition in respect of 'global opportunities' was not thought to be thereby restrained.[96]

**[4.43]** In *Pacifica Shipping*, knowledge of the profit-making opportunity came to the fiduciaries in the course of their company duties. Its nature was such as to be a small expansion of the company's existing business. Could these facts be generalised, so that relevance to a 'line of business' (actual or intended) is a necessary characteristic of all corporate opportunities worthy of protection? What about knowledge of opportunities within the 'line of business' which come to corporate officers otherwise than in their course of duty? Should they, too, be disclosed to the company and/or be made subject to the same rule? Should the scope of the profits rule extend that far? This might be implicit in the (unnecessary) discussion of these issues by Laskin J in *Canadian Aero Services Ltd v O'Malley*[97]—a *dishonest* fiduciary case, to which the rule stated at [4.35] applies. Laskin J spoke generally of the 'standards ... to which the conduct of a director or senior officer must conform'. Application of the standards should be conditioned, he thought, by enumerated 'factors'. These included the–

> position or office [the fiduciary officer] held, the nature of the corporate opportunity, its specificness and the director's or the managerial officer's relation to it, the amount of knowledge possessed, the circumstances in which it was obtained and whether it was special, or, indeed, private.

### 'Corporate opportunity' doctrine

**[4.44]** R P Austin has suggested that Australian law should adopt the 'corporate opportunity' doctrine which obtains in the United States, or a similar principle, to be 'a special supplement' to the conflict and profit rules.[98] 'Appropriation of corporate opportunities' is a matter of state and not federal law in the United States. There are accordingly many versions of the doctrine and substantial State variations.[99] The American Law Institute's *Principles of Corporate Governance* 'Proposed Final Draft' of 1992 is the form of an intended uniform law. Doctrine is there expressed as a rule: §5.05, the rule 'Taking of Corporate Opportunities by Directors or Senior Executives'. It applies to the area which the Australian Corporations Law describes in its Chapter 3 as 'Internal Administration'.

---

[96] Id, distinguishing *CBA Finance Holdings Ltd v Hawkins* (1984) 1 BCR 599 at 604–5.
[97] (1973) 40 DLR (3d) 371 at 391 (curiam).
[98] 'Fiduciary Accountability for Business Opportunities' in Finn *Relationships* 141 at 185.
[99] See 18B *Am Juris* (2d) (1976), §§1770–92 for a summary of these.

**[4.45]** 'Corporate opportunity' doctrine is an overall relaxation of strict trustee standards for certain corporate relationships. It aims to provide a business-like approach to the everyday exigencies and temptations of business.[100] Corporate officers are prohibited by the doctrine (when in the form of a rule) from exploiting corporate opportunities for their own benefit unless the same opportunities have first been offered to and rejected by the corporation.[101] The same doctrine as it exists now in many States of the Union is that a corporate opportunity *does not exist* if the corporation is definitely unable to take it.[102] This is a radical idea. It is at odds with the Anglo-Australian case law we have examined in preceding paragraphs. 'Corporate inability' to take an opportunity may result from the corporate constitution in some cases. An officer of the corporation is then free to exploit opportunities which are ultra vires the corporation.

*Case v Kelly* is a celebrated authority on this point.[103] About a century ago, the inhabitants of a particular locality were prevailed upon to donate land for the building of a railroad. Directors of the railroad company took conveyances of the donated land into their own names. Later the company claimed that the directors were constructive trustees of the land for it. To this, the directors raised the defence that the company had no power to own the land or take title to it. The defence was upheld. Despite the fraud, the company was said (at 29) to be 'not injured' in the circumstances. In other situations, 'corporate inability' may result from financial circumstances. This is a matter on which different state jurisdictions are divided.[104] Even a 'settled business policy' has been held in some States to amount to an exonerating 'inability'.[105]

**[4.46]** The existence of an 'inability or unwillingness' defence demonstrates that avoidance of harm to corporations is what the United States doctrine is directed to. A higher moral imperative does not seem to apply. Avoidance of harm to corporations is less explicitly the basis of the American Law Institute rule. The rationale ignores the prophylactic consideration that fiduciaries' duties in conflict with their personal interests may cause the proper judgement of fiduciaries to be swayed. No strictures are placed on a fiduciary's profit-making when occupying a position of trust. The United States' doctrine instead is guided by an objective view of the corporation's economic interests—expressed by the definition of 'opportunity'.

**[4.47]** Harm to the company is thought likely to occur in the following instances, enumerated in the definition section of the American Law Institute's rule. Section §5.05(b) provides–

> (1) any opportunity to engage in business activity of which a director or senior executive becomes aware, either:

---

[100] R Cooter and B Freedman 'The Fiduciary Relationship: Its Economic Character and Legal Consequences' (1991) 66 *NYUL Rev* 1045 at 1066.

[101] (Paraphrasing) §5.05 (a) *General Rule* of the 'Proposed Final Draft'.

[102] 18B *Am Juris* 2d (1976), §§1788–9.

[103] 133 US 21 (1889) (SC); see also *Urban J Alexander Co v Trinkle* 224 SW 2d 923 (1949) and 18B *Am Juris* 2d (1976), §1789.

[104] See authorities cited at 18B *Am Juris* 2d (1976), §1790.

[105] See *Irving Trust Co v Deutsch* 73 F 2d 121 (1934).

(A) in connection with the performance of functions as a director or senior executive, or under circumstances that should reasonably lead the director or senior executive to believe that the person offering the opportunity expects it to be offered to the corporation; or

(B) through the use of corporate information or property, if the resulting opportunity is one that the director or senior executive should reasonably be expected to believe would be of interest to the corporation; or

(2) any opportunity to engage in a business activity of which a senior executive becomes aware and knows is closely related to a business in which that corporation is engaged or is expected to engage.[106]

Section §5.05 requires senior executives (including executive directors) to offer opportunities that could be advantageous to the corporation before using them themselves. This corresponds to prohibition on the 'use' of an opportunity within Australian jurisdictions. Scope of the prohibition, our present concern, is then definitionally set forth in the sub-paragraphs commencing (A), (B) and (2).

**[4.48]** The definition in sub-paragraph (A) refers to knowledge of an opportunity which is acquired by an officer either in connection with his or her role in the corporation or as a conduit for the corporation, as any reasonable officer would believe. Mainly, it extends the scope of the rule to include an opportunity which is *functionally related* to an officer's duties. This occurs where the opportunity comes to an officer directly in the course of duty. Either the opportunity is apprehended in the course of duty, or a reasonable officer in the circumstances should have realised that the opportunity was meant for the company and not for him. For example,

A, a senior executive of the X Corporation, an oil exploration company, is charged with the responsibility for locating new drilling prospects. X Corporation's geologists give A the result of seismic surveys made by X Corporation in a particular area, and A thereupon personally acquires the most promising prospects. A is obliged to offer the prospects to X Corporation, and has therefore violated §5.05.[107]

Or again,

A is the chief executive officer of X Corporation, which is engaged in the steel manufacturing business. Although X Corporation has no present plans for diversifying its business, A is offered and accepts the opportunity, in connection with the performance of his functions as chief executive officer of X Corporation, to acquire all the stock of Y Corporation, which is engaged in the development of solar energy. If A takes the opportunity for himself, he will have taken a corporate opportunity.[108]

Determination of the scope of this functional type of opportunity raises similar issues to those considered in relation to the 'conflicts' rule, at [4.31]–[4.34] above.

**[4.49]** By the definition in sub-paragraph (B), an officer may become liable for taking a corporate opportunity which the reasonable officer would believe to be 'of interest' to the company. For example,

---

[106] American Law Institute's *Principles of Corporate Governance* 'Proposed Final Draft' (1992).

[107] See 'Proposed Final Draft', *Comment*, 383, Illustration 1.

[108] Ibid, see Illustration 2, at 388.

A, a senior executive of X Corporation, which is engaged in exploring for and producing oil and gas, learns through his position that X Corporation has made promising undisclosed mineral discoveries in a particular location. A acquires drilling rights on adjacent acreage which later proves to be highly productive oil property as a result of X Corporation's drilling operation. [A then possesses a corporate opportunity.][109]

The wording of this provision suggests a corporate 'interest or expectancy' test. A relevant opportunity for the purpose of this paragraph is one which 'fits' the business of the company, as a court might determine. Or the opportunity might be one which is consonant with an established and ascertainable corporate policy. In establishing this 'interest or expectancy', the company's 'line of business' is obviously relevant. The corporation's actual or expected line of business affects whether the corporate officer should be expected to reasonably believe that the opportunity would be of interest to the company.[110] To determine that an opportunity is or would be 'of interest' to a corporation is a forward-looking thing. It involves plans and hopes, as well as concrete designs. The prospective sense of this may be conveyed by those authorities which refer to corporate interests as 'actual' or 'expectant'.[111] One indicium of a corporation having an 'expectant' line of business is the likely profitability for the corporation if the business were pursued. In turn this has required assessment of argument based on market forces and asset prices and a variety of criteria that would be regarded as non-justiciable in Australia.[112] The profit-motive is not so explicitly seen as the spring of rational and reasonable behaviour outside the United States. It may also be as imprecise as it sounds. As Brudney and Clark observe in their scholarly analysis of corporate opportunities, 'the case law offers few useful criteria for determining whether an interest exists'.[113]

**[4.50]**  The third and final type of opportunity for which an officer may be liable is defined in subs (2). The American Law Institute's rule may be triggered by any opportunity to engage in 'business activity' which officers know is 'closely related' to an actual or expected interest of the corporation. It is more clearly than the last a 'line of business' test. 'Relation' to a business that the company engages in or is 'expected' to engage in also seems like a more objective basis for inquiry. The opportunity is equated with what is 'expected' for the corporation and not which might merely 'interest' it. For example,

A is a senior executive of X Corporation, which is engaged in the business of oil and gas production. A is aware of X Corporation's interest in the commercial development of solar cells. A organizes Y Corporation, for the purpose of commercially exploiting solar cells as an energy source. A has a duty to offer the

---

[109] Ibid, see Illustration 5, at 389.

[110] D J Brown 'Note' (1986) 11 *Journal of Corporate Law* 255, 267.

[111] See *Guth v Loft* 5 A 2d 503 (1939), 512–3 and *Equity Corporation v Milton* 221 A 2d 494 (1966), 497 (SC (Delaware)).

[112] See argument in *Equity Corporation v Milton* ibid at 497–8.

[113] V Brudney and R C Clark 'A New Look at Corporate Opportunities' (1981) 94 *Harv LR* 998 at 1014.

investment in Y Corporation to X Corporation and A's failure to do so violates §5.05.[114]

A 'duty of fair dealing' is more easily invoked to phrase the officer's obligation to account for an opportunity defined in this way. This is the main formulation of the United States' doctrine. A corporate officer must not appropriate something which belongs or should 'in fairness' belong to the corporation.[115]

[4.51] In a way the 'corporate opportunities' doctrine is already reflected in the Australian Corporations Law. An officer of a corporation is prohibited by s 232(5) of the Law from making 'improper use of information' to gain an advantage, or to cause detriment to the corporation. Section 232(6) contains a similar prohibition on an officer's improper use of his or her position. The generality of these sub-sections may make them a little unhelpful when 'corporate opportunity' problems arise. It is hard to see that such provisions would entail any predictable outcome in difficult cases. What the United States doctrine offers, additional to the prohibitions, is a flexible standard for what 'improper' means. Our brief examination of 'corporate opportunities' has of necessity omitted some of the doctrine's more contentious applications. These include, first, whether it should apply indifferently between large public companies and 'close' companies.[116] Or should the corporate opportunity doctrine apply differently to the roles of executive director, 'outside' director and senior employee? The American Law Institute has proposals on how different classes of corporate fiduciaries should be covered by the rule.[117]

[4.52] Anglo-Australian authority on the 'conflicts' and 'profits' rules, as noted, takes a 'prophylactic' approach to the private profit-making activities of corporate officers.[118] It categorically prohibits fiduciaries from making personal gains from dealings with the corporation's property or its opportunities. The prohibition will apply even if a transaction would deprive the corporation of nothing and even if the transaction might produce benefits for both fiduciary and the corporation. Various definitions examined of the Anglo-Australian scope of the conflicts and the profits rules, particularly the profits rule, are quite unlike the American Law Institute's formulation. Our prophylactic approach is sweeping. It proscribes *all* modes of a corporate officer making a profit within its scope, not just the ones likely to injure the corporation.

[4.53] 'Scope' in Anglo-Australian fiduciary law , as we saw at [4.1], implies a nexus between a corporate fiduciary's profit and the relevant corporation. This was something which could be expressed in two ways—two alternative

---

[114] Ibid, Illustrations 11 and 12, at 392.

[115] See S Beck 'The Quickening of Fiduciary Obligation: Canadian Aero Services v O'Malley' (1975) 53 *Can Bar Rev* 771 at 778–9.

[116] Argued by V Brudney and R C Clark in 'A New Look at Corporate Opportunities' (1981) 94 *Harv LR* 998 at 1022–42; R P Austin in 'Fiduciary Accountability for Business Opportunities' in Finn *Relationships* 141 at 166–71 takes a contrary view.

[117] Discussed in Brown 'Note' *Journal of Corporate Law* 255 at 267–8; Begert 'Comment' (1989) 56 *Univ of Chicago Law Rev* 827 at 842–5; Brudney and Clark, ibid at 1042–5; R P Austin, ibid 171–5.

[118] See below at [5.71]–[5.73]; concluded also by V Brudney and R C Clark in 'A New Look at Corporate Opportunities' (1981) 94 *Harv LR* 998 at 1002.

routes to the same conclusion. For the purposes of the 'conflicts' rule, scope consists in whether the fiduciaries' duties, properly understood, extended to the making of the personal profits. If they did, then, commerciality aside, a prohibited conflict of interest and duty arose. For the purposes of the 'profits' rule, the nexus between corporation and prohibited officer's profit is even more exiguous. Mere use of corporate assets, information and opportunities, accidental or intended, in order to help the corporation or to harm it, brings the fiduciary within the path of the prohibitory swathe. The Anglo-Australian approach clearly prohibits appropriation of all the corporate opportunities in the American Law Institute definition and many more things as well. Consider, for example, how the *Regal (Hastings) Ltd v Gulliver*[119] case would have been decided under the American Law Institute's version of the corporate opportunity rule. Purchase by Regal directors and others of the outstanding shares in the subsidiary, after the company had purchased all it could, would not have satisfied any of the §5.05 definitions. Negating (A), the opportunity was clearly known to the corporation and availed of by it to the extent that it had the resources to do so. Negating (B) and (2) together, there was no opportunity for the company to purchase the balance of the shares in its subsidiary. Commercial indicators pointed strongly to a corporate benefit by its fiduciary officers acting as they did.

[4.54] In contrast with the absolute nature of Anglo-Australian law on fiduciaries and corporate opportunities, *selective* prohibition is what the United States doctrine tries to achieve. Criteria of 'opportunity' in order to establish a 'corporate opportunity' are connected with the operations, needs, and expectations of companies as business entities. There is no distracting prohibition on profit-making within a fiduciary relationship. The modern conception in the United States of the corporate officer as fiduciary is relatively emancipated. This is despite the disapproving rhetoric of an earlier and less practical age.[120] Cooter and Freedman argue that there is an 'optimal point' in relation to corporate opportunities where a line should be drawn between protection of a corporation's business interests and its fiduciaries' freedom to exploit opportunities on their own account.[121] It is generally recognised by these authors that corporate officers are fiduciaries in commerce who are legitimately motivated by the prospect of profits and financial rewards. Outside the defined criteria of 'corporate opportunity' in the United States, as Brudney and Clark observe, corporate officers are free to use what opportunities they please.[122] 'Indirect' opportunities, ones that arise incidentally from the corporate officer's fiduciary role and not in the course of duty, can usually be exploited without any question of breach of duty.[123] No inner conflict is perceived in a law which permits some sorts of profit-making within the scope of a fiduciary relationship and which prohibits other

---

[119] (1942) [1967] 2 AC 134n.

[120] Dicta of Cardozo J in *Meinhard v Salmon* 164 NE 545, 548; 249 NY 458, 464 (1928) stands apart from modern trends.

[121] R Cooter and B Freedman 'The Fiduciary Relationship: Its Economic Character and Legal Consequences' (1991) 66 *NYULR* 1045 at 1064–6 and Fig 5.

[122] V Brudney and R C Clark 'A New Look at Corporate Opportunities' (1981) *Harv LR* 998 at 1002.

[123] See S M Turnbull 'The Doctrine of Corporate Opportunity: An Economic Analysis' (1988) 13 *Can-US LJ* 185.

sorts. For in the accepted rationale of the applicable fiduciary rule in the United States, a corporate officer should not be *unjustly enriched* at the corporation's expense.[124] Moralising about fiduciary office does not take liability in the United States beyond the point where no injustice to the corporation can be shown.

[4.55] Australia could not adopt the United States doctrine without major change. The Anglo-Australian conception of fiduciary liability in its present form is quite inconsistent. Consider the obvious rationale in any number of Australian fiduciaries decisions. *Green and Clara Pty Ltd v Bestobell Industries*[125] is an example. A corporate officer there had profited from an alleged corporate opportunity in the form of a government tender. Before it was let, the tender was publicly advertised in all states. Ranking of applications for the tender placed the errant corporate officer first and his corporation third. So if the corporate officer had not bid, the tender would have gone to somebody else. Accordingly a submission for the corporate officer was made that no opportunity of the corporation had been appropriated at all. But this was not accepted. The Supreme Court of Western Australia found that the scope of the officer's fiduciary duty was attracted nevertheless. Kennedy J said (at 19–20):

> [the officer] clearly placed himself in a position where his interest and his duty conflicted and he is accountable accordingly ... He put himself in a position in which he might have had personal reasons for not giving [the company] the best advice which it was his duty to give, and, when asked, to give it ... It is not necessary, in a case, such as the present, for [the company] to show that it has suffered damage ... It is also immaterial that [the company] could not have made a profit, as in this case, it be accepted ... that the contract must have gone to the second lowest tenderer ... The reason for this is simply that the rule is, as it has sometimes been expressed, a prophylactic rule and not a restitutionary one.

Profit-making in a fiduciary relationship is castigated in the usual categorical terms, with an undifferentiated invocation of both the conflicts and profits rules. They are couched as inherent wrongs, to be warded against with prophylactic measures. Inappropriateness of restitution of any enrichment subtracted is not to the point in Australia.

[4.56] Consider by contrast how the corporate opportunity doctrine might apply to a similar situation in the United States. We are concerned with the facts of *Green and Clara* and a fiduciary's stealing of customers. In *United Seal and Rubber Co v Bunting*[126] a company sold gaskets, seals, and rubber products in the southeastern United States. Directors of the company resigned in order to start a competing business in the same region. Eventually one-time customers of the company to the value of 50 per cent of the company's former income were attracted to the competing business. The company applied for equitable relief, alleging that the directors had misappropriated the 'corporate opportunity' of its long-standing customer relationships. The nature of the 'interest or expectancy' was explored and found to be that the company's

---

[124] *Hill v Hill* 420 A 2d 1078 (1980); 18B Am Juris (1976) at §1772; R P Austin 'Fiduciary Accountability for Business Opportunities' in Finn *Relationships* 141 at 172–5.

[125] [1982] WAR 1 (FC).

[126] 285 SE 2d 721 (1982).

customers would continue to deal with it. Applying *Southeast Consultants Inc v McCrary Engineering Corp*,[127] this was said (at 723) not to be within the legal sense of 'corporate opportunity'. No existing contract rights had been infringed. Relief was denied as nothing had been subtracted from the company.

---

[127] 273 SE 2d 112 (1980); see also *Sofate of America Inc v Brown* 318 SE 2d 771 (1984) and P K Chew 'Competing Interests in the Corporate Opportunity Doctrine' (1989) 67 *North Carolina Law Rev* 435 at 481–2.

# Chapter 5

# Breach of Fiduciary Duty

## The nature of fiduciary duties

**[5.1]** Fiduciary duties stipulate certain things which fiduciaries cannot be influenced by and *cannot* do. Actions are outlawed by fiduciary duties. Nothing is mandated or prescribed.[1] What fiduciaries should consider and should do in their fiduciary offices is not part of equity's task to regulate. The positive duties of persons who are fiduciaries are governed by other legal regimes and the common law. Tortious negligence is a prime source. We will see below that this *proscriptive* orthodoxy of Anglo-Australian fiduciary law is often a source of confusion. The restricted competence it gives equity does not prevail in the United States and is increasingly under threat in the lower courts in Canada.

Impermissible doings by and influences upon fiduciaries were summed up by Lord Herschell in 1896. In his accustomed peremptory manner, he described—

> an inflexible rule of a Court of Equity that a person in a fiduciary position ... is not, unless otherwise expressly provided, entitled to make a profit; he is not allowed to put himself in a position where his duty and interest conflict.[2]

Almost ninety years later in the Canadian case of *Standard Investments Ltd v Canadian Imperial Bank of Commerce*, this uncompromising canon was repeated:[3]

> the duty imposed on a fiduciary is, in effect, twofold: first, where he has undertaken to act for or on behalf of another, he must refrain from letting any personal interest sway him from the proper performance of his undertaking; second, he must not misuse the position of trust his undertaking gives him to further his own interests. He must not profit from his position of trust.

**[5.2]** Fiduciary duties do not impose positive obligations. This is important enough to repeat. No recommended course of conduct for fiduciaries appears under any of the fiduciary rules. Rather, the rules are cast in terms of the things that a fiduciary must abstain from. Fiduciary obligations in this negative

---

[1] See P Finn 'Fiduciary Principle' Youdan 1 at 25; cf *Biala Pty Ltd v Mallina Holdings Ltd* (1993) 11 ACSR 785 at 832, Ipp J (SC (WA)).

[2] *Bray v Ford* [1896] AC 44 at 57.

[3] (1983) 5 DLR (4th) 452 at 481, Griffiths J (Ont CA).

way bear considerable similarity to some of the more settled obligations of trustees.[4] The same type of equitable liability, it has been said, arises equally for some trustees as for each recognised fiduciary type.[5] The regime for company directors, distributors, joint venturers, receivers and the like is to be understood in this way.

> First, the position held by each of them exists, not for his own, but for another's benefit—in the case of a director, for example, for the company; in the case of the trustee in bankruptcy, for the creditors. Secondly, the duties imposed on, and the powers exercised by, each have a source *other than* in an agreement between him and the person(s) for whose benefit he is required to act—with the receiver, for example, they stem from the order of the court; with the executor, from the will, legislation and the general law. Thirdly, as a general rule, each alone is ultimately responsible for determining how those duties are to be discharged, how those powers are to be exercised.

Duties of fiduciaries merge with the duties of the trustees possessing 'mere' powers or discretions. These are trustees who are not under any specific duty, or 'trust', to act in a particular way. Trustees of this type were referred to by members of the House of Lords in *Re Gulbenkian's Settlements (No 2)*.[6] The 'mere' powers they possess are 'powers collateral', or what Warner J described as a 'category 1', 'category 2' and 'category 4' powers in *Mettoy Pension Trustees Ltd v Evans*.[7] A fiduciary, one could say, resembles a trustee with a 'mere' power—a power of appointment is an example.

[5.3] Similarity between the class of fiduciaries and some trustees can be taken a little further. Still speaking of trustees' 'mere' powers, not being powers coupled with enforceable trusts or directions, equity has traditionally denied itself jurisdiction to intervene in all but a restricted group of cases. Only exceptionally would it intervene to regulate how trustees exercised such powers. General supervision of the process was denied. For unless fraud can be shown, equity will still not compel trustees to explain the way in which their powers have been exercised.[8] Trustees' honest deliberations are of nature exempt from judicial scrutiny. Equity courts will not unmask them. Trustees' incompetence lurking beneath the surface of trusts might be forever concealed.

Sometimes trustees are incautious or confident enough to give reasons for the way they exercise their powers. A court administering trusts will then examine these reasons for quite limited purposes. Namely, seeing whether the reasons disclose that the exercise of power has been formally defective, never considered, or made after the wrong things were taken into account. Claims that the trustees had acted negligently, carelessly or without business sense are alien to this structure. The system was explained by Megarry V-C in relation to a trustees' power of appointment under a deed in *Re Hay's Settlement Trusts*.[9] The only duties he saw incumbent upon the trustees were to:

---

[4] A Scott 'The Trustee's Duty of Loyalty' (1936) 49 *Harv L Rev* 521; A Scott and W Fratcher *The Law of Trusts* 4th edn (1989), 495.

[5] Finn *Fiduciaries* 9.

[6] [1970] AC 508.

[7] [1991] 2 All ER 513, 545; for a traditional analysis, see *Farwell on Powers* 3rd edn, ed C Farwell (1916), 9.

[8] *Re Londonderry's Settlement* [1965] Ch 918 (CA).

[9] [1982] 1 WLR 202, 209.

1. obey the terms of the power;
2. occasionally consider whether to exercise the power;
3. consider the range of possible appointees; and
4. consider the appropriateness of possible appointments.

**[5.4]**  In Part I of Finn's *Fiduciary Obligations* a similar conception of things has been applied to fiduciaries. Regarding their office, fiduciaries are said to be under duties not to delegate discretions, not to act under dictation, not to 'fetter' discretions and to consider whether discretions must be exercised. Regarding beneficiaries, fiduciaries are said to be prevented from acting for their own or some third party's benefit. Fiduciaries must treat beneficiaries equally where they have similar rights; fairly where they have dissimilar rights; and they must not act capriciously or totally unreasonably.[10] This, as said, is to assimilate fiduciary obligations to those regulating trustees' powers. What business sense trustees possess in exercising the powers and how able they are to avoid mistakes are irrelevant. Choice of suitable trustees is a matter for settlors to have considered. Equity courts will not police this. So again, fiduciary obligations are assimilated to the regime where courts will not exercise the powers themselves, nor ensure that the power-holders are competent for the tasks given. The judicial role is only to make the power-holder honest and fair.

**[5.5]**  The nineteenth century case of *Re Beloved Wilkes's Charity*[11] illustrates the point well. Trustees for a charity were involved. The charity was for the occasional selection of a 'poor lad' for education as a clergyman. Preference was to be given to candidates from specified parishes. One year the trustees of the charity nominated a lad who was not from a specified parish. No reason for this departure was given. The plaintiffs, concerned members of a specified parish, sought to overturn the decision and substitute another candidate. He was a lad, they said, who was better qualified. Reversing the court below, Lord Truro LC firmly denied that this claim could be brought. The courts, he said at 333, were not to be able to review a fiduciary's decision simply for the fact that it might have been mistaken. For–

> it is to the discretion of trustees that the execution of the trust is confided, that discretion being exercised with an entire absence of indirect motive, with honesty of intention, and with a fair consideration of the subject. The duty of supervision on the part of this Court will thus be confined to the question of honesty, integrity and fairness with which the deliberation has been conducted, and will not be extended to the accuracy of the conclusion arrived at, except in particular cases.

**[5.6]**  The position has not changed in modern times. The New South Wales Court of Appeal in *Hartigan Nominees Pty Ltd v Ryde*[12] used the same passage in *Beloved Wilkes* to describe the content of fiduciary duties. Interpreting a trustee's exercise of a power of advancement pursuant to a deed of settlement, the following position was taken by the United Kingdom Court of Appeal in *Re Hastings-Bass*.[13]

---

[10]  See also Maclean 46–51.
[11]  (1851) 3 Mac & G 440; 42 ER 330.
[12]  (1992) 29 NSWLR 405, 412–3, Kirby P, 441–2, Sheller JA.
[13]  [1975] Ch 25, 41 (CA) curiam.

The court should not interfere with [the trustee's] action notwithstanding that it does not have the full effect which he intended, unless (1) what he has achieved is unauthorized by the power conferred on him, or (2) it is clear that he would not have acted as he did (a) had he not taken into account considerations which he should not have taken into account, or (b) had he not failed to take into account considerations which he ought to have taken into account.

In *Karger v Paul*,[14] McGarvie J in the Supreme Court of Victoria took the same position in relation to the administration of a discretionary power created by will. He referred to an 'established general principle' that:

unless trustees choose to give reasons for the exercise of their discretion, their exercise of the discretion can not be examined or reviewed by a court so long as they act in good faith and without an ulterior purpose.

### 'Honesty, integrity and fairness'

**[5.7]** Equitable ability to review decisions of trustees or fiduciaries is confined in the *Beloved Wilkes* formula to maintaining the power-holder's 'honesty, integrity and fairness'. These are matters which relate to the deliberations and motives of power-holders making decisions, not the standard of competence or good sense they attain. The power-holders were trustees in that case and we have said that fiduciary duties developed by analogy.

For some types of fiduciaries, the deliberations of decision-making are of central importance. The *Beloved Wilkes* formula is then quite stringent. Decisions of these fiduciaries can be overturned even in the absence of evidence that they profited thereby, served a conflicting interest or did any other corrupt deed. Company directors, for example, are liable to the invalidating effect of fiduciary rules on account of the *purposes* for which they exercised their powers. Fairness of directors' decisions as between competing interests and the adequacy of consideration given to them are justiciable matters. This facilitates a sophisticated evaluation of the way that this important type of fiduciary fulfils the duties of office. We will examine it in detail at [5.89]–[5.112] below. Improper delegation, for example, bias and fettering of discretion are all disallowed, just as they would be for a trustee possessing a 'trust power'.[15] Or in the words of Dixon J, in *Mills v Mills*:

Directors of a company are fiduciary agents, and a power conferred upon them cannot be exercised in order to obtain some private advantage or for any purpose foreign to the power. It is only one aspect of the general doctrine expressed by Lord Northington in *Aleyn v Belchier*.[16] 'No point is better established than that, a person having a power, must execute it bona fide for the end designed, otherwise it is corrupt and void'.[17]

**[5.8]** Fiduciary duties are concerned with the process of decision-making rather than its outcome. The wisdom of decisions made is not generally inquired after. Many of the daily offices of fiduciaries are obviously outside the regime. A careless or negligent fiduciary is not by virtue of negligence or

---

[14] [1984] VR 161, 165.

[15] See L Sealy 'The Director as Trustee' [1967] *CLJ* 83, 95.

[16] (1758) 1 Eden 132, 138; 28 ER 634, 637.

[17] (1938) 60 CLR 150, 185. See also *Howard Smith Ltd v Ampol Petroleum Ltd* [1974] AC 821, 825 (PC), *Whitehouse v Carlton Hotel Pty Ltd* (1987) 162 CLR 285 and *Advance Bank Australia Ltd v FAI Insurances Ltd* (1987) 9 NSWLR 464, discussed at [5.100], below.

carelessness in breach of a fiduciary duty. Instead, breaches of fiduciary duty involve the absence of one of 'honesty, integrity or fairness' on the fiduciary's part. Otherwise, and no matter how reprehensible the fiduciary's conduct has been, the fiduciary regime is broadly inapplicable. One aspect of this is illustrated by the decision of the New South Wales Court of Appeal in *Jones v Canavan*.[18] It concerned a stockbroker who was found to be in a fiduciary relationship with his client for the reasons noted at [3.62]–[3.68]. We are concerned now with the minimum conditions for fiduciary liability. The business of this broker, it will be remembered, involved the 'marriages' of the orders of his buying and selling clients, made off the exchange floor. Without the client's knowledge, purchases and sales of their shares were often completed right in the broker's own office. The report does not disclose whether the broker charged the ordinary commission. One client asserted that with each such 'marriage', a conflict occurred between the broker's own interest and the broker's fiduciary duty. This was alleged in defence to the broker's action against the client for the price of shares purchased and commission earned. The result was said to follow that the broker could not enforce obligations arising out of a 'married' transaction. The New South Wales Court of Appeal found that there was no 'lack of integrity' in the broker's manner of secretly acting for both parties and did not uphold the defence. Jacobs JA held that no breach of the 'honesty, integrity and fairness' requirements had occurred. At 245, with Asprey and Manning JJA concurring, he said:

> I am of the opinion that the custom or usage of marrying transactions in the same broker's office is not unreasonable where the marrying or crossing of transactions does not result in any realistic way in a conflict of duty and interest. The limited function of the stock and share broker makes him an intermediary rather than a negotiating agent. He has the privilege of operating upon a very special kind of market where the commodity is in more or less large supply and the trends of price are governed by a conjunction of factors depending on the actual buying and selling orders held by the brokers. Although no doubt each broker on each order has an obligation to obtain the best price he can, the lowest for the buyer and the highest for the seller, he accomplishes this by nothing which could be described as a negotiation in the ordinary sense of an agent negotiating a sale or purchase.

## Merits are irrelevant

**[5.9]** A fiduciary's decision to act or refrain from acting is usually not considered on its merits. Consider company directors. They are given various discretions by the articles of their companies. These will normally include a power to manage the business of the company, involving the hiring of employees, buying and selling of goods and acquiring of premises. The directors are also given powers which affect the company's ownership, such as the issue and forfeiture of shares. Concerning powers of either type, Professor Ford has said:[19]

> Courts do not hear appeals on the merits of a matter from the decision of a board [of directors] but they will control misuse of discretion.

There is no 'reasonable fiduciary' standard by which to assesses objectively the merits of the decision. Fiduciary principles restrict equitable intervention

---

18  [1972] 2 NSWLR 236 (CA).

19  *Principles of Company Law* 4th ed (1986), [1503] (deleted from later editions); see [5.89]–[5.126] for consideration of company directors' fiduciary obligations in more detail.

to situations of 'disloyalty', where one or more of the 'honesty, integrity and fairness' elements in the context of trust or confidence is found wanting. The criteria of a fiduciary wrong will not exist in many flawed exercises of directors' power to manage a company's business or organise its capital structure. A breach of one of the fiduciary duties described below is needed to establish fiduciary liability. In the United States, as we have noted, the position is otherwise. Stated in *Prosser and Keeton on the Law of Torts*,[20] tortious liability in the United States may arise out of misrepresentation and non-disclosure between parties 'standing in some confidential or fiduciary relation to one another . . . or where trust and confidence is reposed'. Positive duties of disclosure may be imposed. In Canada there is no express extension of tortious liability to fiduciaries. However, the great enlargement of the equitable jurisdiction over fiduciaries in recent times has been accompanied by what J Gautreau (a Judge of the Ontario District Court) has called the new 'functional merging of the fiduciary duty and the duty of care'.[21]

**[5.10]** The United States and Canada are different. There is as yet in Australia no positive rule that a fiduciary must disclose personal interests to a beneficiary, or disclose anything else. Adequate disclosure is a *defence* to each of the conflict and profits rules, as we will see. Any positive disclosure rule would have to have a content. It could not be a mere prohibition. This would be contrary to the scheme of fiduciary duties sketched above.

Equally, there is in Australia no equitable rule that a fiduciary must take care to avoid negligent harm to his beneficiary.[22] Negligence is a matter for the law of torts. The fact that a tortious duty of care has been breached by a person who also happens to be a fiduciary does not constitute a fiduciary wrong. More is needed. Equitable compensation (resembling damages) for loss to a beneficiary must be preceded by a fiduciary wrong. This was the case in the celebrated *Nocton v Ashburton*.[23] A solicitor was found liable in equity for giving bad advice which caused loss to his beneficiary. This appears similar to tortious liability for giving negligent advice. But the critical, additional, fact of the case was that the bad advice was also an 'honesty, integrity and fairness' type of wrongdoing. The advice given had the collateral effect of improving the value of the solicitor's security, in circumstances where a shortfall in recovery was expected. Both common law duties in contract and common law duties of care arise for the fiduciary as well as fiduciary obligations. This can be concurrently with as well as in addition to fiduciary obligations, as has lately been decided by the High Court in *Hawkins v Clayton*.[24] So contract and tort law are not yet outflanked by equity. This is despite what we shall see to be is the remedial attractiveness of fiduciary liability and the occasional

---

[20] W Keeton (ed) 5th edn (1984) 106.

[21] 'Demystifying the Fiduciary Mystique' (1989) 68 *Can Bar Rev* 1, 15; see *Burns v Kelly Peters & Associates Ltd* (1987) 41 DLR (4th) 577, 598, Lambert JA (CA (BC)) and *Tracey v Atkins* (1977) 83 DLR (3d) 47 (SC (BC)).

[22] *Wickstead v Browne* (1992) 30 NSWLR 1, 17–19, Handley and Cripps JJA; *Permanent Building Society (in liq) v Wheeler* (1994) 14 ACSR 109, 160–7, Ipp J, Malcolm CJ and Seaman J agreeing (FC).

[23] [1914] AC 932.

[24] (1988) 164 CLR 539 and see *Waimond Pty Ltd v Byrne* (1988) 18 NSWLR 642 (CA).

mispleaded anomaly like *BLB Corporation of Australia Establishment v Jacobsen.*[25]

**[5.11]**   A caveat should be entered here. We are in a contentious area and remarks on it have a tendency to be not entirely true. In one respect at least, Australian fiduciary law appears to be changing away from the traditional position. The decision in *Whitehouse v Carlton Hotel Ltd*[26], discussed at [5.104] below, may signal a new judicial activism. The limits of what are 'proper purposes' in the exercise of the powers of corporate fiduciaries have been re-defined. A formula which allows for greater intervention has been declared, it will be suggested—in a case concerned with the need to control company directors who use their powers to prevent takeovers.

### Is 'loyalty' the rationale of fiduciary duties?

**[5.12]**   'Conflict of interest' and 'secret profit' prohibitions have been described[27] as 'minimum standards of acceptable conduct for those found to be bound by fiduciary ties'. In fact they are compendious references to a larger body of rules and doctrine, most of which evolved in the nineteenth century. The rules overlap and are indeterminate in number. Paul Finn in *Fiduciary Obligations* deals with some nineteen separate rules. Len Sealy refers to an 'indeterminate' number of traditional equitable claims against a fiduciary 'in cases decided before the Judicature Acts'.[28] Many of the rules indeed pre-date the Judicature Acts and sound strange to our ears.

Both 'conflicts' and 'profits' rules are said to have one thing in common. They each involve the virtue of *loyalty*. A fiduciary must be loyal to the party to whom fiduciary duties are owed. Equity will protect and enforce also the measure of loyalty that beneficiaries are entitled to expect from their fiduciaries. Commentators have developed this idea into a doctrinal category. They maintain that there exists a fiduciary 'duty of loyalty' that a fiduciary owes a beneficiary. 'Loyalty' comprehends the conflicts and profits rules and the several lesser fiduciary rules that have evolved as well. Perhaps the loyalty 'duty' originated in the academic writings of the United States.[29] It seems to have no pedigree in the decided cases.

**[5.13]**   To say that a fiduciary is under a 'duty of loyalty' is not greatly enlightening. 'Loyalty' is defined by the *Concise Oxford English Dictionary*,[30] by reference to 'loyal', which is itself defined as

---

[25] (1974) 48 ALJR 372 (HC), where, on confused pleadings, both negligence and breach of fiduciary duty were disallowed together—suggesting some unity between them; see further at [5.132] and P Finn 'Fiduciary Principle' Youdan 1, 26–31.

[26] (1987) 162 CLR 285.

[27] Finn *Fiduciaries* 4.

[28] 'Some Principles of Fiduciary Obligation, [1963] *CLJ* 119, 132.

[29] See A Scott 'The Trustee's Duty of Loyalty' (1936) 49 *Harv LR* 521, 'The Fiduciary Principle' (1949) 37 *Calif LR* 539, 540f, A Scott and W Fratcher *The Law of Trusts* 4th edn (1989), §495; also L Sealy 'Fiduciary Relationships' [1962] *CLJ* 69, L Sealy 'Some Principles of Fiduciary Obligation' [1963] *CLJ* 119, A McClean 'The Theoretical Basis of the Trustee's Duty of Loyalty' (1969) 7 *Alta L Rev* 218; P Finn 'Fiduciary Principle' Youdan 1, 27–8; 15.2 *Laws of Australia* (1993) 'Fiduciaries' [35-7].

[30] Revised 3rd ed (1973), 648.

'[Fr. O Fr. . . . L. *legalis* Legal] 1. True to obligations of *duty* . . . ' [emphasis added].

Hence the expression 'duty of loyalty' denotes little more than a duty to obey duty—which is a pleonasm. Such question-begging is unlikely to solve many hard cases. The 'loyalty' of a fiduciary to be expected by his beneficiary prohibits in a very general way the type of conflicts and profits that the fiduciary should avoid. But 'loyalty' leaves the reason why equity intervenes in these relationships unilluminated. Nor is it apparent what equity sees at stake in situations where the fiduciary's conduct falls below the minimum standard required by the fiduciary rules. Nevertheless, the loyalty idea is still in vogue. It is sometimes developed in the following sort of way.

> Rules of equity are strict. Courts are astute to find breaches of fiduciary duty. Fiduciary relationships should embody 'loyalty'. For if fiduciaries are loyal, they can be trusted and the rules are intended to protect trust.

The Canadian commentator Ernest Weinrib emphasises that trust is important for the functioning of modern society. Fiduciary principles described as 'loyalty' regulate, primarily, discretions to which others are liable, and, secondarily, the structures of business.[31] Perhaps this is so. But why in particular does *equity* and not the common law become involved? That is to say, does 'loyalty' supply fiduciary law with any specific explanation, or clothe it indiscriminately with the legal imperatives of a modern society? Looking to what happens when a fiduciary relationship is breached, does '*dis*loyalty' best express the result? All this is questionable. Another rationale will now be suggested.

### Is 'deterrence of misappropriation' a better rationale?

**[5.14]**   Misappropriation by the fiduciary, or the threat of it, is the thing which usually occurs when a fiduciary relationship is breached. Deterrence of the misuse of beneficiaries' assets or of their value has been suggested as the real concern of equity in this area. Cooter and Freedman say that this is the kind of wrongdoing that fiduciary rules sanction.[32] Misappropriation describes the kind of wrong that the conflicts and profits rules are directed to. Certainly this deterrence is a plausible enough explanation of the profits rule. A wrongfully obtained profit is almost always a misappropriated profit. But can the misappropriation rationale explain the conflicts rule? Fiduciaries might breach the conflicts rule, we will see below, even though they have taken nothing and have never departed from the course of duty. Misappropriation may be *presumed* in a situation of prohibited conflict. Proof that the fiduciary could be tempted to misappropriate by having inconsistent motives can then equal misappropriation itself. Such a presumption is said not to be inappropriate in the sort of relationship which fiduciaries usually have with their beneficiaries. Usually, there is an information imbalance favouring the fiduciary.[33] The beneficiary is very often reliant and not vigilant to protect his or her own

---

[31] See 'Fiduciary Obligation' (1975) 25 UTLJ 1; also D Waters 'Banks, Fiduciary Obligations and Unconscionable Transactions' (1986) 65 *Can Bar Rev* 37, 55–6: this reasoning is particularly common in Canada.

[32] R Cooter and B Freeman 'Fiduciary Relationship: Its Economic Character' (1991) 66 *NYULR* 1045, 1048–56.

[33] See A Duggan, M Bryan and F Hanks *Contractual Non-Disclosure* (1994), 137–47.

interests. Misappropriation is often hard to prove. Fiduciaries, for their part, can be devious, furtive and shrewd. So, when fiduciaries are proven to have conflicting motives, they are assumed to have done the worst. Or at least, fiduciaries are assumed to be pursuing the worst, if they have not already done it. A breach of the conflicts rule assumes the fact or pursuit of misappropriation from appearances. This justifies the burden of proof shifting to the fiduciary, when it does, to establish the absence of wrongdoing: see [5.113]–[5.126] below.

### 'Unjust enrichment' theory

[5.15] The 'deterrence of misappropriation' rationale is conformable to the 'unjust enrichment' theory of fiduciary liability.[34] Expressed in the words of P Birks–

> a main purpose of [fiduciary] duty is to prevent enrichment. Those who manage the affairs of others must not seek opportunities to line their own pockets. In short, the particular harm to beneficiaries which equity chiefly fears is the harm which consists in the diversion of wealth into the fiduciary's pocket. It is above all to prevent that actual and non-hypothetical evil that equity adopts its anxious prophylactic approach.[35]

The principle of unjust enrichment at its most general may rightly identify equity's major concern here. Namely, the injustice of value passing from a beneficiary to a fiduciary through or by virtue of the fiduciary relationship. The 'loyalty' rationale which speaks of upholding the relationship as an 'institution of trust' is far less focussed. But the wording in the Birks passage is significant. Omissions in his accounts of the law are usually significant. He refers to 'enrichment', rather than the usual 'unjust enrichment'. This may be because a fiduciary's gain will very often not be 'unjust', in the sense of at the beneficiary's expense, especially where the conflicts rule is employed. Hence a fiduciary claim will often not satisfy the condition that all restitutionary claims must satisfy, stated earlier in the work (at 16–22). The 'actual and non-hypothetical evil', mentioned towards the end of the passage, can (grammatically) only relate back to the 'opportunities ... which equity chiefly fears'. But how can an 'opportunity' for doing evil be an evil in itself? Many men possess opportunities for doing evil and still lead blameless lives. Surely evil consists rather in *exploitation* of the opportunity. But if this is so, a large part of fiduciary law is not explained. For equity sanctions the existence of opportunities as well as their exploitation.

[5.16] Modern restitutionary theory based in unjust enrichment requires the enrichment of a fiduciary to be matched by a corresponding detriment suffered by the beneficiary. A 'plus and minus' element appears in the equation. It is not enough that the fiduciary has simply been enriched by his or her breach of duty. In addition, for an 'unjust enrichment' to have occurred, the fiduciary's enrichment must be equalled by the beneficiary's consequent deprivation. For instance, Goff and Jones in their *Law of Restitution* say (at

---

[34] American Law Institute *Restatement of Restitution* (1937), §§160, 190–201; see also Gibbs CJ in *Daly v Sydney Stock Exchange Ltd* (1986) 160 CLR 371, 378–9, describing how unjust enrichment might base the constructive trust as remedy for breach of fiduciary duty.

[35] Birks 339.

p 23), 'The principle of unjust enrichment requires that the defendant be unjustly enriched at the plaintiff's expense'.

There are problems in fiduciary law with this requirement. Correspondence of enrichment and deprivation is not necessitated by any consideration which appears to the writer. Persons are often found to be in breach of fiduciary duty even though they have taken nothing—either from the beneficiary or anyone else. Peter Birks acknowledges that often there is no coincidence between a fiduciary's gain and the loss suffered by the beneficiary. Instead, he contends at 313–14 that a claim to restitution of what the defendant has gained at the plaintiff's expense could be made in a different way. It employs what he calls 'another' sense of enrichment. This widens the 'at the expense of the plaintiff' requirement beyond the mere subtraction of value. The device is a supposed 'commission of a wrong' sense of 'at the expense of'. The *wrong* is the thing said to be at the expense of the plaintiff. This sense can be satisfied without any value passing and, of course, no value does pass in many fiduciaries cases. But what is this 'commission of a wrong' sense? How can one be enriched at someone's expense by taking nothing from them and not leaving them worse off? The 'commission of a wrong' sense of 'at the expense of' has all the hallmarks of a sophistry, an illegitimate attempt to extend the restitutionary canon to include the prophylactic purpose of equity. Equity is not amenable to explanation only in 'benefit-based' restitutionary terms.

[5.17]     Gareth Jones attempts to justify restitution's place in the law of fiduciary obligations by asserting that the 'principle of unjust enrichment' has an important, but subordinate, role to play.[36] This is more sustainable. While 'unjust enrichment' cannot explain the essence of what is going on, it is said to qualify equitable intervention in useful ways. For instance, the unjust enrichment principle can moderate the 'dogmatism' of the rule that fiduciaries in breach of duty must disgorge the whole of their profit. Disgorgement should not be insisted on where there is no 'injustice' in the fiduciary's enrichment, particularly in circumstances where the beneficiary is enriched as well. This is to reverse the majority decision in *Boardman v Phipps*[37] and approve that in *Manufacturers Trust Co v Becker*,[38] as we will see below. Unjust enrichment thus can serve as an antidote to mechanical application of equity's rules.

Other restitutionary theorists come close to denying that the unjust enrichment idea has anything to do with fiduciary obligations. George Palmer, for example, early in his four-volume treatise, states that equity is often not restitutionary.[39] Equity intervenes to reverse profits made by fiduciaries which are clearly not made at a beneficiary's expense, he says, citing the 'corporate opportunity' case of *Pratt v Shell Petroleum Corporation*.[40] The species of unjust enrichment employed there did not involve subtraction from the beneficiary. Rather, any injustice proceeded from the violation of duty. This is similar to the sense that Peter Birks has adopted, but part of a conception which denies that fiduciary law is an instance of restitutionary principle.

---

[36] 'Unjust Enrichment and the Fiduciary's Duty of Loyalty' (1968) *LQR* 472, 473.
[37] [1967] 2 AC 46.
[38] 338 US 304 (1949) (SC).
[39] *Law of Restitution* Vol. 1 (1978), §2.11.
[40] 100 F 2d 833 (1938).

## Hospital Products as an illustration

**[5.18]** The reasoning of Mason J in *Hospital Products Ltd v United States Surgical Corporation*[41] shows the fiduciary rules at work. Like the other members of the Court, Mason J addressed the question of whether HPI, a surgical goods distributor, had acted in breach of the fiduciary rules. At 103 he said:

> McLelland J found—a finding with which I agree—that, as a fiduciary having responsibility for protecting and promoting the market for USSC's products in Australia, HPI was under a duty not to make a profit or to take a benefit by virtue of its position as a fiduciary without the informed consent of USSC and that within the ambit of its fiduciary responsibility it should not act in a way in which there was a possibility of conflict between its own interests and those of USSC.

Mason J then dwelt on the conflicts rule. The 'fiduciary's duty', he said, 'may be more accurately expressed' by calling it—

> an obligation not to promote his personal interest by making or pursuing a gain in circumstances in which there is a conflict or real or substantial possibility of conflict between his personal interests and those he is bound to protect.

**[5.19]** On the broad facts of *Hospital Products*, HPI had profited in a minor way by being a disloyal distributor. By related acts, on a larger scale, HPI had set up a business to pursue similar profits in the future. More complicated realities will be ignored. Principle is unaffected by the attempts of the *Hospital Products* defendants along the way to evade their liabilities by HPI's 'reverse takeover' of Hospital Products Ltd and the interposition of Surgeon's Choice Incorporated.[42] Of importance was the fact that the business of making and selling surgical suturing devices in Australia was set up and ready to go. HPI's structure was evolved in a clandestine way, not obviously constituting a breach of duty in itself. No profits had been made from HPI by the time of the action. If understood literally, the profits rule could not reach a business which had made no profits. It could not touch what the business might yield in the future.

In relation to this structure McLelland J at first instance had made a significant declaration. It was that HPI, in addition to the secret profits it had derived, also breached its fiduciary obligation to USSC–

> (i) by secretly developing a capacity to manufacture copies of USSC's products or components thereof with a view to appropriating for itself at the expense of USSC the whole or a substantial part of the Australian market for USSC products and (ii) by deferring fulfilment of orders for USSC clinical products in anticipation of filling orders with HPI repackaged or competing products and by filling orders for USSC clinical products with such competing products, again with a view to appropriating for itself at the expense of USSC the whole or a substantial part of the Australian market for USSC products.[43]

**[5.20]** McLelland's declaration touched the 'capacity to manufacture copies', which was the critical matter in the case. For the same wrong the New South Wales Court of Appeal ordered the remedy of a constructive trust. This was

---

[41] (1984) 156 CLR 41, 102–7.

[42] See [1983] 2 NSWLR 157, 166 (CA).

[43] [1982] 2 NSWLR 766, 819, McLelland J, extracted by Mason J in his judgement, ibid, 106.

over all the assets and goodwill of HPI in favour of USSC.[44] The same was unanimously disallowed by the High Court.[45] Mason J, in dissent, agreed with McLelland J's characterisation of this wrong as a breach of fiduciary duty. He said of the above declaration that:

> The two breaches described by his Honour need to be understood as involving actions taken by HPI during the term of the distributorship with a view to *appropriating* USSC's market for itself during that term and thereafter. Once the breaches are understood in this light, it is incontestable, it seems to me, that his Honour was correct in finding that the relevant acts constituted breaches of fiduciary duty ... *Neither breach constituted the making of a gain, the intended gain being the appropriation of USSC's local product goodwill. Each breach described in the declaration is a description of the means by which HPI pursued the gain.*[46] [emphasis added]

Appropriation in the future is what the conflicts rule may be a pointer to. This is the *pursuit* of profits, rather than the making of them. By contrast, the profits rule assumes that misappropriation has already occurred and that the plaintiff can actually point to it. The profits rule requires that some specific asset can be shown to constitute the secret profit or advantage which the fiduciary has obtained. A plaintiff alleging breach of the conflicts rule, by contrast, need not be in a position to prove the fiduciary's wrongdoing. Proof of opportunity is sufficient.

#### THE CONFLICTS RULE AND THE PROFITS RULE

**[5.21]**     Conflict or the possibility of it, between the duties of fiduciaries to their beneficiaries and the private interests of fiduciaries, has been said to be the original concern of equity.[47] The conflicts rule was applied in the earliest cases. *Keech v Sandford*[48] is one, involving the trustee of a lease who attempted to renew it for his beneficiary. This the landlord refused, because the beneficiary was still an infant—so the trustee seized for himself the opportunity that this presented and had the lease renewed in his own name. Equity intervened on behalf of the beneficiary and directed that the trustee hold the new lease on trust for the infant. In justifying this finding, Lord Chancellor King seemed to be concerned above all that a finding in favour of the fiduciary might condone a dereliction of duty. At 223 he expressed this matter with remarkable cynicism:

> I must consider this as a trust for the infant; for I very well see, if a trustee, on the refusal to renew, might have a lease to himself, few trust estates would be renewed to the cestui que use.

Chancellor King disregarded the facts that there had been no wrongful appropriation and that the trustee was not shown to be in bad faith or dishonest. It was irrelevant that the opportunity was not even available to the infant. A similar strict regard for attention to fiduciary duty has been cited as the

---

[44] [1983] 2 NSWLR 157, 264.

[45] (1984) 156 CLR 41, 72–5, Gibbs CJ, 101–2, Mason J, 119, Wilson J, 122–3, Deane J, 146–8, Dawson J.

[46] (1984) 156 CLR 41, 106.

[47] A McClean 'The Theoretical Basis of the Trustees' Duty of Loyalty' (1969) 7 *Alta L Rev* 218, 219.

[48] (1726) Sel Cas T King 61; 25 ER 223.

deciding factor in the large number of cases which have followed *Keech v Sandford* expressly.[49]

**[5.22]** The profits rule came to prominence after the rise of the conflicts rule. It dates from the middle of the nineteenth century. Fiduciaries were disciplined for taking private *benefits* or *advantages* as a consequence of their fiduciary offices. Courts awarded relief against fiduciaries after making little and sometimes no reference to conflicts occurring in the deliberative part of fiduciary duties.[50] The new emphasis on profiteering, as opposed to arriving at a decision to take a profit, may have been connected with the introduction of corporate personality. Many of the profits cases concerned companies. In *Regal (Hastings) Ltd v Gulliver* the Law Lords unanimously found company directors liable for breach of fiduciary duty. All bar one of the speeches were based solely in infringement of the profits rule.[51] In modern times, the profits rule has become the pre-eminent justification of fiduciary liability. Without pausing to ask the reason why at this stage, a survey of recent judgements against fiduciaries in Australia confirms the ascendancy of the profit rule.[52] Now some common characteristics of both the rules will be mentioned.

### Are the rules of nature absolute?

**[5.23]** In a striking way it is sometimes said that the conflicts and profits rules are of nature *absolute*. This is what is suggested by the famous rule statements, some of which were referred to by Deane J in *Chan v Zacharia*.[53] Conflicts and profits rules are said to be 'inflexible': they apply 'universally', 'inexorably' and 'however honest and well intentioned' the fiduciary might be. This conception of things may be a residue of 'fiduciary rhetoric', discussed at [2.5]–[2.6]. The statements are unhelpful and not completely true. For the rules do have exceptions, as Deane J noted. For example, a fiduciary's disclosure may avoid breach of the conflicts rule, if it is sufficient and followed by the consent of the person to whom the duties are owed. Or a beneficiary's knowing ratification may avoid breach of the profits rule. These things could not be if fiduciary rhetoric were to be believed.

### Irrelevance of fraud on the fiduciary's part

**[5.24]** Both conflicts and profits rules can still be breached even where there is no fraud, dishonesty, or bad faith on the part of the fiduciaries.[54] Usually

---

[49] Including over the years *Robinson v Pett* (1734) 3 P Wms 249; 24 ER 1049; *Ex parte Lacey* (1802) 6 Ves Jun 625; 31 ER 1228; *Ex parte James* (1803) 8 Ves Jun 337; 32 ER 385; *Wright v Morgan* [1926] AC 788 (PC); *Williams v Barton* [1927] 2 Ch 9.

[50] See *Parker v McKenna* (1874) LR 10 Ch App 96, 118, Lord Cairns LC (referring to both rules), 124–5, Sir W James LJ; *Aberdeen Town Council v Aberdeen University* (1877) 2 App Cas 544 (HL), 549, Lord Cairns LC, 553, Lord Hatherley, 556, Lord O'Hagan; *Re Lewis* (1910) 103 LT 495, Warrington J.

[51] [1967] 2 AC 134n; Lord Sankey alone founded liability in the conflicts rule, at 137–40. See also *Brown v IRC* [1965] AC 244; *Boardman v Phipps* [1967] 2 AC 46, 101, Lord Cohen, 107, Lord Hodson, 117–18, Lord Guest.

[52] Consider, eg, *United States Surgical Corporation v Hospital Products International Pty Ltd* [1983] 2 NSWLR 157 (CA); *Chan v Zacharia* (1984) 154 CLR 178; *United Dominions Corporation Ltd v Brian Pty Ltd* (1985) 157 CLR 1; *Fraser Edmiston Pty Ltd v AGT (Qld) Pty Ltd* (1986) 2 Qd R 1; *Avtex Airservices Pty Ltd v Bartsch* (1992) 107 ALR 539.

[53] (1984) 154 CLR 178, 204.

[54] See the authorities collected in MGL at [522].

this is not the case. Fiduciaries found guilty of breaching a fiduciary duty are typically corrupt, or have acted with at least questionable honesty. But the possibility exists that fiduciaries may be found to be guilty in a transaction where they have worked hard and honestly on behalf of their beneficiaries. What matters is only whether a prohibited conflict of fiduciaries' interests with their duties has occurred, or secret profits have been made. This is enough to constitute the wrong which equity will then sanction with its accustomed vigour. The classic example is *Boardman v Phipps*.[55] Each law lord in the majority in that case found the defendant fiduciaries liable after disregarding evidence of the fiduciaries' good faith. A man of integrity can be a defaulting fiduciary without ceasing to be honest.

## Irrelevance of resulting loss or enrichment

**[5.25]**   For neither the conflicts nor the profits rule does it matter that the beneficiaries were not harmed by what the fiduciary did, or that they were actually better off as a consequence of the action impugned. Secret profits must be disgorged even if they were part of transactions which were irrelevant to any interests of the beneficiaries, or even promoted those interests. For example, in *Moore v Regents of the University of California*,[56] the majority of the Supreme Court of California found that a medical practitioner was liable to an action for breach of fiduciary duty for making secret profits from the sale of a beneficiary's bodily samples. The samples had been taken in the course of life-saving surgery. This finding was independent of a claim that the doctor had violated the claimant's property rights in the things sold. Another profits example is the case of *Estate Realties Ltd v Wignall*.[57] A firm of fiduciary sharebrokers acquired from their client certain publicly listed shares. The brokers paid what was the market price for those shares on the day of purchase. There was no evidence of the client receiving any compromising advice to sell. By use of a scheme which involved a 'high degree of acumen and skill', the brokers were eventually able to sell the shares for a large profit. It was held (at 621) that this was a profit which the brokers were under no duty to their clients to obtain. Nevertheless, the court ordered that the brokers account to the client for the whole of their gain. In *Moore v Regents* and *Estate Realties* the beneficiaries were no worse off as a result of the fiduciary's acts. In *Regal (Hastings) Ltd v Gulliver*[58] and *Boardman v Phipps*[59] the beneficiaries were in fact better off. The cases are examined in detail below at [5.56]–[5.60]. Not only was the fiduciaries' good faith disregarded, but there was also the fact that the beneficiaries were enriched by the act impugned.

The conflicts rule operates in a comparable way. As soon as a prohibited conflict is apparent a fiduciary is accountable, or can be restrained. It is not necessary for the claimant to go further and prove the occurrence of a

---

[55] [1967] 2 AC 46, 104, Lord Cohen, 105, Lord Hodson, 115, Lord Guest.

[56] 793 P 2d 479 (1990) property claim unsuccessful and appeal to the SC denied: 499 US 936 (1991); also *Boardman v Phipps* [1967] 2 AC 46 and *Regal (Hastings) Ltd v Gulliver* (1942) [1967] 2 AC 134n, discussed at [5.56].

[57] [1992] 2 NZLR 615, Tipping J (HC) and see [1991] 3 NZLR 482.

[58] (1942) [1967] 2 AC 134n.

[59] [1967] 2 AC 46, 104, Lord Cohen, 105, Lord Hodson, 115, Lord Guest.

consequential profit or loss.[60] In *Williams v Barton*[61] the trustee of an estate was a sharebroker—held to be in a position of impermissible conflict of duty and interest by accepting payment of brokerage by the estate. Evidence had been received that someone was required to do the broking job and that the broker/trustee charged the going rate. Notwithstanding, Russell J saw the case as:

> clearly one in which [the fiduciary's] duty as trustee and his interest in an increased remuneration are in direct conflict. As a trustee it was his duty to give the estate the benefit of his unfettered advice in choosing stockbrokers to act for the estate; as the recipient of half the fees to be earned . . . on work introduced by him his obvious interest is to choose or recommend . . . [his own firm] to do the job.

## Overlap

**[5.26]** Outcomes are usually the same when either the conflicts or the profits rule is applied. There is only a small class of cases to which only one rule applies and the other is excluded. Accordingly, in appellate cases, where several judgments are delivered, it is common to find the same fiduciaries held both to entertain impermissible conflicts and to derive secret profits.[62] Perhaps this is inevitable.[63] The rules may imply each other, as will be suggested below. R Austin confirms this and says 'the rules cover the same ground and a conclusion expressed in terms of one of them can usually be restated in terms of the other'.[64]

Consider the important wrong of 'self dealing'. A fiduciary acting 'on both sides' of a fiduciary transaction is almost inevitably in breach thereby of both the profits and the conflicts rules. The self-dealer's profit is earned through the fiduciary putting personal interest in conflict with his or her duty. 'Self-dealing' straddles the rules. It could find a home under either one.[65]

**[5.27]** Still, only the conflicts rule may apply in situations where services provided by advisors are affected by their having ulterior motives, while, at the same time, the advisors get no identifiable gain thereby. There is here a pure *risk* of misappropriation. Nothing is taken.

Or, only the profits rule may apply where, unusually, there is no duty or interest disregarded in the making of a secret profit. *Regal (Hastings) Ltd v Gulliver*[66] is said by McClean to be an example.[67] *Regal*, as we saw, concerned

---

[60] *Gemstone Corporation of Australia Ltd v Grasso* (1994) 13 ACSR 695, 703, Prior J, 711–12, Olsson J (SC (SA), FC).

[61] [1927] 2 Ch 9, 12.

[62] See eg *Parker v McKenna* (1874) LR 10 Ch App 96 (CA), 118, Lord Cairns LC (conflicts rule), 124–5, Sir W James, (profits rule); *Jacobus Marler Estates Ltd v Marler* (1913) 114 LT 640n (HL), 640, Lord Parker, *Hospital Products Ltd v United States Surgical Corporation* (1984) 156 CLR 41, 105–6, Mason J, *Avtex Airservices Pty Ltd v Bartsch* (1992) 107 ALR 539, 561 (Fed Ct (FC)), where the rules were applied indiscriminately.

[63] See A McClean in 'The Theoretical Basis of the Trustee's Duty of Loyalty' (1969) 7 *Alta L Rev* 218, 224–9.

[64] 'Fiduciary Accountability for Business Opportunities' in Finn *Relationships* 141, 146.

[65] L Sealy 'Some Principles of Fiduciary Obligation' [1963] CLJ 119, 129–130 and A Scott 'The Fiduciary Principle' (1949) 37 *Calif L R* 539, 544–5, where the organising scheme of 'Consent of Principal' and 'No Consent of Principal' is chosen and these problems are avoided.

[66] (1942) [1967] 2 AC 134n, esp. 156–7, Lord Wright.

[67] 'The Theoretical Basis of The Trustee's Duty of Loyalty' (1969) 7 *Alta L R* 218, 224.

capitalisation of a company's subsidiary by company directors acquiring shares in it personally. This was done so that the whole undertaking could be disposed of. Profit was made when shares in the subsidiary were sold. The directors were not found to owe any duty to the company to arrange for it to make the share acquisition in its name. Indeed, in the circumstances, it would have been a breach of a directors' duty of care to have done so. The company had insufficient funds for the purpose. Liability rested on the profit-making alone.

**[5.28]**  Making a profit implies the existence of a preceding conflict in the decision to take it. Profits and conflicts, in a sense, hunt in pairs, as the following statement by the Full Court of the Federal Court in *Cummings v Claremont Petroleum NL*[68] seems to imply:

> One of the prime duties of a fiduciary is to avoid putting himself in a position of conflict of duty and interest, or at any rate to avoid advancing his personal interest by pursuing a gain in circumstances in which there is a conflict between his duty and his interest. ... In the present case ... a gain [was] pursued ... involving such a conflict.

Concurrent conflicts of interest in what are otherwise profits cases is not at all uncommon. The conflicts rule and the profits rule are very often given as alternative justifications of the same fiduciary liability, which may on occasions be a source of confusion.

**[5.29]**  Consider the following possibilities. First, again, the venerable *Keech v Sandford*.[69] This case could have been decided the same way under the profits in place of the conflicts rule. Disregard for a moment the trustee's deliberations. The same trustee had acquired a valuable asset by virtue of his fiduciary office—the lease of the market profits. He could as easily have been required to account to the trust for this as a profit. Here there was no confusion. The conflicts rule liability has just been transposed into the terms of its cousin, the profits rule.

The second possibility concerns the decision of the House of Lords in *Boardman v Phipps*.[70] Failure to recognise that the outcome in that case under the two rules may not have been the same has been a source of subsequent confusion. A trust solicitor, together with a beneficiary under the trust, took advantage of an opportunity that came their way. They made handsome private profits through the use of information acquired while acting on the trusts's behalf. In the ratio of the case, the majority of the House of Lords held that the trust solicitor and the person acting with him were accountable to the trust for the profit they made. But the reasoning in most of the majority judgments did not keep the conflicts and the profits rules justifications separate. Only Lord Guest decided the case only on the basis of the profits rule, expressly following *Regal (Hastings) Ltd v Gulliver*.[71] Lord Cohen also followed *Regal* and, at 103–4, added the conflicts rule as a further (and unnecessary) basis of his decision. Lord Hodson indiscriminately used conflicts and profits dicta and concluded his judgment (at 112) with a remarkably undifferentiated

---

[68] (1992) 9 ACSR 583, 597.
[69] (1726) Sel Cas t King 61; 25 ER 223.
[70] [1967] 2 AC 46.
[71] (1942) [1967] 2 AC 134n.

restatement of the 'conflict or potential conflict' strictures. The solicitor had made an indisputable profit whilst acting for the trust. Lower courts preferred to base liability exclusively on this fact. Wilberforce J, at first instance,[72] and the Court of Appeal[73] unanimously applied the profits rule, relying on *Regal (Hastings) Ltd v Gulliver*.[74] Denning MR, in the Court of Appeal, at 1020 made a bare allusion to the conflicts rule in connection with subversion of the solicitor's duty to properly advise his client. Evidence in the case of an invalidating conflict of personal interest and the solicitor's duty was much more equivocal. So unlikely was it considered to be, Viscount Dilhorne observed at 92, that the conflicts wrong was not even alleged in the pleadings. However the celebrated dissenting judgment of Lord Upjohn in *Boardman's* case exonerated the trustees and denied the applicability of the conflicts rule in very forceful terms. At 124 he said that 'a real sensible possibility of conflict' did not exist on the facts. For this reason alone, it was implied, the trustees were not liable—which makes no answer to the case as pleaded and supplies no reason why the reasonings of the courts below were incorrect. Nevertheless, the majority view in *Boardman* is often disapproved because it is seen to imply that a sensible possibility of conflict *did* arise on the facts of the case.[75] It should be remembered that no member of the majority took a final view on the application of the conflicts rule to its facts. The profits rule and *Regal (Hastings) Ltd v Gulliver*[76] were relied on instead: by Lord Guest exclusively, Lord Cohen mostly and Lord Hodson in large part. Disapproval of the *Boardman* outcome in terms of the conflicts rule fails to recognise the imperfect rule overlap in that case. It is the sort of problem that arises from failure to keep the rules separate.

### Which rule is more primary?

[5.30] Paramountcy has been and usually is still accorded to the conflicts rule.[77] It has a better case law pedigree. Perhaps equity has always favoured rules, like the conflicts rule, which achieve their purposes indirectly. Direct proscriptions, like the profits rule, tend to be disfavoured. Equity prefers subtlety. Compare the evil that the conflicts rule is directed to with the evil averted by the equitable rule against 'remoteness of vesting'. The most persuasive statement of the purpose of the conflicts rule is possibly the deterrence of actual or threatened misappropriation of value. Other rationales contend. It is less disputed that the rationale of the rule against remoteness of vesting is connected with the evils of inalienability and the perpetual accumulation of wealth.[78] Land should not be rendered sterile. The *points* of each of the conflicts and the remoteness of vesting rules, so established, are

---

[72] *Phipps v Boardman* [1964] 2 All ER 187, 202.

[73] *Phipps v Boardman* [1965] Ch 992.

[74] (1942) [1967] 2 AC 134n.

[75] See remarks on *Boardman's* case of Deane J in *Chan v Zacharia* (1984) 154 CLR 178, 204 and G Jones 'Unjust Enrichment and the Fiduciary's Duty of Loyalty' (1968) 84 *LQR* 472, 486; Ford & Lee [2205]; Jacobs [1736].

[76] (1942) [1967] 2 AC 134n

[77] Eg, in *Consul Development Pty Ltd v D P C Estates Pty Ltd* (1975) 132 CLR 373, 393, Gibbs J; *Williams v Barton* [1927] 2 Ch 9, 12, Russell J; *Re Dover Coalfield Extension* [1907] 2 Ch 76, 83, Warrington J; P Millett 'Bribes and Secret Commissions' [1993] RLR 7, 10.

[78] J H C Morris and W B Leach *Rule Against Perpetuities* 2nd ed (1962) 13–18; R H Maudsley *Modern Law of Perpetuities* (1979), 221–4.

then entirely divorced from the way they work. In the case of the vesting rule, there is a strict and remorseless application of the 'perpetuity period', established at general law by 'class-closing' rules and 'lives-in-being'. Problem cases in such a calculus become complicated. These are resolved entirely apart from how their outcomes bear on the policy of the rule itself. Perpetuities reasoning becomes a self-serving and self-justifying system. Conflicts reasoning is almost the same. It may reflect the jurisprudence of an earlier age. Now it seems to be at variance with an equity based in a policy-responsive, unconscionability standard.

**[5.31]**     On the issue of primacy, Lord Upjohn said in *Boardman v Phipps*[79] that:

> The relevant rule for the decision of this case is the fundamental rule of equity that a person in a fiduciary position must not make a profit out of his trust which is *part of the wider rule that a trustee must not place himself in a position where his duty and his interest may conflict.* [emphasis added]

Lord Wilberforce in *New Zealand Netherlands Society 'Oranje' Incorporated v Kuys* was agnostic on the question of paramountcy.[80] The matter was later addressed by a member of the Australian High Court. This was in *Chan v Zacharia*,[81] where Justice Deane found at 186 that a former partner in a medical practice owed a fiduciary duty to another former partner. This prevented him from taking a personal benefit from the realisation of partnership property when the partnership was being dissolved. Such a benefit was found to be taken when a lease of the former consulting rooms of the practice was renewed by one partner in his own name. The finding was a straightforward application of the profits rule.[82] No conflict of interest and duty was set up in argument, nor needed to be. Deane J did mention the conflicts rule, however, and took the trouble to incorporate it into what he called[83] the 'general principle of equity which requires a person in a fiduciary relationship to account for personal benefit or gain'.

At 198 he said that this was a 'fundamental rule' which 'embodied two themes': the conflicts rule and the profits rule, respectively. 'Notwithstanding authoritative statements to the effect that the "use of fiduciary position" is but an illustration or part of a wider "conflict of interest and duty doctrine" ', he continued–

> the two themes, whist overlapping, are distinct. Neither theme fully comprehends the other and a formulation of the principle by reference to one only of them will be incomplete.

Justice Deane then restated the rules separately, stating that they are alternative means of attracting the general principle whereby equity will intervene. His approach is contrary to the methodology used in this book. Deane J treats a *remedial* obligation to account as the 'principle'. Remedy is put before the rules, by breach of which this principle is surely engendered. Our approach

---

[79] [1967] 2 AC 46, 123.
[80] [1973] 2 All ER 1222, 1225 (PC).
[81] (1984) 154 CLR 178.
[82] See below, at [5.65].
[83] (1984) 154 CLR 178, 198.

puts breach before remedy. The same unities are developed in Chapter 6.

It is significant that Deane J in his *Chan v Zacharia* discussion did not mention the supposed 'duty of loyalty' at all. Instead, at 198, he referred to both fiduciary duties in terms of account and the reversal of gains. Such a 'benefit-based' rationalisation accords well with the above 'misappropriation of value' conception of fiduciary duties. But it says nothing about the rules inter se.

Perhaps, in sum, the paramountcy question is a little needless. There seems to be no useful answer to it. Instead, practical insight may be more likely to come from a question like this. What is the appropriate factual situation for either the conflicts or the profits rule to be argued in? Does each rule have a 'territory', over which it is supreme?

## Particular facts which attract each rule

### The profits rule

[5.32] Profits need to be sanctioned in the majority of situations where fiduciaries are in breach of duty. Some profits, or advantages to fiduciaries (or to the vehicles that they use) are usually identifiable in any fiduciaries litigation where corporate shareholding is not in issue. Secret profits are usually the reason why the parties go to court. The profits rule is a norm which applies directly to the facts. Using *Keech v Sandford*[84] as an example, it is easier to prove that the errant trustee renewed the trust lease into his own name, than to prove that at the time of renewing the lease the trustee failed to consider his duty to renew it for the beneficiary. There is less to establish. No failure to follow duty needs to be shown before the profits rule has been breached. This is to avoid a major difficulty in the cases concerned with corporate officers. Their duties are often contentious. Is any (and, if any, what) private profit-making consistent with a director's duties?[85]

[5.33] The profits rule may also sometimes have a remedial advantage. Assume that the beneficiary is a corporation and the fiduciary is one of its directors. Or the fiduciary might be one of the corporation's promoters. Whichever, the fiduciary causes the corporation to enter a contract which favours the fiduciary's personal interest—perhaps by the corporation agreeing to purchase an asset from the fiduciary at an above-market and unfavourable price. There may be in this both a private profit that the fiduciary derives through self-dealing, and a conflict of interest in the exercise of fiduciary duty. Administration of the corporation and causing it to enter the impugned contract is what the fiduciary duty relates to. A wrongdoing such as this is traditionally seen to involve a fiduciary's breach of the conflicts rule, which equity would sanction by setting the transaction aside in an award of the remedy of rescission.[86] If the beneficiary desires to affirm the transaction, or has lost the ability to rescind, specific remedies of constructive trust and accounting are

---

[84] (1726) Sel Cas t King 61; 25 ER 223.

[85] See R Austin 'Fiduciary Accountability for Business Opportunities' in P Finn (ed) *Equity and Commercial Relationships* (1987), 141, 147 and discussion at [5.71].

[86] *Newbigging v Adam* (1886) 26 Ch D 582 (CA); *Erlanger v New Sombrero Phosphate Co* (1878) 3 App Cas 1218; *Curwen v Yan Yean Land Company* (1891) 17 VLR 745 (FC); *Robinson v Abbott* (1894) 20 VLR 346 (FC); *Guinness plc v Saunders* [1990] 2 AC 663.

available. An impermissible step is usually involved. To award the remedy, the court must establish what the profit to reverse was. This, the magnitude of the 'above market' component of a price, can only be measured by setting a proper price. If 'equity mends no man's bargain', no account of profits is available: *Tracy v Mandalay Pty Ltd*.[87] For an application of the conflicts rule, this may be the law still. In Meagher Gummow Lehane's *Equity* at [534] it is noted that this 1952 finding of the High Court–

> is somewhat difficult to reconcile with such earlier cases as *Bentley v Craven*[88] . . . and *McKenzie v McDonald*[89] . . . but clearly it must be taken to represent the present state of the authorities.

Rescission, as we will see at [6.136], can only be invoked so long as *restitutio in integrum* is possible. So if the corporation wished to retain what it purchased from the fiduciary, or had on-sold that thing to a third party, or was for some other reason unable to avoid the purchase, the remedy was unavailable. No other equitable relief might be available unless the corporation was able to prove loss by the fiduciary's breach of duty.[90]

**[5.34]**   Where, instead of the conflicts rule, the profits rule is invoked, a specific remedy is routinely available to strip the errant fiduciary of his gain. This is the constructive trust. Either this remedy is awarded over the profit, or an accounting may be ordered. Remedies for breach of the profits rule attach to the fiduciary's gain independently of any preceding contract, or loss encountered on the transaction. They are expressions of the 'general obligation', which the authorities 'clearly establish', requiring 'agents not to profit from their position.'[91] *Guinness plc v Saunders*[92] was a recent House of Lords decision which is illustrative of the problems that contracts can make for either rule. The ratio of the case was stated by Lord Templeman at 692. He held that the profits rule applied to make a company director account as constructive trustee for a £5.2m 'consultancy fee' received from the company. This was pursuant to a contract between the director and his company. Consequences of it being too late to rescind the contract for the conflict of interest it entailed were neatly sidestepped by Templeman. He found that the contract was void ab initio for want of authority. It did not need to be rescinded as it was of no effect. Lord Goff gave the only other speech and agreed, but mentioned (at 698) that 'Guinness cannot short-circuit an unrescinded contract simply by asserting a constructive trust'.

Which is to say that there are problems with contractual dispositions and consequent relief for breach of either rule. We will deal with this below, in connection with what Brennan J had to say in *Daly v Sydney Stock Exchange*

---

[87] (1953) 88 CLR 215, 241, Dixon CJ, Williams and Taylor JJ.

[88] (1853) 18 Beav 75; 52 ER 29.

[89] [1927] VLR 512.

[90] See *McKenzie v McDonald* [1927] VLR 512 and generally *Tracy v Mandalay Pty Ltd* (1953) 88 CLR 215, 241, Dixon CJ, Williams and Taylor JJ; *Jacobus Marler Estates Ltd v Marler* (1913) 114 LT 640n (HL), 641, Lord Parker, also discussed below, at [6.125]–[6.130].

[91] MGL [544].

[92] [1990] 2 AC 663.

*Ltd*[93] and the English Court of Appeal decision in *O'Sullivan v Management Agency and Music Ltd.*[94]

### The conflicts rule

**[5.35]** Wherever proof of the fiduciary's profit-making or misappropriation is problematic, the conflicts rule tends to be the more appropriate one to use. It is wiser to allege a conflict in the absence of a profit. This may be the case particularly in two situations. The first is where the fiduciary's wrongful profit is yet to be made, or is a mere possibility. Beneficiaries may in that event still be entitled to injunctive or other relief for infraction of the conflicts rule where they can establish one of the following alternatives. Either the beneficiary must satisfy the court that a prohibited conflict of interest and duty has already occurred, or evidence must be led that the same breach of duty will or may occur, *unless restrained*. In discussing *Re Thompson*,[95] the main authority for this proposition, Mason J said in *Hospital Products Ltd v United States Surgical Corporation* that[96] 'Each breach, had it been discovered in time, might have been restrained by injunction'. It is unclear whether this refers to a *threatened* derivation of a profit or the restraint of a conflict which leads to a profit. The effect is the same.

The second situation is where a fiduciary's profit cannot be established, is exiguous, or even non-existent. This could occur, as we will shortly see, where the conflicts rule is infringed by a conflict of duty with duty, not the more common interest with duty. Or the fiduciaries' acting on a proven conflict of motives might shade into their acting for restrainably *improper purposes*: see [5.88].

### Professionals

**[5.36]** 'No profit' applications of the conflicts rule particularly relate to the situation of the 'information professional'. Also called the 'adviser/information provider', this type of fiduciary may advise wrongfully with an interested motive, but without deriving any identifiable profit.[97] We are referring here to banks, solicitors, investment advisers and the like. Fiduciary liability of these 'professionals', who may entertain simultaneous duties to clients with adverse interests, is regulated by application of the conflicts rule. Fiduciary sanctions are attracted by the conflict of duties, as much as by the conflict of interests and duties. Richardson J, though, said something contrary to this in *Farrington v Rowe McBride & Partners*.[98] A 'sufficient pecuniary "interest"' of the fiduciary, he said, is always necessary in order to attract the conflicts rule. Such an interest was held not to appear from a case where a mere associated investment company of a fiduciary received the beneficiary's business.

---

[93] (1986) 160 CLR 371.

[94] [1985] 1 QB 428, 467–9, Fox LJ and 456, Dunn LJ and see also MGL [534] and *Bentley v Craven* (1853) 18 Beav 75, 76; 52 ER 29, 30.

[95] [1930] 1 Ch 203: see further at [6.10]–[6.14].

[96] (1984) 156 CLR 41, 106.

[97] See the 'advisor/information provider' discussion of P Finn in 'Fiduciary Law and the Modern Commercial World' in McKendrick 1, 10.

[98] [1985] 1 NZLR 83, 90 (CA).

The case of *Standard Investments Ltd v Canadian Imperial Bank of Commerce*[99] is an illustration of the fiduciary liability of 'information-providers'. On the facts, the fiduciary had conflicting duties and no personal interest at stake in the transaction at all.[100] *Standard Chartered*, the plaintiff, was an investment company owned by longstanding customers of the bank. It embarked on a scheme of share purchases intended to yield control of a trust company which was also a customer of the bank. The takeover was contested. Owners of the plaintiff 'bared their souls' to the president of the bank and sought the bank's assistance with the scheme. The president assured them that the bank would do everything it could to help. Simultaneously, the chairman of the bank (not the president) commenced a plan to thwart the plaintiff's endeavour. He caused the bank to itself acquire a strategic shareholding in the trust company. Several years passed. Eventually the bank sold the strategic shareholding to the plaintiff's opponent in the takeover struggle. In the result, the opponent acquired control of the trust company and the plaintiff's large minority shareholding was worth considerably less. The court found (at 436) that the bank was in breach of the conflicts rule on account of its non-disclosure of a conflicting interest it had all along. No financial or equivalent *gain* by the bank, though, was ever established. Wrongful behaviour of the bank chairman and the plaintiff's consequent loss were treated as sufficient justifications for fiduciary sanction.

## The conflicts rule

**[5.37]**    The conflicts rule 'is a rule of universal application', said Lord Cranworth in *Aberdeen Railway Co v Blaikie Bros*,[101] and–

> no one, having [fiduciary] duties to discharge, shall be allowed to enter into engagements [scil. transactions] in which he has, or can have, a personal interest conflicting, or which may possibly conflict, with the interests of those whom he is bound to protect. So strictly is this principle adhered to that no question is allowed to be raised as to the fairness or unfairness of a contract so entered into.

Although avoidance of transactions causing *losses* to beneficiaries is now the most significant use of the conflicts rule, transactions leading to fiduciaries' gains, too, may trigger its application.[102] These tend to be the older cases: see [5.60] below. Mr Blaikie, for example, had been a director of the Aberdeen Railway Co. At the relevant time in 1846 he served as its chairman as well. Acting in his other employment as managing partner in an iron foundry, he accepted a commission from the company to manufacture and supply a large quantity of 'iron chairs'. These were for a new railway line then being built.

---

[99] (1985) 22 DLR (4th) 410 (CA (Ont)).

[100] The view of D Waters in 'Banks, Fiduciary Obligations and Unconscionable Transactions' (1986) 65 *Can Bar Rev* 37, 40.

[101] (1854) 1 Macq 461; [1843-60] All ER 249, 252.

[102] Gains in *Ex Parte James* (1803) 8 Ves Jun 337, 32 ER 385; *Aberdeen Railway Co v Blaikie Bros* 1 Macq 461, [1843–60] All ER 249 (HL); *Re Leeds & Hanley Theatres of Varieties Ltd* [1902] 2 Ch 809; *Jacobus Marler Estates Ltd v Marler* (1913) 114 LT 640n; *Cook v Deeks* [1916] AC 554; *Tracy v Mandalay Pty Ltd* (1953) 88 CLR 215; *Catt v Marac Australia Ltd* (1986) 9 NSWLR 639; L Sealy in 'Some Principles of Fiduciary Obligation' [1963] *CLJ* 119 discusses the conflicts and profits rules under the headings of 'Avoidance of Contracts' and 'Rights to Profits and Advantages' respectively, at 125–32.

Work on the line went much more slowly than expected and the company, having no need for the chairs, declined to accept or pay for the balance of what it ordered. The foundry sued and conflict of interest attributed to Blaikie was asserted as a defence to the claim. On the facts there had been a modest gain for the foundry business, of which he was a member.

[5.38] *Discretions* exercised by fiduciaries in the conduct of fiduciary office are what the rule regulates. Ernest Weinrib says that regulation of these discretions is the 'primary policy' of the fiduciary obligation. It is a 'blunt tool' for the control of a person who has a duty to 'bargain and advise, involving judgement and discretion'.[103] That fiduciaries have uninfluenced judgment is what is important. Our (commercial) concern is particularly with decisions on entry into contracts, agreeing what to pay, deciding whether to enforce the contract against the other party or whether to avoid the exchange. Each involves discretion. Identification of conflict of duty and interest in the exercise of these discretions attracts the rule. It directs attention to the purpose which the decision-maker has and ignores the outcome of the decision taken. Proof of wrongful motive and improper purpose is enough. In *Ex parte James*[104] Lord Eldon LC ordered rescission of a purchase by a solicitor from an insolvent estate for which he acted without any regard to whether it was fair or not. He said:

the purchase is not permitted in any case, however honest the circumstances; the general interests of justice requiring it to be destroyed in every instance; as no court is equal to the examination and ascertainment of the truth in much the greater number of cases.

This outcome assumes that the fiduciary has not been 'immunised' by prior disclosure of the interest to the beneficiary.[105]

[5.39] The conflict of interest and duty rule is almost certainly phrased too strictly by Lord Cranworth. Entry into transactions with a personal interest that conflicts or possibly may conflict with duty is commonplace in commerce. Conflicts like this happen every day. Company directors may quite properly lead their companies to deal with other companies in which they own shares, or of which they are also directors.[106] Or, in 'management buy-outs', directors may legitimately purchase for themselves enterprises that they were appointed to protect. Such considerations may have prompted Sir Frederick Jordan's remarks on how a person 'who occupies a fiduciary position' should–

avoid placing himself in a position in which his duty and his interest, or two conflicting fiduciary duties conflict. This is rather a rule of prudence than a rule of equity; the rule being that a fiduciary must not take advantage of such a conflict if it arises. The conflict necessarily occurs whenever a fiduciary enters into a transaction with a person to whom he owes a fiduciary duty, in a matter connected with the fiduciary relation; yet such transaction is perfectly legitimate if any

---

[103] 'Fiduciary Obligation' (1975) 25 *UTLJ* 1, 4.

[104] (1803) 8 Ves Jun 337, 32 ER 385.

[105] See below at [5.128]–[5.132]; this sense of 'immunise' was discussed in the Senate Standing Committee on Legal and Constitutional Affairs, Report: 'Companies Director' Duties' (November 1989), 46.

[106] Ford [9.090.]

advantage which the fiduciary acquires under it is acquired with the full knowledge and acquiescence of the other party.[107]

The conflicts rule, on this view, is more a 'counsel of prudence' than a prohibition and it is one applicable only in some fiduciary relationships. This is almost to deny that there is any substance in the rule at all. Certainly, the conflicts rule functions in parallel with the profits rule. Fiduciaries are prohibited from taking some profit or advantage in a transaction where they are exposed to a conflict of their own interests with their fiduciary duty.[108] Profits prohibited to a fiduciary are usually preceded by transactions which embody a prohibited conflict. Corrupt deliberations precede corrupt actions. By focusing on the deliberations, breach of fiduciary duty occurs sooner and resulting profit may be prevented.

Some dealings by fiduciaries prohibited by the conflicts rule are listed below.

### Self-employment

**[5.40]**    Fiduciaries may not agree to take remunerative employment while on fiduciary business.[109]

### Self-dealing

**[5.41]**    Prohibited conflict of interest and duty may exist where fiduciaries who are commissioned to buy or sell on behalf of their beneficiaries do so by buying from or selling to themselves. Liability for this may be avoided, as we will see at [5.127]–[5.132], by the fiduciaries obtaining the beneficiaries' consent to the self-dealing. Self-dealing and the making of secret profits is not normally a matter for the conflicts rule. It usually raises the profits rule and we will further examine it under this heading (at [5.61]). The conflicts rule was referred to by Einfeld J in *Combulk Pty Ltd v TNT Management Pty Ltd*[110] to describe the wrong of a 'resources and development manager' of TNT who negotiated and entered contracts on behalf of his employer with a small company in which he was a substantial shareholder. This was without TNT's knowledge. *De Bussche v Alt*[111] is an older example of the conflicts rule doing the same service. A clandestine sale by a fiduciary to himself and resale at a profit was there seen to involve a conflict of interest and duty. Despite that, self-dealing *without* identifiable profit is the form of self-dealing wrong we will discuss under this subheading. In the absence of an obvious profit to implicate the fiduciary, the conflict must be real. An impugned self-dealing will not attract sanction if it is 'independent' of the fiduciaries' conflicting interests: in the sense discussed by Aickin J in *Australia and New Zealand*

---

[107] 'Chapters on Equity in New South Wales', 115, in *Jordan: Select Legal Papers* (1983)

[108] Expressed in *Keech v Sandford* (1726) Sel Cas t King 61; 25 ER 223; *York Buildings Co v MacKenzie* (1795) 8 Bro P C 42, 3 ER 432 (HL); *Parker v McKenna* (1874) LR 10 Ch App 96, 118, Lord Cairns LC; *Boardman v Phipps* [1967] 2 AC 46, 106, Lord Hodson, 129–34, Lord Upjohn (diss); *Chan v Zacharia* (1984) 154 CLR 178, 205, Deane J; *Queensland Mines Ltd v Hudson* (1978) 18 ALR 1, 3 (PC); *Consul Development Pty Ltd v DPC Estates Pty Ltd* (1975) 132 CLR 373, 393, Gibbs J; *Hospital Products Ltd v United States Surgical Corporation* (1984) 156 CLR 41, 103–104, Mason J (diss); *Avtex Airservices Pty Ltd v Bartsch* (1992) 107 ALR 539 (FC), 561, Hill J.

[109] *Bray v Ford* [1896] AC 44; *Bath v Standard Land Co* [1910] 2 Ch 408 affd [1911] 1 Ch 618.

[110] (1992) 37 FCR 45, 52–3—a s 52 'misleading and deceptive conduct' case.

[111] (1878) 8 Ch D 286.

*Banking Group Ltd v Bangadilly Pastoral Co Pty Ltd.*[112] A mortgagee's sale through an assignee was there set aside where the purchaser was shown to be a related company of the assignee. Restrainable conflict may not arise because the *extent* of the fiduciary's conflict is only minor. Assume a transaction where a fiduciary director causes a small company to open a trading account with a national bank. At the time the director owns 100 ordinary shares in that bank. If he or she fails to disclose that interest, it might be thought that a breach of the fiduciary duty to avoid conflict of interest and duty has occurred. This is despite the absence of any identifiable profit resulting. It has been suggested in Ford that the conflict here is too small.[113] It should only be restrained if the fiduciary has *control* of the conflicting interest. Our director would need a controlling shareholding in the bank. Short of that, his interest is not sufficiently *adverse* to his fiduciary responsibilities to be in conflict with them. In *Farrar v Farrars Ltd*[114] it was held that a trustee who sold land to a large public company in which he owned shares was not liable as though he had sold it to a small company that he substantially controlled. Although, the court added, a large shareholding in a public company giving effective control in general meeting might well be a sufficiently adverse interest.

### Purchase of beneficiaries' property

**[5.42]** Fiduciaries will only be permitted to purchase their beneficiaries' property if a fair price is agreed, no improper influence has been exerted and there has been full disclosure to beneficiaries of all relevant information which the fiduciaries possess. Purchases may be set aside unless each of these qualifications is satisfied. *Ex parte James*[115] is a classic authority in this area. Lord Eldon LC set aside the purchase of a bankrupt's estate by the solicitor to the bankruptcy administration. Evidence of proper values and profits was not received. The same wrong was found to be constituted in *Estate Realties Ltd v Wignall.*[116] Sharebrokers had purchased certain of their client's shares and options as part of a scheme to obtain control of a company and on-sell its shares at a considerable profit.

### Competition with the beneficiary

**[5.43]** Fiduciaries cannot enter into transactions with third parties which conflict, or possibly might conflict, with their fiduciary duties.[117] So stated, this sub-rule might on occasion be both unpredictable and too wide. Applications of it have been less than stringent. Consistently with the conflicts rule, it has been held that an executive employee may actively assist a competing enterprise which he intends to join. Byrne J in *McPersons Ltd v Tate*[118] saw 'no critical concept of conflict' arising where the manager of a printing business, while employed, was involved in establishing a competing

---

112 (1978) 139 CLR 195, 225–7.
113 Ford [9.080].
114 (1888) 40 Ch D 395: see also Finn *Fiduciaries* [451].
115 (1803) 8 Ves Jun 337; 32 ER 385, 389.
116 [1992] 2 NZLR 615, Tipping J (HC).
117 *Re Thompson* [1930] 1 Ch 203, 215–16, Clausen J and *Hivac Ltd v Park Royal Scientific Instruments Ltd* [1946] Ch 169, 178, Lord Greene MR (CA); *Rosetex Company Pty Ltd v Licata* (1994) 12 ACSR 779, Young J (SC (NSW)).
118 (1993) 35 AILR 285 (SC (Vic)).

company—including the purchase of a suitable press and encouragement of fellow-employees to become members of the new company's staff. Directors of companies who serve as directors of competing companies, will often not be treated as in breach of this sub-rule. Non-executive directors, certainly, may hold multiple directorships in competing companies. While executive directors are not necessarily prohibited by the conflicts rule either, they are generally subject to contractual restraints which equity will enforce. Service contracts often require substantial attendance and prohibit conflicting engagements. Contractual and fiduciary liabilities of executive directors may be in parallel here.[119] This is despite intersection of the *scopes* of the enterprises of all relevant companies. In other cases, the 'business opportunity' test may supplant delimitation of the opportunity with a criterion of the 'fairness' of what was done. This was noted above at [4.44]. Competition from a corporate fiduciary may not be a wrong ipso facto, but a wrong only where it is 'unfair' to the corporation complaining.

**[5.44]** Conflicts rule reasoning is often used in conjunction with the profits rule. Where profits are made, the conflicts rule is usually subordinate or additional to the profits rule. Profits are often things derived subsequent to a prohibited conflict of interest and duty. We will not deal here specifically with the phenomenon of the conflict (of interest) which causes the fiduciary to make a profit.[120] Breaches of duty which produce ascertainable profits are discussed below under the 'profits rule' heading. We will now consider three more features of the purer type of conflict. It is often of the sort which causes not a profit, but a disappointed reliance and a loss.

### What things must not conflict?

**[5.45]** In the traditional view, certain *influences* on fiduciaries cannot be permitted in the course of their deliberations. Performance of fiduciary duty, the paramount virtue, cannot be deflected by fiduciaries succumbing to contrary persuasion. Rather than sanction lapses as they occur, equity prefers to put temptation out of the way. So inconsistent personal interests are not permissible in the sphere of duty. This is the way that it is intended to avoid a conflict of influences occurring in the minds of fiduciaries. The 'conflict' is between the influence of personal interests, on the one hand, and the influence of fiduciary duty, on the other. So expressed, the conflicts rule is within the reach of the 'honesty or integrity' part of the *Beloved Wilkes's* 'honesty, integrity and fairness' formulation.[121] Here, as there, equity's competence to regulate powers is invoked—although now in a cynical and pre-emptive kind of way. Fiduciaries are not given the chance to be dishonest. It is as though a natural propensity to dishonesty is restrained. Equity forbids the existence of an untoward influence in the minds of fiduciaries, on the assumption that misappropriation is likely otherwise.

### 'Fairness' and the conflict of duty and duty

**[5.46]** The *Beloved Wilkes's* formulation extends to fields of influence which arise from the fiduciary's duties to other beneficiaries. This is what is generally

---

[119] See *On The Street Pty Ltd v Cott* (1990) 3 ACSR 54, 61, Powell J, *Riteway Express Pty Ltd v Clayton* (1987) 10 NSWLR 238, McLelland J, and Ford [9.410].

[120] Eg, in *Cook v Evatt (No 2)* (1992) 1 NZLR 676.

[121] *Re Beloved Wilkes's Charity* (1851) 3 Mac & G 440, 42 ER 330: see [5.7].

referred to as the conflict of duty and duty. Different beneficiaries of the one fiduciary may have interests which conflict as between themselves. The risk is that fiduciaries will prefer one interest to another, or, in attempting to serve all, may be led to sacrifice the fiduciary duty owed to some. The fiduciary is under an obligation to treat beneficiaries of different classes fairly. There are several instances of this. One is where a solicitor acts for parties on both sides of one transaction. Adverse confidential relationships may then be formed. A simple solution to it is that the fiduciary should be prevented from misusing the confidences of either client by being disqualified from acting for both in the future. This will often be an unfortunate solution for the solicitor, who, by trying to service two clients, is left with none. In other cases the obligation of fairness may arise between directors of a corporation and shareholders in different classes.[122] Or trustees may have to be fair to beneficiaries with successive interests in property,[123] or liquidators fair to creditors with differing priorities in insolvency. The fiduciary in each case cannot be adequately sanctioned by disqualification.

[5.47] Obligations of fairness for liquidators and bankruptcy trustees may become quite complicated. Assume that an insolvent businessman dies, leaving many creditors unpaid. His business passes into the hands of an insolvency trustee. The unpaid creditors resolve that they will indemnify the trustee to continue the business, in order that they might be paid. The trustee trades on and more losses are incurred. Now new creditors are unpaid as well as the ones who asked the trustee to keep the business going. Creditors may be said to form two classes. These are 'estate' creditors, with claims originally against the insolvent, and new 'trading' creditors, with subsequent claims against the insolvency trustee. Trading creditors are usually given priority over estate creditors. For the request of the estate creditors that the trustee continue the business is said in fairness to postpone them to creditors thereafter trading with that business. Equity facilitates this outcome by enabling trading creditors to be subrogated to the trustee's right of indemnity. The trading creditors, in effect, have a right to any distributable profits before they are divided between other persons entitled. This doctrine was confirmed by the House of Lords in *Dowse v Gorton*[124] and applied in the High Court decisions in *Vacuum Oil Company Pty Ltd v Wiltshire*[125] and *Octavo Investments Pty Ltd v Knight*.[126] The idea is that the trading trustee's indemnity gives priority to all trading liabilities assented to by the estate creditors. We shall examine the principles of fairness which have developed between directors of corporations and their shareholders separately at [5.102]–[5.105].

[5.48] A different type of fairness issue arises between fiduciaries and beneficiaries who have the same interests. It is notable here that the (equal) rights of many such persons have been codified. In relation to creditors' rights

---

122 See *Mills v Mills* (1938) 60 CLR 150, 164, Latham CJ.

123 See *Howe v Lord Dartmouth* (1802) 7 Ves 137, 32 ER 56 and *Re Chesterfield's Trusts* (1883) 24 Ch D 643, discussed in Ford & Lee chapter 11 and Finn *Fiduciaries* 60–4.

124 [1891] AC 190 and see *Re Oxley* (1914) 1 Ch 604.

125 (1945) 72 CLR 319.

126 (1979) 144 CLR 319.

in bankruptcy, for example, it is provided by the Bankruptcy Act 1966 (Cth) s 108 that:

> ... all debts proved in a bankruptcy rank equally and, if the proceeds of property of the bankrupt are insufficient to meet them in full, they shall be paid proportionately.

For corporate insolvency there is corresponding provision in the Corporations Law s 555 that 'all debts and claims proved in a winding-up [shall] rank equally'. Pursuant to Part 5.6 Div 2 of the Law, members of a corporation must contribute to its winding-up equally, not exceeding amounts unpaid on shares, or amounts guaranteed. However, potential exists for the conflicts rule to be breached outside or contrary to the terms of the statutes. This could be where a bankruptcy trustee or liquidator prefers the interests of some creditors to others. Or it might be like the situation in *Re Batey*.[127] A trustee in bankruptcy carried on the business of the insolvent solely in order to make profits for himself. Continuation of the business was not necessary for the winding-up of the estate. An injunction was issued upon the application of the unpaid estate creditors to restrain this breach of duty.

### Disclosure of the conflict may negate liability

**[5.49]** Disclosure is an exception to the conflicts rule. It is particularly relevant to the 'self-dealing' applications of the conflicts rule we have discussed, where the fiduciary is personally interested in 'contracts and other undertakings' entered on behalf of the beneficiary. For a fiduciary to be exempted from liability, the beneficiary must consent to the transaction after the fiduciary has disclosed:

(a) all special information or 'inside knowledge' that the fiduciary has acquired as to the value of what is being transacted or exchanged, and/or

(b) that the fiduciary is dealing in the transaction as an opposite principal with an adverse interest.[128]

The conflicts rule may be inapplicable if the fiduciary has sufficiently 'shrugged off' the character of his office and the old confidence which existed between the parties has been withdrawn.[129] Disclosure of self-interest in any particular transaction equals notice to the beneficiary that the fiduciary relationship is pro tanto at an end. If the beneficiary is legally competent to consent to that transaction still going ahead, there will be no conflictual liability. An information imbalance between the parties may be redressed by disclosure.

### A 'duty to disclose'?

**[5.50]** Disclosure serves as an exception to the conflicts rule and, discussed at [5.128], to the profits rule as well. Sufficient disclosure may enable the fiduciary to 'shake off the character' of fiduciary office and deal with the beneficiary on a plane of equality. But can it be said that there is ever a fiduciary 'duty to disclose'?[130] There is much dicta in the authorities to suggest

---

[127] (1881) 17 Ch D 35.
[128] L Sealy 'Some Principles of Fiduciary Obligation' [1963] *CLJ* 119, 126.
[129] *Ex parte James* (1803) 8 Ves Jun 337, 32 ER 385, 389, Lord Eldon LC.
[130] See *Ex parte Pye* (1811) 18 Ves Jun 140; 2 Ves Jun Supp 511; 34 ER 271, 1203.

that there is such a duty. For example, in *Tracy v Mandalay Pty Ltd*[131] it was said in the joint judgment that:

> Promoters may sell their property to the new company but they are under a fiduciary duty to disclose . . .

Hope JA said in *Walden Properties Ltd v Beaver Properties Pty Ltd*:[132]

> It is not necessary to analyse or determine the whole of the content of this fiduciary obligation, but undoubtedly it requires Beaver Properties to make full disclosure to Walden . . .

Finally, in *BLB Corporation of Australia Establishment v Jacobsen*,[133] the joint judgment referred to an 'obligation of a fiduciary to make full disclosure' while dismissing a claim in tort wrongly pleaded as a breach of fiduciary obligation.

The 'duty of disclosure' idea seems to be gathering strength. In *Cape v Redarb Pty Ltd*,[134] the court, following *Walden Properties Ltd v Beaver Pty Ltd*,[135] held that the receiver of a company was a fiduciary and thereby under a duty to inform beneficiaries 'whose interests he is to serve'.

Writers on this subject, however, mostly do not share this view. Paul Finn and Len Sealy are two who are of the opinion that there is no disclosure duty.[136] This seems to be the academically orthodox position.

**[5.51]**  It is submitted here, too, that there is no duty to disclose. Such a duty would be inconsistent with the general fiduciaries jurisdiction of equity, noted at [5.1]. Equity forbids things rather than commands them. What may be happening in some authorities is that the conflicts rule is conceived as a double negative. That is, the conflicts rule is treated as a rule to avoid breach of a rule which requires that there be no conflicts. To the extent that the disclosure exception avoids breach of the rule, there is said to be a duty to disclose. A duty to attract the exception to the rule is implied. This is given the same form as the duty to obey the rule itself: not to allow conflicts of interest and duty to occur. This can be seen in *Moore v Regents of the University of California*.[137] It was said there that:

> The duty of disclosure . . . is a fiduciary duty intended to prevent personal interests from affecting the physician's judgement.'

Certainly the virtue of free judgment is a strong rationalisation of the conflicts rule. But it does not directly bear on the disclosure exemption. Disclosure has more to do with honesty than freeing the discloser's judgment.

---

131  (1953) 88 CLR 215, 240, Dixon CJ, Williams and Taylor JJ; and see *Bluecorp Pty Ltd (in liq) v ANZ Executors & Trustee Co Ltd* (1994) 13 ACSR 386, 399, Mackenzie J (SC (Qld)).

132  [1973] 2 NSWLR 815, 835 (CA).

133  (1974) 48 ALJR 372, 378, McTiernan, Mason and Jacobs JJ.

134  (1992) 8 ACSR 67, 80, Higgins J (SC (ACT)).

135  [1973] 2 NSWLR 815; see also dicta in *New Zealand Netherlands Society 'Oranje' Inc v Kuys* [1973] 2 All ER 1222 (PC) and the decision in *Glandon Pty Ltd v Strata Consolidated Pty Ltd* (1993) 11 ACSR 543 (CA (NSW)), considered below.

136  P Finn 'The Fiduciary Principle' Youdan 1, 28–9; L Sealy 'Some Principles of Fiduciary Obligation' [1963] *CLJ* 119, passim.

137  793 P 2d 479 (1990), 483, Panelli J, Lucas CJ, Eagleston, Arabian, Broussard and Kennard JJ concurring.

Consider the duty not to *murder*. From this prohibition, can one infer a correlative duty to kill only in self-defence? Should one apply the considerations that bear upon whether an accused has the intention to murder to the question of whether he only meant to act in self-defence? Or are the things separate? Self-defence is a recognised exception to the murder rule. It is not suggested that one can test the intention requirements needed to uphold a self-defence plea in the terms of the malice aforethought necessary to establish murder. This would be a category mistake. Explained in the joint judgment of Wilson, Dawson and Toohey JJ, delivered in the High Court decision in *Zecevic v DPP*,[138] quite different considerations apply to the constitution of the self-defence exception, as distinct from determining what satisfies the murder rule itself. Murder involves an intention to kill or do grievous bodily harm. Self-defence involves belief about the necessity of the force used, held on reasonable grounds, and the existence of an objective proportion between threats apprehended and the accused's acts in response. The two are not the same. This may correspond to a similar separateness which should exist between the equitable categories of the conflicts rule and the disclosure defence.

**[5.52]**     Out of such elliptical reasoning a fiduciary 'duty to disclose' may have been born. It is understandable that courts are more inclined to adopt this perspective where an information imbalance between fiduciary and beneficiaries is particularly pronounced. The point in this subheading is only that there is no *fiduciary* duty to disclose. Obligations for fiduciaries to disclose arise otherwise, in ways unrelated to equity. For example, corporate officers are obliged to disclose by terms of the Corporations Law and perhaps by the company's articles of association as well.[139] In *Moore v Regents*, the 'bodily samples' case, a beneficiary's ignorance of what was going on was one of the most important facts. Mr Moore had no idea that his physician's judgment in ordering post-operative procedures may have been affected by the same physician's desire to make a private profit. Had he been told the true facts, he might well have refused or qualified his consent to the post-operative procedures.

The reasoning in *Glandon Pty Ltd v Strata Consolidated Pty Ltd* exhibits a similar characteristic.[140] That case involved a claim to set aside a settlement, whereby a dispute between rival company factions was brought to an end. The factions were respectively associated with three persons. Two of these persons were in league and were directors of the disputed company. Pursuant to the settlement, shares in the company belonging to the third person's faction were sold to vehicles owned by the the other two factions. Subsequently, the third person's faction brought a claim for breach of fiduciary duty against the two directors. It was alleged that those directors had, in effect, purchased the third faction's shares themselves and had done so after concealing various important facts. A form of 'self-dealing' contrary to the conflicts rule was alleged. We

---

[138] (1987) 162 CLR 645, 661-5, Mason CJ and Brennan J agreeing.

[139] See, eg, Corporations Law s 231 (directors of proprietary companies to disclose material interests in contracts, property etc); s 232A (directors of public companies who have 'material personal interests' not to vote etc. unless interest is disclosed) also Lumsden 'Conflicts of Interest and Public Company Board Behaviour' (1993) 7 (3) *Commercial Law Quarterly* 9.

[140] (1993) 11 ACSR 543 (CA (NSW)).

have discussed this above at [5.41]. To this claim, as we will see at [5.127], the fiduciary may assert the defence that the beneficiary consented to the purchase after the full facts about it were disclosed. Availability of such a defence was the matter really in contention. The leading judgment in the case, however, determined liability according to whether a 'duty to disclose' existed or not. This duty was illustrated (at 550–1) by only an exiguous pedigree based in various obiter dicta. Nevertheless, the self-dealing that the third person's faction alleged was barely referred to and the disclosure aspect of the defence to the rule was treated as the rule itself.[141] Again consideration of the underlying fiduciary rule and its policy was omitted. There was no consideration given, for example, to the question of *what* should be disclosed pursuant to the supposed duty. If disclosure were part of the fiduciary rule, one might have expected this to have been of central importance.

### Relativity of conflict

**[5.53]**   Older cases sometimes suggest that any conflict of private interest or other duty is sufficient to attract the full invalidating effect of the rule. This can be seen in the above *Aberdeen Railway Co v Blaikie* quotation,[142] where what was forbidden was a 'personal interest conflicting *or which possibly may conflict*'. The idea has since been much criticised. See discussion of authorities above, at [5.31], in connection with Deane J's criticism of equitable 'inflexibility' in *Chan v Zacharia*.[143] In *Boardman v Phipps*[144] Lord Upjohn (dissenting) quite strongly stated the point. 'The phrase "possibly may conflict" ', he said, 'requires consideration':

> In my view it means that the reasonable man looking at the relevant facts and circumstances of the particular case would think that there was a real and substantial possibility of conflict; not that you could imagine some situation arising which might, in some conceivable possibility in events not contemplated as real sensible possibilities by any reasonable person, result in a conflict

This approach was shortly after followed in *Holder v Holder*.[145] In fact the fiduciary rule invoked by all the judges in that case was the profits rule, not the conflicts rule. However the familiar wrongdoing of self-dealing was involved. A fiduciary was relieved from technical liability under the profits rule as it prohibits profits from self-dealing. Victor Holder had accepted appointment as an executor of his father's will. He did some small things on behalf of the estate. Then he renounced probate in order to purchase a farm from the estate for himself. As the Court of Appeal noted (at 389), it is not possible to effectively renounce probate after small, but unequivocal, acts of executorship have been performed. Victor had prima facie made a purchase contrary to the fiduciary self-purchasing rule. Victor's brother sued to challenge the legality of the purchase on this basis. However, in the words of Harman LJ, 'the reasons behind the rule do not exist and I do not feel bound

---

[141]  Ibid, 550, 552, 558–9, Cripps JA, Clark JA agreeing; Mahoney JA, at 547, also agreeing, was less specific.

[142]  (1854) 1 Macq 461; [1843–60] All ER Rep 249, 252, Lord Cranworth LC, at [5.37].

[143]  (1984) 154 CLR 178, 204–5, obiter.

[144]  [1967] 2 AC 46, at 124; following dictum applied recently in *Inge v Inge* (1990) 3 ACSR 63, 70–1, O'Bryan J (SC (Vic)).

[145]  [1968] Ch 353 (CA).

to apply it'. The beneficiaries never looked to Victor to preserve their interests. Victor never influenced the executors who acted after him and was noted at 389 to have paid a good price. For these reasons, the transaction was unanimously upheld by the Court of Appeal. Subsequently, though, the case has been disfavoured. It was distinguished in the similar cases of *Re Thompson's Settlement*[146] and *Re Tabone*[147] and has been disapproved of in both the major Australian textbooks on trusts.[148]

**[5.54]** Why is a very strict view taken of what can be a conflicting interest? Is such a view consistent with the temper of modern times? Stephen Cretney has drawn our attention to the times when the rule originated.[149] In 1726, he said, when Lord King became Chancellor, the South Sea Bubble scandal was at its height. Several Chancery masters became bankrupt, after speculating with £82,301 of litigants' funds. Lord King's predecessor, Macclesfield, was fined £30,000 for trading in offices. Solicitors were then thought to make 'enormous extortions' from their clients. Cretney suggests that the conscience of the age was quite 'ill-developed' and the *Keech v Sandford*[150] decision was of chiefly exemplary significance. It pointed the way to rectitude in an impious age. King himself was said to be–

> a Chancellor, not of the highest genius, but of most respectable talents, and, what is of more consequence, of unblemished virtue ... one of the most consistent and spotless politicians who have ever appeared in England.[151]

Authorities recommending relaxation of strictness in fiduciary rules usually refer to the profits rule.[152] However their reasoning is applicable to conflicts as well. The danger of *rigor aequitatis* setting in is noted all round. Deane J in *Chan v Zacharia*[153] discusses the possibility that principles of equity, including the conflicts rule, are all stated too broadly. He says that it may be 'unconscionable', on the facts of some cases for beneficiaries to assert the conflicts rule against their fiduciaries. This is–

> where ... there is no possible conflict between personal interest and fiduciary duty and it is plainly in the interests of the person to whom the fiduciary duty is owed that the fiduciary obtain for himself rights or benefits which he is absolutely precluded from seeking or obtaining for the person to whom the fiduciary duty is owed.

It may stretch understanding to say that a person can unconscionably claim that another has acted unconscionably to him. Is the court acting unconscionably, too, if it allows the claim? The idea might be restated. Strictness, of fiduciary rules, should defer to the honest judgment of fiduciaries on how best to serve their beneficiaries' interests. Judicial sensibility of conflict (or its possibility) should be subordinate to the maintenance of

---

[146] [1985] 3 WLR 486

[147] [1968] VR 168.

[148] Ford & Lee, [918] and Jacobs, [1738].

[149] 'Rationale of Keech v Sandford' (1969) 33 *Conveyancer* 161, 168.

[150] (1726) Sel Cas Ch 61; 25 ER 223.

[151] Campbell's *Lives of the Lord Chancellors* 4th ed (1857), Ch12, quoted in Cretney supra, 162.

[152] Eg, *Peso Silver Mines Ltd v Cropper* (1966) 58 DLR (2d) 1, 8–9. Cartwright J, curiam (SC), *Chan v Zacharia* (1984) 154 CLR 178, 204–5, Deane J.

[153] (1984) 154 CLR 178, 204.

fiduciary standards. That fiduciaries have the ability to make honest and unfettered judgements is more primary. So the conclusion may follow that wherever the standards are satisfied, then the conflicts rule is excluded. This makes the decisions in *Regal (Hastings) Ltd v Gulliver*[154] and *Boardman v Phipps*[155] look questionable. However, at this point, it should be remembered that the conflicts rule played only a very small part in either.

# The profits rule

**[5.55]** Not just profit-making, but secret profit-making, is what this rule is about. Fiduciaries are not hereby required to eschew all benefits, advantages or gains derived from fiduciary office. They are not made to act gratuitously. Few people would then volunteer for the job. Rather, a fiduciary is prohibited from taking benefits from the office which are not made known to the beneficiary, either before or after they are acquired. 'It is no doubt well settled in equity', said Lord Parker in *Jacobus Marler Estates Ltd v Marler*,[156] that:

> an agent cannot, without the consent of his principal, given with full knowledge of the material facts and under circumstances which rebut any presumption of undue influence, retain any profit acquired by him in transactions within the scope of his agency.

Like the conflicts rule in relation to disclosure, the profits rule is subject to a large exception. It does not reach those profits that the beneficiary is taken to ratify, acquiesce in, or agree to. This is further dealt with at [5.127]–[5.131].

Deane J in *Chan v Zacharia*[157] described the profits rule as the second 'theme' of the 'general principle of equity which requires a person in a fiduciary relationship to account for personal benefit or gain'. The profits rule–

> requires the fiduciary to account for any benefit or gain obtained or received by reason of or by use of his fiduciary position or of opportunity or knowledge resulting from it.

Two more aspects of a prohibited profit are touched upon here, additional to the secrecy consideration. We shall deal with them first.

## 'By reason or by use of'

**[5.56]** This phrase directs attention to the nexus between profits made by fiduciaries and their fiduciary offices. It highlights the *exploitation* of fiduciary office that breach of the profits rule entails. That there is a nexus is important. Incidental profits made by fiduciaries, say, from other employment, from writing books, or from gambling do not usually belong to beneficiaries. That these exempt profits are made when fiduciaries should have been attending to their fiduciary duties makes no difference. In the words of Denning J in *Reading v R*:[158]

---

[154] (1942) [1967] 2 AC 134n.

[155] [1967] 2 AC 46.

[156] (1913) 114 LT 640n, 640 (HL), also *Parker v McKenna* (1874) LR 10 Ch App Cas 96, 124, Sir W M James LJ.

[157] (1984) 154 CLR 178, 198.

[158] [1948] 2 KB 268, 276.

A servant may, during his master's time, in breach of his contract, do other things, to make money for himself, such as gambling, but he is entitled to keep that money for himself. The master has a claim for damages for breach of contract, but he has no claim to the money.

A fiduciary may well argue that no property right or law has been infringed by what he did. Fiduciaries are not universally prohibited from making secret profits whilst serving as fiduciaries. Many aspects of their private businesses or affairs are just not relevant to the fiduciary duties that they owe to particular beneficiaries. The secret profit must be sufficiently connected with the fiduciary relationship to be prohibited. One way of expressing the connection is to say that fiduciary office must be the sole or main cause of the profit being made. This is the link we are looking at. It is a matter of particular significance where the profits are made from the misappropriation of 'soft' property, where a competitive advantage is seized, or a profitable opportunity is used. These are matters that we have already considered, under *Scope* of a fiduciary relationship as 'corporate opportunities': see above at [4.44].

**[5.57]**      Lord Russell used the connective 'by reason of and in the course of' as part of his wider liability formula in *Regal (Hastings) Ltd v Gulliver.*[159] That case involved the sale of a company which conducted a cinema business. Directors of Regal made a profit through their ownership of shares in a subsidiary company, which had been newly incorporated for the sale. Possible unreality of the profit in this case and its questionable outcome are discussed below. We are at present concerned with expression of the *link* between the fiduciary offices of Regal directors and their personal profits derived from sale of shares in the subsidiary. As to this, Lord Russell said (at 147) that:

> shares . . . acquired by the directors were acquired by reason and only *by reason of* the fact that they were directors of Regal and *in the course of their execution of that office.* [emphasis added]

This 'by reason of and in the course of' phrase was generally adopted by other members of the House hearing the case and has since been followed on several occasions.[160]

**[5.58]**      Although a little opaque, 'by reason of and in the course of' as a connective seems to imply some *use* of the fiduciary relationship in order to make a profit. Lord Russell goes on to say, a little self-evidently, that a liability to account 'arises from the mere fact of a profit having, in the stated circumstances, being made'.

This begs the question of what the 'stated circumstances' nexus can be. In *Canadian Aero Service Ltd v O'Malley* the Supreme Court of Canada decided that the 'by reason of and in the course of' formulation of the profit and fiduciary office nexus was a 'straight-jacket' requirement and too narrow.[161] It was said not to include those fiduciaries who resign their offices in order to make profits. In a literal sense this is true. 'Standing in a fiduciary relationship' and other references to the fiduciary relationship *continuing* may

---

[159] (1942) [1967] 2 AC 134n, 143.

[160] (1942) [1967] 2 AC 134n, *semble* 140, Viscount Sankey, 154, Lord MacMillan, 157, Lord Wright, 159, Lord Porter; *Peso Silver Mines Ltd v Cropper* (1966) 58 DLR (2d) 1 (SC).

[161] (1973) 40 DLR (3d) 371, 389–90, judgment of the court.

need to be qualified in Lord Russell's formulation. But that is all. We have noted at [3.83]–[3.86] the problems that attend the 'imprecise ethical standard' that the court in *Canadian Aero* would use to replace Lord Russell's formulation.

### 'Opportunity or knowledge resulting'

[5.59] This expression performs the same function as 'by reason or by use of', that has just been seen. It is another way of describing the nexus between fiduciary office, on the one hand, and fiduciaries' profit-making, on the other. Deane J used this and the previous expression cumulatively in *Chan v Zacharia*.[162] In *Regal (Hastings) Ltd v Gulliver*[163] Lord Wright noted that Lord Russell's analysis–

> shows clearly enough that the opportunity and the knowledge which enabled [the defendants] to purchase the shares came to them simply in their position as directors of the ... company.

Lord Wright brackets opportunity and knowledge together. The word 'knowledge' operates in a similar way to the 'opportunity' link-word, considered at [4.43]. Sometimes it is confusingly referred to as 'information', or more often, as 'confidential information'. The matter is then complicated by involving a different type of equitable intervention as well. 'Confidential information' can serve both as a link-term in establishing breach of a fiduciary duty and also as the key to an independent set of equitable obligations discussed under the heading of 'Breach of Confidence' in Chapter 9. It is the former function only which will concern us here.

### *'Knowledge' as confidential information*

[5.60] A fiduciary wrong, as suggested at [5.14], is ultimately a misappropriation of some kind. Under this heading, we are concerned with where that misappropriation is turned into a profit. If the thing misappropriated is confidential information, the same wrong may also evoke the breach of confidence equity. Assume that a party is an intending joint venturer, similar to the one in *Lac Minerals Ltd v International Corona Resources Ltd*.[164] The venture proposes to exploit a valuable mineral discovery made by the other intending venturer. Before arrangements between the venturers are settled, the first venturer seizes the benefit of the other's discovery for itself. It may be possible to characterise this wrong in at least two ways. Either it can be treated as a breach of an (intending) fiduciary relationship, a denial of the trust which should exist between prospective venturers. Or it can be seen as a breach of confidence, the wrongful use of information imparted by one party to another. In *Lac Minerals*, the court at first instance and the Ontario Court of Appeal analysed similar facts in terms of the *trusting* relationship.[165] In the Supreme Court only two justices were persuaded to see that a fiduciary relationship arose to be breached.[166] The rest of the court denied that a trusting relationship

---

[162] (1984) 154 CLR 178, 198.
[163] (1942) [1967] 2 AC 134n, 156.
[164] [1989] 2 SCR 574.
[165] (1986) 25 DLR (4th) 504 and (1987) 62 OR (2d) 1 (CA).
[166] [1989] 2 SCR 574, La Forest J, 644-67 and Wilson J, 630–1.

existed on the facts and rested liability on breach of confidence.[167] Essentially the same outcome was achieved by either route.

So where a party uses confidential information imparted in a trusting relationship for private gain the wrong might be analysed in terms either of the profits rule or breach of confidence. Fiduciary liability imposed by the majority judgements in *Boardman v Phipps*[168] imposed liability under the profits rule for 'information' acquired in this way. Lord Cohen (at 103) held Boardman liable as would be an agent who profited through the information and opportunity which came to him while acting in the course of duty. Lords Hodson and Guest concurred and began to develop the idea that confidential information used by Boardman was directly equivalent to trust or agency property misappropriated. The alternative 'breach of confidence' type of equity involves a misappropriation of the information in the form in which it was communicated. That it represents a discovery or benefit to be mutually enjoyed need not be proven. Sometimes an advantage may appear from the absence of need to prove a wider transaction: this is considered in Chapter 9. Under the following headings are some typical breaches of the profits rule. A common characteristic of each is that there is an ascertainable profit.

## Breaches of the profits rule

### *Self-dealing with own property*[169]

[5.61]    Fiduciaries who sell their own property to beneficiaries are typically agents, commissioned by beneficiaries to purchase property of the same kind as they sell. By stealth, or with insufficient disclosure, such a fiduciary might receive an excessive price from the beneficiary, or a 'profit'.[170] The present rule focusses on this fact. It specifically reverses the fiduciary's objectionable gain, by making the fiduciary account for its monetary value. This may be allowed regardless of the fate of the sale transaction and despite the inability of the beneficiary to rescind it. Remedial obligations under the profits rule fasten on the profit made through self-dealing, it could be said, and not self-dealing itself.

After the introduction of the Companies Acts in the mid-nineteenth century, this contravention of the profits rule became for a time one of the most litigated breaches of fiduciary duty. Companies were often floated and large funds raised from an unsuspecting public. Promoters of these companies, it was often alleged, sold their own businesses or property to the companies for excessive prices. No independent boards or general meetings would be informed of the full facts, or consent to the sales. Amongst the more notable authorities were *Erlanger v New Sombrero Phosphate Co*,[171] *Re Cape Breton Co*,[172] *North-West Transportation Co Ltd v Beatty*,[173] *Burland v Earle*,[174] *Omnium Electric*

---

[167] Ibid, 599–600, Sopinka and McIntyre JJ, Lamer J agreeing (an 'essential element of dependency or vulnerability' was missing: see above at [3.100]–[3.101]).

[168] [1967] 2 AC 46.

[169] This and subsequent headings are suggested by the scheme in Goff & Jones, chapter 34

[170] See *Grantwell Pty Ltd v Franks* (1993) 61 SASR 390 (FC).

[171] (1878) 3 App Cas 1218 (HL).

[172] (1884) 26 Ch D 221 (CA).

[173] (1887) 12 App Cas 589 (PC).

[174] [1902] AC 83.

*Palaces Ltd v Baines*,[175] *Jacobus Marler Estates Ltd v Marler*[176] and *Tracy v Mandalay Pty Ltd*.[177] Some of the seminal principles of fiduciary law and its remedies were established in these cases. However their facts would not inspire litigation today. Modern companies legislation in the Corporations Law and elsewhere now prevents these fraudulent company promotions from occurring.[178]

**[5.62]** Self-dealing wrongs are also prohibited by the conflicts rule. We saw this at [5.41]. The conflicts rule applies whether the outcome of the misdeed is profitable or not. Good deals as well as bad deals with fiduciaries fall foul of the conflicts rule. Both are liable to be set aside if the beneficiary chooses. Where fiduciaries sell to their beneficiaries and are on both sides of a fiduciary transaction, their personal interests and fiduciary duties will almost inevitably conflict. However, conflicts rule remedies for this are much more limited than what is available under the profits rule. Remedies are essentially one: rescission—the avoidance of the sale. This is only available if the beneficiary meets *restituio in integrum* conditions, such as returning the property sold to the wrongdoer, and if the beneficiary acts promptly. What is more, the conflicts rule remedy system does not allow for specific restitution of the profit itself. This was a doctrinal position discussed and confirmed in *Tracy v Mandalay Pty Ltd*.[179] To obtain the wrongful profit we must employ the profits rule and submit to the necessity of ascertaining and proving it.

**[5.63]** The profits rule does not automatically apply to sales of fiduciaries' own property to their beneficiaries. Indeed, traditional authorities are problematic on whether it applies at all to this fiduciary wrongdoing. The relevant test depends on the property-based reasoning of an earlier age. It looks to the relevant *time* when the fiduciary acquired the property sold, from which an inference as to its ownership status is made.

- If property the fiduciary sold to the beneficiary is property acquired *after* the vendor became a fiduciary, the profit belongs in equity to the beneficiary.[180] Beneficiaries are entitled to ignore the fiduciary's intervening purchase for himself and treat the property as having been acquired for them. Appropriate allowance to the fiduciary is made for the purchase price that he paid.[181] On this basis, the beneficiary is entitled to the fiduciary's profit as to his own money in the fiduciary's hands. The fiduciary is in the same event estopped from denying that the purchase was made otherwise than on the beneficiary's behalf.[182]

---

175 [1914] 1 Ch 332 (CA).
176 (1913) 11 LT 640n (HL).
177 (1953) 88 CLR 215.
178 Eg, *Corporations Law*, Pt 7.12, Div 2—'Prospectuses'.
179 (1953) 88 CLR 215, 239, Dixon CJ, Williams and Taylor JJ, following *North-West Transportation Co v Beatty* (1887) 12 App Cas 589; *Cook v Deeks* [1916] 1 AC 554, *Burland v Eale* [1902] AC 83 and *Jacobus Marler Estates Ltd v Marler* (1913) 114 LT 640n (HL): see above at [5.33]–[5.34] and *Remedies* at [6.136]–[6.137].
180 *Re Cape Breton Co* (1885) 29 Ch D 795, 805, Cotton LJ, Bowen and Fry LJJ agreeing (CA); *Jacobus Marler Estates Ltd v Marler* (1913) 114 LT 640n, 641, Lord Parker (HL).
181 *Jacobus Marler Estates Ltd v Marler* (1913) 114 LT 640n, 640n, Lord Parker (HL).
182 *Re Cape Breton Company* (1885) 29 Ch D 795, 804, Cotton LJ.

• If the property sold was acquired *before* the vendor became a fiduciary, the profit appears to be irrecoverable. Authority for this is based on the idea that a court would be making a new bargain between the parties if the profit component of the sale is to be ascertained and reversed. Equity mends no man's bargain. As the High Court said in *Tracy v Mandalay Pty Ltd*:[183]

> the purchaser ... cannot ask the Court 'to fix a proper price between vendor and purchaser, and estimate the damage with reference to such price. This the Court cannot do'.

Any valuation of the article sold in order to find the profit on sale is conceived to be beyond the equity's competence—a conservative view, perhaps, and one which may not be now followed. For the trend of equity in Australia appears to be to the contrary. The majority decision in *Stern v McArthur*[184] might now instance just such a rewriting of a bargain—there to avert an unconscionable contract forfeiture. That was quite a different equity. Reasoning in the old case of *Bentley v Craven* is inconsistent more specifically.[185] *Bentley* involved a partner in a sugar refining firm who was under a duty to acquire sugar for it. At the same time he speculated in sugar on his own account. In the event the partner sold the firm his own sugar without disclosure. In court, the firm was allowed to elect either to rescind the purchases, or to affirm the purchases *and* to take the partner's profit.

### Diversion of opportunities

**[5.64]**     Fiduciaries may wrongfully appropriate their beneficiaries' contracts, purchases, or other opportunities to profit from third parties. Where they do, the benefits, profits or advantages obtained thereby may be held on constructive trust for the beneficiary. Or the fiduciary may be personally obliged to account for any consequent profits. In *Beatty v Guggenheim Exploration Co*,[186] a fiduciary agent was sent to investigate gold-mining claims in the Yukon. The agent went and later purchased essential adjoining claims in his own name. In such a case,

> [the principal] had the right to say to the agent that he must renounce the profits of the transaction and transfer the claims at cost.[187]

Characterisation of an opportunity as a *fiduciary* opportunity overlaps with characterisation of whether the *scope* of fiduciary duties extends to the opportunity in question. Fiduciaries may contend that the opportunities in question came to them in a private capacity. So conclusions about fiduciary opportunities reached under the *Scope* and *General* headings of this part should be re-emphasised. First, inability of beneficiaries to avail themselves of opportunities presented does not free fiduciaries to take the opportunities personally—see [5.25]. Secondly, good faith and honesty in the fiduciary are

---

[183] (1953) 88 CLR 215, 241, Dixon CJ, Williams and Taylor JJ.

[184] (1988) 165 CLR 489, 526-7, Deane and Dawson JJ, Gaudron J agreeing; as suggested at 514-5, Brennan J, dissenting.

[185] (1853) 18 Beav 75; 52 ER 29 although expressly an application of the conflicts rule: see Romilly MR, at 30, and MGL [534].

[186] 122 NE 378 (1919), 380, Cardozo J.

[187] Goff & Jones 643-8 and L Sealy 'Some Principles of Fiduciary Obligation' [1963] *CLJ* 119, 128-9.

irrelevant—see [5.24]. We have already investigated how these considerations apply to employees, partners and corporate officers. See now the following.

## A. Lessees

**[5.65]** Fiduciaries who are lessees may take beneficiaries' opportunities of gaining lease renewals if they obtain renewed leases in their own names. This is an old example of the 'diversionary' wrong. For hundreds of years the courts have prevented trustees and other fiduciaries from taking renewals of leases personally instead of renewing leases for their beneficiaries. The new lease is an assumed exploitation of the access to the landlord that the previous fiduciary tenancy allowed. The prohibitory rule for trustees is very strict. It applies even though the old lease has expired,[188] or was on different terms from the renewed lease[189] and that renewal was not customary in the circumstances.[190] In form, as Collins MR held in *Re Biss*,[191] this rule is an irrebuttable presumption, sometimes called a 'presumption of law'. For fiduciaries other than trustees, the lessee rule is relaxed somewhat. But it has the same characteristics. Phrased presumptively, the 'lease renewal' sub-rule is a reversal of the usual burden of proof applicable to fiduciary claims. The (non-trustee) fiduciary must establish that lease renewal in the fiduciary's name took place without abuse of his fiduciary position. If this is done, the renewed lease can be retained. This non-trustee rule for lessees has been applied as between mortgagors and mortgagees,[192] joint tenants and tenants in common.[193] It has bound tenants for life[194] and partners.[195] Each of the parties liable may be in what Romer LJ in *Re Biss*[196] meant by persons in a 'special position' to another, to whom, he thought, a rebuttable presumption should apply.

In *Chan v Zacharia*[197] a lease of medical consulting premises was renewed into the name of one of two former partners. The premises were where the partners had conducted their practice. Both applications of the above rule were held to make a former partner a constructive trustee of a renewed lease that he had taken in his own name. First, it was found by Deane J at 197–8 that after dissolution of the partnership each former partner was a trustee for the other in the realization of partnership property. This property included the option to renew the lease which the defendant had exercised in his own name. The strict *Keech v Sandford*[198] trustee rule was held to disallow what the renewing partner did. Secondly, the fiduciary relationship of partnership was held to imply a 'rebuttable presumption of fact' that the renewing partner used

---

188 *Edwards v Lewis* (1747) 3 Atk 538; 26 ER 1110.
189 *James v Dean* (1805) 11 Ves Jun 383; 32 ER 1135.
190 *Killick v Flexney* (1792) 4 Bro CC 161; 29 ER 830—long lease of a farm at low rent.
191 [1903] 2 Ch 40, 57, approved by Deane J in *Chan v Zacharia* (1984) 154 CLR 178, 201.
192 *Leigh v Burnett* (1885) 29 Ch D 231.
193 *Palmer v Young* (1694) 1 Vern 276, [1903] 2 Ch 65n.
194 *Lloyd-Jones v Clark-Lloyd* [1919] 1 Ch 424.
195 *Featherstonehaugh v Fenwick* (1810) 17 Ves 298; 34 ER 115; *Clegg v Fishwick* (1849) 1 Mac & G 294; 41 ER 1278; *Re Biss* [1903] 2 Ch 40 (CA).
196 [1903] 2 Ch 40, 60–1 (CA).
197 (1984) 154 CLR 178.
198 (1726) Sel Cas Ch 61; 25 ER 223.

his former position as partner to obtain the new lease. On the facts, this rebuttable presumption had not been rebutted.[199]

The same principles will apply also to fiduciaries who purchase the reversion of leases held by them in fiduciary capacities.[200] Unless disclosed, a reversion purchased will be a private advantage obtained at the expense of the beneficiary. Waddell J in the Supreme Court of New South Wales examined and distinguished the authorities for this proposition in *Metlej v Kavanagh*.[201] This was concerning the reversion to a lease of solicitors' premises, held by partners as their place of business and then secretly purchased by one partner shortly after the partnership was dissolved. An application by the other partner for a constructive trust of the premises in favour of the partners jointly was refused. In circumstances resembling those in *Chan v Zacharia*,[202] no continuing fiduciary obligations between the former partners were held to exist. On this, probably, the authority of *Metlej* is now questionable.

## B.  Agents

**[5.66]**  Where fiduciary agents are commissioned to employ their principals' property in a certain way, or to make purchases of property for them, the agents may sometimes misapply their principals' property, or make similar purchases for themselves. If this activity is profitable, then the profits will belong to the principal. Meagher, Gummow and Lehane at [527]–[531] deals with the same phenomenon under the heading of 'Cases where a fiduciary is under an obligation not to do for his own benefit what he should have done (if he did it at all) for his principal'.

This is the pre-Judicature Act language discussed by L Sealy.[203] It is a little obscure. We are presumably dealing with the type of liability that the plaintiff argued to exist in *Keith Henry & Co Pty Ltd v Stuart Walker & Co Pty Ltd*.[204] An importer had supplied import licences to the defendant to enable certain goods to pass through customs. The defendant was said to have used the entrusted licences in order to obtain new licences in its own name. The unsuccessful claim in this case highlights that the profit-making must be clearly contrary to the terms of the relevant agency. It may be so if the commission was to make a particular purchase on the principal's account and the fiduciary made it for himself.[205] Or a commodity in short supply may be involved and the agent has increased the scarcity.[206] Or the fiduciary may have made his purchase after holding himself out to the other party as representing the principal.[207]

---

[199]  Ibid, 182-3, Gibbs CJ, 186, Brennan J, 203–4, Deane J, Murphy J dissenting.

[200]  *Protheroe v Protheroe* [1968] 1 All ER 1111; *Thompson's Estate in Bankruptcy v Heaton* [1974] 1 All ER 1239.

[201]  [1981] 2 NSWLR 339, 348–9.

[202]  (1984) 154 CLR 178.

[203]  In 'Some Principles of Fiduciary Obligation' [1963] *CLJ* 119, 132–3.

[204]  (1958) 100 CLR 342, discussed at 351.

[205]  *Robinson v Randfontein Estates Ltd* [1921] AD 168, 179, Innes CJ; *Zwicker v Stanbury* [1952] 4 DLR 344, 357–8 and L Sealy in 'Some Principles of Fiduciary Obligation' [1963] *CLJ* 119, 129.

[206]  *G E Smith Ltd v Smith* [1952] NZLR 470.

[207]  *Boardman v Phipps* [1967] 2 AC 46, especially Lord Guest at 115.

**[5.67]** The agency wrong is illustrated by the case of *Walden Properties Ltd v Beaver Properties Pty Ltd*.[208] A 'co-venture' was involved, between the English investment company, Walden Properties, and two Australian companies. Both Australian companies were owned and controlled by the same person. The venture's purpose was to acquire shares in another company, which was the owner of a valuable building in George Street, Sydney. One of the Australian companies served as agent for the other venturers in negotiations for the share purchase and, it was understood, if the negotiations proved successful, shares purchased by the agent would then be offered to the venturers in equal proportions. In fact Walden was never offered its proportion. A related company of the Australian agent purchased its shares instead. Shortly afterwards, all the shares were sold together for a very substantial profit. Walden as plaintiff argued then that the on-sale to the other venturers which excluded it was in breach of the agent's fiduciary duty. The agent had in effect taken Walden's share in the venture for itself. This the court accepted.[209] In consequence it was ordered that Walden was entitled to receive an accounting of the profit made by both the agent and its related company on the sale.[210] This order was notable, as we will see. Why Walden should have received both the agent's contemplated profit and the wrongful profit of its associated company is not entirely clear.

## C. Partners

**[5.68]** It is provided in the uniform Partnership Acts that:

> Every partner must account to the firm for any benefit derived by him without the consent of the other partners from any transaction concerning the partnership, or from any use by him of the partnership property, name or business connection.[211]

Statute in this way codifies equity's profits rule for partners. The proper 'scope' of partnership obligations, we have seen, is another way to phrase the question about when a personal profit is made within a partnership relation.[212] *United Dominions Corporation Ltd v Brian Pty Ltd*[213] is an instance of the partnership profits rule, when applied to a joint venture not subject to the Partnership Acts. This is a case we have seen before, at [3.12]–[3.13]. Our focus now is upon the opportunity or advantage employed by the profit-making wrongdoer. United Dominions, Brian and Security Projects were three companies that agreed on the joint development of some land in Brisbane. Brian had the idea. Security Projects owned the land. United Dominions was to lend most of the money. Security Projects at the same time owed other money to United Dominions, in respect of borrowing for projects unrelated to the joint venture. When Security Projects executed a mortgage in favour of United Dominions over the development land, the document contained a 'collateralisation clause' in the mortgagee's favour to secure this prior and

---

[208] [1973] 2 NSWLR 815 (CA).

[209] Ibid, 835, Hope JA, applying *Jacobus Marler Estates Ltd v Marler* (1913) 114 LT 640n.

[210] *Ibid.*, Hope JA, 838–839, Kerr CJ agreeing, Hutley JA, 846–8.

[211] NSW, s 29; Qld, s 32; SA s 29; Tas s 34; Vic s 33; WA s 40; ACT s 34 (NZ s 32; UK s 29).

[212] See *Birtchnell v Equity Trustees Executors and Agency Co Ltd* (1929) 42 CLR 384; *Dean v McDowell* (1878) 8 Ch D 345 (CA); *Gibson v Tyree* (1902) 20 NZLR 278.

[213] (1985) 157 CLR 1; see also *Ravinder Rohini Pty Ltd v Krizaic* (1991) 30 FCR 300, 312, Wilcox J, Davies J agreeing (Fed Ct( FC)).

unrelated borrowing as well. The clause purported to secure–

> all amounts from time to time advanced by [United Dominions] to [Security Projects] on any account whatsoever or otherwise owing by [Security Projects] to [United Dominions] and whether advanced to [Security Projects] solely or jointly with another person.

Insertion of such a provision was unknown to Brian. Subsequently, the venture was brought to a successful conclusion and the shopping centre erected on the land was sold at a substantial profit. At this time, for the first time, United Dominions asserted a right to retain all of the profit on the venture because of the other indebtedness of Security Projects. This was pursuant to the 'collateralisation clause'.

[5.69] The venturer Brian was the plaintiff in *United Dominions* and it alleged that United Dominions was unable to rely on a term of the mortgage which had the effect of securing, as against it, what was otherwise part of its profit share. Withholding of the amount of this was said to be a breach of fiduciary duty. Mason, Brennan and Deane JJ (at 13) expressed the relation between the venturers as follows:

> each [venturer] participant was under a fiduciary duty to refrain from pursuing, obtaining or retaining for itself or himself any collateral advantage in relation to the proposed project without the knowledge or informed assent of the other participants.

By the 'collateralisation clause', United Dominions was alleged to have used the land intended for the joint venture to obtain a collateral advantage for itself. In the event, it was destructive of Brian's interest in the venture and secret stipulation for the clause was a breach of the mutual duties that venturers owe.

[5.70] Other members of the High Court in *United Dominions* accepted the contentions in the joint judgment. Referring to the mortgage terms, Gibbs CJ said (at 8) that '[United Dominions] is bound to account to Brian for the improper advantage which it obtained'.

Dawson J agreed with the joint judgment. The consequent remedy was simply to declare that the 'collateralisation clause' was unenforceable against Brian.[214] Entitlement to the profit sum withheld did not require an account or constructive trust to become effective. Fiduciary wrongdoing found to have been committed in United Dominions was to some extent mirrored by that found in *Fraser Edmiston Pty Ltd v AGT (Qld) Pty Ltd*.[215] In that case an optometry shop tenant of a shopping centre had priority in obtaining a lease of new space in the centre. Through its manager, the tenant approached another optometrist with a view to conducting a partnership business in that space. After some inconclusive negotiations, the other optometrist used a 'letter of acceptance' of the new lease that it obtained from the optometrist tenant to take a lease of the new space in its own name. This seizure of an intending partner's opportunity was duly restrained. The wrong argued in *Lac Minerals Ltd v International Corona Resources Ltd*,[216] is also comparable. As described

---

[214] Ibid, 13–14, Mason, Brennan and Deane JJ.

[215] (1986) 2 Qd R 1; see also *Gibb Australia Pty Ltd v Cremor Pty Ltd* (1992) 108 FLR 129 (SC (ACT) (FC)).

[216] [1989] 2 SCR 574 (SC (Can)).

at [3.100]–[3.101], a smaller company's mineral discovery was disclosed to a much larger company in the course of discussing a 'mutual business arrangement' between them. The discovery was then misused. In *Edmiston* the parties had agreed in principle upon a partnership and in *Lac Minerals* a joint arrangement of some kind was contemplated. In each case the wrongdoer took a secret benefit outside the parties' mutual understanding.

## D. Directors

**[5.71]** The principle here is that said to be applicable in *Webb v Stanfield*,[217] that:

> A director of a company who misappropriates to himself property, rights and advantages that ought to have been acquired for the company is liable to account to the company for benefits so acquired.

Although failing on a factual basis, the claim in that case concerned a director's profit-making in contravention of the rule. The company had been set up by persons who became its two directors. The idea was to carry on insurance business in Queensland as agent for the 'Capita Assurance Group'. However, within six months, expectations had not been met and the company entered liquidation. One of the founding directors later arranged for a company of his own to enter an agency agreement with Capita, to the exclusion of the other director and the company in liquidation. The 'opportunity' of agency business was arguably withheld from the original company incorporated to acquire it.

In the taxonomy of reasonings that this book supplies, we will here describe some superseded reasoning in older 'corporate opportunity' decisions. It is mentioned so that it can be avoided. Until recent years, it has been assumed that when opportunities were diverted, wrongs *in personam* were done. 'Property' analysis was seen so to characterise the 'opportunity' subtracted from the beneficiaries. It was in the nature of an expectancy. In the case of company directors, there was always some high authority to the contrary. The agency principle we saw at [5.66] was applied. Namely, if particular property should have been acquired by the agent in the course of the agency, then, if the agent acquires property of that description, he or she is treated as having done so for the principal. Directors seeking business for their companies were treated analogously. Their diversion of companies' opportunities of the kind that they were appointed to seek was treated as a subtraction of the property of those companies. 'In equity', opportunities diverted from companies are thus the property of the companies. The idea corresponds to the 'equity' described in *Jacobus Marler Estates Ltd v Marler*. After the commencement of the agency, a principal can claim property from an agent as his own if the agent was employed to acquire it.[218]

**[5.72]** The Privy Council decision in *Cook v Deeks* is a clear statement of this approach.[219] Deeks and two others were directors of the Toronto

---

[217] (1990) 2 ACLR 283, 285, McPherson J, curiam (SC (Qld) (FC)).

[218] (1913) 114 LT 640n, 641, Lord Parker; application of this reasoning to company directors is discussed in MGL [528]–[529].

[219] [1916] 1 AC 554, see also *Parker v McKenna* (1874) 10 Ch App 96 (CA); *Henderson v Huntington Copper and Sulphur Co* [1877] 5 R 1 (HL); *Albion Wire and Steel Co v Martin* (1875) 1 Ch D 580; *Phosphate Sewage Co v Hartmont* (1877) 5 Ch D 394 (CA); *Re Imperial Land Co of Marseilles Ex parte Larking* (1877) 4 Ch D 566.

Construction Co. This was a company which had for some time done construction work for the Canadian Pacific Railway Co. The work was done satisfactorily and a business relationship was established between the Railway Co and the directors of the Toronto Co. This enabled those directors to recommend to the Railway Co that a certain new construction contract be let to the directors' own company instead of the Toronto Co. Then the directors sought to insulate themselves against claims from the Toronto Co. A general meeting of members was called, at which the directors controlled three-quarters of the votes. That meeting duly ratified the directors' appropriation of the contract opportunity. In these circumstances, a shareholder in the Toronto Co sued. He was also a dissentient director. Other directors were alleged to have diverted business in their own favour which should properly have belonged to the company. Further, the wrong was said to be of a type that could not be ratified or approved. The dissentient's claim was upheld by the Privy Council. The Board began by stating a principle relevant to the profits rule (at 564): where directors who are entrusted with the affairs of a company deliberately try to exclude the company, the directors 'must account to [the company] for profits which they have made out of the transaction.' The exculpatory effect of the members' ratification was then overcome by the Board finding that the diverted contract with the Railway Co was part of the 'property or rights which [the directors] must be regarded as holding on behalf of the company'.

The contract was said to be held for the Toronto Co notwithstanding that it never became a party and the company might never have learnt of the contract, but for the dissentient.

**[5.73]**    The members' exculpatory resolution in *Cook v Deeks*[220] was held to be incompetent. Any 'interest and property' of the company could not be divested from it to the detriment of the minority. As the Board found on the facts,

> the contract in question was entered into under such circumstances that the directors could not retain the benefit of it for themselves, then it belonged in equity to the company . . . a resolution that the rights of the company should be disregarded in the matter would amount to forfeiting the interest and property of the minority of shareholders in favour of the majority, and that by the votes of those who are interested in securing the property for themselves. Such use of voting power has never been sanctioned by the courts . . .

The contract appropriated was, in equity, a bundle of the company's prospective rights. On the basis of this it was said that a proprietary wrong had been committed. Diversion of these expectant rights was treated as equivalent to an improper gift of the company's property, or theft. No meeting of the company's members could thus expropriate a dissentient. This use of property analysis to justify an equitable intervention in corporate affairs was followed in a number of cases.[221] Yet in what sense can anyone be deprived of property in a mere expectancy? The hold of the property paradigm in the

---

[220] [1916] 1 AC 554, 564 (PC).

[221] See, eg, *EBM Co Ltd v Dominion Bank* [1937] 3 All ER 555 (PC); *Maddams v Miller's (Invercargill) Ltd* [1937] NZLR 843; *Peninsular and Oriental Steam Navigation Co Ltd v Johnson* (1938) 60 CLR 189.

'corporate opportunity' cases never was strong. After 1942, this approach to the matter may only be a footnote. It seems to have been entirely displaced by the 'causal' and 'temporal' links proposed in Lord Russell's speech in *Regal (Hastings) Ltd v Gulliver*.[222] These are examined above.

### Competition with beneficiaries

**[5.74]**    Unless a beneficiary consents, a fiduciary may not profit from carrying on a business in competition with that carried on by or for the beneficiary.[223] Partners[224] and corporate officers[225] are the usual type of fiduciary found to have infringed this aspect of the profits rule. The rule, regarding partners, is thus codified in the uniform Partnership Acts:[226]

> If a partner, without the consent of the other partners, carries on any business of the same nature as and competing with that of the firm, he must account for and pay over to the firm all profits made by him in that business.

**[5.75]**    The critical question here is very often whether competition has in fact occurred between the fiduciary and those to whom fiduciary duties are owed. Does, for example, a ship*broking* business carried on by a partner on his own compete with a ship*building* business he carries on in partnership?[227] Does the publication of a morning newspaper compete with the publication of an evening newspaper?[228] P Higgins and K Fletcher observe in their *Law of Partnership in Australia and New Zealand*[229] that:

> The mere fact that the business carried on by a partner is similar in nature to that of the partnership does not render that partner accountable unless it does in fact compete.

First, the allegedly competing activity of a fiduciary director, partner or employee must be isolated. Then the task is to see whether that profit-making activity is within the reach of the relationship's fiduciary obligations. So, in *Hivac Ltd v Park Royal Scientific Instruments Ltd*,[230] an employee who accepted a part-time paying job with a competing firm was held to be in breach of duty. Receiving rewards from the competition was too great a disloyalty. In other cases, the question may be approached from the direction of the relationship itself. Namely, by a determination of the proper *scope* of the relationship, as made in *Trimble v Goldberg*.[231] Some partners in a 'single venture partnership' (which we would now call a joint venture) were held not liable to account for profits they made in a competing venture engaged in on the side. The single venture was not seen to comprehend any other. In relation to competition with the beneficiary, there is also a question as to the effect of a fiduciary's resignation from office prior to commencing the competition. A literal breach of the profits rule might thereby be avoided. We will consider

---

[222] (1942) [1967] 2 AC 134n, 149–52.

[223] Goff & Jones 648.

[224] Eg, *Fleming v McKecknie* (1906) 25 NZLR 216; *Aas v Benham* [1891] 2 Ch 244 (CA).

[225] Eg, *Canadian Aero Service Ltd v O'Malley* (1973) 40 DLR (3d) 371.

[226] NSW s 30; Qld s 33; SA s 30; Tas s 35; Vic s 34; WA s 41; ACT s 35 (cf NZ s 33; UK s 30).

[227] See *Aas v Benham* [1891] 2 Ch 244 (CA).

[228] See *Glassington v Thwaites* (1822) 1 Sim & St 124; 57 ER 50.

[229] 4th ed (1981), 175.

[230] [1946] Ch 169.

[231] [1906] AC 494 (PC).

this in relation to the fiduciary liability of company directors. It should be noted here that there is authority that directors and others who resign from fiduciary office in order to compete will still be in breach of the profits rule to the extent that any profits are earned thereby.[232]

**[5.76]** Fiduciaries' profits from competition may be claimed by the company, a co-partner or any other person to whom fiduciary duties are owed. Either a constructive trust or an accounting may be used for the purpose.[233] This, as we will see, can be either a proprietary or a personal entitlement. It can be justified on the theory that profits made by the fiduciary would have otherwise been made by the person or business wronged. But what of the expenses that the fiduciary incurred in order to derive the profit? Justice would suggest that even though the fiduciary's entire profit was made in breach of duty, the measure of the fiduciary's liability will be reduced by costs that he incurred. We will consider 'just allowances' together with *Remedies* at [6.89]. At this stage one example of what it concerns will suffice.

In *W J Christie & Co Ltd v Sussex Realty & Insurance Agency Ltd*[234] a former director and employee of the plaintiff company started a competing business with a company of his own. He directly solicited property management and insurance agency business from the plaintiff's clients. Defendant company was found liable to pay 'damages' equal to its total receipts from the former clients of the plaintiff. It was argued on appeal that this was excessive for two reasons. First, it was said that some business of the plaintiff would have inevitably moved across to the defendant, regardless of the objectionable solicitation. This reason does not concern allowances. Instead, it objects to the measure of the breach. Disallowing this, the court said that the defendant's wrongful solicitations (at 42) 'forever foreclosed knowledge as to whether and when clients would have transferred allegiance.' Secondly, the damages sum was said to be too large in not reflecting the cost of doing business that either party must have incurred. This reason concerned allowances. As the breach itself was not thereby challenged, this defence was allowed.

### Speculation with fiduciary property

**[5.77]** All profits made from speculation with the property of beneficiaries belong to the beneficiaries and constructive trusts or profit accounting may be ordered to effectuate the right. Liability for this breach of the profits rule differs from the others we have seen. Not only a fiduciary rule may be involved. A legal aspect of property ownership is often asserted. For profits made from the property of another, it has been said, 'are so much fruit, so much increase on the estate or chattel of [the other], and must follow the ownership of the property and go to the proprietor'.

This was in the case of *Docker v Somes*.[235] A beneficiary under an estate made a claim against the executor for an account of trading profits the executor made with moneys not accounted for. It was treated as significant to the

---

[323] See [*Industrial Development Consultants Ltd v Cooley* [1972] 1 WLR 443.

[233] See Goff & Jones 646–7.

[234] [1981] 4 WWR 34 (Manitoba CA), Huband J, curiam.

[235] (1834) 2 My & K 655; 39 ER 1095, 1098, Lord Brougham, LC.

outcome that the beneficiary asserted a right of ownership in respect of the money and not just a personal right to be paid. If the defendant were only a judgment debtor his liability could not exceed the sum plus interest. Proprietary entitlement to the profits was alleged.[236] In *Vyse v Foster*,[237] a similar proprietary entitlement to speculative profits claim was upheld, based on the legal wrong of 'money had and received'. The principle is not a fiduciary one. Property owners are entitled as of course to follow profits derived from their property into the hands of persons who obtain them. Those persons are often wrongdoers. Sometimes they can be classed as fiduciaries. Authorities dealing with fiduciaries who have committed this breach of the profits rule tend to express liability in terms of property rights rather than fiduciary wrongdoing.[238]

**[5.78]**   There is no doubt that this 'proprietary' type of reasoning applies equally to intangible (or 'soft') property, as to property of the more type. Profitable misuse of designs, trade marks or formulae are within this wider sense of the category. So Mason J (dissenting) said in *Hospital Products Ltd v United States Surgical Corporation*[239] that HPI was a 'fiduciary custodian' of USSC's property in 'product goodwill'. Following McLelland J at first instance, he ordered a proprietary constructive trust to make HPI account for profits made from misuse of that interest.

**[5.79]**   The effect of *mixtures* of property on a speculative profits claim is not always clear. We are referring here to the beneficiaries' claim in equity to the profits derived in part from their property and in part from other property, which may include either the fiduciaries' own property, or that of third parties. Mixtures of the beneficiary's property with that of other persons is a subject complicated by an excess of doctrine: in particular, the neighbouring existence of common law and equitable tracing techniques with different rules. Equity has established its own regime to govern whether a plaintiff is able to follow a property entitlement into part of the property held in the name of another. We will examine it in more detail at [6.38]–[6.47].

**[5.80]**   *Scott v Scott*[240] is an illustration of a profits claim made against a fiduciary who mixed profit-making property of the beneficiary with his own. A trustee misappropriated trust moneys in 1942 to purchase a house and added some of his own funds to make up the full price. Many years later he repaid the funds taken to the trust. Shortly after that he died. The land had by this time substantially risen in value. So the incoming trustee sought to recover against the former trustee's estate a sum equal to the proportion of the increase in value in the land which the misappropriated trust funds bore to the original purchase price. The proprietary claim was pro-rated, in effect. Misappropriation was not denied by the estate at trial. As a consequence and

---

[236] See *Yorkshire Railway Co v Hudson* (1853) 22 LJ Ch 529; *Kirkham v Peel* (1881) 44 LT 195: further on proprietary entitlement, see [6.105]–[6.115].

[237] (1872) 8 Ch App 309, 333, Sir W James, LJ.

[238] *Re Patten and the Guardians of the Poor* (1883) 52 LJ Ch 787; *Soloway v McLaughlin* [1938] AC 247 (PC); *Brown v IRC* [1965] AC 244 and authorities referred to in Ford & Lee [1720]–[1725] ('Tracing—Mixture of funds').

[239] (1984) 156 CLR 41, 101.

[240] (1962) 109 CLR 649.

apart from the reimbursement, the former trustee's estate was found liable to concurrent personal and proprietary remedies. At 660 the court allowed the incoming trustee's election to take the proprietary route to the larger sum. The basis of the trust's argument, the court said, was twofold. It rested equally upon:

> the liability of [the former trustee] to make good a breach of trust and also upon his liability to account for a profit which accrued to him, or to his estate, as a result of his misuse of trust funds. These are two different and distinct notions. A trustee's liability to account for profits accruing to him may arise without any positive breach of trust; on the other hand, a trustee may become liable to make good a misapplication of trust moneys with interest even though he has made no profit by the misapplication. But where the expenditure of moneys constitutes a breach of trust the remedies may overlap for the beneficiaries may have both a proprietary and personal remedy and, of course, if they chose to pursue the former this will be the full measure of relief available to them.

The profits rule and proprietary remedies were distinguished along these lines. In *Re Tilley's Will Trusts*,[241] however, on similar facts to *Scott v Scott*, an English court came to an opposite conclusion. The view taken there was that misappropriated trust funds paid into an (overdrawn) bank account could not be treated as the 'source' of funds for profitable speculations that the trustee made. The proprietary remedy was unavailable. When the trustee died, the trust was only entitled to its money back.

**[5.81]**    If fiduciaries make profits by speculation with bribes paid to them whilst on fiduciary business, it seems that profits made on these are also recoverable on a proprietary rationale.[242] The profits may be treated as increase in the value of the beneficiary's property. As appears in the next paragraph, there appears now to be no distinction drawn between a profit directly taken out of a beneficiary's hands and a bribe that the fiduciary receives from a third party. The remedial consequence of an obligation to account is the same. A constructive trust in favour of the beneficiary will be awarded in respect of this type of profit obtained by the fiduciary from fiduciary office. Lord Templeman in *Attorney General for Hong Kong v Reid* drew out the implications of this for the proceeds of speculation with bribes. The case was concerned with a former Crown Prosecutor in Hong Kong who had received substantial bribes over many years. In the names of his wife and solicitor, the prosecutor invested the bribes in three New Zealand properties. The prosecutor was caught and imprisoned and the Hong Kong authorities caveated the relevant land. When application was made to renew the caveats, the New Zealand courts followed established authority in the English Court of Appeal to the effect that the principal of a bribed agent has no proprietary interest in the bribe or property representing it. This was taken to exclude this application of the fiduciary profits rule. The Hong Kong authorities appealed to the Privy Council and Lord Templeman, for the Board, stated that the relevant principle was quite different. It was simply that:

---

[241] [1967] 1 Ch 1179, 1193, Ungoed-Thomas J.

[242] *Attorney General for Hong Kong v Reid* [1994] 1 AC 324, 331–2 (PC); *Sugden v Crossland* (1856) 3 Sm & G 192, 65 ER 620; cf *Metropolitan Bank v Heiron* (1880) 5 Ex D 319; *Lister & Co v Stubbs* (1890) 45 Ch D 1 (CA); *Islamic Republic of Iran v Denby* [1987] 1 Ll LR 367, 370–1, Leggatt J and 15.2 Laws [69].

if the bribe consists of property which increases in value or if a cash bribe is invested advantageously, the false fiduciary will receive a benefit from his breach of duty unless he is accountable for the original amount or value of the bribe but also for the increased value of the property representing the bribe. As soon as the bribe was received it should have been paid or transferred instanter to the person who suffered the breach of duty. Equity considers as done that which ought to be done. As soon as the bribe was received, whether in cash or in kind, the false fiduciary held the bribe on constructive trust for the beneficiary.

This was said to be justified by the decision in *Keech v Sandford*[243] and other basic profits rule authorities that preceded the two main Court of Appeal decisions.[244]

### Receiving bribes and secret commissions

**[5.82]** Bribes and secret commissions are the same thing.[245]

A bribe is a gift accepted by a fiduciary as an inducement to him to betray his trust.[246]

A bribed fiduciary is one who accepts undisclosed advantages to procure actions or decisions in the course of his fiduciary office.[247] Not all secret benefits from trust property, nor all benefits obtained from knowledge acquired in the course of acting as a fiduciary, amount to bribes. In order to qualify, the benefits must have been conferred in order to influence one or more of a fiduciary's decisions taken in the execution of his office. Failure to disclose the receipt of a bribe to the beneficiary or principal is an important aspect of the fiduciary's liability. A necessary characteristic of a 'bribe' in these circumstances is that it is a receipt not actually or impliedly consented to by the person to whom fiduciary duties are owed.[248] But secrecy is not enough. A vendor's undisclosed payment to 'a middleman employed merely to bring the vendor and the purchaser together' may not be a bribe at all. Such a payment by the vendor in *Clark v Hepworth and Michener, Carscallen & Co*[249] was said to be 'common practice' and not such as to knowingly infringe any 'relation of trust and confidence' which might have arisen between the same middleman and the purchaser. The 'middleman' in that case seems to have been an ordinary estate agent and the purchaser was a retired colonel from the British army, who had employed the agent to find a suitable house for his Canadian retirement. The vendor was said to be unaware of this when he paid the agent.

**[5.83]** Receipt of bribes by fiduciaries is ipso facto a breach of their fiduciary duties. This is regardless of whether the beneficiaries are harmed or not.[250] It is presumed 'irrebuttably' that fiduciaries are influenced away from their duties

---

243 (1726) Cas t King 61, 25 ER 223.

244 *Metropolitan Bank v Heiron* (1880) 5 Ex D 319 and *Lister & Co v Stubbs* (1890) 45 Ch D 1.

245 See *Industries & General Mortgage Co Ltd v Lewis* [1949] 2 All ER 573, 575, Slade J.

246 *Attorney General for Hong Kong v Reid* [1994] 1 AC 324, 331, Lord Templeman (PC).

247 Paraphrasing Romer LJ in *Hovenden and Sons v Millhoff* (1900) 83 LT 41, 43 (CA).

248 Goff & Jones 655–6, citing *Great Western Insurance Co of New York v Cunliffe* (1874) 9 Ch App 525, *Baring v Stanton* (1876) 3 Ch D 502 and *Stubbs v Slater* [1910] 1 Ch 632.

249 [1918] 1 WWR 147, 151, Fitzpatrick CJ (SC (Alta) (FC)).

250 *Boston Deep Sea Fishing and Ice Co v Ansell* (1888) 39 Ch D 339, 355, Cotton LJ.

by such receipts.[251] The beneficiary has an equitable right to recover the bribe (or its amount) from his bribed fiduciary. This is old law. In *Mahesan S/O Thambiah v Malaysia Government Officers' Co-Operative Housing Society Ltd*[252] Lord Diplock observed for the Privy Council that:

> By the early years of the nineteenth century it had become an established principle of equity that an agent who received any secret advantage for himself from the other party to a transaction in which the agent was acting for his principal was bound to account for it to his principal: *Fawcett v Whitehouse* . . . The remedy was equitable, obtainable in the Court of Chancery, and there appears to be no reported case at common law for recovery of a bribe by a principal from his agent before the Judicature Act 1875.

We will not be concerned here with the collateral right a beneficiary may have to recover a bribe from the other party—the briber. Nor are we concerned with the action to recover damages in deceit from the briber or the fiduciary for loss that the bribe may have caused.[253]

**[5.84]**    Equity, a little surprisingly, does not figure in the majority of decided cases concerning recovery of bribes. This is even where the bribees are fiduciaries. The equitable claim was for long passed over in favour of the legal action of 'money had and received'.[254] Recovery through the money counts was once believed to be a more straightforward thing. It was until recently part of a more fashionable remedy system. Hence, concerning the legal and equitable routes to the recovery of bribes, Isaacs J said in 1915 in *Ardelthan Options Ltd v Easdown*[255] that:

> Money or money's worth received in that way is received not in trust for, but to the use of the employer. The fraudulent servant or agent, in such a case, is not a trustee of the property, but a debtor in respect of the money or money's worth he has received. The full extent of the benefit he surreptitiously receives, he owes to his employer as an equitable debt, because the mere receipt of the benefit in such circumstances is a fraud on his employer, and he cannot be allowed to retain it if the employer claims it . . . this species of fraud, faithlessness to an employer, is necessarily confined to the employee himself, and its consequences are limited to the benefit he receives.

It is true, nevertheless, that the association of money had and received and equitable recovery was always strong. Here this is perhaps even more marked than in other areas.[256] When a case arose which tested the limits of whether a bribe could be recovered under the money counts, recourse was typically had to equity as a tiebreaker. Equitable relief was sought as an alternative claim

---

[251] *Hovenden and Sons v Millhoff* (1900) 83 LT 41, 43, Romer LJ (CA).

[252] [1979] AC 374, 380.

[253] See C Needham 'Recovering the Profits of Bribery' (1979) 95 L Q R 736 for a more comprehensive account.

[254] In *Ardelthan Options Ltd v Easdown* (1915) 20 CLR 285 (company director); *Metropolitan Bank v Heiron* (1880) 5 Ex D 319 (CA) (company director); *Boston Deep Sea Fishing and Ice Co v Ansell* (1888) 39 Ch D 339 (CA) (company director); *Lister & Co v Stubbs* (1890) 45 Ch D 1 (CA) (purchasing agent); *Andrews v Ramsay & Co* [1903] 2 KB 635 (CA) (auctioneer); *Powell & Thomas v Evan Jones & Co* [1905] 1 KB 11 (CA) (borrower's agent); *Attorney-General v Goddard* (1929) 98 LJKB 743 (police officer); *Reading v R* [1948] 2 KB 268 (army sergeant—first instance only).

[255] (1915) 20 CLR 285, 292.

[256] Goff & Jones c. 1 and 654–8.

in the same suit. *Attorney-General v Goddard*[257] was such a case, where the right tested was that of the Crown to recover bribes taken by a police officer and deposited in the bribee's bank. Could the officer receive money 'for and to the use of' the Crown by acting illegally? Of course, Rowlatt J said, 'the constable was never an agent to receive profits for the Crown'. The Crown does not accept bribes. Common law recovery was thus caught in the travails of its own fiction. The relevant 'use' of the money count was found to arise in equity instead.[258]

**[5.85]**　*Reading v Attorney-General* is a similar and more celebrated example of these two ways of recovering bribes from a bribee.[259] The facts of a sergeant's claim to retain the bribes he received on overseas service have been set out above (at [3.11]). Denning J, at first instance, took a purely common law view of the case. He held that there was no fiduciary relationship between the sergeant and the Crown. Instead, he upheld the Crown's right to the bribes as money had and received and denied that the bribes that the Crown had confiscated should be returned. No precedent was cited for this use of the money count. Denning J simply said at 277 that Reading 'must not be allowed to enrich himself in this way':

> . . . the wearing of the King's uniform and his position as a soldier is the sole cause of his getting the money, and getting it dishonestly.

On appeal to the Court of Appeal the absence of precedent below was referred to, but to no avail. For the Court of Appeal based its reasons for recovery in equity and found a fiduciary relationship to exist between Reading and his employer.[260] At least this was 'in a very loose, or at all events a very comprehensive sense': 'the uniform and the opportunities and facilities attached to it' had been used. Recovery was placed on a more familiar basis. The equitable rule that beneficiaries may recover bribes received by their fiduciaries was applied and then unanimously confirmed by the House of Lords on appeal.[261] This was a use of the profits rule independently of proprietary reasoning.

**[5.86]**　Lord Templeman in *Attorney General for Hong Kong v Reid*[262] has now strongly emphasised that it is appropriate to use fiduciary obligations and the profits rule in order to recover bribes. We have already considered this case in relation to profits earned by a fiduciary in speculating with a beneficiary's property. The nature of a beneficiary's interest in the bribe itself was found to entail ownership of speculative profits. But the case may also have cleared the fiduciary canon of a troublesome qualification relating to the fiduciary's obligation to account. It will now less confidently be suggested that some different juridical basis applies to the account for bribes, as compared to the account for other benefits, for the fact that bribes were originally the property of someone else. The bribee's account is just another species of the

---

[257] (1929) 98 LJKB 743.
[258] At 756, see also *Andrews v Ramsay & Co* [1903] 2 KB 635, 636 (CA), Lord Alverstone CJ.
[259] [1948] 2 KB 268, affd [1949] 2 KB 232 (CA), affd [1951] AC 507.
[260] [1949] 2 KB 232, 236, curiam (Asquith LJ).
[261] [1951] AC 507, 516, Lord Porter, 517, Lord Norman, 517-8, Lord Oaksey, 518, Lord Radcliffe.
[262] [1994] 1 AC 324 (PC).

rule that property which a fiduciary obtains by use of knowledge acquired as fiduciary is held on constructive trust for the benficiary.[263] But the other view has had its defenders in recent times. These are commentators who see 'want of a sufficient proprietary base' in the claim of a bribee's beneficiary[264]— which may take a rather nineteenth century view of what equity can do.

### Misuse of confidential information

**[5.87]** A breach of the profits rule is committed by fiduciaries who profit through the misuse of confidential information acquired in the course of a fiduciary relationship. This is a matter which has been discussed above at [1.24].

# The proper purposes duty

**[5.88]** Both the 'proper purposes' duty and the 'conflicts rule' examine the *purposes* that fiduciaries have in carrying out their duties. Between individuals, fiduciaries' improper purposes almost always take the form of a conflict of their personal interests and their fiduciary duties. Or the conflict may be between fiduciary duties owed to one beneficiary and fiduciary duties owed to another. The 'proper purpose' of a fiduciary equals his or her duty to each claimant. This is quite straightforward. It is assumed every time a conflict is held to have occurred. With an artificial legal person, though, like a corporation, this scheme no longer applies as easily. Much litigation has surrounded the issue of how corporate fiduciaries' duties are to be expressed. Even more litigation has been waged on the subject of whether, in ambiguous circumstances, the duties of corporate fiduciaries have been fulfilled. 'Proper purposes' as a discriminant between different acts of fiduciaries allows for a wider expression of what circumstances are invalidating than 'conflicts' of either type. Conflicts between the fiduciary's interest and duty or between duty and duty are not particularly focussed on the breach of duty which enures to the benefit of third parties. The proper purposes duty is. But the ideas are essentially the same. For this reason we will examine the 'proper purposes' rule and the 'conflicts' rule in separate case studies, which at the same time pertain to fiduciary duties in general.

# Fiduciary duties: two case studies

### 1. FIDUCIARY DUTIES OF COMPANY DIRECTORS

**[5.89]** This is a vexed subject. Company directors are liable to stringent and ambiguous fiduciary duties: duties themselves are often said to be owed to two or more persons or interests. Directorship of a company is unlike other fiduciary capacities. Owing fiduciary duties to a company is unlike owing them to any other beneficiary. The reason is simple. Companies cannot act independently of their directors. At least, this is so whilst companies are not insolvent or otherwise subject to external administration under the

---

[263] Ibid, 5; explicitly approving this view of P Millett in 'Bribes and Secret Commissions' [1993] RLR 1, 23–6.

[264] See Birks, 389; also P Birks 'Obligations and Property in Equity: *Lister v Stubbs* in the Limelight' [1993] *LMCLQ* 30 and R Nolan (1994) *Co Law* 3.

Corporations Law. Directors are part of the company itself, one of its constitutive organs. One of the results is that directors are not subject to the same interference or control that most other fiduciaries are regulated by.[265] Fiduciary wrongs are harder to detect. Our examination for this subject will begin with the second point of difference that we alluded to.

## To whom do directors owe fiduciary duties?

**[5.90]** To find the identity of the person or persons to whom directors' fiduciary duties are owed we will begin with a related proposition—one which has almost axiomatic force. 'Directors', it is often said, 'must act bona fide for the benefit of the company as a whole'. Authority for this is usually associated with what Lindley LJ said in *Allen v Gold Reefs of West Africa Ltd.*[266] Latham CJ endorsed it in *Richard Brady Franks Ltd v Price*[267] and *Peters American Delicacy Co v Heath.*[268] Having cited the authority of the dictum in *Mills v Mills,*[269] Dixon J said that:

> Although 'the best interests of the company' is an indefinite phrase, its meaning admits of little doubt.

The dictum phrased as a norm is partly codified by s 232 of the Corporations Law. Directors must not serve the interests of any one organ of the company to the exclusion of others. They must not serve any one contending faction or interest in the company and not the rest. Directors are obliged to serve the company as a whole. Accordingly, the company 'as a whole' is unquestionably a proper beneficiary of its directors' fiduciary obligations.[270]

**[5.91]** After about a hundred and fifty years of companies, the various aspects of corporate personality seem clear in theory. Distinction without thinking is made between the individuals who compose the corporate entity and the entity itself. Companies are distinct from the directors, shareholders and others in the organs that comprise them. 'Corporate personality' may not now be the jurisprudence conundrum it once was.[271] But corporate personality is yet an idea said still to have only an imperfect hold over the legal imagination. In the words of Len Sealy:[272]

> Nearly a hundred years after it was ruled in *Shalom v Shalom & Co Ltd* ... that Mr Psalmodies' company was in every respect a separate enterprise, we have still not faced up fully to the implications of that decision. The tradition that 'the company' to which directors' duties are owed is the constituency of the shareholders, viewed collectively, has lingered on right into the 1980s.

---

[265] S Worthington 'Directors' Duties, Creditors' Rights and Shareholder Intervention' (1991) 18 *MULR* 121, 151.

[266] [1900] 1 Ch 656, 671–4.

[267] (1937) 58 CLR 112, 135.

[268] (1939) 61 CLR 457, 480.

[269] (1938) 60 CLR 150, 187–8.

[270] Re *Horsley & Weight Ltd* [1982] 1 Ch 442, 453–4, Buckley LJ; also Gower 550–1; *Palmer's Company Law* 25th edn (1992), 8.502.

[271] For older treatments, see *Salmond on Jurisprudence* 12th edn P Fitzgerald (1966), 328–30 and *Textbook of Jurisprudence* 4th edn G Paton and D Derham (1972), 403–25.

[272] 'Directors' Duties—Striking the Right Balance Between Accountability and Freedom of Action', paper presented to the 9th Commonwealth Law Conference, Auckland 1992: *Papers* 99, 102.

Indeed, the expression 'company as a whole' in our axiom is often taken to mean 'the corporators' as a body. The people, that is, in the company's organs. This was the view of the High Court in *Ngurli v McCann*.[273] In principle, it has been said that—[274]

> all powers granted to a corporation or to the management of a corporation, or to any group within a corporation, whether derived from statute or charter or both, are necessarily and at all times extricable only for the rateable benefit of all the shareholders as their interest appears ... in consequence, the *use* of the power is subject to equitable limitation when the power has been exercised to the detriment of such interest ...

**[5.92]** Exclusivity of 'the company' as the object of directors' fiduciary duties has been questioned in recent times. Duties owed to the company have been argued to include protection of the interests other than the company's own interests. Fiduciary duties in this formulation take on a somewhat improbable, 'other regarding' form. Liquidators, particularly, have been successful in pursuing funds misapplied and property diverted through directors' misfeasance for the benefit of creditors. The outcome of the High Court decision in *Walker v Wimborne*[275] is a well known example. It ordered directors to restore certain assets of a company to its liquidator. This was after the assets had been misappropriated by the directors in breach of fiduciary duty that they owed to the company. Creditors were able to assert a wrong done to the company in order to further their own ends. The assets, it was said, would have been available to pay the creditors but for the directors' misappropriation. *Kinsela v Russell Kinsela Pty Ltd*[276] was comparable. The court found, in circumstances where the company was insolvent or nearing insolvency, that directors were under a fiduciary duty to avoid action contrary to the interests of creditors. *Gallardin Pty Ltd (rec and mgr apptd) v Aimworth Pty Ltd (in liq)*[277] was another comparable decision. Perry J in the Supreme Court of South Australia found that an 'asset shuffle' and alterations to intercompany accounts were the product of an evident 'desire to keep assets out of the reach of creditors.' Given the state of the companies at the time of the transfer of assets, he held that the directors' duty to the company required them to take into account the interests of creditors. Again the wider duty was linked to insolvency.

Dyson Heydon has said that the expression 'bona fide for the benefit of the company as a whole' has received at least four inconsistent judicial formulations.[278] Three of these are said to conflate persons interested in the company with the company itself. Courts, it would seem, are in various ways unwilling to conceive of companies in accord with the paradigm of corporate personality. This can particularly be seen in authorities where the expression 'company' is used as a collective noun. If only the corporation as an abstract entity was meant, why confuse the corporation with the corporators?

---

[273] (1953) 90 CLR 425, 438, curiam.

[274] A Berle 'Corporate Powers as Powers in Trust' (1931) 44 *Harv LR* 1049, 1049.

[275] (1976) 137 CLR 1, discussed further below at [5.98].

[276] (1986) 10 ACLR 395; see also *Nicholson v Permakraft (NZ) Ltd* (1985) 3 ACLC 453; *Grove v Flavell* [1986] 43 SASR 410; 4 ACLC 654 and Ford [8.090].

[277] (1993) 11 ACSR 23, 28–9.

[278] 'Director's Duties and the Company's Interests' in Finn *Relationships* 120, 120–34.

**[5.93]**   There is a sense in which it cannot be right that directors' duties are owed only to the company.[279] Think of the typical company. Directors are entrusted with the management of its business. This is what its articles usually provide, in theory, by way of 'statutory contract' between the company's directors and shareholders.[280] To the extent that management of the business imposes fiduciary obligations on the directors, those obligations must be owed to the company. No other person can command the directors' responsibility. That was the point of incorporation: limited liability for shareholders subject to governance according to contract. However, assuming that the articles resemble Table A, the directors will also have a number of other powers. Many of them are not concerned with running the company's business. They include powers which relate to the company's ownership and capital structure, such as:

1. the power to make calls for unpaid capital (Table A, reg 12);
2. the power to issue new shares (reg 37);
3. the power to forfeit shares (reg 26); and
4. the power to refuse to register share transfers (reg 21).

Companies cannot own their own capital in Australia. One consequence of this may be that directors' powers to affect capital ownership cannot be susceptible to effective *corporate* control.[281] What proper 'interest' could the typical company have in the ownership of capital which it is by statute prohibited from holding? Latham CJ said of this in *Mills v Mills*[282] that:

> The question which arises is sometimes not a question of the interest of the company at all, but a question of what is fair as between different classes of shareholders. Where such a case arises, some other test than that of the 'interests of the company' must be applied . . .

**[5.94]**   The 'honesty, integrity and fairness' that Lord Truro LC required of fiduciaries in *Re Beloved Wilkes's Charity*[283] is concerned here, too. 'Fairness' is asked of the corporate director in exercising the powers relating to capital structure. Interests of two or more members inter se must often be balanced. The corporate entity and *its* interests are not employed. To the extent that directors' powers over corporate capital are fiduciary powers, relevant duties must be owed to members and shareholders. They are the only objects who are eligible. Fiduciary duties are said to be owed to them individually. Any ability of the shareholders, collectively, to constitute a general meeting of the company, or some other company organ, is irrelevant.

Directors' discretions relating to the control and ownership of corporations are very often the subjects of litigation. Limited companies are owned and controlled by their members, as a rule. Those members and their interests are what the directors are expected to pay regard to in the exercise of their discretions. Interests of the abstract corporate entity must yield.[284] As

---

[279] I am indebted to Finn *Fiduciaries* [136]–][143] for the following point.
[280] Corporations Law Schedule 1, Table A, reg 66(1).
[281] Corporations Law s 206.
[282] (1938) 60 CLR 150, 164.
[283] (1851) 3 Mac & G 440; 42 ER 330, 333: above at [5.7].
[284] See *Mills v Mills* (1938) 60 CLR 150, 164, Latham CJ.

Megarry J said in the English case of *Gaiman v National Association for Mental Health*:[285]

> The [company] is, of course, an artificial legal entity, and it is not easy to determine what is in the best interests of the [company] without paying due regard to the interests of members of the [company]. The interests of some particular section or sections of the [company] cannot be equated with those of the [company], and I would accept the interests of both present and future members of the [company] as a whole, as being a helpful expression of a human equivalent.

**[5.95]**   Which of the abstract corporate entity and the body of corporators is the proper object of directors' duties? There may be an historical reason for the ambivalence between them. It has been suggested that corporate form in the nineteenth-century developed 'out of phase' with the law of directors' fiduciary obligations.[286] Fiduciary obligations of directors seem to have emerged and been defined in relation to the old 'deed of settlement' companies. With these entities, the members simply *were* the company. So it was conceived that fiduciary obligations were owed, in some ultimate sense, to the members and not the entity. Separateness of corporate identity was recognised some years later. By that time, it has been said, the idea that the members were the proper objects of directors' fiduciary duties was too entrenched to be displaced. The 'duty to the members' supposition exercises a powerful force over our conceptions still.[287] It has an effect comparable to that of 'fiduciary rhetoric'.

**[5.96]**   If companies are seen as the proper objects of directors' fiduciary duties, does it follow that only companies or their controllers can enforce those duties? Yes, appears to be the orthodox answer. The authoritative *Gower's Principles of Modern Company Law* maintains this position. 'Fiduciary duties' were declared to be 'owed to the company and to the company alone', citing *Percival v Wright*.[288] Fiduciary duties are not separately owed to company shareholders. The possibility that such duties might be owed was discussed in *Glandon Pty Ltd v Strata Consolidated Pty Ltd*[289] and the traditional opposition to them was reaffirmed. In the absence of fraud,[290] or misappropriation of the company's assets,[291] it seems to be the rule that only the company (or its liquidator) is the proper plaintiff to sue for a breach of its directors' fiduciary duties.[292] This is significant and affects fiduciary reasoning. As a note, this accepted position has been lately distinguished in the New Zealand case of *Coleman v Myers*.[293] Directors of a small family company were in that decision conceived to owe fiduciary duties directly to shareholders and not to the artificiality that the company represented.

---

[285] [1971] Ch 317, 330.

[286] L Sealy 'The Director as Trustee' [1967] *CLJ* 83, 89–90.

[287] L Sealy 'Directors' "Wider" Responsibilities—Problems Conceptual, Practical and Procedural' (1987) 13 *Mon LR* 164, 166.

[288] At 551, [1902] 2 Ch 421.

[289] (1993) 11 ACSR 543, 555–8, Cripps JA, Mahoney and Clark JJA agreeing (CA (NSW)).

[290] See *Ngurli v McCann* (1953) 90 CLR 425, 447, Williams ACJ, Fullagar and Kitto JJ.

[291] *Burland v Earle* [1902] AC 83, 93, Lord Davey: see above at [5.61]–[5.63].

[292] But cf *Nicholson v Permakraft (NZ) Ltd* (1985) 3 ACLC 453, 459–60, Cooke J.

[293] [1977] 2 NZLR 225 (CA), distinguished to 'close corporations' in *Glandon Pty Ltd v Strata Consolidated Pty Ltd* (1993) 11 ACSR 543, 558.

**[5.97]** In the Australian scheme of directors' fiduciary duties, legitimate claims of shareholders and creditors must be accommodated through the width of the 'benefit of the company' definition. Interests of the company which the fiduciary duty serves have been held to *include* the interests of these parties. Whilst neither shareholders nor creditors may be strictly speaking owed a fiduciary duty themselves, the subject of the duty owed to the company comprehends their interest. Fiduciary duty to the company is thus 'strained' to provide protection to these outside interests. Sarah Worthington notes this point,[294] but goes on to argue (at 133) that the duties owed to the different objects are of separate natures. If there are distinct duties that directors owe to the company, to its creditors and to its members, only the duty to the company can be said to be fiduciary, properly speaking. Duties in favour of shareholders and creditors are instead argued to be in the nature of 'general equitable duties to act for proper purposes'. This certainly simplifies the answer to the question that this sub-heading poses. It would be convenient if fiduciary law could be so quarantined. But the argument must be rejected as contrary to much accepted dicta and, in particular, contrary to the analysis of Lord Wilberforce in *Howard Smith Ltd v Ampol Ltd*.[295]

**[5.98]** The inclusionary approach can be seen in the case of *Walker v Wimborne*, to which we have already referred.[296] Walker was the liquidator of Asiatic Electric Co. Against Wimborne and other directors of the company, the liquidator sought orders that those persons pay losses that the company sustained through payments made to related companies. Despite the existence of interlocking shareholdings, mutual interests between these companies to justify the payments were not shown. So the payments were argued to be 'misfeasances' contrary to directors' statutory duties to the company. Asiatic was insolvent at the relevant time—which may be an important fact. For the principle in the case may be applicable to companies on the eve of liquidation only. In any event, in a judgment with which Barwick CJ agreed, Mason J said at 7 that:

> it should be emphasized that the directors of the company in discharging their duty to the company must take account of the interests of its shareholders and its creditors. Any failure by the directors to take into account the interests of creditors will have adverse consequences for the company as well as for them. The creditor of a company, whether it be a member of a 'group' of companies in the accepted sense of that term or not, must look to that company for payment. His interests may be prejudiced by the movement of funds between companies in the event that the companies become insolvent.

The notion of a fiduciary duty to X 'taking account of' Y was endorsed. Would it not be more direct, though, to acknowledge a duty owed separately to Y? How should the identity of Y, the party to be 'taken account of', be determined? Perhaps non-creditor interests as well should be 'taken account of' as part of the duty to the company. These might include the interests of a company's workers, customers, the interests of beneficiaries of trusts of which

---

[294] 'Directors' Duties, Creditors' Rights and Shareholder Intervention' (1991) 18 *MULR* 121; see also J Corkery *Directors' Powers and Duties* (1987), 69.

[295] [1974] AC 821, 835–6.

[296] (1976) 137 CLR 1

the company is trustee, of the community, the national interest and the interest of the environment.[297] The list is long. As Sealy has said:[298]

the traditional rules and concepts of company law regarding directors' duties have come under challenge. This law, concentrated as it is on the interests of shareholders and no other group, is thought to be too narrowly focussed. It is contended on many sides that the law ought to allow, or even require, directors to have regard to other, wider considerations and interests.

**[5.99]** There is now, as we have said, a body of Australasian authority to the effect that the fiduciary duties of directors protect creditors' interests. In *Walker v Wimborne*,[299] assets were shifted between companies in a group before being recovered from the directors personally. *Ring v Sutton*[300] enabled creditors to recover sums borrowed by a director on an uncommercial basis. A lease to a director on the eve of insolvency was set aside in *Russell Kinsela Pty Ltd v Kinsela*[301] and in *Nicholson v Permakraft (NZ) Ltd*[302] a capital dividend paid to directors was recovered by the liquidator from them, so as to be divided amongst the creditors. In the United Kingdom, Buckley LJ held in *Re Horsley & Weight Ltd*[303] that directors owe an 'indirect duty' to the company not to reduce a company's capital to the detriment of creditors. Or, as Templeman LJ saw the matter in the same case (at 455): if a company is 'doubtfully solvent', certain actions by directors can be a restrained as a 'fraud on the creditors'. Finally in *Lonrho v Shell Petroleum Ltd*,[304] Lord Diplock echoed Mason J in *Walker's* case, in the House of Lords:

it is the duty of the board to consider . . . the best interests of the company. These are not exclusively those of the shareholders but may include those of creditors.

### What duties are owed?

**[5.100]** Exercises of directors' discretions can be set aside despite the absence of any misappropriation or personal gain on their part. At the same time, directors owe duties which mostly stem from the conflicts and profits rules—like other fiduciaries. Directors, for example, must primarily be honest. However, there is a further jurisdiction for examination of the *fairness* of directors' decisions and the *propriety of motive* they had in deciding matters as they did. The recondite doctrine of 'fraud on a power' is applied. It has often been attracted, for example, to exercises of a directors' power to allot shares.[305] *Fairness* of fiduciaries and their *propriety of motive* are in question. Both of these things are implicit in the dictum of Lord Truro LC concerning fiduciaries' discretions that we considered from *Re Beloved Wilkes's*

---

[297] L Sealy 'Directors' "Wider" Responsibilities—Problems Conceptual, Practical and Procedural' (1987) 13 *Mon LR* 164, 169; on interests arising out of trading trusts see also *Hurley v BGH Nominees Pty Ltd* (1984) 37 SASR 499; 2 ACLC 497 and *Inge v Inge* (1990) 3 ACSR 63.

[298] Id; see also F Dawson 'Note' (1984) 11 *NZULR* 68.

[299] (1976) 137 CLR 1

[300] (1980) 5 ACLR 546 (SC (NSW)); see also *Grove v Flavell* (1986)43 SASR 410; 4 ACLC 654.

[301] (1986) 4 ACLC 215 (CA (NSW)).

[302] [1985] 1 NZLR 242 (first instance only).

[303] [1982] Ch 442 (CA), 453–4.

[304] [1980] 1 WLR 627, 634

[305] *Mills v Mills* (1938) 60 CLR 150, 186, Dixon J and *Whitehouse v Carlton Hotel Pty Ltd* (1987) 162 CLR 285, 294, Mason, Deane and Dawson JJ, discussed in McLean 120.

*Charity*.[306] It may be that the closeness of this scrutiny of directors reflects the importance of companies in modern society. We will now examine the duties of directors under the following headings.

### Duty to act in good faith

**[5.101]** Directors are required in the traditional way to act 'bona fide in what they consider—not what a court may consider—is in the best interests of the company'.[307]

Sometimes dishonesty is plain, or an obvious inference to it can be drawn.[308] However the reach of this bona fides duty goes much further. It must be understood in the light of general fiduciary law, where subjective honesty is not all that is required. A director may fail to 'act honestly' without fraud. Honest directors may be in breach of their fiduciary duties to a company, for example, where they act entirely outside the company's interests and act instead in their own, or in some third party's interest.[309] What these 'interests of the company' are and what they might include have been discussed under the heading of '*To whom* are duties owed? The good faith duty also 'overlaps', it has been said,[310] with s 232 of the Corporations Law. Sub-section (2) of that section provides that

> An officer of a corporation shall at all times act honestly in the exercise of his or her powers and the discharge of the duties of his or her office.

For a time there was some uncertainty over whether the term 'honestly' in this subsection of the Corporations Law should bear a more restricted meaning than it would under the general law. We have noted the equitable liability that may attach to a fiduciary who even in good faith acts otherwise than in the company's interests. Penal sanctions attached to s 232(2) were thought to make such an 'absolute' liability too harsh. 'Dishonesty' in the sense of that section (and the equitable rule) seems closer to mere impropriety according to the standards of the criminal law. Dawson J, for one, in *Chew v R*,[311] disapproved of the various 'improper' senses of dishonesty in various recent *Corporations Law* authorities. The problem may now partly be eliminated through the 1993 enactment of Part 9.4B of the Corporations Law. Alternative to the penal sanction, that Part provides civil consequences for breach of the subsection.

### Duty to act for 'proper purposes'

**[5.102]** A 'proper purposes' duty assumes purposes for why each of the fiduciary powers of a given set of directors was conferred. Companies themselves are directed to a great variety of objects. Sometimes they are

---

[306] (1851) 3 Mac & G 440; 42 ER 330, 333, extracted at [5.7].

[307] *Re Smith & Fawcett Ltd* [1942] Ch 304, 306, Greene MR (CA); restated, eg, in *Sydlow Pty Ltd (in liq) v Melwren Pty Ltd (in liq)* (1994) 13 ACSR 144, 147, McLelland CJ in Eq (SC (NSW)).

[308] *Marsden Pty Ltd v Pressbank Pty Ltd* [1990] 1 Qd R 264, 274, Macrossan CJ, Kelly SPJ and Shepherdson JJ agreeing.

[309] *Australian Growth Resources Corporation Pty Ltd v Van Reesema* (1988) 13 ACLR 261 (Sup Crt of SA FC), fol. in *Southern Resources Ltd v Residues Treatment & Trading Co Ltd* (1990) 3 ACSR 207, 226-7, (Sup Crt of SA FC); *Re W & M Roith Ltd* [1967] 1 WLR 432.

[310] See Ford [8.290].

[311] (1992) 173 CLR 626, 641-2, referring to *Marchesi v Barnes* [1970] VR 434, 438; *Morgan v Flavell* (1983) 1 ACLC 831, 838; *Flavel v Roget* (1990) 1 ACSR 595, 606-7; *Corporate Affairs Commission v Papoulias* (1990) 20 NSWLR 503, 506 and particularly *Australian Growth Resources Corporation Pty Ltd v Van Reesema* (1988) 13 ACLR 261.

engines for the production of wealth. At other times, companies are vehicles for the avoidance of tax. The nature of a company will affect the construction of powers that are conferred on its directors.[312] If directors then exercise a power for a different purpose than the one construed, an abuse of the power and breach of duty may have occurred. Acting for improper purposes need not be to 'feather the directors' nests or to preserve their own control'.[313] Self-serving wrongs are adequately sanctioned by the duty to act 'bona fide for the benefit of the company'. Instead, the 'proper purposes' duty applies more aptly to the kind of wrong which looks to the objects of the power and raises 'integrity and fairness' considerations.

**[5.103]**   The 'proper purposes' duty is illustrated by the case of *Howard Smith Ltd v Ampol Petroleum Ltd.*[314] An exercise of a directors' power to allot shares was the trigger of an improper purpose claim. Miller Holdings was a company in need of capital. Millers was also the target of the rival takeover plans of the Ampol and the Howard Smith companies. Ampol and an associate were the majority shareholders in Millers when the story began. Ampol then made a bid for the remainder of the Millers shares. This was considered too low by the Millers board and it advised shareholders against acceptance of the bid. Shortly after, in order to gain control of Millers, Howard Smith made a higher offer for the same shares. Ampol and its associate at this announced that they would thereafter reject any offer made for their own shareholding. In these deadlocked circumstances, the board of Millers decided to make an allotment of new shares to Howard Smith. The Ampol shareholding was much diluted by this and Howard Smith was well positioned to make an effective takeover. Ampol challenged the validity of the directors' decision to issue the shares in order to avoid this outcome. Facts found at first instance (and not challenged on appeal) included the following. First, directors of Millers were not motivated by any purpose of personal gain or advantage, nor by the desire to retain their positions on the board. Secondly, Millers did need capital at the time of the shares issue. Thirdly, the primary purpose of the allotment was not to raise capital, but to dilute the Ampol shareholding so that Howard Smith could proceed with its takeover offer. Street J decided that an improper exercise of directors' powers had been established on this and that Ampol was entitled to the relief it sought. This was affirmed by the Privy Council on appeal.

**[5.104]**   The following passage indicates how the central 'valid purposes of a power' question in *Howard Smith*[315] was approached by the Privy Council.

> In their Lordships' opinion it is necessary to start with a consideration of the power whose exercise is in question, in this case a power to issue shares. Having ascertained, on a fair view, the nature of this power, and having defined as best as can be done in the light of modern conditions the, or some, limits within which it can be exercised, it is necessary then for the court, if a particular exercise of it is challenged, to examine the substantial purpose for which it was exercised, and to

---

[312] See *Buche v Box* (1992) 30 NSWLR 368, 378.

[313] *Whitehouse v Carlton Hotel Pty Ltd* (1987) 162 CLR 285; *Walker v Nicolay* (1991) 4 ACSR 309 (issue conceded); Gower 556.

[314] [1974] AC 821 (PC) (Lord Wilberforce); see also *Wallington v Kokotovich Constructions Pty Ltd* (1993) 11 ACSR 759 and *Lorenzi v Lorenzi Holdings Pty Ltd* (1993) 12 ACSR 398.

[315] [1974] AC 821, 835 (PC).

reach a conclusion whether that purpose was proper or not. In doing so it will be necessary to give credit to the bona fide opinions of the directors, if such is found to exist, and will respect their judgement as to matters of management; having done this, the ultimate conclusion has to be on the side of the fairly broad line on which the case falls.

Validity of the power's exercise thus depends on the answers to two questions. First, what 'on a fair view' is the 'nature' of the power directors possess? At 837 the Privy Council in effect held that the board had invalidly exercised the voting powers of the members in general meeting. Impropriety of the power's exercise followed from a construction of the 'nature' of the allotment power. More specifically, the directors' purpose in the exercise of the power was inconsistent with the Board's perception of 'the constitution of a limited company'. Functions were in effect allocated between the board of directors of a company and a general meeting of its members. This is a matter which is by no means clear, as Len Sealy points out.[316] Overreaching of function within a particular scheme of decision-making disallowed what the directors did. Adjudication of matters relating to a company's ownership is not within the competence of directors entrusted with running its business. At 834 the Board rejected Ampol's argument that the directors' power of share allotment was solely to enable capital to be raised. The second question is more fact-specific. What was the 'substantial purpose' of the impugned exercise of the power? What, therefore, were the directors' motives at the time? This involves a large amount of intuitive judgement, about which it is difficult to generalise. The High Court has said obiter dictum in *Whitehouse v Carlton Hotel Pty Ltd* that the formulation of a 'substantial purpose' test in this area should be replaced by a 'single causative purpose' test.[317] Possibly distinctions between the various expressions canvassed in that judgement are insignificant. The 'substantial object', 'substantial cause', 'significantly contributing cause' and a 'moving cause' may all amount to about the same. Finally, a remedial note. Directors' exercises of power impeached for breach of the 'proper purposes' duty all stand as valid until set aside. They are voidable, that is, and not void.

**[5.105]** The next matter to consider is what difference there is between the 'proper purposes' duty and the 'bona fides' duty. The need to distinguish these duties appears not to have arisen in litigation. Judicial responses, at least, have not been forthcoming. We shall look instead to approaches taken in the established texts. *Ford and Austin's Principles of Corporations Law* at [8.290] suggests that 'bona fides' and 'proper purposes' duties say the same thing from different perspectives. The authors place the two duties in separate chapters in order to reflect their scheme of corporate governance. This separates directors' duties relating to the management of a company by its board[318] from the duties of directors otherwise, taken as individual members.[319]

---

[316] In ' "Bona Fides" and "Proper Purposes" in Corporate Decisions' (1989) 15 *Mon LR* 265, 272

[317] (1986) 162 CLR 285, Mason, Deane and Dawson JJ.

[318] Chapter 8 (Directors' Duties I: Acting in the Company's Interests) see 'Duty to act for proper purposes' [8.200]–[8.280].

[319] Chapters 8 and 9: see 'Duty to act in good faith for the benefit of the company as a whole' [8.070] ff; 'General law and statutory duties of care' [8.310] ff; 'The conflict rule' [9.060] ff; 'Conflicts of interest in transactions with the company' [9.110] ff; 'Misuse of property and information' [9.200] ff; 'Financial benefits to related parties' [9.470].

The pursuit of an improper purpose by a director as board member would also amount to that director not acting for the benefit of the company. On the other hand, both *Gower's Principles of Modern Company Law* at pp 533–9 and *Palmer's Company Law*[320] suggest that the duties are separate things. On this view, they are alternative ways of impeaching a director's exercise of power.

Sealy has said that whilst there may be 'room for debate' on whether these duties are 'one phenomenon or two', such a debate would 'ask the wrong question' and be futile.[321] What is more important, he says, is to see that courts are now much more inclined to take business decisions on judicial review. 'Proper purposes', the duty which used once to be a 'fifth wheel on the coach', merely re-phrasing the 'bona fides' duty, is now a springboard to intervention. This may well be. But the matter may not be quite so political. The 'new interventionism' relates and is essentially restricted to 'fairness and integrity' issues as we have defined them. These are issues like allotment of shares, voting power, members' control and shareholders' rights inter se. The 'bona fides' duty, the conflicts and profits rules perhaps always lacked the resource for resolving these questions.

### Duty to avoid conflicts of interest

**[5.106]**   Directors may not enter transactions where directors' duties to the company conflict or possibly conflict in the two familiar ways. The prohibition applies to directors, either where duty conflicts with directors' own personal interests, or where duty conflicts with duty owed in other directorships.[322] An example of the former was in *Cummings v Claremont Petroleum NL*.[323] Directors who received an unreasonable level of benefits from consultancy agreements with the company were found to be pursuing gains in conflict with their fiduciary duties to the company. Such cases are corporate instances of the conflicts rule considered more generally at [5.37]. Two points will be made. First, conflicts of either type are common amongst directors of companies. An argued conflict of itself may not be enough to attract the courts' attention. Accordingly, the *extent* of the director's adverse interest needs to be demonstrated in order to warrant judicial intervention. A possibility of conflict may be ignored if no reasonable person would think it significant.[324] An exception to this is where a breach of duty is manifest: no additional matters may need to be shown to have an actual conflict restrained. Secondly, disclosure of the offending interest or duty to the board and/or general meeting may immunise a director from the effect of the conflicts rule. The Corporations Law provides a statutory disclosure regime. For proprietary companies, s 231(1) requires a director interested in a transaction to declare the fact, nature, character and extent of the interest to the board and s 231(6) requires that director to disclose to the board any conflicting interest or duty which could arise from the holding of any office or the possession of any property. For public companies, s 232A prohibits a director of a public company from voting on a matter in which he has a 'material private interest', or from being

---

[320] 25th ed (1992), at [8.505]–[8.516].
[321] ' "Bona Fides" and "Proper Purposes" in Corporate Decisions' (1989) 15 *Mon LR* 265, 267–8.
[322] See Ford [9.060]ff; [9.110] ff.]
[323] (1992) 9 ACSR 583 (Fed Ct), 596–7, curiam.
[324] See *Inge v Inge* (1990) 3 ACSR 63, 69, O'Bryan J (SC (Vic)).

present while it is considered, unless the board is apprised of the matter and passes a resolution to permit the director voting.[325] It may be that sidestepping this by 'the simple expedient of leaving the room' will not be permitted. For the power and influence of the interested director may continue to be present. It may be incumbent on a director so placed to actively prevent a flawed transaction from proceeding.[326]

**[5.107]**  *Woolworths Ltd v Kelly*[327] considered a similar disclosure enactment, which has now been repealed. The Woolworths' board had passed a resolution to grant the chairman a long-service pension. Although he did not vote on the resolution, the chairman was a member of the board at the time that it was passed. Later, the management of the company changed and a new board stopped paying the pension. Kelly sued the company and the defence was raised that the resolution for the pension was invalid. This was on the basis that the chairman's interest in the matter had been insufficiently disclosed before the resolution was passed. The majority of the New South Wales Court of Appeal took a large view of what occurred. No *formal* disclosure by the retiring chairman was said to be necessary. The company's defence was disallowed.[328] Whether the board or general meeting of a company is the appropriate organ to be informed depends on the terms of its articles and certain specific provisions in the Corporations Law, detailed in Ford at [9.340]. In *Queensland Mines Ltd v Hudson*,[329] the ambit of an article which gave management responsibilities to the board was in question. The article was construed to allow the board to authorise a director to take a corporate opportunity after the company had declined it. But consent of the board is usually assumed to be inadequate for this and the decision, despite its eminence, has been questioned. There are also certain remedial consequences of directors' breach of fiduciary duty which are peculiar to conflicts of interest in this corporate context. We will consider these at [6.4]–[6.11].

### Duty not to take profits or advantages from company funds

**[5.108]**  This may be put as an independent duty. It is the 'profits rule', in application to directors of companies. Or the prohibition on taking profits and advantages personally is one form of the directors' wider obligation not to apply a company's resources otherwise than for the benefit of the company as a whole.[330] However the source of the duty is conceived, directors must not divert to or use for themselves their company's property, confidential information or opportunities.[331] The obligation is codified by the Corporations Law. Included in s 232 are subs (2)—the directors' duty to act honestly (again); subs (5)—a duty not to misuse information acquired by office; and subs (6)—a duty not to misuse a corporate position to the advantage of one's self or another person.

---

[325] See A Lumsden 'S 232A Conflicts of Interest and Public Company Board Behaviour—New Rules?' (1993) 7 (3) *Commercial Law Quarterly* 9.

[326] *Darvall v North Sydney Brick and Tile Co Ltd* (1989) 15 ACLR 203, 250, Kirby P.

[327] (1991) 22 NSWLR 189 (CA), re s 123 of the Companies Act 1961 (NSW).

[328] Ibid, at 213, Samuels JA and 233–5, Mahoney JA, Kirby P dissenting.

[329] (1978) 18 ALR 1 (PC).

[330] See, eg, *Gemstone Corporation of Australia Ltd v Grasso* (1993) 12 ACSR 47.

[331] Gower 565–71.

Borrowing from the company is a common way for directors to appropriate company property. Borrowing is now a recognised form of the self-dealing abuse. Directors wrongly contract on behalf of the company with themselves as debtors. The Corporations Law prohibits this specifically. By s 234, loans or guarantees may not be given, nor security provided, to directors or associated individuals or companies. An offence is committed under s 234(5) by directors who authorise a contravening transaction. Application of remedial principles of fiduciaries' law to this may have the effect that any property acquired with the proceeds of an improper loan can be treated as belonging to the company. Constructive trust relief will then be available. *Paul A Davies (Aust) Pty Ltd (in liq) v Davies*[332] was an example of this. A restaurant was purchased by company directors in their own names, partly with company money and partly with money borrowed from a financier on the security of company property. A constructive trust in favour of the company was allowed over the whole of profits made from running the restaurant business and the whole of the proceeds which were anticipated from the sale of its premises.

### Duty of care and diligence

**[5.109]** *Gower's Principles of Modern Company Law* at p 585 records a 'striking contrast between the directors' heavy duties of loyalty and good faith and their light obligations of skill and diligence'.

Following *Gower* at 585–90, we will not treat the 'duty of care and diligence' as an equitable duty. It is a common law matter. Cases such as *Re City Equitable Fire Insurance Co Ltd*,[333] *Commonwealth Bank of Australia v Friedrich*[334] and *AWA Ltd v Daniels*[335] treat this duty as based alternatively in contract and tort. It is not equitable. Anderson J in *Permanent Building Society (in liq) v McGee*[336] notes that the duty of care and fiduciary duties are 'different in character' from each other. *Ford and Austin's Principles of Corporations Law* is surprisingly cryptic on the matter, however. At [8.310] it is stated that 'the existence of a fiduciary relationship' is a 'source' of the care and skill duties. No authority or further explanation is given.

### Who can consent to, ratify, or excuse a breach of duty?

**[5.110]** The company is the only entity which can avert or release its directors liability. At least, this is true to the extent that directors' fiduciary duties are owed to the company and not to outsiders. For this we shall assume that the company is solvent. Where it is not solvent, interests of the company's creditors may have to be consulted as well. Shareholders in the company will not then have the authority to absolve directors from their breach of duty. In the practical sense referred to in *Kinsela v Russell Kinsela Pty Ltd (in liq)*,[337] the assets of the company then belong only to its creditors.

---

[332] [1983] 1 NSWLR 440, 448, Moffit P, 451, Hutley JA 454, Mahoney JA, 457–8; see also *O'Brien v Walker* (1981) 5 ACLR 546 and below, at [6.83].

[333] [1925] Ch 407, 428–9, Romer J.

[334] (1991) 5 ACSR 115, Tadgell J.

[335] (1992) 10 ACLC 933, 1005–7, Rogers J—in fact concerning *auditors*, not directors.

[336] (1993) 11 ACSR 260, 287–8 (SC (WA)) and see *Permanent Building Society (in liq) v Wheeler* (1994) 14 ACSR 109, 154–8, Ipp J, Malcolm CJ and Seaman J agreeing (SC (WA) (FC)).

[337] (1986) 4 NSWLR 722, 730, Street CJ.

According to the orthodox position, an ordinary majority of a solvent company's members in general meeting can do any of the following things, subject to two provisos. It may *consent* to directors entering engagements or transactions contrary to their fiduciary duties. It may *ratify* and make binding on the company any (voidable) obligation which resulted from any such transactions contrary to fiduciary duty. And it may *excuse* a director's appropriation of some profit or gain in the process. The provisos are the absence of (1) any 'fraud on the minority' or oppression, discussed at [5.112] below, and (2) there being no contrary provision in the company's articles of association: *Boschoek Proprietary Co v Fuke.*[338] Unanimous agreement of shareholders may even overcome a contrary article.[339]

Any of the foregoing company acts, which we shall term 'authorisations', may be given a past or prospective effect.[340] It has been held, additionally, that the same immunity for directors may be achieved without the need for authorisation. Renunciation of a new venture by a fully informed board of directors (not general meeting) in *Queensland Mines Ltd v Hudson*[341] was allowed to be an enforceable 'consent' by the company to a director taking the venture personally. This may be an exceptional possibility. But the dictum of another, Walters J in *Hurley v BGH Nominees Pty Ltd*,[342] reinforces the view. Thus,

> in the case of a small company, informal consent—evidenced by express or tacit agreement, or by a course of dealing—may be given without a meeting of shareholders.

In general, subject to the absence of 'fraud on the minority', directors who control a company may be able to avoid fiduciary liability so long as they fully disclose to its members what they propose doing and appropriate ratifications are thereafter passed in general meeting.[343]

**[5.111]** Avoidance of liability principles did not arise directly in *Winthrop Investments Ltd v Winns Ltd.*[344] Reasoning in that case was primarily concerned with the enforceability of an impugned transaction. Avoidance of fiduciary liability for company directors was a consequential matter. Directors of Winns made an allotment of shares in the course of an attempted takeover of the company by Winthrop Investments. The allotment would have had the effect of frustrating Winthrop's takeover so long as it stood. Winthrop sought an injunction to invalidate the allotment, based on an allegation that the directors of Winns had voidably exercised the relevant power they exercised for the purpose. Proceedings for this claim were irregular. Winthrop obtained interlocutory relief as a minority shareholder in Winns and the matter came before the court on an application by Winns to have the injunctions discharged.

---

338 [1906] 1 Ch 148.
339 *Grant v John Grant & Sons Pty Ltd* (1950) 82 CLR 1, 50, Fullagar J; *Re Australian Koya Ltd* (1984) 8 ACLR 928.
340 Discussed by Mahoney JA in *Winthrop Investments Ltd v Winns Ltd* [1975] 2 NSWLR 666 (CA), 703–4.
341 (1978) 18 ALR 1, 9–10 (PC) (Lord Scarman).
342 (1984) 37 SASR 499; 2 ACLC 497, 504.
343 Gower 593, citing *Hogg v Cramphorn Ltd* [1967] Ch 254 and *Bamford v Bamford* [1970] Ch 212 (CA).
344 [1975] 2 NSWLR 666 (CA).

At this point, whilst the matter was actually being heard, Winns held a general meeting of its shareholders. The directors' impugned decision to allot the shares was ratified—the resolution for which the majority of the New South Wales Court of Appeal held was invalid for lack of disclosure. But before that conclusion was reached, the whole court concurred in the existence of the following principle. A properly informed general meeting of members *can* ratify a directors' breach of fiduciary duty in the exercise of one of their powers.[345] Further, as Glass JA said at 674, advance authority can be given. In that event no breach of fiduciary duty may occur at all.

Power of the company in general meeting to make the authorisations may not be as firm a rule of law as it is sometimes stated. King CJ in *Residues Treatment and Trading Co v Southern Resources Ltd*[346] made an observation about the decision in *Winthrop Investments Ltd v Wynns Ltd*[347] which indicates that its authority may now be questionable. In reaching its decision in *Wynns*, he said, the New South Wales Court of Appeal was constrained to follow the English Court of Appeal decision in *Bamford v Bamford*.[348] This was a case which allowed that a general meeting of a company's members could ratify an allotment of shares when the relevant directors' power was exercised for an improper purpose. Such English authority need no longer be followed. Pointing to *Ngurli v McCann*,[349] King CJ said that if it was correct that a shareholder has a personal right to have the voting power of his shares undiminished by an allotment of shares made for an improper purpose, then there would still be a 'substantial argument' that the directors' act could not be consented to. Namely, that exercise of the voting power of the majority to ratify an allotment diminishing voting power would be beyond the scope of the purpose for which that power exists.

**[5.112]**   'Fraud on the minority' is an established exception to the avoidance of liability principles. A majority of the members of a company cannot authorise their directors' breach of fiduciary duty if to do so would defraud the minority.[350] *Ngurli v McCann*[351] is the main Australian authority for the proposition. The High Court there assimilated restraints on the powers of directors with restraints on members' voting powers. At 438 the principle stated was:

> powers conferred on shareholders in general meeting and on directors by the articles of association of companies can be exceeded although there is a literal compliance with their terms. These powers must not be used for an ulterior purpose . . . Voting powers conferred on shareholders and powers conferred on directors . . . must be used *bona fide* for the benefit of the company as a whole.

---

[345] Ibid, 672, Glass JA, 683, Samuels JA, 704, Mahoney JA: following *Bamford v Bamford* [1970] Ch 212, Plowman J.

[346] (1988) 51 SASR 177, 204; see also *Colarc Pty Ltd v Donarc Pty Ltd* (1991) 4 ACSR 155, Walsh J (SC (WA)).

[347] [1975] 2 NSWLR 666 (CA).

[348] [1970] Ch 212.

[349] (1953) 90 CLR 425, 438.

[350] Eg, see *J D Hannes v M J H Pty Ltd* (1992) 7 ACSR 8, 11, Sheller JA (CA).

[351] (1953) 90 CLR 425.

A majority of members could not, the court said, authorise the misappropriation of the company's property,[352] nor could it authorise the expropriation of the minority members' shares.[353] A majority of members cannot relieve directors from their fiduciary obligation to act bona fide for the benefit of the company.[354] Perhaps all the exceptions collapse to one, as suggested in the judgment of Evershed MR in *Greenhalgh v Arderne Cinemas Ltd*.[355] Members, as well as directors, must act bona fide for the benefit of the company in authorising abuses of power. Yet the source of such an obligation to bind members is dubious. Further, the proposed obligation on the majority would impose a good faith duty on the members to superintend another good faith duty binding the directors. It may for that reason be a little cumbersome. The suggestion may signal that equitable regulation of corporations has become over-refined. As Gower remarks,[356]

> concepts of 'fraud on the minority' and 'bona fide in the interests of the company' are obsolete and meaningless in relation to activities by members. They were invented by judges to curb the worst excesses of majority rule and at the time of their invention they were needed in the light of the then statute law. Now, however, because of recent statutory reforms, they are needed no longer.

## 2. SOLICITORS AND CONFLICTS OF DUTIES

[5.113] 'Conflict of duties' is the problem of the solicitor who represents clients on both sides of a transaction. The representations involved may be successive: one client's retainer follows another. Or the interests of two or more clients may be served at the same time. In either case, the solicitor will owe fiduciary duties to each client. The duties are owed at the same time and very often to clients whose interests are adverse. Conflict of duties may occur in the absence of adequate disclosure to and the consent of each client. Here we will not be concerned with conflict between solicitors' personal interests and their duties to their clients. Where solicitors enter business transactions with their clients, or where (without adequate disclosure and consent) solicitors are retained in the same matter by two or more clients, fiduciaries problems tend to be resolved on principles specific to the agency relation.[357] At other times, solicitors' pursuit of personal interests over their fiduciary responsibilities may create separate problems of fraudulence or illegality.[358] The Privy Council, though, in dealing with a remarkably innocuous conflict, has recently decided otherwise. *Clark Boyce v Mouatt*[359] held that a claim for

---

[352] *Menier v Hooper's Telegraph Works* (1874) LR 9 Ch App 350; *Cook v Deeks* [1916] 1 AC 554.

[353] See now Gower 596–8, citing *Brown v British Abrasive Wheel Co* [1919] 1 Ch 290 and *Re Bugle Press* [1961] Ch 270 (CA).

[354] Gower 596.

[355] [1951] Ch 286 (CA), Asquith and Jenkins LJJ concurring. Gower at 598–605 discusses and disapproves of the following idea.

[356] Gower 603 (referring in particular to the Companies Act 1985 (UK), s 459, the counterpart of Corporations Law s 260, 'Remedy in cases of oppression or injustice').

[357] See *Farrington v Rowe, McBride & Partners* [1985] 1 NZLR 83 (CA), 96–7, McMullin J, but note Richardson J, contra, at 92 and the agency cases of *Fullwood v Hurley* [1928] 1 KB 498, 502, Scrutton LJ (CA) and *Barr, Leary & Co v Hall* (1906) 26 NZLR 222, 225 Stout CJ.

[358] See *Re Thomas; Jaquess v Thomas* [1894] 1 QB 747 (CA), 749–50, Lindley LJ; *Abdurahman v Field* (1987) 8 NSWLR 158 (CA), 163–4, Hope JA; *Weston v Beaufils* (1994) 122 ALR 240 (Fed C), Hill J, esp at 267.

[359] [1994] 1 AC 428.

breach of fiduciary duty could not be prayed in aid of contractual duties subsisting between solicitor and client. The conflict was only a breach of contract, or negligence. It is unlikely that this reasoning will be persuasive in Australia. The fiduciary relation has too strong a hold.

**[5.114]**  What often highlights a conflict of duties is the need to protect any confidential information that the solicitor has acquired in his confidential relationship with a client.[360] Use of that information to assist another client may trigger the first client's assertion that a restrainable conflict of duties has occurred. Even the perception that such a use might be made, inadvertently or by design, may justify restraint. Alleging a breach of the conflicts rule is only one of several ways for a client to restrain a solicitor in situations like this. Other possibilities include:

1. breach of express/implied term in the contract of retainer;
2. breach of confidence in what is disclosed; and
3. action which attracts the courts' jurisdiction over solicitors under the legal profession practice Acts.[361]

Solicitors' conflicting duties, the conflicts rule and restraint of solicitor fiduciaries will be examined here under the following headings. 'Successive representation' and 'simultaneous representation' make a temporal divide in the subject. Conflicts of duty are classified according to when the duties arise. Either the existence of one duty precedes the other, in a successive representation situation; or the duties both arise more or less simultaneously, as where the solicitor acts for more than one party in the same transaction.[362] Paul Finn adopts a different structure. It is more based in the subject of the conflict and not when the client relationships were formed. His alternative headings of 'same matter conflicts', 'former client conflicts', 'separate matter conflicts' and 'fair dealing conflicts' may be intended to accommodate conflicts in the duties of professional fiduciaries other than solicitors, such as bankers, accountants and the like.[363]

### Successive representation

**[5.115]**  This is the type of conflict where duty conflicts with something done in the past. The 'former client' instance of it is where a solicitor, having once acted for a client in a particular matter, subsequently acts against the client in the same or a related matter.[364] Confidential information imparted by the first client is then at risk. More than sixty years ago, in *Gesellschaft Für Drahtlose*

---

[360] P Finn 'Conflicts of Interest and Professionals' in *Professional Responsibility* Legal Research Foundation Inc NZ (1987) 9, 27.

[361] Generally, see J Disney et al *Lawyers* 2nd ed (1986), chapter 21 and F Reynolds 'Note' (1991) 107 *L Q R* 536, 537.

[362] It reflects the scheme of 'Developments in the Law—Conflicts of Interest in the Legal Profession' (1981) 94 *Harv LR* 1292–314.

[363] 'Fiduciary Law in the Modern World' (in) E McKendrick (ed) *Commercial Aspects of Fiduciaries and Trusts* (1992), 7, 19–39; solicitors are said to be 'not of immediate concern' to this publication.

[364] See M Dean and C Finlayson 'Conflicts of Interest: When May a Lawyer Act against a Former Client?' (1990) *NZLJ* 43; P Kryworuk 'Acting Against Former Clients—a Matter of Dollars and Common Sense' (1984) 45 CPC 1.

*Telegraphie mbH v Brown*,[365] this was said to be governed by a 'well established rule of public policy' in the United States that:

> where an attorney has acted for a client he cannot thereafter assume a position hostile to the client concerning the same matter, or use against the client knowledge or information obtained from him whilst the relation subsisted.

The 'separate matter' instance of 'successive representation' conflict is where a solicitor obtains information from a client relevant to one matter, then uses it in favour of another client on another matter. No conflict of interests between the clients is then necessary. In both cases, the central matter is the possibility of unauthorised use of the confidential information imparted by the first client. There is another signal fact about the law in this area: solicitors' conflicts from successive representation are quite common:

> Merger, partial merger and the movement of lawyers from one firm to another are familiar features of the modern practice of law.[366]

There may even be a public interest in promoting such fluidity in a legal profession. However, when knowledge of a migrating lawyer passes to lawyers in other firms, mergers may have an undesirable effect. A client's confidential information imparted to one firm is arguably communicated to a firm to which the lawyer transfers, or to one with which the first firm merges. If a solicitor employed in a firm which represents one party to a transaction leaves that firm and joins a firm which represents another party, prima facie the second firm is in conflict of duties and can be restrained.[367] If a firm which represents a client merges with a firm that represents an adverse party to that client, it also may be in conflict.[368]

**[5.116]**   The once leading authority in the area is the now aged English Court of Appeal decision in *Rakusen v Ellis, Munday & Clarke*.[369] An unusual kind of two-man firm was there involved. Rakusen was the client. He consulted one of the solicitor partners about an action against his employer and gave him some confidential information on the subject. The other partner was overseas at the time and knew nothing about what the partner at home was doing. This was shown to be a normal state of affairs. The firm later ceased to act for the client. Subsequently, the other partner commenced acting for the employer. When the former client sought an injunction to prevent the other partner from continuing to represent the employer, and to protect the confidences he had imparted, the court held that there was no rule to prevent this 'conflict' occurring. There was said to be no prohibition on a solicitor's successive representation of opposing sides in litigation. Instead, it was up to the client in each case to show what Cozens-Hardy MR referred to at 835 as the 'probability' of 'real mischief and real prejudice' occurring. Or, as Fletcher Moulton LJ put it at 841, the client had to show that 'mischief is rightly

---

[365]  78 F 2d 410 (1935).

[366]  *MacDonald Estate (Gray) v Martin* [1991] 1 WWR 705 (SC of Can), 712, Sopinka J.

[367]  *In the marriage of Magro* (1988) 93 FLR 365, Rourke J (Fam Ct of Aust); *In the marriage of Thevanaz* (1986) 84 FLR 10, Frederico J (Fam Ct of Aust); *Royal Bank of Canada v Appleton* (1987) 17 CPC 209 (SC (Ont)); *Morton v Asper* (1987) 45 DLR (4th) 374 (CA (Man)).

[368]  *Supersave Retail Ltd v Coward Chance (a firm)* [1991] 1 All ER 668.

[369]  [1912] 1 Ch 831.

anticipated'. As the client in this case failed to do these things, he was unsuccessful and the firm was not restrained.

**[5.117]** Under the *Rakusen* test, a plaintiff bears the onus of proving a 'probability' of mischief occurring. This is quite different from the typical United States position. Courts in that country have mostly adopted the stricter 'possibility of real mischief' test to determine what is a restrainable conflict of duties. Once it is established that there is a 'substantial relationship' between a matter out of which the confidential information is said to arise and the retainer to be restrained, there is an irrebuttable presumption that the attorney received the relevant information.[370] If the attorney practises in a firm, there is a further (rebuttable) presumption that lawyers who work together will share each other's confidences. All members of the firm are imputed with knowledge of that confidential information.[371] There are two common methods of rebutting the second, the shared information, presumption. First, the firm may establish that it placed an effective 'Chinese Wall' around the information. A Chinese Wall is a screening device, within a firm, intended to prevent communication between lawyers who are tainted and those who are not.[372] Secondly, 'cones of silence' may be used. These are undertakings by tainted lawyers to the effect that they will not disclose a client's confidential information.[373]

**[5.118]** In *MacDonald Estate (Gray) v Martin*[374] the Canadian Supreme Court adopted a modified form of this United States position. Several matters were seen to require something stricter than the *Rakusen* test. That justice should appear to have been done was one. Clients were entitled to expect something better from those in whom they invested trust. In the relevant formulation of the majority, two issues were seen to arise in particular. Did the lawyer receive any relevant confidential information? Would that lawyer now use it prejudicially? The American irrebuttable presumption in answer to the first question was rephrased in rebuttable form. As Sopinka J expressed it (at 724): lawyers in a 'substantial relationship' are assumed to receive confidences 'unless the reasonably-informed person would [otherwise] be satisfied'. The second presumption was also phrased rebuttably. It allowed that the likelihood of communication and misuse within a firm may be disproved. 'In the age of the mega-firm', Sopinka J said at 725, the 'knowledge of one is the knowledge of all' principle is 'unrealistic' and amounts to an 'overkill'.

---

[370] See 'Developments in the Law—Conflicts of Interest in the Legal Profession' (1981) 94 *Harv LR*, 1315–34, discussed by Sopinka J in *MacDonald Estate (Gray) v Martin* [1991] 1 WWR 705, 715–18.

[371] Id, criticised 1355–9; *Analytica Inc v NPD Research Inc* 708 F 2d 1263 (1983, 7th Circ), Posner J.

[372] See F Costigan 'Conflict of Interest—Chinese Walls and Bamboo Curtains' in C Coady and C Sampford (eds) *Business Ethics and the Law* (1993), 113; M Keith 'Information Barriers Must Face Tough Tests' (1993) 15 *Law Soc Bulletin* 23; L Aitken ' "Chinese Walls" and Conflicts of Interest' (1992) 18 *Mon L R* 91; M Keith 'Berlin Wall Down, Chinese Walls Next?' (1992) 14 *Law Soc Bulletin* 12; R Tomasic 'Chinese Walls, Legal Principle and Commercial Reality in Multi-Service Professional Firms' (1991) 14 *UNSWLJ* 46; (Note) 'The Chinese Walls Defence to Law-Firm Disqualification' (1980) 128 *U Penn LR* 677.

[373] *MacDonald Estate (Gray) v Martin* [1991] 1 WWR 705, 715. See *Analytica Inc v NPD Research Inc* 708 F 2d 1263 (1983 7th Circ), 1269, Posner J—affidavits denying that improper communication has taken place, or will take place, are 'difficult to verify objectively'.

[374] [1991] 1 WWR 705, 726–7, Sopinka J, Dickson CJC, La Forest and Gonthier JJ concurring.

'Chinese Walls' and 'cones of silence' were given a Canadian lease of life. The minority position in the case is notable, too. It would have made both presumptions irrebuttable. This was because of a perceived paramountcy in the policy which preserves the integrity of the judicial system and the seeming justice of its institutions.[375]

**[5.119]**  Courts in England and Australia have yet to formally emancipate themselves from the authority of *Rakusen v Ellis, Munday & Clarke*.[376] *Re a firm of solicitors*[377] was a decision where the English Court of Appeal restrained a large unnamed firm from acting against a former client—the sometime manager of a Lloyds' syndicate. Members of the majority of Lords Justices at 363 assimilated the *Rakusen* 'probability' of mischief test to one which was activated by the mere 'risk' of it. They enforced, in effect, the irrebuttable bar contained in the *Law Society's Guide to the Professional Conduct of Solicitors*.[378] A 'Chinese Walls' defence against imputation of knowledge of the confidence to others in the firm was rejected as unsatisfactory. The second 'prejudicial use' question, isolated by Sopinka J in *MacDonald Estate (Gray) v Martin*,[379] was found against the firm. The 'principal case' of *Rakusen v Ellis, Munday & Clarke* was distinguished to its 'very special' facts, but the burden of proof upon resting on the client was left untouched.[380] Of course, the English Court of Appeal is unable to overrule its own decisions and the task of courts below is to loyally apply them. Notwithstanding, unclarity in the *Rakusen* test has allowed some 'leeway of choice'. In the first instance decision of *Re a solicitor*[381] the report attributes to Hoffmann J a preference for 'mischief rightly anticipated' to the 'probability' of mischief—the more moderate phrasing of Fletcher Moulton LJ in *Rakusen* being preferred.

**[5.120]**  An Australian court as long ago as 1882 took a view of the matter close to the current United States' position. In *Mills v Day Dawn Block Gold Mining Co Ltd*[382] a former client sought to restrain a solicitor from using confidential information the client had allegedly imparted to him. The solicitor denied ever having received such confidences. In these circumstances, the court found for the client simply on the basis of a prima facie case. No conflicting evidence of the solicitor was admitted in evidence.

The authority of *Rakusen* has recently been both approved and questioned. It was approved in *D & J Constructions Pty Ltd v Head t/a Clayton Utz*,[383] where the court refused to restrain a solicitor because the client did not establish that the solicitor possessed any confidential information 'worthy of protection by injunction'. This was a conservative decision. *Rakusen* was

---

[375]  Cory J, 728–9 (Wilson and L'Heureux-Dube J concurring).

[376]  [1912] 1 Ch 831.

[377]  [1992] 1 All ER 353 (CA).

[378]  (1990), [11.02].

[379]  [1991] 1 WWR 705 (SC (Can)), 725–6.

[380]  Confirmed in *C S Low Investment Ltd v Freshfields (a firm)* [1991] 1 HKLR 12 (CA (HK)).

[381]  (1987) 131 SJ 1063–the following point being observed by Parker LJ in the Court of Appeal: [1992] 1 All ER 353, 361.

[382]  (1882) 1 QLJ 62, 63–4, Lilley CJ, Harding and Pring JJ concurring (SC (Qld) (FC)).

[383]  (1987) 9 NSWLR 118, 124, Bryson J (SC (NSW)).

approved also in *Australian Commercial Research and Development Ltd v Hampson*.[384] This was another conservative decision, which this time went in favour of the applicant. The case is worthy of note for two reasons. First, its facts concerned protection of confidences given in a brief to a barrister, rather than in instructions to a solicitor. This was said to be a matter which made no difference. Secondly, it appeared that the defendant QC, whom the applicant sought to restrain from subsequently acting against it, was one of 14 QCs from the Queensland bar that the applicant had briefed in respect of the matter. It was alleged that the applicant had, through the dissemination of its 'confidences', attempted to 'corner the market' for legal services and ought for this reason to be unsuccessful in its claim. 'Unclean hands' for the applicant were said to result. This was considered at some length. Evidence was received that the applicant's tactic of covering itself in 'shark repellant' even extended to a successful challenge to the judge first listed to try the case. He, too, had been briefed when at the bar. In the end it was found that only a 'suspicion' was raised as to the applicant's motive and that was not enough to deflect the 'probability of real mischief' which otherwise appeared. *Rakusen* was questioned in dicta by Gummow J in the Federal Court in *National Mutual Holdings Pty Ltd v Sentry Corporation*.[385] Inconsistency between the 'probability' requirement in *Rakusen* and other statements of the conflicts rule was noted.

[5.121] Finally, *Rakusen* was distinguished in *Mallesons Stephen Jaques v KPMG Peat Marwick*[386] and not followed in *Wan v McDonald*.[387] Ipp J said in the *Mallesons* case that 'disassociation and separation of [one partner] from the firm is essential to the decision in *Rakusen v Ellis, Munday & Clarke*'. A test involving the mere 'possibility' of conflict was there preferred to the *Rakusen* 'probability of mischief' requirement. A 'Chinese Walls' defence was found to be unavailing. *Mallesons* concerned an application to restrain the firm of that name from representing the Commissioner for Corporate Affairs against its former client, the auditor of the Rothwells merchant bank. Using a military metaphor, it was said in response that the Commissioner's work would be done by a Mallesons 'task force', situated in a different building. At 371–4 this was examined and found not to be a 'true wall'. Possibilities of 'wordless communication' were not removed. 'Walls' were rejected also in the 'successive representation' case of *Fruehauf Finance Corporation Pty Ltd v Feez Ruthning*.[388]

*Wan v McDonald*[389] reached its conclusion on facts that did not involve the supposition of any confidential information at all. The former client was a Hong Kong resident, who was inveigled to invest in a scheme to evade requirements of the Australian Government's 'Business Migration Plan'. The scheme was promoted by another of the solicitor's clients. Mrs Wan trusted

---

[384] [1991] 1 Qd R 508, Mackenzie J (SC (Qld)).
[385] (1989) 87 ALR 539, 558–61, referring to *Boardman v Phipps* [1967] 2 AC 46, 103–4, Lord Cohen (*possibility* of conflict); *Chan v Zacharia* (1984) 154 CLR 178, 199, Deane J (*significant possibility* of conflict).
[386] (1990) 4 WAR 357, 373 (SC (WA)).
[387] (1992) 105 ALR 473, Burchett J (Fed Ct).
[388] [1991] 1 Qd R 558, 571, Lee J (SC (Qld)).
[389] (1992) 105 ALR 473.

the solicitor to obtain an interest for her in a Gold Coast property she believed she was investing in. A caveat was lodged in her name over the property. In the event, many irregularities occurred with her investment, culminating in Mrs Wan commencing proceedings against the promoter through a different solicitor. Those proceedings were then transferred from state to federal courts. The first solicitor used the fact of this transfer of courts to misrepresent to the Registrar of Titles that the litigation had concluded. Removal of the caveat followed, which facilitated the property's resale by the other client. The proceeds of this were not accounted for. Burchett J found that the manner of removal of the caveat amounted to a breach of the solicitor's fiduciary duty. The solicitor had acted to his former client's detriment by falsely representing to the Registrar a transaction wherein he had once acted on the client's behalf. This was treated as equivalent to his abuse of confidential information. Only the need for restraint was all the more obvious here. Burchett J notes (at 496) that the focus of attention was shifted from the (contingent) conflicts inherent in amalgamation or partnership changes to the more actual conflicts of duty engaged in by a solicitor who continues to act for one client, having previously acted for both. In the present case, he says, 'the issues of loyalty and propriety seem ... to loom more largely'. To require Mrs Wan to prove a 'probability of mischief' in this case is both onerous and unnecessary. The facts sufficiently spoke for themselves.

**[5.122]**  Finn has supplied four reasons why *Rakusen* and cases like it should be allowed to 'sink into oblivion'.[390] First, *Rakusen* is said to ignore 'unconscious' use of information. Use, that is, when the breach of confidence is 'embryonic'. Secondly, the *Rakusen* placing of the burden of proof on the client is said to undermine the policy of the law which protects the professional relation. Thirdly, the *Rakusen* assumption that a solicitor *can* act successively without breaching confidences of the first client is inconsistent with the duty of full disclosure to the second client. Fourthly, *Rakusen* may be inconsistent with the public policy that justice should be seen to be done. Finn accordingly recommends that Australia adopt a position similar to that in the United States. An irrebuttable presumption is proposed, that the lawyer has always acquired client confidences in the prior retainer, combined with a rebuttable presumption that those confidences are communicated to the entire firm. This is stricter than the position now obtaining in Canada, where both presumptions are rebuttable.

## Simultaneous representation
**[5.123]**  Clients are entitled to receive their solicitors' loyalty, unimpaired by the pressures of conflicting interests.[391] This is a consequence of the parties' fiduciary relationship. Protection of confidential information may be relevant too, but it takes a subordinate place. It is not necessary for the substantiation of fiduciary liability. Conflict in a solicitor's duties may occur without any abuse of the client's confidential information or opportunities. Obviously a solicitor cannot act for opposing parties in contentious matters. 'Serving two

---

[390] 'Conflicts of Interest and Professionals' in Legal Research Foundation Inc *Professional Responsibility* (1987), 9, 16–21.

[391] Note 'Developments in the Law; Conflicts of Interest in the Legal Profession' (1981) 94 *Harv LR* 1244, 1293.

masters in a single matter' is the subject even of biblical injunction.[392] It is a sort of self-evident wrongdoing. Reported cases of solicitors having to be restrained from so doing are relatively uncommon.[393] A client can, however, waive the protection that fiduciary law affords and retain a solicitor who otherwise acts in conflict of duty. Such a solicitor, in order not to be in breach of the conflicts rule, must disclose the full extent of his conflicting duties to the client and firmly advise that client to take independent legal advice.[394]

**[5.124]** In *non-contentious* business, by contrast, there is no general law prohibition on a solicitor representing more than one party. Statutes, though, are sometimes to the contrary.[395] In the United States there are a number of judicially supervised codes of professional ethics relating generally to attorneys' 'simultaneous multiple representation'.[396] Such simultaneous representation is generally permissible in Australian jurisdictions before actual conflict arises. This is so long as both clients are fully informed by the solicitor and each consents to his or her acting for the other.[397] Most commonly this is where one solicitor acts for both vendor and purchaser in conveyancing transactions. It is not uncommon for country solicitors to act for both parties in various transactions and, indeed, that practice may add to the efficiency of much conveyancing.[398] Notwithstanding, it is often condemned as an undesirable practice. In the words of Wootten J in *Thompson v Mikkelsen*[399]–

> It seems to me that the practice of a solicitor acting for both parties cannot be too strongly deprecated. It is only because of the possibility that something may be wrong in a transaction, or may go wrong during its implementation, that the employment of highly trained professional people at professional scales of remuneration can be justified. To scrutinize a transaction to discover whether something is wrong in a way that may affect his interests, or to notice and deal with something that goes wrong during the transaction, is what a party employs such a person for. He is entitled to assume that that person will be in a position to approach the matter with nothing [in mind] but the protection of his client's interests against [those] of the other party. He should not have to depend on a person who has conflicting allegiances and who may be tempted either consciously or unconsciously to favour the other client, or simply to seek a resolution of the matter in a way which is least embarrassing to himself.

**[5.125]** What in non-contentious business amounts to the client's 'fully informed consent' is important here. First, do clients in all cases have the legal

---

[392] Matthew 6:24.

[393] See *Woodruff v Tomlin* 616 F 2d 924 (6th Circ 1980); *United States Fidelity & Guarantee Co v Louis Rosner & Co* 585 F 2d 932 (8th Circ 1978); *Jedwabny v Philadelphia Transport Co* 390 P 231, 135 A 2d 252 (1957).

[394] *Clark Boyce v Mouatt* [1994] 1 AC 428, 437 (PC) (Lord Jauncey); *Garofoli v Kohm and Raimondi* (1989) 77 CBR 84, 98.

[395] Eg, Sale of Land Act 1962 (Vic) s 33; Law Soc of the ACT also conditions the right of solicitors to act for both parties in sales of land (quoted in J Disney et al *Lawyers* 2nd ed (1986), 763–4).

[396] R Aronsen et al *Professional Responsibility* (1985), 344–58.

[397] J Disney ibid, 758–9; stated in the Law Institute of Victoria *Members' Handbook* (1993), 'Professional Ethics', 3-1420.

[398] Submission to the NSW Law Commission on 'Conveyancing of Land and Conflicts of Interest' (1979), quoted in J Disney, ibid, 765–6.

[399] Unreported (SC (NSW) 3 Oct 1974), quoted in *Wan v McDonald* (1992) 105 ALR 473, 492–3; see also *Commonwealth Bank v Smith* (1991) 102 ALR 453, 478 (FC) 'an undesirable practice'; *Farrington v Rowe, McBride & Partners* [1985] 1 NZLR 83, 90 Richardson J.

expertise and judgment to consent? There is obviously a difference between the consent of a large client that is able to rely on the advice of its corporate legal department on the one hand, and the consent of many sole traders on the other. Secondly, is a solicitor who has a personal interest in the transaction able to procure a valid consent? The answer to this should perhaps be no.

> The consent of an individual litigant cannot be presumed to be fully informed when it is procured without the advice of a lawyer who has no conflict of interest.[400]

Thirdly, what things need to be disclosed? Certainly more, it seems, than simply the fact of the solicitor having double employment in the task in hand. Every adverse and every prior retainer which may affect the solicitor's discretion should perhaps also be disclosed.[401] Finn suggests that the disclosure should be sufficient to allow the beneficiary to make an intelligent decision about whether to retain independent counsel.[402] Perhaps—

> the attorney [should] not only inform the prospective client of the attorney's relationship to the seller, but also explain in detail the pitfalls that may arise in the transaction which would make it desirable that the buyer have independent counsel.[403]

**[5.126]** Neither the 'Chinese Walls' nor the 'cones of silence' defence is usually allowed when the simultaneous species of a solicitor's conflict of interest is alleged. United States courts have been said to 'demonstrate a judicial hostility to screening devices in concurrent representation cases.'[404] A confidential information 'trigger' is not needed to activate a solicitor's fiduciary duty.

# Defences to fiduciary claims

### 1. CONSENT, RATIFICATION AND EXCUSE[405]

**[5.127]** Consent, ratification and excuse have been described as a fiduciary's only defences to breach of fiduciary duty claims. Lord Wright referred to them in *Regal (Hastings) Ltd v Gulliver*[406] in connection with the profits rule. 'An agent, a director, a trustee or other person in an analogous fiduciary position', he concluded, is not entitled to defeat a claim to account on any ground, 'save that he made profits with the knowledge and assent of the other person.'

Consent, ratification and excuse are defences which 'confess and avoid' the application of fiduciary obligations. Each of the existence, scope and apparent

---

[400] *Aetna Casualty & Surety Co v United States* 438 F Supp 886, 888 (approved in 94 *Harv L Rev* 1243, 1314).

[401] *Williams v Reed* 3 Mason 405, 418 (1824), Story J (CC Maine).

[402] P Finn 'Conflicts of Interest and Professionals' in *Professional Responsibility* (1987), 9, 25–7.

[403] *Re Kamp* 194 A 2d 236, 240, Proctor J (1963), concerning conflict in a conveyancing transaction.

[404] (Note) 'The Chinese Wall Defence to Law-Firm Disqualification' (1980) 128 *U Penn LR* 676, 690, referring to *Fund of Funds Ltd v Arthur Anderson & Co* 567 F 2d 225 (2nd Circ 1977) and *Westinghouse ElectricalCorporation v Kerr-McGeeCorporation* 580 F 2d 1311 (7th Circ 1978).

[405] See MGL [537]; J Kearney 'Accounting for a Fiduciary's Gains in a Commercial Context' in Finn *Relationships* 189–91.

[406] (1942) [1967] 2 AC 134n, 154; repeated by Lord Hodson in *Boardman v Phipps* [1967] 2 AC 46, 105 and Connolly J in *Maxmore Engineering Pty Ltd (in liq) v Walsh* (1980) 5 ACLR 358, 363 (Qld SC).

breach of fiduciary duty are not contested. Liability for the breach is avoided by reason of something represented or held out by the party to whom the duty is owed. Specifically, a consent to or ratification or excuse of what the fiduciary did is alleged.[407] They raise exonerations that the fiduciary bears the onus of proving.[408] Consent, it is said, is only a 'prima facie' defence.[409] It is up to the court to see whether it is just and reasonable in the circumstances that the beneficiary should not succeed.[410]

## Exculpatory defences and disclosure

**[5.128]**  Disclosure is an important aspect of these defences which proceed from the beneficiaries' acts. Beneficiaries can only be said to have consented to, ratified or excused breaches of fiduciary duty after they have had disclosed to them all the relevant facts known by the fiduciary. We must distinguish the extent to which (non) disclosure is a constituent of each of the profits and the conflicts rules. Noted at [5.55], liability only attaches to the fiduciaries' derivation of *secret* profits in connection with fiduciary office. Not all profits are included in this. Noted at [5.49], (non) disclosure is also a primary component of the conflicts rule. The duty with which an interest may conflict is defined in relation to what has been previously disclosed to the beneficiary. This might be relevant, as Sealy says,[411] in order to determine whether a fiduciary's purchase from or sale to a beneficiary should be allowed to stand. Emphasis on disclosure in fiduciary law appears to have had its origins in the conflict of duty and interest cases.

**[5.129]**  In relation to the profits rule, Lord Hodson said in *Boardman v Phipps* that:

> Nothing short of fully informed consent which the learned judge found not to have been obtained could enable the appellants in the position which they occupied having taken the opportunity provided by that position to make a profit for themselves.[412]

This mixes the senses of disclosure. The sense, that is, in which (non) consent is an integral part of the cause of action based on the profits rule is mixed with the sense in which consent is a defence to any fiduciary liability. We are here concerned with defensive applications. Consent (ratification or excuse) must be 'informed' by disclosure. A fiduciary is not exonerated from fiduciary liability for a profit because the beneficiary is 'on notice' of the fact that the fiduciary is making it. The profit-making must be explicitly brought to the beneficiary's attention. Disclosure is not relevant in relation to 'improper purposes' or 'not for the benefit of the company' types of breaches by company directors. These are examined above at [5.101]–[5.102]. Directors

---

[407] MGL [523]; Finn *Fiduciaries* [560]–[567]; *Bowstead on Agency* 14th ed (1976), 130–40.

[408] *Clegg v Edmonson* (1857) 8 De G M & G 787, 44 ER 593, 602, Turner LJ; *Birtchnell v Equity Trustees Executors and Agency Co Ltd* (1929) 42 CLR 384, 398, Isaacs J.

[409] *Spellson v George* (1992) 26 NSWLR 666, 669, Handley JA.

[410] *Re Paulings Settlement Trusts* [1961] 3 All ER 713, 730, Wilberforce J.

[411] L Sealy 'Some Principles of Fiduciary Obligation' [1963] *CLJ* 119, 135; see also *Boardman v Phipps* [1967] 2 AC 46, 91, Viscount Dilhorne.

[412] [1967] 2 AC 46, 109.

may have acted honestly and openly at all times and still be in breach of the duty to exercise their powers for proper purposes.[413]

We will here briefly examine the disclosure requirements where they are necessary for exoneration by way of consent, ratification or excuse.

### To whom should disclosure be made?

**[5.130]** Disclosure should be made to the person to whom fiduciary obligations are owed.[414] Made to a person, that is, who is able to consent to or excuse the fiduciary's profit or conflict, or ratify a transaction which results. This creates few problems where the beneficiary is an individual. It is obvious who that person is. Principles of ratification of fiduciary breach where the beneficiary is a company were examined at [5.110]. These might be applicable to the other defences as well.[415]

### What should be disclosed?

**[5.131]** A 'full and frank disclosure of all material facts' is needed. This is also before beneficiaries can be said to have adequately consented to what fiduciaries propose to do, or have done, inconsistently with their obligations.[416] Disclosure must be of all the relevant facts which fiduciaries know of. 'Knowledge' includes what fiduciaries wilfully close their eyes to. There would seem to be no positive obligation, however, that the fiduciary go further and discover facts which a prudent inquiry might have revealed.[417]

**[5.132]** Sufficiency of a fiduciary's disclosure was disputed in the case of *Grantwell Pty Ltd v Franks*[418] and a very high standard was imposed. The facts concerned an estate agent whom certain of his clients relied on as a financial adviser. In 1988 the clients sought the agent's advice on the purchase of a 'negatively geared' investment. He suggested a suitable property, disclosing that two of his companies owned it. A sale of the property 'at valuation' was agreed upon. In fact the 'valuation' was a document prepared in the agent's office and his companies had purchased the property for considerably less about a year before—facts that were put before the clients at the time of signing the agreement, in statutory and other forms. The Full Court of the Supreme Court of South Australia found that these disclosures were not enough to prevent the agent from being a fiduciary in breach of duty. They were insufficient, King CJ said at 398, because there had been no specific mention that 'the price was greatly in excess of the price paid by the vendors the year before' and that 'persistent efforts to sell at the [sale] price had been unsuccessful'. This position was related to the stringency of the fiduciary duties of a financial adviser in particular and a proposition of more general application may not be implicit. The vigour of the decision is remarkable.

---

[413] As in *Howard Smith Ltd v Ampol Petroleum Ltd* [1974] AC 821 (PC) or *Whitehouse v Carlton Hotel Pty Ltd* (1987) 162 CLR 285.

[414] *DPC Estates Pty Ltd v Grey and Consul Development Pty Ltd* [1974] 1 NSWLR 443, 466, Hutley JA.

[415] See reasoning in *New Zealand Netherlands Society 'Oranje' Incorporated v Kuys* [1973] 2 All ER 1222 (PC).

[416] *New Zealand Netherlands Society* ibid, 1132.

[417] *BLB Corporation of Australia Est v Jacobsen* [1974] 48 ALJR 372 (HC), 378, (curiam)

[418] (1993) 61 SASR 390 (FC), King CJ and Bollen J, Mohr J dissenting.

Trading between some fiduciaries and their beneficiaries seems to be permitted only on a wholly uncommercial basis.

More conservatively, limitations on what needs to be disclosed are illustrated by the decision of the High Court in *BLB Corporation of Australia Est. v Jacobsen*,[419] although mainly in the cause of action sense and not the defensive sense. Jacobsen was the fiduciary agent of BLB, an Italian company (incorporated in Liechtenstein) which set up a textile factory in Australia. On behalf of BLB, Jacobsen supplied much of what the Australian factory produced on credit to Bel-Knit Pty Ltd. Bel-Knit was a company in which Jacobsen had a ninety per cent interest. When Bel-Knit became insolvent, it owed BLB a substantial amount of money. BLB commenced proceedings against Jacobsen, alleging that he had 'failed to disclose' various things. These included both 'the nature and extent of his interest in Bel-Knit' and 'that Bel-Knit was unable to pay its debts'. As to the first, the High Court confirmed a finding of fact against BLB that BLB had at all times a 'comprehensive picture' of Jacobsen's interest in Bel-Knit. Pleading in the case was elliptical. The fiduciary wrong which appeared to base this part of the claim was an alleged conflict between Jacobsen's duty to BLB and his personal interest in Bel-Knit. At 376, BLB was found to have consented to Jacobsen acting with this interest and not to be in breach of fiduciary duty thereby. A 'failure to disclose' in the defensive sense would have to be subordinate. The second non-disclosure was independent of BLB's consent to the subject of the first. Jacobsen as a fiduciary was bound to disclose all further information acquired 'in his capacity as agent'. It was held, though, that this did not extend to what Jacobsen did not know of. He did not know of the over-valuation of assets in Bel-Knit's books of account and substantial trading losses it had incurred. Hence he was not liable for not passing that information on and the consequent loss suffered by BLB. Meagher, Gummow, Lehane's *Equity* is critical of this approach to the doctrine of notice. It asks (at [537]):

> But what of the case where the defendant has no relevant knowledge, either because he has deliberately refrained from acquiring it or because by his negligence he has failed to acquire it? In the first case it is not difficult to attribute to the defendant a degree of unconscientiousness equal to that of a defendant who actually knows but does not reveal. In the other case, the degree of unconscientiousness is less, but one would have thought that if a fiduciary is negligent, and by his negligence is enabled to profit from a dealing with his principal, he should be equally called to account.

## 2. EXEMPTION CLAUSES

**[5.133]** Exemption clauses are enforceable as contract terms. We have already considered at [3.26]–[3.31] one aspect of the interrelation between contract and the fiduciary relation. A contract may regulate a fiduciary relation coming into existence and, sometimes, can prevent a fiduciary obligation from arising.[420] The competence of a particular 'exemption clause' to nullify an existing fiduciary liability is a different thing. Such a clause represents the waiver of an obligation implied by law. A court would give binding effect to

---

[419] [1974] 48 ALJR 372 (HC).

[420] *Woolworths Ltd v Kelly* (1991) 22 NSWLR 189 (CA), 225, Mahoney JA; *Noranda Australia Ltd v Lachlan Resources NL* (1988) 14 NSWLR 1, 17, Bryson J.

such a waiver if it enforces the exemption clause. Whether it would do so raises a number of further considerations of the contractual kind. These include the relative bargaining powers of the parties, the existence of information disparities between them, and 'fairness', generally, of the clause to the beneficiary affected.[421] A fiduciary's breach of duty will often amount to unconscionable conduct on his or her part. It is hard to imagine any Australian court giving effect to the 'natural and ordinary meaning' of a clause that shelters a fiduciary from the consequences of such acts.[422]

---

[421] Criteria suggested in A Anderson 'Conflicts of Interest': Efficiency, Fairness and Corporate Structure' in 25 *UCLA Law Rev* 738 (1978), 755–6, where the possibility of an enforceable waiver in the US is doubted.

[422] See *Darlington Futures Ltd v Delco Australia Pty Ltd* (1986) 161 CLR 500, 510, curiam.

# Chapter 6

# Remedies Against Fiduciaries

[6.1]   Equitable remedies for commercial wrongs have several characteristics which distinguish them from the corresponding remedies at law. Treatises are written on the subject.[1] Remedies in equity are largely defined in relation to common law remedies. It might be said that equity always lacked autonomy in the way that its remedies developed. Most equitable remedies took their form as supplements to perceived inadequacies of common law damages. At this stage, we shall draw attention to just two defining characteristics. The first is that equitable remedies are always discretionary. Spry says in *Equitable Remedies* that common law remedies are quite 'strict and inflexible' by contrast.[2] Another commentator says that the difference between the two remedy systems is greatly exaggerated: both are qualified to about the same extent.[3] The second characteristic is that equitable remedies are not available against persons who acquire legal interests for value and without notice of the equitable claim. This works as a kind of mechanical loss-splitting device between innocent parties. However, it underlines the old political division between equity and law.

## Discretion

[6.2]   Equity may withhold its relief from any litigant who seeks it.[4] No one possesses a right to an equitable remedy. Beneficiaries in fiduciary relationships can never be completely assured of equitable intervention, no matter how strong their claims might be. All relief is subject to overriding discretions. In the first place, discretions can be 'conduct-based'. Relief may be withheld on account of the way that the claimant has acted. Equity, for example, may deny a claim on account of the claimant's delay, which was why the claimant failed in the celebrated *Erlanger v New Sombrero Phosphate Co.*[5] The facts of *Baburin v Baburin (No 2)*[6] were said to disclose an 'even stronger case' for denying relief. The plaintiff in *Baburin* had waited some twenty-four years before seeking to rescind a sale of shares in a small

---

[1] Eg, Spry, esp chapters 1–2; MGL chapters 19–28; Tilbury chapter 6.

[2] At 25; see also W Gummow 'Compensation for breach of Equitable Duty' in Youdan, 57, 75.

[3] J Beatson *Use and Abuse of Unjust Enrichment* (1991), 250–1.

[4] See Snell's *Equity* 29th ed (1990), 582; Tilbury [6028]–[6047].

[5] (1878) 3 App Cas 1218, 1238, Lord Cairns LC.

[6] [1991] 2 Qd R 240, 245, McPherson J (FC), referring to the decision in *Erlanger*.

company. In that time the buying-power of the price paid for the shares had dramatically eroded in value. Also, though the actual shares had not changed, the nature and value of the underlying business had been transformed. The balance of justice was found to be such that equitable relief should be refused entirely. The 'conduct-based' discretion to disallow relief takes other forms as well. It is attracted where claimants have not done equity to the defendant themselves.[7] They may have acted harshly or improperly instead. Or the claimant may not have come to equity with 'clean hands'.[8]

**[6.3]** A second class of discretion can be described as 'result-based'.[9] The prospect of an objectionable outcome may prompt courts to deny relief. Often this is because unacceptable hardship will be imposed on the defendant. Or, relief may be withheld because it is futile, or the performance of personal services will have to be enforced. Remedies at law may be quite adequate, providing a result which is not substantially different from what equity might provide. Finally a third class of discretion may be appropriate to describe the more general application of policy in withholding of relief. For example, in *Jones v Canavan*,[10] a share broker who was in a prima facie conflict of interest and duty was not sanctioned because the 'customs and usages' of the Sydney Stock Exchange negatived any realistic infringement of equity's rule.

# Direct enforcement of fiduciary duties

## INJUNCTIONS

**[6.4]** An injunction is a court order available in equity which restrains a person from performing a specified act.[11] It may, exceptionally, require a person to perform an act. Injunctions are relief in specie for threatened or continuing wrongs. Performance of fiduciary duties is directly enforced thereby. Kerr describes injunctions as a 'judicial process' whereby a party is required to do or refrain from doing a particular thing.[12] Meagher, Gummow and Lehane's *Equity* says something to the same effect at [2101]—injunctions are 'court orders forbidding or commanding the person to whom they are addressed to do something'. A breach of fiduciary duty might be the act or thing that an injunction restrains. Or the act commanded might be performance of such duty. The fiduciary can be ordered not to break, or to perform, his duty, as the case may be.

Duties of fiduciaries produce equitable rights in their beneficiaries. Injunctions enforcing these rights are an exercise of equity's exclusive jurisdiction. Spry at 327 notes of injunctions enforcing equitable rights that 'on a strict analysis the right to the injunction represents pro tanto the equitable right in question'.

---

[7] *Hewson v Sydney Stock Exchange Ltd* (1967) 87 WN (Pt 1) (NSW) 422; MGL [311]–[321].

[8] MGL [322]–[327].

[9] Tilbury [6037]–[6043].

[10] [1972] 2 NSWLR 236 (CA), 245, Jacobs JA and Tilbury [6044]–[6047].

[11] Spry 317.

[12] *Kerr on Injunctions* 6th ed (1927), 1.

This is a little formalistic, perhaps inspired by Maitland and the in personam conception of equity. Whether equitable rights correspond with the remedies to enforce them is yesterday's jurisprudence. What is important is that common law damages for breach of fiduciary duty are definitely not available. An injunction to restrain a fiduciary's breach of duty cannot be denied on the basis that damages at law are adequate. They are never adequate. There is one less discretionary (or jurisdictional) hurdle for the claimant to surmount.[13] Injunctive relief is available almost as of right once the beneficiary's case is established.[14]

**[6.5]** Prevention of a fiduciary's breach of duty is something that an injunctive remedy can particularly achieve. No other remedy has this function. Only the injunctive remedy can order the discontinuance of an existing breach of duty—a 'continuing breach', as this is sometimes called. Another use of the injunction is 'restorative'. This refers to an order that a fiduciary return his beneficiary to the state of affairs which obtained before the breach was committed. Other remedies share this ground. In each of these uses of the injunction, *coercion* is involved.[15] The fiduciary is commanded to do things or not to do them. Coercion is effective only if it 'bites' in time. It is critical to the effectiveness of injunctions that the means to the relief be both effective and amenable to the court's power. Legal restraint or command can scarcely be useful otherwise. There would have been no point, for example, for the New South Wales Court of Appeal in *United States Surgical Corporation v Hospital Products International Pty Ltd*[16] to have ordered injunctive relief against the dishonest distributor. Restraining appropriation of the supplier's 'local product goodwill' would have been difficult, after the distributor had set up its own business to achieve the result. The horse had bolted. Misappropriation of the goodwill had occurred before the action commenced. When the case reached the High Court, Mason J (in dissent) accepted McLelland J's first instance findings of breach of fiduciary duty. This looks to the consequence of the wrongs. He added (at 106) that each of the appropriations might have been restrained by injunction, but only if 'discovered in time'.

In addition to being coercive, injunctions are also specific to the things complained about. This is another signal feature of equitable remedies. Injunctions do not substitute, say, the payment of damages for an act which should have been performed.[17] The act itself is commanded or enjoined. Fiduciary duties are directly enforced.

**[6.6]** Injunctions, in summary, are coercive, specific and appropriate only if sought in time. Their main use for the beneficiary in a fiduciary relationship is defensive. Injunctions ward off harm which is apprehended. This is known as the *quia timet*, or 'because he fears', use of the remedy. Beneficiaries claim injunctions here because of the fear that the fiduciary will, unless restrained,

---

[13] Spry 374–80 (discretionary); MGL [2107] (jurisdictional)

[14] 15.8 Laws [14], citing the express trust cases of *Park v Dawson* [1965] NSWR 298 and *Ackerly v Palmer* [1910] VLR 339.

[15] See Tilbury chapter 6.

[16] [1983] 2 NSWLR 157.

[17] F Lawson *Remedies of English Law* 2nd ed (1980), 14–15.

breach his fiduciary duty. For example, a solicitor's former client may be aggrieved that the same solicitor now works for an adverse party in the same matter. She is worried that confidential information she once imparted might be divulged.[18] Or a person might run a business in the capacity of a fiduciary executor of an estate. The executor could threaten to commence a competing business and employ for his own benefit what he learnt in acting for the estate.[19] Injunctions can be used to restrain the solicitor from continuing to act for the new client, or to restrain the executor from opening up the competing business. Injunctions can be more backward-looking. The 'harm' may have already occurred and is in need of reversal. Injunctive relief, for example, could be part of the strategy of a takeover raider. This was dealt with at [5.102]–[5.105]. Fiduciary directors of a target company can be prevented by injunction from giving effect to an allotment of new shares to a 'white knight', which will frustrate the takeover. For this the disappointed raider needs to have standing to assert the directors' 'improper purpose'. An existing minority shareholding in the company may be needed to base injunctive proceedings.

**[6.7]**  Injunctions are most commonly sought to prevent breach of either the 'conflicts rule' or the 'proper purposes' duty. The 'profits rule' is much less commonly the basis of an injunctive application. Fiduciaries typically do not threaten to earn secret profits. They simply do. By its nature, the 'secret' wrong of profiteering is usually not apparent until after the profit has been made. An injunction by way of a restraint may be useless in this event for the fact that it comes too late. Restoration of the profit made is better achieved by the remedy of having the fiduciary account for that profit as a constructive trustee. It is considered below at [6.81].

An example of appropriate injunctive relief in a fiduciary context can be seen in *Pacifica Shipping Co Ltd v Anderson*.[20] An employer sought an injunction to restrain its former employees from misusing its 'business opportunity'. *Pacifica Shipping* raised a *scope* of the fiduciary relationship question which was discussed at [4.42]. Breaches of both the conflicts and the profits rules were threatened. The court restrained 'usurpation' of a business opportunity by an injunction which imposed a nine month postponement of the time when the defendants' competing business could commence. This was intended to approximate the preparatory time that it would have taken the defendants had they not misappropriated the advantage of the plaintiff's opportunity. Injunctive relief was tailored to the wrong committed. Specific relief here nearly equalled the flexibility of damages.

**[6.8]**  Other cases where injunctions have involved fiduciaries have also involved the threat of competition. In *Re Thomson*[21] Clausen J restrained an executor from pursuing his threats to compete with the estate which employed him. In *Surveys & Mining Ltd v Morison*,[22] a consulting geologist who was 'making applications' for mining leases in his own name and preparing to compete with his employer was also restrained by injunction. Matters had gone

---

[18]  *Mallesons Stephen Jaques v KPMG Peat Marwick* (1990) 4 WAR 357.

[19]  *Re Thomson* [1930] 1 Ch 203.

[20]  [1986] 2 NZLR 328, Davidson CJ (HC).

[21]  [1930] 1 Ch 203.

[22]  [1969] Qd R 470, 472, W B Campbell J.

even further in *Timber Engineering Co Pty Ltd v Anderson*,[23] described at [6.86]. Injunctions were issued to restrain former employees from further competing with their one-time employer. This was in addition to the defendants being obliged to account for the past profits of their wrongful acts.

**[6.9]** Injunctions can restrain fiduciaries from misusing business names of their beneficiaries: a *continuing* species of breach of fiduciary obligation. An allegation of this was considered in the Privy Council decision in *New Zealand Netherlands Society 'Orange' Incorporated v Kuys*.[24] 'Oranje' was a society of Dutch settlers in New Zealand. It was held entitled to an injunction to prevent the publication of Kuys's newspaper under the society's 'Windmill Post' banner. Lord Wilberforce delivered the opinion of the Board and said, with engaging frankness, that he was not sure whether this was a breach of the conflicts or the profits rule (at 1129). *Aas v Benham*[25] illustrates another continuing restraint. A partner was there enjoined by his co-partners from conducting a private business under the partnership name.

**[6.10]** Injunctions may issue to prevent an employee from misusing his employer's confidences. There are many cases on this, some of which are referred to at [9.30]. In *Attorney-General (UK) v Heinemann Publishers Australia Pty Ltd*,[26] for one, the plaintiff claimed an injunction to restrain the publication of the book *Spycatcher*. This was based, inter alia, on the allegation that 'Mr Wright, at all relevant times, stood, and still stands, in a fiduciary relationship to the British Government'.

Closely related are the injunctive awards which vindicate the interests of a solicitor's former client when the solicitor acts or threatens to act for a client with an adverse interest. This is where the duties of solicitors conflict. Each of the following solicitors' conflicts of duty cases commenced with the former client's application for an injunction: *Mills v Day Dawn Block Gold Mining Co Ltd*,[27] *Rakusen v Ellis, Munday & Clarke*,[28] *D & J Constructions Pty Ltd v Head t/a Clayton Utz*,[29] *National Mutual Holdings Pty Ltd v Sentry Corporation*,[30] *Mallesons Stephen Jaques v KPMG Peat Marwick*[31] and *Re a firm of solicitors*.[32]

**[6.11]** Declaratory rather than injunctive relief is more common in the company directors' 'proper purposes' cases. Alternatively, summary proceedings pursuant to the Corporations Law can be taken. Declarative or summary, the 'proper purposes' proceedings have a common preventative object. For example, the plaintiff in *Ampol Petroleum Ltd v R W Miller*

---

[23] [1980] 2 NSWLR 488, 503, Kearney J.
[24] [1973] 1 WLR 1126.
[25] [1891] 2 Ch 244 (CA).
[26] (1987) 8 NSWLR 341, Powell J.
[27] (1882) 1 QLJ 62.
[28] [1912] 1 Ch 831 (CA).
[29] (1987) 9 NSWLR 118.
[30] (1989) 87 ALR 539.
[31] (1990) 4 WAR 357.
[32] [1992] 1 All ER 353 (CA).

*(Holdings) Ltd*[33] came to court claiming a declaration that a particular share allotment was invalid and should be set aside. Now the Corporations Law s 212—'Power of the court to rectify register [of members]'—provides a summary way of overturning share allotments. A corresponding provision of earlier companies legislation framed the claim in *Whitehouse v Carlton Hotel Pty Ltd*.[34] Declarations can avert undesired fiduciary outcomes as aptly as injunctions where there are no compliance problems; although declarations can rather less easily put unjust outcomes right. Declarations apply equally to fiduciaries' gain-making and loss-causing acts and to acts performed for improper purposes. Like injunctions, declarations binding fiduciaries need not always take a preventative form. The 'preventative possibility' was not evident, for example, in the fiduciary aspects of the declaration claim in *Mabo v Queensland (No 2)*.[35] Liability was declared notwithstanding.

## Recovery of property misappropriated

**[6.12]**  Recovery of the beneficiary's *pre-existing* property interests is the subject here. These are claims against fiduciaries for the return of beneficiaries' misappropriated money, or other property. Beneficiaries assert that they have never been divested of equitable, or legal and equitable property in the assets that they seek, or they may claim an additional right to undo previous dispositions whereby property has already passed. Claims may take two forms. Either the property is said never to have ceased to be part of the beneficiary's estate, or the property is such as should be re-vested in that estate. An unjustified diminution of the beneficiary's assets has occurred.

**[6.13]**  There is a significant complicating factor in this type of claim. Fiduciaries may become insolvent. This is something which may occur at any time between a fiduciary's misappropriation of the beneficiary's property and the case coming to court. A trustee in bankruptcy or a liquidator becomes the defendant in this event. Unsecured creditors of the fiduciary are effective adverse parties to the action. The creditors have not caused the misappropriation and also have claims against the fiduciary. Equities in the litigation are then quite different and there is the possibility that secured creditors might overreach the beneficiary's claim. Secured creditors, too, have not caused the misappropriation and have claims against the fiduciary.

**[6.14]**  A recovery of pre-existing property claim can take several forms, in equity or at law. Consider first the celebrated facts of *In Hallett's Estate*.[36] Russian bonds belonging to a solicitor's client were wrongly sold by that solicitor when he was in financial difficulties. Proceeds were placed in a much-used personal bank account, together with his own moneys. He died a bankrupt three months later. Estate creditors asserted that only a debt was due to the client and it abated with all other debts owed by the estate. Surmounting certain tracing difficulties, the client succeeded in recovering the proceeds of

---

[33]  [1972] 2 NSWLR 850, Street CJ in Eq (first instance); also *Re Horsley & Weight Ltd* [1982] 1 Ch 442 (CA) and *Re Halt Garage* (1964) Ltd [1982] 3 All ER 1017: see above at [   ].

[34]  (1987) 162 CLR 285.

[35]  (1992) 175 CLR 1, 199–205, Toohey J.

[36]  (1879) 13 Ch D 696 (CA).

the wrongly sold bonds in specie from the fiduciary's account. This was in priority to the claims of the estate's general creditors.

## Claims at law

**[6.15]**   Claims against fiduciaries at law are not often made. Legal claims do not proceed against the defendants in their capacity as fiduciaries. 'Fiduciary' status is irrelevant. It is as the recipients or converters of property that fiduciaries are liable at law. Legal claims for the recovery of property from third parties are examined at [7.8]–[7.14] and the point is made that the legal claim based in receipt of money has certain economies of proof compared to the analogous equitable claim. Recipients do not have to be shown to have acted dishonestly, or with 'want of probity' in order for the claim to be made out. However this is a small advantage against fiduciaries. After breach of fiduciary duty their wrongdoing is not often in doubt. More significantly, claims at law against fiduciaries are undesirable because they yield personal, and not proprietary, judgments.

## Proprietary remedies and insolvency

**[6.16]**   It is an established principle of insolvency law that trust property is not available for distribution amongst the insolvent's own creditors.[37] Only property in which the insolvent has a beneficial interest is 'divisible property' within the meaning of the insolvency statutes. Trust property is excluded. This is so whether the trust is express,[38] resulting[39] or constructive.[40] If a remedy to effectuate the claimant's *recovery of pre-existing property* type of claim either recognises or re-vests title to the property in the claimant, then its operation is immune from the effect of the insolvency statutes. This is a significant matter. Proprietary remedies are more desirable than personal ones, as a rule, whenever the fiduciary is bankrupt or in liquidation. Proprietary remedies do not abate in an insolvency administration.

## Money claims

**[6.17]**   Most fiduciaries' misappropriations are of their beneficiaries' money. It is convenient to speak of the beneficiaries then 'getting their money back'. But the expression is misleading, as Lord Musthill reminds us in *Re Goldcorp Exchange Ltd*.[41] When money is voluntarily paid to fiduciaries by their beneficiaries, the money becomes what his Lordship described as the fiduciaries' own 'unencumbered property'. Legal property in the money passes at the time when its possessor intends it to pass, subject to the intent being vitiated by a factor like mistake or duress.[42] This is so even if the payment transaction is later rescinded. Property in the money has irretrievably gone.

---

[37] *Halsbury's Laws of England* 4th ed (1973), vol 3, [636]; W Lee 'Trusts and Bankruptcy' (1973) 47 ALJ 365, 372; D Waters 'Trusts in the Setting of Business, Commerce and Bankruptcy' (1983) 21 *Alberta LR* 395, 401–2; Goode 55–6: see [6.49]–[6.51].

[38] Eg, *Scott v Surman* (1742) Willes 400, 403; 125 ER 1235, 1237.

[39] See Ford & Lee [2119].

[40] Eg, *Re Goode* (1974) 24 FLR 61, 68.

[41] [1994] 2 All ER 806, 825–6, (PC).

[42] *Ilich v R* (1987) 162 CLR 110, 117, Gibbs CJ, 129, Wilson and Dawson JJ; *Miller v Race* (1758) 1 Burr 453, 457; 97 ER 398, 401; *Banque Belge v Hambrouck* [1921] 1 KB 321 (CA), 330, Scrutton LJ.

Money which the fiduciary steals from the beneficiary, or takes without any authorisation, may not be in this category. And, anomalously, a mistaken payer of money was said to retain an equitable 'proprietary interest' after its payment in *Chase Manhattan Bank NA v Israel-British Bank (London) Ltd.*[43] To the same effect the fiduciary might mix the money with his own money so as to be indistinguishable from it, or pay it to innocent third parties. If money is recovered, whether in a mixed condition or from a third party, an *equivalent* sum and not the money misappropriated will be what is repaid.

So proprietary rights in the whole or any part of a misappropriated sum of money are rarely available. The justice of some cases perhaps inclines the courts to grant the insolvency advantage of a lien over the fiduciary's fund or funds. A security right over a larger sum will be what is enforced, not a right to the money misappropriated. Nevertheless, in recovery of money situations, the language of constructive trusts of particular sums is often used. This is more than a doctrinal footnote. Most cases concern money. The juridical nature of money recovery is closer to a lien over an identifiable fund than a right *to* any part of it.

## CONSTRUCTIVE TRUSTS

**[6.18]** Constructive trusts are an equitable device. One of their uses is to compel a person who unfairly holds a property interest to transfer it to the person better entitled.[44] When a court finds that a fiduciary holds a property interest unjustly, unconscionably or unlawfully against a beneficiary, it takes the interest from the fiduciary and vests it in the beneficiary. A constructive trustee is not treated for all purposes as though he were a trustee. The formula 'constructive trust' is really just an efficacious way of compelling the defendant to surrender property. The numerous other fiduciary obligations of an express trustee are not imposed.

A constructive trust is not a fiduciary relation in itself. Circumstances that give rise to a constructive trust may, but need not necessarily, involve a fiduciary relation.[45] A fiduciary obligation must arise prior in time to the remedy which enforces it. Fiduciary relationships may be a source of rights which are protected and enforced by the constructive trust. Following *Scott on Trusts* 4th ed (1989) and the American Law Institute's *Restatement of Restitution* (1937), we shall also deal with the equitable devices of the lien and subrogation under the constructive trust heading.

### Liens

**[6.19]** An equitable lien is a proprietary remedy.[46] It is like the proprietary constructive trust to that degree. The two can be argued for in similar terms. But unlike the constructive trust, a lien does not confer property rights in the things to which it applies. Nor does a lien confer a right to obtain possession

---

[43] [1981] Ch 105, Goulding J: mentioned but expressly not approved in *Re Goldcorp Exchange* [1994] 2 All ER 806, 826.

[44] *Trusts and Trustee* G and T Bogert 2nd ed (1978), 471.

[45] *Scott on Trusts* ed W Fratcher 4th ed (1989), 462.1

[46] Generally, see *Pomeroy's Equity Jurisprudence* 5th ed (1941), 1223–4; *Snell's Equity* 29th ed (1990), chapter 10.

of those things.[47] *Hewett v Court* imposed an equitable lien over a part-built house sitting on a bankrupt builder's premises.[48] The claimant had no right to demand possession of it. Liens operate as judicially imposed charges to secure the performance of personal obligations owed by the legal owner.[49] Fiduciaries and beneficiaries do not create liens by mutual dealings or voluntary acts. Both liens and constructive trusts are ordered by the courts. After a lien is decreed, its subject property can be proceeded against by the beneficiary obtaining an order for judicial sale.[50] Proceeds of sale will then be available to him for satisfaction of the obligation that the lien was inferred to protect.

**[6.20]** Liens have not been the usual relief sought in beneficiaries' claims for breach of fiduciary duty. Claimants usually attempt to satisfy the various criteria of a proprietary constructive trust. Liens are awarded in an adjunctive kind of way. Where property sought cannot be traced, but the claimant is deserving nevertheless, a lien may be ordered. It is a way of reaching the property of another as a security for the value of a claim where, for one or other reason, an equitable proprietary interest in it cannot be established. Liens may be allowed as equivalents to the constructive trust. This particularly applies to restitutionary interests in money sums. Money, for example, might have been misappropriated and then unidentifiably mixed in a larger fund.[51] Or a claim might be made to money spent on making improvements to the defendant's property.[52] The fund augmented or property improved can be charged with satisfaction of the claimant's monetary entitlement so long as that fund or property is sufficiently identifiable.[53] Liens stand as an exception to the tracing rules. But, for the purposes of the insolvency statutes, interests in liens obtain the full proprietary exemption. It is notable that recent academic writings and judicial pronouncements have promoted the utility of this remedy. What Lord Templeman has said in the House of Lords is a particular example.[54]

## Subrogation

**[6.21]** Subrogation is a transfer of rights ordered by the court.[55] As such it is a personal remedy.[56] Sometimes it can have a proprietary effect. It applies to many situations, including where the claimant's property has been used by the fiduciary in discharging an obligation. By order of the court, the claimant may be placed in the prior position of the person to whom the obligation was owed. The position, that is, of being entitled to enforce the obligation before it was satisfied. Where the obligee's rights transferred were secured rights, or are otherwise of a proprietary nature, the claimant may succeed to proprietary

---

[47] *Stephenson v Barclays Bank Trust Co Ltd* [1975] 1 WLR 882, 891, Walton J.

[48] (1983) 149 CLR 639.

[49] *Pomeroy's Equity Jurisprudence* 5th ed (1941), §1234; *Snell's Equity* 29th ed (1990), 456.

[50] *Pomeroy* ibid §1233.

[51] *Space Investments Ltd v Canadian Imperial Bank of Commerce Trust Co (Bahamas) Ltd* [1986] 3 All ER 75, 76–7 (Lord Templeman in dicta).

[52] *Re Diplock* [1948] 1 Ch 465, 529–39, curiam; *Hewett v Court* (1983) 149 CLR 639.

[53] *Lord Napier and Ettick v Hunter* [1993] AC 713, 738–9, Lord Templeman.

[54] In *Space Investments Ltd v Canadian Imperial Bank of Commerce Trust Co (Bahamas) Ltd* [1986] 3 All ER 75, 76–7 (PC); *Lord Napier v Hunter* [1993] AC 713, 738–9.

[55] *Orakpo v Manson Investments Ltd* [1978] AC 95, 104, Lord Diplock.

[56] *Lord Napier v Hunter* [1993] AC 713, 744, Lord Goff.

advantages. This will be permitted if it is just and equitable that such a thing should occur. The justice of this depends on what was intended by all parties at the time that the obligation was discharged. If the fiduciary paid out a mortgage with the claimant's money, for example, there is a presumption that all parties intended that the mortgagee's rights should be kept alive for the claimant's benefit.[57] But the intention must appear from the whole facts. Accession to a proprietary interest by subrogation cannot be fortuitous.[58]

## Tracing

**[6.22]** Tracing is incidental to most kinds of property rights, not including the lien and the proprietary uses of subrogation. It annexes the claim of a constructive trust to particular property which lies in the defendant's hands. If a sufficient interest for a constructive trust is raised, that interest is followed into an asset in the defendant's possession. Tracing to property in specie is an alternative to the imposition of a lien on that property.[59] There are complicated rules which regulate whether and how a property interest can be followed, which are discussed at [6.38]–[6.48].

### Remedy or institution?

**[6.23]** This is not really a live question these days. Constructive trusts are *remedial*, as they have been introduced here. However in a recent essay with the encouraging title of 'Property and Unjust Enrichment',[60] Roy Goode has said:

> Anglo-Australian jurisprudence adheres to the concept of the constructive trust as institutional, that is, a true property trust . . . By contrast, case law in the United States and, more recently, in Canada considers the trust to be remedial in character.

And at 220 he says that the 'substantive property-based constructive trust' is one where:

> P merely seeks the return (in its original or changed form) of that which was always his, so that [the remedy] merely upholds P's title and does not itself effect any transfer of beneficial ownership.

Justice Deane had discussed this in *Muschinski v Dodds*,[61] in a judgment with which Mason J agreed. To date a further High Court pronouncement on the subject has not been made. Deane J noted that 'the area of breach of fiduciary duty' has been the 'principal operation of the constructive trust in the law of this country'. Then he said:

> Some text writers have expressed the view that the constructive trust is confined to cases where some pre-existing fiduciary relationship can be identified . . . Neither principle nor authority requires however that it be so confined to that or any other category or categories of case . . . Once its predominantly remedial character is accepted, there is no reason to deny the availability of the constructive trust in any case where some principle of law or equity calls for the imposition on the legal

---

57 *Ghana Commercial Bank v Chandiram* [1960] AC 732, 745 (PC); *Paul v Speirway* [1976] 1 Ch 220, 234, Oliver J.

58 See *Evandale Estates Pty Ltd v Keck* [1963] VR 647, 652, Hudson J and *Nottingham Permanent Building Society v Thurston* [1903] AC 6.

59 *Trusts and Trustee* G & T Bogert 2nd ed (1978), §865.

60 'Property and Unjust Enrichment' in Burrows, 215, 216.

61 (1985) 160 CLR 583, 616–17 and see *Bryson v Bryant* (1992) 29 NSWLR 188 (FC), 200–2, Kirby P, 217–19, Sheller JA.

owner of property, regardless of actual or presumed intention, of the obligation to hold or apply the property for the benefit of another.

**[6.24]**   Our concerns in this section can be outlined in the terms of Justice Deane's exposition. First, we are concerned with both 'pre-existing' and the more instrumental varieties of fiduciary relationships. This is the 'pre-existing fiduciary relationship', not pre-existing property. The view that constructive trusts are to be limited to 'pre-existing' fiduciary relations can be rejected as too narrow in general and not relevant to the concerns of this book. The 'predominantly remedial' constructive trust can be accepted without demur. The idea seems even more applicable now than in 1985. We are dealing in this chapter with the consequences of a fiduciary's breach of an equitable duty. Defence of property rights is relevant under this 'recovery of property' sub-heading. 'Disgorgement of gains' is dealt with in the following section. Thirdly, most constructive trusts arising from a fiduciary's breach of duty invoke one 'principle of law or equity'. This is the *profits rule*. It was discussed at length at [5.55]–[5.87]. Trustees' gains may be made by the subtraction of property, or the derivation of improper gains.

## CLAIMING A CONSTRUCTIVE TRUST

**[6.25]**   Where the claimant seeks to recover property that the fiduciary has misappropriated by assertion of a constructive trust, there are *two steps* that must be taken. Separate rules apply to each.
1. An equitable interest must be raised in the property misappropriated ('raising the interest'); and
2. The interest must be followed into that or other property which exists in the defendant's hands ('tracing').

The separateness of the second step should be emphasised. The tracing or 'identification' rules are not conditions for determining whether the equitable interest should be recognised. Only after the interest is raised are the tracing rules called into play. From the fact that an interest is raised it does not follow that a constructive trust over particular property can be asserted. A constructive trust claim may fail to satisfy either step.

**[6.26]**   Simple cases exist where there is scarcely any need to trace the remedy to its subject. Constructive trusts, once raised, directly and unambiguously apply to the relevant property. This is the *Muschinski v Dodds*[62] type of case. Ownership of a domestic home, it will be remembered, was disputed between former de facto spouses. The home had been purchased in joint names with the resources of the woman and transferred to the man and woman jointly. There was no dispute about which house was referred to. There was no question of who was entitled to anything additional which went with the house, or whether the man's interest in it was susceptible to the order made. In short, there was no question additional to the entitlement question for the court to deal with. The only process corresponding with the above second step was mechanical annexure of the contribution obligation to the man's registered proprietorship.

**[6.27]**   The way that the property interests were vindicated in the decision noted at the beginning of this section can be contrasted. Tracing was of much

---

[62] (1985) 160 CLR 583, 623–4, Deane J, Gibbs CJ and Mason J agreeing.

more importance in *Re Hallett's Estate*.[63] The claimant asserted a beneficial title in her Russian bonds after they had been misappropriated. This corresponds to the first step in our analysis. The Official Receiver did not bother to deny that it was satisfied. The solicitor never had an interest in the bonds. The case is of interest for the way in which the claimant satisfied the second step. At the time of trial the bonds were represented by part of the value of a chose in action which the solicitor's insolvent estate held against a bank. This was the account that the deceased had operated. Withdrawals from that account made during the deceased's lifetime meant that, on the view Fry J took at first instance, the bond proceeds had been removed and dissipated. However, the claimant was not relegated to the status of unsecured creditor. Application of the tracing rule described at [6.40] allowed her full recovery.

### 'Raising the interest'

**[6.28]** We are concerned here with pre-existing property interests. The constructive trust to vindicate these is straightforward. A claim to make the fiduciary surrender the beneficiary's property is based in that property. That is the interest concerned. It is a small step to say that this type of constructive trust operates as a substantive institution. Restoring property restores the status quo. However, this is perilous ground. Elsewhere in the book the constructive trust idea clearly does remedial service. How can a part-substantive and part-remedial institution be suffered to exist? A much better case can be made for saying that a constructive trust is remedial in *all* its applications. Even here it is not a substantive trust. Indeed–

> a quasi-contractual obligation ... is about as similar to an actual contractual obligation as a constructive trust is similar to an express trust.[64]

If a 'substantive' constructive trust means a real trust, it clearly is not that. The 'trustee' never, or nearly never, intends it. If 'substantive' means based in the claimant's property interest, a lot of cases have been wrongly decided. *Keech v Sandford*[65] is one early example. If 'substantive' means based in a recognised relation like the fiduciary relation, one should refer back to [2.24], where the idea of the 'instrumental fiduciary relation' was explored. The thing had no substance to it at all. If to be substantial means based in the prevention of fraud, then the game is up. It is clearly remedial. Notwithstanding, the view that the constructive trust is a 'substantive institution—analogous to the express trust' still has its modern adherents.[66]

**[6.29]** United Kingdom authority once seemed firmly committed to the constructive trust as a substantive institution. A century ago, the Court of Appeal in *Lister & Co v Stubbs*[67] drew a clear distinction between a debtor–creditor relationship and the sort of relationship necessary for proprietary relief. The *Lister v Stubbs* approach was re-affirmed in the United Kingdom Court of Appeal several times, including in *Attorney-General's Reference*

---

[63] (1879) 13 Ch D 696 (CA).
[64] *Scott on Trusts* 4th edn, ed W Fratcher (1989), 462.4.
[65] (1726) Sel Cas T King 61; 25 ER 223.
[66] Eg, A Burrows *Law of Restitution* (1993), 39; Birks 377–85.
[67] (1890) 45 Ch D 1, Lindley, Cotton and Bowen LJJ.

*(No 1 of 1985).*[68] Now *Lister v Stubbs* has been disapproved by the Privy Council in *Attorney-General for Hong Kong v Reid*.[69] Lord Templeman upheld an equitable proprietary interest based in no more than breach of a fiduciary duty. Sufficient property interest to lodge a caveat for flowed from an employee's duty to account for bribes received. The Court of Appeal in England may be re-thinking the basis of constructive trusts, too. *Metall und Rohstoff AG v Donaldson Lufkin & Jeanrette Inc*[70] and *Council of the London Borough of Islington v Westdeutsche Landesbank Girozentrale*[71] (the 'swaps case') both seem to indicate that the institutional constructive trust has entered a decline. In an otherwise conservative case, the Privy Council in *Re Goldcorp Exchange Ltd*[72] countenanced the fact that constructive trusts sometimes exist independently of property rights.

**[6.30]**   Australian courts now take a policy-oriented approach to the raising of interests to justify constructive trusts. Remedial and result-oriented considerations guide the inquiry. 'Property interest' simulacra of the express trust are no longer appropriate. Judges in recent times have wrestled with several alternative ways to express the basis of the remedy. Wide scope beyond the restoration of property interests makes this a difficult task. Perhaps the most common formula to date is the question-begging 'unconscionable retention of title'. Or as it is sometimes put, 'unconscionability'. The writer believes that 'unjust enrichment' is preferable. It has slightly more heuristic potential. The grounds which attract it are a little more apparent. But the matter is not of great consequence. The policy-oriented approach of the courts will continue under whatever rubric and the words themselves imply very little. Policy considerations are considered separately. Insolvency is considered at [6.49]–[6.77] and the disgorgement of improper gains is considered at [6.105]–[6.115]. Under the present 'misappropriation of property' heading the justice of the case is fairly plain. The property of one has been misappropriated by another. The claimant is entitled to his property back. He has a sufficient interest in getting it back. *Tracing* that interest and the second step commands more attention.

### Constructive trusts and unjust enrichment

**[6.31]**   The 'principle of unjust enrichment', according to Goff and Jones, involves a 'reasonably developed and systematic complex of rules'. It requires three things:[73]

> First, the defendant must have been enriched by receipt of a *benefit*. Secondly, the benefit must have been gained *at the plaintiff's expense*. Thirdly, it would be *unjust* to allow the defendant to retain that benefit.

In situations where the claimant's property has been misappropriated, there is no difficulty in satisfying the first requirement. Benefit to the misappropriator

---

[68] [1986] 1 QB 491.

[69] [1994] 1 AC 324 (Lord Templeman): see [6.107].

[70] [1990] 1 QB 391 (CA), 479, Slade LJ.

[71] Unreported, Court of Appeal, 17 December 1993, Dillon, Leggatt and Kennedy LJJ, 12–13, Dillon LJ, 27–8, Leggatt LJ, affirming *Westdeutsche Landesbank Girozentrale v Council of the London Borough of Islington* [1993] 1 Bank LR 1, Hobhouse J.

[72] [1994] 2 All ER 806, 822–3 (Lord Musthill).

[73] Goff & Jones 16.

is manifest.[74] In the restitutionary canon of Peter Birks's *Introduction*, at pp 114–16, any property the defendant retains is assumed to be beneficial without being valued. No reasonable man could deny being enriched by money or what can be turned into money. The second requirement is easily satisfied too. Subtraction of property is the paradigm sense of an 'at the expense of' enrichment. It is where a 'plus to the defendant' as Birks says at 132, 'is a minus to the plaintiff'. A transfer of wealth from the plaintiff to the defendant has occurred.

**[6.32]** The third element, the 'unjust factor', is a little more problematic. Goff and Jones's *Law of Restitution* does not really supply the need here. To the extent that the claimant is seeking his chattels back, the claim would probably be classified as a 'pure proprietary' one and outside the scope of the book.[75] To the extent that the claimant seeks to get his money back, Goff and Jones says that he will only succeed if the (equitable) title is otherwise his. Which is self-evident. It is not what the book would describe as a 'restitutionary proprietary claim', whereby property interests are re-vested or vested anew on a discretionary basis. Birks is also silent on the point. No applicable unjust factor is apparent from his *Introduction*. In fact there is no proprietary unjust factor. Proprietary recovery, or the 'second measure of restitution', is assumed to function according to substantive property rules. Compendiously these are referred to as a 'continuing proprietary interest'— collapsing the interest step with the tracing step.[76] A property interest must exist and be continuously traceable. Andrew Burrows' *Law of Restitution* seems to be more helpful. A specific unjust factor is suggested for our situation. 'Retention of property belonging to the plaintiff without his consent' is suggested.[77] At first sight, this seems tailor-made for misappropriation. Burrows says (p 374):

> it would be very odd to deprive a plaintiff, who has identified his property as retained by the defendant, of the priority advantage that an available proprietary remedy would give him.

When a claimant can 'satisfy the title and tracing rules' and show that he has a better title than the defendant, it would be *unjust*, he says, that the claimant should not recover that property and enjoy whatever priority it entails. This all seems very convenient. But it tells you little. The function of unjust enrichment here was to describe the process whereby the interest base for a constructive trust was raised. According to Burrows, a claimant must prove his 'title' before it can be traced and recovered. Is not 'title' another word for interest? The 'retention of property' unjust factor is assuming what we are trying to prove. For is not a 'title' to be unjustly retained something which must be determined by the existing law of property and constructive trusts? The 'unjust factor' cannot tell us how to derive constructive trusts.

**[6.33]** Writing before the Burrows book was published, W Gummow remarked that the principle of unjust enrichment provides no rationale for the

---

[74] Burrows *Restitution* 362.
[75] Goff & Jones 73–4.
[76] Birks 378–85.
[77] Burrows *Restitution* 362–9.

award of proprietary as opposed to personal remedies.[78] It seems that this is still true. The prevalence of the constructive trust remedy seems almost an embarrassment to some English restitution scholars. Constructive trusts resolutely do not conform to a number of axioms. There is no equivalence, for example, between a defendant's enrichment and the measure of the remedy which reverses it.

**[6.34]** This is not a problem by which the American restitutionary scholars seem much troubled. A less doctrinaire approach to remedies is taken in the American Law Institute's *Restatement of Restitution* (1937) and the authorities which follow it. Authoritative texts on the subject like George Palmer's *Law of Restitution* (1978) are relaxed in the same way. Palmer says of the constructive trust at §1.4 that it is no more than 'a technique to be used in working out the problems of unjust enrichment.' He refers to a statement from *Latham v Father Divine*,[79] where the constructive trust was said to be–

> limited only by the inventiveness of men who find new ways to enrich themselves unjustly by grasping that which does not belong to them.

What is recommended here is that the 'unjust enrichment' formulation functions as a basic indicator that a constructive trust is due. Attention is then to be directed to the appropriate measure of relief.[80] Answers to hard cases are rarely forthcoming from the benefit and detriment calculus. The world is not that simple. And as we have noted, 'unjust enrichment' tells us nothing in insolvency cases. It is as only a rude framework for describing the constructive trusts entitlement that we must assess the idea. 'Unjust enrichment' in this context is perhaps a small advance on 'unconscionable retention of title' and suchlike self-evidencies.

### Avoiding earlier dispositions of beneficial interests

**[6.35]** Beneficiaries will sometimes need to undo dispositions to fiduciaries before being entitled to have the property restored. A beneficial interest disposed to a fiduciary must be set aside or rescinded before it can be claimed. Only after the beneficiary's title is re-established can a proprietary right in the property or money be recognised and enforced. Of course, equitable title has not passed and there is nothing to set aside where there has been a theft by the fiduciary, or a taking without claim of right.

**[6.36]** 'Rescission' is what this heading refers to. The word is very confusing. It may refer to the final equitable relief that a beneficiary seeks in a proceeding. This is a form of the doctrine which we will consider at [6.131]–[6.136]. Or 'rescission' may be a pre-condition of other relief. This is more the form we are concerned with here. Our inquiry is directed to the need for rescission of dispositions, usually contracts, which alter beneficial interests in the property to be recovered. Rescission of such dispositions may be necessary before a constructive trust can be imposed. It has been so held several times. Property or money cannot be the subject of specific relief until contracts inconsistently disposing of it have been avoided. In *Guinness plc v Saunders*[81]

---

[78] 'Unjust Enrichment, Restitution and Proprietary Remedies' in Finn *Restitution*, 47, 75.
[79] 85 NE 2d 168, 170 (1949) (CA (NY)).
[80] See J McCamus 'Unjust Enrichment: Its Role and Limits' in Waters 129, 155–6.
[81] [1990] 2 AC 663, see 697–8, Lord Goff, Lord Griffiths concurring, see [6.93].

this was argued to mean that before Mr Ward could be made a constructive trustee of the £5.2m 'consultancy fee' that he received from the company, a secret contract whereby he was paid this sum for his services had to be rescinded. The problem then was that rescission was impossible. The requirement of *restitutio in integrum* could not be met. Parties could not be replaced to their former positions. Guinness could not rescind the contract and restore Mr Ward to his former position after he had done the work contracted. Lord Goff acknowledged the force of this. 'Guinness', he said, 'cannot short-circuit an unrescinded contract by simply alleging a constructive trust'. Fortunately for the company, Lord Goff was able to overcome this rescission hurdle by finding that the contract was not properly authorised in the first place.

**[6.37]** The judgment of Brennan J in *Daly v Sydney Stock Exchange Ltd*[82] was to a similar effect. Daly's case concerned Dr Daly's deposit of a sum of money with a firm of share brokers. This was pending purchase of shares through that firm. Dr Daly had been told when the deposit was made that the time was not then right for the purchase of shares. An investment with the firm would in the meantime be 'as safe as a bank'. At this time in fact the firm was in a parlous financial position. It became insolvent shortly afterwards and unable to pay its debts. Dr Daly applied to recover compensation from a fidelity fund established by the Securities Industry Act 1975 (NSW). That Act provided compensation only where the claimant could show that the stock broking firm received the money 'as trustee'. The firm was argued to be a constructive trustee. In a judgment with which Wilson J agreed, Brennan J held that this could not be allowed if the broker had received the money beneficially under a contract of loan and that contract had not been avoided. At 390 he said that–

> it is incumbent on the claimant to show that, at the time when the stockbroker received the moneys in question, he received them on behalf of another as trustee. The criterion is not satisfied if he received the moneys under a contract which gave him a beneficial title recognized by equity, albeit a beneficial title that is imperfect and liable to be divested by relation back in the event of avoidance of the loan. In the absence of evidence of avoidance of the contracts of loan, there is nothing to show that Dr Daly or Mrs Daly has the equitable interest in the moneys lent by Dr Daly to Patrick Partners which might have arisen by relation back.

The reasoning could be extended to other dealings where contractual regulation of the transfer of property between the parties has occurred. Equity respects and will give effect to the contractual disposition of beneficial interests. For this reason a beneficiary cannot raise an inconsistent equity in what a contract has disposed of until the contract is avoided. The idea accords with the reasoning of Kitto J in *Latec Investments Ltd v Hotel Terrigal Pty Ltd (in liq)*.[83] Where a constructive trust is asserted over property sold, Kitto J said, the purchaser's beneficial title remained consistent with the contract of sale as long as it stood.[84] Authority for the proposition is impeccable. Yet the necessity for rescission supposed in *Guinness's* and *Daly's* cases has a formalism which

---

[82] (1986) 160 CLR 371, 382–91.
[83] (1965) 113 CLR 265, 290–1.
[84] (1965) 113 CLR 265, 277–8.

seems inappropriate beside many conceptions of the constructive trust. The idea was not mentioned, for example, by Lord Templeman in *Space Investments Ltd v Canadian Imperial Bank of Commerce Trust Co (Bahamas) Ltd*,[85] or by the other members of the High Court in *Daly's* case itself.

### 'Tracing the interest'

**[6.38]**    The constructive trust as a proprietary remedy is not constituted where the tracing step cannot be satisfied. The constructive trust interest must be annexed to particular property in the defendant's possession, or it has no effect. We will now assume that an interest sufficient to base a constructive trust has been raised. We are concerned here to see whether that interest can finally be asserted. This is a live question in a great number of misappropriation cases. Annexure is problematic.

### *Identification rules: mixtures and changes in form*

**[6.39]**    'Tracing' refers to the equitable regime for determining whether the identity of property can be followed as that property is confounded with other property, or as it passes from one form to another. Where the money or a thing has either been exchanged or had its character altered, the claimant may succeed to rights to or over the end-product.[86] Sometimes the end-product has become a mixture of the claimant's money or things and those of other claimants. At other times the money or things are mixed with the defendant's own things. In such cases, equity has evolved a number of rules. They provide authoritative resolution of whether and how the claimant is able to identify and trace to the form which the property eventually takes.

**[6.40]**    1. A fiduciary who has used the beneficiary's money or thing (and none other) in exchange for some other money or thing gives the beneficiary an election. Either the beneficiary can identify and take the other property in specie. Or the beneficiary can assert a lien over the property toward the satisfaction of a claim for the value of what was taken. This is known as 'the election in *Hallett's* case'.[87]

**[6.41]**    2. A fiduciary may mix his own property with the beneficiary's money or thing so that they are unidentifiable separately. Then part of the mixed fund is re-invested or dissipated. The fiduciary will be treated as having re-invested or dissipated that part of the fund which provides the greatest recovery for the beneficiary. This statement connects the principle in *Re Hallett's Estate*, at 709, that a fiduciary is presumed to draw out and dissipate his own money first, with the principle in *Re Oatway*[88] that a trustee is unable to claim any part of a mixed fund until he has restored trust money.

**[6.42]**    3. A fiduciary may mix his own with the beneficiary's money or things so that they are unidentifiable separately. Then the fiduciary may dissipate all or part of the mixed fund. Later again, the fiduciary may restore all or part of what he dissipated. Whether then the beneficiary is able to identify any part

---

[85] [1986] 3 All ER 75 (PC).

[86] *Banque Belge v Hambrouck* [1921] 1 KB 321 (CA), 330, Scrutton LJ.

[87] *Re Hallett's Estate* (1879) 13 Ch D 696 (CA), 709, Jessel MR, explained in *Scott v Scott* (1962) 109 CLR 649, 660–4, curiam.

[88] [1903] 2 Ch 356, 361, Joyce J.

of his claim in the restored fund depends on what the fiduciary's intention was at the time of the restoration. Sometimes he may have intended to reconstitute the original property subject to the relationship. It will then be available to the beneficiary accordingly.[89] At other times it will be clear that the original trusts are exhausted.[90]

**[6.43]** 4. If the fiduciary mixes the money or things of two or more beneficiaries, then dissipates part of the mixed fund, the loss will be borne equally by the beneficiaries in proportion to their claims. This is unless the fund constitutes a running account, like a bank account. Losses on a running account will be borne by the beneficiaries on the 'first in, first out' basis. This is known as the 'rule in *Clayton's* case'.[91] There is little authority on this. Principle suggests that the loss should be borne by the beneficiaries equally and the rule in *Clayton's* case has been much disapproved. It was seen to work an injustice and rejected in the New Zealand Court of Appeal in *Re Registered Securities Ltd*.[92] The United States 'rateable' distribution, or proportionate sharing basis, was preferred. The English Court of Appeal in *Barlow Clowes International Ltd (in liq) v Vaughan*[93] recently applied the rule with the greatest reluctance. The 'North American solution' of rateable distribution was said to be 'manifestly fairer'. Unfortunately in *Barlow* it was impracticable on the facts.

**[6.44]** 5. If the fiduciary innocently mixes his money or thing with the money or thing of the beneficiary so that they cannot be identified separately, the parties are then entitled to participate in the mixed fund in the proportions of their separate values mixed. This is unless the fund is a running account, when 'first in, first out' rule may apply.[94]

**[6.45]** 6. A fiduciary may mix his own money or things with those of the beneficiary so that the interests are unidentifiable separately. If he therewith purchases an investment which appreciates in value, the beneficiary and the fiduciary are entitled to share in that increased value proportionately to their original contributions.[95] However *Paul A Davies (Australia) Pty Ltd (in liq) v Davies*[96] has held that this 'tracing rule' defers to the profits rule where both are applicable. Noted at [5.55], the profits rule requires a fiduciary to disgorge the entire profit made in breach of fiduciary duty.

**[6.46]** 7. Identification is impossible and the beneficiary's proprietary right will be extinguished in the following circumstances.

---

[89] *James Roscoe (Bolton) Ltd v Winder* [1915] 1 Ch 62.

[90] *Lofts v McDonald* [1974] 3 ALR 404 (SC (Qld)).

[91] *(Devaynes v Noble)* (1817) 1 Mer 572; 35 ER 781; see Jacobs [2717] and LRCBC 'Report on Competing Rights to Mingled Property', 48.

[92] [1991] 1 NZLR 545, 553, curiam.

[93] [1992] 4 All ER 22, 35, Woolf LJ, discussing *Re Schmidt (Walter J) & Co* 298 F 314 (1923) (US DC SD NY).

[94] *Re Diplock* [1948] 1 Ch 465 (CA), 551–2, 554–6.

[95] *Re Tilley's Will Trusts* [1967] 1 Ch 1179, 1189, Ungoed-Thomas J.

[96] [1983] 1 NSWLR 440 (CA).

- The beneficiary's money or thing reaches the hands of a bona fide purchaser.[97] This is particularly applicable to third party claims: see [7.15]–[7.19] below.
- The beneficiary's money or thing is consumed, either without residue or without discharge of an existing liability of the fiduciary.[98]
- If it would be inequitable to allow the beneficiary to trace or be subrogated to a creditor's rights.[99]

**[6.47]** These traditional identification rules are often criticised for being arbitrary. Or, as the Canadian David Stevens puts it, the rules are not 'causal' or 'congruent' with the way in which traceable interests are acquired.[100] There certainly is no reversal of an unjust enrichment in the 'first in first out rule'. However the point of the rules is not evident from their form. In a similar way the tracing rules are criticised for operating on the basis of 'accidental' features of a transaction. Rules are unrelated to the substantial merits of a claim.[101] But does this matter? The rule that cars must drive on the left-hand side of the road is comparable. To criticise that rule as arbitrary or lacking in congruence would be to ignore the 'channelling' function it performs. Expecting tracing rules to operate causally within a proprietary claim is a little like expecting the traffic rule to be congruent with a tendency of drivers to drive on a particular side of the road.

### Declining significance of identification rules

**[6.48]** Application of the foregoing identification rules may be in decline. Sometimes, despite the most favourable application of the above rules, deserving plaintiffs are unable to identify their pre-existing property in the confusion of defendants' affairs. Facts may cry out for 'equitable priority' and yet a right to trace cannot sensibly be upheld. This is a feature of the rules we shall deal with in the insolvency context.

### The effect of insolvency

**[6.49]** The modern importance of equitable proprietary claims is mostly associated with defendants' insolvency. Where a court is asked to protect a pre-existing proprietary interest, Roy Goode says that it is a 'matter of indifference' to the insolvent's creditors whether the court grants a proprietary remedy.[102]

> This is because P's interest is not dependent on the court order, so that if P's claim for specific return is upheld the assets available for D's secured or [unsecured] creditors are not diminished in any way by the court order, whilst if P's claim is refused and he is required to be content with a money judgment his interest in the asset continues until such time as the judgment is satisfied, so that D's estate can only acquire the asset by paying its monetary value. Thus the economic effect of the court's decision to grant or refuse a real remedy is essentially neutral.

---

[97]  *Brady v Stapleton* (1952) 88 CLR 322, 332–3, Dixon CJ and Fullagar J.
[98]  *Re Diplock* [1948] 1 Ch 465, 521.
[99]  Ibid, 547–50; see [7.20]: Third parties and 'Change of position'.
[100]  'Restitution, Property and the Cause of Action in Unjust Enrichment Pt I' (1989) 39 *UTLJ* 258, 271–6.
[101]  D Oesterle 'Deficiencies in the Restitutionary Right to Trace' (1983) 68 *Cornell LR* 172, 174–5.
[102]  R Goode 'Property and Unjust Enrichment' in Burrows 215, 223–4.

In some moral sense, perhaps, the claimant is only claiming what was always his. But from the claimant's perspective, the difference in the remedy being allowed or not may be quite dramatic. The statutory regimes are as follows.

## Bankruptcy

[6.50]  Where the defendant is an individual and he is adjudged a bankrupt, s 58(1) of the Bankruptcy Act 1966 (Cth) provides that the 'property of a bankrupt' vests in the Official Trustee in Bankruptcy. The 'property of a bankrupt' is defined in s 5(1) of the Act to be 'property divisible amongst the creditors of the bankrupt'. Section 116(2)(a) then specifically excludes from the definition of what property is divisible amongst the creditors of the bankrupt 'property held by the bankrupt on trust for another person'.

In other words, only property in which the bankrupt holds a beneficial interest is divisible amongst his creditors. A creditor of a debtor is protected from the rateable distribution consequences of his debtor's bankruptcy to the extent that he can successfully claim an equitable interest in the nature of a trust in property which the debtor possesses. For the subject of a constructive trust effective at the date of bankruptcy does not form part of the bankrupt estate. The property passes in specie to the claimant, unless it is part of another creditor's security interest which precedes the trust, or unless the property is intercepted by a bona fide purchaser for value.[103] When the trust becomes effective is critical. Prima facie, a constructive trust is effective from the time of the unconscionable conduct which occasions it.[104] After observing this, Deane J in *Muschinski v Dodds* went on to say that the timing aspect of the remedy may not be beyond development.[105] For,

> in this country at least, the constructive trust has not outgrown its formative stages as an equitable remedy and should still be seen as constituting an in personam remedy attaching to property which can be moulded and adjusted to give effect to the application and interplay of equitable principles in the circumstances of the particular case. In particular, where competing common law or equitable claims are or may be involved, a declaration of constructive trust by way of remedy can properly be so framed that the consequences of its imposition are operative only from the date of judgment or formal court order or from some other specified date.

Remarks like this may well be a straw in the wind. But, as legal doctrine had not so evolved at the date of writing this book, we will ignore these possibilities and assume that a constructive trust as remedy for a breach of fiduciary duty is effective for all purposes as from when the breach occurred.

[6.51]  Where the claimant cannot or does not raise for himself an equitable interest in any of the debtor's property, all of that property passes to the Official Trustee. However it does so subject to all the liabilities and equities which affected the property in the debtor's hands.[106] Neither a bankruptcy trustee nor a general creditor of the bankrupt is a 'bona fide purchaser' within

---

103  McDonald, Henry and Meek *Australian Bankruptcy Law and Practice* 5th ed (1977), [567/1] ff.

104  *Muschinski v Dodds* (1985) 160 CLR 583, 614, Deane J; *Re Jointon* [1992] 2 Qd R 105, 107–8 and see *Re Osborn* (1989) 91 ALR 135, 142, Pincus J.

105  (1985) 160 CLR 583, 615.

106  *Re Goode* (1974) 24 FLR 61, 68, White J; *Daly v Sydney Stock Exchange* (1986) 160 CLR 371, 389, Brennan J.

the meaning of this exception to the competence of equitable remedies.[107] Potential constructive trusts are unaffected by bankruptcy of the possible constructive trustee. Constructive trusts may be claimed before or after the property of a bankrupt debtor passes to the Official Trustee. When they are successfully claimed before bankruptcy, the claimant will be able to invoke para 116(2)(a) of the Act to prevent the subject property from becoming 'property of the bankrupt'. When they are successfully claimed after bankruptcy, the claimant's equity becomes an equitable interest governed by the same provision. Liability of the Official Trustee is the same whenever the equity is asserted, although priorities with other creditors may vary.

### Corporate insolvency

**[6.52]**    This is analogous to the bankruptcy of an individual. It is governed by the Corporations Law, Part 5.6 'Winding up generally'. 'Property of a company' referred to in that Part does not include property that the company holds on trust for another. This much has been assumed in much litigation. However it is not expressly stated in either the Corporations Law or in the Corporations Regulations. Unlike the sequence of events in the bankruptcy of an individual, there is no transfer of the assets of the insolvent company to an insolvency official. The official is a liquidator who displaces the board and acts in right of the company. Liquidators distribute the available assets in the company's name. The company name is given a suffix to indicate the new regime.[108] Perhaps the draftsman thought it was too obvious to say that liquidators can only distribute assets which are vested in companies beneficially. Of course an insolvent company cannot distribute someone else's property as its own. Trust assets then are only referred to obliquely. For example, the Corporations Law s 577(1) excludes from the commission's residual power of disposal 'any estate or interest in property . . . merely held in trust'.

### 1.    Priorities between beneficiaries and unsecured creditors

**[6.53]**    One of the central uses of the constructive trust in insolvency is to enable its beneficiaries to obtain priority over a debtor's unsecured creditors. *Scott on Trusts* makes a rather dry observation at this point.[109] 'Most of the writers of monographs on the subject of priorities', he says, 'and many of the judges', think that 'there is something essentially commendable in giving one claimant priority over others.'

> This is a peculiar psychological phenomenon. It is doubtless due to a comfortable feeling of generosity to the victim, and it has the peculiar advantage that the generosity is wholly vicarious. It is not the writer of the monograph who pays the bill but the general creditors of the wrongdoer.

From the beneficiary's perspective, the difference that priority can make is between specific recovery of his property, on the one hand, and an abated personal claim, on the other. Abated personal claims are often of negligible value. From the unsecured creditors' perspective, if a claim abates it means more value available for pari passu distribution. More abated recovery for all

---

[107] Explained in American Law Institute *Restatement of Restitution* (1937), [173], comment *j*.
[108] See *Re Matheson* (1994) 121 ALR 605, 611–12, Spender J (Fed C).
[109] 4th edn ed W Fratcher, §521.

unsecured creditors, in other words. The opposite is the case when beneficiaries prevent the value of their property from becoming part of the divisible 'property of the company'.

**[6.54]** Section 116(2)(a) of the Bankruptcy Act 1966 (Cth) and the general law provide that persons entitled to interests under constructive trusts have priority over an insolvent's unsecured creditors. This is a positive matter. The problem is that this priority often seems unjust. Such was the appearance of the decision of the Federal Court in *Re Stephenson Nominees Pty Ltd*.[110] A mortgage-broker had loaned money on behalf of various investors and promised them that they would obtain first mortgage security status in return. Irregularities occurred in the course of his business. Securities were not always linked to the correct lenders or amounts. One of the investors was Stephenson Nominees. It already had moneys with the broker secured by a mortgage shortly to be discharged. A proposal for the re-deployment of those moneys was agreed to. They were to be invested in a loan to a Mr and Mrs Roberts and secured by a mortgage given by them. The broker in fact drew the money for the Roberts advance from an undisclosed fund he administered. In this fund the moneys of many investors were unidentifiably mixed. A mortgage document was signed by the Roberts in favour of Stephenson Nominees, witnessing the advance of a similar amount to what had been agreed. It was then registered in legal form by the broker and handed to Stephenson Nominees. The company thereby obtained a legal right to the mortgage re-payments made by the Roberts. At about this time the broker was adjudged a bankrupt. A substantial shortfall in the mixed fund came to light. No client could establish from whose moneys any loan (including the Roberts loan) had been made. The Roberts later paid the mortgage moneys into court in order to obtain their discharge. Stephenson Nominees appeared to be entitled to the sum. However the Official Trustee sought an order that Stephenson Nominees held its legal right to the moneys on trust for himself, as the person standing in the broker's shoes. This was said to be because no investor could identify or trace the funds in the mortgage advance as its own. Stephenson Nominees was argued to be a 'volunteer' in relation to a mortgage which secured funds really advanced by the broker. The argument was upheld by the majority. Spender J at 494 (with whom Forster J agreed) said that Stephenson Nominees was a constructive trustee of its rights under the mortgage for the Official Trustee. It was said to be 'unjust and unconscionable for [Stephenson Nominees] to assert a beneficial title' to the payments.

**[6.55]** A persuasive dissent was entered in the Stephenson Nominees case by Gummow J. At 500–1 he saw no trust to arise in favour of the broker. So far, he said, that inference of a trust depended on the broker's intention, all evidence of it pointed the other way. The broker had plainly intended that Stephenson Nominees should have the security which the mortgage allowed. This was a possible 'appropriation' of the type we will examine under a following sub-heading. Nor, at 506–10, did Gummow J see that there was any equity for the court to impose a constructive trust in favour of the broker. The

---

110 (1987) 76 ALR 485: see also *Re Australian Home Finance Pty Ltd* [1956] VLR 1, Herring CJ; *Windsor Mortgage Nominees Pty Ltd v Cardwell* (1979) ACLC 40-540; *Australian Securities Commission v Melbourne Asset Management Nominees Pty Ltd* (1994) 12 ACLC 364, Northrop J (Fed Ct).

facts, as he saw them, did not indicate that Stephenson Nominees had acted 'unconscionably' in the transaction. Gummow J did acknowledge that recovery of property by constructive trust might be based otherwise than on identification of proprietary interests in the plaintiff's claim. 'Unequal acceptance of risk' was suggested. On this point dicta from the decision were quoted at length and followed by Northrop J in *Australian Securities Commission v Melbourne Asset Management Nominees Pty Ltd.*[111] We shall examine the idea at [6.61]–[6.66].

**[6.56]**  Of course, the facts of *Stephenson Nominees* were a little unusual. The constructive trust was in reverse of that usually imposed. Instead of being in favour of a creditor to defeat the Official Trustee, it was in favour of the Official Trustee to defeat a creditor. Yet the majority reasoning is a good example of the process whereby a constructive trust may now arise even though the claimant is unable to identify any property interest in the assets claimed. For the broker was not able to identify the loan funds as his own, by reason of the obvious fact that he had no beneficial interest in funds invested on behalf of clients. The court was unanimous on that. Perhaps the majority justices were moved to act on behalf of the other clients by reason of their plight. It was not *fair*, it was *unconscionable*, that *Stephenson Nominees* should enjoy a fortuitous advantage. The company claimed the fruits of legal rights as mortgagee when the creditors were all really in the same boat. But this is not an application of principle. As Gummow J pointed out, other principles of equity pointed away from a constructive trust. We shall now examine some different approaches to the question of whether priority should be allowed.

*Ability to trace*

**[6.57]**  The view in the United States is that a claimant's ability to trace his property into the defendant's hands is the decisive test of whether to allow the claimant priority over unsecured creditors. We have said that this is an orthodoxy in Anglo-Australian law as well. Tracing rules are the traditional basis of 'fairness' to unsecured claims.[112]

**[6.58]**  A need for tracing does not carry the implication that constructive trusts must be based in (traceable) property. Remedial constructive trusts have too strong a hold on the judicial imagination for that. In the present context there are usually no tracing problems, though. For claims in this part are ones where property is to be 'recovered'. Property, that is, which is definitionally pre-existing. We have noted above some of the ways that constructive trusts can be justified besides being based in property. 'Unjust enrichment' is pre-eminent amongst these.

**[6.59]**  A body of older Australian authorities dealing with identifiability and equitable proprietary relief supports the need for tracing for this insolvency purpose. Tracing is perhaps the most significant of the general law additions to the ranking of creditors of an insolvent estate in Part 6 of the Bankruptcy Act 1966 (Cth). Now that interests to justify constructive trusts can be raised by result-oriented formulae, tracing may be more needed than before. For all

---

[111] (1994) 12 ACLC 364, Northrop J (Fed Ct).

[112] See R Goode 'Ownership and Obligation in Commercial Transactions' (1987) 103 *LQR* 433, 444.

the intuitive justice and revendicatory virtue that unjust enrichment implies, it is virtually *blind* in insolvency terms. Because it eschews proprietary reach or competence, unjust enrichment supplies few ways of discriminating between several claimants who have suffered injustices. Two stockbroker cases show how tracing can supply this need. In the case of *Re Docker*,[113] the broker was a member of the Sydney Stock Exchange. He had become contractually liable to other members of the exchange for the prices of shares purchased from them. These shares the broker had re-sold and the proceeds were placed in a special account. Upon that member becoming insolvent and ceasing to trade, the other members of the exchange argued that because of one of the exchange rules they were entitled to an equitable lien over the account. This was in priority to the general creditors. It was allowed in part only by Lukin J. At 105 he held that the other members were entitled to succeed to the extent that they were able to specifically identify and trace their moneys into the special account.

**[6.60]** Another example is *Re Ward & Co*,[114] also a stockbroker case. The bankrupts had been partners in a firm trading on the Stock Exchange of Melbourne. At the date of bankruptcy there was the usual shortfall of assets over liabilities. A mixed collection of share scrip certificates existed. They were held for various clients of the firm. At 44–5 Lukin J discussed the possibility that the collection was the subject of a constructive trust held in proportionate shares for the whole body of clients. 'The relationship between the bankrupts and their clients' he said, 'was that of principal and agent'–

> the shares or moneys of the clients were given for a special and limited purpose and the brokers held such moneys or shares or the proceeds of such shares in a fiduciary capacity, and thereby trusts were created.

However the judge went on to hold at 49 that the trust failed in respect of all the scrip which a client was not able to 'trace and identify as his property in its converted and changed form and/or condition'. It was insufficient that the clients could prove that the share broker owed them equitable obligations, flowing from receipt of the shares as a fiduciary. The tracing rules had to be satisfied as well in order to enable the share broker's clients to enjoy the priority advantage of taking their shares in specie from the broker's scrip collection.

## *Character of the wrong and acceptance of risk*

**[6.61]** Another basis for awarding priority over the general body of creditors proceeds from the type of wrong which brings the claimant to court. Are breach of fiduciary duty claims of higher merit than the claims of unsecured creditors? On one view, the assets of the wrongdoing fiduciary have been 'swollen' by the improper gain. The insolvent estate is larger than it would have been but for the wrong.[115] But as against this, it might be said that unsecured creditors have been wronged by the insolvent, too. They have not been paid. Some unsecured claims may have arisen in circumstances at least as deserving as those of the putative beneficiary. As a rule, unsecured creditors

---

[113] (1938) 10 ABC 97.

[114] (1937) 10 ABC 42 and *Re Hodgetts* (1949) 16 ABC 201.

[115] *Scott on Trusts* ed W Fratcher 4th edn (1989), §521.

have given value to the debtor. Goods were delivered or work was done. Beneficiaries in fiduciary relationships have only occasionally given value. Or an unsecured creditor may seek to enforce a judgment for personal injury damages. This could be on account of the insolvent's driving, or a vicious assault. It is hard to generalise that unsecured claims are always inferior. Perhaps, as David Paciocco says, a wrong's nature and a defendant's behaviour are insufficient bases for the award of proprietary relief.[116]

**[6.62]** The 'acceptance of risk' criterion is comparable. It looks to the nature or source of contending claims. Unsecured creditors who lend money without security or who sell goods on general credit are said to take the risk that their debtors may become insolvent and unable to pay the debts. Those, by contrast, who entrust their property to others are said to be entitled to believe that no risk of the others' insolvency is being run. Entrustors are entitled to assume honesty in their fiduciary. Persons trusted should have segregated the trusted property from their own, so that it is identifiably separate from any insolvent estate and not liable to abate with claims upon it. At least, this is the way that George Palmer and the Americans explain the 'acceptance of risk' justification.[117] It is used to justify the priority that is given to an interest which can be traced into existing property. This is the very thing that some English and Australian authorities believe that 'acceptance of risk' can supplant.[118] It will be contended here that the 'acceptance of risk' criterion is not an autonomous alternative to the tracing requirements.

**[6.63]** We shall examine the pedigree of the 'acceptance of risk' principle. *Re Kountze Bros*[119] was the main authority for it given in the English and Australian cases. *Re Stephenson Nominees Pty Ltd*[120] described *Kountze* as—

> an authority expressed in wider terms that bases the priority given to a fiduciary claimant over general creditors on the footing that inherent in the nature of the fiduciary relationship was the reposition of trust in the honesty of the fiduciary, whilst the general creditors took the risk of his solvency.

It is hard to see that the decision in *Kountze Bros* framed any such principle. The facts were as follows. Los Angeles city was a customer of a New York bank which failed in the depression. The city claimed an entitlement to trace the proceeds of cheques that the bank was collecting on its behalf. A 'constructive trust' was asserted over a fund said to contain them. This was the bank's own account with another bank. However, on the relevant day, that account was technically overdrawn. This would normally have extinguished the city's tracing claim. The result was avoided because the defendant's banker extended credit to the defendant on a basis additional to the overdraft. Assuming that this additional basis had been used up first, the defendant was

---

[116] 'The Remedial Constructive Trust: A Principled Basis for Priorities over Creditors' (1989) 68 *Can Bar Rev* 315, 348.

[117] *Law of Restitution* vol 1 (1979), §2.14; *Law of Trusts and Trustees*, rev 2nd ed, G & G Bogert (1982), §926; *Scott on Trusts* ed W Fratcher 4th edn (1989), §518.

[118] See *Space Investments Ltd v Canadian Imperial Bank of Commerce Trust Co (Bahamas) Ltd* [1986] 3 All ER 75, 78 (PC, Lord Templeman); *Re Stephenson Nominees Pty Ltd* (1987) 76 ALR 485, 505–6, Gummow J; *Australian Securities Commission v Melbourne Asset Management Nominees Pty Ltd* (1994) 12 ACLC 364, 382–3 Northrop J (Fed Ct).

[119] 79 F 2d 98 (1935) (CA (2nd circ)), 102, Swan J, Chase and L Hand JJ agreeing.

[120] (1987) 76 ALR 485, 506, Gummow J.

taken not to have depleted the account into which the city's cheques were paid. This enabled a constructive trust to be impressed upon the account to secure the collected proceeds. Swan J said:

> Equity marshalls the withdrawals against the fiduciary's own funds so long as it can because that result is deemed fairer. There is good reason for this because the fiduciary's creditors have *accepted the risk of his solvency*, whilst his cestui have accepted the risk only of his honesty. [emphasis added]

This remark was made relative to tracing the interest that the city had raised to the relevant fund. It was the only reference that the court made to the 'acceptance of risk' idea. The idea was to justify what we would call 'the rule in *Hallett's case*', a tracing rule.[121] Fiduciaries are assumed to act honestly by withdrawing first their own moneys from a mixed fund. *Hallett's case* was one of the authorities the New York Court considered.

**[6.64]** The first time the English courts discussed the 'acceptance of risk' idea appears to have been in *Space Investments Ltd v Canadian Imperial Bank of Commerce Trust Co (Bahamas) Ltd*.[122] A bank had been made trustee pursuant to various deeds of trusts. Each of these contained a clause permitting the trustee to deposit trust moneys in a savings account maintained by any bank, including itself. In accordance with the power, the bank itself took trust moneys on deposit. A petition was later presented for the winding up of the bank and liquidators were appointed. Beneficiaries of the trusts argued on a liquidator's summons that trust moneys deposited with the bank were impressed with a constructive trust in their favour. They claimed an entitlement to trace and recover their money in specie, in priority to the claims of other depositors. The Privy Council rejected this. It held that the beneficiaries were unsecured creditors of the bank without priority rights. According to the law of banker and customer, Lord Templeman said (at 76), a customer who is a trustee is still only an ordinary creditor of the bank without any trust interest in the bank's assets. Since the deposits by the bank as trustee were made in conformity with the terms of the trusts, the beneficiaries could not have any greater rights than any other unsecured customer had against the bank.

**[6.65]** The decision itself in *Space Investments* does not bear as much on this subject as the following obiter dicta in the Board's opinion. Lord Templeman (at 97) considered the position which would have obtained had the bank's deposit with itself been in breach of trust. It should be remembered that the facts supposed included a 'proprietary base' for the claimants in the trust moneys deposited.

> Whether a bank trustee lawfully receives deposits or wrongly treats trust money as on deposit from trusts, all the moneys are in fact dealt with and expended by the bank for the general purposes of the bank. In these circumstances it is impossible for the beneficiaries interested in trust money misappropriated from their trust to trace their money to any particular asset belonging to the trustee bank. But equity allows the beneficiaries, or a new trustee appointed in place of the insolvent bank trustee to protect the interests of the beneficiaries, to trace the trust money to all the assets of the bank and to recover the trust money by the exercise of an equitable charge over all the assets of the bank. Where an insolvent bank goes into liquidation

---

[121] (1879) 13 Ch D 696 (CA).
[122] [1986] 3 All ER 75.

that equitable charge secures for the beneficiaries and the trust priority over the claims of the customers in respect of their deposits and over the claims of all the other unsecured creditors. This priority is conferred because the customers and other unsecured creditors voluntarily accept the risk that the trustee bank might become insolvent and unable to discharge its obligations in full. On the other hand, the settlor of the trust and the beneficiaries interested under the trust never accepted any of the risks involved in the possible insolvency of the trustee bank.

This has been criticised as an illegitimate disregard of the *Re Diplock* tracing requirements.[123] Something equivalent to tracing was distilled out of the beneficiaries' disappointed expectations. Whether this is sufficient for the purpose is highly questionable. In the fourth edition of Goff and Jones the sufficiency question was side-stepped. A claimant's acceptance of the risk of the defendant's insolvency is at 98–9 elevated into a criterion above and *additional* to the identification rules. Identification of assets in insolvency, Jones says, 'is not enough to capture their value'. This does not appear to be what Lord Templeman intended. Templeman contemplates that the beneficiaries might have been able to assert equitable proprietary rights over unidentifiable funds. An interest under an equitable lien would thus override the passing of the beneficial interest in the money to the bank according to the usual terms of the banker and customer relationship.[124] This reasoning has since been disapproved by the same tribunal in *Re Goldcorp Exchange Ltd*.[125] We note at [6.73] how the English courts have reaffirmed the identification rules where equitable proprietary interests in insolvency are claimed.

**[6.66]**   If *Space Investments* is followed in Australia, it will hasten the demise of the identification rules. Obiter dicta of Gummow J in *Re Stephenson Nominees Pty Ltd*[126] have unearthed the idea for other courts to consider. Gummow J says, a little obscurely, that after *Daly v Sydney Stock Exchange Ltd*[127] unequal acceptance of risk 'may not always suffice' to yield priority on its own. However, Northrop J treated 'acceptance of risk' as sufficient on its own to award a constructive trust in *Australian Securities Commission v Melbourne Asset Management Nominees Pty Ltd*.[128] This was another mortgage-broking case and the claimants were unable to trace their entitlements. Maybe it is better not to see the idea as sufficient rationale of a constructive trust, but rather as the beginning of an undefined 'equity' in insolvency.[129] This seems to be closer to what Goff and Jones propose.

*Specific appropriation*

**[6.67]**   This is a different way to argue for the annexure to misappropriated property of an interest raised. Equitable significance that an appropriation of

---

[123] R Goode 'Ownership and Obligation in Commercial Transactions' (1987) 103 *LQR* 433, 445–7, referring to [1948] Ch 465, 521 (CA).

[124] Cf S Stoljar in 'Re-Examining Sinclair v Brougham' (1959) 22 *MLR* 21, 31.

[125] [1994] 2 All ER 806, 827 (PC), followed by *Bishopsgate Investment Management Ltd v Homan* (unreported, UK Court of Appeal, 12 July 1994).

[126] (1987) 76 ALR 485, 502.

[127] (1986) 160 CLR 371.

[128] (1994) 12 ACLC 364, 44–7, Northrop J (Fed Ct).

[129] Cf M Neave and M Weinberg 'The Nature and Function of Equities (Part II)' (1978) 6 *U of Tas L Rev* 115, 136 and J Glover 'Bankruptcy and Constructive Trusts' (1991) 19 *ABLR* 97, 120–3.

assets may have was described in the following passage from the judgment of Gibbs ACJ in *Australasian Conference Association Ltd v Mainline Constructions Pty Ltd (in liq)*:[130]

> when money is advanced by A to B, with the mutual intention that it should not become part of the assets of B, but should be used exclusively for a specific purpose, there will be implied (at least in the absence of a contrary intention) a stipulation that if the purpose fails the money will be repaid, and the arrangement will give rise to a relationship of a fiduciary character, or trust.

Gibbs J was commenting on *Barclays Bank Ltd v Quistclose Investments Ltd*[131] and the principle that a constructive trust for a person may arise where money is appropriated to a purpose, given to another and the purpose fails. *Quistclose* concerned an express trust, but the reasoning in the speech of Lord Wilberforce seems to relate to constructive trusts as well.[132] There have been several Australian cases which follow the *Quistclose* principle which do not strictly distinguish whether express or constructive trusts are being upheld. See *Re Veli*[133] and *Re Travel House of Australia*[134] and favourable comments of L Priestly in Finn's book on *Equity and Commercial Relationships*.[135]

**[6.68]** *Re Goode* was a case where the 'appropriation' idea was used in combination with more normal 'tracing' requirements. Goode traded on the Stock Exchange of Adelaide. He operated a share scrip 'pool', into which he placed share certificates belonging to his clients together with those relating to his own speculations. A trust account for moneys of clients which Goode possessed from time to time was not used. Instead, he mixed his clients' with his own moneys in an account which was at all material times overdrawn. Bankruptcy caught up with him. One of the issues in the insolvency administration was how the pool of scrip should be distributed and whether, in particular, any client could assert a trust interest in the scrip to take it outside the body of assets to be distributed generally. Whilst all scrip or money given by a client to a broker as fiduciary was seen to be potentially trust property, White J (at 68–9) held that only *identifiable* trust property did not pass to the Official Trustee upon the broker's bankruptcy. All those clients who conducted a running account with the broker were unable to identify their scrip. Only those clients who could show that the broker had specifically appropriated scrip to them from his 'pool' were entitled to stand outside the insolvency administration.

The result of *Goode's* case contrasts with that in *Windsor Mortgage Nominees Pty Ltd v Cardwell*.[137] Windsor was an insolvent mortgage-broker whose affairs were being tidied up. Again there had been a wrongful mixture of funds. Money and securities could not be unravelled as appointed to any investors in particular. Yet the broker had 'declared trusts' in favour of some

---

130 (1978) 141 CLR 335, 353.
131 [1970] AC 567.
132 S Scott 'The remedial constructive trust in commercial situations' [1993] *LMCLQ* 330, 347.
133 (1988) 18 FCR 204, Ryan J (Fed Ct).
134 SC (Vic), Murray J, 31 August 1978, unreported.
135 'The Romalpa clause and the Quistclose Trust', in Finn *Relationships* 217.
136 (1974) 24 FLR 61, White J (Ct of Insolvency).
137 (1979) ACLC 40-540, 32,199, Dunn J (SC (Vic)).

investors and supplied them with written details of securities and sums invested. No trust priority was allowed on this account. They were appropriations by 'accident', it was held, and to give effect to them was not a principled way to discriminate between claimants.

### United States approaches

**[6.69]**  United States approaches to the constructive trust differ from state to state. Jurisdictions mostly draw a similar distinction to that between the above two steps. Interests under constructive trusts are mostly *raised* according to flexible criteria. But *tracing* is needed to obtain advantages in insolvency. This is how the remedy-based idea is restrained and the insolvency laws are not overwhelmed. The 'raising the interest' step is explicitly result-oriented and performed according to an orthodoxy of 'unjust enrichment'. 'Raising of an interest' has no necessary relation to property interests, pre-existing or otherwise. As early as 1920 Roscoe Pound described the constructive trust as a 'purely remedial institution' which afforded, he said, 'specific restitution of a received benefit in order to prevent unjust enrichment.'[138] The 1937 *Restatement of Restitution* put it thus:

> **§160  Constructive Trusts**
> Where a person holding title to property is subject to an equitable duty to convey it to another on the ground that he would be unjustly enriched if he was permitted to retain it, a constructive trust arises.

The restatement plan was to deal with constructive trusts in the *Restatement of Restitution* and not in the *Restatement of Trusts*. For it no doubt was and is still believed by most American jurists that 'the differences between the express trust and the constructive trust are greater than the similarities.'[139]

**[6.70]**  In the scheme of the Restatement, the tracing step is dealt with subsequently. The ability to follow the constructive trust property into mixtures and other forms appears at §§202-15.

> **§215  Necessity of Tracing Property**
> (1) . . . where a person wrongfully disposes of the property of another but the property cannot be traced into any product, the other has merely a personal claim against the wrongdoer and cannot enforce a constructive trust or lien upon any part of the wrongdoer's property.

Almost every constructive trust case referred to in this book would be subject to these tracing rules if it were heard in the United States. Tracing's importance is mirrored by the position that it occupies in *Scott on Trusts* 4th ed (1989) and Bogert's *Trusts and Trustees* rev 2nd ed (1978). Raising the interest and tracing the interest are treated as separate things. Bogert even puts them in different volumes. 'Unjust enrichment' and purely remedial constructive trusts on the American model may not be the charter for indiscriminate recovery that some fear. If a fiduciary wrongly misappropriates the property of a beneficiary, the beneficiary is not entitled to recover merely because of the character of the wrong done. Just because fiduciaries are unjustly enriched at their

---

[138] 'The Progress of Law' 33 *Harv LR* 420, 421 (1920).

[139] *Scott on Trusts* 4th edn, ed W Fratcher (1989), §461, also *Law of Trusts and Trustees* 2nd ed G & G Bogert (1978), §471.

beneficiary's expense does not mean that the court will order constructive trust relief. The claimant must additionally prove that the subject property is in existence and that either it or its product is held by the defendant.[140] Tracing rules and the established procedure of identification must still be followed. The difference is in how the equitable interest is raised.

## 2. Priorities between beneficiaries and secured creditors

[6.71]   Secured creditors will also be concerned by constructive trust claims if they are not bona fide purchasers of legal security interests. Both constructive trust beneficiaries and secured creditors will be claiming equitable property rights. Priority is the question. Claimants' interests under constructive trusts may well take priority over any secured entitlement. This was the outcome in the breach of fiduciary duty claim made against a third party in *Linter Group Ltd v Goldberg*.[141] The decision highlights a feature of modern financing. For various reasons, including the minimisation of stamp duty, commercial security interests are often equitable in form. Unforeseen conflict of equities will result when a constructive trust enters the scene. Assume for the moment that the equities of a secured creditor and the beneficiary are equal and neither is better than the other.[142] The prima facie rule of priority is that the first interest in time prevails.

### When the constructive trust arises

[6.72]   This is relevant to the operation of the prima facie rule. Interests of secured creditors arise upon the execution of the documents creating them. At least, this is where the interests are created by document. For a few transactions, like 'dealer floor-plans' and bill discounting, the interest may arise at other times—perhaps the time of some action that the documents contemplate. But the answer is usually simple. It is the date of the deal. When interests under constructive trusts arise is more complicated. It has been argued that an interest under a constructive trust arises at the time that the court decrees the trust to exist. This is so, it is said, even though the interest may be given retrospective effect to the time of the breach of duty.[143] The argued consequence is that the interest is analytically a 'mere equity' and not an equitable interest until the decree is made. It could not become retrospective before the court so orders. Hence if the priority question arises prior to the constructive trust decree, the equities are not equal and the lender's interest should prevail.[144] A constructive trust must be established before the interest which it confers is made retrospective. This is an idea which seems to be implicit in the reasoning of Menzies J in *Latec Investments Ltd v Hotel Terrigal Pty Ltd*.[145] However the view of Ford & Lee at [2213] and the weight of most authority is to the contrary. The better view may be that interests under constructive trusts arise independently of court orders.[146] A claimed

---

[140]  See *Restatement of Restitution* (1937), 215 (1), comment *a*.
[141]  (1992) 7 ACSR 580: see further at [7.38].
[142]  *Latec Investments Ltd v Hotel Terrigal Pty Ltd* (1965) 113 CLR 265, 276, Kitto J; MGL [803].
[143]  Eg, *Muschinski v Dodds* (1985) 160 CLR 583, 614, Deane J; *Re Sharpe* [1980] 1 WLR 219.
[144]  See *Phillips v Phillips* (1861) 4 De G F & J 208; 45 ER 1164.
[145]  (1965) 113 CLR 265, 290
[146]  See *Queensland Mines Ltd v Hudson* (1976) ACLC 40-266, 28,708–9.

beneficial interest in the property is from the beginning in the person who has been wronged.[147] No suit in equity is needed to create it. Constructive trusts are 'construed', not 'constructed' at trial. Their name is said to imply as much.[148] Priority in time between constructive trusts and secured creditors depends on when the constructive trust was caused.

### Character of the constructive trust interest

**[6.73]** Although the beneficiary of a constructive trust has an equitable interest in property and one which arises independently of a court order, it is not in all respects comparable to the interest of a beneficiary under an express trust. A defendant constructive trustee, for instance, commits no wrong by withholding the property from the claimant prior to the court order being made.[149] The sense of 'property' is much more instrumental. The decision of the Privy Council in *Re Goldcorp Exchange Ltd*[150] illustrates this use. Goldcorp was a New Zealand gold dealer. Prior to becoming insolvent it had engaged in the following scheme. Goldcorp sold investors quantities of gold bullion, for delivery in the future. After each sale the buyer was issued with a 'Non-Allocated Metal Certificate'. The bullion itself was said to be 'stored and insured' by Goldcorp without charge. Buyers had a right to take physical delivery of the gold upon seven days' notice and the payment of certain charges. Few exercised that right. Goldcorp also bound itself to a floating charge in favour of the Bank of New Zealand. This had the effect of securing the bank over whatever supplies of bullion Goldcorp owned. As Lord Musthill said at 827:

> The bank relied on the floating charge to protect its assets; the customers relied on the company to deliver the bullion.

Goldcorp became insolvent. It transpired that supplies of gold held were quite inadequate to meet the buyers' claims. More money was in fact owed to the bank than the value of all the bullion that Goldcorp had on hand. So buyers asserted proprietary interests. These were to give them priority over the bank charge. As Lord Musthill put it at 827, a 'means' had to be found, 'retrospectively to create a situation' whereby the bullion was not an asset of Goldcorp that was charged to the bank. Or, alternatively, a way had to be found whereby the prices paid to Goldcorp for the bullion never became part of its assets. For both purposes the buyers were looking for an equitable interest 'deemed to come into existence from the moment when the [purchase] transaction was entered into'.

**[6.74]**   The critical interest in *Goldcorp*[151] could not be obtained by the sale itself. The Privy Council was definite about that. Each purchase contract related to 'unascertained goods' to which legal title would not pass under the Sale of Goods Act 1908 (NZ). It was impossible to have title to goods when it was not known to which goods the title related. Equitable title was also

---

[147] *Scott on Trusts* 4th edn, ed W Fratcher (1989), §262.4.

[148] Ibid, §462.4.

[149] *International Refugee Organization v Maryland Drydock Co* 179 F 2d 284 (1950 4th circ.); *Scott on Trusts* 4th edn, ed W Fratcher (1989), §462.4–5.

[150] [1994] 2 All ER 806 (Lord Musthill).

[151] [1994] 2 All ER 806 (Lord Musthill).

unavailable, relying on the authority of *Re Wait*.[152] This venerable decision made it clear that under a simple contract for the sale of unascertained goods, no equitable title passes. The buyers had to rely on what the Privy Council described at 17 as a 'remedial constructive trust, or ... restitutionary proprietary interest'.

> Such a trust or interest ... would not arise directly from the transaction between the individual claimants, the company and the bullion [sic], but would be created by the court as a measure of justice after the event.

However the Board considered that the facts in *Goldcorp* were insufficient to raise a restitutionary proprietary interest. Lord Musthill said at 827 that none of the buyers' arguments could displace the bank's security. So the identification rules which operated adversely to the claim continued to apply. This approach of the Privy Council has since been followed by the Court of Appeal in *Bishopsgate Investment Management Ltd v Homan*.[153] Consequences of the Robert Maxwell defalcations were involved. A large amount of Bishopsgate's pension moneys were misappropriated and placed in the overdrawn account of Maxwell Communication Corporation ('MCC'). Insolvency administrators of MCC proposed to make an interim distribution in favour of that corporation's creditors. Bishopsgate pensioners took action to forestall this, claiming an equitable charge over MCC assets with priority in respect of the misappropriated moneys. All members of the Court of Appeal held that this claim must fail on the *Goldcorp Exchange* reasoning. Tracing requirements were the insuperable obstacle. The pension moneys ceased to be amenable to the equitable relief when they were paid into an overdrawn, and therefore non-existent, fund. We shall deal further with the alternative 'remedial constructive trust' claim under the 'Disgorgement of gains' heading, at [6.105].

*Factors which might postpone a secured interest*

**[6.75]** This is a large subject. Meagher, Gummow and Lehane's *Equity: Doctrine and Remedies* at [807]–[818] suggests that factors for the purpose come in ten categories. Assessment of conduct is important in determining the merits of a claim. Both the parties asserting interests are liable to have their behaviour examined. Has the secured creditor, for example, done anything *negligent* which would warrant its postponement? A common case of this is in facilitation of the fraud of others. Conveyancing transactions are largely where relevant principles have been stated. One needs to ask whether the secured creditor has done anything analogous to 'arming' rogues with 'indicia of title', enabling them to pass themselves off as true owners?[154] Action of secured creditors may have created the risk of reasonably foreseeable misconduct on the part of another. In the event of any loss thereby occurring, beneficiaries may be treated as possessing 'better equities'.[155]

**[6.76]** Secured creditors may also have acted *unconscionably* enough towards the claimant or the world to have their security interest postponed. This refers

---

152 [1927] 1 Ch 606 (CA).
153 Unreported, Court of Appeal, 12 July 1994, Dillon, Leggatt and Henry LJJ.
154 *Lapin v Abigail* (1934) 51 CLR 58, 71 (PC, Lord Wright).
155 *Heid v Reliance Finance Corporation Pty Ltd* (1983) 154 CLR 326, 345, Mason and Deane JJ.

to equitable wrongs. Estoppel may be alleged. This can be as an alternative to negligence, for the type of representation that would 'arm' a rogue. Or representations may be made to the beneficiaries themselves. When *Goldcorp* was in the New Zealand Court of Appeal,[156] the buyers of gold bullion alleged that a proprietary estoppel bound Goldcorp and forced it to recognise their interests. This was because Goldcorp invited buyers 'to look on and treat stocks vested in it as their own'. Southwell J in *Linter Group Ltd v Goldberg*[157] also examined the conduct of secured creditors fairly closely. This was in order to confirm the priority that the constructive trust was given over various share mortgages taken by lenders. While he did not base constructive trust priority on conduct assessments, Southwell J did note at 603–4 that the share mortgage in favour of Occidental Life Nominees had been back-dated. This was said to be a 'sharp practice', enough to deprive that company of status as a bona fide purchaser for value.

### 3. Priorities between beneficiaries inter se

**[6.77]** Recovery does not have to be shared between those entitled to proprietary constructive trusts. Persons who are successful in claiming this remedy get their property back unabated. They take it in specie. If the property cannot be reached or separated from other entitlements, the remedy is unavailable. It has failed at the tracing step. Equitable liens and subrogation have the potential to operate differently. We saw at [6.19]–[6.21] how each of these remedies is an exception to the tracing requirements. Equitable liens may award successful claimants something rather less than in specie recovery. Assume that the fund over which a lien is impressed is insufficient to satisfy all the equitable entitlements. Equity need not regard the claims as defeated by this, but is able to order recovery proportionate to the size of each claim.[158] It is not unlike the way that the Bankruptcy Act 1966 (Cth) s 140 operates. There was such a division made in *Australian Securities Commission v Melbourne Asset Management Nominees Pty Ltd*.[159] Some investors with an insolvent mortgage-broker were given priority over ordinary creditors by way of lien on an 'unequal acceptance of risk' basis. The fund in court, as it happened, was too small to recoup all the investors in full. They were satisfied proportionately instead.

# Disgorgement of a fiduciary's gains

**[6.78]** A beneficiary's claim that a fiduciary disgorge a gain to him is specifically based in the fiduciary's wrongdoing. The obligation to disgorge is a personal one. Rights to property in the gain are rarely asserted. This is because the gain is not related to any property which the beneficiary possesses or once possessed. Profits, bribes and prohibited advantages come from third parties. Breach of duty in making the gain is the thing which obliges a fiduciary to disgorge it. At the same time the disgorgement obligation may be

---

[156] *Liggett v Kensington* [1993] 1 NZLR 257, 268, Cooke P.

[157] (1992) 7 ACSR 580: see [7.38].

[158] *Lord Provost, Magistrates and Town Council of Edinburgh v Lord Advocate* (1879) 4 AC 823, 833, Lord Blackburn.

[159] (1994) 12 ACLC 364, 384–5, Northrop J (Fed Ct).

given a proprietary reach. Cases like *Keech v Sandford*[160] and *Attorney-General for Hong Kong v Reid*[161] make it clear that equity may reverse the gains of fiduciaries by creating proprietary interests. It is done remedially. Beneficiaries are given property rights where they never had them before. Money or things which constitute the profits are made their property. A long-standing reluctance to annexe gains based in wrongs to the property gained seems to have been overcome.[162] Probably the analytic need for a proprietary base has never existed in any 'disgorgement of profits' type of case.[163]

## CONSTRUCTIVE TRUSTS

**[6.79]** Disgorgement of gains is primarily achieved by use of the constructive trust. This, we have seen, is a fictional device. Here a non-proprietary kind of fiction is involved. Personal *obligations* of trusteeship are imposed in respect of particular losses and gains. Constructive trustees may be ordered to account for profits they have made just as though they were profiteering trustees.[164] This accounting obligation is closely related to breach of the profits rule. When imposing a constructive trust to make a fiduciary account for a gain in *Hospital Products Ltd v United States Surgical Corporation*,[165] Mason J said that we were employing one principle. It was that–

the fiduciary cannot be permitted to retain a profit or benefit which he has obtained by breach of his fiduciary duty.

**[6.80]** The conflicts rule, too, has been bent to an appropriate shape where a fiduciary is obligated to account. *Re Jarvis* records such an event.[166] A constructive trust claim was argued before Upjohn J—who was always a great friend to the conflicts rule in fiduciary disputes. In his judgment he found that the applicable principle upon which to base a constructive trust was that–

A trustee must not place himself in a position where his duty and his interest conflict, and if he does so he must *account for any profit thereby made or for the property thereby acquired*. [emphasis added]

Trust-engendering gains and liability to restore property may thus follow from conflicts of interest and duty. But the centrality of the *gain* is present always.

### PERSONAL OBLIGATIONS

**[6.81]** To repeat, obligations of trusteeship may be imposed over losses and gains made by persons analogous to trustees. Fiduciaries are the archetype of this trustee-like category. They are made liable to account for profits just as are profiteering trustees in similar circumstances. Perhaps it would be more accurate to refer to this aspect of the remedy as constructive trustee*ship*, rather

---

[160] (1726) Sel Cas t King 61; 25 ER 223.

[161] [1994] 1 AC 324 (PC).

[162] See R Goode 'Recovery of a Director's Improper Gains: Proprietary Remedies for Infringement of Non-Proprietary Rights' in McKendrick 137, 142–5.

[163] Cf Birks 313–4; R Goode 'Property and Unjust Enrichment' in Burrows 215, 232.

[164] Hayton 441–2.

[165] (1984) 156 CLR 41, 107, Mason J.

[166] [1958] 2 All ER 336.

than the constructive trust.[167] For the imposed personal obligation is unrelated to the existence of a trust estate. It attaches to the defendant personally and is liable to abate in the event of the defendant's insolvency. Implication of constructive trustee*ship* need not be annexed to any res or thing. Indeed, the disappearance of property or the fact that the fiduciary never received it may be the reason why relief is claimed.

## 1. Identifying a fiduciary's gain

**[6.82]** Isolation of the subject is necessary for both personal constructive trusts and those that involve proprietary annexure of the gain. It resembles the *tracing* step in the other type of constructive trust. The task is to identify what the court should reach. A gain itself must be defined. Then a decision can be taken on whether the gain can be appropriately reversed by a constructive trust. There may also be the further question as to whether the constructive trust should have a personal or proprietary operation.[168]

**[6.83]** *Paul A Davies (Australia) Pty Ltd (in liq) v Davies*[169] illustrates several of these matters. The case began with a liquidator's claim that the directors of a company had misappropriated its funds. Existence of a fiduciary relationship between the directors and the company was conceded by the directors. That the facts of this case were within the scope of the relationship was also conceded, as was the fact that the resulting duty had been breached. Even the constructive trust as the appropriate remedy was not disputed. What was in question corresponds to the stage that the present inquiry is now at. Moffitt P said (at 444):

> a breach being proved, inquiry is directed to a determination of the gain or profit flowing from the breach, the remedy being to require the fiduciary to account to the beneficiary, in this case the company, for the gain. There is not conferred, as there is in the case of some other sanctions penal or criminal against wrongdoing, a discretion to quantify the penalty so as to match the circumstances mitigating or otherwise.

At this point Moffitt quoted Lord Wright in *Regal (Hastings) Ltd v Gulliver*.[170] An 'agent, director, trustee or other person in an analogous position' must account for all secret profits acquired by him in the course of the position. After the profits rule was stated, he continued:

> Where there is a breach of fiduciary duty, the first question which arises is as to what is the gain from the breach. The relief is that which is considered appropriate in the circumstances to take that gain from the fiduciary. If property has been acquired with trust money then it will normally be appropriate, if sought, to declare a trust over the asset acquired. If such property has been sold, it will normally be appropriate, if sought, to order the fiduciary to account for the profit.

**[6.84]** The fiduciary's gain is the focus of this constructive trust. A gain was constituted in *Regal (Hastings) Ltd v Gulliver*[171] by the directors' profit from

---

[167] Suggested in Hayton 441.
[168] J Kearney 'Accounting for a Fiduciary's Gains in a Commercial Context' in Finn *Relationships* 186, 191.
[169] [1983] 1 NSWLR 440 (CA).
[170] (1942) [1967] 2 AC 134n, 154.
[171] (1942) [1967] 2 AC 134n.

buying and selling shares. That profit was one which, on the face of things, should have gone to the company and not to its directors. In *Chan v Zacharia*[172] the gain consisted in the goodwill attached to a lease. A fiduciary took it all even though his former partner was equally entitled. In *Lac Minerals Ltd v International Corona Resources Ltd*[173] the gain was mineral-rich land that Lac acquired. Lac's prospective co-venturer would have acquired the valuable land but for Lac's breach of fiduciary duty. The same inquiry in *Paul A Davies (Australia) Pty Ltd (in liq) v Davies*[174] identified a gain in the capital appreciation of a Sydney guest-house. These were all cases where identification of the gain was straightforward.

### Business profits or the business itself?

**[6.85]**　Accounting for a gain equal to the value of the fiduciary's business is a special case. The assistance of a proprietary remedy may be needed to subtract it fully. For the gain is identified with the business as a productive asset. A business has a profit-making potential. Its value is not reflected in a sum of profits previously made. Non-proprietary remedies fail to reach the profit-making asset. They 'bite upon the fruit rather than the tree'. In this the traditional distinction is maintained between profit-making structure and profits generated.[175]

This problem does not occur in the type of situation which arose in *Re Jarvis*.[176] All that was needed there was a declaration of right regarding beneficial ownership and an accounting of profits which had been received. The case involved a business comprised in an estate. After that business was re-started by one executor and run for her exclusive benefit, the other executor sought a declaration that the business was still part of the estate and that the defendant was under a (personal) liability as constructive trustee to account for profits derived.

**[6.86]**　*Timber Engineering Co Pty Ltd v Anderson*[177] is a case where the profit was said to be in part the value of a non-fiduciary business undertaking. Two employees of the plaintiff set up the company 'Mallory Trading'. This was to conduct a business in competition with that of their employer. Fortunes of Mallory Trading were secretly promoted with the resources and facilities of the claimant. Telephones, motor cars, expense accounts, marketing methods, customer lists, goodwill and other things were used. In the end, the employees resigned in order to pursue their interest in the competing business full-time. That business was transferred to the new entity of 'Mallory Timber Products', which was alleged to conduct a fresh and unrelated venture. At trial, the finding was made (at 496–7) that:

> Every opportunity which Mallory Trading has received is directly traceable to
> resources and benefits provided by [the claimant], even to the extent of time and

---

[172] (1984) 154 CLR 178.

[173] [1989] 2 SCR 574, 669, La Forest J (Wilson J agreeing).

[174] [1983] 1 NSWLR 440 (CA).

[175] See *London Australia Investment Co Ltd v FCT* (1977) 138 CLR 106; *FCT v Myer Emporium Ltd* (1987) 163 CLR 199 and J Waincymer Australian *Income Tax Principles and Policy* 2nd ed (1993), 212–6.

[176] [1958] 2 All ER 336, Upjohn J.

[177] [1980] 2 NSWLR 488, Kearney J.

efforts expended by [the employees] for which [the claimant] was paying. Every advance made by Mallory Trading was due to the advantages of the tangible and intangible resources and facilities provided by [the claimant]. In truth, the business of Mallory Trading was carved out of the business of [the claimant], and thus ought to be treated as being ... held on trust for [the claimant].

On the basis of these findings it was seen to follow (at 499) that the Mallory companies were accountable to the claimant as constructive trustees of the business. Liens were ordered in the claimant's favour over the shares in the Mallory companies held by the employees and their spouses. The gain's nature and extent was seen to dictate this outcome.

**[6.87]**    A comparable result occurred at the penultimate stage of appeal in the *Hospital Products* litigation.[178] It had been found at first instance that the fiduciary distributor of an overseas supplier had misused its distributorship and appropriated the supplier's market to itself.[179] The New South Wales Court of Appeal drew a further inference. It found that the distributor's profit earned in breach of duty equalled the value of the entire business that the distributor had set up.[180] In consequence, at 233–5, a (proprietary) constructive trust was imposed in favour of the supplier over all the assets of the distributor as at a particular day. In *Clegg v Edmondson*,[181] some of the partners in a mining partnership were wrongly excluded from participation in the profits of certain mining leases. This led to the court imposing a constructive trust over the mining leases, as well as requiring an account of profits actually made. Future profits were captured in this way.

## 2.   Measurement of a fiduciary's gain

**[6.88]**    Measurement is the next step in moulding the accounting remedy. It, too, is applicable to both personal and proprietary recovery. We are now concerned with the dimensions of a gain. It will have been identified according to the procedure outlined in the preceding paragraphs. The gain identified, say, is the value of a fiduciary's business. Or perhaps it is the profit on a transaction that the fiduciary has wrongly entered. *Measurement* considerations concern whether the whole or some lesser part of the business or profit should be accounted for. Two 'mechanisms' of equity may be employed. Inputs may be 'apportioned' and a fiduciary's efforts can be the subject of a 'just allowance'.[182] To an extent, the apportionment and just allowance mechanisms overlap and could be treated together.[183] But the majority of commentators view the ideas separately and we shall do so here.[184] A rough distinction of them is as follows. Just allowances relate to the value of services and matters

---

[178] *United States Surgical Corporation v Hospital Products International Pty Ltd* [1983] 2 NSWLR 157 (CA).

[179] [1982] 2 NSWLR 766, 809–11, McLelland J.

[180] [1983] 2 NSWLR 157, 224–5, curiam.

[181] (1857) 8 De G M & G 787; 44 ER 593.

[182] See J Kearney 'Accounting for a Fiduciary's Gains in Commercial Contexts' in Finn *Relationships* 186, 195.

[183] Eg, as in *United States Surgical Corporation v Hospital Products International Pty Ltd* [1983] 2 NSWLR 157, 242–3, *curiam* (CA); J Kearney ibid 191–201.

[184] See G Jones *Restitution in Public and Private Law* (1991), 60–8; Goff & Jones 652–3; MGL [551].

in personam. Apportionment tends to deal with the segregation of proprietary inputs.

### 'Just allowances' for skill and industry

**[6.89]**   A gain to be reversed may in part represent the fiduciaries' own efforts. Fiduciaries will often have worked hard to exploit opportunities for themselves, before the court finds that they should have abstained from the attempt. In many cases fiduciaries will have been honestly mistaken. Their own and their beneficiaries' entitlements may not be clearly demarcated. It may not be fair, in many cases, for vindicated beneficiaries to succeed to the benefit of their fiduciaries' hard work without giving credit for it. The sum accounted for may need to be reduced to reflect the value of the fiduciaries' work. 'Just allowances' is the name of the unstructured principle by which this is achieved. 'Just allowances' are said to include 'everything which the Court thinks just and proper'.[185] Which is obviously apt to include the 'apportionment' of money and property inputs as well. Just allowances and apportionment are alike in being computed differently as between honest and dishonest fiduciaries, as we will see. Nevertheless we will persist in examining the just allowance for personal services separately.

**[6.90]**   *Boardman v Phipps*[186] involved fiduciaries who used 'commendable skill' for their beneficiaries whilst acting in breach of fiduciary duty. The result they achieved was advantageous both to their beneficiaries and to themselves. They acted with complete honesty. Wilberforce J at first instance ordered that an allowance for their work and skill be made on 'a generous scale'. He thought that it would be 'inequitable' for the beneficiaries to take the profit without paying for any of the work and labour which produced it.[187] In the Court of Appeal, Denning MR treated this aspect of the case in a restitutionary way.[188] The beneficiaries' claim, he said, did not extend to the value of the fiduciaries' work. Rather, in an 'action for restitution'–

> the defendant has unjustly enriched himself, and it is against conscience that he should be allowed to keep the money. The claim for repayment cannot, however, be allowed to extend further than the justice of the case demands. If the defendant has done valuable work in making the profit, then the court in its discretion may allow him a recompense. It depends on the circumstances. If the agent has been guilty of any dishonesty or bad faith, or surreptitious dealing, he might not be allowed any remuneration or reward.

Also in the Court of Appeal, Pearson LJ at 1030–1 was firmly in favour of making an allowance for the good work done. He regretted that the court did not have the power to apportion profits. When the case reached the House of Lords, two members of the majority of law lords confirmed the allowance ordered by Wilberforce J.[189] The power to make 'just allowances to honest fiduciaries is thus firmly established. Equity's prophylactic rules for fiduciaries are mitigated to this small extent.

---

[185] *Lord Provost of Edinburgh v Lord Advocate* (1879) 4 App Cas 823, 839, Lord Hatherley.
[186] [1967] 2 AC 46.
[187] *Phipps v Boardman* [1964] 1 WLR 993, 1018.
[188] *Phipps v Boardman* [1965] Ch 992 (CA), 1020.
[189] [1967] 2 AC 46, 104, Lord Cohen, 112, Lord Hodson.

**[6.91]** The 'just allowances' principle was also argued in *O'Sullivan v Management Agency and Music Ltd*.[190] O'Sullivan was once an unknown composer and performer of popular music. He was also, as Waller LJ said at 470, 'a young man in his early twenties, of very limited experience, and employed as a postal worker'. O'Sullivan entered an exclusive management agreement with the defendant management company. It was confirmed by the English Court of Appeal that the company was in a fiduciary relationship with O'Sullivan and that the management agreement was obtained through the company's exercise of undue influence. The company claimed credit for itself nevertheless. Adept management, it was argued, as much as the young man's talent, led to his eventual commercial success. On the basis of this the company claimed an appropriate allowance for its care and skill.

**[6.92]** Dunn LJ noted in *O'Sullivan's* case at 443 that, at the time of trial:

> Raymond O'Sullivan (professionally known as Gilbert O'Sullivan) ... is a well known composer and performer of popular music. The retail sales of records of his music between 1970 and 1978 realised a gross figure of some £14.5 million. In addition he has received world-wide fame as an artiste playing to packed houses in this country and the United States.

Relevantly to the just allowance he added:

> it is significant that until O'Sullivan met Mills [acting for the defendant] he had achieved no success, and that after he had effectively parted company with Mills in 1976 he achieved no success either. During the years that he was working with Mills his success was phenomenal. Although equity looks at the advantage gained by the wrongdoer rather than the loss to the victim, the cases show that in assessing the advantage gained the court will look at the whole situation in the round ... This point was made forcibly by Mr Miller at the conclusion of his address in reply, when he relied on the maxim 'He who seeks equity must do equity' and submitted that equity required that the position of O'Sullivan was relevant in considering the appropriate remedy.

Each member of the United Kingdom Court of Appeal thought that the justice of this case demanded a recognition of the manager's skill and labour. The approaches of Fox and Waller LJJ put the matter so high as to suggest that the equivalent of profit-sharing between these parties was appropriate.[191] This, according to Gareth Jones, implicitly recognises that the law in the past has treated fiduciaries too harshly.[192]

**[6.93]** The same liberal approach to the efforts of defaulting fiduciaries has subsequently been denied in the House of Lords. *Guinness plc v Saunders*[193] included the claim of a 'just allowance' set-off to a constructive trust claim. Mr Ward, a director of Guinness, was paid a £5.2m fee for personal services that he supplied in connection with a takeover of Distillers plc. However, payment of the fee was authorised by only a committee of the Guinness board. The full board of Guinness later authorised proceedings to have the money restored and the payment was held to be void for want of authority. Summary judgment against Ward for return of the amount paid was confirmed by the

---

[190] [1985] 1 QB 428 (CA).
[191] Ibid, 468–9, Fox LJ; 472–3, Waller LJ; see Underhill 315.
[192] *Restitution in Public and Private Law* (1991), 61.
[193] [1990] 2 AC 663.

House of Lords.[194] Any allowance for Mr Ward's services was refused. *O'Sullivan v Management Agency and Music Ltd*[195] was cited in argument but not referred to in either of the leading speeches. The director in *Guinness* was made a constructive trustee of the whole unauthorised payment for the company. His claim for a quantum meruit for services rendered was disallowed. Lord Templeman said (at 694) that the equitable jurisdiction to grant allowances for 'skill and labour' existed only in 'exceptional' cases. If, as Lord Goff said (at 701), *Boardman v Phipps* was such an exceptional case–

> The present case is ... very different. Whether any such allowance might ever be granted by a court of equity in the case of a director of a company, as opposed to a trustee, is a point which has yet to be decided; and I must reserve the question as to whether the jurisdiction could be exercised in such a case.

### Relevance of fraud or moral turpitude

**[6.94]** The fiduciary who claimed an allowance in Guinness was far from honest. He had fled overseas whilst his associates faced criminal trials at home. The Guinness takeover was one of the great City of London scandals of the eighties and received extensive coverage in the press.[196] Minor dishonesty, though, may not bar a fiduciary from obtaining an allowance. Meagher, Gummow and Lehane's *Equity* observes at [551] that in the case of minor dishonesty the *degree* of liberality may be what is affected. This has been said to be on a sliding scale to the point where a fiduciary's conduct has been so unconscionable as for equity to decline to order an allowance altogether.[197]

A similar approach was taken by Tipping J in *Estate Realties Ltd v Wignall*.[198] In that case a firm of share brokers secretly purchased certain shares from one their clients, whilst purporting to act for another of their customers who 'preferred to remain anonymous'. The prevailing market price was paid on the day of purchase. Earlier proceedings had found that a fiduciary relationship subsisted at the time between the broker and its client.[199] After obtaining the shares, the broker expertly accomplished a scheme to gain control of the company. Shares in the company were then sold at a considerable profit. The facts are a little reminiscent of the 'liberal allowance' case of *Boardman v Phipps*.[200] However one difference was that the fiduciary here had somewhat deceived the beneficiary. Tipping J decided at 630–1 that the nature and circumstances of the deception in the *Estate Realties* case, while possibly 'deserving of censure', should not deprive the fiduciaries of an allowance entirely. It was not the overwhelming factor and–

> if the defendants had not played their blighted hand with considerable skill then there might well have been no profit at all.

---

194 Ibid, 684, 694–5, Lord Templeman, 701, Lord Goff, Lords Keith, Brandon and Griffiths agreeing.
195 [1985] 1 QB 428 (CA).
196 G Jones *Restitution in Public and Private Law* (1991), 62.
197 *Story on Equity* 3rd edn (1920), [679]; *Berridge v Public Trustee* (1914) 33 NZLR 865, 872, Edwards J; *United States Surgical Corporation v Hospital Products International Pty Ltd* [1983] 2 NSWLR 157 (CA), 242–3, curiam.
198 [1992] 2 NZLR 615 (HC).
199 [1991] 3 NZLR 482, Tipping J; see above at [3.63].
200 [1967] 2 AC 46.

In these circumstances the judge thought that no 'exceptional circumstance' needed to be shown before a court of equity could make an allowance to the fiduciary. Lord Templeman's remark to the contrary in *Guinness plc v Saunders* was described as 'overstated'. On other occasions, as Tipping J noted, the improper conduct of the fiduciary could be more significant. It could sometimes be inconsistent with the fiduciary's right to be rewarded in any measure.

**[6.95]**  So a fiduciary who has committed serious fraud should forfeit an allowance entirely.[201] In *Australian Postal Corporation v Lutak*[202] the defendant had received stamps stolen from Australia Post. He turned the stamps into cash. Some of it was used to pay part of the price of a house that was transferred into his own and his wife's name. The remainder of the price was paid from an ordinary bank mortgage. A modest appreciation in the value of the house occurred with the passage of a few years. Bryson J said at 596 that the only basis on which Lutak could receive any share of the proceeds of this 'unauthorized investment' with Australia Post's money was what he and his wife could establish an entitlement to as a 'just allowance'. The amount of the bank loan was subtracted from what had to be accounted. Beyond that, both allowances and apportionment were denied. As Bryson J said:

> a [just allowance] claim by persons such as the Lutaks who applied stolen money to the purchase of a property with the apparent intention of owning it themselves and were later brought to account when their dishonest conduct was revealed is a very poor one. People who use stolen trust money, and are in effect laundering it and concealing what has happened to the money, and who are found out and have a constructive trust imposed on them cannot expect much consideration.

### Apportionment of profits made from mixed monetary and property inputs?

**[6.96]**  Apportionment to reflect the amount of profit attributable to the fiduciary's own inputs is sometimes factually possible. But principles contend on whether the fiduciary should ever be credited with the amount. One is a strict interpretation of the profits rule. It suggests that a fiduciary must account for *all* of the profits made from breach of fiduciary duty—regardless of their source. The other is the older idea that entitlement to gains made with property of the beneficiary mixed with property of the fiduciary should be apportioned according to the contribution of each.[203] We saw this as a tracing rule at [6.45]. Lord Brougham relied on the older rule in *Docker v Somes*.[204] The case concerned a trustee who wrongly mixed trust funds with his private moneys and employed the resulting sum in a 'trade or adventure'. The trustee was held to be liable to the beneficiary for only a proportion of the adventure's profits. The proportion was that which the invested trust money bore to his own money. The defendant was given not only his own money back, but part of

---

[201] *Paul A Davies (Australia) Pty Ltd (in liq) v Davies* [1983] 1 NSWLR 440 (CA).

[202] (1991) 21 NSWLR 584.

[203] *Scott v Scott* [1964] VR 300, 309–12, Hudson J; *Paul A Davies Pty Ltd (Australia) (in liq) v Davies* [1983] 1 NSWLR 440, 444, Moffitt P; *Re Pumphrey, deceased* (1882) 22 Ch D 255, 262, Kay J relying on *Phayre v Peree* (1815) 3 Dow 116, 3 ER 1008.

[204] (1834) 2 My & K 655, 39 ER 1095, 1098–9 (HL).

the wrongful profit. Things may have changed in modern times.[205] The ascendency of the profits rule is such that the prima facie rule may be that a profit from mixed sources must be accounted for in its entirety. Invested resources of the fiduciary's own may be overlooked. Money borrowed from a bank could be regarded as a merely collateral source of a wrongful profit. It does not change its nature.

Apportionment of profits may on other facts not be possible at all. The gain in question is then not of nature 'severable' into apportioned parts.[206] Where separate inputs to a gain cannot be valued, the whole will usually belong to the beneficiary. The fact that a gain is eventually liquidated does not mean that the same is then severable. Even though the asset has been sold for a money sum, the contributions to that quantum cannot always be apportioned. For a gain of that size may not have been available to each of the contributors to it had they acted alone. Certainly the interest on a deposit could be apportioned and so could the appreciation of publicly listed shares. But the purchase of a profitable business or a valuable parcel of land often requires large resources. The investments are not available in parcels the size of the separate contributions. For this reason, as Bryson J said in the *Lutak case*, proportionate entitlement may be unsusceptible of valuation. The whole, perhaps, is greater (and more profitable) than the sum of its parts: an apportionment question that has arisen in a few cases.

**[6.97]** *Paul A Davies (Australia) Pty Ltd (in liq) v Davies*,[207] as we saw, involved a directors' breach of fiduciary duty. The directors' nominee company agreed to buy a large guest-house with the assistance of company funds. There was no 'straight substitution' of what was taken for the property. Instead, the misapplied funds were used as a kind of holding deposit for several years. During that time a capital gain was found to have been made. Realisation of the gain was to have been achieved through use of a bank 'bridging' loan. This would be used to pay the full price shortly before the conveyance to the purchaser and receipt of the sale price. The bridging loan was taken out and secured by a mortgage over the property. Directors asserted that, in these circumstances, the measure of the gain for which they were accountable was the proportion of the sale price that the company funds represented. This was not a big proportion, of course. The critical significance of the company funds as the 'holding deposit' was argued to have no bearing on the matter of profit apportionment. If the constructive trust took the form that the directors argued for, it would have left the larger part of the gain still in their hands. The Court of Appeal would not allow the constructive trust in support of the profits rule to be so limited. The directors were found liable to pay the whole capital gain to the company.[208] For this, some figure as to the true value of the property had to be assumed. It was taken to be what a buyer had agreed to pay for the guest house shortly before the appellate hearing. As things happened, the contract of sale 'went off' during the course of argument. No other evidence of value was adduced. So the case may be a little suspect

---

[205] See *Attorney-General for Hong Kong v Reid* [1994] 1 AC 324 (PC); *Australian Postal Corporation v Lutak* (1991) 21 NSWLR 584, Bryson J (below).

[206] *Australian Postal Corporation v Lutak* (1991) 21 NSWLR 584, 597, Bryson J.

[207] [1983] 1 NSWLR 440 (CA); see [6.83]

[208] [1983] 1 NSWLR 440, 448, Moffitt P, 452, Hutley JA, 459, Mahoney JA.

on this account as well as in some of its reasoning, as we shall see.

**[6.98]** The result in *Paul A Davies (Australia) Pty Ltd (in liq) v Davies*[209] was reached after the High Court authority of *Scott v Scott*[210] was discussed and distinguished. *Scott* was a similar case. A trustee of a deceased estate wrongly used trust moneys together with his own money for the purchase of a house where he lived until his death. Shortly before dying the trustee repaid the estate the amount of trust moneys wrongfully used. The house had substantially appreciated in value by that time. On a beneficiary's application, the High Court approved an apportionment of the profit between the trustee's own deceased estate and the estate of which he was formerly trustee. The court denied that the estate was *limited* to a claim for the misused sum with interest. Apportionment was made after the house had been sold and a sum of easily divisible proceeds was in hand. The question of whether recovery should be limited to a proportion of the profit, or otherwise be the whole profit, was not argued in the High Court. Appeal was only on the question of whether the beneficiary deprived should get only its money back, or get a rateable proportion of the increase in value. The plaintiff sought no more than a proportion of the profit and made no claim to the whole of it. Merely proportional recovery was something that the directors in *Paul A Davies* were prepared to concede.

**[6.99]** *Scott v Scott* at first instance in the Supreme Court of Victoria,[211] did examine the plaintiff's contention that the whole of the value of the land acquired from mixed funds should be accounted for. Hudson J rejected the idea as contrary to established authorities, including *Docker v Somes*[212] earlier referred to. This was ignored by the Court of Appeal in *Paul A Davies*. Moffitt P at 447 and Hutley JA at 451 said there that *Paul A Davies* had two features which distinguished it from *Scott's* case. First, they said, the bank 'bridging' loan in *Davies* could not be equated with *Scott's* 'personal moneys of the fiduciary'. Yet the first instance report of *Scott* shows that the defaulting fiduciary in that case also borrowed a similar proportion of the funds for purchase of the house. He borrowed them from his brother. Secondly, in *Paul A Davies* the amount of the appreciation of the land, fixed at the time of sale, was said to be almost solely attributable to the holding deposit paid with misapplied funds. *Scott* on the other hand was seen to involve an appreciation occurring through the deployment of mixed funds for seventeen years. Whether this is an adequate distinction or not, it might be thought, the point required affirmative evidence as to value.

**[6.100]** In this way, the Court of Appeal in *Paul A Davies* held that the 'entirety or proportion' question was free of authority. Moffitt P at 444 emphasised the 'penal' nature of the profits rule. This was how an otherwise unlikely result in the case was justified. Apportionment of the gain in favour of its primary source was seen to be a discretionary matter. The benefit of the discretion was denied to the directors who stood to benefit from it in this case.

---

[209] [1983] 1 NSWLR 440 (CA)
[210] (1963) 109 CLR 649.
[211] [1964] VR 300, 312.
[212] (1834) 2 My & K 655, 39 ER 1095.

The decision has been followed in *In the Marriage of Wagstaff*[213] and *Australian Postal Corporation v Lutak*.[214] Again the profits rule with its prophylactic overtones has triumphed over a non-penal conception of equity's role. *Wagstaff* involved a claim arising from breach of express trust. A divorced wife used funds in a trust fund set up for her children in order to purchase a house for herself and her new partner. Misused trust funds provided the deposit and the rest was borrowed from the bank. The court followed *Paul A Davies* and held at 86–7 that the children were entitled to the whole profit made when the house was realised some years later. *Lutak* was the receiver of stolen stamps. Facts of the case were set out at [6.95]. He and his wife failed in their claim to obtain part of the appreciated value of a house purchased with both the proceeds of the stolen stamps and funds borrowed from a bank. In both *Wagstaff* and *Lutak* the purchases were preponderantly funded by borrowed funds. What was subtracted from the beneficiary was a deposit, or less. Should at least a de minimis principle limit this new competence of the profits rule?

## 3. Personal liability to account as a constructive trustee

**[6.101]** This is the *in personam* form of the constructive trust remedy for breach of fiduciary obligation. It is sometimes referred to in this context simply as the equitable obligation to 'account'. An order to account as a constructive trustee is obtained against the fiduciary individually.[215] It is satisfied by the defendant paying the monetary sum found due. The quantum of this may be agreed between the parties or fixed in subsequent judicial proceedings. Procedural steps involved in a fiduciary accounting of profits were explained in the intellectual property cases of *Leplastrier and Co Ltd v Armstrong Holland Ltd*[216] and *Colbeam Palmer Ltd v Stock Affiliates Pty Ltd*.[217] The sum to be accounted for in these fiduciaries cases is computed by reference to a specified gain made, either in,[218] or by reason of,[219] a fiduciary relationship. Identification and measurement of gain exercises were dealt with in previous paragraphs. It will be assumed that an appropriate form of words has been settled to describe what the defendant must account for.

**[6.102]** Beneficiaries must formally choose the accounting form of the constructive trust. It is an 'election' and the remedy is taken in lieu of other remedies.[220] One convenient feature of the account is that the transaction under review need not be set aside. The beneficiary, in effect, adopts what the fiduciary has done—and takes the benefit of it. Another feature of account is

---

213 (1990) 14 Fam L R 78 (Fam Ct (FC)).

214 (1991) 21 NSWLR 584, Bryson J.

215 See Underhill Art. 33 (301–25).

216 (1926) 26 SR (NSW) 585.

217 (1968) 122 CLR 25 and see F Patfield 'The Modern Remedy of Account' 11 *Adel LR* 1, 16–18.

218 Eg, *Cook v Deeks* [1916] AC 554, 565 (PC); *McLeod and More v Sweezey* [1944] 2 DLR 145, *Industrial Development Consultants Ltd v Cooley* [1972] 2 All ER 162, *Canadian Aero Service Ltd v O'Malley* (1973) 40 DLR (3d) 371, *Consul Development Pty Ltd v DPC Estates Pty Ltd* (1975) 132 CLR 373, *Green and Clara Pty Ltd v Bestobell Industries Pty Ltd* [1982] WAR 1 (FC), *Avtex Airservices Pty Ltd v Bartsch* (1992) 107 ALR 539.

219 Eg, *Regal (Hastings) Ltd v Gulliver* (1942) [1967] 2 AC 134n, 149, Lord Russell.

220 Ford & Lee [1714]–[1714.2].

that it is enough that the fiduciary is shown to have made the profit, not that he or she still holds it.[221] It is analogous to the need only to prove a receipt for the purposes of 'money had and received'. This could be advantageous where the gain is of nature untraceable or has ceased to exist.[222]

**[6.103]** Distinction between personal remedies, such as the account, and proprietary remedies was once said to be brought out in the bribery cases.[223] A bribe received by a fiduciary was untraceable by the beneficiary on the much criticised authority of *Lister & Co v Stubbs*.[224] Its investment 'exchange-product', be it land or other things, could not be followed into the fiduciary's possession. This would have prevented the army sergeant in *Reading v Attorney-General*[225] from being liable to any proprietary remedy, had this been sought. But the example of untraceable property may not now be a good one. For whether beneficiaries obtain property rights in bribes their fiduciaries receive is questionable after the Privy Council decision in *Attorney General for Hong Kong v Reid*.[226] *Lister & Co v Stubbs* has now been disapproved of by a high tribunal.

**[6.104]** Another way of distinguishing a personal accounting for profits as constructive trustee from a proprietary constructive trust over the same has been suggested. A proper case for the personal remedy may only arise where the fiduciary has taken advantage of his or her *position* to make the profit. By contrast, the proprietary constructive trust is appropriate where the fiduciary has taken advantage of *property* in the relationship.[227] Such a distinction corresponds with some of the older United Kingdom authorities and supplies a relatively clear guide for courts faced with this problem. However the distinction fails to explain remedial aspects of the modern proprietary constructive trust.

The better view may be that the courts in modern times possess a *discretion* to award proprietary relief. Where a personal obligation to account for a profit is awarded by a court, this may not mean that a proprietary constructive trust was inappropriate. The reason may be simpler. Proprietary relief, perhaps, was not needed. Cases where fiduciaries' personal accounting was ordered and proprietary relief was not sought include *Cook v Deeks*,[228] *Birtchnell v Equity Trustees Executors and Agency Co Ltd*,[229] *Regal (Hastings) Ltd v Gulliver*,[230] *Walden Properties Ltd v Beaver Properties Pty Ltd*,[231] *Canadian Aero Service Ltd v O'Malley*,[232] *English v Dedham Vale Properties Ltd*,[233] *Green and Clara*

---

[221] See *Estate Realties Ltd v Wignall* [1991] 3 NZLR 482, 496, Tipping J.

[222] Suggested in Ford & Lee [2212].

[223] In Underhill 303.

[224] (1890) 45 Ch D 1 (CA).

[225] [1951] AC 507.

[226] [1994] 1 AC 324 (PC), Lord Templeman: discussed at [5.86].

[227] Discussed (and disapproved) in Underhill 314–5.

[228] [1916] AC 554.

[229] (1929) 42 CLR 384.

[230] (1942) [1967] 2 AC 134n.

[231] [1973] 2 NSWLR 815 (CA).

[232] (1973) 40 DLR (3d) 371.

[233] [1978] 1 WLR 93.

*Pty Ltd v Bestobell Industries Pty Ltd*[234] and *Avtex Airservices Pty Ltd v Bartsch.*[235] There is less to prove with personal accounting and, in the absence of the defendant's insolvency or some other exceptional factor, the result in each case is exactly the same.

**PROPRIETARY RELIEF**

**[6.105]** Constructive trusts of the property in profits are proprietary applications of the profits rule. They may be imposed on property of two descriptions. First, the beneficiary's property in the profit may be created anew. Money or things that the fiduciary receives from third parties are turned into the beneficiary's property for the first time. Secondly, the remedy may be an extension of the beneficiary's pre-existing rights. If the fiduciary invests the beneficiary's money, for example, the beneficiary may be entitled to its product as 'fruit' of the thing invested. Both the 'newly created' and the 'pre-existing property' constructive trusts of fiduciaries' profits apply to property that the fiduciaries possess when the order is made. Profits may have changed in form from the time that they were made. Bribes, say, may have been invested in land. The beneficiary's proprietary entitlement may be given a retrospective effect in an appropriate case. This is something that we examined at [6.72]. It may improve the beneficiary's priority position with other persons interested in the property. Retrospectivity can be justified as giving the remedy effect at the time of the wrongful act which based it.

**[6.106]** *Annexure* of property in the profit is involved here. Proprietary reach of this variety of the constructive trust takes effect in this way. It is an exercise which corresponds to the *tracing* of pre-existing entitlements. Gains to be accounted for are annexed to particular property. Just as property to be recovered is traced to the form in which it is retained. Property in the profit rather than the defendant personally becomes the subject of the account. Proprietary constructive trusts of profits are satisfied from the profits. Prior to this being done, the obligation to account will have been defined and measured. The obligation here merges in a particular gain, or where necessary, an appropriate proportion of the gain.

**[6.107]** An image of 'identification' might describe the annexure process. The gain is identified with particular property. So the 'corporate opportunity' in *Timber Engineering Co Pty Ltd v Anderson*[236] was identified with a business the fiduciaries had secretly commenced. Analysis has moved on a step from determining that the opportunities equal the gain. Now we are led from the gain to specific property. From abstract 'opportunities' we arrive at a business or its value that the court can reach. In *Attorney General for Hong Kong v Reid,*[237] a Crown prosecutor in Hong Kong had corruptly received bribes in carrying out his official duties. He invested them in New Zealand real property, in his own and other names. The prosecutor was caught and imprisoned. After the Attorney-General learnt of the investment he desired to caveat the properties in the Crown's name. This is how litigation over the existence of a

---

[234] [1982] WAR 1.
[235] (1992) 107 ALR 539.
[236] [1980] NSWLR 488.
[237] [1994] 1 AC 324 (PC).

proprietary interest in the Crown's name arose. The first determination referred to here would identify the prosecutor's obligation to account for the bribes he received. Obligation is identified with gain. The present inquiry would link the gain with land in New Zealand. For this is what the gain now represents. Gains are identified with specific property. This is what the Privy Council in *Reid's case* decided. The Crown did have an interest in the land flowing from the receipt of bribes contrary to the terms of the profits rule. We will outline the present step again. An obligation to restore a defined gain is now annexed to particular property. That property can be reached and is now in the defendant's hands.

## In theory

[6.108]    Constructive trusts with this annexure process are entirely remedial. Property is created out of thin air. Or at least, property is created out of abstract obligations without any *locus* of value. But what kind of abstract obligations? Could a common law obligation suffice? Deane J suggested as much in *Hospital Products Ltd v United States Surgical Corporation.*[238] A remedial constructive trust could be based on a 'calculated' breach of contract. It would be 'unconscionable', he said at 125, for a person to retain a benefit appropriated 'in breach of his contractual or other legal or equitable obligations to another.' The possibilities of this are disturbingly large.

[6.109]    Senior counsel for the Reids in *Attorney-General for Hong Kong v Reid*[239] made some interesting submissions on the point. He assumed that the general basis of equitable proprietary interests lies in policy. Members of the House of Lords in *Lord Napier and Ettick v Hunter*[240] had recently indicated this was so. Once upon a time, it was submitted, *Lister & Co v Stubbs*[241] had tried to limit the interest to an 'original proprietary basis'. But wrong-based proprietary remedies had existed since long before. Obviously not all wrongs could qualify, or every victim and unsecured creditor might claim. A line had to be drawn. *Reid's* case was an appropriate place to draw one. An a priori limit had to be imposed, which the reasoning of Roy Goode was adopted to supply. Goode said that an eligible obligation for this purpose has first to be equitable.[242] It is the analogue of an American 'unjust enrichment'.

> There is no basis for the imposition of a constructive trust on one who owes no fiduciary or other obligation to P in relation to the gain-producing activity.

Interrupting counsel for a moment, we might note that the ultimate reason for this is probably historical. It is difficult to contest that the obligation must be equitable. We are the lawyers that our legal history has made us. Judicial politics of seventeenth-century England has defined the legal consciousness of common law countries. At 239, Goode said that there was a further limitation. Profits in the defendant's hands had to result from 'deemed agency activities in breach of [the defendant's] equitable obligation to P'. This is where the line was really drawn. Breach of not every equitable obligation will do. Only if

---

[238] (1984) 156 CLR 41, 124–5.
[239] [1994] 1 AC 324, 328–9.
[240] [1993] AC 713, 738, Lord Templeman, 744, Lord Goff, cf. 750–2, Lord Browne-Wilkinson.
[241] (1890) 45 Ch D 1.
[242] 'Property and Unjust Enrichment' in Burrows 215, 238.

the fiduciary in breach of duty acquired for himself a benefit which ought to have been acquired for his beneficiary can he be made a constructive trustee of it. If the fiduciary acts wholly outside the scope of his duties or ambit of his legitimate activities the remedy should not be forthcoming. A bribe is outside that scope and is illegitimate, too.

**[6.110]** The submissions in *Reid* were not accepted. At 332 Lord Templeman said that the 'rule', derived from *Keech v Sandford*[243] must be that 'property which a trustee obtains by the use of *knowledge* acquired as trustee becomes trust property'. [emphasis added]

This is much broader than the 'deemed agency gain' idea. It has no proprietary implications at all. 'Knowledge' is not said to be property. Where a fiduciary profits 'by or in the course of' a fiduciary relation, a property in the profit can be allowed wherever the profits rule applies. A fiduciary profiting by knowledge acquired as fiduciary is virtually the scope conclusion reached at [4.43]. So the opening sentence at [6.105] is confirmed. Constructive trusts of fiduciaries' profits are proprietary applications of the profits rule—a 'proprietary overkill', as it has been called.[244]

### Annexing property in the fiduciary's profits

**[6.111]** Profits from fiduciary office can be the subject of proprietary constructive trusts. Breach of the fiduciary's equitable obligation to account for gains is a sufficient justification for award of the proprietary remedy.[245] Accounting obligation are annexed to the gains. Proprietary constructive trusts can then be *of* and *over* the profits themselves, whether they take the form of money or something else. It has been decided that each of a business undertaking,[246] a lease renewed,[247] or what was bought with the amount of the profit[248] can be made liable to the claim of a proprietary constructive trust 'of profits'. The property either was or represented the gain. Like the cousin to this remedy, the personal obligation to account as constructive trustee, no pre-existing interest in the gain need be shown. The two forms of the remedy are interrelated. A proprietary constructive trust may give rise to a concomitant personal liability to account as constructive trustee, as it was found to do in *Re Montagu's Settlement Trusts*.[249]

**[6.112]** *Boardman v Phipps*[250] is an unlikely example of the proprietary constructive trust. The plaintiff was a beneficiary with an interest in a large estate, for which Boardman was the solicitor. Boardman was found to have profited by using information which came to him whilst doing the estate's business. With his own money, Boardman had made some advantageous purchases of shares for himself. It was legally impossible at the time for the

---

[243] (1726) Sel Cas T King 61; 25 ER 273.

[244] P Birks [1993] *LCMCLQ* 30, 31; other English critics include P Watts (1994) 110 *LQR* 178; R Pearce [1994] *LMCLQ* 189 and D Crilley [1994] *RLR* 73.

[245] Ford & Lee [2112]; Hayton 446–50.

[246] *Timber Engineering Co Pty Ltd v Anderson* [1980] 2 NSWLR 488.

[247] *Chan v Zacharia* (1984) 154 CLR 178 and see *Gibb Australia Pty Ltd v Cremor Pty Ltd* (1992) 108 FLR 129 (SC (ACT)).

[248] *Attorney General for Hong Kong v Reid* [1994] 1 AC 324 (PC).

[249] [1987] Ch 264, Megarry V-C.

[250] [1967] 2 AC 46.

estate to have made these purchases instead. The estate lacked the power to purchase more shares without court approval. Nevertheless, a combination of the profits and the conflicts rules was invoked to find that Boardman held the shares he purchased on constructive trust for the plaintiff. The majority confirmed the order of Wilberforce J at first instance, which included a declaration of proprietary constructive trust.[251] The plaintiff was a beneficiary of the estate. Boardman was decreed to hold his shares on constructive trust for the plaintiff in proportion to the plaintiff's interest in the estate.

[6.113] Of course the plaintiff in *Boardman* had no pre-existing proprietary interest in the shares that Boardman purchased. Boardman had dealt at arm's length with third parties and the estate, as we said, had no power to commission anyone to acquire the shares on its behalf. Yet in the consistent reasoning of the majority law lords, the plaintiff was awarded a proprietary interest in the shares. This can only have been by annexure of the property that the profits represented. The proprietary nature of the remedy ordered was something not directly considered. Whether the remedy had a personal or a proprietary reach made little difference. Boardman was a wealthy man. He later became the chairman of the Conservative party and a member of the House of Lords.

[6.114] Proprietary results based in no more than the duty to account have occurred in Australia. Consider the New South Wales Court of Appeal decision in *United States Surgical Corporation v Hospital Products International Pty Ltd*.[252] The defaulting fiduciary there was made to account by way of proprietary constructive trust for the value of a competing business which it had secretly formed. The beneficiary, United States Surgical Corporation, was a long way from having a pre-existing interest in the business. Part of its case was that the existence of the business had been kept a secret from it until shortly before the issue of proceedings. Property interests in a fiduciary's gains are very often *created* for beneficiaries, we have said, out of nothing more than the obligation to account for them. This was once described as the signal 'unsoundness consisting in confounding ownership with obligation'. It was so deprecated by Lindley LJ in *Lister & Co v Stubbs*,[253] in the related context of an employee receiving bribes in the course of his employment. It is not unsound now to recognise that a proprietary remedy may flow from a personal wrongdoing.

### Annexing profits made from the beneficiary's pre-existing property

[6.115] Profits from fiduciary office may have been earned in several ways. One is through the misuse of the beneficiary's pre-existing property. That property and profits derived therefrom as its traceable product can both be recovered from the fiduciary if they are identifiable in his hands. Principles regarding recovery of property and derivative profits are the same were described by Mahoney JA in *Paul A Davies (Australia) Pty Ltd (in liq) v Davies*.[254] Company directors who misapply the funds of their company and

---

[251] [1964] 2 All ER 187, 208; cf parallel report at [1964] 1 WLR 993, 1018 and D Hayton 'Developing the Law of Trusts for the 21st Century' (1990) 106 *LQR* 87, 101–3.

[252] [1983] 2 NSWLR 157.

[253] (1890) 45 Ch D 1, 13 (CA).

[254] [1983] 1 NSWLR 440 (CA), 445–6.

purchase land will hold whatever appreciated value that land has on constructive trust for the company. Or it has been held that a fiduciary engaged as agent to buy property on behalf of his principal will hold that property on constructive trust if he wrongfully buys it for himself.[255] This is because the property bought has been in equity deemed to belong to the principal from the moment the agent acquired it. Obligations to disgorge the profit are annexed in these cases to the property wherefrom it is derived. Property and profit are then recovered together. This type of annexure employs constructive trusts which have a more traditional proprietary base. The fiduciary's gain is recovered either as a misappropriation of profits derived from fiduciary property, or that property itself.

The 'entrusted property or its product' species of the constructive trust is probably not of great significance. Relief under this heading is characteristically sought against fiduciaries who are also express trustees. This is a use of the constructive trust as a 'remedial adjunct' to an express trust, which was one of its earliest employments. A feature of these 'adjunct' cases is that no property need in theory be 'created' at all. Misappropriated assets are identified as their exchange products. Property rights asserted pre-exist the making of the claim.

## ACCOUNT

**[6.116]**  We have already dealt with this remedy. It is the same as the form of the constructive trust we described at [6.81]. Namely, a personal obligation of a fiduciary to account for gains as though he were a constructive trustee. Issues of jurisdiction on which most treatments of the remedy focus are irrelevant in a fiduciary context. Where the plaintiff and the defendant are the opposite parties in a fiduciary relationship, there is always sufficient jurisdiction to order the account. For equity, as *Snells' Equity* points out, has an exclusive jurisdiction to order an account in aid of a purely equitable right.[256] Breach of fiduciary obligation is perhaps the foremost species of this purely equitable jurisdiction.

# Restoring a beneficiary's losses

## COMPENSATION

**[6.117]**  Compensation implies a loss. Equitable compensation in the present context is an indemnity for losses suffered by a beneficiary as the result of his fiduciary's breach of duty.[257] A loss that can be compensated for under this heading must usually be financial.[258] Payment of money is the means by which

---

[255] *Longfield Parish Council v Robson* (1913) 29 TLR 357; *Bentley v Craven* (1853) 18 Beav 74, 52 ER 29, 30.

[256] *Snell's Equity* 29th ed (1990), 637; see also MGL [2503]; *Pomeroy's Equity Jurisprudence* 5th ed (1941), §1424; F Patfield 'The Modern Remedy of Account' (1987) 11 *Adel LR* 1, 3; S Stoljar 'The Transformations of Account' (1964) 80 *LQR* 203, 216–21.

[257] See MGL [552]–[554] and [2302–4]; I Davidson 'The Equitable Remedy of Compensation' (1982) 13 *MULR* 349, 372–91; W Gummow 'Compensation for Breach of Fiduciary Duty' in Youdan 57.

[258] Davidson ibid, 349; but see *Norberg v Wynrib* (1992) 92 DLR (4th) 449 (SC), 484–502, McLachlin J (equitable compensation for mental distress).

indemnities are effected. Fiduciaries are placed under an equitable personal obligation to satisfy an award of pecuniary compensation. 'The Court of Chancery never entertained a suit for damages', James and Baggalay LJJ observed in *Re Collie*,[259]

> The suit [for compensation] was always for an equitable debt or liability in the nature of a debt. It was a suit for the restitution of the actual money or thing, or value of the thing . . .

For equitable compensation, despite its name, is computed on a restitutionary rather than compensatory basis. This is a fact which often makes for a significant difference between the quantum of a damages award and the quantum of compensation for the same wrong.

The jurisdictional basis of the compensation remedy is the same as for the other equitable remedies in the exclusive jurisdiction. Equity courts have inherent power to award compensation in a fiduciary context.[260] Breach of fiduciary duty invokes rights over which a court of equity has exclusive authority. Fiduciary rights are equitable rights and breach of a fiduciary duty is a purely equitable wrong. Statutory power to award damages is not needed. This avoids the controversy which has attended such wrongs as breach of confidence over the correct interpretation of the various statutory powers to award damages 'in lieu of or in addition to' other equitable remedies.

## Utility of the remedy

**[6.118]** Many types of fiduciaries' misconduct have been the subject of equitable compensation awards. They include losses suffered from the following wrongs: a solicitor's pursuit of a secret interest when advising on the discharge of his client's securities,[261] a fraudulent exchange between an estate agent and his principal,[262] bad advice given by a bank manager on the purchase of a business,[263] misrepresentations by the promoters of an investment scheme,[264] misrepresentations by share brokers inducing their customers to purchase of shares,[265] a prospective partner's unlawful use of a business opportunity,[266] fraudulent employees causing the loss of a franchise for Japanese engines,[267] termination of a distributor's agency through the disloyalty of its employee,[268] investment in a business after misrepresentations by its promoters,[269] fraudulent sale of shares by a solicitor to his client,[270]

---

[259] (1878) 8 Ch D 807, 819 (CA), approved in *Wickstead v Browne* (1992) 30 NSWLR 1, 14, Handley and Cripps JJA (CA) and *Gemstone Coproration of Australia Ltd v Grasso* (1994) 13 ACSR 695, 703, Prior J (SC (SA) (FC)).

[260] MGL [2302].

[261] *Nocton v Ashburton* [1914] AC 932.

[262] *McKenzie v McDonald* [1927] VLR 134.

[263] *Commonwealth Bank of Australia v Smith* (1991) 102 ALR 453 (Fed Ct (FC)).

[264] *Catt v Marac Australia Ltd* (1986) 9 NSWLR 639.

[265] *Burke v Cory* (1959) 19 DLR (2d) 252 (CA (Ont)); *Culling v Sansai Industries Ltd* (1974) 45 DLR (3d) 456 (BCSC).

[266] *Fraser Edmiston Pty Ltd v AGT (Qld) Pty Ltd* (1986) 2 Qd R 1.

[267] *Markwell Bros Pty Ltd v CPN Diesels Queensland Pty Ltd* [1983] 2 Qd R 508.

[268] *Dwyer v Warman International Ltd* (SC (Qld) (FC), 23 February 1994, unreported).

[269] *Hill v Rose* [1990] VR 129.

[270] *Robinson v Abbott* (1894) 20 VLR 346 (FC).

solicitors' unprofessional and interested advice[271] and a solicitor's failure to disclose a fraud to a client.[272]

**[6.119]** Interrelation of the compensation remedy with equitable rescission is illustrated by the decision of the Supreme Court of Victoria in *McKenzie v McDonald*.[273] A widow from the Great War was induced by an estate agent to sell her farm and buy his shop on very unfavourable terms. Later she sued to have these transactions rescinded on account of the agent's abuse of trust and confidence in the transaction. However the agent had by this time sold the farm to a third party. This meant that, in terms of rescission, even 'substantial restitution' could barely be achieved. Only half the transaction could be 'unpacked'. Compensation was said to offer another route to the same result. Dixon A-J (at 146) ordered that the widow be paid a money sum equalling what she had been deprived of in the exchange of the farm for the shop. The order allowed the possibility of 'partial rescission' to occur at the election of the agent, by return to him of his shop at its true valuation.[274] In passing, Dixon A-J noted (at 146) that a 'fiduciary's gain' rather than 'beneficiary's loss' remedy might have been applied to achieve the same result. For there was here what restitutionary theorists might describe as a 'perfect quadration': the widow's loss was matched by the agent's gain. The agent could as easily have been made accountable for his profit on the exchange.

**[6.120]** *McKenzie's* case brings out the following features of compensation as a remedy. First, compensation may be an alternative way of recovering losses in situations where rescission is unavailable. On the principles of compensation stated by Lord Haldane LC in *Nocton v Ashburton*,[275] compensation and rescission are independent remedies and the availability of one does not depend on the availability of the other. Secondly, compensation may be an alternative way of making fiduciaries account for gains where those gains are subtracted from beneficiaries. No doubt for this reason, the plaintiff cannot normally recover both compensation and an account of profits.[276] But the possibility of this double recovery is unlikely. Compensation is usually awarded where no gain is evident on the facts at all. It is more likely to be awarded in situations where the beneficiary, or the fiduciary and the beneficiary together, has or have made losses and the dispute is over which party should bear them.[277] Thirdly, a *fiduciary* wrong is needed to base the award. If the estate agent in *McKenzie v McDonald* had simply failed to exercise reasonable care, then equitable compensation would not have been available. No fiduciary duty would then be breached, as discussed above. Perhaps for the same reason, W Gummow has recently suggested that a

---

[271] *Brickenden v London Loan & Savings Co* [1934] 3 DLR 465 (PC); *Day v Mead* [1987] 2 NZLR 443 (CA); cf *Mouatt v Clark Boyce* [1992] 2 NZLR 559 (CA).

[272] *Jacks v Davis* (1983) 141 DLR (3d) 355 (BCCA).

[273] [1927] VLR 134, Dixon A-J.

[274] At 146–7, following *Robinson v Abbott* [1894] 20 VLR 346, 365–8.

[275] [1914] AC 932, 952.

[276] I Davidson 'The Equitable Remedy of Compensation' (1982) 13 *MULR* 349, 354; but cf *Cook v Evatt (No 2)* [1992] 1 NZLR 676.

[277] As in *Nocton v Ashburton* supra; *Catt v Marac Australia Ltd* (1986) 9 NSWLR 639; *Hill v Rose* [1990] VLR 129; *Canson Enterprises Ltd v Boughton & Co* (1991) 85 DLR (4th) 129 (SC).

'conflict of interest' may be needed before any compensatory award can be made.[278] Conflict of interest, of course, is one species of fiduciary wrong.

## The effect of insolvency on personal claims

**[6.121]**   We noted the (limited) effect of insolvency on *proprietary* claims against fiduciaries (at [6.49]–[6.77]). By contrast, a personal claim for compensation under this heading, or an account claim, or , in some circumstances, rescission and the constructive trust claims, are all significantly affected. That is, where individual fiduciaries are bankrupted or corporate fiduciaries are put in liquidation before the entry of judgments on personal claims against them. Administrations for individuals pursuant to the Bankruptcy Act 1966 (Cth), and pursuant to the Corporations Law for corporations, refer to the claims which can be proven against an insolvent as 'debts'. Once proven, debts are to be ranked and satisfied proportionately. Not all claims are eligible. As we will see, breaches of fiduciary duty are admitted to the regime of provable debts, but they are often not extinguished upon completion of the insolvency administration, like the rest of a fiduciary's debts.

Regarding debts provable in an individual bankruptcy, the Bankruptcy Act provides:

SECTION 82   DEBTS PROVABLE IN BANKRUPTCY

**82(1)** . . . all debts and liabilities, present or future, certain or contingent, to which a bankrupt was subject at the date of the bankruptcy, . . . are provable in his bankruptcy.

**82(1A)** . . .

**82(2)** Demands in the nature of unliquidated damages arising otherwise than by breach of contract, promise or breach of trust are not provable in bankruptcy.

Claims for compensation for breach of fiduciary duty have been held on several occasions not to be 'demands in the nature of unliquidated damages'. Personal torts like defamation and assault are the only claims consistently identified within this 'unliquidated' category.[279] Breach of fiduciary duty has sometimes been equated with breach of trust and hence specifically included in the class of what is provable.[280] This is a little more questionable, or at least may seem so to the more conservative courts. Status of a breach of fiduciary duty as a 'breach of trust' is not necessary to secure 'provable' status for it against an individual fiduciary. Debts or claims are provable in the winding up of corporate fiduciaries pursuant to s 553(1) of the Corporations Law. This section clearly includes breach of fiduciary duty claims: claims without exception can be proven as debts of a corporation in liquidation.

Upon completion of an insolvent individual's bankruptcy administration, the policy of bankruptcy law is that a bankrupt should be made a 'freed man', released from all the debts, liabilities and duties proven or provable against

---

[278] In 'Compensation for Breach of Fiduciary Duty' in Youdan 57, 66–7.

[279] *Chittick v Maxwell* (1993) 118 ALR 728, 738–9, Young J (SC) (NSW)); *Re Vassis* (1986) 9 FCR 518, 527, Burchett J (Fed C); *Cornelius v Barewa Oil Mining NL (in liq)* (1982) 42 ALR 83, 89, Wickham J, other JJ agreeing (FC); *Emma Silver Mining Co v Grant* (1880) 17 Ch D 122, 130, Jessel MR; see *McPherson on Company Liquidation* 3rd edn, J O'Donovan ed, 379.

[280] Eg, *Britter v Sprigg* (1900) 26 VLR 65 (FC), 82, curiam.

him.[281] This is what s 153(1) of the Bankruptcy Act provides. Bankrupt fiduciaries must usually wait five years for a discharge from bankruptcy. However, by entering a deed of arrangement or assignment, or by making a composition with creditors, defaulting fiduciaries can obtain a release from provable debts and their fiduciary obligations in a relatively brief time.[282] Possibilities for abuse of the Act are reduced by the next subsection, which provides:

**153(2)**   The discharge of a bankrupt from a bankruptcy does not–
(a) ... ;
(b) release the bankrupt from a debt incurred by means of a fraud or fraudulent breach of trust to which he was a party or a debt of which he has obtained forbearance by fraud;
(c) ... ;
(d) ...

So some equitable debts of fiduciaries remain on foot notwithstanding discharge from and termination of the bankruptcy regimes. If the fiduciaries have engaged in 'fraud' or 'fraudulent breach of trust' in their breach of duty, the resultant debts survive as personal equitable obligations against them.[283] It is not clear whether either or both of 'fraud' and 'fraudulent' in these contexts includes constructive, as well as actual fraud. This may become important in claims against insolvent fiduciaries who have been honest, or negligent at most. The Act gives little indication and the matter has not been decided by the courts. Commentators are not concerned.[284] It is suggested that the expression 'fraudulent breach of trust', when used in addition to 'fraud' generally, includes the constructive sense of fraud applicable to a 'breach of trust' and liabilities which are assimilable. Many if not most breaches of fiduciary obligation are then 'fraudulent' in the s 153(2)(b) sense.

## Computation of the award

**[6.122]**   The *restitutionary* measure, as we have said, is the appropriate basis of a compensation award. Compensation in this context is broadly intended to restore beneficiaries to the positions that they enjoyed prior to the breach of fiduciary duty occurring. Whatever is the cost of achieving restitution at the date of hearing is said to quantify a compensation award.[285] This involves a fairly primitive idea of 'compensation', as we shall see.

It is sometimes observed that the money sum awarded to the beneficiary may be computed by reference to the fiduciary's profit.[286] This assumes that a 'plus and minus' equation applies: the fiduciary has made a profit and

---

[281] *Ex parte Llynvi Coal and Iron Co: Re Hide* (1871) LR 7 Ch App 28 (CA in Ch), 31, W James LJ.

[282] See Bankruptcy Act 1966 (Cth): s 230 (assignment); s 234 (arrangement); s 240 (composition).

[283] *Cornelius v Barewa Oil & Mining NL (in liq)* (1982) 42 ALR 83, 85, Burt CJ, 89, Wickham J, 92–3, Kennedy J (SC (WA) (FC)); *Chittick v Maxwell* (1993) 118 ALR 728, 740, Young J (NSW SC); *Emma Silver Mining Co v Grant* (1880) 17 Ch D 122, 129–30, Jessel MR.

[284] See, eg, Lewis' *Australian Bankruptcy Law* (9th edn 1990), D Rose ed, 101; the Insolvency Act 1986 (UK) s 281(3) restates the exception in the same terms and I Fletcher *The Law of Insolvency* (1990) makes no comment, at 296.

[285] MGL [2304]; I Davidson 'The Equitable Remedy of Compensation' (1982) 13 *MULR* 349, 352–3.

[286] MGL [2304].

subtracted it from the beneficiary. Profits are otherwise things that can be subtracted from the fiduciary by the more direct means of the constructive trust, in either of its forms, or the equitable lien. Usually, though, it is a loss that the beneficiary suffers that justifies the remedy. Measurement of that loss brings out compensation's restitutionary features.

**[6.123]** The decision in *Re Dawson*[287] highlighted the nature of this remedy and the differences there are in effect between damages at law and compensation in equity. In 1939 an express trustee committed a breach of fiduciary duty in New Zealand. Improper payments of trust moneys in New Zealand pounds were made, a currency then at exchange parity with Australian pounds. A new trustee was later sued for the wrong in New South Wales. This was in 1966. By this time the Australian pound had declined in value as against the New Zealand pound. Street J entered judgment in Australian pounds for the sum necessary in 1966 to return to the trust the New Zealand pounds that the trustee had misappropriated in 1939. This was a larger sum of Australian pounds than the subtracted sum expressed in New Zealand pounds. Had the action been brought as a parallel common law claim in conversion, the 'date of liability rule' would have led to a different result. The appropriate exchange rate between the two currencies under that rule would be the one which prevailed when the debt became payable. This was when the currencies were at par. So by holding that the appropriate exchange rate to apply was that obtaining at the date of his order, Street J (at 216) provided for a higher figure in Australian pounds. This was consistent with the restitutionary nature of the award. It equalled the amount of money that it took to restore the trust estate at the time of restoring. Street J rejected the argument that the decline in the Australian pound was too remote an event for the wrongdoer to have foreseen. The trustee's primary liability was to restore the trust estate to the same position as though no breach had occurred. In consequence, he said at 215,

> Considerations of causation, foreseeability and remoteness do not readily enter into the matter.

**[6.124]** This was not followed in *Jaffray v Marshall*.[288] A trustee was again found liable to compensate his beneficiaries for a wrong that had been committed some years before. A mortgage over a domestic home owned by a trust was executed by the trustee to secure an unauthorised debt. Eventually the home was sold by the mortgagee when the debt was not paid. Restitution in respect of this continuing breach was said to enable the trustee to take advantage of his own wrong. For the home was worth more at the time proceedings were issued than when judgment was finally obtained. In these circumstances, a 'proper measure of the remedy' was said to be the house's highest intermediate value between the date of the breach and the date of the action.

One aspect of *Re Dawson*[289] deserves further examination. This is remoteness of loss, not what was actually decided. The facts of the case are insignificant. As Sykes and Pryles observe, the currency problem would probably not now arise, or arise differently, given that many Australian

---

[287] [1966] 2 NSWLR 211, 215, Street J.
[288] [1994] 1 All ER 143, 154, Nicholas Stewart QC.
[289] [1966] 2 NSWLR 211.

jurisdictions have been conferred with the power to award judgments in foreign currencies.[290]

## Problems with the remedy

### Remoteness of loss

**[6.125]**  Equitable compensation, at least in theory, ignores all immediate causes such as fire, lightning, accidents and other forms of the *novus actus interveniens* if they are preceded by a breach of fiduciary duty.[291] 'Restoring' beneficiaries to their pre-breach of duty positions, or restitution, seems to imply 'but for' causation in an unreconstructed form.[292] Fiduciaries in breach of duty for the purpose of this remedy may be held indiscriminately responsible for the effects of all operative causes leading to their beneficiaries' loss.

The 'restitutionary' measure of compensation has traditionally been married to a remarkably crude theory of causation. Taken to its logical extreme in the Canadian case of *Canson Enterprises Ltd v Boughton & Co*,[293] the majority of the Supreme Court declined to support the orthodox position. The facts of the *Canson* case concerned a solicitor who acted for the purchaser of an urban development site. The purchaser intended to erect a warehouse on the land. In breach of fiduciary duty, the solicitor concealed the fact that another client had interposed itself between purchaser and vendor and was making a secret profit on the purchase transaction. At trial the finding was made that the purchaser would not have gone ahead with the deal had it known the true facts about the interposition. In the event, the purchaser did go ahead and commenced erection of the warehouse. It then encountered a problem of quite a different kind. Negligent contractors caused the warehouse foundations to be defective. Repair work that this caused led to the purchaser incurring considerable extra expense. The contractors were duly sued, but judgments obtained against them were not fully satisfied. The purchaser then made a further claim for the loss. This time it sued in equity and made a claim against the firm of solicitors that had concealed the secret profit of the intervening purchaser. The theory of the claim might be guessed at. If the solicitor had not concealed the profit, the land would not have been purchased. If the land had not been purchased, the foundations would not have been dug. If the foundations had not been dug, the loss would not have been made. The solicitors were said to be responsible for the loss.

**[6.126]**  Of course the *Canson* claim was unsustainable. It was a wonder that it rose so high in the Canadian appellate system. The plaintiff's argument seemed to involve what Glanville Williams laughingly described as 'Adam and Eve causation'. This is where 'cause' is defined so widely that 'it goes back to the primaeval slime'.[294] Hart and Honore remind us that notions of 'cause' used in the attribution of responsibility for harm must be supplemented

---

[290]  E Sykes and M Pryles *Australian Private International Law* 3rd ed (1991), 634, 642–3.

[291]  *Caffrey v Darby* (1801) 6 Ves Jun 488; 31 ER 1159, 1162, Sir W Grant; *Bennett v Minister of Community Welfare* (1992) 176 CLR 408, 426–7, McHugh J.

[292]  Cf. *Re Dawson* [1966] 2 NSWLR 211, Street J, 215–6.

[293]  (1991) 85 DLR (4th) 129 (SC).

[294]  'Causation in the Law' [1961] *CLJ* 62, 64

by criteria of intention and a process of reasoned judgment.[295] Which is what the 'considerations' of 'foreseeability and remoteness' rejected by Street J in *Re Dawson*[296] really amount to.

**[6.127]**   The majority judgment in *Canson* took the view that the solicitor was not liable because in common law terms the harm was 'too remote'.[297] Equitable principles, it was said, should borrow the remoteness idea from the common law. Applicable policy considerations were thought to be the same in both jurisdictions. The minority judgment of McLachlin J reached the same conclusion (at 154), but eschewed borrowing from the common law. Policy considerations applicable to the 'unique foundations and goals of equity', she said at 155, could never be so assimilated. Rather–

> the better approach is to look to the [equitable] policy behind compensation for breach of fiduciary duty and determine what remedies will best forward that policy.

Common sense, reasonableness and fairness were prominent in this equitable 'policy'. They suggested that 'the losses in the construction of the warehouse did not "result or flow" from the breach of fiduciary duty'. Both majority and minority approaches achieved the same result. Coke P in *Mouat v Clark Boyce*, presiding over the New Zealand Court of Appeal, has said that the majority approach in *Canson* is 'more direct and natural'.[298] The minority view in that case, perhaps, was unable to discriminate between causes. For this reason it was obliged by common sense to conclude that the solicitor's breach of duty was not really a 'cause' at all. Which was obviously contrary to the fact. Is it right here that the fusionist reasoning of the majority should be rejected like Satan?

### *Contribution and mitigation of loss*

**[6.128]**   As with remoteness and the notion of proximate cause, contribution between causative agents and the duty of the victims to mitigate their loss are also alien to the theory of equitable causation. Compensation theory has been questioned similarly here, as under the previous heading. Remoteness, contribution and mitigation are perceived as something of a doctrinal series by the Canadian and New Zealand courts. Those jurisdictions have now plainly adopted the idea of contributory negligence in the computation of a compensation award. This is evident from the Canadian Supreme Court decisions in *Laskin v Bache & Co*[299] and *Canson Enterprises Ltd v Boughton & Co*[300] (the majority view). *Day v Mead*[301] witnesses the same development in the New Zealand Court of Appeal. This will not necessarily be followed in Australia. For in addition to equity possessing its own jurisdiction where contribution between wrongdoers is concerned, the matter is also governed by

---

[295] H Hart and H Honore *Causation in the Law* 2nd ed (1985), chapter 3 'Causation and Responsibility'.

[296] [1966] 2 NSWLR 211, 216.

[297] *Canson Enterprises Ltd v Boughton & Co* (1991) 85 DLR (4th) 129, 135–53, La Forest J, Sopinka, Gonthier, Cory JJ agreeing.

[298] [1992] 2 NZLR 559, 568 (CA).

[299] (1973) 23 DLR (3d) 385.

[300] (1991) 85 DLR (4th) 129, 149–50.

[301] [1987] 2 NZLR 443 (CA).

statutory provisions in the Australian states.[302] There may be no need to take the stand that Canadian and New Zealand courts have done. A comparable contribution regime already applies.

Australian courts have also as yet to take a stand on whether the mitigation idea should be incorporated into compensation doctrine. There is, of course, considerable familiarity with the tortious principle that the victim of a wrong should minimise his loss and is unable to prove for it to the extent that he does not. It seems intuitively just and the 'medieval' jurisprudence of equity has yet to express a corresponding limitation. Yet dicta of Street J in *Re Dawson*[303] are clearly opposed to the idea. Is this a sufficient reason not to borrow from the common law?

### Exemplary damages

**[6.129]** Fiduciary obligations are strict. Fiduciary obligations and their sanctions are expressed with prophylactic vigour—in large part to deter the disloyal fiduciaries at large. This is for the encouragement of others. It is not to do justice between the parties. Accordingly, *gains* that fiduciaries make may sometimes have to be accounted for to beneficiaries, even though they are made honestly and not at anyone's expense.[304] Where fiduciaries cause *losses*, the prophylactic counterpart is exemplary damages. It is not compensation. A thief cannot be deterred simply by being required to return stolen goods whenever he or she is caught. Thieving may then on the balance of probabilities be a profitable business. For a corresponding reason, a fiduciary cannot be deterred from cynically causing losses by the prospect, in some cases, of being required to put the losses right. More is needed. Fiduciaries who cause loss to a beneficiary in a cynical, malicious or particularly reprehensible manner need to be deterred in an exemplary way. If this is accepted, then the ultimate rationale of a fiduciary's duty of loyalty is not restitution, or not only restitution. It is prophylaxis as well. 'A prophylactic rather than a restitutionary principle' underlies fiduciary duties, as Gareth Jones says, and as much has been acknowledged by several other restitutionary scholars.[305] Earlier authorities we examined in Chapter 2 on the nature of the fiduciary relation are not explicable otherwise.

**[6.130]** Compensation in an exemplary measure has yet to be awarded for a fiduciary wrong in Australia. New Zealand and Canadian courts have done so.[306] Perhaps the right case has not presented itself. Some commentators have suggested that exemplary awards of compensation are inappropriate to sanction defaulting fiduciaries in all cases.[307] Although disapproving dicta are to be

---

[302] See 15.3 Laws [4-13] for citations to state and territory laws.

[303] [1966] 2 NSWLR 211, 215–6.

[304] R Cooter and B Freedman 'The Fiduciary Relationship: Its Economic Character and Legal Consequences' 66 *NYUL Rev* 1045, 1051–2.

[305] G Jones 'Unjust Enrichment and the Fiduciary's Duty of Loyalty' (1968) 84 *LQR* 472, 474; also G Palmer *The Law of Restitution* (1978), §2.11; P Maddaugh and J McCamus *Law of Restitution* (1990), 613–5; Birks *Introduction* 341–3 (some cases only).

[306] *Cook v Evatt (No 2)* [1992] 1 NZLR 676 (CA)); *Norberg v Wynrib* (1992) 92 DLR (4th) 449 (SC), 505–507, McLachlin J (alone); *Szarfer v Chodos* (1986) 27 DLR (4th) 388 (HC (Ont)).

[307] Eg, L Aitken 'Developments in Equitable Compensation: Opportunity or Danger?' (1993) 67 *ALJ* 596, 599–600.

found in authorities relating to the requirements of equitable rescission[308] and the setting of interest rates in lieu of accounts for profit,[309] a better view and one which best reflects equity's rationale in the fiduciaries area may be that of Ian Spry. 'The court may', he says, referring to equitable damages pursuant to an undertaking, 'order the payment of exemplary or punitive damages in an appropriate case'.[310]

## RESCISSION

[6.131]   When a rescission order is made a transaction which has legal consequences or under which benefits pass is set aside. The claimant obliges the defendant to restore him to his pre-transactional position. Or at least, restoration is ordered so far as it can be through the court's grant of personal orders. Usually the legal effect of the transaction is set aside together with the re-delivery of property which has passed and/or the payment of money. *Restitutio in integrum*, or substantial restitution for all parties, is essential to avoid unjust enrichment. Defendants, too, will receive back anything they gave in the transaction, or be appropriately compensated instead. Lord Wright explained this even-handed, non-penal approach in *Spence v Crawford*.[311] Parties are each to be restored so far as is 'practically just', except where the defendant has behaved fraudulently or been otherwise reprehensible. Where there is evidence of the defendant's fraud, he said–

> the court will exercise its [rescission] jurisdiction to the full in order, if possible, to prevent the defendant from enjoying the benefit of his fraud at the expense of the innocent plaintiff.

Against a fraudulent defendant the rescission remedy will be employed to more drastically undo the transaction and subtract profits or other benefits that may have been acquired. Compound interest may be awarded against a defendant in combination with the rescission order if the wrongful profits cannot be measured.[312] In *Koutsonicolis v Principe (No 2)*[313] the court used the authority of *Spence v Crawford* to justify an unusual order. Pensioners who purchased a house for residential purposes sought to rescind the contract of sale some six years later. Building defects had been fraudulently concealed from them before they signed the contract. Rescission was allowed subject to the pensioners making allowance for the fact that they had occupied the house for six years. The value of this occupation was not computed as the proper market value over the time. Rather it was a 'modest sum', in recognition of the fact that the occupation was unwanted and the pensioners did not take action sooner because they lacked the means. Prevention of the pensioners' unjust enrichment was seen to require no more.

---

[308] Eg, *Spence v Crawford* [1939] 3 All ER 271, 288–9, Lord Wright.

[309] Quoted in MGL [2304].

[310] Spry 621, referring to *Smith v Day* (1882) 21 Ch D 421, 428, Brett LJ.

[311] [1939] 3 All ER 271 (HL) 271, 288, Lord Wright.

[312] *Re Hatton Developments (Australia) Pty Ltd* (1978) 3 ACLR 484, Needham J; *Southern Cross Commodities Pty Ltd (in liq) v Ewing* (1988) 91 FLR 271, 285, White J (SC (SA) (FC)).

[313] (1987) 48 SASR 328, 331, White J.

**[6.132]** Of the several senses of 'rescission' that commentators have isolated, 'equitable rescission' is what we are dealing with here. 'Equitable' rescission is what the court orders when it sets aside a specified transaction and puts the parties back in their previous positions.[314] Transactions set aside are usually contracts. However, equitable and contractual senses of 'rescission' are quite distinct things. Contractual rescission, by contrast, is a creature of common law. It refers to the avoidance of a contract that a party to it may accomplish without even coming to court.[315] A vendor may rescind a contract for the sale of land pursuant to a rescission notice. The notice is drawn and served by the party himself, or his or her solicitor. The court simply enforces the vendor's act. Equitable rescission does not occur before the court makes its order. The transaction is set aside only to the extent that the court directs it. Any purported prior avoidance of a transaction by a party to it pertains only to the exercise of equity's remedial discretion.[316] Finally, rescission is of nature a personal and not a proprietary remedy. The orders bind the defendant in personam.

**[6.133]** The rescission remedy could have been placed under any of the 'direct enforcement', 'disgorgement of gains' or 'restoration of losses' headings. Depending on the transaction rescinded, rescission could have any of these effects. So the undoing of a transaction may make fiduciaries *disgorge gains* that they thereby make, or *restore losses* to beneficiaries that they incur. *Direct enforcement* of a fiduciary duty may occur when the wrong to be reversed changes the rights and liabilities of parties at law. The change is set aside.

**[6.134]** Rescission was at one time the cardinal relief for breach of fiduciary duty. It reflected the nineteenth-century preoccupation with breach of the conflicts rule as the pre-eminent fiduciary wrong. When Lord Chancellor Cranworth gave his celebrated exposition of the 'universal' conflicts rule in *Aberdeen Railway Co v Blaikie Bros*, the right to rescind was the only sanction mentioned.[317] The conflicts rule and the sanction of rescission were applied to fiduciary law's then archetypical rogue, the profiteering company promoter. Promoters were often found to be fiduciaries acting in breach of the conflicts rule.[318] Contracts between promoters and the companies promoted were sometimes rescinded on the application of a liquidator and sometimes that of a reconstituted board. Rescission was how the promoters' gains were recovered. Dishonest deals were set aside. Excessive prices were repaid. But as a remedy, rescission now seems to be regarded as of more limited usefulness. Rescission is associated with breach of the conflicts rule and that rule, as noted at [5.53]–[5.54], is now itself in decline. Claimants for rescission as primary relief are now usually persons who allege that they have been unduly influenced, or that they have entered transactions vitiated by another's

---

[314] MGL [2416]; *Snell's Equity* 29th ed (1990), 616.

[315] See *Shevill v Builders Licensing Board* (1982) 149 CLR 620; [MGL], [2416]; *Snell*, ibid, 616–7.

[316] *Latec Investments Ltd v Hotel Terrigal Pty Ltd* (1965) 113 CLR 265, 277, Kitto J.

[317] (1854) 1 Macq 461; [1848–60] All ER 249, in the passage quoted at [5.37].

[318] Eg, *Erlanger v New Sombrero Phosphate Co* (1878) 3 App Cas 1218; *Curwen v Yan Yean Land Co* (1891) 17 VLR 745; *Re Cape Breton Co* (1884) 26 Ch D 221 (CA); *Transvaal Lands Co v New Belgium (Transvaal) Land and Development Co* [1914] 2 Ch 488 (CA); *Jacobus Marler Estates Ltd v Marler* (1913) 114 LT 640n (HL); *Tracy v Mandalay Pty Ltd* (1953) 88 CLR 215.

unconscionable conduct. Rescission is sought by way of *direct enforcement*. We will deal with remedies for these and other claims arising out of the fiduciary relationship of *influence* in Chapter 8. Profits and losses tend to be reversed by more direct means of constructive trusts and compensation.

### Rescission and gains

**[6.135]**   The ability of rescission to redistribute gains is small, which may follow from the limited effect of rescission in only setting transactions aside. Assume that a fiduciary's gainful transaction with his beneficiary is rescinded. A sale of the fiduciary's own property to a beneficiary is avoided. The whole gain that the fiduciary makes is at the beneficiary's expense and will be restored to the beneficiary. Assume then that the fiduciary engages in a secret transaction with a third party in fraud of the beneficiary, but which causes the beneficiary no loss. The gain is one that the beneficiary did not possess or have a likelihood of making in his original position. Rescission cannot pass to the beneficiary any of the profit that the fiduciary has made. The third party is restored. This difference highlights rescission's inappropriateness to reverse many of the gains that fiduciaries make in relationships with their beneficiaries—namely, gains made by dealing with third parties and not at the beneficiaries' expense.

Rescission was nevertheless used effectively to strip a self-dealing company director of his wrongful profit in the old case of *Transvaal Lands Co v New Belgium (Transvaal) Land and Development Co*.[319] In the circumstances it was hard to tell which of the various companies that the director held interests in was the one that had enjoyed a gain which had unquestionably been made. It was easier to undo the transaction itself.

### Rescission and *restitutio in integrum*

**[6.136]**   The need for restoration of both parties to their pre-transactional positions is a firm brake on availability of the remedy. Defendants' changes of position, or the introduction of third party rights,[320] will deny rescission in many situations. This is despite equity's 'greater readiness' to 'pull a transaction to pieces' if the defendant has been fraudulent[321] and despite equity's very considerable flexibility to avoid an injustice to either party.

Change of position is illustrated by the case of *Erlanger v New Sombrero Phosphate Co*.[322] The majority of law lords in that case took a robust view on the liability of fraudulent company promoters. They were confirmed as fiduciaries in relation to the company by Lord Cairns LC at 1236 and by Lord Blackburn at 1268–9, who had made the usual kind of improper gain. Erlanger and others had purchased a phosphate island for £55,000 and sold it not long after to a company they promoted for £110,000. Some years later a new board of the company brought proceedings in equity for rescission of the sale. This entailed return of the island to the syndicate and repayment to the company of the £110,000, with interest. The problem was that in the years which had elapsed the company had mined a substantial portion of the island's phosphate.

---

[319] [1914] 2 Ch 488 (CA), 496–497, Astbury J (at first instance, affirmed by CA).
[320] *McKenzie v McDonald* [1927] VLR 134, 146, Dixon J.
[321] *Spence v Crawford* [1939] 3 All ER 271, 288, Lord Wright.
[322] (1878) 3 App Cas 1218.

Whatever the true value of the island had been at the time of sale, it was worth a good deal less when rescission of the contract was sought. Lord Blackburn was undeterred by these things. Rescission would be available, he held, on equitable terms. Account should be taken of phosphate profits which the company had made and of deterioration which the island had suffered. Money sums arrived at for these things should adjust the £110,000 price to be returned. For, as he said at 1278–9:

> a Court of Equity [should] give this relief whenever by the exercise of its powers, it can do what is practically just, though it cannot restore the parties precisely to the state they were in before the contract.

**[6.137]**  In the ancient case of *York Buildings Co v Mackenzie*[323] equity was said to be able to award rescission on terms, even 'very favourable' terms. In that case, counsel for the fiduciary were Lord Eldon and Sir William Grant. So possibly the advocate's skill contributed to this favourable outcome. Jurisdiction to grant these terms has been confirmed on several occasions. Yet it still does not mean that rescission, the remedy, is in good health. *Coleman v Myers*[325] indicates what may be a more modern attitude. Father and son were directors of a large private company. They recommended to the shareholders that they sell their shares to a particular purchaser. In breach of fiduciary duty, the directors did not disclose the true state of the company's assets at the time and the fact that the purchaser was a company associated with the son. The shares were sold. Between that time and when the enlightened former shareholders brought applications to rescind their sale contracts, the value of the shareholders' funds had doubled. Substantial capital dividends could then be paid, of which the original shareholders had no reasonable expectation. Cooke J (for the New Zealand Court of Appeal) said that in these circumstances 'it would not be practically just' to grant rescission.[326] The shareholders would be put in a much better position than if there had been no breach of duty—a thing, as we have seen, that has not troubled equity judges in the past. Instead, 'fair compensation' was awarded: a remedy said to be more directly proportionate to the wrong committed.

---

[323] (1795) 8 Bro PC 42; 3 ER 432 (HL).

[324] Eg, *Newbigging v Adam* (1886) 26 Ch D 582 (CA); *Curwen v Yan Yean Land Co* (1891) 17 VLR 745; *Robinson v Abbott* (1894) 20 VLR 346 (FC); *Spence v Crawford* [1939] 3 All ER 271 (HL).

[325] [1977] 2 NZLR 225 (CA).

[326] At 361, referring to the dictum of Lord Blackburn in *Erlanger v New Sombrero Phosphate Co* (1878) 3 App Cas 1218, 1278–9, quoted at [6.136].

# Chapter 7

# Remedies Against Third Parties

**[7.1]** Beneficiaries can make several claims where fiduciaries are in breach of duty. Not all involve proceeding against the fiduciaries themselves. Claims against third parties may be brought for any of the following reasons. First, property that the beneficiary seeks to recover is in a third party's hands: that party is the proper defendant to a proprietary claim.[1] Secondly, the fiduciary may be insolvent or of doubtful solvency and an eligible third party is a bank or person whose solvency is assured.[2] Thirdly, the fiduciary may have absconded, or otherwise not be amenable to the court's jurisdiction, which is often the case with commercial fraud.[3] Fourthly, third parties may have profited by the fiduciary's breach: beneficiaries may claim such profits for themselves.[4] Fifthly, the beneficiary may be still associated with the fiduciary, despite the wrong, and recovery from an outsider is preferred.[5]

Recovery of misapplied assets or misdirected funds is sometimes how this phenomenon is described. Fraudulent fiduciaries have largely left the picture. Beneficiaries claim instead against the third parties who have 'laundered' their money, or against those who ultimately received the fraudulent gains. One English Chancery judge recently estimated that about 80 per cent of the time of the Chancery Division is now taken up with recovering the proceeds of fraud. Proceedings for this, he said, are usually brought against third parties.[6] The shape of modern fiduciaries litigation may now be in this chapter. Unfortunately it is still a little obscure.

---

[1] *Black v S Freedman & Co* (1910) 12 CLR 105; *Banque Belge v Hambrouck* [1921] 1 KB 321 (CA) and see *Cowan de Groot Properties Ltd v Eagle Trust plc* [1992] 4 All ER 700, 767.

[2] Eg, *Stephens Travel Service International Pty Ltd v Qantas Airways Ltd* (1988) 13 NSWLR 331 (CA); *Baden v Société Générale pour Favoriser le Dveloppement du Commerce et de l'Industrie en France SA* (1983) [1992] 4 All ER 161.

[3] Eg, *Linter Group Ltd v Goldberg* (1992) 7 ACSR 580; *Polly Peck International plc v Nadir (No 2)* [1992] 4 All ER 769 (CA).

[4] Eg, *Consul Development Pty Ltd v DPC Estates Pty Ltd* (1975) 132 CLR 373; *United States Surgical Corporation v Hospital Products International Pty Ltd* [1983] 2 NSWLR 157, 247-59 (CA).

[5] Possibly in *Barnes v Addy* (1874) LR 9 Ch App 244 (CA) and litigation related to *Equiticorp Industries Group Ltd v Hawkins* [1991] 3 NZLR 700.

[6] P Millett 'Recovering the Proceeds of Fraud', 2, unpublished paper presented at 'Insolvency and Banking Law' seminar, Hong Kong, March 1993.

**[7.2]**  We shall begin generally. Claims against third parties can be seen to fall into two groups. First there is the proprietary type of claim. Tracing claims leading to the recovery of misappropriated property in specie are dealt with under the second heading below. Advantages described at [6.50]–[6.51] in relation to the *third party's* insolvency are applicable. The other group comprises personal claims of both legal and equitable varieties. They are dealt with under the first and third headings. The first heading includes the legal actions of 'money had and received' and the proprietary torts. Both supply personal remedies based in property rights. So also does the first claim in heading three: the equitable liability to account for the 'knowing receipt' of property. The other liability to account in heading three is unrelated to property. Third parties can be liable under it for just their 'knowing assistance' in fiduciaries' fraud. At [7.54] there is a diagram which summarises the range of remedial possibilities.

# 1.  Legal remedies

**[7.3]**  Property forms a nexus between defrauded beneficiaries and persons who are their legal strangers. Actions against strangers often vindicate beneficiaries' property rights, accordingly. At the same time these legal remedies almost never have a proprietary reach. This is so in the insolvency sense, discussed at [6.49]–[6.51]. Beneficiaries can alternatively seek an award of damages pursuant to one of the 'proprietary torts' at common law. Conversion is the most common. For this the beneficiary must have been entitled to immediate possession of what is said to have been converted. And the property must be identifiable at trial. In the case of money, this means that the beneficiary must show that the particular notes, coins or negotiable instruments misappropriated are now held by the third party and have not been negotiated along the way, or had their value confounded in some larger mass. Money needs to have been kept separate.[7] This usually means kept in some particular bank account, fund or bag. The third party cannot have been paid a cheque as a holder in due course pursuant to s 79 of the Cheques and Money Orders Act 1986 (Cth).[8] Most third party claims involve money as their subject, which tends to rule out tortious relief.

## 'Money had and received'

**[7.4]**  The action at law for 'money had and received' is specifically adapted to the fungible nature of money. The passing of title is irrelevant. Liability of the defendants can be established upon proof of little more than that they *received* the claimant's money. The cause of action is then complete, subject to the defence that recipients were agents who have accounted to their principals.[9] Defendants may be made personally liable to account. Dishonesty

---

[7]  F Mann *Legal Aspect of Money* 5th ed (1992), 7-8

[8]  See S Fennel 'Misdirected Funds: Problems of Uncertainty and Inconsistency' (1994) 57 *MLR* 38, 39-40.

[9]  See *Australia and New Zealand Banking Group Ltd v Westpac Banking Corporation* (1988) 164 CLR 662, 684, curiam.

or 'want of probity' on their part need not be shown. A regime of strict liability for receipts is imposed.

It does not matter for this action whether the money was retained after it was received. Indeed, defendants do no wrong by mixing the money with their own, spending it, or giving it away. It is their own affair. The money belongs to them. But they cannot rid themselves of the obligation to account, which receipt of the money has imposed upon them.[10] In this way the action is an alternative to tracing claims. And it need not be fruitless where tracing fails, as Millett J remarked in *Agip (Africa) Ltd v Jackson*.[11] Liability is based in receipt and not retention. Dismissing the action in that case because a 'receipt' could not be proven, Millett said at 287 that a defendant to the action also needs to be an 'immediate recipient' from the beneficiary. In his later article he mentioned this again. 'There is something distinctly odd', he said, 'about a personal receipt-based remedy lying against successors in title of the original recipient.'[12] A potentially serious limitation is highlighted here. The majority of third parties to fiduciaries' breaches of duty are subsequent recipients of the beneficiaries' money. Fiduciaries will often have received cheques from beneficiaries, banked them and drawn their own cheques in favour of third parties.

**[7.5]** Most of the advantages that the action of 'money had and received' has were evident in the House of Lords decision in *Lipkin Gorman v Karpnale Ltd*.[13] A firm of solicitors alleged that the Playboy Club in Mayfair had received their money. One of the partners had misappropriated the money from the firm and gambled it away. Money was taken from the firm by the partner drawing cheques on the firm's trust account and cashing them with the firm's cashier. With that money he purchased chips at the casino. Nearly all the money was lost. After the partner absconded overseas, the firm sued the casino in money had and received. Money received by the casino was conceded to be the firm's money. This meant that a prima facie case was made out. It was then no defence for the casino to say that it was an innocent recipient. The action imposed a regime of strict liability. Finally, reversing the courts below, the House held that no value was given by the casino. This was because of the unusual status of gambling chips. An exchange of these could not be good consideration because of the void status of gambling contracts. The firm succeeded, though the casino was not shown to have knowledge, or notice, or mala fides at all. The case should be noted for having several less than typical features. First, the defendant was solvent and there was no need for proprietary relief. Secondly, problems with tracing at common law were averted by the defendant's concession. Thirdly, though the casino was honest and unaffected by the partner's frauds, it gave no value for the money it received. The last feature would rarely recur.

---

[10] P Millett 'Tracing the Proceeds of Fraud' (1991) 107 *LQR* 71, 78-9.

[11] [1990] 1 Ch 265, 270 (in arguendo).

[12] 'Tracing the Proceeds of Fraud' (1991) 107 *LQR* 71, 77.

[13] [1991] 2 AC 548.

## Common law tracing

**[7.6]** 'Tracing at common law', as Peter Millett says, 'is neither a cause of action nor a remedy but serves an evidential purpose.'[14] It is not part of a proprietary regime.[15] Actions for legal proprietary relief have now almost all fallen into disuse. This excepts the (exceptional) discretion to order specific return of a thing detained[16] in detinue and the common law lien.[17] Both of these have limited application to fiduciary claims. Common law tracing is otherwise a technique to facilitate personal judgments, of which conversion and 'money had and received' are instances.

Common law tracing has signally failed to keep up in the age of electronic banking. The value of money can be followed at law only so long as it is represented by a money order, or some physical equivalent. Where amounts of money are transmitted between computer terminals the common law has no resource. For nothing more tangible passes between the parties then than a 'stream of electrons'.[18] In *Agip (Africa) Ltd v Jackson* tracing was used in an attempt to establish the 'receipt' element of a 'money had and received' action. The plaintiff oil company had been defrauded by a Mr Zdiri. Millett J at first instance said (at 290) that Zdiri was one of Agip's 'senior and responsible' corporate officers 'in a fiduciary relationship' with the company. Large cheques had the names of payees fraudulently altered so that their value was paid to persons associated with Zdiri. Over $10.5m US was taken in this way. After each fraud, the value of a cheque drawn on a Tunis bank was telegraphically transferred to a company's account at Lloyds bank in London. Agip sued the partners in 'Jackson & Co', a firm of accountants practising on the Isle of Man who had assisted in this process. They were third parties who controlled the account through which the money had passed to various untraceable individuals. In the alternative to an equitable 'knowing receipt' claim, examined below, a 'money had and received' action was brought in respect of one cheque. Millett J at 278–82 closely examined the sequence of events whereby Lloyds bank received and passed on the value of the cheque. In addition to the electronic instruction to credit the transferee, he found that Lloyds bank actually obtained value by transfer made to it by Citibank in New York. An international set-off arrangement had been employed. Citibank had also been instructed electronically by the Tunis bank. It was 'not possible' then, Millett J said (at 286):

> to treat the money received by Lloyds bank in London or its correspondent bank in New York as representing the proceeds of the payment order or of any other physical asset previously in its hands and delivered by it in exchange for the money. The Bank du Sud merely telexed a request to Lloyds bank to make a payment to [the holder of the account] against its own undertaking to reimburse Lloyds bank in New York.

---

[14] 'Tracing the Proceeds of Fraud' (1991) 107 *LQR* 71, 72.

[15] See Kurshid and Matthews 'Tracing Confusion' (1979) 95 *LQR* 78; A Scott 'The Right to Trace at Common Law' (1966) 7 *UWALR* 463; Pearce 'A Tracing Paper' 40 *Convey* (1976), 278-84; B Fitzgerald 'Tracing at Law (etc)' (1994) 13 *Uni of Tas LR* 116.

[16] See *McEown v Cavalier Yachts Pty Ltd* (1988) 13 NSWLR 303, 307-8, Young J; F Trindade and P Cane *Law of Torts in Australia* 2nd ed (1993), 164-6.

[17] See D Stevens 'Restitution, Property and the Cause of Action in Unjust Enrichment: I' (1989) 39 *UTLJ* 258, 275.

[18] *Agip (Africa) Ltd v Jackson* [1990] 1 Ch 265, 286, Millett J.

This may imply that the value of a cheque cannot be followed at law if the drawer and the payee of the cheque maintain accounts at different banks. Attempts to follow money through inter-bank clearing house systems are likely to fail. As this will be necessary in the majority of situations, the regime becomes 'unacceptably haphazard'.[19]

## Conversion

**[7.7]**　Anomalously, and apart from money claims, an action against a third party in conversion consequent on breach of fiduciary duties can sometimes approximate a proprietary effect. *Coleman v Harvey*[20] was one such case. An action in conversion was brought against a solvent co-tortfeasor for a bankrupt fiduciary's wrong. Silver in particular coins was traced into ingots produced by an insolvent refining company. Or, in other cases, an action in conversion could be brought against the misappropriator's bankruptcy trustee. Judgments against bankruptcy trustees personally do not abate. Bankruptcy trustees can be affected by the fiduciary's misappropriation because, if the converted property has not been disclaimed, they must assume it with all the liabilities that it had in the fiduciary's hands. Conversions remain exible as continuing wrongs.[21] They are not prevented by the stay of proceedings provided by s 60 of the Bankruptcy Act 1966 (Cth).

# 2. Equitable proprietary remedies

### TRACING PROPERTY INTO THE HANDS OF STRANGERS

**[7.8]**　Equity works in personam. It acts upon third parties' consciences. Where, say, third parties have their bank balances inflated by fiduciaries' fraud, third parties may in conscience be obliged to refund the superfluity. Good conscience here is a matter of rules. Beneficiaries will be able to make third parties liable and recover their money if they can raise and trace interest into this balance. The raising and tracing an interest steps set out at [6.28]–[6.48] are applicable. Insolvency advantages in proprietary relief will follow, where claims are brought against insolvent third parties. There are many similarities between proprietary relief against fiduciaries and proprietary relief against third parties. However, there are two important defences available to third parties which fiduciaries do not have. These are (1) bona fide purchase for value and (2) change of position. We will examine the defences separately after the following general discussion. Neither defence is limited to proprietary relief—although they apply conspicuously in this context.

**[7.9]**　*Black v S Freedman & Co*[22] illustrates a proprietary claim against a third party, made to recover the proceeds of theft. John Black was employed by the claimant. He stole cash from his employer and paid it into his own bank account. Then he drew cheques on the account which were paid into the account of his wife Isabella. After John Black had been prosecuted, the employer brought a claim against Isabella to recover the balance in her

---

[19] P Millett 'Tracing the Proceeds of Fraud' (1991) 107 *LQR* 71, 73-4.
[20] [1989] 1 NZLR 723, noted (1990) 106 *LQR* 552.
[21] *Scott v Surman* (1742) Willes 400, 125 ER 1235
[22] (1910) 12 CLR 105

account. That money was identified as the employer's and the claim succeeded, upon it being inferred that the only possible source of Isabella's credit was her husband's theft.[23] In a similar connection, see also *Newton v Porter*,[24] *Spedding v Spedding*,[25] *Goodbody v Bank of Montreal*[26] and *Lane County Escrow Service Inc v Smith*.[27] An advantage of the Australasian and United States jurisdictions in the 'proceeds of theft' cases is that the thief does not formally need to be a fiduciary. Unjust retention of title will suffice. The fiduciary requirement seems to be applicable in the United Kingdom still.[28]

## Raising interests and tracing them

**[7.10]** Equitable proprietary remedies are equitable interests annexed to property. Beneficiaries are able to raise constructive trust entitlements and other equitable interests as against third parties comparably to the way they can against fiduciaries. Third parties have been just as unjustly enriched as fiduciaries, when they retain property which they do not own. Third parties may additionally have been accessories in fiduciaries' breaches of duty. They may then serve as what Ford & Lee calls 'substitute fiduciaries'.[29] The regime for the tracing of interests raised to third parties is also comparable to that in claims against fiduciaries. Rules set out at [6.38]–[6.47] are, as we have said, equally applicable here.

## Third parties as defendants

### Third parties and value

**[7.11]** The following principle applies to third parties dealing with wrongful fiduciaries. Assume that the beneficiary's misappropriated assets are in the hands of a fiduciary who took them. Whether or not the beneficiary's beneficial title has been judicially recognised, a third party who purchases those assets from the fiduciary can obtain good title from the fiduciary if the purchase is for value and without notice of the beneficiary's claim. Any proprietary claim of the beneficiary must then follow whatever are the proceeds of the asset's sale or exchange that the fiduciary received. No proprietary liability on the part of the third party arises.

### Subsequent third parties

**[7.12]** Further to the preceding paragraph, consider what happens when one third party transfers property to another. A third party purchaser from a fiduciary has either failed to give value or has notice of the beneficiary's claim. The third party with a defective title can still pass good title to another third party who takes from him for value and without notice. This, too, will convert

---

[23] Ibid, 109, Griffith CJ, Barton and O'Connor JJ agreeing; see also *Banque Belge v Hambrouck* [1921] 1 KB 321 (CA).

[24] 69 NY 133 (1877).

[25] (1913) 3 WN (NSW) 81.

[26] (1974) 47 DLR (3d) 335.

[27] 560 P 2d 608 (1977).

[28] Restated by Fox LJ in *Agip (Africa) Ltd v Jackson* [1991] Ch 547, 566 (CA); see also P Millett 'Tracing the Proceeds of Theft' (1991) 107 *LQR* 71, 76; E McKendrick 'Tracing Misdirected Funds' [1991] LMCLQ 378, 387.

[29] Ford & Lee [2216].

the tracing claim. Either identifiable proceeds are sought, or the claim is extinguished.

The High Court dealt with a related situation in *Brady v Stapleton*.[30] The facts of the case were in parallel to a breach of fiduciary obligation. In 1949 one Charles Coward made a number of 'alienations of his property with the intent to defraud creditors'. Real estate, motor vehicles, race-horses, some shares and 'a large quantity of tobacco' were all transferred to one of his associated companies. Property legislation in most states provided then and still provides that alienations to defraud creditors are 'voidable at the instance of any person thereby prejudiced'.[31] Coward had been earlier found to have been engaged in tax evasion and he had been presented with large amended assessments and penalty assessments pursuant to the Income Tax Assessment Act 1936 (Cth). The purpose behind the alienations was obviously to defeat the commissioner's claim to his estate. Shortly after disposing of most of his property to the company, Coward was declared a bankrupt. The company then on-sold the property to bona fide purchasers for value before the bankruptcy trustee got around to avoiding Coward's alienations.

[7.13] The High Court's analysis of the situations of Coward and the company is applicable here. A fiduciary's disposition of property in breach of duty is voidable by a beneficiary in the same way as Coward's alienation. We shall treat the company in *Brady's* case as a third party. Coward plays the part of a fiduciary who misappropriates assets. The bankruptcy trustee will serve as the beneficiary. In these terms, a fiduciary transferred property to a third party who either took with notice of the beneficiary's rights and/or gave no value for the property received. The report of the case does not record whether the company gave value. Dixon CJ and Fullagar J said at 332–3:

> The company in this case must be taken to have received the property with notice of the fraudulent character of the assignment to it, and, the proceeds of a sale of any of that property by the company to a bona fide purchaser for value could be identified in the company's hands, the case of *In re Mouatt; Kingston Cotton Mills Co v Mouatt*[32] would be authority for saying that the [bankruptcy] trustee would be entitled to have handed over to him any asset in the company's hands which represented the proceeds of sale; ... But the learned judge has found (what is not surprising) that the proceeds cannot be identified, and his finding is not challenged.

The beneficiary, or the representative of the 'person thereby prejudiced', could not go behind a sale to a bona fide purchaser from the company as third party. Therefore a proprietary claim to the proceeds of sale was not maintainable. Further relief could only come from the third party personally.

[7.14] In *Cowan de Groot Properties Ltd v Eagle Trust plc*[33] a claim to go behind a third party sale was made by Eagle Trust. It tried to trace and recover certain properties on-sold by the Cowan de Groot company. De Groot had

---

[30] (1952) 88 CLR 322.

[31] See Conveyancing Act 1919, s 37A(1) (NSW); Property Law Act 1958, s 172(1) (Vic); Property Law Act 1974, s 228 (Qld); Law of Property Act 1936, s 86(1) (SA); Property Law Act 1969, s 89(1) (WA); Conveyancing and Law of Property Act 1884, s 40(1) (Tas): largely duplicated by s 121 of the Bankruptcy Act 1966 (Cth).

[32] [1889] 1 Ch 831.

[33] [1992] 4 All ER 700, 767.

purchased the properties from Eagle Trust extremely cheaply, by reason of the fraud of Eagle Trust directors. The purchaser from de Groot was said to have notice of the wrong, even if it gave value. Knox J upheld the necessity for prior rescission in these circumstances, where the beneficial interest had passed. We examined this at [6.35]–[6.37]. The requirement in Knox J's view had to be satisfied by the plaintiff, even where a bona fide purchaser defence could not be made out. For there could be–

> no independent right to trace against a purchaser for value under a contract for sale where the contract is not liable to be set aside and there is [then] no valid claim to impose a constructive trust.

## DEFENCES
### Interests acquired for value without notice
**[7.15]** This is sometimes referred to as the 'bona fide purchaser' defence. Third parties are immune from proprietary and other claims if they acquired the relevant property for value and without notice of the beneficiary's claim.[34] This doctrine has the effect of 'cutting-off' an already existing constructive trust. In other cases it may prevent a constructive trust from arising. One who acquires property for value and without notice of the beneficiary's claim, speaking remedially, may not be 'unjustly enriched' if he is permitted to retain it.[35] Only third parties can avail themselves of the 'bona fide purchaser' defence. Fiduciaries cannot be heard to say that they were unaware of their duty. Andrew Burrows says that the rationale for the defence is–

> maintaining the sanctity of contracts. The courts are generally not prepared to disturb a contract unless the purchaser for value was contracting in bad faith.[36]

The exercise of tracing equitable interests to where they can be asserted must stop where the property interests of bona fide purchasers for value is reached. We saw in *Brady v Stapleton*[37] that either then there is a conversion to a proceeds claim, or the proprietary interest is extinguished. Bona fide purchase is also a defence to the *personal* equities which may be brought against third parties. This can be seen from judgments handed down in *Lipkin Gorman v Karpnale Ltd*[38] when the case was in the Court of Appeal. Because gambling chips were found to constitute valuable consideration given for the cash the casino received, the purchaser for value defence was made out.

**[7.16]** Receipt of equitable interests by bona fide persons for value without notice of equitable wrongdoing bars an equitable remedy. The definition of 'purchaser' in s 18 of the Law of Property Act 1925 (Imp) or equivalents is a reference to such persons. Purchasers who acquire legal interests in property are immune from equitable interference. For they have undertaken no obligation to anyone in the acquisition. Nor have they succeeded to any

---

[34] See Ford & Lee [2221.1].
[35] *Scott on Trusts* ed W Fratcher 4th edn (1989), 474.
[36] *Restitution* 472
[37] (1952) 88 CLR 322: at [7.].
[38] [1989] 1 WLR 1340 (CA), 1349-50, May LJ, 1364-5, Parker LJ, Nicholls LJ dissenting.

obligation through taking a voluntary title. No equity can arise to affect their consciences.[39]

**[7.17]**  What amounts to 'notice' in this definition is fairly settled. 'Notice' for conveyancing purposes includes what persons actually know, or would know if reasonable inquiries and inspections had been made. Most Australian states have legislation to this effect.[40] There is an established procedure for investigating title to land. Whether, though, the same sort of 'constructive' notice applies in commercial transactions is not resolved.[41] It might be a sufficient reason for depriving a bona fide purchaser of land in a hard case. But the pace of commerce is swifter. Conveyancing notice assumes an established procedure for investigating title. There is no counterpart in many commercial dealings. Nor will it always be reasonable to expect inquiries in the absence of a duty to inquire.[42]

**[7.18]**  The related issue of what is 'constructive knowledge' for the purpose of imposing personal constructive trust obligations on third parties has lately attracted a deal of attention. Megarry V-C said in *Re Montagu's Settlement Trusts*[43] that one could not assimilate what is sufficient for conveyancing 'notice' to the 'knowledge' needed to impose a personal liability. Liabilities are too conscientious to be imposed on the basis of 'notice'. One does not behave unconscientiously because one 'forgets' things or because of what one's agents once knew. Lindley LJ in *Manchester Trust v Furness*[44] said that 'constructive knowledge' in commerce is something that the courts have always 'resolutely set their faces against'–

> The equitable doctrines of constructive knowledge are common enough in dealing with land and estates, with which the court is familiar; but there have been repeated protests against the introduction into commercial transactions of anything like an extension of those doctrines, and the protest is founded on perfectly good sense. In dealing with estates in land, title is everything, and it can be leisurely investigated; in commercial transactions possession is everything and there is no time to investigate title; and if we extend the doctrine of constructive knowledge to commercial transactions we should be doing infinite mischief and paralysing the trade of the country.

After citing the above passage, Vinelott J said in *Eagle Trust plc v SBC Securities Ltd*[45] that–

> The courts have always been particularly reluctant to extend the doctrine of constructive notice to cases where moneys are paid in the ordinary course of business.

---

[39] F Maitland *Equity: A Course of Lectures* rev ed (1949), 114-5.

[40] Conveyancing Act 1919 (NSW) s 164; Property Law Act 1958 (Vic) s 199; Law of Property Act 1936 (SA) 117; Conveyancing and Law of Property Act 1884 (Tas) ss 5, 35A.

[41] M Bryan in 'The Meaning of Notice in Tracing Claims' (1993) 109 *LQR* 368, 371.

[42] P Millett 'Recovering the Proceeds of Fraud', 8-9, unpublished paper presented at 'Insolvency and Banking Law' seminar, Hong Kong, March 1993.

[43] [1987] 1 Ch 264, 277-84.

[44] [1895] 2 QB 539, 545.

[45] [1992] 4 All ER 488, 507.

**[7.19]** It was suggested by Scott LJ in *Polly Peck International plc v Nadir*[46] that 'notice' in a commercial connection will be limited *conscientiously*, in the same way as he thought 'knowledge' should be. He was dealing with a tracing alternative to a personal constructive trust claim. A third party purchaser could then be permitted to avail itself of the purchase for value defence whenever its conscience is not affected by notice received. But this makes life much more complicated. If the constituents of the 'bona fide purchaser' defence to a proprietary claim are a little like the constituents of a personal claim of 'knowing receipt or assistance' then the uncertainty that surrounds the 'receipt and assistance' claims may also be imported. There is, as we will see, no one view of what must be known or to what degree it must be known for the purposes of the personal claim. It may be wisest to conclude that the notice or knowledge requirements are a matter of degree in all cases. Allowing them to be established by fictions like the imputed cognisance of agents, or what the reasonable man might have discovered, is fairer in some cases than others. But when, it may be asked, can it be appropriate that commercial outcomes are to be determined by fictions?[47]

## Change of position

**[7.20]** It may be unjust to allow the beneficiary to recover property traced into a third party's hands. Third parties may have acted to their detriment on the faith of an earlier status quo. The bona fide purchasers' defence may assert that a detriment was incurred in their money payment.[48] 'Change of position' has a universal quality. Two proprietary examples of it concerning innocent volunteers were given in *Re Diplock*.[49] Money in that case, belonging to the Diplock estate, had been mistakenly distributed under a will. Over 130 charities were found to be liable in rem (and personally) to repay gifts which had been made pursuant to a void provision. Guy's Hospital, for one, had used its gift to construct two new children's wards: the Caleb ward and the Diplock ward. To require the hospital to 'disentangle' money used in this alteration or improvement of its assets was said not to be fair. The Leaf Homoeopathic Hospital used its gift to pay off a secured loan. To impose the relevant proprietary remedy of a charge by subrogation was treated as unfair for the same reason.

**[7.21]** The change of position defence to the more restitutionary type of claim has been accepted in the House of Lords in *Lipkin Gorman v Karpnale Ltd*[50] and in the High Court in *David Securities Pty Ltd v Commonwealth Bank of Australia*.[51] A mistaken payment was concerned in each case. Its recipient was said to have acted to its detriment on the faith of what was paid. The casino in *Lipkin Gorman* had paid the gambling partner on those (few) occasions when he was in luck. Lord Goff said (at 582–3) that a change of position defence should be allowed to this extent. To require the casino to

---

46 [1992] 4 All ER 769, 782.

47 See *Eagle Trust plc v SBC Securities Ltd* [1992] 4 All ER 488, 501-2, Vinelott J.

48 See P Birks 'Persistent Problems in Misdirected Money: A Quintet' [1993] *LMCLQ* 218. 229.

49 [1948] Ch 465 (CA), 545-50, curiam.

50 [1991] 2 AC 548, 558, Lord Bridge, 568, Lord Ackner, 578-80, Lord Goff.

51 (1992) 175 CLR 353, 385-6, Mason CJ, Deane, Toohey, Gaudron and McHugh JJ, noting acceptance also in Canada and the United States.

repay the firm in full notwithstanding these winnings would be 'inequitable'. In *David Securities* a borrower mistakenly paid withholding tax on a transaction when the relevant liability really lay with the lender. It was said (at 384–6) to be a good defence for the lender to allege that it relied on the payment to the extent of not stipulating for a higher interest rate. Neither the *Lipkin Gorman* nor the *David Securities* decision defined the scope of the defence. It is as yet a very general equity.

## 3.   Equitable personal remedies

### ACCOUNTING AS CONSTRUCTIVE TRUSTEES

**[7.22]**   This is a complicated area. The remedies we will call 'recipients' and 'accessories'[52] describe third party liability for *participation* in fiduciaries' breaches of duty.[53] They occupy overlapping ground and are commonly bracketed together. Some common elements are shared. But in several significant respects they are different.

Looking at 'recipients' first, it is where third parties knowingly 'receive and become chargeable with the trust property'. Or it is where they acquire notice subsequent to receipt of the property and then deal with it inconsistently. Defendants are made liable to account for the value of that property as constructive trustees. Liability is generated in each case out of the property's receipt. It has an objective ring to it. Retention of the property received in either case is irrelevant. The liability of 'recipients' closely resembles that of defendants to the action of 'money had and received'. This was an action at law, we saw at [7.4], imposing strict liability on the defendant. No 'knowledge' on the part of the recipient needed to be shown. Possibly 'money had and received' was what Lord Selborne LC meant when he described the 'recipients' equity in *Barnes v Addy*.[54] For the Judicature Act had just been passed, he did not qualify the nature of the receipt as 'knowing' and he failed to give any pedigree for the principle he expressed.

'Accessories', the other wrong, is more like a tort.[55] Third parties commit it where they 'assist with knowledge in a dishonest and fraudulent design on the part of the trustees'.[56] They are made to account to beneficiaries: supplying restitution or compensation to them as constructive trustees. Any trust property concerned in the third party's transgression may have disappeared. Although it must, on one view, have existed at some stage.[57] What matters is that the third party has participated in a fiduciary's iniquity with a certain state of mind. The 'accessories' wrong has been said to be founded in the third party's

---

[52] Terms used by P Birks in 'Trusts in the Recovery of Misapplied Assets: Tracing, Trusts and Restitution' in McKendrick, 149, 151.

[53] P Finn 'The Liability of Third Parties for Knowing Receipt of Assistance' in Waters, 195, 212-3.

[54] (1874) LR 9 Ch App 244, 251.

[55] P Birks 'Trusts in the Recovery of Misapplied Assets: Tracing, Trusts and Restitution' in McKendrick, 149, 152.

[56] *Barnes v Addy* (1874) LR 9 Ch App 244, 252, Lord Selborne.

[57] *Baden v Société Générale* (1983) [1992] 4 All ER 161, 233, Peter Gibson J.

'unconscionability',[58] 'dishonesty'[59] or 'lack of probity'.[60] By contrast with 'recipients', 'accessories' has a subjective ring to it. A sort of civil conspiracy is alleged.

## Common themes

### Use of the constructive trust remedy

**[7.23]** Under both types of remedy, the third parties come under a personal obligation to account to the beneficiary for the value of the beneficiary's misappropriated property passing through their hands. Personal constructive trusts serve as an alternative to tracing claims where the subject property cannot be identified. 'Recipients' is usually the variety for this. Or the personal constructive trust may be to make a third party disgorge a gain. This is something not normally traceable. The 'accessories' claim in *Consul Development Pty Ltd v DPC Estates Pty Ltd*[61] was of this type. 'Accessories' may also make a third party compensate the beneficiary for a loss which has been incurred.

### Insolvency, third parties and secured creditors

**[7.24]** Personal constructive trusts do not have proprietary advantages in a third party's insolvency. Yet the beneficiary will not always rank as an unsecured creditor behind bank floating charges and other proprietary securities. This is partly because of the particular feature of modern commercial financing, noted at [6.71]. The interests of secured creditors are often equitable in form. This means that there is no automatic answer to the question of priority between security interests and personal constructive trusts of either of the present sorts. Assume that a secured creditor has taken an equitable charge. The law of priorities tells us that this charge, in the absence of special circumstances, will be subject to a prior interest under a constructive trust.[62] We saw at [6.72] that constructive trusts come into being at the time of the unconscionable conduct to which they are a response. The charge then will be subject to the constructive trust if the breach of fiduciary duty occurred before the time when the charge was created. There are a number of other relevant priority principles, some of which were discussed at [6.73]–[6.76], as well as a possible distinction between an 'equity' to obtain a constructive trust and an equitable interest.

**[7.25]** The possibility of an equitable priorities dispute between a 'recipients' constructive trust and a line of creditors who had taken equitable securities is illustrated by the decision in *Linter Group Ltd v Goldberg*.[63] One security in that case preceded the time of the unconscionable conduct and two were created subsequently. However, on a working out of the priority rules, the party entitled to the constructive trust took priority over each. This was

---

[58] *Powell v Thompson* [1991] 1 NZLR 597, 607, Thomas J (HC).

[59] *Agip (Africa) Ltd v Jackson* [1990] 1 Ch 265, 293, Millett J affd [1991] Ch 543 (CA).

[60] *Carl Zeiss Stiftung v Herbert Smith & Co (No 2)* [1969] 2 Ch 276, 300, Edmund Davies LJ (CA).

[61] (1975) 132 CLR 373: see [7.].

[62] See R Austin 'Constructive Trusts' in Finn *Equity* 196, 214-5.

[63] [1991] 7 ACSR 580, Southwell J (SC of Vic).

particularly remarkable in view of the structure of the transaction. Facts of the case are discussed more fully below under the 'knowledge' heading at [7.38].

### 'Trusts'

**[7.26]** One common element between 'recipients' and 'accessories' constructive trusts is the supposed prior existence of a 'trust' between the claimants and their fiduciary. This is a quaint way of putting it. 'Recipients' and 'accessories' originally applied to third party participation in breaches of formal trusts. Misappropriations by express trustees were the usual background wrongs. It is now sufficient that a fiduciary relationship subsisted between the 'trustee' and the property of the claimant and was breached. Company directorship is probably now the paradigm. Because of the fiduciary character of directors' duties to their company, they are treated as though they were trustees of any of the company's property under their control.[64] In *Consul Development Pty Ltd v DPC Estates Pty Ltd*[65] the High Court saw a 'breach of trust' sufficient to attract the 'accessories' liability to arise from breach of the fiduciary duty owed by an employee to his employer. 'Trusts' to base 'recipients' and 'accessories' remedies may be expressed even more remedially. R P Austin puts the matter like this.[66] Fiduciaries may be liable to account as constructive trustees to their beneficiaries because they have breached the profits rule. A third party who deals with such these fiduciaries in a way prohibited by the 'recipients' or the 'accessories' rules may be liable to account as a constructive trustee, too.

### Imposition of (personal) constructive trusts

**[7.27]** Remedies for either the 'recipients' or the 'accessories' wrongs are the imposition of a remedial form of the constructive trust on the third party. It is not surprising that 'constructive trust' is the chosen vehicle for this relief. For we saw at [6.23]–[6.24] that the idea of a constructive trust has little institutional content. It may be just a convenient way to signify the 'nature and measure' of liability.[67] Of course, in many if not most claims against third parties there will be no property to annexe the claimant's equitable interest to. Only the accounting and compensatory obligations of constructive trustees set out at [6.81]–[6.84] will be applicable. The fact that the third party is described as a 'constructive trustee' is only of concern to those whose theories lead them to favour the old, institutional, property-based constructive trust. Peter Birks and Andrew Burrows deprecate the law's 'constructive trust' description of this relief accordingly.[68]

### 'Knowledge'

**[7.28]** What the third party actually knew or is taken to have known of the wrongful participation is the kernel of liability. 'Knowledge' has several elements. The first concerns knowledge attributed to third parties that are corporations. A company will be attributed with the mind and will of any

---

[64] *Selangor United Rubber Estates Ltd v Craddock (No 3)* [1968] 2 All ER 1073, 1094, Ungoed-Thomas J.

[65] (1975) 132 CLR 373.

[66] In 'Constructive Trusts' in Finn *Equity* 196, 222-3.

[67] Ford & Lee [2216].

[68] P Birks 'Trusts in the Recovery of Misapplied Assets: Tracing, Trusts and Restitution' in McKendrick 149, 153-6; A Burrows *Restitution* 150-6.

natural person who controls its actions. One must, for this, precisely identify the natural person who has the management and control of the act of the corporation in question.[69] There may be an exception to this imputation idea, where the corporation's controller acquires the knowledge confidentially in some other organisation. In this circumstance, the corporation as third party may not be attributed with it.[70] Secondly, knowledge must first have a certain content. *What* the third party must know is relevant here. Must, for example, the third party know of the whole scheme by fraudulent company directors in order to be liable for it, or only part? Thirdly, knowledge has different *qualities*. The *degree* to which requisite things must be known tends to differ.[71] Must the scheme be actually known, or what if a reasonable man would only suspect it? It would be logical to deal with these second and third matters now, in a way applicable to both 'recipients' and 'accessories'. However the law has developed in a way which makes this difficult. Different 'knowledge' tests may be applicable to each remedy. Before looking to the remedies separately, we shall set out a quality of knowledge taxonomy that cases on both remedies often refer to. It relates to knowledge *quality* and was counsel's suggestion in the marathon 'accessories' case of *Baden v Société Générale*.[72] The relevant 'types' of knowledge were said to be:

> (i) actual knowledge; (ii) wilfully shutting one's eyes to the obvious; (iii) wilfully and recklessly failing to make such inquiries as an honest and reasonable man would make; (iv) knowledge of circumstances which would indicate the facts to an honest and reasonable man; (v) knowledge of circumstances which would put an honest and reasonable man on inquiry.

We will refer to these states of knowledge as the *Baden* categories, by number. The main divide is between categories (i) to (iii) and categories (iv) and (v). The former are different species of *actual* knowledge. They refer to things which an honest third party is presumed to know. The latter categories (iv) and (v) each involve *constructive* knowledge. They refer to things which third parties are negligent, but not necessarily dishonest, in not knowing.

**'RECIPIENTS'**

## Knowing receipt or dealing

**[7.29]** 'Recipients' was the sort of liability imposed in two banking cases, *Stephens Travel Service International Pty Ltd v Qantas Airways Ltd*[73] and *Westpac Banking Corporation v Savin*.[74] Stephens was a travel agent. It had made certain arrangements with IATA in return for being allowed to validate airline tickets itself. In particular, Stephens agreed that moneys that it received from the sale of tickets would be held in trust for the airlines concerned. However, as things happened, those moneys were regularly paid into Stephens'

---

[69] *El Ajou v Dollar Land Holdings plc* [1994] 2 All ER 685, 695-7, Nourse LJ (CA), applying *Lennards Carrying Co Ltd v Asiatic Petroleum Co Ltd* [1915] AC 705, 713, Vis. Haldane LC.

[70] See *Harkness v Commonwealth Bank of Australia* (1993) 12 ACSR 165, 175-6, Young J (NSW SC).

[71] Distinction suggested by R Austin 'Constructive Trusts' in Finn *Equity* 196, 235-8.

[72] (1983) [1992] 4 All ER 161, 235, Peter Gibson J.

[73] (1988) 13 NSWLR 331 (CA), followed in *Re Air Canada and M & I Travel Ltd* (1993) 108 DLR (4th) 592 (SC of Can).

[74] [1985] 2 NZLR 41 (CA).

overdrawn general account with the ANZ bank. Twice a month, to the knowledge of the bank, Stephens accounted to the airlines by cheque drawn on the account. Matters proceeded smoothly until 1984, when the Stephens indebtedness exceeded the bank's permissible limit. An accounting cheque in favour of Qantas was dishonoured. The account was then closed and the bank appointed receivers to the Stephens business. Qantas claimed that the bank was liable to account to it as constructive trustee for the amount of the accounting cheque. Stephens, as part of the claim, was alleged to have misapplied trust moneys by paying them into the overdrawn account. The bank was alleged to have received the moneys with knowledge of the trust in favour of Qantas. Receipt was beneficial to the ANZ to the extent that the overdraft was reduced. It was unanimously found by the New South Wales Court of Appeal that the bank in these circumstances was liable as third party for participation in Stephens' breach of trust. It had *received* trust moneys with the requisite knowledge.

*Westpac Banking Corporation v Savin* was a New Zealand case where the fiduciary was Acqua Marine, a boat-seller. Acqua Marine agreed to sell Savin's boat on commission. After the boat was sold, Acqua Marine paid the proceeds of sale into its overdrawn account with the Westpac bank. Savin never received them. Acqua Marine went into liquidation first and left no funds available to satisfy the claims of unsecured creditors like him. So Savin sued the bank, claiming that it was personally liable to account for the proceeds from his boat. This claim was also allowed. Proceeds of sale were said to be held on trust for Savin and, in breach of trust, they were paid in reduction of Acqua Marine's overdraft. The bank was found to have sufficient knowledge of both trust and breach to justify being made to account.

**[7.30]**   There are three main constituents of 'recipients' claims. The claimant must prove:
• a trust (of the claimant's property);
• the property's receipt (by the third party, in breach of trust); and
• the third party's knowledge (that receipt was in breach of trust).

### (i) 'Trust'

**[7.31]**   This was discussed at [7.26]. The word describes a relationship between the claimant and another concerning the claimant's property. Participation with another in breach of the trust is the spring of the third party's liability. An express trust affecting the claimant's property was clear in the *Stephens case*. It was what had been agreed between Stephens and IATA. Ticket proceeds would be held in trust for each airline. In *Savin's case*, a trust-equivalent was derived from the fact that Acqua Marine received money as agent on behalf of Savin. Savin thereby obtained an equitable interest in the proceeds, as Richardson J found at 49, in the sort of situation we examined at [3.72]–[3.81].

### (ii) 'Receipt'

**[7.32]**   The 'receipt' constituent defines the type of participation which this remedy sanctions. Knowing receipt of trust property by a non-trustee is a sort of self-evident wrong. A trustee must have been in breach of trust for this to occur. It is not always clear, though, whether agents of trustees receive trust property, or are merely conduits between trustees and others. Consider the case of *Agip (Africa) Ltd v Jackson* again.[75] Agip had been defrauded by Mr Zdiri and its funds were paid to the credit of London bank accounts operated by the partners in Jackson & Co. Those partners were sued for particiaption, but 'recipients' liability did not apply. This was for the reason that moneys in the London bank accounts were not held by the partners beneficially. The partners as agents of the wrongdoer had, by the time of trial, accounted to their client for nearly the entire balance passing through their hands. Millett J stated that an 'essential feature' of 'recipients' was that 'the recipient must have received the property for his own use and benefit'. And he added:

> This is why neither the paying nor the collecting bank can normally be brought within it. In paying or collecting money for a customer the bank acts only as his agent. It is otherwise, however, if the collecting bank uses the money to reduce or discharge the customer's overdraft. In doing so it receives the money for its own benefit.

The bank in both *Stephens'* case and *Savin's* case used the money which their customer had paid in to reduce that customer's overdraft. A 'receipt' in the appropriate sense was therefore made out.

### (iii) 'Knowledge'

**[7.33]**   The 'knowledge' constituent of both 'recipients' and 'accessories' is critical. The point was made at [7.22] that 'recipients' is the more objectified sort of wrong. Proceeding from this one might think that if third parties definitely either do or do not receive trust property to which they are not entitled, perhaps 'knowledge' could be similarly objectified? Unfortunately, the cases are in considerable disarray. Courts seem to have stipulated for generally applicable 'knowledge' tests which are really only appropriate to the class of defendant before the court. Sometimes third parties are honest but unlucky agents, like banks. At other times they are associated companies of a rogue fiduciary. The authoritative formulation of 'recipients' knowledge has not been enunciated by the High Court.

### Content and quality of knowledge distinguished

**[7.34]**   The 'content' of knowledge requisite for 'recipients' liability is straightforward. Guilty third parties should be shown to have known of the existence of a trust in respect of the claimant's property and of the fact that their receipt or dealing was in breach of the trust. So in the circumstances of the *Stephens*[76] case it was said that:

> [the] ANZ must be held to have notice both of the existence of a trust in respect of the moneys it received for Qantas tickets not already paid for, and that the use of those moneys by Stephens to reduce its debt to the ANZ would be a breach of trust.

*Savin's* case[77] gave limited consideration to the question of what a third party must know, as distinct from the degree to which it must be known. Richardson J however did say at 52 that a breach of fiduciary duty in the 'misapplication by a customer of funds entrusted to the customer' is that 'notice' which disentitles a bank from making beneficial use of a deposit. We

---

[75] [1990] 1 Ch 265, 292, Millett J, affd [1991] Ch 543, 567 (CA): above at [7.6].

[76] (1988) 13 NSWLR 331, 359, Hope JA (CA).

[77] [1985] 2 NZLR 41 (CA).

will deal under the 'accessories' heading with the question of whether knowledge must always be of facts, or whether sufficient knowledge might be of claims only. Moving now to the quality of knowledge requisite for 'recipients', we can see that there are at least three eligible possibilities.

## Dishonesty

**[7.35]**     The first possibility is that the degree of knowledge possessed by third parties must lead to an inference of dishonesty on their part. Third parties are dishonest where they actually know of a trust concerning the claimant's property and its breach, or they wilfully shut their eyes to the obvious, or they wilfully and recklessly fail to make inquires that an honest and reasonable person would make. *Baden* categories (i) to (iii) are applicable. It need not entail third parties knowing everything about the trust of the claimant's property and the circumstances of its breach. This is a content point. They must have known sufficient to make it dishonest for them to have received or dealt with the property as they did. The dishonesty approach has been taken in a number of United Kingdom authorities. Disallowing the claim made in *Carl Zeiss Stiftung v Herbert Smith & Co (No 2)*, judgments in the English Court of Appeal put it that there must be a 'consciously acting improperly' or 'want of probity' on the third party's part.[78] The case arose as part of a wider claim made by East German Carl Zeiss against West German Carl Zeiss to the effect that the West German company was an impostor and possessed assets as constructive trustee for the claimant. Herbert Smith were the solicitors for the West German company. It had been alleged that a 'recipients' claim could be made out based on the knowledge of the claim that the firm had from the court pleadings. Sums the firm received by way of its professional costs were then said to be received in the knowledge that a trust in favour of the claimant had been breached. It was not really surprising that this claim failed. Perhaps the situation of the defendants as solicitors justified their immunity.

**[7.36]**     *Eagle Trust plc v SBC Securities Ltd*[79] was a stronger 'recipients' claim, where again the 'dishonesty' criterion was applied. Eagle Trust made a takeover offer for the shares in a group of companies. Under the terms of an offer which included a rights issue, shareholders in the target group were offered new shares in Eagle Trust or a cash alternative. SBC agreed to underwrite the cash alternative and the rights issue. Later SBC sought sub-underwriters to share its liability to Eagle Trust. The chief executive of Eagle Trust, a Mr Ferriday, provided SBC with a list of willing sub-underwriters. This included himself to the extent of 25 million £1.80 shares. Then the 1987 'Black Friday' occurred. The stock market crashed. Ferriday's wealth dramatically declined and the underwriting risk loomed larger. Ferriday in these circumstances was called upon and found £13.5m to satisfy his sub-underwriting obligations. Control of Eagle Trust changed soon after. A new board of the company discovered that the £13.5m had been taken from Eagle Trust itself. Recovery proceedings were commenced against SBC. It was alleged that SBC must have known that Ferriday would meet his obligation

---

[78] [1969] 2 Ch 276, 298, Sachs LJ, 299, Edmund Davies LJ (CA).

[79] [1992] 4 All ER 488, Vinelott J; see also *Polly Peck International plc v Nadir (No 2)* [1992] 4 All ER 769, 777-80, Scott LJ (CA); *Cowan de Groot Properties Ltd v Eagle Trust plc* [1992] 4 All ER 700, Knox J.

from the only source of funds available to him—the coffers of Eagle Trust. SBC was said to be a constructive trustee for Eagle Trust and liable to account for the £13.5m because of its knowing receipt. Vinelott J considered that the claim should be struck out. He saw (at 492) that it all depended on the *degree* of knowledge that SBC had. This was nothing like conveyancing 'notice', he said. It was something more related to the third party's conscience. What was fair to ask of third parties in commerce? Should they be expected to 'play the detective'? Should SBC have informed the board of Eagle Trust and asked the company to investigate its own chief executive? With conscientious considerations in mind he analysed the *Baden* categories (at 501–2), finding only (i) to (iii) to be applicable. He said in conclusion (at 511):

> [SBC] may have felt some anxiety, and even have entertained some suspicion, as to how Ferriday had managed to arrange for the £13.5m to be paid ... But it is to my mind going altogether too far to say that any honest and reasonable man would either have inferred that ... the £13.5m was Eagle's money which had been misappropriated by Ferriday in gross breach of his duty as a director.

Michael Bryan summarised this approach neatly by saying that these dishonesty cases are a 'restructuring of the *Baden* criteria in terms of commercial morality'.[80]

*Fault*

**[7.37]** An undifferentiated kind of 'fault' is the second possibility for knowledge quality. Third parties will be liable where they are negligent as regards the beneficiary's rights, as well as if dishonest. Both actual and constructive knowledge are now comprehended. This was what the property legislation referred to at [7.17] provided. We discussed there how applicable this might be to commercial situations. On the *Baden* scale, fault comprehends categories (i) to (iv), and possibly (v) as well. It is favoured in New Zealand. Both *Westpac Banking Corporation v Savin*[81] and another 'recipients' case of *Powell v Thompson*[82] have opted for this broad test. The current edition of *Halsbury's Laws of England* appears to do the same.[83] Objective factors are used to justify it—like a third party's 'unjust enrichment' that the *Powell v Thompson* facts were said to disclose (at 609).

**[7.38]** Australian authority is not settled. It appears to favour the 'fault-based' test, although a little obliqely. A recent example from the Supreme Court of Victoria is *Linter Group Ltd v Goldberg*.[84] In 1990 Linter Group Ltd engaged in the takeover of Brick and Pipe Ltd and an attempted takeover of Tootal Ltd. Borrowed funds were used on both occasions. A corporate vehicle named Arnsberg was used in the successful Brick and Pipe takeover. It was the nominal share purchaser with funds on-lent by Linter Group. The attempt was too highly leveraged. All companies in the group were soon after placed in liquidation. Newly acquired Brick and Pipe shares were sold and the

---

[80] 'Cleaning Up After Breaches of Fiduciary Duty: The Liability of Banks and Other Financial Institutions as Constructive Trustees' unpublished paper presented at Bond University conference 23.7.94.

[81] [1985] 2 NZLR 41.

[82] [1991] 1 NZLR 597, Thomas J (HC).

[83] 4th ed (1984) vol. 48, [592].

[84] (1992) 7 ACSR 580, Southwell J (SC of V)

proceeds were paid into court. It was held by the court that Linter Group was entitled to be repaid the loan it had made to Arnsberg out of these proceeds first. This was in priority to the (equitable) security interests over the shares possessed by each of the lenders. Priority rules determined the outcome of the case. The lenders, in fact, had provided Linter Group with the funds to lend to Arnsberg. Such a result was pursuant to a 'recipients' constructive trust in favour of the Linter Group. 'Tracing' and proprietary relief were irrelevant to the outcome, despite some dicta and argument to the contrary. Linter Group's liquidator claimed that the company's directors breached a fiduciary obligation by lending, unsecured, some $205m from the company's (borrowed) resources to a $2 company. Apparently the directors' idea had been to enable Arnsberg to pass on the shares purchased to the directors' private family trusts. What knowledge Arnsberg had of this, as third party, was not much discussed. Arnsberg had Linter Group's misappropriating directors as its own and was assumed to be privy to the design. At 623 Southwell J quoted and approved a passage from *Belmont Finance Corporation v Williams Furniture Ltd (No 2)*[85] which maintained the sufficiency of actual or constructive knowledge for a 'recipients' claim.

**[7.39]**   The 'recipients' claim of *Stephens Travel Service International Pty Ltd v Qantas Airways Ltd*[86] is on its face of little assistance here. The ANZ was found at 359 to have actual knowledge of the tickets trust for Qantas and its breach. This was said, uncommonly, not to involve any 'dishonesty' or even the possibility of an 'accessories' claim as well. The ANZ officers apparently had never thought about the facts they 'knew'. This is very close to constructive knowledge and fault. It is, by another name, a negligent failure to advert to the legal consequences of a transaction's facts.

*Strict liability*

**[7.40]**   This is the third possibility for what can amount to 'recipients' knowledge. It is a subject canvassed by restitutionary scholarship. Peter Birks and others see no reason in principle why 'recipients' in equity should stand outside the strict liability scheme of the common law.[87] We saw at [7.4]–[7.5] how 'money had and received' and conversion do not require proof of any intent or state of mind in the defendant. A comparable equitable liability based in objective criteria is not entirely without precedent, although it is uncommon.[88] Strict liability elevates the claimant's property interest into one which leaps over all the in personam factors which the ordinary claimant must negotiate. What is so special, though, about this party's interest?

**[7.41]**   One case which seems to support the strict liability idea is the New Zealand decision in *Powell v Thompson*.[89] Remarks on strict liability were

---

[85] [1980] 1 All ER 393, 405, Goff and Waller LJJ.

[86] (1988) 13 NSWLR 331, Hope JA, Kirby P and Priestly JA agreeing (CA).

[87] P Birks 'Trusts in the Recovery of Misapplied Assets: Tracing, Trusts and Restitution' in McKendrick 149; 'Misdirected funds: restitution from the recipient' [1989] LMCLQ 296; 'Persistent problems in misdirected money: a quintet' [1993] LMCLQ 218; P Burrows *Restitution* 150-6.

[88] Re Diplock [1948] Ch 465 (CA) and see *GL Baker Ltd v Medway Building and Supplies Ltd* [1958] 3 All ER 540 (CA).

[89] [1991] 1 NZLR 597, Thomas J (HC); also *El Ajou v Dollar Land Holdings plc* [1993] 3 All ER 717, 739, Millett J (revd on another point).

really dicta. The third party had actual knowledge. But the facts are interesting. Mrs Powell and her two daughters owned a house as tenants in common. Some years earlier, the daughters had gone overseas and left their mother with powers of attorney which they did not revoke on their return. Mrs Powell worked for a small business run by Mr Thompson. Over several years she managed, undetected, to embezzle from it some $289,000. Eventually Thompson discovered her. He was prevailed upon not to take the matter to the police and to accept her offer of substantial repayment, including transfer of the jointly owned house. Transfer formalities were completed by Mrs Powell without her daughters' knowledge. She used the old powers of attorney. Mr Thompson was good enough to allow the original occupants to remain there as tenants and the whole thing was kept a secret. Even the unmarried daughter who continued to live in the house was fooled. She thought that rent payments were being made towards a mortgage. About a year later the true facts emerged. The daughters made a 'recipients' claim against Mr Thompson, alleging that he held the house as constructive trustee for them in their former shares. Allowing the claim, Powell J said at 607 that 'recipients' was really based in unjust enrichment of the third party at the expense of the claimant. The knowledge requirement for a remedial constructive trust, he said at 608–9, was certainly 'all five' of the Baden categories. Indeed, he added, the state of the third party's conscience was really irrelevant. The claim was analogous to an equity in conveyancing. A third party has to be a bona fide purchaser to escape it. Thomas went on at 616–17 to decide the case in the traditional way. Thompson the third party had actual knowledge of the trust affecting the claimants' rights (co-ownership). A 'necessary inference' was that he also knew of its breach (being secret use of the powers of attorney).

## 'ACCESSORIES'

### Assisting with wrongful designs

[7.42] 'Accessories' is closer to the paradigm of participation liability.[90] Whether or not third parties have received any of the 'trust' property, they may become personally liable if they knowingly assist the 'trustees' in a fraudulent design. 'Accessories' in this way is different from both tracing and 'recipients'. It is not concerned with misappropriation of property. It focusses instead on the deterrence of fraud.[91] 'Accessories' thus overlaps with 'recipients' and goes further by applying to situations where no property is present. 'Accessories' is also a more normal sort of equitable claim. It makes explicit appeal to the wrongdoer's conscience.

R P Austin says that 'recipients' should perhaps now 'melt away'. The whole field of participation wrongs could then be served by 'accessories'.[92] For each case of 'recipients' also attracts the liability of 'accessories'. And there are a lot of problems with 'recipients', as we have seen. Liability is based on what is often a neutral or haphazard event. Receipt of property is scarcely adequate as a basis for generating equitable liability. When are misapplied funds 'received' by the third party in the course of electronic

---

[90] *Scott on Trusts* §321 and see dicta of Kirby P in *Equiticorp Finance Ltd v Bank of New Zealand* (1993) 32 NSWLR 50, 103-4 (CA).

[91] *Agip (Africa) Ltd v Jackson* [1990] 1 Ch 265, 292-3, Millett J.

[92] R Austin 'Constructive Trusts' in Finn *Equity* 196, 217.

banking? Is it when a computer operator keys in the appropriate information? Is it when an answering impulse is received? The significance of the moment of receipt is nugatory.

**[7.43]** 'Accessories' was the form of participatory liability considered by the High Court in *Consul Development Pty Ltd v DPC Estates Pty Ltd*[93]. Jack Walton was the managing-director of DPC Estates and a solicitor. DPC conducted a business of acquiring run-down properties, renovating them and selling them at a profit. Grey was employed by DPC as its full-time manager. He had the job of finding the right properties to buy. Walton as solicitor employed an articled clerk named Clowes, with whose father he had once engaged in property ventures. Clowes decided to enter the property market himself after his father died, through a family company named Consul Development. Grey volunteered details to Clowes of suitable properties which DPC was not in funds to purchase. Clowes and Grey then agreed that Consul would buy the suitable properties and any profit from resale would be shared equally between Consul and Grey. Walton became aware of the arrangement after Consul had purchased and sold a number of the properties. DPC then sued Grey and Consul, alleging that they both were constructive trustees and liable to account for the profits that had been made. Liability of Consul was based in its knowing assistance in Grey's fraudulent breach of his fiduciary duty to DPC. For this the knowledge imputed to Consul through Clowes was critical. A majority of the High Court found that Clowes did not have sufficient awareness that Grey was acting in breach of duty in order to make Consul liable to account. We will now separately examine the constituents of the 'accessories' liability that Consul Development was argued to be under. They are that:

  (i) a 'trust' or fiduciary relation exists for the claimant's benefit;
 (ii) the trust is breached;
(iii) the third party assists in the wrong; and
(iv) the third party is shown to have possessed sufficient knowledge of what was happening.

### (i) 'Trust'

**[7.44]** This is the same as for 'recipients', except that property of the claimant is not of importance. A fiduciary obligation standing alone will suffice. What was DPC's 'trust property' in the *Consul Development*[94] case? There was none at all, as Gibbs J acknowledged at 395. Breach of obligations to found the remedy was a purely in personam thing—despite what Peter Gibson J seemed to say in *Baden v Société Générale.*[95]

### (ii) Fraudulent breach of duty

**[7.45]** The fiduciary's act must have been fraudulent. Not all breaches of duty will suffice. If, for instance, the trustee of a superannuation deed misreads an investment power he may have acted in breach of trust. Such a breach will almost certainly not fix a merchant bank assisting him with 'accessories' liability. Some 'fraud' on the beneficiary is a necessary characteristic of acts

---

[93] (1975) 132 CLR 373.
[94] (1975) 132 CLR 373.
[95] (1983) [1992] 4 All ER 161, 233.

assisted in.[96] Acts of the 'trustee' must be lacking in probity. It is important to isolate this issue from what the mental state of a guilty third party must be. The third party's necessary mental state is dealt with under the next sub-heading.

**[7.46]** There is also a need to reconcile the recent United Kingdom authorities with an established Australian position on whether breach and lack of probity should be associated. Should a fiduciary's breach of duty always have ramifications for third parties who assist? To say that a 'breach of trust', without more, can generate an 'accessories' liability would be to give the wrong a very wide ambit. It has a potentially disastrous application to banks. Gibbs J discussed the width of 'accessories' in *Consul Development Pty Ltd v DPC Estates Pty Ltd*.[97] He said first that the wrong should apply to third party participation in wrongs by fiduciaries and not just trustees. Next he said that 'the maintenance of a very high standard of conduct on the part of fiduciaries' needed to be supported by a rule which deterred third parties from assisting fiduciaries and taking benefits from the breach of their obligations. He concluded (at 397)–

> that a person who knowingly participates in a breach of fiduciary duty is liable to account to the person to whom the duty was owed for any benefit he has received as a result of such participation.

Perhaps this pitches the rule rather too widely. Participation in any breach of fiduciary duty should not attract 'accessories'. A different line has been taken in the United Kingdom. It appeared to the Court of Appeal in *Belmont Finance Corporation Ltd v Williams Furniture Ltd*[98] that nothing short of dishonesty and fraud on the trustee's part would suffice. Two subsequent United Kingdom decisions are notable here.[99] Both involved commercial fraud, although in neither was this proven. The relevant fiduciaries preferred to abscond, rather than face cross-examination and committal at home. The 'fraudulent *and* dishonest' qualification of the trustees' design in *Barnes v Addy*[100] was repeated without much light being shed. 'Accessories' was said to be 'plainly inapplicable' in *Re Montagu's Settlement Trusts*,[101] where the trustee was honest. It is submitted that the 'want of probity' qualification provides the fairest reinforcement of the fiduciary profits and conflicts rules. It binds third parties where they have been wilfully breached.

### (iii) 'Assistance in the wrong'

**[7.47]** To 'assist', the third party must be shown to have had the intention of furthering the fraudulent breach of duty.[102] It is not enough that the third party just permitted or allowed the fraud to occur.[103] Sufficient assistance must

---

[96] P Millett 'Recovering the Proceeds of Fraud', 5, unpublished paper presented at 'Insolvency and Banking Law' seminar, Hong Kong, March 1993.

[97] (1975) 132 CLR 373.

[98] [1979] Ch 250, 267.

[99] *Baden v Société Générale* (1983) [1992] 4 All ER 161; *Polly Peck International plc v Nadir (No 2)* [1992] 4 All ER 769—Millett J at 1st instance.

[100] (1874) LR 9 Ch App 244, 252, Lord Selborne LC (CA).

[101] [1987] 1 Ch 264, 270, Megarry V-C.

[102] *Biala Pty Ltd v Mallina Holdings Ltd* (1993) 11 ACSR 785, 832, Ipp J (SC of WA).

[103] *Wickstead v Browne* (1992) 30 NSWLR 1, 16, Handley and Cripps JJA.

be an act or acts which are *part* of the fiduciary's design and not things of minimal importance.[104] This is widely interpreted. Even banks' ministerial execution of their customers' payment orders has been held to be a sufficient 'assistance'. This was what was decided in *Selangor United Rubber Estates Ltd v Craddock (No 3)*[105] and *Karak Rubber Co Ltd v Burden (No 2)*[106]—the 'financial assistance' cases—where fiduciaries caused companies to make wrongful payments in connection with the purchase of their own shares.

### (iv) 'The third party's knowledge'

[7.48] Whether the third party has assisted with sufficient is the largest question in most 'accessories' cases. There are many parallels with 'recipients' on the subject, even if knowledge is closer to the heart of the 'accessories' wrong. Knowledge 'content' and knowledge 'quality' components can be separated, as was done at [7.34].

### 'Content' of knowledge

[7.49] Content directs us to *what* the third party must know. For 'accessories' this means two things in particular. First 'the trust': the third party must be aware that a fiduciary owed obligations to the claimant, in same sense as at [7.26]. Secondly, the third party must know of a fiduciary's breach of the duty, discussed at [7.28]. This prompts three questions. How does a third party come to know of these things? What if the third party becomes aware only of *claims* that fiduciaries have breached their duties? And, which seems a little less likely, what if the third party is only aware of *claims* that fiduciary duties are owed to the claimant? *Carl Zeiss Stiftung v Herbert Smith & Co (No 2)*[107] is in point again. In that case it was decided, at least by Sachs LJ, that if a third party had knowledge only of claims, then a 'breach of trust' for 'recipients' purposes could not be established. Becoming aware of a disputed claim or a 'doubtful equity', he said at 296, was different from possessing knowledge of the facts claimed. A third party has no obvious way of assessing the validity of claims. There may indeed be differences between the two things. Knowledge derived from the apprehension of fact is distinguishable from knowledge derived from hearsay. Notice only and not knowledge may result from the awareness of claims. However, whether this potential distinction is material for present purposes has not yet been established.

[7.50] The sufficiency of knowledge of claims arose in Australia, when *Hospital Products* was in the New South Wales Court of Appeal.[108] Background facts to the third party participation issue were as follows. USSC commenced several breach of fiduciary obligation proceedings against Hospital Products International ('HPI') in 1980. In mid-1981 HPI sold its entire Australian 'surgical suturing business' to a moribund and loss-making company called Aquila Investment Corporation. In return for the business, Mr Blackman and his associates obtained a majority shareholding in the purchaser. The effect was to leave Blackman still in control of his business which was

---

[104] *Baden v Société Générale* (1983) [1992] 4 All ER 161, 234, Peter Gibson J.
[105] [1968] 2 All ER 1073, 1104-5, Ungoed-Thomas J.
[106] [1972] 1 All ER 1210, 1232-3, Brightman J.
[107] [1969] 2 Ch 276 (CA).
[108] [1983] 2 NSWLR 157, 255-8 (CA): for full facts see [3.9]–[3.10].

then nominally conducted by a listed public company. The Court of Appeal described this arrangement as a 'reverse take over'. Some time later Aquila was renamed 'Hospital Products Ltd ('HPL'). The question thereafter arose whether HPL had knowingly acquired the assets of HPI in a way which made it accountable as constructive trustee for USSC.

**[7.51]**  During the time that the 'reverse takeover' in *Hospital Products* was pending, USSC served Aquila with a statement of claim alleging fraudulence on the part of HPI and also that HPI's intended sale was an attempt to defeat USSC's claim. Aquila therefore was informed of USSC's claims. But it did not acquire knowledge of the facts on which those claims were based. Nature of the knowledge was the main problem with inferring either a 'recipients' or 'accessories' constructive trust against Aquila. Characterisation of things that HPL could be attributed with knowledge of suggested that the knowledge constituent of the claim was not satisfied. This was not allowed to stand in the way of the Court of Appeal's disallowal of HPI's strategem. *Carl Zeiss*[109] was distinguished to its 'solicitor and client' facts: the court purportedly following the *Consul Developments*[110] approach of Gibbs J in this rather than Stephen J. The court concluded (at 257):

> We cannot suppose that claims of this kind, made in such circumstances, are incapable of constituting facts amounting to knowledge in the relevant sense.

The outcome that the Court of Appeal reached in *Hospital Products* on this point was undoubtedly right. It would seem to be an instance of justice prevailing over doctrine.

## Quality of knowledge

**[7.52]**  The 'dishonesty', 'fault, and 'strict liability' taxonomy of the quality of knowledge advanced at [7.35]–[7.41] is applicable again, although the matter is now less speculative. There is explicit High Court authority on the point. Stephen J, with whom Barwick CJ agreed, adopted a modified 'fault' position in relation to the quality of knowledge needed in *Consul Developments Pty Ltd v DPC Estates Pty Ltd*.[111] He ruled out the need for that sort of knowledge which 'serves to expose a party to liability because of negligence in failing to make an inquiry'. *Baden* category (v) was regarded as excessive. He continued:

> If a defendant knows of facts which themselves would, to a reasonable man, tell of fraud or breach of trust the case may well be different, as it clearly will be if the defendant has consciously refrained from inquiry for fear lest he learn of fraud. But to go further is, I think, to disregard equity's concern for the state of conscience of the defendant.

Clearly *Baden* category (iv), and as well categories (i) to (iii), are included in Stephen J's formulation. Knowledge of circumstances which would indicate the facts to an honest and reasonable man is sufficient. To this extent, actual *or* constructive knowledge suffices. Knowledge can be inferred from criteria which pay no regard to the third party's state of mind. Gibbs J made a similar

---

[109]  [1969] 2 Ch 276.
[110]  (1975) 132 CLR 373, 398-9.
[111]  (1975) 132 CLR 373, 412.

point at 398. In a judgment which substantially concurred with Stephen, he said that:

> it does not seem to me to be necessary to prove that a stranger who participated in a breach of trust or fiduciary duty with knowledge of all the circumstances did so actually knowing that what he was doing was improper. It would not be just that a person who had full knowledge of all the facts could escape liability because his own moral obtuseness prevented him from recognizing an impropriety that would have been apparent to an ordinary man.

**[7.53]**     The High Court has not again since *Consul Development* considered the quality of knowledge required for 'accessories'. The majority decision may be assumed to state the current Australian position. What *Consul* decided may be inconsistent with the High Court's slightly earlier decision in *BLB Corporation of Australia Establishment v Jacobsen*.[112] Although *BLB* was concerned with the liability of a non-disclosing fiduciary, and not that of a third party, the case imposed a knowledge test which went no further than the first three *Baden* categories. We may assume that the law has become stricter. Recent New Zealand[113] and United Kingdom[114] authorities which describe 'accessories' liability as a matter of conscience and restrict knowledge to 'dishonesty' and the first three *Baden* categories can be assumed not to be persuasive until the High Court is seised of the matter again.

---

[112] (1974) 48 ALJR 372: see D Heydon 'Recent Developments in Constructive Trusts' (1977) 51 *ALJ* 635, 642–3.

[113] See *Powell v Thompson* [1991] 1 NZLR 597, 611, (HC); *Equiticorp Industries Group Ltd v Hawkins* [1991] 3 NZLR 700, 728; *Marshall Futures Ltd v Marshall* [1992] 1 NZLR 316 and *Lankshear v ANZ Banking Group Ltd* [1993] 1 NZLR 481.

[114] See *Agip (Africa) Ltd v Jackson* [1990] 1 Ch 265, 293; affd [1991] Ch 547 (CA).

**[7.54]  Equitable liability of third parties**

| Factual situation | Nature of defendant's liability | Equity | | Common law | |
|---|---|---|---|---|---|
| Where the defendant received the property and still has it | Property-based | The proprietary or tracing claim | *Liability:* Strict *Defence:* Bona fide purchaser for value without notice | Not applicable | |
| Where the defendant received the property but has parted with it | Property-based | 'Recipients' | *Liability:* Requires fault ie actual or constructive knowledge of a fraudulent breach of duty | Money had and received | *Liability:* Strict *Defence:* Innocent purchaser for value |
| Where the defendant did not receive the property but actively assisted in its misdirection | Delictual | 'Accessories' | *Liability:* Requires fault ie actual or constructive knowledge of a fraudulent breach of duty | Not applicable (Conspiracy to defraud) | |

The table above was suggested by one which appeared in Peter Millett's unpublished paper 'Recovering the Proceeds of Fraud', presented to 'Insolvency and Banking Law' seminar, Hong Kong, March 1993.

# Part Two

# The Fiduciary Relation of Influence

# Chapter 8

# Undue Influence

[8.1] 'Undue influence' concerns fiduciary relationships of a kind different from the confidential fiduciary relationship of previous chapters. A fiduciary relationship for undue influence purposes implies the exercise of wrongful persuasion, influence or pressure by one party to a transaction upon another. The fiduciary concept is used a little differently. It is only a background fact to a wrong. Though fiduciary relations are the most common source of influence misused, rights do not arise from the relationship itself. They arise from the influence the relationship creates. In *Johnson v Buttress*,[1] Dixon J said that the basis of the doctrine was the prevention of 'unconscientious use of any special capacity or opportunity' concerning another party's 'will or freedom of judgment'. This looks to whether the influenced party really consented or not. Undue influence deals more particularly with motives, with the 'production' of the influenced party's consent, rather than the fact of it.[2] It regulates the inducements which the other party may lawfully give. Relationships which are capable of creating influence for these purposes cannot be easily categorised. The idea rests on a principle. One person, as Dixon said, occupying a position of ascendancy over another, will be attributed with the power to wrongly influence the other.[3]

[8.2] The principle underlying both forms of undue influence has been authoritatively said to be the prevention of the 'victimisation' of one party by the other.[4] Undue influence is not based in 'vague public policy' or designed to protect people from the consequences of their own folly. It is focussed on the wrongful exercise of influence, either by the influencer in fact, or by attribution of the power to do so. Parties influenced usually suffer a disadvantage in the transactions overturned. A sale at an undervalue is a common example. The question has arisen whether the victim of the undue influence should have to establish this disadvantage, in addition to the influence itself. Or should the victim of undue influence, in a correlative way,

---

[1] (1936) 56 CLR 113, 134.
[2] *Huguenin v Baseley* (1807) 14 Ves Jun 273, 300; 33 ER 526, 525, Lord Eldon.
[3] *Johnson v Buttress* (1936) 56 CLR 113, 134–5; *National Westminster Bank plc v Morgan* [1985] AC 686, 709, Lord Scarman.
[4] *Allcard v Skinner* (1887) 36 Ch D 145, 182–183, Lindley LJ, as approved by the House of Lords in *National Westminster Bank plc v Morgan* [1985] 1 AC 686, 705, Lord Scarman, Lords Keith, Roskill, Bridge and Brandon agreeing.

need to show that the influencer obtained some benefit by means of the influenced transaction. These are some of the difficulaties of the commercial wrong.

**[8.3]** Undue influence was primarily shaped as a way of challenging gratuitous dispositions. Donees were called upon to deny that their imposition had any part in the obvious disadvantage that donors or settlors incurred in giving away their property. Contracts or commercial transactions are different. There is then no inevitable disadvantage to the influenced party. Commercial transactions are not one-sided in the way that gifts are. Consideration moving from both parties is the thing which binds deals together. Deals are species of exchange. Fairness of the exchange must dictate whether the deal is to be unpacked. Unfair advantage-taking might occur where a person, through exercise of influence from a previous relationship, procures another to enter into a transaction on unfavourable terms.[5] Or a transaction might be obtained by what equity regards as the stronger party's unconscionable persuasion.[6] Less subtle forms of commercial pressure might be exercised where one party to a sale of shares agreement threatened to have the other murdered unless he agreed.[7] All these are potential cases of undue influence. The remedy is concurrent, we will see, with other remedies in equity and at law. But it has its own special territory.

## Categories of undue influence

**[8.4]** That a power to influence was unduly exercised may be apparent from the facts of a transaction. This is actual undue influence. Influence is manifest. Obvious sway of one party over the mind of another may mean that the other has not entered into the transaction through exercise of his own will and judgment. No pre-existing relation may be needed to see this influence at work. In other cases the influence can only be appreciated as something which has developed over time. Facts of the transaction itself may be equivocal. Where parties have developed a relationship of trust and confidence whence influence ordinarily flows, the wrong presumes influence to inform the transaction impugned. Presumed influence flows from a species of pre-existing fiduciary relationship, the sort which gives the trusted party the ability to direct the actions of another. Two broad categories of undue influence exist. First, *actual undue influence*: the sort which develops with the transaction under review. The claimant affirmatively shows it. Secondly, *presumed undue influence*, which involves the presumed effect of a 'trusting and confidential' relationship over time. Following *Bank of Credit and Commerce International SA v Aboody*[8] we shall call these 'class 1' and 'class 2' undue influence respectively. *Aboody* then classifies the relationships which create a presumption within the second class. 'Class 2(A)' relationships are those where influence arises as a

---

[5]   *Tomson v Judge* (1855) 3 Drewry 306; 61 ER 920, 923, Kindersley V-C.

[6]   *Wright v Carter* [1903] 1 Ch 27, 61, Cozens-Hardy LJ (CA); *Phillips v Hutchinson* [1946] VLR 270; argued in *Berk v Permanent Trustee Co of New South Wales Ltd* (1947) 47 SR (NSW) 459.

[7]   *Barton v Armstrong* [1973] 2 NSWLR 598, 631 (PC), adopting Mason JA (dissenting), 617–8 (CA).

[8]   [1990] 1 QB 923, 953 (CA), also in *Barclays Bank plc v O'Brien* [1994] 1 AC 180, 189, Lord Browne-Wilkinson.

matter of law from the trust and confidence they embody. 'Class 2(B)' relationships are those others where the claimant must prove that trust and confidence were reposed.

## CLASS 1: ACTUAL UNDUE INFLUENCE

**[8.5]** The actual form of undue influence is 'overreaching, some form of cheating' in a transaction whereby the influencer gains a benefit.[9] The source of influence does not come from any antecedent relation. It arises from the circumstances of the transaction itself. The claimant must prove that the impugned disposition or engagement was not his free act.[10] The parties' relation in the transaction does not have to be characterised as 'fiduciary' or of 'trust and confidence' in order for influence to be shown. 'Class 1' undue influence is therefore not, in a sense, within the scope of this book. But we shall examine it a little further all the same. The ambit of the class bears on the proper sense of 'class 2' and that clearly does have a fiduciary source.

Commercial varieties of actual undue influence involve exchanges improperly obtained: dispositions or obligations extracted by improper persuasions. So a bank's threat to prosecute a son if a mortgage were not executed was held to amount to undue influence in *Williams v Bayley*.[11] Lord Westbury found there that the influenced party was not a 'free and voluntary agent' after the threat was made. A wife or her successors might prove that her husband wrongly pressured her into making a disposition favourable to himself,[12] or into entering an engagement required by the financier of his business.[13] Parents of an importunate son might be able to establish that the security they provided for his business was obtained in circumstances which severely disadvantaged them.[14] Whether the influence is 'undue' in all these cases raises questions which we shall deal with below.

A point to note about 'class 1' undue influence is that it functions very similarly to the common law doctrine of 'duress', now that the scope of duress has been extended in this century. Duress was once limited to actual or threatened violence to the person and the 'established categories'. Now it extends to the exercise of economic pressure and threats to interfere in business relations as well.[15] Members of the High Court in *Commercial Bank of Australia Ltd v Amadio*[16] virtually assimilated duress and class 1 undue influence in order to distinguish undue influence from unconscionable dealing. Undue influence, Deane J said, deals with the 'quality of consent' and other voluntariness factors, viewed from the weaker party's perspective. Such a reconciliation of doctrinal developments may be at the expense of subtlety that

---

[9] *Allcard v Skinner* (1887) 36 Ch D 145, 181, Lindley LJ (CA).

[10] *Johnson v Buttress* (1936) 56 CLR 113, 134, Dixon J; *Barclays Bank Plc v O'Brien* [1994] 1 AC 180, 189, Lord Browne-Wilkinson.

[11] (1866) LR 1 HL 200, 219; also *Mutual Finance Ltd v John Wetton & Sons Ltd* [1937] 2 KB 389 and *Kaufman v Gerson* [1904] 1 KB 591.

[12] *Farmers' Co-operative Executors & Trustees Ltd v Perks* (1989) 52 SASR 399.

[13] *Bank of Credit & Commerce International SA v Aboody* [1990] 1 QB 923 (CA).

[14] *Coldunell Ltd v Gallon* [1986] 1 QB 1184 (CA).

[15] See Goff & Jones 255–75.

[16] (1983) 151 CLR 447, 461, Mason J, 474, Deane J, followed in *Louth v Diprose* (1992) 175 CLR 621, 627, Brennan J.

the remedy has in its United Kingdom form. In *Goldsworthy v Brickell*,[17] a decision of the United Kingdom Court of Appeal, it was found that an 85-year-old man's will was not dominated in the relevant transaction. Indeed, he was said at 389 to be–

> in good health and physically strong . . . remarkably well preserved for his age . . . not at all the sort of person who could be overborne in argument, or influenced by the strength of personality.

Yet his undue influence claim was still upheld. A gift of most of his assets to a neighbour was set aside. Such concurrent findings of voluntariness and undue influence would not seem to be possible in Australia. M Cope has suggested in the circumstances that common law duress should be subsumed under the equity (here called) 'class 1 undue influence'.[18] Economy of concepts would suggest as much. But something is lost in the austerity.

## CLASS 2: PRESUMED UNDUE INFLUENCE

**[8.6]**   These are situations where the onus of proof is reversed. The defendant is given the task of disproving that a transaction resulted from influence, rather than the claimant having to prove that it was influenced. Presumptions arise where the parties were previously involved in a relationship where one party was ascendant over another. The attributed influence is presumed to continue and affect the impugned transaction. This type of relationship has 'fiduciary characteristics'. It involves ascendancy or influence, on the part of the stronger party, and dependence or trust on the part of the weaker party.[19] It is distinct from the 'confidential' type of fiduciary relationship that this book has previously examined. The fiduciary relationship specific to the wrong of undue influence is such as to confer the indicia of authority or influence on one party over another.[20] It is in no sense constructive. It is not such as the law might impose to reflect parties' expectations of honesty or fidelity.[21] Employees, for example, undoubtedly fiduciaries, will not usually be in a position to influence and dominate their employer. They are within the wider canon of fiduciaries, but not the undue influence wrong.

In Australia there is no requirement that the claimant prove a 'manifest disadvantage' before raising a presumptive undue influence claim. Things are otherwise in the United Kingdom, although the idea has recently been restricted.[22] 'Adequacy of consideration' tends to raise the same considerations as manifest disadvantage in commercial situations. Undue influence may not be disproved by showing that the claimant was 'paid the going rate'. There are all sorts of reasons why a person who has been offered a fair price might not wish to enter an exchange.[23] Unconscionability may consist in forcing an unexceptionable deal upon an unwilling contractor.

---

[17] [1987] 1 Ch 378, 402–3, Nourse LJ (CA).

[18] *Duress, Undue Influence and Unconscientious Bargains* (1985), [124], [132].

[19] *Johnson v Buttress* (1936) 56 CLR 113, 134–5, Dixon J.

[20] W Winder 'Undue influence and fiduciary relationships' (1940) 4 *Convey (NS)* 274, 274–5.

[21] See [3.87]–[3.88].

[22] *National Westminster Bank plc v Morgan* [1985] AC 686, as explained in *CIBC Mortgages plc v Pitt* [1994] 1 AC 200, 207–9.

[23] *Commercial Bank of Australia Ltd v Amadio* (1983) 151 CLR 447, 475, Deane J; D Tiplady 'Note' (1985) 48 Mod LR 579, 581.

**[8.7]**    Commercial application of the presumptive wrong is illustrated in the Queensland case of *Cowen v Piggott*.[24] The defendant was an accountant, retained by a mining engineer to advise on the development of gold-mining leases. The engineer needed money. He was aware that the accountant had some wealthy Asian clients. An agreement with some of the clients was entered whereby they became entitled to proportions of the engineer's venture in return for making a capital investment. The accountant himself took an interest in a very small proportion, in addition to his normal professional fees. All interests in the venture were later sold and the investors were repaid their investments with handsome interest. The engineer was unhappy about this. He believed that the accountant should have advised him to borrow money on his own account rather than give an equity interest to the investors. In court the engineer argued that the accountant was a fiduciary, who bore the burden of disproving the exercise of undue influence over him. No indicia of the accountant's dominion or ascendancy over the engineer, though, were shown, either relationally or in fact. No other case of breach of fiduciary duty was made out, nor was it shown that the accountant was the engineer's 'confidential advisor' in relation to the financing of the venture. The transaction was at 'arm's length'. No relationship of trust and confidence which might engender influence over the engineer was evident at all. 'In my opinion', McPherson J said, the claim–

> mistakes the principles involved and blurs the distinction between contracts induced by undue influence and those made with a person to whom fiduciary duties are owed. It is true that a person in a position to exercise undue influence owes duties to the other party that are the same as, or similar to, the duties owed by a fiduciary to a person whom he advises. But the converse is not necessarily true. The mere fact that a person occupies a fiduciary position does not mean that any contract he enters is presumed, without further proof of reliance, to be the product of that relationship.

**[8.8]**    This is the point we examined at [1.23], referring to the decision of the United Kingdom Court of Appeal in *Re Coomber*.[25] The facts of the case were that a son administered the liquor business of his deceased father for a short time after the father died. This was on behalf of his mother, the person absolutely entitled to the father's estate. During the son's administration the mother executed an assignment of the business to him by way of gift. Apparently this was done in accordance with the father's wishes. However, after the mother died, the son's brother and sister brought an action to have the son declared constructive trustee of the business for the mother's estate. For the son had taken a transfer of the business from the mother personally, when he was at the time running it as her fiduciary agent. The doctrine of undue influence was said to supply a presumption against the validity of this gift. The court unanimously held that the presumption of undue influence did not apply. The fact that the son was a fiduciary agent of the mother at the time he was did not entail his being presumed to have the influence that the wrong was founded upon. It was a mistake to suppose that all fiduciary relationships will supply that interest. An agent, for example, must be loyal to

---

[24]  [1989] 1 Qd R 41, 44 (first inst).

[25]  [1911] 1 Ch 723 (CA); point made also by Starke J in *Harris v Jenkins* (1922) 31 CLR 341, 367.

his principal and deal honestly with him, but cannot be supposed to possess any ascendancy or influence through the relation. So equally for a fiduciary agent conducting a business on behalf of the estate. Buckley LJ said at 730:

> This doctrine of equity does not rest upon the existence of a fiduciary relationship whatever be its nature. It rests upon the existence of such a fiduciary relationship as will lead the court to infer undue influence.

## Class 2(A): 'the established relationships'

**[8.9]**   Certain well known relationships are considered likely of nature to involve the influence of one party over another. A burden of disproving influence is imposed on the presumptively stronger party as soon as the benefit of some disposition or engagement is taken and the relation is shown to exist between the relevant parties.[26] 'Established relationships of influence' is a somewhat dated idea, of which only a few categories now clearly exist. These are:[27]

- parent and child;
- guardian and ward;
- spiritual adviser and adherent;
- solicitor and client; and
- doctor and patient.

In each relation, the first party is presumed to obtain any substantial benefit he or she does from the second party by means of influence that the relationship has created. This is a matter of law.[28] It is the up to the party who bears the burden to show that the other party is emancipated from the presumption's effect, or has not been disadvantaged, as the case may be.[29] If an unemancipated child contracts with a parent to dispose of property or an inheritance, the parent's influence over the child is presumed to make the contract unfair. The law will avoid it without further proof.[30] Parties not infrequently do business with their legal advisors. This happened in *Wright v Carter*.[31] A solicitor failed to justify a deed he entered with his client, even though he gave evidence that the deed was part of a plan to enable the client to avoid his creditors. 'The onus', Vice-Chancellor Kindersley said in *Tomson v Judge*,[32]

> lies on the solicitor to show that the transaction was perfectly fair, that the client knew what he was doing, and in particular that a fair price was given, and of course that no kind of advantage was taken by the solicitor.

The relationship of husband and wife is not a class 2(A) relationship.[33] This is an important point. Mere proof of a married union does not raise the

---

[26] *Johnson v Buttress* (1936) 56 CLR 113, 134, Dixon J.

[27] Laws 35.25; MGL [1511].

[28] *Barclays Bank plc v O'Brien* [1994] 1 AC 8180, 189, Lord Browne-Wilkinson.

[29] *Barr v Union Trustee Company of Australia Ltd* [1923] VLR 236; *Lamotte v Lamotte* (1942) 42 SR (NSW) 99.

[30] *West v Public Trustee* [1942] SASR 109; *Phillips v Hutchinson* [1946] VLR 270.

[31] [1903] 1 Ch 27 (CA).

[32] (1855) 3 Drewry 306; 61 ER 920, 923.

[33] *Barclays Bank plc v O'Brien* [1994] 1 AC 180, 190, Lord Browne-Wilkinson.

presumption. Nor is the relationship of a man and a woman whom he is engaged to marry now within the class.[34]

### Class 2(B): 'the proven relationships'

[8.10] A relationship sufficient to establish the presumption of undue influence may be proven as a matter of fact. A party seeking to set aside a transaction may factually demonstrate that

- the other party assumed a position of ascendancy, power or domination over him; and/or
- he or she had taken a position of dependence or subjection in relation to that party.[35]

If the claimant establishes a relation of ascendancy or dependence successfully, that relationship is taken to be a presumptive source of influence on the impugned transaction. It is given effect in the same way as a relationship within one of the 'established categories'. The onus of proof passes to the defendant to rebut the presumption. The claimant will be able to have the transaction set aside in the absence of further proof.

[8.11] Some of the factors courts have taken to identify the influence of one party over another are as follow:

(i) the standard of intelligence and education and the character and personality of the disponor;[36]

(ii) the age, state of health, blood relationship, experience or lack of it in business affairs of the disponor;[37]

(iii) the length of friendship or acquaintance between the disponor and the disponee and the intricacy of their business affairs;[38]

(iv) the relative strength of character and personality of the disponee; the period of closeness of the relationship and the opportunity afforded the disponee to influence the disponor in business affairs.[39]

This expression of the undue influence doctrine deals with a particular type of fiduciary relationship. *Facts* of the relationship are important for their ability to raise the presumption of influence. Most of the fiduciary relationships examined in this book will be inadequate for the purpose. In seeing whether relationships suggest the influence of one party over another, the courts use the concept in a new way. Liability is not imposed for the relationship's breach. Rather, the relationship presumptively identifies influence. Influenced dispositions are set aside. Undue influence, the wrong, can be proven in the absence of fiduciary relationships altogether. Influence can be demonstrated in another way.

[8.12] Inadequacy of consideration passing to the weaker party is not so much a characteristic of the present 'proven' type of fiduciary relationship as it is a consequence of the relationship. Inadequate consideration is the 'benefit'

---

[34] Cf. *Johnson v Buttress* (1936) 56 CLR 113, 134, Dixon J.

[35] *Johnson v Buttress* (1936) 56 CLR 113, 134, Dixon J; MGL [1521].

[36] *Johnson v Buttress* (1936) 56 CLR 113.

[37] *Poosathurai v Kanappa Chettiar* (1919) LR 47 Ind App 1 (PC).

[38] *Brusewitz v Brown* [1923] NZLR 1106.

[39] *Bank of New South Wales v Rogers* (1941) 65 CLR 42; *Union Fidelity Trustee Co Ltd v Gibson* [1971] VR 573.

received by a stronger party, rather than something to describe the relationship it came from. This appears from *Brusewitz v Brown*.[40] Brusewitz was 66 years of age and dying of alcoholism, separated from his wife and boarding in a hotel. He entered a contract to dispose of almost all of his property to Brown, the companion who drank with him every day. The consideration Brusewitz received from Brown was a small annuity, both insufficient for his daily purposes and such as to deprive his wife of all inheritance on his death. Salmon J noted the inequality of the exchange, but ignored it when assessing the facts leading to the presumptive relationship of 'confidence and influence'. Brown, he found, was a retired jeweller who did not entirely share Brusewitz's drunken habits. Brown performed minor offices for Brusewitz and secured his trust over several years. It was obvious by the time of the contract that Brusewitz did not have long to live. In fact he died four months later. Salmon J said:

> The mere fact that a transaction is based on an inadequate consideration or is otherwise improvident, unreasonable or unjust is not in itself any ground on which this Court can set it aside as invalid. Nor is such a circumstances in itself even a sufficient ground for a presumption that the transaction was the result of . . . undue influence.

The stronger party's benefit, the absence or inadequacy of consideration for the transfer of the property, had to be combined with what Salmon J described as a 'special relation of confidence, control, domination, influence, or other form of superiority' before the law would presume that something unconscientious had occurred.

**[8.13]**     The banker and customer relationship in Australia has generally not been interpreted as suppling the basis for an undue influence claim. We noted this at [3.110]. This is despite the relationship being treated as fiduciary in the confidential sense.

One of the few Australian cases where undue influence has been argued was in *James v Australia and New Zealand Banking Group Ltd*.[41] The Federal Court was there concerned with the financial demise of a long-established farming family in Western Australia. The bank's obtaining by undue influence was pleaded in the alternative to its breach of fiduciary duty. Undue influence was said to be constituted by the bank's exploitation of an inequality of bargaining power. This was done so that the bank could obtain an advantage for itself in the form of a high-earning loan facility supported by substantial securities. At the same time the bank was said to have knowledge that the customers had no alternative source of finance and were in jeopardy of defaulting under a contract to purchase farming land. It appeared that the customers were unhappy about their need to find a great deal of money quickly. On account of their market disadvantage, one could say, the customers were obliged to accept unfavourable borrowing terms. Toohey J disallowed their claim (at 390), finding that the bank was itself 'a reluctant lender' to these troublesome customers. Also, the finance package offered was not

---

[40] [1923] NZLR 1106, Salmon J.

[41] (1986) 64 ALR 347, 388–91, Toohey J; also *Nobile v National Australia Bank Ltd* (1987) ASC ¶55-580.

unreasonable in the circumstances. No unduly influencing wrong could be spelt out of this ordinary commercial dealing.

## Rebutting the presumption

[8.14]   The party who seeks to uphold a presumptively influenced transaction bears the burden of proof in denying either that the influence existed, or that it had the presumed effect. Inducements which led the weaker party to the deal must be justified separately. Dixon J said in *Johnson v Buttress*[42] that the stronger party must 'satisfy the court' both that no advantage was taken of the weaker party and that the allegedly influenced behaviour was—

the independent and well understood act of a man in a position to exercise a free judgment based on information as full as that of [the stronger party].

This gives the stronger party an almost impossible task. Another party's independence of mind and freedom of judgment are matters which the court may infer, but a litigant can scarcely prove. In a commercial context the question is slightly different. Commerce concerns reciprocal, rather than voluntary behaviour. Fairness of exchange, we saw, rather than the freedom of judgment is the yardstick by which a business transaction must be assessed. The presumption of undue influence in a commercial case is rebutted if the stronger party proves that the dealing was at arm's length and that the other's will was not overborne by a preceding fiduciary relationship.[43] This is one way of expressing fairness. It avoids making any finding about the motives which inspired the transaction. Motives are much more important when gifts and voluntary settlements are impugned. When undue influence arises in commerce, motives are almost irrelevant. Or, at least, they are an assumed and non-reviewable aspect of commercial interaction. Courts dealing with commercial undue influence intervene when a transaction is unfair. The fact that a transaction is inexplicable by ordinary commercial motives suggests that some unfairness has been practised. But it is not an impropriety in itself. Instead, commercial unfairness has its own indicia.

[8.15]   Inadequacy of consideration is associated with unfairness in commercial dealings, as we noted at [8.3]. It is almost an assumed fact in this sort of case. There is little point in alleging commercial undue influence, usually, if the price is fair. *Westmelton (Vic) Pty Ltd (rec app) v Archer and Schulman*[44] was one of the few cases where the stronger party, a firm of solicitors, managed to justify the consideration exchanged in a presumed transaction. The claimant was a client of the firm, a property developer. An 'established' presumption of undue influence was held to arise in relation to a dealing between the firm and its client. In lieu of outstanding professional fees, the firm agreed to take a share of the developer's profits. Seven and a half per cent of the project was exchanged for $10,000 in overdue fees. At 319 the court noted that to the 'hard headed businessmen' involved, this was

---

[42] (1936) 56 CLR 113, 134.

[43] *Westmelton (Vic) Pty Ltd (rec app) v Archer and Schulman* [1982] VR 305, 312–13 (FC).

[44] [1982] VR 305 (FC); also *Blaikie v Clark* (1852) 22 LJ (Eq) 377, 384, Romilly MR and *Berk v Permanent Trustee Co of NSW Ltd* (1947) 47 SR (NSW) 459.

not unfair. *Wright v Carter*[45] typifies the more normal situation. The solicitor there failed to justify the sale and it was set aside, when both insufficient consideration and lack of independent advice were asserted.

**[8.16]**  The presence of independent advice is a factor more commonly argued in the rebuttal of presumptions. Independent advice arguably removes the weaker party from the 'suspected atmosphere' of an influencing relationship. Misapprehensions may be counterbalanced by an 'independent mind' directed to the subject.[46] A solicitor, briefed separately, is the usual person whose advice is used to rebut the presumption. The absence of this sort of independent advice was the primary reason why the singer's management agreements were set aside in *O'Sullivan v Management Agency and Music Ltd*.[47] The claimant entered into undertakings designed to last for several years when he was a young and unknown musician. Some time later, and after efforts of the manager, the claimant became a considerable commercial success. Yet the claimant was successful in having the agreements set aside. They were, the claimant alleged, on disadvantageous terms and he did not have independent advice when he agreed. Dunn LJ concluded (at 448) that—

> [the managers] knew that it would be unjust and unfair to expect O'Sullivan to know where his best interests lay without independent legal and professional advice. They did not advise him to seek such advice because they knew that they would not have been able to tie O'Sullivan to their organisation and get his services on such bargain basement terms if they had.

## THIRD PARTIES

**[8.17]**  A party may have unduly influenced another (or be presumed to have done so) and not obtain any or all of the benefit thereby. The benefit may pass instead to a third party. Where this occurs, an equity which the influenced party obtains against the influencer can in some circumstances be enforced against the benefiting third party. On first principles, the 'bona fide purchaser for value without notice' defence comes into question. An interest in the influencer's benefit purchased by a third party who can assert the defence has priority over the equitable claims of the influenced party.[48] Third party liability is in this way described by the availability of the defence. Given that third parties in commerce are almost always purchasers for value and given that we will only deal with third parties who are in good faith, only notice is left outstanding. Whether the third party is affected by an equity directs attention to this element of the defence. Did the third party have any notice of what went on? Did that notice extend to particulars of what the undue influencer did, or the constituents of the presumption against him?

**[8.18]**  The usual type of third party in undue influence cases is a bank, or other lending institution. A guarantee or other security is taken by the lender from a party who is subjected to undue influence (or who can raise the

---

[45] [1903] 1 Ch 27 (CA), applying *Tomson v Judge* (1855) 3 Drewry 306; 61 ER 920; also *Phillips v Hutchinson* [1946] VLR 270.

[46] *Re Coomber* [1911] 1 Ch 723, 730, Fletcher Moulton LJ (CA).

[47] [1985] 1 QB 428 (CA).

[48] See *Barclays Bank plc v O'Brien* [1994] 1 AC 180, 195–6, Lord Browne-Wilkinson and discussion in N Chin 'Undue Influence and Third Parties' (1992) 5 *Jo of Contract Law* 108, 116–20.

presumption). The equity arising will affect the lender if the 'bona fide purchaser' defence cannot be raised. Notice may be actual or constructive, as in a conveyancing transaction.[49] The 'rule' stated by Dixon J in *Yerkey v Jones*,[50] is—

> that where there is a relation of influence and the dominant party is the person by or through whom an instrument operating to his advantage is obtained from the other, the instrument is voidable even against strangers who have become parties to the instrument for value if they had notice of the existence of the relation of influence or of the circumstances giving rise to it.

In terms of our analysis, the permutations of disqualifying notice include actual or constructive notice of the constituent facts of either class 1 or class 2 claims. The notice must be of undue influence in fact, or it must be of the circumstances from which the presumption of undue influence is said to arise.[51] Actual notice needs little elucidation, apart from 'imputed' knowledge which we deal with as 'agency theory' below. Constructive notice includes what a party did not have notice of in fact, but would have reached that party's attention had all proper inquiries been made. What are 'proper inquiries' is something affected by the existence of exceptional and suspicious facts that should attract attention.[52]

**[8.19]**   *Bank of New South Wales v Rogers*[53] was a presumed influence case which based the third party's liability on notice. It concerned a transaction which occurred between a spinster aged 64 and the 88-year-old uncle with whom she lived. The uncle induced his niece to give the bank a charge over nearly all her property in order to secure his overdraft. Starke J (at 52)– described the niece as

> an intelligent woman with a will of her own, not an aggressive woman, or one who yielded too easily, but in matters of business she relied upon and followed her uncle's advice without question.

He went on to say that there could be 'no doubt' that—

> [the uncle] stood in *loco parentis* towards [the niece], and therefore in the special class of relationship from which undue influence is presumed until rebutted.

A presumption arising from an established category was therefore made out. Justice McTiernan at 70–1 examined what the bank knew or could be taken to know of the circumstances in which the presumption arose. The bank, he said, through its manager, was aware that the niece lived with her uncle and that she frequently gave him her cheques. The bank was also aware that the security provided by the niece would probably never be redeemed. For the uncle's affairs were in a parlous state. All this, he said, was enough to put the bank on inquiry. If the manager had thought about the matter at all, he must have realised that the niece was not acting prudently.

---

[49]  A J Duggan *A Financier's Guide to the Law of Guarantee in Australia* 3rd ed (1994), 30–1; MGL [1530].
[50]  (1939) 63 CLR 649, 677.
[51]  *Bank of Credit & Commerce International SA v Aboody* [1900] 1 QB 923, 975 (CA).
[52]  *Bank of New South Wales v Rogers* (1941) 65 CLR 42, 64, McTiernan J and [7.28] above.
[53]  (1941) 65 CLR 42.

There were strong grounds for suspecting that there was some special or peculiar relation between [the uncle] and [the niece] which enabled him to dominate her will, and also that she had no independent advice.

**[8.20]**  The House of Lords approach in *CIBC Mortgages plc v Pitt*[54] was not dissimilar, although a different outcome was reached. *Pitt* concerned actual undue influence exercised by a husband over his wife. Mr and Mrs Pitt jointly owned a house in London. It was encumbered by a small mortgage. The husband wanted a 'better standard of living for them both' and thought that he could provide this through speculation on the stock market. For the purpose of funding his plan he put pressure on the wife to execute a large mortgage over the house. An application for finance made to CIBC falsely stated that the purpose of the loan was long-term financing for a holiday home. CIBC made the appropriate checks of the couple's joint income and approved the loan applied for. All went well for Mr Pitt for a time. He became a millionaire on paper. To maximise his gains he mortgaged the securities he had purchased and, in consequence, owed a lot of money at the time of the 1987 stockmarket crash. All the securities were then sold and the Pitts could not even afford to pay interest on the CIBC loan. So CIBC commenced an action to realise its security over the house. Mrs Pitt established in those proceedings that her husband's pressure concerning the transaction was a species of actual undue influence practised upon her. She argued that CIBC should be affected by it. Lord Browne-Wilkinson, at 211, with the agreement of the other Law Lords, confirmed that the bank had no actual or constructive notice of any irregularity which would put them on inquiry. The bank had no reason to believe other than that this was a normal borrowing for the couple's joint benefit. Given the appearance of mutual benefit in the loan application that the bank had received, to expect inquiry about the husband's importunity would be unreasonable.

**[8.21]**  Principles expressed in *Barclays Bank plc v O'Brien*[55] and the decision in *CIBC Mortgages plc v Pitt*[56] represent the current state of authority in the United Kingdom in the bank guarantee cases. In the preceding eight years, it was noted in *Barclays*, there had been 11 reported decisions of the Court of Appeal on the subject. In the *Barclays* formulation, a financier holds its contractual rights against the guarantor subject to notice of any equity that the guarantor may have against the debtor to set the transaction aside. This is a refinement of the approach of the High Court in *Bank of New South Wales v Rogers*,[57] though analytical problems may still exist. Browne-Wilkinson developed a 'right to set aside the transaction against the husband', which was asserted in *Turnbull & Co v Duvall*,[58] into the prima facie right of a wife to set aside the transaction against the bank. In *Barclays*, the contract was a mortgage charge given to the bank by the husband and wife jointly. Browne-Wilkinson said at 191 that the bank became subject to the wife's right to set that transaction aside when it acquired notice of the husband's equitable delinquency. The judgment does not really explain how the wife's rights

---

[54] [1994] 1 AC 200.
[55] [1994] 1 AC 180, 191, Lord Browne-Wilkinson.
[56] [1994] 1 AC 200, 210–1, Lord Browne-Wilkinson.
[57] (1941) 65 CLR 42.
[58] [1902] AC 429.

against a co-disponor can set the transaction aside against the disponee.[59]

Two alternative 'theories' to determine the bank guarantee cases were discussed and discarded in *Barclays Bank plc v O'Brien*. The first was 'agency theory'. A person who procures the surety's liability is treated as agent of the third party creditor, so that knowledge of the agent is imputed to the third party. Such an agent might be an independent adviser employed by the third party,[60] or a debtor to whom the third party has entrusted the procurement of the surety's execution of the guarantee instrument.[61] At 194 this was seen to involve an unnecessary fiction. Agency doctrine implies the principal's vicarious liability and is an idea which has no resonance in equity. The other theory was 'an invalidating tendency'. This is still the subject of High Court authority in Australia and has not been overruled. For that reason, it justifies separate treatment.

## An 'invalidating tendency'

[8.22] In a judgment which has been questioned in modern times,[62] Dixon J in *Yerkey v Jones*[63] held that three equitable presumptions of an 'invalidating tendency' existed in parallel to undue influence. The important one for present purposes arose where the wife's confidence in her husband gave him opportunities of 'unfairly or improperly procuring her to become surety'. A husband, in that case, entered a contract to purchase a poultry farm. One of the conditions of this was that he would procure a mortgage of his wife's property in favour of the vendor. A solicitor was employed and it was found that he explained the mortgage transaction to the wife in an adequate way. It was also found that the husband did not exercise any undue influence over his wife. Nor, in the circumstances, could he be presumed to have done so. Nevertheless, the woman gave evidence that she failed to comprehend the transaction at the time she agreed. Dixon J examined whether an equity in her favour could still arise. Even if no 'established' presumption of undue influence existed between husbands and wives, Dixon J said (at 674),

> courts of equity examine every transaction between husband and wife with an anxious watchfulness and caution, and dread of undue influence.

Dixon J extolled the matrimonial state and outlined what was said to inspire the tendencies at 675–6. The second tendency was that strangers who dealt with the wife through the husband, in transactions to the husband's advantage, might by that fact alone be affected with any equity as between the husband and the wife arising from his conduct. This articulates the link we observed to be missing from *Barclays Bank plc v O'Brien*.[64] The third tendency concerns voluntary dealings by the wife to the husband's advantage, like signing guarantees for his companies. Such guarantees must be adequately understood

---

[59] See discussion in J Cartwright *Unequal Bargaining* (1991), 188–92.
[60] *Bank of Credit & Commerce International SA v Aboody* [1990] 1 QB 923 (CA).
[61] *Coldunell Ltd v Gallon* [1986] 1 QB 1184 (CA).
[62] Eg, *Warburton v Whiteley* (1989) NSW Conv R 55-453, Clarke JA esp. (SC (NSW) (FC)); *European Asian of Australia Pty Ltd v Kurland* (1985) 8 NSWLR 192, 200; N Chin 'Undue Influence and Third Parties' (1992) 5 Jo of *Contract Law* 108, 123–5; L Gerathy 'Yerkey v Jones Revisited' [1993] 2 *Commercial Law Quarterly* 16, 19.
[63] (1939) 63 CLR 649, 675.
[64] [1994] 1 AC 180: see [8.21].

by the wife in order to be enforceable. The idea behind this was associated by
Dixon J with the Australian case of *Bank of Victoria Ltd v Mueller*.[65] A
doctrine was stated there for cases where the wife's consent to become a surety
for her husband's debt was procured by the husband. If the wife executed a
guarantee without sufficient understanding and the creditor accepted it without
ever dealing with her directly, then she possessed a prima facie right to have
the instrument set aside.

[8.23]  Dixon J's *Yerkey* formulation may be a little problematic in a sexually
liberated age. The 'apparent concern' of Dixon's view, says one commentator,
'is to encourage women's selflessness in marital relationships rather than to
promote equality'.[66] Lord Browne-Wilkinson in *Barclays Bank plc v O'Brien*[67]
was careful to incorporate gender-neutrality in his undue influence
formulation. 'Cohabitation', he said, was the relationship which needed
protection. This could be married or unmarried, heterosexual or homosexual.
'Tenderness' of the law was not now to be based on wedding ceremonies. But
at 196 he expressed the 'reasonable steps which a creditor should take if it is
not to have notice of the wife's rights' in quite a gender-specific way. It was
some contrast and may have been called for because it was in a part of his
judgment where juristic categories and not generalities were used. Sixty years
after it was decided, *Yerkey* is still being discussed . Doubtless this is because
of the juristic precision with which the tripartite rights and liabilities are
described. Precision of this kind is unattainable where a class of 'cohabitees'
is concerned. Rights of cohabitees are various, context-specific and uncertain.
This is in large part because the rights do not proceed from an 'act in law',
like a marriage ceremony. Kirby P said in *Warburton v Whiteley*[68] that 'the
law has moved to a higher level of abstraction' since the *Yerkey* decision. A
'more appropriate, modern and satisfactory' general principle, he thought,
arose from the decision in *Commercial Bank of Australia Ltd v Amadio*.[69] To
this we shall now turn.

## Unconscionable dealing or undue influence?

[8.24]  Although there has been a proliferation of cases where guarantors
assert equities to avoid finance liabilities, there has been virtually no recent
Australian decision where 'undue influence' was the dominant legal category.
The equitable doctrine of 'unconscionable dealing' seems to have supplanted
it. Third party liability is replaced by the idea that a financier may do an
actionable wrong itself by proceeding with a transaction that it knows has been
vitiated by another's wrong.[70] One party may, it is said, 'unconscientiously
take advantage' of the opportunity presented by another party, who contracts
with the former whilst being at a 'special disadvantage', defined in various
ways. *Commercial Bank of Australia Ltd v Amadio*[71] is the locus classicus of

---

[65] [1925] VLR 642, 656, Cussen J.

[66] D Otto 'A Barren Future? Equity's Conscience and Women's Inequality' (1992) 18 *MULR* 808,
819.

[67] [1994] 1 AC 180, 198.

[68] (1989) NSW Conv R 55-453, 58,287.

[69] (1983) 151 CLR 447.

[70] A J Duggan *A Financier's Guide to the Law of Guarantee in Australia* 3rd ed (1994), 31.

[71] (1983) 151 CLR 447.

this theory, when applied to bank guarantee facts. Two elderly migrant farmers there, a husband and wife, were improperly persuaded by their son to give security for his company overdraft. The impropriety itself, if not the likelihood of it, should have been evident to the manager who dealt with the couple on behalf of the bank. At that time, Mason J said at 467–8, the manager should have made certain disclosures to them and required that the Amadios obtain independent advice. Entering the transaction in the absence of these things, the bank was held to have dealt unconscionably.

One salient point about the *Amadio* facts should be noted. The case was eminently suited to the making of an undue influence claim. Indeed, such a claim appeared in the plaintiffs' pleadings. As an alternative to unconscionable conduct, undue influence was alleged on the part of the bank. However there was no allegation that the bank was implicated in the undue influence as a third party. Mason J said of this (at 464) that–

> it is to be hoped that [the Amadios'] statement of claim does not find its way into the precedent books.

On the pleadings, the bank could not be affected by any notice of undue influence on the part of the son. Its manager, as it happened, was found to have this notice. Only an unconscionability claim could exploit the fact. A pleader's mistake may have directed the formation of Australian doctrine which has followed in look-alike ways. The United Kingdom, it should be borne in mind, has experienced very similar difficulties with spousal bank guarantees to those in Australia. It must be doubted whether there is any substantial difference in outcome between the undue influence and unconscionable dealing approaches to the problem. The same social policies contend. Recently stated by Lord Browne-Wilkinson, these are the need to legally protect the many wives who are still subject to their husband's wrongful persuasions, whilst not hindering business access to 'the high proportion of private wealth invested in the private home'.[72]

# Remedies

[8.25] Rescission of influenced transactions is the primary remedy for undue influence. It is of nature equitable. As we noted at [8.17], the remedy cannot be effective against the holder of a legal interest who is a bona fide purchaser without notice. This is the main thing which defines the liability of third parties. Most influencers, by contrast, have notice of the wrong they perpetrate.

Rescission is where a transaction is set aside. A condition of the remedy's availability is that the parties to a transaction can be restored to their pre-transactional positions. Equity does not enforce this too strictly. Even where it is impossible to place the parties in the positions they were in prior to their entering the influenced transaction, equity may still order rescission. *O'Sullivan v Management Agency & Music Ltd*[73] held that the remedy was available where 'practical justice' could still be done. The influencer, it was said, should be ordered to give up advantages that he obtained and also be compensated for all work performed. On the basis of 'reasonable remuneration

---

[72] *Barclays Bank plc v O'Brien* [1994] 1 AC 180, 188.
[73] [1985] QB 428, 458, Dunn LJ, (CA).

including a profit component', it was held appropriate to rescind a singer's management agreement and redistribute profits earned over several years.

Beyond rescission and account, it is not clear what other undue influence remedies there are. Compensation would seem available on the general grounds mentioned at [6.118]–[6.119]. Restitutionary proprietary remedies of the type discussed by Lord Musthill in *Re Goldcorp Exchange Ltd (in rec)*[74] are potentially available, although the question is untried. A successful assertion of the undue influence equity confers, on a traditional classification, only a right to have a transaction set aside. Such equities have been postponed to nearly all other equitable claims, according to the reasoning in *Phillips v Phillips*,[75] followed in *Latec Investments Ltd v Hotel Terrigal Pty Ltd (in liq)*.[76]

---

[74] [1994] 2 All ER 806, 823–9 (PC).
[75] (1861) 4 De GF & J 208; 45 ER 1164.
[76] (1965) 113 CLR 265.

Part Three

# Fiduciary Relations and Confidential Information

# Chapter 9

# Breach of Confidence

**[9.1]** A person who receives information of a confidential nature from another in what the law regards as circumstances of confidence may not make unauthorised use of that information.[1] In equity and at common law, the recipients of confidential information are restricted in what use they can make of it. We shall call the recipient of confidences 'the confidant' and the person who claims protection, 'the confider', although there has sometimes been no 'confiding' and the information was obtained by eavesdropping,[2] or theft.[3]

Almost any variety of technical or commercial information in any form can be protected if it is identifiable, secret and the requirements of contract law and/or the principles of equity are met. Contract and equity are the two main regimes for the protection of confidential information.[4] Equitable remedies predominate for both. Injunctions are the most common remedy for enforcement of a right of confidentiality. This is even where the right arises from agreement. For breach of a specifically equitable duty, the whole body of equitable restitutionary relief is available. This includes the constructive trust, accounts of profit and equitable damages. Some courts and commentators have been led to predict a jurisdictional coalescence in the area of breach of confidence.[5] Essentially, it is said, the same remedies are sought for the same wrongs and the only difference is in how the claims originated.

## Contractual confidentiality: express and implied terms

**[9.2]** An obligation not to use or disclose confidences may be expressly agreed. Patent or trade mark licences and agreements relating to 'know-how' and trade secrets often have terms to this effect. Confidentiality stipulations may also appear in employment agreements, sometimes in combination with provisions in restraint of trade and against employment by competitors. In

---

[1] See Ricketson chapters 43–5; Gurry passim; MGL chapter 41; Finn *Fiduciaries* chapter 19.

[2] Eg, *Francome v Mirror Group Newspapers Ltd* [1984] 2 All ER 408; *E I duPont deNemours & Co Inc v Rolfe Christopher* 431 F 2d 1012 (1970): see [9.17].

[3] Eg, *Franklin v Giddins* [1978] Qd R 72: see [9.17].

[4] And see P North 'Breach of Confidence—Is there a new Tort?' [1972–3] *JSPTL* 149; Gurry 46–56, Ricketson 852–5.

[5] Eg, F Gurry 'Breach of Confidence' in Finn *Equity* 110, 113–15.

*Wright v Gasweld Pty Ltd*[6] an employee of a hardware importing firm was obliged to enter a restraint of trade agreement as a condition of being allowed to undertake a business trip to visit his employer's Taiwanese suppliers. He agreed with the company that he would not disclose or use any information obtained during the course of employment concerning who those suppliers were. After the employment later terminated, the company obtained an injunction to prevent its former employee from using the same Taiwanese suppliers in his own business.

**[9.3]**    An obligation of confidence may alternatively be implied into contracts between persons between whom confidential information passes. Confidentiality stipulations must be 'reasonable and equitable' and 'necessary' for reasons of business efficacy.[7] Implied terms of confidentiality are sometimes upheld in sub-contract agreements. Information about a process, idea or design may have been communicated in order to describe a sub-contracted task. In *Mense and Ampere Electrical Manufacturing Co Pty Ltd v Milenkovic*[8] the plaintiff was a plastics manufacturer. It confided information concerning a specially designed die, pursuant to an oral request that the confidant manufacture an accessory to it. An enforceable obligation prohibiting the defendant's misuse of the die information was derived from a term implied in this arrangement. Obligations of confidence may also be implied into contracts of employment, though enforceability of these terms is complicated by the common law restrictions on restraint of trade. *Faccenda Chicken Ltd v Fowler*[9] involved an employer's breach of confidence claim based on an implied term. A man who had been employed to deliver refrigerated chickens was held to come under a duty of confidence which outlasted the continuance of his employment. He had learned the identities and requirements of his employer's customers. An injunction was obtained to restrain the ex-employee from supplying those customers on his own account.

## The equitable obligation

**[9.4]**    There is a principle of equity, apart from contracts, that a court will 'restrain the publication of confidential information improperly or surreptitiously obtained or of information imparted in confidence which ought not to be divulged.'[10] In either its general law or codified[11] forms, the principle

---

[6]  (1991) 22 NSWLR 317, 337, Kirby P, 339, Samuels JA (Gleeson JA dissenting) (CA); see also *Commercial Plastics Ltd v Vincent* [1965] 1 QB 623 (CA) and *Mainmet Holdings plc v Austin* [1991] FSR 538.

[7]  *United States Surgical Corporation v Hospital Products International Pty Ltd* [1983] 2 NSWLR 157 (CA), 196 curiam; *Saltman Engineering Co Ltd v Campbell Engineering Co Ltd* (1948) 65 RPC 203 (CA), 211, Greene MR, Somervell and Cohen LJJ agreeing.

[8]  [1973] VR 784, 801, McInerney J and see *Deta Nominees Pty Ltd v Viscount Plastic Industries Pty Ltd* [1979] VR 167.

[9]  [1987] Ch 117 (CA) and see *Robb v Green* [1895] 2 QB 315 (CA), *Amber Size Chemical Co Ltd v Menzel* [1913] 2 Ch 239, *Ormonoid Roofing and Asphalts Ltd v Bitumenoids Ltd* (1930) 31 SR (NSW) 347 and *Schindler Lifts Australia Pty Ltd v Debelak* (1989) 15 IPR 129; cf *Pacifica Shipping Co Ltd v Anderson* [1986] 2 NZLR 328, 342.

[10]  *Commonwealth of Australia v John Fairfax & Sons Ltd* (1980) 147 CLR 39, 50, Mason J, adopting the words of Swinfen Eady LJ in *Ashburton v Pape* [1913] 2 Ch 469, 475.

[11]  Under the Corporations Law s 232(5), where corporate officers or employees acquire the information by virtue of their positions: examined in *Rosetex Co Pty Ltd v Licata* (1994) 12 ACSR 779, 793–4, Young J (SC (NSW)).

will protect confidential information in many situations beyond the reach of the contract. This may be where information is communicated confidentially during negotiations for a contract which never eventuates. 'Concept' cases like *Talbot v General Television Corporation Pty Ltd*[12] are an instance. Talbot was a film producer who conceived of a series of television programmes to be entitled 'To Make a Million'. In the course of negotiations with the defendant Channel 9 Network with a view to sale of the programmes, the producer disclosed most of his production concept. Several months elapsed and no agreement was reached. When the network later advertised its intention to broadcast a similar programme without reference to the producer, the purely equitable obligation supplied jurisdiction for an interim injunction to restrain it. No contract between the parties existed to be enforced.

In other cases, confidential information may pass from the confidant to a third party with whom the confider never intended to contract. This is the classic breach of confidence situation. Information imparted to the confidant for a specific purpose is wrongly disclosed to a third party. The third party may then use or intend to use the information to the confider's detriment, or contrary to his wishes. In *Saltman Engineering Co Ltd v Campbell Engineering Co Ltd*,[13] Saltman commissioned Campbell to manufacture certain tools to be used in repetition engineering. Design drawings were supplied to Campbell for the purpose. Campbell did not do the work itself, but employed a subcontractor. The subcontractor used the drawings for its own purposes, despite being aware that the drawings had been supplied by Saltman only to enable the tools to be manufactured. On the basis of this knowledge on the part of the subcontractor, the Court of Appeal was prepared to find that it was bound by an equitable duty to respect Saltman's confidentiality in the drawings.

**[9.5]** *Attorney-General (UK) v Observer Ltd*[14] contained a very broad statement of this equitable duty by Lord Goff. It arose, he said, where confidants had simply had notice that the information was confidential, combined with the fact that it would be just to prevent them from disclosing it. Usually confidentiality arises in the course of a pre-existing transaction or relationship between the parties. The equitable obligation extends further and may come into being in the absence of such things. 'Knowledge' (or notice) of confidentiality can be inferred from the means that the defendant employed to obtain the information. Consider an Australian example. The genetic secret of an orchardist's nectarine trees was furtively removed as a tree cutting. Sufficient knowledge of a confidence and its breach was found to be disclosed.[15] Or the same knowledge might be inferred from the defendant's use or disclosure of what any reasonable man would have realised was

---

[12] [1980] VR 224 see also *Seager v Copydex Ltd* [1967] 2 All ER 415 (CA), *AB Consolidated Ltd v Europe Strength Food Co* [1978] NZLR 515 and *Lac Minerals Ltd v International Corona Resources Ltd* [1989] 2 SCR 574.

[13] (1948) 65 RPC 203, 213, Greene MR (CA); see also *Ansell Rubber Co Pty Ltd v Allied Rubber Industries Pty Ltd* [1967] VR 37; *Castrol Australia Ltd v EmTech Associates Pty Ltd* (1980) 51 FLR 184; *Smith Kline & French Laboratories (Aust) Ltd v Secretary, Department of Community Services and Health* (1990) 22 FCR 73.

[14] [1990] 1 AC 109, 281.

[15] See *Franklin v Giddins* [1978] Qd R 72.

confidential, whether he adopts reprehensible means to get the information or not.[16] To use Lord Goff's examples of this from the *Observer* case (at 281), if a folder containing obviously secret formulae is mislaid in a lift, or an obviously confidential report is wafted by electric fan out of a window and into a crowded street below, then strangers finding the information could make themselves liable to the duty.

### Should equitable principles apply to the contractual obligation?

**[9.6]**   Equitable and contractual obligations of confidence are surely different things.[17] There is no obvious reason why contract should subordinate itself to equitable requirements. Meagher, Gummow and Lehane at [4104] announce an intention to avoid this question, together with the contractual obligation of confidence and the associated jurisdiction of equity in aid of contractual rights. This is to ignore the majority of decided cases. Other writers say that with both the contractual and equitable obligations the courts are dealing with 'the same phenomenon' and 'no operative difference' exists.[18] Which is to say that subordination or assimilation is necessary.

**[9.7]**   Courts in several cases have taken the step of assimilating the contractual duty of confidence to the equitable one.[19] The contractual obligation is required to conform to the conditions applicable to the equitable duty. It is doubtful whether this is correct. No reason in principle is supplied why equity, acting in aid of contractual rights, should employ additional conditions when enforcing terms which embody confidentiality stipulations. These, like any other stipulations, may be specifically enforceable if in the appropriate form and certain enough. Equitable requirements of 'confidentiality', or what amounts to a confidence's 'use', seem analytically irrelevant to the enforcement of contractual obligations. Assimilation may also obscure substantial differences in effect. Kirby P said something to the point in *Wright v Gasweld Pty Ltd*,[20] in the course of deciding what the limits of 'confidential' should be for an expressly agreed confidentiality clause. 'With limited experience in the operation of particular businesses', he said, 'courts should give wider effect to what parties agreed to be confidential than equity acting alone'. Fullagar J in *Deta Nominees Pty Ltd v Viscount Plastic Products Pty Ltd*[21] found a remedial difference between contractual and equitable rights. He held that an injunction awarded for an employee's infringement of the

---

[16]  *Coco v A N Clark (Engineers) Ltd* [1969] RPC 41, 47–48, Megarry J.

[17]  *Deta Nominees Pty Ltd v Viscount Plastic Products Pty Ltd* [1979] VR 167, 191, Fullagar J; see also *Coco v A N Clark (Engineers) Ltd* [1969] RPC 41, 47, Megarry J, *Faccenda Chicken Ltd v Fowler* [1987] Ch 117 (CA), 135 curiam and cf *Vokes Ltd v Heather* (1945) 62 RPC 135, 141.

[18]  Finn *Fiduciaries* 166; Ricketson 814–5, Gurry 58–61 and F Gurry 'Breach of Confidence' in Finn *Equity* 110, 118; *United Sterling Corporation Ltd v Felton and Mannion* [1974] RPC 162, Brightman J.

[19]  In *Peter Pan Manufacturing Corporation v Corsets Silhouette Ltd* [1963] 3 All ER 402; *Surveys and Mining Ltd v Morison* [1969] Qd R 470; *Mense and Ampere Electrical Manufacturing Co Pty Ltd v Milenkovic* [1973] VR 784; *Conveyor Co of Australia Pty Ltd v Cameron Bros Engineering Co Ltd* [1973] 2 NZLR 38; *United Sterling Corporation Ltd v Felton and Mannion* [1974] RPC 162; *Thomas Marshall Ltd v Guinle* [1979] Ch 277 and *G D Searle & Co Ltd v Celltech Ltd* [1982] FSR 92.

[20]  (1991) 22 NSWLR 317 (CA), 333–334, 334.

[21]  [1979] VR 167, 194–196

equitable duty should be for about a year, limited by consideration of what 'commercial advantage' the plaintiff was entitled to. However, he went on to order a perpetual injunction as being appropriate to a contractual entitlement. The contractual obligation is submitted to function independently of equitable requirements.

## Constituents of an equitable claim

**[9.8]**   These are the things that the plaintiff must prove if a purely equitable claim for breach of confidence is to succeed. The absence of any contractual obligation is assumed. Gummow J in *Corrs Pavey Whiting & Byrne v Collector of Customs*[22] described a list of factors which is set out below. With the addition of the first, the list is reminiscent of the 'elements' of a breach of confidence action described by Megarry J in *Coco v A N Clark (Engineers) Ltd*[23]. The authority of the *Coco* elements has now been approved by the highest tribunals.[24]

### 1.   Information must be specific

**[9.9]**   The plaintiff in a breach of confidence action must supply a sufficiently precise definition of the information said to be confidential.[25] This sounds rather self-evident. Nevertheless it was the main reason why the plaintiff's confidential information claim failed in *O'Brien v Komesaroff*.[26] In that case a solicitor in sole practice evolved a unit trust deed and the articles of association of a trustee company. These were for use in tax minimisation schemes. The solicitor alleged that, together with preparing the documents, he orally communicated confidential information on how to evade an Act of Parliament and its regulations. The High Court held that such a claim did not particularise any information capable of being the subject of a confidence. It was too general. As Mason J said at 326–7, the plaintiff's oral communication showed only that he had exercised 'knowledge, skill and experience in a particular field', without giving the court any specifics for a confidentiality order.

### 2.   Information must be confidential

**[9.10]**   Any formula, pattern, design, or compilation of information of any kind can be the substance of confidential information which is protected in equity. There is no restriction on the mode or medium through which

---

22   (1987) 14 FCR 434, 443, citing *Saltman Engineering Co Ltd v Campbell Engineering Co* (1948) 65 RPC 203, 205; *Commonwealth v John Fairfax & Sons Ltd* (1980) 147 CLR 39, 50–51 and *O'Brien v Komesaroff* (1982) 150 CLR 310, 326–328; see also *Smith Kline & French Laboratories (Aust) Ltd v Secretary, Department of Community Services and Health* (1990) 22 FCR 73, 87.

23   [1969] RPC 41, 47–8.

24   In Australia, *Commonwealth v John Fairfax & Sons Ltd* (1980) 147 CLR 39, 51 Mason J; in the United Kingdom, *Attorney-General (UK) v Observer Ltd* [1990] 1 AC 109, 268, Lord Griffiths; in Canada, *Lac Minerals Ltd v International Corona Resources Ltd* [1989] 2 SCR 574, 611, Sopinka and McIntyre JJ, Lamer J agreeing, 635, La Forest J, Wilson J agreeing.

25   *International Writing Institute Inc v Rimla Pty Ltd* (1993) AIPC 39,736, 39,750, Lockhart J (Fed Ct); *Carindale Country Club Estate Pty Ltd v Astill* (1993) 115 ALR 112, 120–1, Drummond J (Fed Ct); *Independent Management Resources Pty Ltd v Brown* [1987] VR 605, 609.

26   (1982) 150 CLR 310

protectable information can be conveyed. Information may be placed in a permanent or oral form.[27] It may be expressed by words or diagrams.[28] It may appear from photographs,[29] the design of a product,[30] or the genetic structure of a tree.[31] The necessary 'quality of confidence' in information protected is sometimes a novel combination of commonplace or well known things. No intrinsic secrecy in the information is required before protection is given. A protectable confidence is pitched well short of the 'inventive step' required for a patent.[32] It has been said that the information itself need not be secret at all, so long as it tends to reveal something of a confidential nature. In *Falconer v Australian Broadcasting Corporation*[33] some legitimately obtained photographs were held to be confidential, as they tended to reveal the identity of police informers. Confidential information in commerce includes the following types.

### 'Profit-making ideas'

**[9.11]** Such things might be a questionnaire and other documents submitted in the form of a tender for a survey of solicitors' firms;[34] the concept of a television series to be entitled 'To Make a Million', with a pilot script for one programme;[35] the idea of how to manufacture a type of plastic furniture from known processes;[36] the uses of hydraulic pressure control valves in gymnasium equipment;[37] or the identity of Taiwanese suppliers of a hardware importing firm.[38] What is protected is the entitlement to make a profit from an idea. Nothing specially secret needs to inhere in the idea, just the value of labour, time, effort and skill spent in its derivation. Ideas may be embodied in things tangible or intangible. They can be in letter form, or in discussions, or in the design of a chattel manufactured.[39] Confidential information of this 'profit-making' type will give its possessors an advantage over competitors who do not possess it. The task of the courts is to recognise and protect that advantage. A gain to the confidant from breaching this type of confidence often correlates with a market loss to the confider. The court's consultation of hypothetical market forces enables a figure to be put on the value of the breach and restitution by way of money order.

---

[27] See *Seager v Copydex Ltd* [1967] 2 All ER 415 (CA).

[28] See *Fractionated Cane Technology Ltd v Ruiz-Avila* [1988] 1 Qd R 51; *Saltman Engineering Co Ltd v Campbell Engineering Co Ltd* (1948) 65 RPC 203 (CA).

[29] See *Pollard v Photograph Co* (1889) 40 Ch D 345.

[30] See *Ansell Rubber Co Pty Ltd v Allied Rubber Industries Pty Ltd* [1967] VR 37.

[31] See *Franklin v Giddins* [1978] Qd R 72.

[32] *Mense and Ampere Electrical Manufacturing Co Pty Ltd v Milenkovic* [1973] VR 784, 799, McInerney J.

[33] [1992] 1 VR 662.

[34] *Interfirm Comparison (Australia) Pty Ltd v Law Society of New South Wales* (1975) 5 ALR 527.

[35] *Talbot v General Television Corporation Pty Ltd* [1980] VR 224.

[36] *Deta Nominees Pty Ltd v Viscount Plastic Products Pty Ltd* [1979] VR 167.

[37] *Titan Group Pty Ltd v Steriline Manufacturing Pty Ltd* (1990) 19 IPR 353, 379, O'Loughlin J (Fed Ct).

[38] *Wright v Gasweld Pty Ltd* (1991) 22 NSWLR 317 (CA)

[39] F Gurry 'Breach of Confidence' in Finn *Equity* 110, 116.

## 'Harmful' confidences

**[9.12]** An example of this is where the defendant discloses, or threatens to disclose, some compromising information about the claimant.[40] It does not matter that the information is also available in fragmented form from a series of obscure public sources. The information in its disclosed form must be economically deleterious to the confider if disclosed. Breach of a confidence of this type may bring commercial loss to the confider unmatched by a gain to the confidant. For example, the disclosure of product flaws to consumers, or of competitive weaknesses to firms that compete, has a very indirect relation to the discloser's gain. There is, compared to the 'profit-making idea', a notable lack of restitutionary correspondence between the value of what is taken and the value of what is wrongfully used. Nor, often, will any measure of a compensatory remedy apply, so that relief by way of money orders will usually be inappropriate. Equity protects confidences here not so much to reverse gains, or redistribute losses, as to vindicate rights. The next type of information protected may be its logical extension.

## 'Worthless' confidences

**[9.13]** Examples of these are not easy to find. Drawings for a failed pig-rearing machine were the basis of one case.[41] Neither harm to the claimant nor subtraction of any worth from him was threatened. Marketplace considerations suggest that no protectable confidence existed. The pig-rearing machine was described as 'a loss to anyone who has ever had anything to do with it'— including the confidence-breaker. Yet a confidence still existed. Equitable protection for the confidence is a legitimate exercise of the confider's rights: rights which may be exercised in such a case for some altruistic or sentimental reason.

**[9.14]** 'Secrecy' or confidentiality in a piece of commercial information must involve its being neither public knowledge, nor general knowledge within an industry or trade. 'Confidentiality' in most cases is a relative thing. It has been denied, and information treated as 'public', even though it was known only to a small group.[42] Equally, the fact that the public at large could be said to have the means of knowing certain information, or knew it in a disjointed way, has been held consistent with information remaining confidential.[43] The idea is one of accessibility. If special labours have to be performed before a member of the public can reproduce the information, then the information is likely to be confidential.[44] Design information published to the world in the form of a finished commodity can be confidential even though it could be obtained by anyone who took the trouble to 'reverse engineer' it. So in *Saltman Engineering Co Ltd v Campbell Engineering Co Ltd*,[45] Greene MR was

---

[40] *Schering Chemicals Ltd v Falkman Ltd* [1982] 1 QB 1 (CA).

[41] *Nichrotherm Electrical Co Ltd v Percy* [1956] RPC 272, 273, Harman J.

[42] *O'Brien v Komesaroff* (1982) 150 CLR 310, 326, Mason J, Murphy, Aickin, Wilson and Brennan JJ agreeing: see Finn *Fiduciaries* 146.

[43] *Schering Chemicals Ltd v Falkman Ltd* [1982] 1 QB 1 (CA) and *Robb v Green* [1895] 2 QB 1, 315 (CA).

[44] See Gurry 70–2.

[45] (1948) 65 RPC 203 (CA)

concerned with the confidentiality of machine tool drawings which could have been duplicated in this way. At 215, he said—

> No doubt, if they had taken the finished article, namely, the leather punch, which they might have bought in a shop, and given it to an expert draughtsman, that draughtsman could have produced the necessary drawings for the manufacture of the machine tools required for making that particular finished article. In at any rate a very material respect they saved themselves that trouble by obtaining the necessary information either from the original drawings or from tools made in accordance with them. That, in my opinion, was a breach of confidence.

**[9.15]**   Listed below is a set of confidentiality 'factors', contained in an American *Restatement of Torts*.[46] These are applicable to the main type of confidence, the 'profit-making idea', and exclude the 'harmful' and 'worthless' confidences. The factors emphasise the relativity of the subject. They are:

(a) the extent to which the information is known outside the claimant's business;[47]

(b) the extent to which it is known by employees and others involved in the business;[48]

(c) the extent of measures taken to guard the secrecy of the information;[49]

(d) the value of the information to the claimant and to competitors;

(e) the amount of effort and money expended in developing the information; [50] and

(f) the ease or difficulty with which the information could be properly acquired or duplicated by others.[51]

A further possibility of publication is that the wrongful confidence-breakers could, by their own wrong, take once-confidential information outside the equitable jurisdiction and into the public domain. If the confidence is of the 'profit-making idea' this should affect the remedy which it would be appropriate to order rather than the jurisdiction to make it.[52] Where it is of the other types, the matter is not clear. There is authority from the law relating to the protection of governmental confidences that governments may not be able to protect information which has passed into the public domain through the confidence-breaker's wrong.[53] This makes sense for a harmful confidence which causes no assessable loss. Otherwise, perhaps, a denial of relief should be scaled down to become the inappropriateness of an injunction. Loss is still caused by the confidence-breaker's revelations.

---

[46] The US *Restatement of Torts*, 1st (1939) 757, Comment b.

[47] See *Amway Corporation v Eurway International Ltd* [1974] RPC 82, 87, Brightman J, *Interfirm Comparison (Australia) Pty Ltd v Law Society of New South Wales* (1975) 5 ALR 527, 542–3, Bowen CJ in Eq; *O'Brien v Komesaroff* (1982) 150 CLR 310, 325–6, Mason J and *Snell v Pryce* (1989) 99 FLR 213, 218–9, Angel J (SC (NT)).

[48] See *Ansell Rubber Co Pty Ltd v Allied Rubber Industries Pty Ltd* [1967] VR 37, 40, Gowans J; *United Sterling Corporation Ltd v Felton and Mannion* [1974] RPC 162, 173, Brightman J.

[49] See Fractionated *Cane Technology Ltd v Ruiz-Avila* [1988] 1 Qd R 51, 67, McPherson J, affirmed (1988) 13 IPR 609.

[50] See *Ohio Oil Co v Sharp* 135 F 2d 303 (1943), 306, Murrah J.

[51] See *Franklin v Giddins* [1978] Qd R 72, 80, Dunn J.

[52] As in *Talbot v General Television Corporation Pty Ltd* [1980] VR 224, Harris J.

[53] *Commonwealth of Australia v Walsh* (1980) 147 CLR 61, 62, Mason J and the 'Spycatcher' cases: *Attorney-General (UK) v Heinemann Publishers Australia Pty Ltd* [1987] 8 NSWLR 341, Powell J (point considered at first instance only); *A-G (UK) v Observer Ltd* [1990] 1 AC 109, 260, Lord Keith, 267, Lord Brightman, 276–277, Lord Griffiths, 290, Lord Goff.

## 3. Circumstances importing the duty: knowledge of restrictions

**[9.16]** Equitable duties to respect the confidentiality of confidential information will be owed if confidants knew (or ought to have known) of restrictions placed on the use of the information. The restrictions are those placed by confiders, or persons in whose hands the information was originally confidential. Usually, persons who own or originate the information are the persons from whom defendants acquired it.[54] The equitable duty arises from the circumstances in which the information was received, rather than those in which it was disclosed.[55] Protected information may be deliberately confided to the defendant or a third party who reveals it.[56] Or the information may be surreptitiously acquired, or acquired serendipitously—by being picked up in the street.[57] Innocent recipients of unintended confidences can be restrained once they know (or are taken to know) that the information was originally held in confidence.[58] What matters in either case is that the defendant is treated as knowing of the restrictions placed on the use of the information.

**[9.17]** This knowledge of restrictions requirement was exemplified by the decision of the Supreme Court of Queensland in *Fractionated Cane Technology Ltd v Ruiz-Avila*.[59] An inventor of a machine designed to dehydrate sugar-cane invited a potential purchaser to see it demonstrated. Samples of the machine's product were provided. No mention of confidentiality was made. Subsequently, the purchaser patented a dehydration process similar to that in the machine. This the inventor sought to restrain. However, the inventor was unable to establish that an obligation of confidence existed in respect of the design of the machine, for he had imposed no restriction on the use of details he imparted. Such a result is to be compared with that in *Franklin v Giddins*.[60] It was another Queensland case that we have noted already. Claimants there conducted an orchard where they grew nectarines of a specially bred variety. This type of nectarine had a substantial commercial value and the plaintiffs were known to keep its genetic make-up a secret. The defendant entered the orchard by night and stole tree cuttings. It was held (at 80) that by 'unconscionable behaviour' the defendant had knowingly infringed the plaintiffs' secret. The defendant's manner of learning the information implied the guilty knowledge. So, on the one hand, the inventor's failure to make an express reservation of confidentiality was sufficient to negative the other's knowledge in *Fractionated Cane*. On the other, the employment of reprehensible means to acquire the confidential information in *Franklin v Giddins* was sufficient to show it. A significant fact about the latter case was

---

[54] See *Smith Kline & French Laboratories (Aust) Ltd v Secretary. Department of Community Services and Health* (1990) 22 FCR 73, 87, Gummow J; *Saltman Engineering Co Ltd v Campbell Engineering Co Ltd* (1948) 65 RPC 203, 213, Greene MR and MGL [4111].

[55] H Carr and R Arnold *Computer Software: Legal Protection in the United Kingdom* 2nd ed (1992), 33.

[56] *Attorney-General (UK) v Observer Ltd* [1990] 1 AC 109, 281, Lord Goff.

[57] Noted in H Carr and R Arnold *Computer Software: Legal Protection in the United Kingdom* 2nd edn (1992), 31.

[58] *Fraser v Evans* [1969] 1 QB 349, 361.

[59] [1988] 1 Qd R 51, 66 McPherson J, affirmed (1988) 13 IPR 609.

[60] [1978] Qd R 72, Dunn J; see also *E I duPont deNemours & Co Inc v Christopher* 431 F 2d 1012 (1970) and *Francome v Mirror Group Newspapers Ltd* [1984] 2 All ER 408.

that the acquirer was knowingly evading the orchardist's restrictions on publication.

### Implied restrictions

**[9.18]** It is sometimes not clear that the confider placed any restrictions on use of the information by the defendant or anyone else. Defendants will as a general rule be found liable for breach of restrictions which should have been apparent to them. Restrictions may be implied after the court has made an objective assessment of circumstances surrounding the obtaining of the information. An approach like this was taken in *Coco v A N Clark (Engineers) Ltd*,[61] concerning a confidentiality claim arising out of a course of pre-contractual negotiations. The plaintiff was the designer of a moped engine who disclosed details of the engine to the defendant manufacturing company in the course of protracted negotiations for a production contract. In fact no contract resulted and the defendant proceeded to manufacture a moped with an engine of its own design. However, that engine had some features which resembled what the plaintiff had disclosed. One of the questions which arose was whether the design information was obtained in circumstances where a restriction on use was implied. Or, in other words, did the circumstances of disclosure import an obligation of confidentiality? Megarry J at 46 suggested that the matter depended on what a reasonable man standing in the defendant's shoes would have realised.

**[9.19]** *Seager v Copydex Ltd*[62] was another instance of the equitable obligation arising circumstantially. Details were volunteered in a pre-contractual setting. A manufacturer and an inventor, who was said to be 'a very difficult man to stop talking', negotiated about the right to manufacture a type of carpet grip which the inventor had devised. In the course of discussions, the inventor volunteered the details of another of his carpet grips. Negotiations eventually broke off without agreement. The manufacturer decided to make a carpet grip of its own. The grip which resulted was found at 416–17 to embody an idea that the inventor had mentioned, when talking about the other carpet grip. Both of the officers of the defendant company at the time, Denning MR said at 416, 'realised' that the information as to the other grip was 'given to them in confidence', wherefrom the restriction and obligation of confidence was implied.

### 4. Breach of duty

**[9.20]** The equitable obligation is breached by unauthorised use of the information. This includes a disclosure made contrary to the owner's restrictions. In *Saltman Engineering Co Ltd v Campbell Engineering Co Ltd*[63] the defendant was held to know that the plaintiff had given it some confidential drawings only for the purpose of making machine tools for it. When the defendant used those drawings in order to make tools for itself it breached the plaintiff's confidence. The following headings were suggested by Gurry at 256–8.

---

[61] [1969] RPC 41.

[62] [1967] 2 All ER 415 (CA).

[63] (1949) 65 RPC 203 (CA), Greene MR: above at [9.4].

*Information must be obtained from the claimant*

**[9.21]** Defendants who find confidential information through their own endeavours, by independent rediscovery, or from a public source, breach no confidence in obtaining it.[64] An instance of this is where a defendant goes to the length of 'reverse engineering' the claimant's product in order to discover its design secret. If the secret is found, it is not treated as having been obtained from the confider.[65] Endeavours to find the information have been those of the defendant. This is distinct from the defendant having mere access to the information from sources other than the confider. If defendants use the confider as their information source, a confidence may have been breached even if the defendants had access to the information from a public library.[66]

*Use or disclosure contrary to restriction*

**[9.22]** Delinquent use or disclosure is often obvious on the facts.[67] Confiders sometimes impart information to defendants for only one use. Breach occurs where the defendant is proved to put the information to another use. In *Castrol Australia Ltd v EmTech Associates Pty Ltd*[68] Castrol sent the Trade Practices Commission a confidential report by consulting engineers on a new grade of engine oil. This was so that the Commission could approve a forthcoming marketing campaign. Subsequently the Commission sought to rely on the report in order to prosecute Castrol, in connection with the same campaign. Castrol's claim that this was a breach of confidence was upheld. At 204, the relevant information was said to have been supplied for the sole purpose of having the campaign approved. Liability for making a prohibited use or disclosure is strict.[69] It is irrelevant that the defendant did not mean to infringe the claimant's rights,[70] or that he was entirely honest[71] or in good faith[72] in acting as he did. A number of authorities have held the defendant liable for 'unconscious' copying of the confider's ideas.[73]

# Defences to the claim

**[9.23]** Whether the action to protect confidential information is based on the independent action in equity, or on equitable remedies to enforce a contract

---

[64] G Jones 'Restitution of Benefits Obtained in Breach of Another's Breach of Confidence' (1970) 86 *LQR* 463, 482.

[65] *Cranleigh Precision Engineering Ltd v Bryant* [1966] RPC 81, 89–90 and see *United States Surgical Corporation v Hospital Products International Pty Ltd* [1982] 2 NSWLR 766, 776–7, McLelland J (first instance).

[66] See *Schering Chemicals Ltd v Falkman Ltd* [1982] 1 QB 1, 36, Templeman LJ (CA).

[67] Eg, in *Seager v Copydex Ltd* [1967] 2 All ER 415 (CA) and *Surveys and Mining Ltd v Morison* [1969] Qd R 470.

[68] (1980) 51 FLR 184, Rath J.

[69] See Gurry 261–6.

[70] See *Interfirm Comparison (Australia) Pty Ltd v Law Society of New South Wales* (1975) 5 ALR 527, 154, Bowen CJ in Eq.

[71] See *Seager v Copydex Ltd* [1967] 2 All ER 415.

[72] *National Broach & Machine Co v Churchill Gear Machines Ltd* [1965] RPC 61, 78, Cross J.

[73] *Talbot v General Television Corporation Pty Ltd* [1980] VR 224, 239, Harris J, affirmed by FC; *Seager v Copydex Ltd* [1967] 2 All ER 415, 417, Denning MR, 418, Salmon LJ; *Terrapin Ltd v Builders Supply Co (Hayes) Ltd* [1960] RPC 375, 390, Roxburgh J.

term, the standard equitable defences will be available. That a confider behaved improperly and consequently had 'unclean hands' is a familiar assertion.[74]

## Bona fide purchase and change of position

**[9.24]** These are related defences we examined at [7.15]–[7.21]. They mostly involve third parties. Should confiders be prevented from enforcing their rights against innocent defendants who have been deceived through the wiles of others? Defendants may have purchased the information in question by paying a large price to a confidence-breaker. This is an old problem in breach of confidence claims.[75] Helsham CJ in Eq considered the position of the bona fide purchaser in *Wheatley v Bell*.[76] A confider had conceived of a 'Teleguide' system of advertising licences, for the marketing of advertising within particular localities. He communicated the idea to the first defendant in confidence. The first defendant breached that confidence by establishing an identical system in another city. By the date of hearing, this party had sold licences in the system to various persons. The second, third and fourth defendants were licence purchasers who had paid for their licences without knowing that the first defendant had pirated the claimant's idea. Injunctions to restrain use of the 'Teleguide' concept were awarded against all defendants. Helsham CJ at 549–50 found that the bona fide purchaser defences were inefficacious to displace a non-proprietary liability of good faith. A similar equity may arise by way of 'change of position'. Defendants may not only have paid for, but also set up businesses to exploit ideas to which they are not entitled. Substantial research and development expenditure may have been incurred, or plant and machinery acquired, perhaps in an effort to improve or develop them.[77] Several learned commentators have recommended that a defence of change of position should be allowed to a breach of confidence claim.[78] Gareth Jones suggests that the idea of change of position is already pervasive in the law. This is because of the flexible nature of equitable remedies and their amenability to being moulded to the individual justice of a case. Detriment to the defendant may be valued and taken account of in the measure of relief given to the confider. Relief may even be denied if the defendant's detriment is sufficiently substantial. To allow the defence might be to explicitly recognise the remedial latitude that equity has always had.

---

[74] *Hubbard v Vosper* [1972] 2 QB 84 (CA); *Church of Scientology of California v Kaufman* [1973] RPC 627, Goff J; *Corrs Pavey Whiting & Byrne v Collector of Customs* (1987) 14 FCR 434, Gummow J 456–8 (diss) (Fed Ct (FC)).

[75] See *Morison v Moat* (1851) 9 Hare 241, 263, 68 ER 492, 501, Turner V-C; *Stephenson Jordan & Harrison Ltd v MacDonald and Evans* (1951) 68 RPC 190, 195, Lloyd-Jacob J and in *Printers and Finishers Ltd v Holloway* [1965] RPC 239, 253, Cross J and see G Jones 'Restitution of Benefits Obtained in Breach of Another's Confidence' (1970) 86 *LQR* 463, 478–9.

[76] [1982] 2 NSWLR 544.

[77] American Law Institute *Restatement of the Law of Torts* 1st edn (1939), §758 'Comment' at 22; G Jones 'Restitution of Benefits Obtained in Breach of Another's Confidence' (1970) 86 *LQR* 463, 477–8.

[78] Eg., the Reporters for the American Law Institute *Restatement of the Law of Torts* 1st edn (1939), §758(b); G Jones 'Restitution of Benefits Obtained in Breach of Another's Confidence' (1970) 86 *LQR* 463, 477–478; J Stuckey 'The Liability of Innocent Third Parties Implicated in Another's Breach of Confidence' (1981) 4 *UNSWLJ* 73, 77–9.

**'Public interest'**

**[9.25]** This is an umbrella term for policy limitations on the duty. Public interests are normally in favour of maintaining commercial confidences.[79] Secrecy serves socially useful ends. Confidentiality is an incentive to invention. Protectable relationships of 'trust and confidence' may involve secret information. At the same time, 'the public interest' has been said to 'define the content' of the confidences which can be subject to enforceable obligations.[80] Or 'public interest' is a named exception to what can be an equitably protected confidence.[81] To the extent that the conduct of the confider is involved in the public interest defence, the idea may be no more than a restatement of the old 'unclean hands' defence by another name.[82] But categories of the public law lie unhappily beside equitable rights. 'Public interest' may be too blunt an instrument with which to regulate assertion of a private right. The expression 'disclosure in the public interest' shall be understood here as a reference to the following sanctioned disclosures.

**[9.26]** A disclosure may excusably 'uncover crimes, frauds and misdeeds', as Denning MR said in *Initial Services Ltd v Putterill*.[83] That was a case concerning an ex-employee's alleged breach of a contractual obligation of confidence through disclosure of his employer's breach of the Restrictive Trade Practices Act 1956 (UK). Disclosure was justified because it disclosed his former employer's false attribution of price rises to a tax increase. Disclosure of a crime is an even stronger case.[84] Authority conflicts, though, on whether this extends to a *past* crime, as equally to a prospective wrong which disclosure might avert.[85] Disclosure cannot be allowed to perpetuate a private grievance, as Gurry says at p 334. The definition of what is a 'misdeed' will be more contentious than what is a crime or civil wrong. Denning MR has extended the sense of misdeed to include a deception of the public which does not amount to a civil wrong. On this rationale, the public may have a corresponding right to 'know the truth' about dangerous drugs,[86] or to be told

---

[79] See J Pizer 'The Public Interest Exception to the Breach of Confidence Action: Are the Lights About to Change?' (1994) 20 *Mon LR* 67, 100–1.

[80] *Gartside v Outram* (1856) 26 LJ Ch (NS) 113, 114, Wood V-C, followed in *Corrs Pavey Whiting & Byrne v Collector of Customs* (1987) 14 FCR 434, 451–456, Gummow J; *Smith Kline & French Laboratories (Aust) Ltd v Secretary, Department of Community Services and Health* (1990) 22 FCR 73, 110, Gummow J and *Attorney-General (UK) v Observer Ltd* [1990] 1 AC 109, 268–269, Lord Griffiths.

[81] *Initial Services Ltd v Putterill* [1968] QB 396; *Attorney-General (UK) v Observer Ltd* [1990] 1 AC 109, 282–3 per Lord Goff; P Finn 'Confidentiality and the "Public Interest" ' (1984) 58 LQR 497, 505–8.

[82] See *Hubbard v Vosper* [1972] 2 QB 84; *Church of Scientology of California v Kaufman Ltd* [1973] RPC 627; *Corrs Pavey Whiting & Byrne v Collector of Customs* (1987) 14 FCR 434, 456–458, Gummow J; P Finn 'Confidentiality and the "Public Interest" ' (1984) 58 *LQR* 497, 506 at n 81.

[83] [1968] QB 396, 406, Denning MR, 410, Salmon LJ, 410, Winn LJ (CA), applying *Gartside v Outram* (1856) 26 LJ Ch 113.

[84] *Malone v Commissioner of Police of the Metropolis (No 2)* [1979] 2 All ER 620, 646, Megarry V-C; Gurry 331.

[85] Compare *Initial Services Ltd v Putterill* [1968] 1 QB 396, 405, Denning MR with *Weld-Blundell v Stephens* [1919] 1 KB 520, 529, Bankes LJ.

[86] Disapproved in *Schering Chemicals Ltd v Falkman Ltd* [1982] 1 QB 1, 27, Shaw LJ.

of the private lives of public figures.[87] Such a wider use of the *Putterill* formula has secured little approval in Australia.[88]

**[9.27]** Disclosure can vindicate what we might call 'a higher interest'.[89] Certainly the following public interests may be more significant than (and 'trump') the interests of individuals that their confidences are respected. Avoidance of public danger is one.[90] If information disclosed relates to something which may in the avoidable future be 'medically dangerous to the public', a breach of confidence to disclose it is justifiable.[91] Where the disclosure is not preventative of harm, however, and merely a 'wide and vital public interest' is gratified, no justiciable public interest may arise.[92] The 'thalidomide' birth defects litigation in *Distillers Co (Biochemicals) Ltd v Times Newspapers Ltd* was an example.[93] A related idea is expressed as the 'avoidance of public deception'. It is rather more doubtful. The proper administration of justice is an unquestionable 'higher interest'. Confidentiality will always yield to the interests of justice, as Lord Diplock said in *D v National Society for Prevention of Cruelty to Children*.[94] The status of information as 'confidential' gives it no privilege in a court of law. Only a more important public interest than the administration of justice, if one can be found, will confer on confidential information its own public interest immunity.[95]

# Remedies

**[9.28]** What remedies are available for a breach of confidence may still depend on whether the confidence is protected solely in equity, or whether it has otherwise a common law contractual (or tortious) base. This is the orthodox view.[96] Cases like *Saltman Engineering Co Ltd v Campbell Engineering Co Ltd*,[97] *Franklin v Giddins*[98] and *Smith Kline & French Laboratories (Aust) Ltd v Secretary, Department of Community Services and Health*[99] awarded no damages because no legal wrong had been committed. Equitable relief was awarded instead. Where defendants have breached

---

[87] *Woodward v Hutchins* [1977] 1 WLR 760, 764, Denning MR.

[88] Not accepted by Rath J in *Castrol Australia Pty Ltd v EmTech Associates Pty Ltd* (1980) 51 FLR 184, 214–5; see also S Ricketson 'Public Interest and Breach of Confidence' (1979) 12 *MULR* 176, 198 and P Finn 'Confidentiality and the "Public Interest" ' (1984) 58 *ALJ* 497, 507.

[89] *Weld-Blundell v Stephens* [1920] AC 956, 965–6, Bankes LJ; F Gurry 'Breach of Confidence' in Finn *Equity* 128–30; cf P Finn 'Confidentiality and the "Public Interest" ' (1984) 58 *ALJ* 497, 506–7.

[90] See Gurry 335–8.

[91] *Beloff v Pressdram Ltd* [1973] 1 All ER 241, 260, Ungoed-Thomas J.

[92] Finn *Fiduciaries* 158 and Gurry 336–7.

[93] [1975] 1 All ER 41, Talbot J.

[94] [1978] AC 218, 230.

[95] S McNicol *Law of Privilege* (1992), 375 and see *Australian Securities Commission v Zarro (No 2)* (1992) 10 ACLC 553, Drummond J (Fed Ct).

[96] See MGL [4127].

[97] (1948) 65 RPC 203, 211, Greene MR.

[98] [1978] Qd R 72.

[99] (1990) 22 FCR 73, affirmed (1991) 28 FCR 291.

contractual obligations of confidence, or the wrong can be regarded as a tort,[100] damages will be available as of right. Whether nominal or substantial compensation is then allowed depends on the extent to which the breach of confidence has caused loss.[101]

**[9.29]** We will concentrate on equitable remedies first. In Chapter 6 we examined the goals of equitable remedies. *Restitution* is a primary idea. Claimants should be restored to the position that they would have been in had confidences not been breached. A secondary goal is *redistribution*. The latter idea was discussed in *Hospital Products* by the New South Wales Court of Appeal.[102] Persons who misuse confidential information are answerable to the claimants wronged for any gain they make. The following three situations may illustrate some of the inter-relations of these goals in a market context.

1. Confidence-breakers may wrongfully pirate an idea in one market and introduce it to another where the confider does not operate. Profits are made. This was the situation in *Peter Pan Manufacturing Corporation v Corsets Silhouette Ltd*.[103] A restitutionary goal was served by the defendant being permanently prevented from using the idea in the new market. Redistribution required that the profits should be accounted for.
2. Confidence-breakers may appropriate only an unrealised idea. No profits needing redistribution might have been made. The claimant in *Coco v A N Clark (Engineers) Ltd*[104] was an inventor and the defendant was a company to whom he unsuccessfully tried to sell his idea. The inventor's restitution interest was treated as equivalent to the likely return that he could have expected if sale had occurred. This was satisfied with a compensatory remedy. An award of damages equal to a fair royalty payment was made.
3. Confiders and confidence-breakers may compete in the same market. Relief can and should be directly proportioned to market forces. In *Deta Nominees Pty Ltd v Viscount Plastic Products Pty Ltd*[105] a manufacturer and its tool-making sub-contractor both sold plastic drawers in Melbourne. The defendant threatened to compete with the confider's idea. This was the advantage of a secret design, although it was not something over which the confider enjoyed any patent or monopoly rights. The manufacturer's competitors were free to pull the drawer apart and 'reverse engineer' it for themselves. The court defined the advantage that the manufacturer possessed to be the *time* that this reverse engineering would take. This was what had to be restored. An injunction preventing the competition for the duration of this 'headstart' or lead-time advantage was granted.

## 1. Injunctions

**[9.30]** Injunction is the primary remedy for a breach of confidence. Defendants can be prohibited from using or further using the confidences that

---

100 See MGL [4127], discussing *Seager v Copydex Ltd (No 2)* [1969] 1 All ER 718.
101 *London & Provincial Sporting News Agency Ltd v Levy* [1928] Macg Cop Cas 340 (nominal) and *Mechanical and General Inventions Co Ltd and Lehwess v Austin and the Austin Motor Co Ltd* [1935] AC 346 (substantial) and Gurry 430–1.
102 [1983] 2 NSWLR 157, 233, curiam.
103 [1963] 3 All ER 402, 410, Pennycuick J.
104 [1969] RPC 41, 53–54, Megarry J.
105 [1979] VR 167, 194–5, Fullagar J.

they have breached. No distinction has been drawn in the award of this remedy between the contractual and purely equitable rights of confidentiality.[106] Discretion will be significant here, as it was noted to be at [6.2]. Courts will be motivated by their assessment of the defendant's conduct. Fewer equities can be asserted on behalf of a dishonest confidence-breaker.[107] If the defendant has acted in good faith, and perhaps changed his position as well, an injunction may be withheld. Some less drastic remedy like damages will be ordered instead.[108] Injunctive relief may also be withheld because of the nature of the information upon which the claim is based. If there is 'nothing very special' about what was confided, as in situation (2) above, a court may decline to grant an injunction. It may instead award a remedy which restores the plaintiff's loss with less inconvenience to the defendant. Injunctions will not protect 'trivial tittle-tattle'[109] or 'pernicious nonsense'.[110] Finally, the time during which the defendant should be subject to injunctive restraint must be considered. The injunction may be expressed to last forever, or it may last a very short while. Relief, we saw above in situation (3), can be tailored to reverse the size of the market advantage that the confidence-breaker has seized. 'Headstarts' and 'springboards' are metaphors sometimes used to describe it. Behind them is an idea of the wrongful use of an idea to 'steal a march' on a rival, or to compete on unfair terms.

## 2.  Account of profits

**[9.31]**   Where the defendant makes an identifiable profit from the wrongful use of confidential information, a court may order that this be accounted for to the plaintiff. This is said to be the paradigmatic 'restitutionary' entitlement.[111] It is not often claimed. Whether of nature restitutionary or redistributive, the effect of an account on the defendant is onerous. By electing to take an account rather than compensatory damages, the confider retrospectively treats the defendant as his agent—a person working for the confider's gain and not his own. The remedy is extraordinarily difficult and expensive to administer.[112] Profit accounting has been granted in a surprisingly small number of reported cases and there where the equities were strongly in the confider's favour.

## 3.  Damages

**[9.32]**   Damages for breach of confidence are monetary compensation awarded by the courts to restore confiders to the position they would have been in had the breach not occurred. A proven loss, or injury or damage occurring is restored. Damages are a flexible and convenient remedy. They have been awarded where the purely equitable obligation of confidence is

---

[106] Finn *Fiduciaries* 162.

[107] See *Wright v Gasweld Pty Ltd* (1991) 22 NSWLR 317 (CA) and *Franklin v Giddins* [1978] Qd R 72.

[108] *Seager v Copydex Ltd* [1967] 2 All ER 415, 419 (CA).

[109] *Coco v A N Clark (Engineers) Ltd* [1969] RPC 41, 48, Megarry J.

[110] *Church of Scientology of California v Kaufman* [1973] RPC 635, 658, Goff J.

[111] Eg, G Jones 'Restitution of Benefits Obtained in Breach of Another's Confidence' (1970) 86 LQR 463, 486–8; Birks 315–6 and MGL [4127].

[112] Ricketson 841–2.

involved,[113] as well as where equity assists in the enforcement of contractual rights.[114] In some cases, a loss consequent on a breach of confidence must either be compensated in damages, or it will go unremedied.[115] For there may be no gain to make the defendant account for. Nor is any conduct still being pursued which might be enjoined.

The proper basis, or 'jurisdiction', for a court of equity to award damages has for some time been a contentious matter. This treatment will not enter the minefield of doctrine on the subject. We will focus instead on some of the compensatory problems which can arise with confidences particularly. 'Damages', it will be assumed, can be awarded whether the basis of the confidential obligation lies in equity, contract or tort. A substantial body of the cases now fails to distinguish between the sources of 'damages' for breach of confidence.[116]

### Valuation of the information

[9.33] A familiar idea may assist with valuation. For a breach of confidence, as for other wrongs, the 'nature of the loss' can be said to define the way in which the damages for that loss are assessed. The loss on breach of confidence will usually be deprivation of what the information is worth. Assuming that the information is in some way transmissible or alienable, abstract 'worth' of the information is quantified as its market value.[117] This approach will be inadequate where confidants claim more than the value of the information. They may have lost as well the possibility of acquiring the subject of the confidence—perhaps a business opportunity[118], or mining prospect.[119] Or the confidant may additionally or instead suffer consequential loss of profits, or loss of custom in a business.[120] The assessment task in this event is to value the consequences of a breach of confidence separately from, or in addition to, the subject of the confidence. We shall deal first with the situation where the loss equals the market value of specific information. Our inquiry then becomes how that value can be established.

### Form of the information

[9.34] Confidential information may include things as various as a series of disconnected insights, a concept for human interaction, or the design of a tool. Before information can be assigned a value for the purposes of compensation, it must be attributed with a form. Information needs a 'nature' before the court

---

113 Saltman *Engineering Co Ltd v Campbell Engineering Co Ltd* (1948) 65 RPC 203; *Seager v Copydex Ltd* [1967] 2 All ER 415.

114 *Schindler Lifts Australia Pty Ltd v Debelak* (1989) 15 IPR 129; *Wright v Gasweld Pty Ltd* (1991) 22 NSWLR 317.

115 As in *Aquaculture Corporation v New Zealand Green Mussel Co Ltd* [1990] 3 NZLR 299 (CA): see [9.36] below.

116 Including *Seager v Copydex Ltd* [1967] 2 All ER 415, 419, Denning MR; *Coco v A N Clark (Engineers) Ltd* [1969] RPC 41, 51, Megarry J; *Aquaculture Corporation v New Zealand Green Mussel Co Ltd* [1990] 3 NZLR 299, 301 (CA); *Ansell Rubber Co Pty Ltd v Allied Rubber Industries Pty Ltd* [1967] VR 37, 50, Gowans J.

117 *Seager v Copydex Ltd (No 2)* [1969] 2 All ER 718, 719 and Gurry 448–51.

118 *Aquaculture Corporation v New Zealand Green Mussel Co Ltd* [1990] 3 NZLR 299.

119 *Lac Minerals Ltd v International Corona Resources Ltd* [1989] 2 SCR 574, 614–26, Sopinka and McIntyre JJ.

120 See *Robb v Green* [1895] 2 QB 1, affirmed [1895] 2 QB 315.

can make an inference as to its worth. Should the information be characterised as an inventor's creation, say, a designer's process, or simply what a repetition engineer might be paid to achieve? The differences between these as bases of valuation may make a dramatic difference to the quantum of the award. Which basis applies will depend upon the court's view of the form which the information took. So Denning MR said in *Seager v Copydex Ltd (No 2)*[121] that the market value of the item of confidential information 'will depend on the nature of it'. Referring to the design for a carpet grip which was the subject of the confidence, he continued (at 719–20):

> If there was nothing very special about it, that is, if it involved no particular inventive step but was the sort of information which could be obtained by employing any competent consultant, then the value of it was the fee which a consultant would charge for it; because in that case the defendant company, by taking the information, would only have saved themselves the time and trouble of employing a consultant. But, on the other hand, if the information was something special, as, for instance, if it involved an inventive step or something so unusual that it could not be obtained by just going to a consultant, then the value of it is much higher. It is not merely a consultant's fee, but the price which a willing buyer—desirous of obtaining it— would pay for it. It is the value as between a willing seller and a willing buyer.

The court then considered whether to characterise the design as a draftsmanlike skill such as a consultant could supply, or whether the design was inventive. It found the latter. Inventors are usually given an interest in the invention's commercial success. In a 'once for all' damages award, this was expressed by the allowance to the designer of a capitalised royalty.

**[9.35]** *Interfirm Comparison (Australia) Pty Ltd v Law Society of New South Wales*[122] was a comparable case. It concerned the wrongful use of questionnaire forms that the claimant had devised. An award was made of what would have been an appropriate licensing fee for the claimant to have required, had it been asked to give its consent to the use. In both *Seager* and *Interfirm* it was apparent that the claimants had no intention of manufacturing or using the relevant articles for themselves. The designers in each case had an expectation of exploiting the relevant invention or information by way of royalty, licence fee, consultancy, or other similar remuneration. This assumes another's beneficial use of the information. No manufacturing *profit* was ever anticipated by the person who originated the confidence. In *Dowson & Mason Ltd v Potter*,[123] by contrast, the claimant was a manufacturer in a line of business in which the second defendant was a competitor. The first defendant was a disloyal employee who wrongly gave some of the plaintiff's confidential information to the competitor. It was found that as the firm was intending to manufacture and sell the relevant article for itself, even if it would have parted with the information about it for a fee, the appropriate measure of damages was a loss of manufacturing profit.[124] Market value of what was confided cannot be assumed to be the measure of loss where the claimant intends to make use of the information other than by way of sale.

---

[121] [1969] 2 All ER 718, 719, Salmon and Winn LJJ agreeing.

[122] (1975) 5 ALR 527, Bowen CJ in Eq.

[123] [1986] 2 All ER 418 (CA).

[124] Ibid, 422, Sir E Eveleigh, 423–424, Stocker LJ, 424–425, Slade LJ; see the discussion of this in *McGregor on Damages* 15th edn (1988) H McGregor (ed), [1709].

## Consequential loss

**[9.36]**   Recovery of loss beyond the market value of the information depends on the principles of remoteness of damages.[125] The forms which consequential loss from breach of confidence may take being several, we will limit our consideration to recoverable economic losses—that is, trading losses incurred by breach of confidence and profits foregone. Consider, for example, the claim made in *Aquaculture Corporation v New Zealand Green Mussel Co Ltd*.[126] A manufacturer incurred research and development expenditure in respect of a remedy for arthritis involving New Zealand mussels. It had been hoped that the drug could one day enter the large and lucrative United States market, for which the prior approval of that country's 'Food and Drug Administration' was required. The confider communicated some confidential information to the defendant about how the mussel extract was produced. Wrongly, the defendant breached the confidence and used the extract in a product of its own. This was extensively advertised in the American market—both as a food supplement and 'cure for arthritis.' A mortal blow was said to have been dealt to the confider's enterprise. The mussel specific was branded a quack remedy by the American Arthritis Foundation and was banned by the Food and Drug Administration. So the confider sued the defendant for compensatory and exemplary damages, as well as injunctive relief for breach of what was argued to be an equitable obligation of confidence. Reversing the court below on the damages point, the Court of Appeal at 302 allowed the confider a compensatory damages award of $1.5m.

## 4.   Constructive trusts

**[9.37]**   Cases where the proprietary constructive trust has been awarded for breach of confidence have been few and the remedy has attracted little academic support.[127] Two Canadian cases are the main ones to illustrate it. *Pre-Cam Exploration and Development Ltd v McTavish* was the first.[128] The claimant was a prospector who had staked certain mining claims in a mineralised zone of Canada. He thereafter commissioned a survey company to perform exploratory work in the area surrounding the claims. The defendant was a junior employee of the company. His only responsibility was the taking of readings from a magnetometer and recording them in a log book. In the course of the survey for the claimant, it became apparent to the defendant from his magnetometer work that the land to the north and east of the claims was on the 'strike' of the mineralised zone. So, after he had delivered the log book of readings, the defendant terminated his employment and staked several claims in his own name. These were all north and east of the claimant's claims and contiguous to them. It was held by the court that the defendant had, in the course of his employment, acquired highly confidential information. This was the claimant's information, being used by him in order to acquire other claims to be held advantageously with the existing claims staked. By using

---

[125] See *McGregor on Damages, supra*, [1357] ff.

[126] [1990] 3 NZLR 299 (CA)

[127] *Ohio Oil Co v Sharp* 135 F 2d 303 (1943); see Goff & Jones at 694–5; P D Maddaugh and J D McCamus *The Law of Restitution* (1990), 676; MGL [4127]; Gurry, Ricketson and G Jones in 'Restitution of Benefits Obtained in Breach of Another's Confidence' (1970) 86 *LQR* 463 do not refer to this remedy.

[128] [1966] SCR 551, curiam.

that information for his own advantage, the defendant was (at 555) found to be in breach of an implied obligation of confidentiality in his contract of employment. This amounted to a 'fraud' and a remedial constructive trust in favour of the claimant was imposed.

**[9.38]** A constructive trust was also awarded in the Canadian Supreme Court decision of *Lac Minerals Ltd v International Corona Resources Ltd*.[129] It was also a confidentiality claim arising out of a mining prospect, a variant on the theme of *Pre-Cam*[130]. The facts, however, differ from Pre-Cam in the following ways. First, the confidence that Lac Minerals abused was disclosed by Corona in pre-contractual negotiations, not a relationship of employment. Secondly, Lac Minerals was a large company rather than a junior employee and, thirdly, Lac Minerals purchased title to and spent money developing the mineralised site. That still leaves a lot of sameness between the cases. In neither was any pre-existing property right of the confider vindicated. Constructive trusts were of the remedial variety. Property in confidences is problematic in any event.[131] Each case involved the remedy being imposed over property acquired from third parties at the defendant's expense. Neither case involved reliance on a pre-existing 'special' or fiduciary relationship between the parties. Such a relationship in the form of a fiduciary relationship of employer and employee did exist in the *Pre-Cam* facts; but it was not referred to in the Supreme Court. In *Lac Minerals*, Lac and Corona had not had any dealings before the negotiations commenced and hence had between them no pre-existing relationship.[132] So, if based neither in property nor in a pre-existing relationship, the constructive trust must have flowed from the breach of confidence wrong itself. The problem in this may be with identification of the property over which the trust is impressed.[133] Very often an 'acquisitive' wrong involves no subtraction and leaves no product.

**[9.39]** The singular *effectiveness* of the constructive trust awarded was notable in both *Pre-Cam*[134] and *Lac Minerals*.[135] The fiduciary 'profits rule' was applied to confidence-breakers. Analogously to exploitation of an opportunity in breach of fiduciary duty, the acquisition was treated as one made on behalf of the party to whom the duty is owed. Particularly in the *Lac Minerals* decision, the party wronged received a seemingly inequitable net benefit through the constructive trust. Corona was much better off at the end of the day for the fact that Lac had committed the wrong. This was justified on exemplary grounds. Confidence-breakers are treated with harshness in order to deter others. In the background facts to *Lac Minerals*,[136] Corona had entered the negotiations for a minerals joint venture at a time when it had the expectations of a non-funding minerals discoverer. The corresponding interest

---

129 [1989] 2 SCR 574: Sopinka and McIntyre JJ dissented and, at 617, disapproved of the *Pre-Cam* decision.

130 [1966] SCR 551.

131 See *Nichrotherm Electrical Co Ltd v Percy* [1957] RPC 207, 209, Lord Evershed MR.

132 Noted by Sopinka J (diss) at [1989] 2 SCR 574, 516; cf *Ontex Resources Ltd v Metalore Resouces Ltd* (1993) 103 DLR (4th) 158.

133 See G Jones *Restitution in Public and Private Law* (1991), 91–3.

134 [1966] SCR 551.

135 [1989] 2 SCR 574.

136 Ibid, 618–626, Sopinka J (diss), 668–679, La Forest J.

in a venture would not normally have exceeded 30 per cent. It was transformed by the award of a constructive trust into the sole beneficial owner of a 100 per cent share in mineralised land—less allowance for the additional benefit that, by the time of trial, Lac had substantially developed the land. An award of a constructive trust in these circumstances approached the punitive. This was a point with which La Forest J dealt at 672–3. He praised the 'utility' of the constructive trust for the 'promotion and preservation of desired social behaviour and institutions'. Though the constructive trust is perhaps the most stringent of equity's restitutionary remedies, still it must sometimes be justified by other goals. The moral quality of the defendant's conduct is a useful pointer to its application.

# Index

**References are to paragraphs**

**References are to paragraphs**

**References are to paragraphs**

**References are to paragraphs**

**References are to paragraphs**

**References are to paragraphs**

**References are to paragraphs**

**References are to paragraphs**

**References are to paragraphs**